Meal Management

Meal Management

Fourth Edition

Faye Kinder

Associate Professor Emeritus
Michigan State University

The Macmillan Company, New York
Collier-Macmillan Limited, London

THE MACMILLAN COMPANY
866 THIRD AVENUE, NEW YORK, NEW YORK 10022
COLLIER-MACMILLAN CANADA, LTD., TORONTO, ONTARIO

Library of Congress catalog card number: 79–189679

Printing: 1 2 3 4 5 6 7 8   Year: 3 4 5 6 7 8 9

Preface to the Fourth Edition

This fourth edition of *Meal Management* is extensively rewritten and updated. New material has been added in response to widespread and vigorous interest in developments in food technology, standards for foods, the inspection of food, the marketing of food, and legislation that affects the food-buying process. The chapters on food buying have been enlarged and strengthened because of the influence of the economic situation in the United States in the early seventies on the food-buying practices of families. Nearly all of the line drawings have been redesigned.

The suggested problems that were formerly included in certain chapters have been omitted because the author believes that, from among the almost endless possibilities that suggest themselves, students and/or their instructors can better develop problems of interest and relevance.

Legislation in response to consumerism has been rapidly enacted, but much is in process. For the last word, the reader will find it necessary to consult proper sources. Investigations of the agencies responsible for administering protective laws—the Food and Drug Administration, the United States Department of Agriculture, and the Federal Trade Commission—have had some effects. The reader may wish to seek current and more recent information than could be included here on the policies and effectiveness of these agencies.

The author has attempted to provide information basic to decision-making, but she has left the decision-making to the meal manager. Guidelines for action are suggested; they are not, however, definitive.

I am grateful to the several persons who assisted in the typing of the manuscript. To the companies who provided photographs and to the many persons in federal agencies who provided information, I express my appreciation.

F. K.

Contents

TABLES   ix
FIGURES   xiii
PHOTOGRAPHS   xvi

Introduction   1

CHAPTER 1. Meal Management—Some Concepts and Definitions   5
CHAPTER 2. The Marketplace and the Consumer   19
CHAPTER 3. Science, Technology, and Food   58
CHAPTER 4. Food Laws and the Regulation of the Food Supply   77
CHAPTER 5. Purchasing Food—Some General Precepts   120
CHAPTER 6. Purchasing Food—Meat, Poultry, and Fish   150
CHAPTER 7. Purchasing Food—Cheeses   206
CHAPTER 8. Purchasing Food—Dairy Products, Nondairy
             Products, and Eggs   233
CHAPTER 9. Purchasing Food—Fruits   257
CHAPTER 10. Purchasing Food—Vegetables   284
CHAPTER 11. Purchasing Food—Grain Food Products and
              Miscellaneous Food Products   303
CHAPTER 12. Meal Management Goals—Good Nutrition   323
CHAPTER 13. Meal Management Goals—Planned Spending   353
CHAPTER 14. Meal Management Goals—Satisfying Meals   400
CHAPTER 15. Meal Management Goals—Controlled Use of Time   419
CHAPTER 16. Timing Meal Preparation   427
CHAPTER 17. Styles of Meal Service   435
CHAPTER 18. Setting the Table   444
CHAPTER 19. Waiting on the Table   470
CHAPTER 20. Etiquette of the Table   483
CHAPTER 21. Managing Guest Meals   501
CHAPTER 22. Managing Buffet Meals   513

vii

CHAPTER 23.   *Teas, Receptions, and Other Occasions with
              Light Refreshments*   535
APPENDIX A.   *Format for Menus*   561
APPENDIX B.   *Quantity Food-Purchasing Guides*   563
INDEX   569

Tables

5– 1.   Cost of Selected Items as Purchased in Different Types of
        Food Stores   123
5– 2.   Cost of a Market Basket of Items as Purchased in Three
        Supermarkets at Minimum Cost   124
5– 3.   Two Plans for Selecting Meats   126
5– 4.   Two Plans for Selecting Vegetables   127
5– 5.   Two Plans for Selecting Dairy Foods and Nondairy Foods   128
5– 6.   The Cost of Pastry Purchased Ready-Rolled, as a Mix,
        and Home-Prepared   129
5– 7.   Package Size and Unit Costs   132
5– 8.   Preparation Time for Some Meat, Fish, Poultry, and
        Cheese Dishes   138
5– 9.   Average Cost per Serving of Selected Homemade and
        Convenient Main Dishes and Dinners   139
5–10.   Average Cost per Serving of Selected Homemade and
        Convenient Baked Products   140
5–11.   The Cost of the Convenience of Plain Cake Mix   145

6– 1.   Quantity of Meat Bought, Money Value of Meat Bought,
        and Money Value per Pound of Meat Bought per
        Urban Household, Spring, 1965, According to Income   152
6– 2.   Estimated per Serving Costs of Selected Kinds and
        Cuts of Meat, Poultry, and Fish   153

7– 1.   Cheese-Making Techniques and the Resultant Cheeses   209

8– 1.   The Cost of One Quart of Selected Fluid Milk Products
        as Purchased in Containers of Different Sizes from
        Different Sources   231
8– 2.   Cost per Quart of Nonfat Dry Milk as It Varies with
        Purchase of Different Brands and Different Packages   241

8– 3.   Summary of United States Standards for Quality of
        Individual Shell Eggs   248

9– 1.   Per-Serving Cost of Some Fresh Fruits   258
9– 2.   Cost per Pound of Canned Peaches as Cost
        Differs with the Kind, Quality, and Size of Can
        Purchased   273
9– 3.   Cost per Pound of Selected Canned Fruits   274
9– 4.   Per-Serving Cost and Vitamin-C Content of Four-Ounce
        Servings of Some Citrus Juices and Citrus-Flavored
        Beverages   279

10– 1. Per-Serving Cost of Selected Vegetables, Fresh and Frozen   287
10– 2. Per-Serving Cost of Some Frozen Ready-made
        Vegetable Dishes   299
10– 3. Per-Serving Cost of Selected Canned Vegetables   300

11– 1. Cost per Pound of Selected Breads, Rolls, and
        Baked Goods   307
11– 2. Cost per Pound of Some Selected Ready-to-Eat Breakfast
        Cereals and of Two Cook-Before-Eating Cereals   308

12– 1. Desirable Weights   331
12– 2. Values for a Quick Method of Estimating Protein
        Content of Meals   334
12– 3. Recommended Dietary Allowances—Seventh Revised
        Edition, 1968, Abridged   342–343
12– 4. A Model for Use in Planning Meals   344
12– 5. The Nutrient Content of Foods Selected According to
        a Model for Use in Planning Meals   346
12– 6. The Total Nutrient Content of Foods Selected According
        to a Model for Planning Meals Plus Foods Added in
        Meal Planning   350

13– 1. Per Capita Civilian Consumption of Major Food
        Commodities   356
13– 2. Basic Low-Cost Family Food Plan   363
13– 3. Second Low-Cost Family Food Plan   364
13– 4. Moderate-Cost Family Food Plan   365
13– 5. Liberal Family Food Plan   366
13– 6. Economy Family Food Plan   367
13– 7. Weekly Quantities of and Cost of Food for a Family of
        Four According to All Plans   370
13– 8. Three Plans for Selecting Meat, Poultry, and Fish in
        Accordance with Guides to Decision-Making When the
        Basic Low-Cost Plan Is Used   374

13– 9. Differences in the Quantities of Food Provided by the
Two Low-Cost Plans   378

13–10. Weekly Quantities of Food for the Same Family According
to the Moderate-Cost and Basic Low-Cost Plans and
Differences Between Plans   379

13–11. Quantities of Food for the Same Family According to
the Liberal-Cost and Moderate-Cost Plans and
Differences Between Plans   381

13–12. Market Baskets of Three Food Plans for a Family of Four   384

13–13. Market Baskets of the Basic Low-Cost Plan and the
Economy Plan for a Family of Four Showing
Differences Between Plans   387

13–14. Food Selections for the Economy Plan with
Estimated Costs   388–391

13–15. Food Plans by Family Income and Size, 1970   395

15– 1. Time Used by Urban Housewives for Household Work
and Food-Related Activities   420

16– 1. Steps 1 and 2 in Timing Meal Preparation   429

16– 2. Step 3 in Timing Meal Preparation—Tasks Listed in
Descending Order of Total Time Required   431

16– 3. The Time Schedule for Preparing the Meal   432

16– 4. Steps 1 and 2 in Timing Meal Preparation   433

16– 5. Step 3 in Timing Meal Preparation—Tasks Listed in
Descending Order of Total Time Required   433

16– 6. The Time Schedule for Preparing Dinner for Four   434

B–1. Guide to the Use of Foods in Cooking and
Meal Preparation   564–565

B–2. The Measure of One Pound   566

B–3. How Much There Is in a Can   567

Figures

2– 1. Farmer's share of the market-basket dollar, by food group   36

2– 2. Shares of the market-basket dollar   36

4– 1. Meat inspection marks   111

4– 2. Poultry inspection mark   112

5– 1. Index of food prices   121

5– 2. Preparation times, including active and total time, for angel food, devil's food, and yellow cakes and pies   137

5– 3. Expenditures for convenience foods   141

6– 1. Meat consumption per person   151

6– 2. Per capita consumption of poultry and eggs   151

6– 3. Beef chart—wholesale cuts of beef and their bone structure   156

6– 4. Veal chart—wholesale cuts of veal and their bone structure   156

6– 5. Pork chart—wholesale cuts of pork and their bone structure   156

6– 6. Lamb chart—wholesale cuts of lamb and their bone structure   157

6– 7. The seven basic retail cuts of meat   157

6– 8. Bones identify seven groups of retail cuts   158

6– 9. Retail cuts of beef and where they come from   159

6–10. Unboned steaks   160

6–11. Unboned cuts from the chuck and the round   161

6–12. Retail cuts of pork and where they come from   163

6–13. Retail cuts of veal and where they come from   164

6–14. Retail cuts of lamb and where they come from   165

6–15. Meat inspection marks   169

6–16. Poultry inspection mark   169

6–17. Rib roasts of USDA yield grades 2 and 4   172
6–18. USDA yield grade and quality grade symbols   173
6–19. Combination grade and inspection symbol for poultry
       showing class of bird   177
6–20. U.S. Grade A and U.S. Grade B turkeys   178
6–21. Ready-to-cook chickens of U.S. Grade A, U.S. Grade B,
       and U.S. Grade C qualities   178

7– 1. The "Quality Approved" symbol that may appear on
       cottage cheese and process cheese products   217

8– 1. Grademark for instant nonfat dry milk   240
8– 2. Grade symbols for graded butter   244
8– 3. Grademark for graded eggs   247
8– 4. Grade symbol for Fresh Fancy Quality eggs   249
8– 5. Measuring the thickness of the thick white of eggs   250
8– 6. Appearance of broken-out eggs   251
8– 7. Weight classes for eggs   252

9– 1. Noncitrus consumption per person   257
9– 2. Citrus consumption per person   257

10– 1. Vegetable consumption per person   285
10– 2. Per capita consumption of potatoes   285

11– 1. Approximate retail cost per serving of tea and coffee   316

12– 1. Quality of diets, 1955–1965   323
12– 2. Diets meeting allowances for nutrients, 1955 and 1965   324
12– 3. Income and diets below allowances   325
12– 4. Calcium from one day's diet, as a per cent of the
        Recommended Allowances   326
12– 5. Iron from one day's diet, as a per cent of the
        Recommended Allowances   326
12– 6. Nutrients less than the Recommended Dietary Allowances   327
12– 7. Meat group   328
12– 8. Milk group   328
12– 9. Bread cereal group   329

13– 1. Food expenditures and income   353
13– 2. Food of U.S. families. Values per week, 1955 and 1965   354
13– 3. Income and food spending per family per week, 1965   354
13– 4. Quantities of food used per person per week, 1955 and 1965   355
13– 5. Meat group. Use and money value up in 1965   356
13– 6. Cost of a week's food by family type, June 1971   358
13– 7. Food at home. Average value per family per week   361

18– 1. Formal service—individual cover   448

18– 2.   Alignment of napkin, flatware, and plate within a cover   449
18– 3.   Possible positions of the dinner fork when no dinner
         knife is laid   451
18– 4.   Possible positions of the butter spreader on the
         bread-and-butter plate   451
18– 5.   Position for the butter spreader when no
         bread-and-butter plate is placed   452
18– 6.   A possible position for the dessert fork and the
         beverage spoon   453
18– 7.   Position for the fruit knife and fork and the beverage spoon   455
18– 8.   Serving pieces laid beside serving dishes   456
18– 9.   Serving pieces laid at the server's cover   457
18–10.   Possible positions of the water glass   457
18–11.   Position of the bread-and-butter plate   459
18–12.   Position of the salad plate when there is no
         bread-and-butter plate in the cover   459
18–13.   Possible positions of the salad when a bread-and-butter
         plate appears in the cover   460
18–14.   Possible positions of the salad service at the server's cover   461
18–15.   Possible arrangements of a beverage service at the
         hostess's cover—beverage served during the meal and
         no tray used   463
18–16.   A tray arranged for beverage service   464
18–17.   Dining table set for service of food at the table   466
18–18.   A serving table arranged for convenient use   468

19– 1.   Dessert placed for serving at the table   475
19– 2.   Possible arrangements of the beverage service at the
         server's cover   476

20– 1.   Order of serving persons at the table   487

21– 1.   Tray arranged for offering a beverage in glasses   507
21– 2.   Tray arranged for offering accompaniments to a beverage   507
21– 3.   Tray arranged for serving coffee in demitasse   508

22– 1.   Small chest set for buffet service—table service at
         dining table   514
22– 2.   Small chest or table set with trays, appointments, and
         beverages   515
22– 3.   Buffet arranged so that guests proceed around it—
         table service   521
22– 4.   Buffet arranged so that guests proceed from end to end—
         plate service   522
22– 5.   Arrangement for self-service of a hot beverage   527
22– 6.   A self-serve dessert buffet   528

23– 1.   Tray arranged for afternoon tea or coffee   541
23– 2a. A small table arranged for tea or coffee—finger food   545
23– 2b. A small table arranged for afternoon tea or dessert—
         food requires the use of a fork   546
23– 2c. A small table arranged for afternoon tea or morning
         coffee—food requires the use of a butter spreader   547
23– 3.   Table arrangement for a large tea—a single service on
         one side of table and cups and saucers used   548
23– 4.   Table arrangement for a large tea—duplicate services on
         one side of table, cups and plates used   549
23– 5.   Table arrangement for a large tea—duplicate services on
         the two sides of the table, cups and saucers used   552
23– 6.   Table arrangement for a large tea—guest takes food,
         then receives beverage   554
23– 7.   Table arrangement for serving punch   556

Photographs

1.   Cover of formally set table   437
2.   A table arranged for the serving of food at the table   439
3.   A table arranged for the self-serving of food—
     American style of table service   440
4.   Table setting that shows placement of the dessert
     flatware above the cover   454
5.   Buffet arrangement—guests to dine at tables   524
6.   Buffet supper table—plate service   525
7.   Dessert buffet   529
8.   Tray arranged for afternoon tea or coffee   543
9.   Small table arranged for afternoon tea   544
10. Large table arranged for afternoon tea   555
11. Table arranged for serving punch   558

Introduction

Change is inevitable; it is a law of life. Man has always lived with change; he has accepted it and adapted to it, or he has perished. What disturbs man today is the rapidity of change. It has been said that persons who became fifteen years old in 1967 have seen more change than had occurred in all of previous time. The decade of the 1960's—perhaps a little more, perhaps a little less than half of the lifetime of the average student attending an institution of higher learning—witnessed great change, not only in the United States but worldwide. Man went to the moon. The common man became aware of ecology, although he had long known that the air he breathed was dirty. The merits of pesticides became suspect. By early 1970, 42 per cent of all women sixteen years old and older were in the labor force. They made up almost 40 per cent of the labor force. About 60 per cent of the female labor force consisted of married women. Forty per cent of married women were in the labor force (3). The women's liberation movement gained momentum. There was rebirth of long hair, whiskers, and sideburns, and male fashions again cast the male in the role of peacock. By actual measurement it was discovered that young women were taller and more slender than those of the 1940's.

Americans in the United States became a nation of snackers eating some 4.17 times per day. The consumer price index for all items went up some 35 per cent. The price of Coca-Cola increased 50 per cent in the last half of the 1960's. It was established statistically that husbands do engage in housework and that women who work outside of the home spend fewer hours in household work than nonworking wives. Americans living at home ate more meals and snacks away from home, perhaps as many as 13 per cent of them. At the end of the decade they were spending 20 per cent of their food expenditure for food eaten away from home. Ralph Nader became the champion of the consumer.

There was too much change during the 1960's, especially for those over thirty. But, man continues to eat, sometimes he truly dines. Where he eats

1

or dines may change; what he eats may be new and/or different; nonetheless, meals remain. They are essential to all persons for physical well-being; for many persons they are essential for social and psychological reasons as well. There must be a manager of meals in every household, even of one only person; in every human institution whether commune, prison, or nursing home; and in all the diverse kinds of places where meals and snacks can be eaten away from home. Meal management has changed too; it has become a responsibility requiring far more knowledge and skills than formerly.

The causes of change are many; some have come from outside the United States; others are the outcome of developments within the United states. The world has become a global village (1). We have travelled it widely as tourists, workers, and members of the armed forces. We have come to know the foods and food customs of other cultures. We have adopted and adapted so-called foreign foods and dishes, especially those of Oriental countries. They have been added to our cuisine, already a melding of the food customs of many cultures, although the decade of the 1960's revealed that in the United States regional differences in food culture were fast disappearing (4).

We became aware of hunger in the world and at home. We are equally aware that hunger on a far larger scale threatens not only because of the population-food imbalance but also because man has misused and polluted his total environment: the air, the land, and the waters of his rivers, lakes and seas. There has never been enough food for all; cruel as it may seem, population increases were held in check by famine in the past. For the first time in history, nations are dedicating resources—time and energy, knowledge and skills, and money—in the endeavor to prevent famine. Abundant food crops are shared, thereby introducing new and different foods to peoples in all parts of the world. The developments of new and better varieties of grains, vegetables, and fruits; of crossbreeds of animals and of poultry; of new and different food sources, such as bacteria, yeasts, and algae; of designed foods like the meat analogs, nondairy foods, and cereal mixtures like Incaparina change meals now and will change them further in the future.

Developments from within the United States that have affected meals and their management are several. Some developments have had more effect than others; some have acted together to effect change. Our affluence, as much if not more than any other factor, changes our meals and the meal management task. However, it could not have effected the impact that it has were it not that technological and agricultural developments produced a prodigious food supply. A study made by the United States Department of Agriculture in 1965—it will often be referred to in the text—disclosed that urban families in the lowest third of income were eating more meat, poultry, and fish than families in the highest third were in the spring of 1942 (4). We can spend more for food, we can buy expensive foods. Affluence has encouraged an ever-increasing sophistication about food and wine. Cooking schools flourish. "The French Chef" and "The Galloping Gourmet" have extensive television audiences. New cookbooks are published monthly, some are best sellers. For several reasons, one of which is affluence, more persons know more about more foods (from abalone and buffalo meat to zucchini) and about more dishes (from *arroz paella* and *boeuf à la Bourguignonne to zabaglione*) than ever before. Fondues, *sukiyaki,* and cheese and wine tastings have become commonplace. Growing sophistication about food is also attributable to increased leisure, man's need to be creative, higher levels of education, and travel outside of the United States.

Research and development by the food industries have produced all kinds of semiprepared and ready-prepared foods that an affluent society can purchase. Meals of the 1970's, whether eaten at home or elsewhere, will be composed from mass-produced foods and dishes. Home-cooked meals—our literature abounds in descriptions of them—have entered the realm of nostalgia along with other facets of life "of the good old days." This statement is not a contradiction of the earlier statement about our increasing interest in food. The preparation of time-consuming and elaborate dishes has been made easier because of the availability of ready-made products and convenient ingredients that provide shortcuts in cookery. Working housewives find the convenience products indispensable.

Families eat more meals away from home than formerly: at school, company cafeteria, restaurant, and drive-in. Families eat fewer meals together than they did just a few years ago, partly because of the availability of meals at school for children but also because homemakers work outside the home.

The food markets in which we shop have changed some in recent years; supermarkets have increased the variety of offered services. Discount food stores and convenience stores were developments of the 1960's. The number of items offered in supermarkets increased to an average of eight thousand in 1970. Because there are different types of food stores and many items to choose among, the meal manager has to make many decisions that she was spared just a few years ago.

The cost of food at home rose by 27 per cent during the 1960's. Rising food prices alter the meals of some families; more hamburger and less steak, more beans and bread and less meat, and so on. Antipoverty programs resulted in making available more and better meals for some families through educational and other measures.

Though formal and informal education produced an awareness of nutritive needs both qualitative and quantitative, diets of the mid-1960's were not as good as those of the mid-1950's (2). Mass communication about heart disease effected an awareness of the need for maintenance of a desirable weight and for regulation of the kinds of fat consumed; in turn, the character of meals was altered for many persons. Further, the sedentary nature of the lives of most persons also altered the character of meals, even of children.

Decision-making by the meal manager has become increasingly complex as change occurred. The complexity of this problem has been recognised in a consumer movement, described as consumerism, that has been generated and is gaining in strength. Important to the manager of meals is the trend toward the unit pricing of foods and the open dating of perishable foods. Important achievements of the 1960's were passage of the Fair Packaging and Labeling Act of 1966, amended laws regulating the wholesomeness of meat and poultry products, and the study of the Food and Drug Administration by Ralph Nader's Raiders.

In the chapters of this text, we shall explore further the changes that have occurred in recent years. We shall define meal management and explore in depth the decisions the meal manager must make. We shall provide some information for decision-making and for carrying out the decisions made. In spite of some changes in the character of our meals, they remain sources of pleasures of different kinds for different persons. One such pleasure is the sheer enjoyment of food. One of the changes of recent years for many persons is that meals no longer taste as good as formerly. We continue to share our food in the gesture of friendship. We continue to celebrate great occasions with special meals. We continue to use the food we eat and the meals we serve as symbols, perhaps of our real or imagined status and sophistication. And finally, we continue to socialize through meals. What matter if our meals are smaller, or are simpler, or are more quickly prepared, or are prepared from ready-made dishes, or are more sophisticated, or include exotic foods and dishes, or are more simply served?

REFERENCES CITED

1. McLuhan, Marshall. *Understanding Media: The Extensions of Man.* New York: McGraw-Hill Book Company, 1964.
2. "Quality of Diets in U.S. Households in Spring, 1965," *Family Economics Review*, Consumer and Food Economics Research Division, United States Department of Agriculture, Washington, D.C. (March 1968), p. 6.
3. Walman, Elizabeth, "Changes in the Labor Force Activity of Women," *Monthly Labor Review*, Bureau of Labor Statistics, United States Department of Labor, Washington, D.C. (June 1970) , pp. 9-12.
4. "What Americans Eat . . . Why It Is Important to Know," *Toward the New*, Agriculture Bulletin No. 341, Agricultural Research Service, United States Department of Agriculture, Washington, D.C. (April 1970), p. 8.

Chapter I

Meal Management— Some Concepts and Definitions

In 1970, personal expenditures for food in the United States were $114.3 billion in contrast to $70.1 billion in 1960, an increase of 60 per cent. The former was, however, an expenditure of only 16.7 per cent of disposable personal income compared with 20 per cent in 1960. During the decade, the food price index for food eaten at home rose from 100.6 to 127.7 and for food eaten away from home from 105.5 to 155.4. Reported sales of food in grocery stores in 1970 were $88.415 billion. This is the expenditure for meals and snacks eaten in the home or carried out of the home for consumption. It was about 80 per cent of household food spending, the remaining 20 per cent was spent for meals and snacks eaten away from home. A study of household food consumption made in 1965 revealed that the percentage of meals eaten away from home ranged from 9 to 16 per cent as income rose from $3,000 to $8,000 and over; the average was 13 per cent (4). Similarly, the percentage of snacks eaten away from home ranged from 14 to 20 per cent; the average was 18 per cent. These data would seem to suggest that to eat is to spend and that, by and large, Americans eat at home. Thirteen per cent of meals away from home, assuming that 21 meals are eaten each week, averages out to be only 2.7 meals per week.

A recently reported study of housewives in Seattle, Washington (3) revealed that the average homemaker spent 18.5 hours per week on food preparation and dishwashing, almost twice as much as for house care. This was 37.5 per cent of the time devoted to household tasks and it was 5.2 hours more than were utilized by homemakers for food preparation and dishwashing in 1920. The authors of the study suggested that the reasons for the increased use of time in 1968 were less help from children and less hired help available than formerly. Another study (6), though it established that husbands spend time in household work, disclosed that they do not provide much help in meal-related activities: only six to twelve minutes per day. It appears that in spite of the economic, social, and technological developments of this twentieth century, the contemporary homemaker, or housewife, devotes not only more hours but a higher percentage of her household-work hours to meal-related activities than did her grandmother.

Meal-related activities include both decision-making and action. We shall call the person who carries the responsibility for providing meals the meal manager; the responsibility, meal management. The meal manager makes decisions *ad infinitum:* what to serve, how much to spend, where to shop, how much to buy, how to prepare food, how much time to spend on meals, how to serve meals, at what hour to serve meals, how to equip the kitchen, how to furnish the dining area, and so on. She makes decisions in her kitchen and in the marketplace. She makes decisions that affect the family, and she makes decisions that affect only her. Her decisions are not all the same this week, nor will all be the same next week. Many of her decisions are routinely made, as if by habit. Others are thoughtfully made.

The meal manager engages in a variety of tasks: she is a hostess, a dietitian who plans the family meals, a purchasing agent, an organizer of things, an organizer of tasks, and a supervisor of others when she receives assistance. She is chef, waitress, maid in the kitchen, and janitor in both the kitchen and the dining area. She may also be an artist when she sets her table and serves her meals. As manager of meals she has and well deserves the most expensive room in the house.

DECISION-MAKING

When a variety of goods and services is available, we are forced to choose from among them—a kind and cut of meat, a way of preparing potatoes, a kind of vegetable, a brand of canned peaches, a kind of breakfast cereal, a kind and brand of cake mix, and so on. When more than one course of action is open, we are forced to decide—to shop where stamps are given or at a nonstamp store, to shop Wednesday or Friday, to serve dinner at six or at eight o'clock, and so on.

It is possible to map the sequential steps in arriving at choice, that is, in decision-making. First is the recognition that there is a condition of choice. Next is the discovery of what choices. Then would come the weighing of the relative merits of possible choices, that is, of alternative choices. Finally, would come the choice from among alternatives. This sequence of steps can be illustrated by a decision as to which potato product to buy. A trip through the supermarket brings the knowledge that potatoes may be purchased other than in bags of fresh potatoes.

Potatoes are available canned in various styles; frozen in various styles for cooking at home and frozen precooked; and dehydrated for mashing and in mixes for preparing various kinds of potato dishes. From information given on packages, it is possible to estimate the cost of comparable numbers of servings of potatoes and to estimate the time required for the preparation of a particular potato dish. A choice can be made solely on the basis of cost, or it may take into account the amount of time required for preparation, or it might be made on the basis of palatability. All choices are made from some frame of reference or set of criteria. They are made for something, goals to be achieved or satisfactions wanted. The meal manager's goal may be maximizing her food dollars; in this situation, she would choose to buy bags of fresh potatoes most months of the year. Her goal could be saving her time; in this situation, she might buy a canned, or a frozen ready-prepared, or an "instant" potato product. Or, her goal could be the maximum enjoyment of the potato as a food; in this situation, she might purchase fresh potatoes of a given variety and grade.

Many decisions of all meal managers are rational ones made objectively to achieve a recognized end, such as maximizing the dollars allocated for food. For example, beef is bought when it is cheaper than pork; pork when it is cheaper than beef; nonfat dry milk instead of bottled milk; frozen peas instead of frozen asparagus; bananas instead of strawberries; and tuna instead of shrimp. Or, the meal manager chooses corn, not beets; beef, not lamb; hamburger, not beef liver; cornflakes, not oatmeal because of food preferences. Decisions made on the basis of food likes are rational decisions. The decision to buy a ready-made cherry pie instead of baking one from basic ingredients would be a rational decision if a limited supply of time for meal preparation directed it. Rational decisions are thought-out decisions; they make use of information. The meal manager makes nonrational decisions too. These are decisions affected by the feelings of people, beliefs, reactions to past experience, what people think of us, what people anticipate, the self-image, sentiment, and so on. These decisions effect emotional satisfactions. Meals planned and prepared for special occasions and for guests are very often fashioned by nonrational decision-making. They often require greater expenditures of time, energy, and money than is realistic in terms of resources; however, these expenditures are amply rewarded in such personal satisfactions as being recognized as a great cook, as a gracious hostess, or as having great sophistication regarding food.

Man has many wants, he is a seeker after satisfactions. Few men can satisfy all wants; we must decide which ones to strive for—these are goals. We contrive within the limits of our means or resources to achieve them. Our wants and resources provide the frame of reference for making decisions. To paraphrase, one can say that decision-making forces us to manipulate what we have to get what we want. What we have, we shall discuss next; what we want, after we discuss resources.

RESOURCES

The homemaker's resources are nonhuman and human. For the great majority of families, money is the one nonhuman resource that is readily recognizable, measurable, and controllable, that is, manageable. First, and foremost, the money resource is used to purchase food. Second, it is used to equip a kitchen. Equipping a kitchen involves expenditures for some or all of the following: range, refrigerator, freezer, dishwasher; small equipment like toaster, electric frypan, mixer, electric can opener, and automatic coffee maker; pots and pans for cookery; tools for cookery like good knives for cutting and spoons for stirring; and small items like dish towels, potholders, paper goods, soaps, cleansers, and so forth. Third, the money resource is used for the dining area and its furnishings, including linens, dinnerware, flatware, beverageware, and assorted accessories. Fourth, the money resource can be used to buy service—in convenience foods, in the employment of a maid or a cook, and in meals eaten away from home.

All else being equal, different families allocate their nonhuman resources in different ways—they spend different sums for food and for the kitchen and dining areas because families differ in their value systems and goals. What families eat, where they eat it, and how they eat it are personal and private decisions, made by the homemaker alone or with other family members.

Human resources include time, energy, knowledge, skills, and abilities. To provide meals for a family, time must be invested in planning meals, shopping for food, the care and storage of food, preparing and serving meals, clean-up after meals, the care of the kitchen and its equipment, and the care of the dining area and its furnishings. The time available and decisions on how to use it partly determine the character of any family's meals, both as to the kind of food eaten and the manner of dining.

In addition to time, one or more persons must expend energy—that is, do the hand-and-foot work of preparing and serving meals. Energy is expended in shopping, the care of food, cooking, table setting, waiting on the table, clean-up after meals, and the care of the kitchen and its equipment and of the dining area and its furnishings. Here, too, the available supply of energy and the willingness to use it partly determine the character of meals. Time and energy may be equally available to many families, yet they may eat dissimilar meals, served quite differently, because willingness to devote time and energy to meals depends on the values placed on them. If, at the one extreme, the goal is that mealtime is merely for refueling the body, any food is satisfactory, and any quick manner of eating suffices. Food may go from range to plate to dining counter—and as soon as it is empty, the plate may be taken to the sink and deposited as the eater departs. If, on the other hand, the goal is that mealtime provides a period of relaxed interaction and opportunity for congenial conversation for the family, whether guests are present or not, each dish may be meticulously prepared, the table painstakingly set to provide a soul-satisfying background for the meal, the food served from the dining table, the table cleared between courses, and the meal prolonged over a last cup of coffee.

Very important among the homemaker's resources are her knowledge, skills, and abilities. They determine, to no small extent, how much money, time, and energy she expends on the meal responsibility, for the uses of her resources are interrelated. The more knowledge, abilities, and skills she has, the less money, time, and energy she need spend to achieve a given end. The better she knows how to shop in today's markets, the better she can control food expenditures. The less money she has to spend, the more time and energy she may have to spend. The more money she has, the more ready-prepared and quick-cooking foods she can buy, thereby reducing expenditures of time and energy. And the better she knows how to organize the tasks involved and the more skill she has in food preparation and meal serving, the more control she has over the expenditures of money, time, and energy.

It has been suggested that how families use the resources of money, time, energy, knowledge, skills, and abilities depends on their goals and values. Given similar resources, similar families may use them very differently. For example, the Smiths may spend more money than the Browns. Let us say that the Smiths enjoy eating foods that are expensive to purchase and that they dine from a table set with exquisite appointments in a dining room expensively furnished. The Smiths' expenditures bring them such satisfactions that they may be willing to provide for other wants less expensively. On the other hand, the Browns may dine on frugal fare in Spartan simplicity because they prefer to spend money for books, travel, a rose garden, two homes, or, in fact, any number of things. In the same vein, the Smiths may dine together leisurely once each day, regardless of each member's commitments, which are of secondary importance to them. At the Browns, meals may be of the eat-and-run variety, rarely occasions when all dine together.

Beyond satisfying the need for food, meals satisfy other wants: the sensuous enjoyment of good food, the aesthetic experience provided by food and surroundings, the need to be with people, the need to be part of a group, the desire to emulate those held in high regard, the search for prestige and status. Meals may be the symbol of something a homemaker wants for her family or that the family itself wants. When meals mean more than simply meeting physiological needs, the family dedicates resources accordingly in order to satisfy other wants. Meals that are intended merely to fill the stomach may be described as sloppy, slipshod, or impossible by the meticulous. The meals of those with high standards for food and service may be described as fussy, ridiculous, or impossible by others. Differences in meal habits and customs among families result from differences in value systems.

So much for resources—now let us examine the values and goals that influence decisions on the use of resources.

GOALS

It is probably easier to talk about goals than values. Goals are wants; they are close and meaningful. On the other hand, the values that prompt us to select specific goals are much less evident and are neither visable nor touchable. In fact, awareness of just what values motivate us is less common than unawareness. Keeping in mind that values determine goals and that the two belong together, we will first consider the home-maker's goals for family meals—perhaps it would be fairer to say the family's goals for family meals.

At least four general goals related to meals can be cited. The first goal is good nutrition. Study of the national diet reveals that some families are well fed—although not all persons within each family are equally well fed. During this century perceptible changes in national food habits would suggest that lip service only is paid to the principles of nutrition. That our personal diets do not reflect our knowledge is difficult to explain because nonrational factors influence one's choice of what to eat. Perhaps, personal experience and preference, social and emotional maturity, desire to conform or deviate, and personal values and goals are some explanations for the failure of some members within a family to take advantage of nutritionally adequate meals. In an era during which attention is focused on good nutrition during the prenatal period, the child is fed according to strict pediatric practice during infancy and early childhood, and nutrition education continues through the early school years, it is difficult to be unaware of the significance of good nutrition. It would be strange, indeed, were good nutrition not a goal of the modern homemaker.

A second goal in meal management is that meals not cost too much; that is, a goal of planned spending for food. This goal is real for almost all meal managers whether they are responsible for the meals for the small nuclear family, the members of a commune, an army, persons in a retirement home, prisoners, hospital patients, or the general public eating meals in school lunchrooms, drive-ins, or gourmet restaurants. How much is "too much" depends on the extent of the money resource and the debt commitments and spending plans of a given family. There is a minimum essential cost for the nutritionally good diet; however, nutritionally adequate meals can be purchased at widely different levels of spending. The amount of money essential for feeding a family depends on the size of the family, the age composition of the family, and the region of residence. The estimated cost per week—United States average—of a low-cost plan for a family of four with school-age children was approximately $30.70 in March, 1971; of a liberal-cost plan, approximately $48.20. The range in cost of a low-cost plan was from $28.70 in the South to $34.70 in the Northeast; the costs of the plan for the West and the North Central region were similar and about $31.50 (1).

In general, the character of family meals and snacks is determined by the amount of money available to buy them or the amount of money set aside to buy them. Inflation paralleled with rising costs for goods and services, unemployment, and recession in 1970 forced families to regulate spending for food. Two surveys were made during 1970 by a large advertising agency to determine how women economized in their food and nonfood spending. The second survey revealed that three out of four housewives cut back on food expenditures in 1970 compared with 1969. Some thrift measures practiced were comparison shopping; patronage of discount markets; buying less expensive items within food classes, such as pot roast instead of steak; switching from national brands to store brands; more careful menu planning; and finally, cooking and baking from scratch. Homemakers under twenty-five years old, those with one or more years of college education, and those with incomes of $15,000 and more were the sharpest shoppers who got the most for the dollars they spent (2).

There was in 1970, a spate of books, magazine essays, newspaper articles, booklets, brochures, supermarket leaflets, United States Department of Agriculture leaflets, and radio and television discourses on how to spend wisely and how to save money in food buying. There is still no end in sight to the movement.

In 1970, 16.7 per cent of disposable personal income was used for food. According to the Bureau of Labor Statistics' budgets for three standards of living, the percentage of the cost of family consumption for food ranges from about 33 per cent to 25 per cent for the lower and higher budgets respectively. Rising incomes in the United States have been paralleled with an ever increasing number of wants and needs. According to 1970 census data, 65 per cent of families owned a home; 30 per cent owned two or more cars; 40 per cent, a color television set; 40 per cent, a clothes dryer; and 17 per cent, a dishwasher. Some families limit spending for food in order to satisfy other wants and some families spend what they can; but for almost all, limited spending, that is, planned spending, is a goal.

A third goal for meals is that they be the kind the family wants to eat. This goal offers explanations as to why we spend more for meals than is required to purchase the nutritionally good diet; why some persons over-eat; why some persons do not consume a nutritionally good diet; and why some families spend more time and energy on meals than others do. All persons have some food preferences; these are learned and not quickly changed. The kinds of meals we like are established by such influences as ethnic background, family customs, region of residence, socioeconomic background, education, religion, and the experiences we have had.

Meals provide satisfactions such as the enjoyment of food per se. We eat what we like and we like what we eat. Fortunately, food preferences do change; for example, millions have learned to like instant coffee and store-bought bread. In the 1970's and 1980's, it is quite probable that the foods and dishes of which meals are now composed will undergo change whether we like it or not. It has been suggested that, with the exception of the beliefs and practices associated with a religious concept, resistance to new and different foods is not strong if economic or labor-saving advantages are to be gained (5). Perhaps the goal that meals satisfy will, before the end of the century, like so much else, just fade away.

The meal manager's last goal is to fit the responsibility for meals into her planned use of time and energy. Time is required for planning meals and organizing the hand-and-foot work of meals; time and energy are required for shopping, meal preparation, and clean-up after meals. The ready acceptance of convenience foods, the mixes and ready-mades, is evidence that we place a high value on time and wish to save it; it also indicates that we wish to bypass the tedious tasks of cooking. In essence, today's homemaker tailors her meals to her time. She serves thirty-minute dinners when her time is short; she may spend the better part of a day preparing a meal when time permits. Time and energy are budgeted as is money. As different families budget their money differently, so do they budget their time and energy differently. But, out of necessity or design, all families place limits on the use of time and energy.

VALUES

Man is a valuing animal. He does not find all things equally good or equally desirable; he prizes some things more highly than others. At any moment in time, all men do not find things of equal value. And, what man or any man values can change with time. What each person prizes are his values and not all of these are of equal importance to him. He organizes his values into a structure according to relative importance—a hierarchy of values. The decade of the 1960's is presumed to have witnessed some changes in such values as the attainment of material success, of racial equality, of freedom from poverty, and of equal rights for women.

Values and their relative importance establish wants and goals and

thereby pattern behavior. Through history man has valued many different things: success as measured in a given culture, equality, peace, religious freedom, genuine love of fellowman, the high regard of peers,
self-esteem, prestige, status as determined in a given culture, beauty,
plumpness—a happy stomach, piety, health, loving and being loved,
being of service to mankind, thrift, work, leisure time, safety of person,
sensuous pleasures, freedom to be oneself and do one's own thing, and so
on *ad infinitum*. We have symbols for our values: long hair, love beads,
the car we drive, the kind of house in which we live, the neighborhood
in which we live, the kinds of food we eat, the kinds of meals we eat and
serve, the music we listen to, the way we dress, the art objects we own,
and, again, so on *ad infinitum*. Our wants are symbols of our values.

We do not always know what we value. The more we seek to know and
understand what we value the better we understand our wants and
behavior. Not infrequently our values are in conflict. For example, the
desire to maintain a desirable body weight and the desire to eat apple pie
à la mode for dessert are not always compatible. We are torn between the
values of health and pleasure. Similarly our goals are often in conflict. We
live in an era of "gracious living" and "casual but elegant dining"—if we
believe the magazines and the advertising—but the supply of time and
energy to devote to meals is not consistent with such a goal for many
families except for occasional meals.

It is not difficult to postulate ways in which family meals reflect the
values of the family and/or the meal manager. The allocation of resources
to meals is a clue; goals are another. The value we place on health
explains the goal of good nutrition for meals. When material wants are
many, money may be conservatively allocated for the purchase of meals,
and the kinds of food eaten reflect this. When the enjoyment of food,
especially expensive food, takes first place, both dollars and time and
energy may be allocated inordinately to meals that will surely display this
enjoyment. When little time is allocated to the preparing or the eating of
meals, it may tell us that meals per se are little valued but that other
activities, either leisure-time or service-oriented, are highly valued. In an
era of ready-mades, the home preparation of meals may reflect that the
meal manager intends to live up to her image of herself as a "good
mother," or that she needs to be creative, or that the family has fallen on
bad times economically. Meals can be symbols of love and affection; all
persons—father, mother, child—occasionally use resources extravagantly
to this end.

ACHIEVING MEAL MANAGEMENT GOALS

Meal management is making decisions; it is also action, that is,
planning meals, shopping for food, storing food, meal preparation, table

setting and waiting on the table, dishwashing, care of the kitchen and its equipment, and care of the dining area and its furnishings.

Random reading gives the impression that housewives in the United States neither plan their meals nor know how to shop for food. Probably nothing is further from the truth. Admittedly, many select a miscellany of foods for the next meal within minutes of the meal hour and from resources on hand. And, admittedly, many persons make unanticipated purchases while shopping for food. That is not to say that these impromptu decisions are less wise than premeditated ones. Indeed, it would be strange if experience did not enable the manager of meals to behave in just that manner.

Some experienced housewives shop from a prepared list, partly because it suggests possible purchases, but more importantly, because it is a reminder of needs. Others shop without lists; they rely on memory and reminders received as they progress through the market. Often decisions are delayed until they see what the market has to offer: whether beef or pork is the better buy and whether the broccoli or the cauliflower is of superior quality that particular day. Some accomplished homemakers shop with specific meal plans in mind; others have only general ones, which crystallize into clear plans as they shop. Still others simply buy an assortment of foods from which they ultimately design meals. Through happy and unhappy experiences in food purchasing and menu planning, plus continual repetition, shopping for food and planning meals can become routine. Both come to be accomplished more or less effortlessly because they become habitual.

However, this text has been written for beginners. For them, it is desirable to discuss the role and value of planning in meal management. It is undeniable that concrete plans, made in relation to goals, are of utmost importance until experience makes it possible to make proper decisions more or less spontaneously. Further, it is desirable to point out that some kinds of plans, especially those related to the production of special meals, may be done in great detail even by those who have had much experience. In fact, in such situations it is quite likely that those with the most experience will do the most planning.

Planning is for something—in this instance, it is for meals that are what the homemaker and her family want them to be. Because these goals are several, planning to achieve them involves decisions among many alternatives: when to serve which foods, so that meals may be varied and pleasing; how best to use available time; what foods among those on the market are right for the budget; which convenience items fit the budget, and which are too expensive at this time.

Such questions are answered in planning meals. Perhaps *planning for meals* better suggests the nature of the task. Planning for meals is planning that begins before shopping for food, and continues during shopping and preparation. It often does not end until the meal is over, for a person may revise the plan for dessert while eating the main course. In a more restricted sense, meal planning involves nothing but menu planning, that is, selecting the foods for a given meal. In the broader sense, meal planning includes menu making in accordance with goals plus plans for shopping, preparing, and serving meals. Let us agree again that housewives with long experience may accomplish this planning without apparent plans or shopping lists; they plan, shop, prepare, and serve meals according to habit. The beginner, on the other hand, has to make many decisions; she or he even has to learn the fundamentals that provide the bases for making decisions. It is ironical that the decisions of the beginner who has the fewest resources of money, time, knowledge, and skill are more critical than those of the experienced housewife who probably has more of these resources. The shorter the supply of resources, the more important it is that decisions be the right ones.

Young homemakers soon, if not immediately after marriage, discover that expenditures for food must be limited if the young family is to satisfy its many wants. Limiting this resource may preclude the purchase of much convenience food, which means that time and energy have to go into the production of meals. Further, a limited budget means more careful selection of foods to derive a nutritionally good diet. The young homemaker will progress more rapidly to the habit stage of handling the meal responsibility and will manage it more effectively if she begins by planning for meals in concrete fashion in advance of shopping. She can accomplish this by tentatively drafting the menus of meals to be eaten at home for several days ahead. To use her time efficiently, she should plan for an entire week, so that shopping time can be limited to one weekly trip to the supermarket. Each day of the week, one or more markets advertise; from these ads she can learn what foods are in good supply and what are featured "specials" for the week. Using this information, which can help her spend her food budget skillfully, paying attention to nutritive needs, keeping in mind her work schedule, and working around food likes and dislikes, she can compose her menus. From these she can draw up her shopping list. During marketing, she may alter choices in relation to the quality of available foods and to bargains espied. On her return from shopping, her tentatively composed menus can be revised and completed in accordance with the best use of her time and with her plans for serving.

Many homemakers will argue that such planning of meals in advance is not only time consuming but wastes time because emergencies arise which require alterations of plans. The latter is true—it does happen. However, there are at least five benefits to be derived from thoughtful preplanning of the family's meals.

First, an hour or so spent in planning—that is, composing menus and shopping lists and drafting plans for preparing and serving meals—saves time and energy in shopping, cooking, and planning each meal as the hour for it approaches. Time and energy are saved in shopping because the number of shopping trips can be calculated and restricted. The meal manager saves time by the dovetailing of preparations in the kitchen— making ready one or more parts of tomorrow's meals while preparing and cleaning up after today's dinner, for example. Finally, having made careful plans for the meals of the week, the homemaker need spend no more time in decision-making. And, if she keeps her plans from week to week, she finds that planning becomes easier and less time consuming each successive week because each old plan is evaluated in the light of its merits and gives ideas for new plans.

A second reason for planning meals is that precise planning makes it easier to control the expenditure of money for food in at least four ways. First, food choices can be made deliberately to conform to the planned level of spending. Second, choices of more and of less expensive foods can be juggled to arrive at a final total expenditure consistent with spending plans. Third, planned menus lead to planned shopping, a practice that minimizes waste. Fourth, spending can be regulated because meals planned in the market on the spur of the moment tend to be costly. They are apt to be composed of favored foods or ready-to-eat dishes. Quick, uncalculated decisions by the beginner often account for her failure to control spending.

A third reason for planning for meals is to achieve the goal of good nutrition. Meals planned on the spur of the moment may or may not provide for good nutrition. No meal stands alone in meeting nutrient needs; the three for the day must be considered as a unit. For that matter, as more and more members of the family eat the noon meal away from home, the two meals eaten at home become more important. The homemaker, unless she packs lunches, has little control over meals consumed away from home. To ensure good nutrition, she may find it desirable to consider the two meals eaten at home as a unit. She may plan to include in them most of the foods suggested in the model proposed in Chapter 12 for planning nutritionally good meals. It is not difficult to plan nutritionally good meals, nor is it difficult to consume the foods essential to a good diet. It is desirable, however, to plan for good nutrition because no one instinctively eats the nutritionally good diet.

By the late 1970's or 1980's the enrichment of foods and the designing of foods to meet nutritive needs may have progressed to the point where it will no longer be necessary to plan for good nutrition—good nutrition will have become inescapable.

A fourth reason for advance planning for meals is that planned meals can include a wider variety of foods than meals hurriedly composed and prepared. There are several arguments in favour of a varied diet. First, the nutritionally good diet can be more easily planned when many instead of a few foods can be included in meals. All foods make some nutrient contribution to the diet, but few are precisely alike, the nutrient content of the diet is the sum total of the nutrient contributions of many different foods. Second, the nutritionally good diet can be more inexpensively purchased when many different foods can be used so that inexpensive choices can balance more expensive ones. Last, it is easier to plan meals that provide eating satisfactions when a variety of foods is included. There are persons who are satisfied with a diet composed of a few foods; however, the great majority of persons do not like a monotonous diet.

A last reason for planning meals is to help form good meal-planning habits. Experience in deciding what to serve, how much to spend, and how much time and energy to invest in meals favors the development of good judgment in meal management. Habits result from repetitious behavior.

Summary. To sum up, meal management is decision-making and action. Decisions are made in accordance with desired satisfactions; but they must realistically recognize resources: the available supply of money, time and energy, and the knowledge, skills, and abilities of one or more persons. General goals for meals are that they provide good nutrition; that they not exceed in cost an established plan for spending; that they be satisfying; and that they not exceed established limits on the use of time and energy. Meals are sources for satisfactions that are not alike for all persons or families. Neither the decisions made nor the action engaged in in meal management will be universally the same, even of very similar family groups.

Chapters 5 through 11 provide information of use in making decisions relative to food buying. Chapters 12 through 15 provide assistance in planning meals to match established goals. Later chapters are concerned with the action of meal management: meal preparation, table setting, and serving meals. Chapters 2 through 4 are descriptive of the world in which the manager of meals operates.

REFERENCES CITED

1. "Cost of Food at Home," *Family Economics Review,* Consumer and Food Economics Research Division, United States Department of Agriculture, Washington, D.C. (March 1971), pp. 34–36.
2. "The Cost of Food: How Women Are Trying to Stretch Their Food Budgets," *Monthly Information Service,* Foote, Cone, and Belding Advertising, Inc., New York (June 1970).
3. Hall, Florence, and M. P. Schroeder, "Time Spent on Household Tasks," *Journal of Home Economics* 62:23 (1970).
4. LeBovit, Corinne, "Foods Eaten Away from Home," *National Food Situation,* Economic Research Service, United States Department of Agriculture, Washington, D.C. (May 1970), pp. 25–31.

5. Niehoff, Arthur, "Food Habits and Cultural Patterns," in *Food, Science, and Society,* Nutrition Foundation, Inc., New York (1969), p. 68.
6. "Time Used by Husbands for Household Work," *Family Economics Review,* Consumer and Food Economics Research Division, United States Department of Agriculture, Washington, D.C. (June 1970), p. 8.

Chapter 2
The Market Place and the Consumer

Food retailing in the United States is the largest of all retailing enterprises; it has more customers and takes in more dollars than any other. It is also the most efficient retail distributor. In 1970, sales in retail food outlets reached an all-time high of $94.53 billion. Of this vast sum, $88,415 million were spent in grocery stores; the remainder, in such specialty stores as bakeries and meat markets. We spent 22.7 per cent of the retail dollar in food stores versus 7.7 per cent of the retail dollar in eating and drinking places. This means that approximately 75 per cent of the food expenditure was spent in food stores (42).

TYPES OF FOOD STORES

The food store industry classifies food stores as follows: specialty stores —in general, small units that offer only one type of food, such as bakeries, meat markets, fish markets, cheese shops, vegetable markets, fast food outlets; grocery and combination stores—departmentalized stores offering different classes of foods and groceries, i.e., the supermarket and the convenience store; and the new combination store which is a supermarket and a department store with common checkouts. Specialty stores had only about 6.5 per cent of sales in 1970. They offer the consumer variety as in the cheese shop and, sometimes, price advantage as in the dairy store.

Stores are classified on the basis of annual volume of business as supermarkets, superettes, and small stores. The *supermarket* is a departmentalized retail food store with at least the grocery department fully self-service and with annual sales of $500,000 or more; the *superette* is a store with sales of from $150,000 to $500,000 per year; and a *small store* has sales of less than $150,000 per year. In 1970, small stores far outnumbered the others but they had only 12 per cent of grocery store sales. In 1970, 38,300 supermarkets had 75 per cent of grocery store sales; 33,500 superettes had about 13 per cent of sales, just slightly more than the small stores.

Food stores are independents or units of chains. A *chain* operates eleven or more retail stores. An independent store is one of a group of ten or less. In 1970, as in preceding years, the number of independent stores far exceeded the number of chain stores, 174,100 to 34,200. However, the volume of sales of the independents was only about 52.4 per cent of total sales.

On the basis of ownership, stores are corporately owned or retailer owned. Corporately owned chains are numerous; among the top ten are the Great Atlantic and Pacific Tea Company (A&P), Safeway Stores, Food Fair, Jewel Companies, and National Tea Company. Although retailers may operate wholly independently, many affiliate with a wholesaler or a retailer-owned cooperative for advantageous buying and other services. The retailer who affiliates with a wholesaler does so voluntarily; hence, the designation *voluntary group* for stores affiliated with a wholesaler. The retailer member of such a group has the same name and follows the same advertising and merchandising policies as other stores of the group. There are about seven hundred voluntary groups; well-known voluntary groups include Red and White Stores, Independent Grocers' Alliance (IGA) stores, Clover Farm stores, Super Valu stores, and Spartan Stores. *Retailer-owned cooperatives* are organizations set up to accomplish low-cost buying and other services for retailers. Affiliates of these organizations use names of their own choice and follow their own established practices in advertising and merchandising. Shop-Rite Super Markets of New Jersey and Certified Grocers of California are two such cooperatives. Both voluntary groups and retailer-sponsored groups may be so large as to become chains. Units within these groups may be supermarkets, superettes, or small stores.

The *convenience* store is a miniature supermarket. It is a development of the sixties and represents a return to the "corner grocery store." There were an estimated 14,000 of them in 1971. They offer a wide range of products, but offer a fourth to half as many items as larger markets. They feature convenience of location, long hours, and quick service. They are patronized for items needed between trips to the supermarket. They have a higher margin than supermarkets, they are more expensive stores in which to shop, but an affluent society is willing to pay for their convenience.

A development of the late 1960's was discounting in food retailing. The first discount-type food markets featured low prices; they were either free standing or were departments in discount department stores. By 1970, 30 per cent of all stores, 47 per cent of chain stores, and 27 per cent of independent stores were operating under discount programs. By 1971,

33 per cent of chain supermarkets, 36 per cent of independent super-markets, and 34 per cent of all supermarkets were operating under discount programs. Discounting is selective low pricing. Groceries and certain nonfoods are discounted; perishables are less affected, though the trend of the early 1970's is to discount these also.

The Supermarket

Supermarkets had 75 per cent of grocery store sales in 1970. These departmentalized food stores are a development of the twentieth century. Many conditions and factors—technological, economic, agricultural, social, and psychological—favored the phenomenal growth of the super-market and its smaller versions, the superette and convenience store. We shall mention only a few of these factors. The first and of great significance was the automobile, which made shopping possible beyond the immediate neighborhood. Second were technological advances in refrigeration, food processing, and food packaging. These made possible self-service and the sale of a diversity of products within the supermarket. Further, shopping could be reduced to one trip per week as soon as families had refrigerators and freezers. Third was the development of a vast body of knowledge within the industry of how to retail food—and, later, non-food merchandise—efficiently at low cost. Fourth, women entered the labor market in ever-increasing numbers. They wanted self-service to minimize the time and work investment in shopping; they wanted one-stop shopping; and they wanted low prices and quality. Fifth, families moved to the suburbs. Lastly, incomes rose and food consumption habits changed.

Supermarket Development.   Large food markets in the United States date back to 1658 and the Faneuil Hall Market in Boston, Massachusetts. By 1918, there were 174 of these large markets in cities of over thirty thousand in population. They were conglomerates of retailers of diverse kinds of foods. Each retailer occupied a booth or stall in an open-air market or an enclosed structure designated often as "the market." At these large markets, although they purchased from many different retailers, consumers could shop for all their food needs. Three evolving concepts culminated in the supermarket, though it was very like the trading post or general country store that had long been a part of the American scene. These were centralization of management, self-service by the customer, and the cash-and-carry concept. Centralization of management came first. The first departmentalized food store under one ownership was established in Lowell, Massachusetts before the Civil War; it was known as the Lowell Public Market. It was also the first market to precut meat before sale. By the turn of the century, such markets as Ralph's Grocery Company of Los Angeles and Frank Munsey's Mohican Stores had been established under central management. Clerk service and delivery service were the general rule, but self-service had been introduced. It was popularized by Clarence Saunders in the Piggly Wiggly Stores opened in 1916, in Memphis, Tennessee, where he also introduced the turnstile, the checkout, and cash payment for groceries. The idea of self-service succeeded from the beginning. Much to the surprise of many operators, it was discovered that the customer liked to browse and choose. John Hartford of the Great Atlantic and Pacific Tea Company is credited with the cash-and-carry concept. He established, in 1912, economy stores without delivery or credit. But chains were not the inventors or developers of the supermarket. The first market that could be called a supermarket was opened in Jamaica, New York by Michael Cullen in August, 1930.

The depression of the 1930's favored the rapid growth of large self-service markets described as "cheapy" markets. They were departmentalized with meat, bakery, dairy, produce, and grocery departments. Established in low-rent locations on the fringes of densely populated areas, they occupied abandoned warehouses and empty department stores, garages, and factories. Interiors had crude floors, bare ceilings, glaring lights, gaudy signs, and merchandise piled everywhere. Most of the space was allocated to food merchandising although some operators leased space to dealers in hardware, paint, auto accessories, and so on. These "cheapy" markets offered abundant parking space and one-stop shopping. They featured low food prices, a policy they could adopt because of the low cost of their facilities and because of buying practices. King Kullen Stores sold some items at cost, others at 5, 15, and 20 per cent above cost (8). Their success markedly affected the volume of business of independents and chains. By the mid-1930's, the chains started supermarket operations; the Kroger Company in 1935 and the Great Atlantic and Pacific Tea Company in 1937.

Small independent merchants were threatened by both the supermarkets and the chains. They were forced to adopt the supermarket principle. This they accomplished by affiliating either with wholesaler-sponsored or retailer-sponsored groups. There was rapid increase in the number of supermarkets in the late 1930's. There was little expansion during World War II, but an important change in merchandising policy occurred. To hold and expand volume, supermarkets took on nonfood lines, products not previously sold in grocery stores.

There were many developments in the supermarket industry following World War II: larger chains; more and larger supermarkets; more emphasis on nonfood merchandise; more services to consumers; more competition; rising margins and smaller profits; acquisition of food-manufacturing plants, such as bakeries, dairy plants, and slaughter plants by corporate chains and wholesaler-owned affiliations; and studies of the industry both from within and without. Mergers by the chains and within affiliated groups resulted in billion-dollar organizations of which there were ten in 1970. In order of diminishing volume of sales they were the Great Atlantic and Pacific Tea Company, Safeway Stores, the Kroger Company, Acme Markets, Food Fair, the Jewel Companies, the National Tea Company, Lucky Stores, the Winn-Dixie Company, and Grand Union. The Great Atlantic and Pacific Tea Company was the giant with 4,575 stores; Safeway had 2,274, and the Kroger Company, 1,898. The other chains had less than 1,000 stores each in 1970.

By the 1960's the market was saturated. There was a period of nonprice competition during which there was extensive use of stamps, games, and numerous other kinds of promotions. During the 1960's, price competition returned via discounting, and stamps and games declined in use. Inflation and the rising cost of goods and services during the 1960's contributed to these developments.

The food store industry researched itself diligently for two decades. It became knowledgeable on matters of store location, store layout, stock arrangement, pricing, display, checkouts, department location, contribution to sales and margins by department and product category, and advertising and promotion. The principles of efficient operation became well understood and were widely applied. All food markets, whether large or small, came to look alike. During this era, in which the industry matured, it assumed that all customers were average or alike. During the 1960's, the customer was researched and it was discovered that different stores have different kinds of customers; further, that the customers of any one store are not all alike. The trend in the 1970's will be the continued customizing of supermarkets to the predominant clientele; the mix of goods and services will be in response to customer wants. To effect these changes, the managers of supermarkets will have been given incentives and power, as well as sophisticated know-how.

Organization of the Supermarket.   The usual departments of the supermarket are seven: meat, produce, dairy, frozen foods, bakery, grocery, and nonfood. In 1970 the "average" shopper spent each $10.00 in these departments as follows:

Meat, fish, poultry	$2.83
Produce	.76
Dairy foods, including eggs and margarine	1.03
Frozen foods, including ice cream	.45
Baked goods	.50
Groceries	4.05
Nonfood merchandise	.38
	$10.00

The grocery, meat, and dairy departments account for 80 per cent of sales. The nonfoods department and the nonedibles in the grocery department—such items as pet foods, household supplies, paper products, and laundry supplies and soaps and detergents—account for about 20 per cent of sales, about the same as the meat department. The high margin departments are nonfoods, produce, and frozen foods including ice cream; low margin departments are the grocery and dairy departments. *Margin* is the difference between the cost and the selling price of an item expressed in percentage of the retail price; the cost includes the cost of doing business. Average department margins are: meat, 20 per cent; produce and nonfoods, about 30 per cent; frozen foods and ice cream, 25 per cent; baked goods, 20 per cent; dairy, 17 per cent; and grocery, 14 per cent (42). However, department margins vary among different organizations; for example, one may have a low grocery margin and high margins on meat and produce; another may have a low margin on meats and a high margin on groceries. Within departments there is great range in the margins of individual items. For example, within the grocery department the following are high margin items: candy, gum, crackers and cookies, snack foods, and household supplies. Low margin items include sugar, canned soups, detergents, coffee, and canned and nonfat dry milk. The meat and grocery departments offer the most specials; the nonfoods department, few.

Supermarket Buying and Selling. Our interest in the buying and selling functions of the supermarket differ. Our interest in the buying function is academic; our interest in the selling function is personal. Buying is an area of specialization and must be efficient if selling is to take place in a competitive market. Chains have bargaining power, and the larger they are, the greater is this power. Large chains use specialized buyers for routine buying; small organizations may have only one agent for routine buying. The majority of organizations use buying committees made up of a buyer and top advertising, promotion, merchandising, and sales executives for the purchase of new products. Buying by committees favors decision-making unbiased by personal likes and dislikes. Store profits are contingent on selections from among new products that customers will buy. Some companies use consumer panels to assist in the selection of new products. To avoid stocking a new product that may not be accepted by consumers, some chains put new products on trial in test stores.

Food store profits depend on good buying practices, but also on efficient and low-cost selling. Gross margins of stores must cover the cost of store operation and permit profit. Factors that affect costs to retailers and the cost of retailing affect prices paid by customers. Gross margins have trended upward in food stores from an average 18.12 per cent in 1955 to an average 22.48 per cent in 1964. Margins trended downward during the last half of the 1960's in spite of rising wages and costs. In 1970, the average margin of independent stores was 18.8 per cent, the same as in 1969; of chain stores, 19.5, the same as in 1969. For fiscal 1969–1970, the total net income before taxes of a cross-section of chains was 1.86 per cent; net income after taxes was 0.92 per cent. Profits were 9 to 10 per cent of net worth. Independent supermarkets reported 2.5 per cent net income before taxes for 1970. Discounting during 1970 reduced margins to about 17 per cent in markets under discount programs. The food retailing industry is a low-profit industry; for this reason, only sales volume makes it profitable (42).

Price competition among supermarkets declined during the 1950's and early 1960's as a result of retailer affiliations and growth in the size of chains. Further, consumers were affluent and less price conscious than prior to World War II. Competition for the consumer's dollars was so keen that store policies and sales strategies were of utmost consequence. To find ways to expand and hold volume, the industry studied itself extensively. Some of the means it devised for getting and holding customers will be discussed. These include strategies in pricing, strategies in traffic routing and in the art and science of display, advertising and promotions, and customer services.

The National Commission on Food Marketing studied pricing policies of several chains in different cities. The commission found that in two cities each chain's price level for 121 food and nonfood items weighted in accordance with consumption patterns was similar to that of its competitors. Prices were irregular from week to week, with the chains switching places with regard to high and low pricing levels. In two other cities, one chain had a consistently higher price level, two others were similar in pricing policy to the chains in the first-mentioned cities. There did not appear to be a consistent low price store. The commission indicated that specials accounted for pricing irregularities (32). Similar findings (46) were published of a study made by the United States Department of Agriculture. The average weekly cost of a market basket of food over a three-month period was $32.13 as purchased in one store; $32.11, in another. However, a consumer shopping both stores for items advantageously priced would have purchased the market basket at a weekly cost of $28.84 or approximately 10 per cent less. Specials are a form of price competition; they are also a socially beneficial kind of promotion. Only a few hundred out of the eight thousand or more items a supermarket stocks are offered as specials. They are items with high turnover rates and high margins; they are also the items that consumers know the regular cost of—hamburger, sirloin steak, chuck beef roast, coffee, bananas, cake mixes, chicken pot pies, head lettuce, and so on. Consumer studies have shown that consumers read the weekly food store ads and that they buy specials, frequently patronizing more than one store to purchase the best offerings of each. Obviously, stores must price nonspecial items so as to cover the cost of selling specials—each chain and supermarket has a pricing policy that permits profitable operation.

Price competition returned in the 1960's with discounting. By 1971, 34 per cent of all supermarkets, 36 per cent of independent supermarkets, and 33 per cent of all chain supermarkets were discounting. Sales gains were reported by 84 per cent of independents operating under discount policies; the average gains were 25 per cent (42). Two studies reported in the late 1960's revealed price competition in food retailing. A study of food prices in the four major cities of Ohio—Cleveland, Cincinnati, Columbus, and Toledo (37)—revealed that there were statistically significant differences in the cost of a market basket of food as it was purchased in different types of stores. The cost of the market basket was lowest in the discount food store. The cost of the market basket increased in this order: national chain, local chain, regional chain, and affiliated independent. The cost of the market basket was highest in the store that had the biggest share of the market. A study was reported by Kammer and Shawhan (21) of chain supermarkets, chain discount stores, chain convenience stores, and independent stores in Cincinnati, Ohio. Prices in high- and low-income areas were similar but there was price difference by type of store. In order of increasing cost by store type they were chain discount market, chain supermarket, independent store, and, finally, chain convenience store.

Another kind of price competition between supermarkets is in the extent and diversity of private label offerings. Supermarkets got their start in the self-service of nationally or regionally known brands of food products. The supermarket of the 1970's offers national brands but also its own private label items, as well as products manufactured by local and little-known companies. A chain may produce in its own plants its private label merchandise or the chain may acquire it from manufacturers. The big food companies engage in dual branding of their products, that is, such foods as cornflakes, canned milk, or frozen peas may bear the food company's label or they may bear the label of a chain. The same product may be name brand and it may also be private label with a price differential in favor of the item bearing the private label. The original intent of the private label was to establish store loyalty; the intent of the name brand, to establish brand loyalty. Brand loyalty does exist. Product parity also exists in food items as well as other merchandise. Its brand image is carefully nutured by a company and it is for many consumers a symbol of the quality they seek and a guide to decision-making in the supermarket. Private label items sell at lower prices; at equal prices, consumers seem to prefer nationally known brands. Retailer-brand merchandise can undersell advertised brands because the latter must be priced to cover the cost of development, advertising, and promotion. Private label food products include soups, baking mixes, gelatin desserts, pudding mixes, canned milk, nonfat dry milk, cereals, crackers and cookies, canned and frozen vegetables, canned fruits, canned and frozen fruit juices, and so on. Some private labels include such names as Ann Page, Whitehouse, Shurfine, Kroger, Spartan, Thrifty Maid, and Country Club. In general, private label items offer quality at lower cost than comparable national brand products.

To hold and expand volume, supermarkets use strategies in routing traffic through the store and in the art and science of display and detaining the customer. The two areas of the store, the perimeter area and the midstore area, are shopped differently. Positioning of the meat, produce, bakery, and dairy departments around the store perimeter assures heavy perimeter traffic. Midstore displays receive much less customer attention. To divert traffic into midstore aisles strategies are used: good signs that identify product locations, lighted shelving, brightly lettered signs, blinking lights, positioning of the products that draw heavy traffic—coffee, bread, cookies and crackers, baking needs, paper products, canned soups, laundry supplies, cereals, and sugar—to achieve maximum coverage of midstore aisles, and placing advertised specials in light traffic areas. Techniques of display that favor increased sales include full shelf stocking with every available item visible and reachable; "sore-thumb" displays that dramatically call attention to products; multiple pricing of units; the display of go-togethers in adjacent positions, such as potato chips and pretzels beside soft drinks; the display of candies, health and beauty aids, and nonfood goods beside such traffic-drawing items as cereals, soft drinks, and coffee. We are detained, that is, encouraged to spend more time in the supermarket, by such facilities as a snack bar, a kiddie corner, a bakery shop, a gourmet shop, a "wine cellar," a restroom, and free coffee. The longer customers stay in a store the more they spend (9).

Advertising and promotions are means of increasing sales. Together they use 2.4 per cent of the sales dollar when the cost of trading stamps is included, 1.1 per cent when stamps are excluded. Direct advertising uses somewhat less than 1 per cent of the sales dollar (39). Additional advertising costs are paid by food manufacturers through deals offered, especially to the large chains. Media used for advertising include printed matter—newspapers, magazines, circulars, posters—radio, and television. Newspaper advertising uses 52 per cent of the advertising budget. Weekly and biweekly advertisements apprise consumers of sales, specials, and seasonal food supplies. Dickens (15) reported that 59 per cent of white homemakers and 41 per cent of black homemakers were influenced in their food buying by food store advertisements. Roberts (34) summarized the results of a Southern Regional Food Marketing Project: 37 per cent of black homemakers and 46 per cent of white homemakers indicated that they purchased specific foods as a result of newspaper advertising. The higher the income and the higher the educational level, the more the homemakers were influenced by store ads. Twenty-six per cent of white and 21 per cent of black homemakers responded positively to television advertising, only about 7 per cent to radio advertising. In a 1971 study by Burgoyne, Incorporated, almost 80 per cent of queried shoppers stated that they read newspaper food ads in contrast to about 57 per cent in 1954; about 80 per cent read two or more ads (32). According to a 1969 study by the same group, about 40 per cent viewed food store advertising on television; and 14 per cent heard food store advertising on radio (38).

Promotions. Promotions are intended to—and must—bring in customers and to keep them coming, that is, establish store loyalty. Promotion practices include trading stamps, premiums, sales, specials, loss leaders, store coupons, sweepstakes, special offerings of such merchandise as dinnerware, beverageware, and kitchenware at low cost, and, finally, low food prices. During the late 1950's and early 1960's, because of intense competition among supermarkets, there was an explosion of promotions; however, by the end of the 1960's, only low prices, coupons, and stamps remained, and stamp use had declined. Rising food prices and inflation of the dollar caused customer dissatisfaction that focused on promotions. Customers decided nothing was free and that they were paying for the cost of promotions in higher food prices. Food discount stores grew in number and volume of sales; but by this time, saving stamps had become a habit with housewives. Because no one is certain of their future, a brief discussion of the trading stamp follows.

Lures or premiums in the mercantile business are as old as recorded history; the baker's dozen was an early premium of a food merchant. The B. T. Babbitt Company is credited with using the first systematic premium plan in the United States. Beginning in 1851, it placed a coupon inside the wrapper of its soap. Accumulated coupons could be redeemed for pictures. The Great Atlantic and Pacific Tea Company is credited with being the first food retailer to give premiums on a regular and systematic basis. In the 1860's it gave premiums of glassware and crockery to customers. Other tea and coffee companies followed suit, a "me too" policy in business that remains in use in the 1970's.

The first trading stamps were issued by the Schuster Department Store of Milwaukee, Wisconsin, in 1891. The stamps, when a sufficient number had been accumulated, could be redeemed for store merchandise or cash. In 1896, Thomas B. Sperry and Shelley B. Hutchinson founded as an independent business the first trading-stamp company to supply stamps, stamp books, premium catalogs, and merchandise for the redemption of the filled books. The stamps were sold to retailers as a plan for giving their customers a discount on cash purchases. The stamps were a success. An estimate by the Sperry and Hutchinson Company indicated that stamps were being given for about 7 per cent of all retail trade by 1914.

During World War I, this dropped to about 2 per cent of retail trade. Until World War I, the Great Atlantic and Pacific Tea Company was one of the largest users of the S&H green stamp; but, interestingly enough, this company was the last of the large chains to hold out during the resurgence of stamp use in the 1950's. Stamp use increased but little during the 1920's, and it decreased during the Depression of the 1930's and during World War II. Beginning with 1945, but particularly since 1951, the stamp industry experienced phenomenal growth in the number of stamp companies and in sales (18). In 1965, supermarkets and other food stores accounted for 61 per cent of the revenue of stamp companies. The percentage of food store sales by stamp-giving stores rose from 1 per cent in 1950 to 47 per cent in 1963. The percentage of supermarkets owned by members of the Super Market Institute giving stamps rose from 13 per cent in 1954 to 78 per cent in 1962; by 1965, this percentage had declined to 69 per cent. According to *Progressive Grocer,* the percentage of chain supermarkets giving stamps rose to 90 per cent in 1962; it declined to 41 per cent in 1964; by 1969, the percentage was 36 per cent. That same year, 1969, only 27 per cent of independent supermarkets and superettes were giving stamps. In 1970, 31 per cent of local and regional chains and 22.4 per cent of independent supermarkets and superettes used stamps.

The cost of trading stamps to a supermarket was, in 1968, between $25,000 and $35,000 per year; the national average was $27,000 or 2 per cent of the store's gross sales. For stamps to pay their way, they must produce at least a 12 per cent increase in sales. If an increase in sales does not materialize, then a supermarket must raise its prices or cover the cost of stamps by such means as reducing expenditures on advertising or offering customers fewer specials and services. Fox (18) states that empirical research has not definitively established that stamp adoption increases food prices in a food store nor that stamp defection decreases prices. He further states that "trading stamps seem obvious and simple, but they reflect an inextricable conglomeration of consumer motivations and market dynamics" and are categorically neither good nor bad. All of which would seem to put the burden of proof on the consumer. Comparison shopping in stamp and nonstamp stores would disclose the situation locally and would force her to decide in favor of lower prices, if they existed, or stamp acquisition.

In addition to or in place of stamps, games were greatly used in the early 1960's but had declined in use by 1967. In 1966, Mrs. Esther Peterson asked the Federal Trade Commission to investigate them. In a two-year study, the commission found them deceptive, though not actually fraudulent, in overstatement of the chances of winning. In October, 1969, regulations governing games of chance in food retailing became effective. The regulations, among other stipulations, required disclosure of the odds of winning, of the termination date of a game, of the complete list of winners, of the number of prizes available, and of the number of prizes awarded. The use of games in food retailing has faded away.

It is not likely that the 1970's will see an end to promotions. It is quite probable that they will be "part and parcel" of the mix of merchandise and services that the sophisticated consumer of the 1970's demands.

The Supermarket and New Food Items. The supermarkets of 1970 stocked about eight thousand items or more. Not all of them stocked the same number of items and not all of them the same items. The estimated numbers of items handled in food stores since World War I are as follows (42):

Year	Number of Items
1928	867
1946	3,000
1950	3,750
1955	4,723
1962	6,600
1964	6,900
1967	7,350
1968	7,525
1969	7,700
1970	7,800

About one half of all items now on supermarket shelves were introduced during the 1960's. Eighty-two per cent of all frozen food items were not in existence at the beginning of the 1960's. *Progressive Grocer* reported that during 1969 the average store added 490 items and discontinued 335 items for a gain of 155 items (41). Critical to the success of new items is the speed with which they are distributed to retail food stores. *Progressive Grocer* estimates that of all new items successfully introduced each year, 35 per cent receive automatic distribution from warehouses, while 65 per cent are received at the store's option. Of food chains reporting to *Progressive Grocer,* 77 per cent indicated major new items were automatically shipped to retail stores and that other items with special sales appeal to certain demographic groups were distributed at the option of the manager. In independent stores, the majority of new items are ordered by managers.

The failure of 80 per cent of new introductions is ascribed to both the food manufacturer and the supermarket. Buyers and/or buying committees reject some introductions and store managers reject some of the acceptances. In the supermarket, new products can fail because managers fail to display them properly or to inform customers of their availability. The establishment of new product centers in some supermarkets has pleased customers and improved the sales of new products. Customers can influence the adoption of new products by food stores. When queried, about 72 per cent of shoppers stated that it was fairly important that they be able to purchase new products as soon as they were available. About 50 per cent said they would patronize another store to buy an item if they were unable to purchase it in the store in which they regularly shopped (27). The supermarket has a role in making new products available to the consumer, but the ultimate success or failure of new items probably lies in the hands of the consumer.

The Supermarkets of the 1970's.   Although predictions are risky at any time, they are especially so when change comes as rapidly as it has in the twentieth century. However, here are some of the predictions for the supermarket of the 1970's. The newly built supermarkets of the 1970's will be larger than those built in the 1960's; because of the scarcity and cost of land, some of them will be storied. Established stores will be remodeled and refurbished. Supermarkets will cease to have the warehouse look; they will be beautified and some will be stylized as "Early American," "Old West," "Spanish," "Oriental," and so on. Decor will, however, be matched to the clientele to avoid what might appear as extravagance—equated with high price—to some customers; but also to give the prestigious appearance favored by some customers.

There will be a break from traditional store layout patterns. Meat and produce may move from the perimeter locations. There will be small shops—the boutique look—within the supermarket, such as the flower shop, the candle shop, the wine cellar, the cheese shop, the gourmet food shop, the liquor store, the ice cream parlor, the bakery, and others. There will be a fast foods shop, accessible from both the inside and the outside of the supermarket. There may be an attached convenience store with a separate entrance to assist the customer in shopping quickly for only a few items. A diet center and a new-food-products center as well as a center for cooking classes may appear in some supermarkets. As manufacturers adopt a universal code for marking items, partially automated checkouts will come into use; however, checkers and baggers will be present. Customer benefits of semiautomation would be the elimination of cash register errors, speedy checkout service, and the receipt of an itemized list of purchases with per unit and per package prices. The intent of changes in the supermarket is to make shopping more pleasurable and to reduce the time and energy costs of shopping.

Each year of the 1970's supermarkets will offer more items, a number that will become 10,000 or more by 1980. Some predictions as to the merchandise of the 1970's are these: more frozen red meat and chicken; more frozen ready-to-eat dishes; more out-of-season produce; more frozen breakfasts; more single-service prepared foods and dishes, including entrees and desserts; more filled and imitation dairy foods; and less expensive meat analogs. Unit pricing will expand in use. This means that items will carry two prices, one for the package and one for a unit, such as ounce, pound, pint, or other applicable unit. Further, open dating of perishables is certain to become widespread. Much more grade labeling of food may come in the 1970's, and labeling to reveal nutritional content is certain to come. The latter developments are responsibilities of the food industries and will be further discussed subsequently.

More services may be available in some supermarkets; however, as long as low food pricing is policy, services may have to be curtailed. Some services that may be introduced are educational programs for men shoppers and young women shoppers, catering service, a postal substation, a utility payment substation, dry cleaning pickup service, a child-care center, a lunch counter, a watch repair shop, and so on.

Supermarkets of the 1970's will pattern merchandise and services to the predominant clientele. Customers will be younger and less experienced as the percentage of the population twenty to thirty-four years old increases. More husbands will shop alone or with the housewife. Further, the number of working wives will increase. All this means that there will be an ever-expanding demand for convenience foods; home-cooked meals may become only a memory of those well over thirty.

The managers of the supermarkets of the 1970's will have authority and stature. They will be trained for, motivated for, and rewarded for the responsibility they assume. Because of the keen competition between markets and the compelling need for volume business, they will be decision-makers in their respective supermarkets instead of relying on the former practice of decision-making at headquarters.

The Discount Food Store

Discount stores began as closed membership stores. This gave them an aura of exclusiveness because those who shopped in them belonged to a select group. Undoubtedly, this situation favored the quick patronage of the open discount store and the discount food store. The development of and increase in numbers of discount supermarkets were a phenomenon of the 1960's, particularly of 1969 and 1970. By the end of 1969, 60 per cent of all chains had discount operations; and 47 per cent of all chain stores, 27 per cent of all independent stores, and 30 per cent of all food stores were operating under discount plans. By mid-1970, the percentage of all stores had risen to 40 per cent because of consumer price-consciousness and competition. By early 1971, 70 per cent of all chain companies had stores operating under discount programs and 34 per cent of all supermarkets were discounting. In 1970, about 50 per cent of small chains were discounting in all stores, while only about 25 per cent of the large chains were discounting in all stores. The sales gains of discount operations have been 15 to 30 per cent, gains similar to those experienced by supermarkets that adopted stamps in the late 1950's. The average sales gain in 1970 was about 25 per cent. The extent of discounting is from 2 to 5 per cent with 2.8 per cent the average. In 1970, the average gross margin of discounting stores was about 17 per cent (42).

In general, when supermarkets became discount supermarkets, stamps were dropped and often the name was changed; for example, Food Fair stores became Pantry Pride stores. The discount supermarket introduced price competition into the food retailing business. Historically, the chain store and the supermarket had performed this same function.

A survey conducted by the United States Department of Agriculture (23) in which the prices of thirty identical food items were compared in chain supermarkets, independent food stores, and discount food stores revealed that discount store prices were lower. Some strategies of discount operations that permit lower prices are summarized as follows.

1. They may be open fewer hours per week, thereby cutting the costs of operation.

2. They may have everyday low prices in contrast to weekend specials, thereby equalizing store traffic.

3. They do not stock "smalls" but do stock large, family-sized, and economy-sized packages.

4. They rarely offer stamps, games, or gimmicks.

5. They do much multiple pricing.

6. They may stock fewer numbers of brands.

7. They may stock less variety in the styles and sizes of a product. For example, one might find canned peach halves only in cans of sizes No. 303 and No. 2½.

8. They may discount name brands but not private label, local, or regional brands.

9. They may reduce the amount of newspaper advertising and eliminate mailers and store coupons.

10. They may stock fewer numbers of items than other supermarkets and favor fast-moving items with rapid turnover, such as coffee, canned soups, breakfast cereals, and canned vegetables.

11. They may adopt a policy of slow adoption of new food items because new items reduce stockturns and increase costs and margins.

12. They may broaden product lines, particularly nonfoods, to permit

the maintenance of some low prices and at the same time maintain a suitable gross margin.

Initially, price reductions were in the grocery department and in health and beauty aids in the nonfoods department. The trend, now evident, is to apply price cutting very selectively within store departments, with some below-cost merchandising. Meats tend to be offered at the lowest economically feasible prices but with maintenance of such quality as the shopper of the 1970's demands. Although, as polled in 1969, about 60 per cent of shoppers thought discount food store prices were about the same as those of other supermarkets, about one third patronized the discounting supermarket because of its lower prices (38). Differences in opinion as to the price level of discounting supermarkets would arise because of different consumption practices, that is, the particular mix of goods purchased. The discount store is probably here to stay, at least as long as the dollar continues to inflate.

The Convenience Store

The convenience store is a miniature supermarket, that is, a minimarket. Convenience stores are a food retailing development of the 1960's. They increased in number from about 500 in 1957 to 11,620 in 1969 and nearly 14,000 in 1971. Their sales volume increased from $75 million in 1957 to $2,610 billion in 1970; the percentage of increase in their share of grocery store sales was from 0.2 per cent in 1957 to 3 per cent in 1970. The average pre-store sales volume in 1970 was $182,250, a figure that would place some convenience stores in the superette category. About 25 per cent of chains operate convenience stores. In 1970, 22 per cent of convenience stores were franchise operations. Convenience stores engage in little advertising and in few such promotions as stamps. Store margins are higher than in supermarkets, about 25 per cent in 1970. Net profit before taxes is also higher, 4 per cent in 1970 (42).

The convenience store represents a return to the "corner grocery store." It is close by; it is small; its personnel are friendly and known; it is open from early morning until late evening for seven days of the week; and it has frequently been customized to the neighborhood. It meets the need of the working housewife for quick and convenient shopping between trips to the supermarket and for meeting emergencies. The names of the different stores reflect their character: "Minit Market," "Quick Stop," "Jiffy Shop," and "Pick Kwik," for example. The average number of items carried in the convenience store is about three thousand in contrast to the eight thousand of the supermarket. Generally, neither fresh meats nor produce is stocked. About two thirds of the sales are derived as follows: groceries, 25 per cent; beer and soft drinks, 20 per cent; dairy, 15 per cent;

and frozen foods, 4 per cent. This 4 per cent for frozen foods is about the same as the percentage in the supermarket. Though prices are higher in the convenience store and though the shopper is aware of this, it is predicted that convenience stores will further increase in number and gain in patronage in the 1970's at the expense of supermarkets, as the latter gain in size and become more impersonal and as more housewives enter the labor market.

The New Combination Store

The new combination store is a development of the 1960's that will probably develop further in the 1970's. It marks a return to the general country store. The new combination stores may be described as family center stores because both food and such nonfood departments as appliances, auto accessories, clothing, footwear, giftwear, hardware and paints, housewares, health and beauty aids, household linens, school supplies, and others are housed under one roof. They succeed because they favor one-stop shopping; and because the concept of self-service has been widely accepted. These stores developed as discounting in food stores and rising costs of doing business reduced the profits of supermarkets. The high margins and low operating cost of merchandising nonfoods favor a profitable enterprise. Some corporations that have new combination stores include Kroger Company, Red Owl Stores, Jewel Companies, and Food Fair.

THE FOOD MANUFACTURING INDUSTRY

Although the meal manager is most interested in and operates in the supermarket or other retail food store, she cannot ignore the other elements of the food marketing system, especially the food manufacturing industry. The system is complex; we shall simplify it by stating that between site of original production—farm, feed lot, or chicken ranch—and purchase at the retail level, basic food matrials must be transported one or more times, stored one or more times, and, most importantly in the 1970's, processed and packaged. The farm value of food purchased by the consumer in 1970 was about 39 per cent and the marketing cost about 61 per cent of the consumer's dollar (see Figures 2–1 and 2–2). However, the farm value and the marketing cost differ with products; the farm value being as much as 54 per cent for poultry and eggs and as little as 19 per cent for bakery and cereal products. The more foods are processed and packaged, the smaller is the farmer's share of the consumer's food dollar and the wider is the farm-retail price spread. This spread increased 37 per cent from 1950 to 1965 (17). The United States Department of Agriculture calculated (June, 1966) that the costs of a loaf of bread were as follows:

	Cost (Cents)
For the wheat farmer	3.1
For the miller	1.0
For transportation and miscellaneous	2.1
For the baker	11.6
For the retailer	4.0
Total	21.8

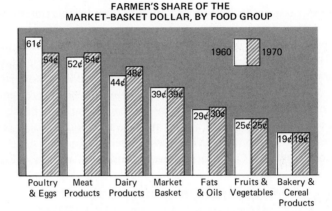

FIGURE 2–1. Farmer's share of the market-basket dollar, by food group. (*United States Department of Agriculture photograph.*)

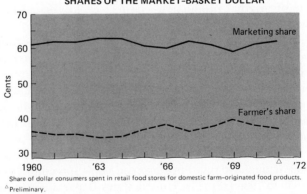

FIGURE 2–2. Shares of the market-basket dollar. (*United States Department of Agriculture photograph.*)

Although a small proportion of the cost of a loaf of bread is for basic ingredients, few consumers would have it otherwise.

Chain Store Age (20) estimated how a six-ounce can of orange juice derived the retail value of 15.5 cents per can—a six-pack retailed for 93 cents. Their estimates follow.

	Cost (Cents)
For growing and picking oranges	6.04
For processing, storing, and marketing	4.96
For transport to food warehouse	1.24
Cost of retailing	3.26
Total	15.50

The cost of the basic food ingredient is less than half the cost of the final product; but the convenience of and the year-around availability of the product make it a bargain. Further, it would be almost impossible anywhere in the United States to buy the nine oranges required to make that quantity of concentrate for the cost of the frozen concentrate.

We consumers have indicated by our purchases that we want food extensively processed, that is, the soup ready-made, pastries ready-baked, cereals ready-to-eat, and breakfasts and dinners ready-to-heat. In fact, it would appear that we want all foods either instant or ready. The food manufacturing industries provide, for a price, the convenience of the foods we purchase. They also preserve the food supply by canning, freezing, and dehydration and by food manufacturing. Further, they introduce new and/or improved—though this is debatable—items at the rate of some 7,000 per year (30). Predictions are that 120,000 new products will be introduced during the decade of the 1970's. Actually, few of them will be truly new, that is, innovations such as were potato flakes. They will, in general, be only minor modifications of older products; "me toos"; and products preserved by different or improved processing techniques. The research and development of new products is costly. Failures are costly too. Angelus (3) reported that 80 per cent of the items introduced in 1968 failed and that 90 per cent of the failures had successful test results. A modest failure can cost $100,000; a big failure, $20 million. His analysis of a number of failures placed the burden of responsibility on the manufacturer. Similarly, Borden (5), though he could point to no definitive causes of failure, suggested that the manufacturer might be at fault. Some reasons that have been proposed to explain failures are summarized. (1) Products did not receive prior market testing that would have predicted consumer acceptance. (2) The results of market tests were poorly analyzed and evaluated. (3) Products performed poorly; for example, the cereals with freeze-dried fruits failed because the fruits rehydrated so slowly that the cereal became soggy by the time the fruit was ready for eating. (4) Products did not have universal taste appeal, for example, some of the dry soup mixtures. (5) Products were me-too items in a market where others were known and established. "Me-toos" can lower the cost of products however. (6) Supermarket buyers and buying committees reject some new products, rejections dictated by both wisdom and expediency. The cost of failures is borne by the consumer in the price paid for other products of the line. Further, successes are not immediately profitable because of high advertising and promotion costs as well as the costs of research and development, again affecting the price paid by the consumer.

The scale of and the quality of the advertising and promotions of the food industries have directed much criticism toward them. Advertising and promotion by food, beer, soft drink, and candy manufacturers cost about $2.9 billion, or $14.50 per capita, in 1968 (12). In addition to extensive advertising via the different media, especially television, the food industries offer coupons, refunds on purchases, "cents-off" promotions on established products, "bonus gifts" redeemable for cash or trading stamps, and so on. Consensus is that high promotional spending does not ensure the success of new introductions. There is as yet no proof of correlation between advertising volume and sales increases (12). A study made in early 1970 by Foote, Cone and Belding Advertising, Incorporated (11) of the ways housewives were trying to stretch their food budgets would seem to confirm this. They were switching to less-known brands and they were forsaking convenience products for the preparation of dishes from scratch, particularly the younger and better educated housewives. The White House Conference on Food, Nutrition, and Health urged mandatory limitations on the promotional and advertising expenditures of food companies to effect reductions in food costs.

The food manufacturing industries are also criticized for their opposition to such consumer benefits as truth in packaging, the promulgation of definitions and standards of identity for food products, the mandatory listing of ingredients and percentages thereof, the honest and truthful labeling of dietary foods, the open dating of food products, the grade labeling of foods, and limitations on the use of food additives. The cereal industry, the baking industry, and the producers of instant breakfast products and some juice drinks were singled out for criticism because of nutritional claims made in their advertising during 1970 and 1971.

Although, there is more that could, and probably should, be said pro and con the food manufacturing industries, we shall conclude discussion of them with the following observation. About 23.3 per cent of the $1,950 food bill of a family of four (1969) bought inedibles: 18.3 per cent for packaging, including the cost of its pickup; 3 per cent for advertising and promotion; and 2 per cent for new product failures and supermarket thefts (12). Packaging costs are big and packaging is no small factor in the fight against pollution. Only time will tell what the 1970's will accomplish regarding packaging and advertising wastes.

Summary. In summary, it can be said that the marketplace for food offers some variety in sizes and kinds of stores. There is some price differential between stores. The marketplace offers a bewildering assortment of edibles and nonedibles. There is some price differential between like or near-like items. The marketplace is nearby. It is dynamic. Shopping there requires decision-making. Dollars spent there purchase more than food, namely, packaging, advertising, research and development, brand name, and convenience.

The Consumer in the Marketplace

The food store industry researched itself diligently for two decades. It became knowledgeable on matters of store location, store layout, stock arrangement, pricing, display, checkouts, department location, contribution to sales and margins by department and product category, and advertising and promotion. The principles of efficient operation became well understood and were widely applied. All food markets came to look alike. During this era in which the industry matured it assumed that all customers were "average" or alike. The *Progressive Grocer Colonial Study* (33) made in 1962 was the first *Progressive Grocer* study to focus attention on the customer; the second was the *Consumer Dynamics Study* (9) made in 1965; the third was a two-part study of the A&P customer and her shopping habits. One study was conducted in May, 1970, in seven cities: Atlanta, Louisville, Boston, Paterson (New Jersey), Philadelphia, Cleveland, and Kansas City (Missouri). To establish a demographic profile of the A&P customer, shoppers were interviewed in stores in five types of neighborhoods—upper income, industrial, black, suburban middle class, and apartment dweller—and in discount stores of the A&P company. A second study was made in the Detroit area because metropolitan Detroit typifies the demographic diversity represented in the national food market. Customer habits and product performance were studied in stores serving six distinct types of neighborhoods—apartment dweller, black, industrial (blue collar), young family, small town, and upper income—plus a discount store. The profiles developed from the Detroit study were quite similar to those derived from the study made in seven cities. These studies will be referred to as the Seven Cities Study and the Detroit Area Study (1, 2). These studies and others have revealed that there is no "average customer," though studies average findings for the purpose of comparing different socioeconomic groups. There are differences between the customers who patronize one store as compared with the customers of another store, and also between the customers shopping in the same store. Obviously, consumers differ in age; their families differ in size; they have different resources, different wants, different personalities, different educational and cultural backgrounds, and different lives in the world of work; they have had different experiences; and they live in different kinds of neighborhoods, for example, the inner city versus the suburbs. The findings of the earlier-mentioned studies provoked changes in the food store industry; stores studied their customers and began customizing stores to the predominant clientele.

The Consumer's Choice of Food Store

Retailers would very much like to know why consumers shop at one or two stores to the exclusion of others almost identical in size, arrangement, pricing policy, and merchandise offered. The respondents in the *Colonial Study* believed that stores differed greatly in personnel, in services offered, and in the quality of meat and produce available, but less markedly in grocery, dairy, and nonfood offerings. When queried as to why they patronized a Colonial Store, they replied as follows: 73 per cent, because of friendly personnel; 52 per cent, because of wide variety of products and brands; 50 per cent, because stamps were given; and about 40 per cent, because of the quality of meat and produce.

In the *Consumer Dynamics Study,* reasons for shopping a particular store varied with socioeconomic groups; however, all groups but one gave as their first reason good store housekeeping. In ordering other reasons, most groups considered quality of meat, variety of goods and services, and friendliness and courtesy of personnel above low prices. But low-income consumers rated stamp giving of greater significance than high-income families, and small-town shoppers rated courteous personnel higher than all other groups. Socioeconomic groups of the *Consumer Dynamics Study* were five: upper-middle-income white-collar families, middle-income blue-collar families, young married middle-income families with young children, black families, and small-town families.

A 1965 study (44) of the food shopping habits of 4,210 supermarket shoppers in a widely scattered sample revealed that 86 per cent of the shoppers mentioned one of the following as the first consideration in choosing a food store: the quality and freshness of meats, low prices on groceries, convenient location, store housekeeping, the variety and selection of the grocery department, and the quality and freshness of fruits and vegetables.

A study of shoppers who had recently moved and their subsequent choice of a food store revealed that three to four weeks were required to make a choice; that 26 per cent visited two stores before making a choice; nearly a third, three stores; and about one third, four stores. Reasons for choosing a favorite store were in decreasing order of frequency: the quality of meat, the cleanliness of the store, the location and convenience of the store, brand selection and variety, and the friendliness of the personnel. Prices and stamps as reasons were mentioned by less than 16 per cent of the shoppers (9).

According to the 1971 annual study of supermarket shoppers conducted by Burgoyne, Incorporated (32), the six leading reasons for the choice of a favored supermarket were low prices on groceries, 30.8 per cent; the quality and freshness of meats, 25 per cent; the attractiveness and cleanliness of the store, 15 per cent; convenient location, 10.5 per cent; the variety and selection of grocery merchandise, 7.4 per cent; and the quality and freshness of fruits and vegetables, 3.9 per cent. These percentages are increases in the preference percentages for low prices on groceries, quality and freshness of meats, and the attractiveness and cleanliness of the store; they are decreases (since 1958) in the preference percentages for the variety of grocery merchandise, convenient location, and the quality and freshness of vegetables. The 1971 percentages would seem to reflect the inflation of the 1960's and the upgrading of some departments within the supermarket. According to this same 1971 study, the main customer complaints about stores remained slow checkout service, poor store housekeeping, and inadequate stocking of brands and sizes. The percentage of shoppers who would prefer a store with a 2-per-cent-lower pricing policy over one giving trading stamps increased from 45 per cent in 1963 to 84 per cent in 1971. However, R. H. Bruskin Associates reported that about 20 per cent of shoppers chose a specific store because it gave stamps (7). The principal reason for patronizing discount-food-store departments given by one third of the patrons was lower prices, again reflecting the economic situation of the late 1960's. More than half of the young homemakers studied by Lamkin (22) gave prices and sales or specials as their first consideration in grocery store selection.

In 1969, the A. C. Nielsen Company reported to the supermarket industry on the likes and dislikes of shoppers about supermarkets (26). Inevitably, the shoppers' likes and dislikes influenced their choice of a supermarket. Likes were as follows: everyday low prices, convenient store location, high quality and fresh meats, a wide variety and selection of merchandise, friendly personnel, more and better maintenance of express lanes, help in unloading carts, rest areas with coffee bars, clean and well-kept aisles and shelves, and stable merchandise location. Dislikes were aisles that were too long, narrow, and cluttered; too many items out of stock; shelf stocking done during rush hours; poor bagging; carts too small for today's shoppers; limited item selection; price marking that was often unreadable and confusing; stores that were out of advertised items;

and wrong prices rung up on the cash register. Thompson (43) concluded that the location of a supermarket was less important than formerly, and that price, quality, and certain aesthetic factors have come to be more valued than convenient location. It has been reported, however, that when the customer patronizes a convenience store, it is one that is nearby or within walking distance.

The two A&P studies of 1970 profiled customers but did not report why these customers shopped A&P stores. High percentages—66.5 per cent of upper-income shoppers to 80 per cent of blacks and apartment dwelling shoppers—shopped for the most part at the store where they were interviewed. About 40 per cent rated A&P prices lower when compared with those of other stores, but 50 per cent felt that all prices were about the same.

Frequency of Shopping

There was a trend to greater frequency of shopping during the decade of the 1960's. According to the studies of shoppers made by Burgoyne, Incorporated, in 1961, 59 per cent of shoppers shopped in a supermarket once weekly or less often; 23 per cent, twice weekly; 12 per cent, three times weekly; and 6 per cent, more frequently (44). In 1971, 41 per cent shopped in a supermarket once weekly or less; 27 per cent, twice; 18 per cent, three times; and 11 per cent more frequently (32). According to the Consumer Dynamics Study, the average number of shopping trips per shopper per week was about three; two to a supermarket, one to another type of store. The Seven Cities Study of shoppers showed that 62 per cent shopped at a supermarket once a week or less; 19 per cent, twice weekly; and 18.7 per cent, three times or more weekly. The Detroit Area Study —one that profiled shoppers by neighborhood of residence—showed that almost half of blue-collar and upper-income shoppers shopped more than once weekly, while only a third or slightly more of black shoppers, apartment dwellers, and young families shopped more than once weekly.

Some explanations for frequent shopping are that milk and bread are store bought and require repeated purchase; that storage resources, particularly of apartment dwellers, are limited; that meal planning in the 1970's is done in the store and is based on specials rather than planned ahead for a period of time; that the numbers of convenient markets make for convenient stops to pick up small numbers of items; and, finally, that uncertainties created by the increase in the number of meals eaten away from home and the decrease in the number of family meals at which all members of the family are present may make one weekly trip to the food store impractical. In defense of frequent shopping, it may be said that it is less likely to lead to overbuying and food waste than infrequent shopping accompanied by overbuying.

Store Loyalty

The frequency of shopping trips by consumers causes store managers to work toward developing store loyalty among consumers. The Burgoyne studies (32) revealed that the percentage of consumers patronizing only one supermarket decreased from 41 per cent in 1954 to 10 per cent in 1971. In 1971, about 90 per cent of consumers shopped at two or more food stores during one week; 54 per cent, three or more supermarkets; and 20 per cent, four or more. The *National Survey of Supermarket Shopping* (24) made by *Look* magazine in 1963 reported that 70 per cent of shoppers were loyal in that they bought more food at one store than at any other store. The study further noted that loyalty decreased as income increased and was lower in metropolitan than nonmetropolitan areas. The *Seventh DuPont Consumer Buying Habits Study* (36) reported, in 1965, that 61 per cent of shoppers patronized more than one store. Lamkin's young homemakers were not loyal—87 per cent had shopped at more than one store the week previous to the survey. The Seven Cities Study showed that 29 per cent of the shoppers interviewed shopped only at the market where they were interviewed, that is, were loyal shoppers. In the Detroit Area Study, the range in loyalty was from one third for blue-collar shoppers to nearly two thirds for apartment dwellers; the composite was 53.2 per cent loyalty. The forty-seventh annual "Milwaukee Journal Consumer Analysis" (28) disclosed that during one week the number of different stores patronized by shoppers was as follows: one store only, 19 per cent; two, 48 per cent; and three or more, 31 per cent. Differing degrees of store loyalty are conditioned by available market resources and transportation means, as well as shopper preferences and the search for bargains.

The 1969 Burgoyne study reported that 28 per cent of shoppers patronize a convenience market once weekly or more often because of its convenience. The rapid growth of these minimarkets during the late 1960's would appear to be indirect evidence both that consumers shop frequently and that they are not loyal to any one food store. Further, the housewife's acceptance of and the availability of such fast foods as "take-home" fried chicken undermines loyalty and increases shopping trips. Shoppers have a favorite store where they buy most of their food—about one half of the respondents in the Burgoyne Index Study of 1969 (38) had patronized a favorite store for over five years; 11 per cent, from three to five years; 10 per cent, from two to three years; 14 per cent, from one to two years; and 14 per cent, for less than one year. In the *Consumer Dynamics Study,* 64 per cent of those who had moved three miles or less returned to a favorite store; but the loyalty to a chain of those who moved greater distances varied between 39 and 58 per cent. The Seven Cities Study reported that 51.5 per cent of the shoppers surveyed had shopped at the same store for five years or longer; 31.5 per cent, for from one to five years. About half of the shoppers surveyed traveled one mile or less to the store and about 30 per cent, from one to three miles. In the Detroit Area Study, there was wide divergence in the percentage of shoppers patronizing one store more than five years: 62 per cent for shoppers in the upper-income neighborhood to 20 per cent for apartment dwellers and those from the blue-collar neighborhood.

When asked why she quits one market for another, the typical food shopper gives the following reasons: the quality of the meat and produce, unsatisfactory prices, poor store housekeeping, rude personnel, and waiting too long in checkout lines.

The Consumer's Shopping Habits

The "average" family of 3.8 persons spent between $25 and $30 per week or between $1,300 and $1,500 per year for food in 1965. It bought three thousand items annually in an "average" three trips weekly to food stores, two of which were supermarkets (9). In 1970, the composite A&P weekend shopper as profiled by the Seven Cities Study spent an average of $17.80; the range was $15.36 spent by apartment dwellers to $20.66 spent by discount supermarket shoppers. The total weekly expenditure was an average of $36.37. The weekend shopper was in the store twenty-seven minutes and selected between 20 and 50 items. Shopping habits as revealed in different studies and surveys are presented.

1.   Stores do 75 per cent of their sales volume on Thursday, Friday, and Saturday, indicating that these are the favorite shopping days of consumers.

2.   About 15 per cent of shoppers do most of their food shopping Monday through Wednesday; about one fourth on Thursday; about one third on Friday; and the remainder on Saturday.

3.   As profiled in the Seven Cities Study, the homemaker shops alone 62 per cent of the time; with her husband, 6.3 per cent of the time; and with her children, 13 per cent of the time. However, there are differences according to the neighborhood: 68 per cent of upper-income housewives shop alone versus 53 per cent of black housewives; 16.7 per cent of blue-collar housewives shop with children; while 18 per cent of apartment-dwelling shoppers are men shopping alone.

4.   About 30 per cent of shoppers use shopping lists; however, it has been observed that nearly 50 per cent of upper-income shoppers shop with shopping lists (9). About 50 per cent of shoppers, though they have no written lists have intended purchases in mind. Only 16 per cent of shoppers make all their decisions in the store (24). Shoppers with lists stay in the store longer, they buy more items, and they spend more than shoppers without lists (9). Although there is no evidence that these customers shop less frequently, it might be presumed that they do. Fifty-two per cent of

Lamkin's young homemakers almost always made a list, either general or specific. Such choices as of fresh fruits and vegetables, of bakery products, of snack items, and even of meats are practical in-store decisions. Among the A&P shoppers, an average of 35.6 per cent used shopping lists; the range was from 24.7 per cent for black shoppers to 41.8 per cent for upper-income shoppers. The upper-income shoppers are better educated, they buy more, and they are less likely to consult advertising in making up lists.

5.   According to the *Progressive Grocer Colonial Study* made in 1963, men shopping alone spend less time and less money than women shoppers. Men shoppers in the nineteen to thirty age bracket spend more than shoppers in the thirty-one to fifty age bracket, and these spend more than shoppers older than fifty (2). According to the Detroit Area Study, the percentage range of men shoppers was from 4.9 per cent in the discount store to 27.1 per cent in the black neighborhood; the average was 15.6 per cent. Suggested reasons for the appearance of more men as food store shoppers are the number of wives in the labor market and the shorter work week.

6.   The average expenditure of shoppers in stores in different types of neighborhoods are given below for the Seven Cities Study.

Types of Neighborhood	*Weekly Expenditure*
Discount store	$36.68
Black	34.32
Upper-income	41.58
Suburban middle-class	40.90
Apartment dwellers	31.61
Industrial	33.22
Average	36.37

Because no data on family size were given, it is not possible to know which group spent the most or the least per person for food, though the spending surely reflects the income level.

7.   In the conduct of the study of shoppers in the Detroit Area Study, the sales of every item in each of the seven stores were monitored for thirteen weeks. From these data, it was possible to profile the food purchase practices of different socioeconomic groups. In each type of neighborhood, there were white-collar and blue-collar families; large, small, and intermediate family sizes; and families with incomes under $5,000 to over $15,000; but in each there was a predominant group. Here is how they differed in food purchases when the sales of each store were compared with the average sales of all stores.

(a)   In the high-income store, the produce, ice cream, dairy, bakery, and frozen foods departments exceeded the average in sales; the meat, dry groceries, and nonfood departments were under the average in sales. This high-income shopper bought above the average in lamb and veal; frozen turkey, frozen fish, frozen entrees, frozen cakes and pastries, frozen fruits and vegetables; nationality foods, such as Chinese, Greek, or Mexican dishes; fresh fruits and vegetables, especially the less common ones like artichokes; salad greens and salad mixes; specialty cheeses, dips, and spreads; low-calorie dairy foods like skim milk, cottage cheese, and yogurt; and variety breads. She was an average buyer of beef, but she was not a buyer of poultry, sausages, and pork, nor of frozen dinners.

(b)   In the suburban, young family neighborhood, about 25 per cent of shoppers were under thirty as well as up to fifty years old. In this store, the produce, bakery, and nonfood departments exceeded the average in sales; the meat department was lower in sales; and the remaining departments were about average in sales. Housewives in this neighborhood were great buyers of convenience foods: frozen pot pies, pizza, and dinners; canned hams; toaster pastries, bakery cakes, cookies, and pies; frozen vegetables in sauce and vegetable specialties. They purchased more beef than any other group. They bought above the average in luncheon meats and frankfurters; eggs; processed cheese; and ice cream novelties.

(c)   The blue-collar shopper is conservative and traditional in tastes —she equates eating and the good life. She shops ads, compares prices, buys specials. She is the most cost conscious of the groups, but does not favor private label brands. Her conservatism is mirrored in her larger purchase of waxed paper and smaller purchases of aluminum foil, poly sandwich bags, and plastic wraps. She bought more fresh and canned foods than frozen foods. She exceeded the average in the purchase of butter, cream, and whole milk; eggs; process cheese; and cakes and pies. She bought more fresh fruit than any other group, but she was the second lowest buyer of fresh vegetables; however, this was because she very likely had a garden. She bought beef and pork but was a poor buyer of veal, lamb and fish. In the blue-collar store, only the produce, dairy, and bakery departments were average or better in sales; meat, ice cream, frozen foods, dry groceries, and nonfood departments were under average in sales.

(d)   The population mix patronizing the apartment dwellers' store was 40 per cent nonwhite and 60 per cent white. The white shoppers of this store were big buyers of convenience foods, gourmet items, delicatessen items, and party foods. The store was below the average in sales in all departments except meat and frozen foods. The shopper in this store showed a preference for veal and lamb. She wanted variety in fresh fruits, salad greens, and such salad vegetables as cucumbers, green peppers, and tomatoes. In the dry groceries department, she bought less than the average of almost every item excepting condiments, juices and drinks, canned and dry milk, snacks, and soft drinks. The black patrons of the store followed the practices of those who shopped at the store in the predominately black neighborhood.

(e)   In the store in the black neighborhood, about 77 per cent of shoppers were nonwhite. Though 57 per cent of the shoppers interviewed shopped that store exclusively, only about 26 per cent thought A&P prices were lower. Of these shoppers, 55 per cent had incomes under $10,000; family size ranged from one to four persons in 70 per cent of the families. In this store 25 per cent of shoppers were men shopping alone; 25 per cent, couples; and the remainder, women shopping alone or with children. This fact is accounted for by the high employment rate of black women and the high unemployment rate of black men. Excepting the meat department, all the departments of this store had sales of less than the composite or average store. The store was second only to the apartment dwellers' store in meat sales; but it was first in sales of pork and fresh poultry. Sales of fresh pork, bacon, smoked pork, and sausage meats were extensive. The produce department and ice cream did almost as well as the average. Some big-selling items in the store were hot cereals, canned luncheon meats, canned greens and okra, canned peaches, rice, and canned punches and powdered soft drinks. Purchases reflected the traditional cultural food pattern of blacks.

(f)   Shoppers in the small-town store were above-average buyers of dairy products, including ice cream, dry groceries, and nonfood; they were below-average buyers of meat and produce because they had their own food resources. They were good buyers of frozen dinners and pot pies, luncheon meats, and frankfurters. They were second to the discount shopper in purchase of nonfood items.

(g)   At the beginning of 1970, nearly one half of all chain stores and 20 per cent of independent stores were operating on a discount basis. Obviously, there are many shoppers who patronize discount stores. The profile of the customers of the discount store in the Detroit area follows: 70 per cent had incomes from $7,000 to $15,000; 75 per cent were under fifty years old; the family size ranged from three to more than seven for almost 80 per cent; more than half thought that A&P prices were lower than those of other stores; and there was a half-and-half mix of white-collar and blue-collar families. Only the produce, dry groceries, and nonfood departments of the store exceeded the average in sales; all others were nearly average or less than average. The discount store shopper bought large-size packages, was price conscious, and shopped more frequently than the average.

8.   The shopper for food is a coupon user. Billions of cents-off coupons are distributed annually by the food industries by mail, in magazines, in newspapers, and in or on packs. In addition, coupons redeemable for short

periods of time appear in the newspaper advertising of supermarkets. These latter are manufacturer-paid or partly manufacturer-paid coupons with the supermarket paying or partly paying for the advertising. The average value per coupon was eight cents in 1970, however, some coupons had greater and some lesser value. Couponing is a form of promotion that is considered socially beneficial by shoppers who particularly favor redeeming them for trial of new and/or improved products.

9. A study (32) done for the National Commission of Food Marketing suggested that only about 25 per cent of shoppers knew the difference between name brand and retailer brand goods; another 25 per cent recognized the difference between well-known and less well-known brands. The majority of women shoppers, 82 per cent, thought well-known brands were better; 50 per cent thought private label products were bought for budgetary reasons. Actually about one half of the shoppers had brand preferences, with name brands being favored about three to one. The other half selected both types of brands on the basis of specific knowledge. According to the 1966 Burgoyne Study, only 15 per cent of the respondents did not buy private label brands, 12 per cent bought mostly private label brands, and 73 per cent bought some. Sixty per cent thought private label brands equal to nationally advertised brands and 68 per cent thought private label or store brands a good value when priced lower than other brands. Better-educated consumers had less brand loyalty than less well-educated consumers (25). The *Better Homes and Gardens* Consumer Questionnaire (4) reported in 1967 that an average 78 per cent of housewives felt that nationally advertised brands cost more; this percentage increased to 80 per cent as the level of education rose from high school level; and it was 82 per cent for those under age thirty-five; and it was 65 per cent for those over fifty-five years of age. Forty-eight per cent thought the quality of national brands was better, but almost the same percentage thought the quality was about the same. Day (15) reported that one third of users switch brands every ninety days and that 53 per cent of shoppers change attitudes toward brands within a six-month period. Brand loyalty is positive for different food products of a given brand name, for example, Ann Page, Del Monte, or Thrifty Maid (29). *Progressive Grocer* reported (1970) that the private brand share of sales in groceries increased in 54 per cent of chains in 1969. Several surveys of the practices of food shoppers made during 1970—when food prices were high and rising—revealed that housewives were switching from name brands to private label goods. Warwich & Legler Associates of New York found that 45 per cent of the 811 homes questioned had switched from advertised brands to store brands. Foote, Cone, and Belding Advertising, Incorporated discovered that among strategies for stretching the food dollar, housewives were buying lesser known brands.

10.   In 1971, about 86 per cent, a percentage that remained fairly constant during the 1960's, of supermarket shoppers saved stamps when they received them (32). In the late 1950's, almost 95 per cent saved them. The percentage of shoppers who thought supermarkets giving trading stamps charged higher prices rose from 35 per cent in 1955 to 65 per cent in 1971. In 1971, 84 per cent of shoppers would have preferred a store discounting food prices by 2 per cent to one giving stamps; this percentage was 43 per cent in 1963 (32). According to R. H. Bruskin Associates, stamp enthusiasts are low-income consumers, housewives under age twenty-five, Westerners, and Southerners. Older and more affluent consumers are less interested in stamps (7). By 1971, stamps and games had given way to discounting, though some stores continued to give stamps.

When queried as to a favorite promotion, 65 per cent of shoppers (in 1969) expressed a preference for bonus stamps to offers spread over several months whereby such items as books, dinnerware, beverageware, and kitchenware could be purchased at reduced prices from week to week; or special values on such items as lawnmowers, vacuum cleaners, steam irons, blenders, coffee makers, and other special equipment in one-time promotions (38). The rationale for this seeming contradiction is that stamp books provide a greater choice in acquiring things; further, all the named promotional items are almost always available at reduced prices at discount department stores.

It has been suggested that some of the disenchantment with stamps has come about as a result of the recognition that the cost in stamps for merchandise is much higher than the cost of the same merchandise on the retail market. For example, the cost of a General Electric spray-steam-dry iron was $14.89 in a department store (in 1963). Seven and one-half books of a well-known kind of stamp were required to obtain this iron. The stamp company evaluated a book as being worth $3.00; that is, the cost of the iron in stamps was $22.50. The consumer had to spend $900 to acquire that number of stamps. A 2 per cent discount in the cost of food would have saved the consumer $18.00; she could have purchased the iron and had $3.11 left over (32). The assignment of a value of $3.00 to a book of stamps was for the purpose of collection of sales taxes on redemptions.

11.   Observations of supermarket shoppers in the supermarket would reveal them to the picky and choosy. They handle and rehandle cuts of meat, packages of fresh fruits and vegetables, loaves of bread, jars of instant coffee, cartons of margarine, packages of cheese, and so on. Yet studies reveal them to be quite uninformed. Fifty per cent of Lamkin's young homemakers associated the meat inspection stamp with wholesomeness and 40 per cent related it to quality. *A Study of Consumers' Knowledge and Use of Government Grades for Selected Foods* (10) can be summarized as follows:

(a)   Information was sought from shoppers on their purchases of beefsteak, bacon, eggs, butter, white bread, margarine, fresh milk, fresh potatoes, fresh apples, and whole turkey.

(b)   The percentages of buyers who looked at the labels when purchasing the above items ranged between 80 per cent for turkeys to 58 per cent for fresh potatoes.

(c)   Forty per cent looked for the price, 27 per cent for the weight, 25 per cent for the grade, and 11 per cent for the inspection mark when buying beefsteak.

(d)   About 30 per cent looked for grade and size when purchasing eggs.

(e)   More than half of the buyers looked for brand names when purchasing butter, white bread, and margarine; about 40 per cent, when buying milk.

(f)   Knowledge of grades as displayed by the surveyed group was incomplete and inaccurate. Most respondents stated rightly that there were government grades for beeksteak, turkey, and eggs; 60 per cent, for butter; and about 40 per cent, for fresh apples and potatoes. Seventy per cent thought there were government grades for fresh whole milk, an assumption easily made because milk is described as Grade A, a description of its sanitary qualities. Almost 70 per cent or more of the respondents who said there were grades for products stated that they were buying graded products, including bacon, white bread, margarine, and fresh milk, for which there are no USDA grades. Excepting for eggs, few respondents were able to correctly state the grade they purchased and one third or more did not know the grade purchased. One fourth incorrectly identified beefsteak, bacon, white bread, margarine, and fresh apples as Grade A. Respondents generally scored zero in their ability to name the grades for a food from highest to lowest.

(g)   The author ascribes some results of the study of knowledge of grading to the "halo effect": such foods as beef and eegs are graded, therefore all foods must be graded; Grade A is the grade for high quality eggs, therefore Grade A must be the grade for all other items of high quality.

(h)   Respondents were asked to identify the USDA inspection and grade marks from among a group of shapes including the square and triangle, in addition to the circle and shield. Thirty-eight per cent did not know the shape for the grade mark, 22 per cent correctly identified it, and 30 per cent identified the circle as the grade mark. Forty-two per cent did not know the inspection mark, 30 per cent correctly identified it, and 18 per cent identified it as the shield.

(i)   In response to a directive to rank the importance of brand names when shopping for the ten items of the study, "very important" was the rank given by more than half in buying bacon, butter, white bread, fresh milk, and whole turkey; by 30 per cent or less in buying fresh apples and fresh potatoes; by almost 50 per cent in buying margarine and beefsteak;

and by about 40 per cent in buying eggs. This finding gives credence to the concept held by some that brand names fulfill some of the same functions as consumer grades.

12.   Though there was phenomenal growth in the use of credit cards during the 1960's, only 10 per cent of supermarket shoppers queried in 1969 would be interested in buying groceries on a credit plan. Of those interested in buying groceries on credit, 70 per cent would be willing to pay a service charge of 1½ per cent if the bill were not paid within thirty days (38).

13.   Two recently reported studies point out that planned spending for food is a contemporary practice. Lamkin (22) reported that 70 per cent of the group had some kind of spending plan, usually of a weekly expenditure. A larger proportion of those under thirty, with incomes less than $10,000, and with weekly expenditures of less than $35 had a spending plan. Davis (13) reported that 59 per cent of student wives at the University of New Mexico reported that they had food budgets.

14.   The contemporary shopper believes that the food manufacturer should make food more nutritious but that the government is responsible for food safety (41).

Present-day supermarket shoppers equate "new," "changed," and "improved" with quality; an evaluation not difficult to understand in a decade that follows so closely man's trip to the moon. The shoppers surveyed in the *Consumer Dynamics Study* did not all embrace the new with equal enthusiasm. Percentages of shoppers who bought something on one shopping trip that they had never purchased before were young marrieds, 44 per cent; high-income shoppers, 37 per cent; small-town housewives, 29 per cent; blue-collar shoppers, 25 per cent; and black housewives, 19 per cent. Store audits showed that most of these purchases were new store items. A later survey (19) indicated that about 72 per cent of shoppers felt it was very important or fairly important that they be able to purchase new items as soon as they come on the market. Fifty per cent stated that they would patronize another store in order to buy it. Significant factors in the purchase of new items are the desire for more convenience and the desire for variety in foods. The first mix for a bakery product was a pancake mix introduced in 1880; a gingerbread mix was introduced in the 1930's. Both were slowly adopted, but after World War II, many kinds of mixes were developed and adopted. Instant coffee was introduced at the turn of the century; it remained unknown until World War II. Consumption gradually increased until in 1970 about 16 per cent of coffee beans roasted in the United States were processed to prepare instant coffee. The development of freeze-dried coffee and the improvement in the quality of regular instants resulted in the consumption of about two pounds of green beans as an instant product and about eleven pounds as regular coffee per capita in 1970. It has been postulated that one of several reasons for the slow acceptance of instant coffee—and of some other convenience products as well—was that its acceptance challenged the housewife's position as an expert in the brewing of coffee. Further, use of an instant coffee robbed her of the personal satisfaction she derived from being an expert. Finally, because Western culture defined one of the houswife's responsibilities as that of preparing meals, the use of a time-saving product could be looked upon as negligence of a responsibility. Of course, the instant product had to produce a good cup of coffee, and even with the super technology of its production in the 1970's not all persons think it does. To oversimplify what may be a big bundle of attitudes and feelings, the supermarket shopper buys and tries new products. If they are acceptable to her and her family tastewise and not too expensive for her food budget, she may continue to buy the product until something better comes along. And, she expects new products to be time-saving and work-saving. She has come a long way in changing her feelings about her role and responsibilities.

Food store shoppers in the 1970's will be buyers of new food products. The *Nielsen Alert Report* (30) reported that an average of six hundred new items—flavors, sizes, containers, brands, and so on—are introduced to supermarkets each month, or about seven thousand per year. *Progressive Grocer* reported in January 1970 that 82 per cent of frozen food items were not in existence at the beginning of the 1960's. About one half of all items now on supermarket shelves were introduced during the 1960's. The life cycle of new items is short: 15 per cent achieve long-time success; one third peak out within three years; and one half, within two years. Of all the new products introduced since World War II, 80 per cent failed. Angelus (3) predicts that 120,000 new items will be introduced in the 1970's and that 100,000 will fail with consequent great waste. Although there may be many explanations for failures, there is fundamentally only one cause for failure: the customer does not buy the product. There may likewise be many explanations for why she does not buy it; but there is only one reason: she does not like it. Borden (5) states that if a product does not fulfill a consumer's legitimate need or want, it will fail; and that no amount of advertising, coupons, deals, or other promotions will save it.

Who and What Influence Buying Decisions

Roberts (34) in a summary of studies done in seven southern states stated that recent food purchases were influenced by the following in decreasing order of consequence: information on boxes, cans, or containers; requests of children and family members; and newspaper advertising. Store specials and bargain counters appealed to homemakers in the younger age brackets and to homemakers with above-average incomes and education. VandeMark (45) interviewed shoppers in cities of different population densities. She discovered that consumers were more influenced by newspaper advertising in the smallest and largest cities, but that in medium-sized cities—25,000 to 100,000 population—stamps were of greater influence. In small towns—10,000 to 25,000 population—the following were influences in decreasing order of importance: newspaper advertising, recipe booklets, children's requests, the butcher's assistance, stamps, and in-store sampling of products. In middle-sized cities, the order was stamps, newspaper advertising, and children's requests. In larger cities, the order was, from most to least influential: newspaper advertising, stamps, in-store samples, and butcher assistance. In the *1969 Consumer Analysis of the St. Paul Market* (48), questionnaire respondents rated forms of advertising as being most helpful as follows: 84 per cent, newspapers; 6.6 per cent, direct mail; 6.2 per cent, television; 3.6 per cent, coupons; 1 per cent, magazines; and radio, less than 1 per cent.

Eighty-six per cent of consumers interviewed in the *Consumer Dynamics Study* responded that they read store ads in preparation for the major shopping trip of the week. In a study by the A. C. Nielsen Company, 66 per cent said they used newspaper food ads for shopping. In the 1965 Burgoyne Study, 72.4 per cent of respondents had read food store advertising during the previous week, and each ad reader read 2.8 ads; in 1966, 73.8 per cent were ad readers and they read an average of 2.6 ads each; in 1969, 78 per cent of shoppers were ad readers and they read 2.7 ads each. From the reading of advertising the consumer acquires knowledge of the different prices for similar items at different stores; she identifies specials and foods in abundant supply; she learns about new food products; and, if she is a stamp collector, she discovers how to select purchases so as to maximise stamp acquisition.

Decisions are influenced by other people: mothers and mothers-in-law, other relatives, neighbors, friends, husbands, and children. Seventy-seven per cent of homemakers shopping with children buy something at a child's suggestion. Some children-influenced purchases include cereals, soups, and ice cream among food items and toothpaste among nonfood items. Children are influenced by television, grocery store visits, and experiences at school and in the homes of friends (16). Lamkin's young homemakers were much influenced by the food requests of preschool children. The foods requested and generally bought by the majority were cereal, certain dairy products, cookies, crackers, fruit juices, dry beverage mixes, and fruits. Television programs seemed to influence children's desires, but children were also introduced to foods through store visiting. A study of home makers made for *Better Homes and Gardens* revealed that about 70 per cent of husbands under age twenty-five and about two thirds over age twenty-five influenced food choices because they either purchased or asked that certain foods be purchased (47).

Probably all shoppers in a supermarket made some in-store decisions: they are responses to recalled food and nonfood needs; they are specific decisions in response to generally planned purchases as of "oatmeal bread" for "bread" as listed on a shopping list; but they are also in response to merchandise displays in the different departments of the supermarket and to in-store advertising. According to the *Seventh DuPont Consumer Buying Habits Study* (36), almost 70 per cent of purchases resulted from an in-store decision: 17 per cent were generally planned but finalized in the store, 2 per cent were substitute purchases, and 50 per cent were purchases made without preplanning. As might be anticipated the lowest percentages of in-store decisions were made in the dairy, meat, and produce departments. The greatest percentage of in-store decisions were on frozen foods, bakery products, and cookies, crackers, and snack foods. However, a relatively small percentage of the food dollar is spent for the last-named foods. It might be presumed that the 30 per cent of planned purchases were the major purchases that used the largest proportion of the food dollar.

Summary. In summary, the behavior of supermarket shoppers is complex and varied. It is not static but changes as attitudes change, as income rises, as educational level rises, and with experience; it also responds to economic conditions as it did during the years 1969 and 1970. There is no average shopper. Food store buyers are loyal, and they are not loyal. They shop once weekly or less. They shop several times weekly. They patronize a nearby store. They travel several miles to a favorite store. They prepare shopping lists, and they made in-store decisions. They are brand loyal, and there is no brand loyalty. They prefer name brands, and they buy store brands. They are penny pinchers, and they patronize convenient stores where they know prices are higher. They have food budgets, and they do not. They demand a variety of goods and services. They have food preferences. They read food store ads, they buy specials, and they redeem coupons. They buy new products when introduced, and they are slow to accept new products. They like to shop. They like to pick and choose, see, and feel. Electronic shopping for food would be for most supermarket shoppers an abdication of pleasure and loss of power.

REFERENCES CITED

1. "The A & P Study: Part VI. How A & P Wins Its Millions of Customers," *Progressive Grocer* 49:42–55 (August 1970).
2. "The A & P Study: Part VIII. How Different Customers Shop the Modern Supermarket," *Progressive Grocer* 49:35–55 (October 1970).
3. Angelus, T. L., "Improving the Success Ratio in New Food Products," *Food Technology* 24:333 (1970).
4. "Better Homes and Gardens Questionnaire," in *The Food Industry*

—Indices 42, Better Homes and Gardens, Des Moines, Iowa (1970), p. 57.

5. Borden, Neil H., Jr., *Acceptance of New Food Products*. Boston: Division of Research, Graduate School of Business Administration, Harvard University, 1968.

6. "Business Highlights," *Progressive Grocer* 49:41 (August 1970).

7. "Business Highlights," *Progressive Grocer* 49:64 (September 1970).

8. Charvat, Frank J., *Supermarketing*. New York: The Macmillan Company, 1961, Chapter 2.

9. *Consumer Dynamics in the Supermarket: A Study of Food Retailing in the Supermarket*. New York: Progressive Grocer, 1966.

10. *Consumers' Knowledge and Use of Government Grades for Selected Food Items*, Marketing Research Report No. 876, Economic Research Service, United States Department of Agriculture, Washington, D.C. (1970).

11. "The Cost of Food: How Women Are Trying to Stretch Their Food Budgets," *Monthly Information Service*, Foote, Cone and Belding Advertising, Inc., New York (1970).

12. Cross, Jennifer, *The Supermarket Trap*. Bloomington, Indiana: Indiana University Press (1970), Chapters 2 and 3.

13. Davis, J. G., et al., *Food Buying Practices of Students' Wives at New Mexico State University*, New Mexico State University, Agricultural Experiment Station, Bulletin 547, LaCruces, New Mexico (1969).

14. Day, C., "Mandate to P-O-P: Make Message Match Supermarket Image," *Supermarketing* 25:29 (1970).

15. Dickens, Dorothy, *Sources of Information Which Influence Homemaker's Food Purchases*, Home Economics Series No. 2, Agricultural Experiment Station, Mississippi State University, State College, Mississippi (1962).

16. Dickens, D., and A. Johnston, *Children's Influence on Family Food Purchase Decisions*, Bulletin 671, Agricultural Experiment Station, Mississippi State University, State College, Mississippi (1963).

17. *Food from Farmer to Consumer*, Report of the National Commission on Food Marketing, Superintendent of Documents, Washington, D.C. (1966).

18. Fox, Harold W., *The Economics of Trading Stamps*. Washington, D.C.: Public Affairs Press, 1968.

19. "How Different Consumers Respond to Lure of New Items," *Progressive Grocer* 46:74 (June 1967).

20. "How Prices Are Made," *Chain Store Age* 43:37 (April 1967).

21. Kammer, J. B., and G. L. Shawhan, "Comparison of Food Prices in High and Low Incomes Areas," *Journal of Home Economics* 62:56 (1970).

22. Lamkin, E., et al., "Food Purchasing Practices of Young Families," *Journal of Home Economics* 62:598 (1970).

23. Leiman, Martin, *Food Retailing by Discount Houses,* Marketing Research Report No. 785, Economic Research Service, United States Department of Agriculture, Washington, D.C. (1967).

24. *Look National Survey of Super Market Shopping.* New York: Cowles Magazine and Broadcasting, Inc., 1963.

25. Lyon, David G., *Off Madison Avenue.* New York: G. P. Putnam's Sons, 1966, Chapter 6.

26. *Marketing Changes in the 70's—A Special Report to the 32nd Annual Convention, Super Market Institute.* Chicago: A. C. Nielsen Company, 1969.

27. "Merchandising New Items at Retail: The Payoff at Point of Purchase, Part I. New Items in Action," *Progressive Grocer* 47:46 (1968).

28. "Milwaukee Journal Consumer Analysis," The Journal Company, Milwaukee (1970).

29. Newman, Joseph W., *On Knowing the Consumer.* New York: John Wiley & Sons, Inc., 1966, p. 17.

30. *Nielsen Alert Report,* Nielsen New Product Service, A. C. Nielsen Company, New York (August 1970).

31. "1969 Consumer Analysis of the St. Paul ABC City Zone," St. Paul Dispatch-Pioneer Press, St. Paul, Minnesota (1969).

32. *1971 Study of Supermarket Shoppers,* Burgoyne, Incorporated, Cincinnati, Ohio, 1971.

33. *Organization and Competition in Food Retailing,* Technical Study No. 7, National Commission on Food Marketing, Superintendent of Documents, Washington, D.C. (1966).

34. *Progressive Grocer Colonial Study: A Report on Supermarket Operation and Customer Habits.* New York: Progressive Grocer, 1963.

35. Roberts, John B., *Source of Information and Food Buying Decisions,* Southern Cooperative Series Bulletin 85, University of Kentucky Experiment Station, Lexington, Kentucky (1963).

36. *Seventh DuPont Consumer Buying Habits Study, The Family Shopper—Here's How She Buys,* E. I. DuPont de Nemours & Co., Wilmington, Delaware (1965).

37. Simonds, Lois A., "Variations in Food Costs in Major Ohio Cities," *Journal of Consumer Affairs* 3:52 (1969).

38. *Sixteenth Annual Study of Supermarket Shoppers,* Burgoyne Index, Incorporated, Cincinnati, Ohio (1969).

39. *Special Studies in Food Marketing,* National Commission on Food Marketing, Superintendent of Documents, Washington, D.C. (1966).

40. *Thirty-fifth Annual Nielsen Review of Retail Grocery Store Trends,* A. C. Nielsen Company, Chicago (1970).

41. "Thirty-seventh Annual Report of the Grocery Industry," *Progressive Grocer* 49:47–86 (April 1970).

42. "Thirty-eighth Annual Report of the Grocery Industry," *Progressive Grocer* 50:59–106 (April 1971).

43. Thompson, B., "Intraurban Retail Structure: The Supermarket Sector," *Journal of Retailing* 45:69 (1969).

44. *Twelfth Annual Study of Supermarket Shoppers*, Burgoyne Index, Incorporated, Cincinnati, Ohio (1966).

45. VandeMark, M. S., "Influence of Media on Food Marketing," *Journal of Home Economics* 54:219 (1962).

46. "Variations in Food Prices in One Shopping Area," *Family Economics Review*, Consumer and Food Economics Research Division, United States Department of Agriculture, Washington, D.C. (June 1965).

47. *Women and Food*, The Food Industry Indices, Vol. 42, Better Homes and Gardens, Des Moines, Iowa. (1970), p. 49.

Chapter 3

Science, Technology, and Food

The next several chapters after this one are devoted to the presentation of some kinds of information that will assist the consumer in decision-making in the marketplace. The intent of this chapter is to review briefly the scientific and technological developments that have created the market mix that demands informed decision-making. Almost up to the time of World War II, the manager of meals had relatively few decisions to make. She prepared meals out of what was at hand and in season from quite a limited variety, whether she utilized what was home grown and preserved or she bought her supplies in food stores. We shall discuss agricultural developments first, then the technological developments. These have often gone hand in hand, as, for example, the development of the mechanical harvester for tomatoes and the development of tomatoes that would withstand the rigors of mechanical harvesting.

AGRICULTURE, SCIENCE, AND TECHNOLOGY

Agricultural advances in this century have been so great both qualitatively and quantitatively as to beggar description. Agricultural developments can be credited to scientists who have developed crossbreeds of meat animals and poultry and new and improved varieties of fruits, grains, and vegetables; to the scientists who have studied and determined the optimum environmental conditions for food animals and plants; to the scientists who have assisted in the development of disease resistance in plants and animals as well as the prevention and control of diseases; to the scientists who have aided in the development of pest resistance and in the control of pests in the environment; and to many other scientists who have altered purposely or adventitiously the raw agricultural products that are man's food. The sum total of the efforts of all concerned is more food of better quality; some specific accomplishments are worthy of note.

First, the season for many fruits and vegetables has been extended naturally through the development of early- and late-maturing varieties and varieties that store well, and through the adaptation of varieties to different environments, such as to the temperate zone as well as to warm zones and vice versa. For example, peach varieties better adapted to warmer climates have been developed. Such advances plus environmental control during storage have all but eliminated season, and most fruits and vegetables are available fresh all the year. Varietal changes have resulted in such improvements as better color, or shape, or fleshiness, or size, or juiciness, and so on. However, flavor and aroma have not always been improved; for example, there are those who are critical of the flavor of the newer varieties of tomatoes and corn-on-the-cob. Improvements of recent decades are to be seen in peaches, apricots, plums, strawberries, potatoes, sweet corn, carrots, celery, cucumbers, and others. Varietal improvements coupled with increased knowledge of the cultural requirements of plants both in the field and in the greenhouse have increased production.

Developments in animal husbandry have given us the low-cost broiler or fryer; abundant egg production; broad-breasted turkeys; small turkeys; tender, lean beef from meat-type steers; and lean pork from meat-type hogs. Breeding has been an important factor in these developments; and disease control, feeding management, and environmental control have also been important.

Science, or know-how, continues to be exceedingly important when production is complete, so that fruits and vegetables are harvested at the optimum time, and animals are slaughtered when of the best size and quality. Mechanical harvesting of fruits and vegetables has replaced hand harvesting extensively and will ultimately replace it almost entirely. At-harvest treatments like vacuum cooling and hydrocooling maintain garden freshness for days in such vegetables as carrots, celery, corn-on-the-cob, and lettuce and in fruits like peaches and nectarines. These processes provide wide distribution of fresh fruits and vegetables. In vacuum cooling, produce is cooled in a partial vacuum from the field temperature to 35°F in minutes. Dipping in ice water effects cooling in hydrocooling. This sudden drop in temperature is significant in the maintenance of the quality of freshness. Some items are packaged and go to market at this point; others are stored for future distribution, such as apples and pears. Some freshly harvested fruits and vegetables are immediately frozen; others are processed by other methods, including canning and dehydration. The storage and prevention of spoilage of fruits especially has become so effective that apples harvested in November may remain in good condition until the following June. To deter spoilage, fruits may receive very mild heat treatments in water or steam; lemons, peaches, blueberries, strawberries, and fresh figs are some fruits so treated. Other fruits are treated with solutions containing such chemicals as are effective for the specific organisms to which a fruit is susceptible: apples are dipped to prevent storage scald, a skin disorder; citrus fruits, to prevent mold damage. Grapes, pears, and potatoes also receive chemical treatments. Storage facilities wherein the temperature, humidity, and atmosphere—that is, the carbon dioxide-oxygen ratio—are controlled extend the storage life of fruits and vegetables, such as apples, grapes, and pears.

All turkeys and a great proportion of the broiler crop are frozen after slaughter. Some, but not much, beef is frozen for the consumer trade; more is frozen for institutional use. It goes without saying that all food is transported in vehicles with refrigeration facilities.

SCIENCE, TECHNOLOGY, AND FOOD PROCESSING

Thus far discussion has been of science and technology in the production, the harvest, and the storage of food consumed fresh; it is, however, in the science and technology of food preservation and processing that food products derive their stability and convenience. Canning, cooking, dehydration, and freezing and combinations of these are the methods by which today's convenience foods are processed.

Canning Preservation

Canning leads other methods of food preservation; it effects good storage life and convenient food products. Canned foods have been heat processed at sufficiently high temperatures to destroy pathogenic and spoilage organisms present in the raw food, and the food has been sealed in a container to prevent contamination. Foods are canned in metal cans and glass containers. Recently, flexible packages made from laminated films as well as laminated films and aluminum foil have been developed. It is predicted that in the 1970's, the flexible package will come into greater use; it will favor canned products of better flavor because of possible shorter processing times. Further, it will be less expensive and shipping costs will be reduced because of lighter weight. Currently, metal cans of aluminum or tin exceed other containers in use. Tin cans are steel with a thin coating of tin on both the external and the internal surfaces. Cans for some products are further coated with enamels formulated from oleoresins to protect brightly colored fruits like cherries and raspberries from fading; to prevent sulfur-bearing vegetables like corn from becoming black as a result of interactions between constituents of the food and elements in the metals; and to prevent detinning action by such foods as tomato juice and some fish products. High-temperature, short-time canning has improved the quality of some canned products. Aseptic canning wherein the food and the container are separately sterilized has been used for canning whole milk, whipping cream, coffee cream, half-and-half, and ready-to-eat puddings. The dairy products are packaged in foil-lined cartons. Dehydro-canning is the canning of foods that have had their water content reduced by 50 per cent before processing. Canning modifies unfavorably the flavor, the color, and the texture of vegetables, fish, poultry, and other foods for some persons; they prefer many food products frozen instead. Although canning does give storage stability, canning does not preserve food indef-initely because there are changes in color and flavor during storage. The 1970's will probably see the enactment of a law that will require the mandatory open dating with the date of processing for all canned foods. Familiar ready-to-heat and ready-to-eat canned foods include familiar soups, fruits and vegetables, meats, fish, poultry, sauces, and mixed dishes, and less familiar ones, like caviar, smoked oysters, pickled mushrooms and artichokes, and papaya juice. It is quite probable that the 1970's will see the production of more single-serving foods in cans than are now available—juices, desserts, and a few entrees.

Dehydration

More and more foods processed by dehydration are to be found in the supermarket. They are visible as the many instants to which one adds water to make them ready to eat or to heat; they are also present and less visible in assorted foods and mixes. There are naturally dehydrated foods, such as nuts, grains, beans and peas, and sun-dried fruits. Because of the vagaries of the weather these are often finished commercially with arti-ficial drying. There are several techniques for the dehydration of food, more than for preservation by canning or freezing. An advantage of dehydration is weight reduction by water loss. Water removal occurs both at high temperatures and at low temperatures in a vacuum; quality is better in the latter instance.

In tunnel drying, food passes through chambers into which heated air is blown. In spray drying, liquid foods are sprayed into cone-shaped cham-bers into which hot air is blown. The food is instantly dried. Milk, coffee, juices, and coffee creamers are dried in this way. In roller or drum drying, food slurries or purees are heated in a thin layer on the surface of a heated revolving drum. The dry film is removed and flaked or pulverized. Instant potato flakes, instant cereals, and instant sweet potatoes, applesauce, and pumpkin are some foods processed in this way. In foam-mat drying, the puree is released under pressure from a nozzle into a heated chamber for drying as in spray drying. This process is used for milk, instant flour, coffee and tea, fruit and vegetable juices, and fruit purees.

Freeze drying has so expanded in use that in 1970, some five hundred million pounds of more than fifty products were processed by this technique. The two-step process includes the initial quick freezing of the pre-pared product, followed by drying in a vacuum chamber. The final product retains its original cell structure, is light in weight, is shelf storable, and is of good color and flavor. The freeze-dried product is fragile and requires special packaging to protect it from shattering. Research has demonstrated that freeze-dried foods can be compressed for purposes of bulk reduction and that on hydration they are restored to normal appearance and texture. Freeze-dried foods take up water rapidly and some are subject to deterioration in oxygen; they must be packaged in an inert atmosphere in moistureproof and vaporproof wraps. Products dehydrated by freeze drying include coffee; raw and precooked meats, fish, poultry, and shellfish; such precooked vegetables as peas, spinach, corn, and carrots; cottage cheese; such fruits as peaches, strawberries, cherries, and pears; such fruit juices as orange, grapefruit, and pineapple; shrimp, chicken, and tuna salads; casserole dishes like beef Stroganoff; and so on. The armed forces use the following freeze-dried entrees: beef hash, beef stew, beef with rice, pork and escalloped potatoes, chili con carne, spaghetti with meat sauce, chicken stew, and chicken with rice. With the addition of boiling water these are ready to eat within five minutes. In the early 1970's, some similar products are being test-marketed for consumers and have been introduced for institutional feeding.

The reverse of freeze drying is dehydrofreezing. It combines the economy of dehydration with the flavor-holding advantages of freezing. The water content of fruits and vegetables is reduced by 50 per cent; the product is then frozen. The process is used for processing fruits and vegetables for food manufacturing, for example, apple slices for pies and potatoes and vegetables for soups and stews. Explosion puffing, first used to puff cereals, has been applied to vegetables, including the potato, and fruits. Products are first partially dried; they are then placed in a pressure chamber; release of pressure in the chamber causes the pieces to explode, much as corn pops. The finished pieces are about the same size as they were before processing. Flavor is good, and the products reconstitute readily. Reverse osmosis is a process whereby water is removed from fruits placed in a concentrated sugar solution; when the water content is reduced to the desirable level, the fruit is further dried to low water content by vacuum drying.

Freezing Preservation

Millions of pounds of more than two thousand items were processed by freezing in 1970. This poundage included many and diverse products; some to thaw and eat, some to heat and eat, others to cook and eat. Many varieties of plants are grown especially for preservation by freezing, notably peas and strawberries. New frozens are introduced all of the time; old ones fade away. Many include maid service and chef service, such as precooked dinners and ready-to-bake pies.

Foods preserved by freezing are either quick frozen at temperatures from minus 10°F to minus 40°F or instant (or cryogenic) frozen at minus 100°F to minus 320°F, depending on the refrigerant. Refrigerants include liquid nitrogen, liquid or solid carbon dioxide, liquid air, and Freon. Freon, developed by DuPont, has been approved by the Food and Drug Administration as a refrigerant. It is sprayed on food and subsequently recovered. Prepared foods frozen in consumer-sized packages are quick frozen between metal plates or in cold air blasts. Products that are packaged after freezing are spread on a wire mesh belt and either pass through a freezing tunnel or are subjected to a current of icy cold air that passes up through the mesh belt, causing the food to tumble and freeze in the air. Freezing is rapid and the individual pieces do not stick together but are individually quick frozen (IQF). The IQF fruits, vegetables, and other products so frozen are readily pourable from the package and handy to use in the kitchen.

Instant (or cryogenic) freezing improves the appearance, color, and palatability of some frozen foods, especially of such vegetables as asparagus, green beans, corn-on-the-cob, and peas, and of such fruits as strawberries and peaches. Further, it is possible to freeze instantly food that cannot be satisfactorily quick frozen, such as tomatoes, green peppers, avocados, mushrooms, and watermelon. Some foods do not require instant freezing to be of good quality, such as precooked meats and vegetables and prepared meals. Meat patties and meat cuts instantly frozen must be cooked from the frozen state.

Microwave Processing

The Food and Drug Administration approved in March, 1968 radiofrequency radiation (including microwave frequencies) for the heating of food. Microwaves are a form of electromagnetic energy that is intermediate in frequency and wavelength between radio waves and infrared waves. Microwaves are absorbed by food, causing agitation of molecules and friction; hence, rapid heating. Water selectively absorbs the energy. Commercially, microwave heating is being used in processing potato chips and in frying chicken. Its use permits control of browning. The microwave oven is used extensively for cooking and heating food in restaurants and institutional feeding. Though not in extensive home use yet, it is anticipated that home use will expand in the 1970's. In 1970, the Food and Drug Administration approved as safe the microwave ovens of major manufacturers.

Radiation Preservation of Food

Regulation of the use of radiation preservation or treatment of food is under the Food and Drug Administration by authority of the Food Additives Amendment of The Food, Drug, and Cosmetic Act of 1938. The preservation of food by radiation has been extensively researched worldwide since World War II. High radiation dosage effects complete and total sterilization of food; "cold sterilization" at a lesser dosage level effects sterility comparable to canning. Low-radiation doses pasteurize, disinfest, and inhibit sprouting. Pasteurization reduces spoilage and extends the shelf life of such perishable foods as fresh fruits and vegetables, and fish and shellfish. Unfortunately, radiation treatment of food reduces acceptability by affecting color and flavor and aroma. Even pasteurization causes flavor change described as "radiation flavor." It has been discovered that cooking or freezing food before radiation results in fewer undesirable changes.

In February, 1963 the Food and Drug Administration authorized the radiation sterilization of canned bacon. This product did not reach the consumer market; but it was consumed by the armed forces. In August, 1968 approval was withdrawn on the basis of adverse effects produced in animals fed irradiated foods. There is as yet no consensus on the safety of radiation-treated food. There is some loss of nutrient content, but it is comparable to the losses caused by heat treatment. Food does not contain induced radioactivity. However, there is the possibility of the production of toxic agents in the food by radiation. Radiation preservation is expensive and it will probably not be introduced in food processing unless it can offer some unique advantage over established methods. It remains in use for disinfestation of wheat and wheat flour and for the inhibition of the sprouting of potatoes. The use of ultraviolet radiation for the processing and treatment of food is permitted by the Food and Drug Administration for surface microorganism control as in the fast ripening of beef and for sterilization of water for food processing.

Food Packaging

Advances in food technology have required advances in food-packaging technology, and, on the other hand, developments in food-packaging materials and packing technology have made possible advances in food technology. The consumer asks that the package be convenient, informative, and protective; the food processor, that it sell his product or products and that it be protective; and the supermarket manager, that it be all of these plus pilferproof.

Convenient packages are easy to open, easy to reclose if this is desirable, easy to carry, easy to handle and use, and convenient to store if this is important and relevant. Consumers want the package to inform them through its labeling what a product is and how to use it; also, to reveal the nature of the contents as in window-boxed products when this is feasible. Lastly, consumers require that packaging protect the contents of the package from contamination and deterioration. Shrewd shoppers may choose between products and product lines because of the quality of packaging: film versus paper or string bag, opaque versus transparent pouches, and plastic versus paperboard egg cartons.

The package is the silent salesman of a product in the supermarket. A package communicates; consumers select it or they pass it by. If we pass it by, an otherwise good and useful new product may fail—not because it was not good; but because in some way the package failed the product. Food packaging is both art and science. In addition to selling his product, the processor wants the package to protect the product from the rigors of transport and handling and the adverse factors in the environment. And he wants all of these at economical cost.

The prime purpose of packaging is protection: protection from physical damage during transport and handling, protection from contamination, and protection from deteriorative changes effected by environmental factors. Protection during shipping and handling is easily obtained by the use of strong cartons that have stacking strength, special wrappings and liners, fillers, and moulded trays or containers. Materials used for food packaging include wood, wood veneer, fibreboard, paperboard, kraft paper, packaging films of great variety, aluminum foil, laminates of films and other materials, steel and aluminum for cans, glass for containers, and plastic for containers of diverse kinds. Protection from contamination means prevention of the entry of insects, dust, filth, and microorganisms. Insect infestation of food is common. The presence of insects and the presence of filth in food is considered adulteration by the Food and Drug Administration. To prevent it, in-plant insect control and the use of insect resistant containers are essential; rodent control is required; and maintenance of a high level of sanitation is necessary. Only food that has been processed to destroy all organisms and is packaged in hermetically sealed containers is free from the danger of contamination by microorganisms. All other foods must be packaged according to kind and properly stored. At best, packaging and storage conditions simply delay the reactions that lead to deterioration and ultimately to spoilage.

Factors in the environment that cause the deterioration and spoilage of food are heat, oxygen or air, moisture or humidity, and light. Through effects on enzymes in plant and animal foods and on the growth rates of microorganisms, some or all of these environmental factors cause loss of crispness, loss of flavor, development of rancidity, loss of color, drying, moldiness, fermentation, and putrefaction. Packaging that removes one or more of the environmental factors delays these changes. It includes the use of the best packaging material for the processed product; proper sealing of the package; packaging in a vacuum; packaging in an inert gas; the use of additives, such as antioxidants, desiccants, mold inhibitors, and preservatives in the packaging material or in or on the food itself. A problem of the 1970's is the disposal of the waste that packaging creates. Though some of the materials can be recycled, not all can be. No-return bottles pose a special problem because they are difficult to destroy. It is quite likely that a method for their destruction will be discovered or that a method of producing them that modifies them to make them destructible will be developed in the 1970's.

Some examples of good packaging are perforated film bags for fresh fruits and vegetables to control respiration and moisture loss; shrink-film packaging for lettuce, fresh and frozen poultry, and cheese; opaque, oxygen-impermeable films for ground beef and fresh and cured meats; opaque labels on one side of cured-meat packages if packaged in air-permeable films; vacuum- and nitrogen-backfilled packages for luncheon meats and dried beef; skintight vacuum packs for bacon; oxygen impermeable film for hotdogs; shrink-film vacuum packs for frozen fish; moisture- and vapor-proof packaging for frozen foods to prevent drying, i.e., freezer burn; and opaque packaging for frozen vegetables to protect against color loss. Some favorite consumer packages are boil-in-the-bag pouches, containers that serve as a baking pan or a serving dish, pull-tab cans, cans with plastic covers, see-through trays for meat packaging, window-box cartons, no-return bottles, paperboard containers for ready-to-bake pastries, and aerosols.

Substitutes and Synthetic Foods

No discussion of science and technology and food in the 1970's can omit mention of substitute and synthetic foods and designed or engineered foods. *Synthetic products* have been defined as those that include at least one major ingredient derived from nonfarm sources. A *major nonfarm ingredient* is any substance that displaces natural agricultural materials in a food product's set of basic attributes, particularly flavor, texture, viscosity, and color. Usually petroleum provides the bulk of material for synthetic ingredients. Some synthetics are fruit juice drinks, fruit juice powders and concentrates, and fruit punches. About 20 per cent of the retail citrus beverage market is of orange-flavored drinks that contain no citrus derivatives. *Substitute food products* have been defined as those that contain one or more major ingredients derived from unconventional agricultural resources. Some foods considered to be substitutes are margarine, the meat analogs, nondairy coffee creamers, and nondairy whipped toppings. At the present time, substitutes exceed synthetics in number. The currently projected future food-population imbalance favors the continued development of both. If meat analogs were to replace meat in our diet, current agricultural capacity would feed four to five times as many persons as it now does; or if we consumed dairy products at the pre-World War II level, dairy production would have to be 50 per cent greater at this time. Producing agricultural products to feed animals in order to feed meat and other animal foods to man is less efficient and more costly than if man were to consume the primary crops. In general, only in the Western, or advanced countries has it been possible to feed the primary crops to animals; the rest of the world's people eat diets composed of grains, yams, roots, legumes, and other vegetables, that is, the primary food products.

In the United States substitutes have been accepted because of the frequent replacement of animal fat with vegetable fats as in margarine, filled milk and cheese, and the nondairy coffee creamers. The meat analogs are accepted because of religious beliefs that forbid the eating of meats. The soybean meat analogs number about sixty now; they are used by vegetarians and in institutional feeding. The food processors use textured vegetable proteins in such dishes as chili with beans, spaghetti sauce with meat, meat loaf, and Spanish rice to name but a few.

Designed or engineered foods include those developed for overcoming malnutrition in the developing countries. They are fabricated from agricultural products with or without the addition of minerals and/or vitamins. Some are intended for the feeding of children especially. They are formulated from cereal grains, soybeans and other legumes, cottonseed meal, and fishprotein concentrate. They are prepared for eating as gruels, soups, breads, and whatever other dishes are peculiar to the diet in a given place. In general, small quantities of the product provide a high proportion of nutrient needs other than calories.

The threat of starvation as a result of population-food imbalance has led to the research and development of unconventional sources of protein. Bacteria, yeasts, and fungi have been cultured in a variety of substrates to provide great quantities of protein and other nutrients. Fish-protein concentrate; oil-seed protein concentrate derived from the press cake that remains after the pressing of oil from oil-bearing seeds; leaf protein concentrate; and protein concentrate derived from the culture of algae are other unconventional food sources. The Food and Drug Administration has approved fish-protein concentrate for limited use by humans; the use of the remaining unconventional sources remains in the future for man, though some are in use in animal feeding.

Food Additives

Just as an abundant agriculture is dependent on the use of a host of chemicals, so is the abundant supply of high quality food and processed food found in the supermarket of the 1970's dependent on a host of chemicals. These are the food additives the uses of which are both maligned and applauded. Their proper use presupposes that they are safe, that their use effectively serves an intended purpose, that the quantity used is no more than is required to accomplish a given purpose, that their use does not supplant good manufacturing practice, and that their use does not provide an opportunity for deception. The legal aspects of food-additive use will be discussed in Chapter 4; the discussion here is limited to the purposes of use and to the kinds of compounds in use. The use of additives increased in food processing by 50 per cent during the 1960's, per capita consumption in 1971 was three pounds per year.

There is a long history of adding substances to food to preserve it, such as the salting of meat and fish; to make it taste better, such as the use of spices, herbs, and sugar; and to color it to make it look better. In the 1970's, science and technology have made possible the presence in a food of one or several of some ten thousand substances, either intentionally or unintentionally. Unintentional additives can derive from agricultural production (these are the chemicals that are necessary for an abundant agriculture); they can derive during processing from the equipment itself or from the substances used in maintaining the equipment; or lastly, they can derive from packaging materials. In illustration of the latter, pigments, inks, waxes, adhesives, resins, and the gases of aerosols can migrate to and enter a food. The presence of some of these constitutes adulteration; for others regulations are in effect. But, in general, the additives present in a food are put there intentionally for specific purposes: to color, to flavor, to enhance flavor, to produce a proper mouthfeel of a food, to produce a smooth texture, to keep a food crisp, to keep a food moist, to preserve, to emulsify, to aid in foaming, to prevent foaming, to prevent the development of rancidity, to sweeten, and so on, *ad infinitum*.

Some classes of additives will be described according to function and it may be noted that some additives function in more than one capacity, i.e., nitrates and nitrites and sulfur dioxide and sulfites.

Preservatives or antimicrobial additives extend the shelf life of foods; they are important in preventing food waste and in maximizing the food supply. Salt, sugar, acids, and wood smoke have been in use for centuries. They remain in use as antimicrobial agents, but chemical preservatives have superseded them in use. The use of chemical preservatives cannot, by law, result in deception, or adversely affect the nutritive value of a food, or permit the growth of food poisoning organisms while suppressing the growth of other organisms that would make spoilage evident. Label statement of the use of chemical preservatives in standardized foods is mandatory. Further, the label statement must specify the nature of the preservative action, for example, "added to retard mold growth." Benzoic acid and sodium benzoate are active against many bacteria, yeasts, and molds. Their use is permitted in carbonated and still beverages, fruit drinks and juices, margarine, prepared salads and salad dressings, mince-meat, and pickles. The parabens (para-hydroxybenzoate esters) are similar in action and used in the same products, except margarine, and also in chemically leavened baked goods, pastries, icings, toppings, and dried fruits and vegetables.

Sorbic acid and its sodium and potassium salts are effective for molds and yeasts especially; they are used in the foods already mentioned and also for cheese and cheese products, dry sausages, and salted or smoked fish. In addition to being used directly on a food, the sorbates may be present on wrapping materials. Proprionic acid and its sodium and calcium salts are mold inhibitors especially. They are used mainly for this purpose for breads and cheese and cheese products. Proprionates are sprayed on brown-and-serve rolls and butter wrappers are impregnated with them. Sulfur dioxide and the sulfites are antimicrobial for bacteria, yeasts, and molds; they also protect the color of fruits and vegetables by actions that deter browning. Sulfur is applied as fumes, in a dip, or by spray. Though nitrates are antimicrobial, their main use is in curing mixtures for meats, where they function to develop and fix the red color that is unique to cured meats. The safety of the nitrate additives is suspect. After proper study, a decision on their safety will be made in the 1970's. Acetic acid, acetates, and vinegar are effective against yeasts and bacteria. They are used in catsup, mayonnaise, pickles, and pickled sausages.

Antioxidants also preserve food by preventing the development of rancidity, browning, loss of color, and loss of flavor. A moderately long list of these has been approved for foods and for packaging materials. Some of them, the names of which appear in full or in abbreviated form on labels, are butylated hydroxyanisole (BHA), butylated hydroxytoluene (BHT), propyl gallate (PG), gum guaiac, tocopherols, and lecithin.

A group of compounds known as sequestrants function similarly to antioxidants in that they protect against the development of rancidity and color and flavor losses, but in a different manner. They are chelating agents that react with metals to alter the effects of metals in substances. Some sequestrants, the names of which appear on labels, are oxystearin, sorbitol, EDTA (ethylenediaminetetra acetate), and citric, tartaric, and pyrophosphoric acids. Their use extends the shelf life and stabilizes the flavor of salad dressings, french fried potatoes, fried and baked goods, roasted nuts, and margarine, that is, products containing fats and oils. They protect the vitamin content, especially vitamin C, of fruit juices; the color of canned vegetables and fruits and of frozen fruits; and the color and flavor of fish and shellfish processed by canning and freezing.

One of the prime requisites of a food is that it taste good; hence, an extremely important group of food additives is one that includes flavorings and flavor enhancers and potentiators. The nature of flavor and, likewise, the nature of flavor perception are complex. Food flavors range from delicate to robust, from labile to relatively stable. We have already noted that a number of food additives are used for the purpose of protecting flavor. Spices introduced in Europe during the Crusades and herbs introduced during the Middle Ages were the first flavoring agents. Their function was twofold: to mask the bad flavor of nearly spoiled food and to provide pleasing flavors. A glance at the labels of almost any prepared food on supermarket shelves reveals that flavor agents are both natural and artificial, generally the latter only. Artificial flavor agents that closely resemble natural ones can be made more economically, more uniformly, and in greater concentration than the natural flavor agents. Man-made flavorings are of two types: the synthetic ones that have the same chemical composition as natural flavor agents, and simulated, or imitation, flavorings that taste like the natural flavor agents. Both are used in foods and would be described on labels as artificial flavorings. The development of meat analogs was contingent on the availability of flavor agents to provide the beef, chicken, and other flavors that cause the analogs to taste like the real thing. Likewise, cake mixes, imitation dairy foods, margarine, dessert mixes, and a host of other foods require the use of prodigious quantities of artificial flavorings.

In addition to the use of flavor agents per se, there is wide use of compounds known as flavor enhancers and flavor potentiators. These are compounds that when used in small quantities have no sensory effect but that affect the ways in which flavor is perceived. A number of naturally occurring flavor enhancers have been identified; those in commercial production and use include monosodium glutamate (MSG), maltol, 5'-inosine monophosphate (IMP), and 5'-guanine monophosphate (GMP). They intensify flavor and appear to suppress some undesirable flavor notes. All are used in minute quantities, and the amount of MSG used to produce certain effects can be reduced by the use of the 5'-nucleotides, which act synergistically with it. The flavoring of processed foods is both science and art; an otherwise convenient food may fail because of unacceptable flavor, for though flavor is an experience short in duration, it is lasting in memory.

Gums comprise a group of compounds in extensive use in processed foods. Gums derived from seaweeds were in use for centuries as thickening and gelling agents but it took twentieth-century food technology to give them the importance they now have. They are, excepting gelatin, complex carbohydrates composed of sugar units. Dissolved in water they produce viscous solutions or gels. They function as thickening, gelling, emulsifying, suspending, water-binding, and stabilizing agents. Gums from natural sources are, in decreasing order of use, gum arabic, guar gum, gelatin, carrageenan, locust bean gum, and agar. The natural sources of gums, excepting gelatin, are plants. Gums derived from seaweeds are agar, algin, carrageenan, and furcellan; from seeds, locust bean gum and guar gum; and from tree sources, gum arabic, gum tragacanth, and karaya gum. Semisynthetic gums are derived by treatment of starch and cellulose; several have been approved by the Food and Drug Administration for use: methyl cellulose, carboxymethyl cellulose, and propylene glycol alginate. Pectins are derived from fruits, especially citrus fruits. The names of gums appear abundantly on food labels; however, carob bean gum, gum karaya, gum tragacanth, guar gum, and oat gum may be designated as "vegetable gum." Gums, almost all of them, are used in the production of the following dairy products: ice cream and ice milk, sherbets, chocolate milk drink, cottage cheese, cream cheese, cheese spreads, whipped cream, and yogurt. Some or all of the named gums are used in bread doughs and mixes, cake mixes, cake fillings and toppings, pie fillings, puddings, cookies, and others. Further, they are used in salad dressings and French dressing; in white sauces and gravies; in syrups and toppings; in spaghetti sauces; in canned meat, fish, and poultry; as sausage binders; and in low-calorie foods and others.

Some other groups of food additives will be discussed only briefly in this miscellaneous grouping.

The color additives are both artificial and natural colors. The natural ones include annatto, an extract from the seeds of a tropical tree; beta carotene; caramel; paprika; saffron; turmeric; and grapeskin extract. All artificial colors must be certified as safe by the Food and Drug Administration. A group of compounds called polyglycerol esters is interesting because they are defoaming agents and antispattering, antisticking, antiweeping, antilumping, and anticlouding agents. They also make peanut butter and margarines more spreadable; further, they are emulsifiers, thickeners, and stabilizers. Surfactants are extremely important in food processing: they are emulsifying agents and wetting agents and they retard the staling process in yeast-raised baked goods, as well as performing other functions. Important ones are the mono- and di-glycerides, propylene glycol monostearate, and polysorbate 60. These surface-active agents give shortenings and oils their easy-to-use properties. The addition of food nutrients, as in the enrichment of flour, bread, cereals, fruit beverages, milk, and salt, is important nutritionally. It is quite probable that as more foods are designed, the addition of nutrients will become increasingly important.

The following appeared in 1970 on the label of a breakfast toaster-pastry: "Made from flour, shortening, sugar, eggs, water, brown sugar, yeast, raisins, nonfat dry milk, dough conditioners, salt, mono- and di-glycerides, corn flour, honey, cocoa, cinnamon, artificial flavors and colors, agar, polysorbate 60, sorbitan monostearate, sodium proprionate, potassium sorbate-preservatives." In summary, it may be stated that twentieth-century food technology makes extensive use of food additives for various purposes: to fabricate foods of acceptable quality, that is, good flavor, color, and texture; to maintain quality, that is, prevent deterioration and spoilage; to enhance nutrient content; and, of course, to provide the consumer with built-in maid and built-in chef services.

FOOD SAFETY

Agricultural and technological advances, increased populations of man and animals, and increased consumption of meals away from home have expanded the opportunities for the pollution of food by harmful biological and chemical agents. Chemical agents include the pesticides, herbicides, fumigants, germicides, fungicides, antibiotics, and others used in agricultural production; direct and unintentional additives introduced during food processing; and radio-nuclides arising from nuclear testing. In addition, there is growing concern that industrial chemicals that pollute the environment may ultimately find their way into man's food —for example, the recent discovery of toxic amounts of mercury in freshwater fish, tuna, and swordfish as a result of the contamination of bodies of fresh water. The provisions of the Food, Drug, and Cosmetic Act of 1938 and its subsequent amendments prohibit the presence in food of poisonous, deleterious, and unsafe substances. Milk and plant foods are vehicles for radio-nuclide pollution. Radioactive elements that may be present include strontium-89, strontium-90, cesium-137, and iodine-131. Monitoring of food by the Atomic Energy Commission, by the Department of Health, Education, and Welfare, and by the United States Department of Agriculture is presumed to assure their presence in food only at safe levels. Biological pollutants are more prevalent in food and drink than chemical pollutants, although the latter do occur. The provisions of the Food, Drug, and Cosmetic Act are relevant for biological pollutants. The meat and poultry inspection acts were enacted to ensure clean meat foods from healthy animals. Be that as it may, the incidence of foodborne disease in man is increasing; and will perhaps become worse, not better.

Biological agents include bacteria, mycotoxins, viruses, and parasites; of these, bacteria are the most serious offenders. Opportunities for bacterial contamination are numerous; a partial list would include animal pens, feeds, slaughterhouses, packing plants, warehouses, processing plants, transportation vehicles, drive-in kitchens, institutional kitchens, and home kitchens. Vectors of the polluting organisms are insects, rodents, birds, animals (including household pets), and man himself. The usual route of contamination is oral-fecal. Food infection of bacterial origin is caused by the *Salmonellae*. Illness and infection result from their presence in the gut. Food introxications are caused by toxins that have been introduced into food by *Staphylococcus aureus, Clostridium botulinum,* and possibly *Clostridium perfringens.* In 1969, *Clostridium perfringens* food poisoning affected nearly 65 per cent of all persons involved in foodborne outbreaks; staphylococcal gastroenteritis, 12 per cent; and salmonellosis, 6.6 per cent. The major vehicles of infection were turkey, chicken, beef, pork, and/or gravy, and/or dressing. *Clostridium perfringens* is a spore-forming anaerobe, and there are many types. The mode of action of this organism is not clearly understood; it may be by infection or by toxin or by both. The spores are resistant to curing and smoking; some are heat resistant. *C. perfringens* is widely distributed in feces, sewage, soil, and water. It is so widespread that researchers generally concede that it is a probable contaminant of nearly all foods. Food is safe only when it has been handled in accordance with maximum sanitation standards and has been maintained at temperatures above and below the critical zone. Meats, poultry, and gravies must be quickly cooled and refrigerated.

Staphylococcal intoxication was the second ranking foodborne illness in 1969. Though a food is the vehicle for the toxin, this foodborne illness is generally of human origin; that is, the food was contaminated by man. *S. aureus* is present on the skin, in nose and throat discharges, and in the pus of infected lesions. It produces a heat-stable enterotoxin that causes the illness. Poor sanitation standards in food handling result in the contamination of the food. Then, when food is improperly chilled or heated, it becomes an excellent medium for the rapid multiplication of the organisms and the consequent production of the toxin. Foods that are most commonly incriminated in outbreaks of staphylococcal intoxications include meat and meat products; eggs and egg products; salads, such as chicken, tuna, egg, and potato; cream-filled pastries and pies; and milk and milk products. Meals eaten away from home, delicatessen foods, and foods improperly handled and stored in the house can be unsafe because of the organism.

Salmonellae, there are one thousand two hundred or more types, are ubiquitous in air, soil, and water. Their home is the intestinal tract of animals and man, and they are distributed via feces. A partial list of the foods in which they have been found to occur includes red meats, processed meats, poultry, eggs and egg products, dried milk, coconut, dried yeast, chocolate candy, dietary supplements, and animal feeds. Avoidance of the contamination of food by *Salmonellae* requires the maintenance of maximum sanitation standards throughout the food production and processing chain and the maintenance of food temperatures above or below the critical temperature range of 40°F and 140°F, within which there is rapid growth of any bacteria present. It is required that liquid, frozen, and dried eggs be pasteurized or subjected to equivalent heat treatment to destroy this organism. The Communicable Disease Center of the United States Public Health Service has established a surveillance program covering the fifty states, Puerto Rico, and the Virgin Islands. The program records the incidence of salmonellosis and acts to control outbreaks. Participation has been extended to Canada and some European countries.

Clostridium botulinum is a ubiquitous spore-forming anaerobe. During growth, the organism produces toxins lethal to man if a sufficient quantity is consumed. Botulism—the disease caused by the toxin—is not common: only about 50 deaths were ascribed to it in the 1960's. The toxin is rarely present in commercially canned foods. The danger of this food contaminant has long been considered to be home-canned nonacid foods, such as corn, peas, or meats, because processing at a high temperature is essential for the destruction of the heat-resistant spores. Commercially canned nonacid foods are presumed to have been sufficiently processed to effect the destruction of all spores. However, during the summer of 1971, one death occurred from botulism as the result of the eating of a commercially canned soup—vichyssoise, a potato-leek soup eaten cold. All products of the company that processed the soup—Bon Vivant, Incorporated of Newark, New Jersey—were recalled by the Food and Drug Administration and the company closed its plant. The fact that the company had sold its gourmet line under 21 different labels made recall difficult. Also during the summer of 1971, the Campbell Soup Company recalled one lot of chicken-vegetable soup because of contamination by the botulinum toxin. The toxin is heat-destructible when food is boiled for ten minutes; however, few persons boil canned foods for that long, and some canned foods are eaten unheated. Cans of food should be discarded when they show even slightly bulged ends or any other evidence of spoilage such as souring, gas formation, discoloration, or leaks. Under no circumstances should suspect food be tasted.

Hepatitis and poliomyelitis can be caused by viruses linked to contaminated food and water polluted by sewage. Several parasitic infections can be contracted from food, but trichinosis is the one most likely to occur. Pork is the carrier of the causative organism, *Trichinella spiralis*. The infection of swine is prevented by maintaining them in rodent-free pens and by feeding them infection-free rations. Infected meat is made safe by holdin freezing storage for twenty to thirty days and by heating to a temperature of not less than 137°F; however, pork should be cooked to a temperature of not less than 150°F.

Mycotoxins are produced by molds. Until the early 1960's there was no concern about molds in food. In fact, molds are purposefully introduced in cheese-making to develop desired flavors. (See Chapter 7.) In 1961, thousands of turkeys died of an unknown cause in Great Britain. It was subsequently established that death was caused by toxin produced by *Aspergillus flavus*, now known as aflatoxin. Aflatoxin is acutely toxic to many animal species and is a potent carcinogen; consumed by animals it appears in tissues and milk. Molds occur throughout the world but develop more abundantly where heat and humidity are high. Cereals and nuts if not properly dried after harvest become moldy. The presence of aflatoxin has been established in animal feeds, peanuts and peanut products, Brazil nuts, pecans, corn, copra, and cottonseed. To maintain a safe food supply, methods of prevention and control of mold growth in foods and feeds must be practiced; moldy foods and feeds must be removed from the marketplace, and susceptible and suspicious foods must be tested for the presence of aflatoxin. A no-tolerance level has been established for their presence in food. Formerly, it was stated that molds were harmless and that when the unsightly moldy parts were removed from a food the food was edible. Now it is recommended that with few exceptions moldy food be discarded.

Antibiotics

The Food and Drug Administration has ruled that the use of antibiotic drugs in the preservation of food constitutes a public health hazard. The presence of antibiotic drugs in foods intended for human consumption, or the direct or indirect addition of such drugs to foods, is deemed adulteration. This statement of policy does not however, bar the establishment of safe tolerances in or on raw agricultural commodities if there is evidence of the usefulness of the antibiotic and of the safety of the residue. Antibiotic drugs are components of animal feeds and antibiotics are in use to control animal diseases. Their use in animal feeding effects increased efficiency in the utilization of feeds and greater and more rapid growth than occurs when they are not used. The mechanism of their action in oral feeding is not fully understood.

Good Manufacturing Practice

To promote the safety of food, the Food and Drug Administration, in 1969, promulgated regulations for good manufacturing practice. Its authority to do so derives from the Food, Drug, and Cosmetic Act, which deems a food adulterated "if it has been prepared, packed, or held under insanitary conditions whereby it may have been contaminated with filth or whereby it may have been rendered injurious to health." The regulations provide criteria for use in "determining whether the facilities, methods, practices, and controls used in the manufacture, processing, packing, or holding of food are in conformance with or are operated or administered in conformity with good manufacturing practices to assure that food for human consumption is safe and has been prepared, packed, and held under sanitary conditions." The criteria are applicable to grounds; plant design and construction; water supply, sewage disposal, plumbing, toilet facilities, hand-washing facilities, and rubbish and offal disposal; sanitary operations (including animal and vermin control), sanitation of equipment and utensils, and storage and handling of cleaned portable equipment and utensils; and, lastly, the supervision, education and training, cleanliness, and disease control of personnel. A notable requirement of the regulations is that a person knowledgeable in sanitation concepts be assigned the responsibility for assuring compliance of all personnel with all requirements. Failure to comply with the regulations is grounds for seizure, injunction, and prosecution. Further, as the law intended, conditions of insanitation alone are now sufficient for the condemnation of food as adulterated.

Summary. During this century, our food supply has been vastly increased by developments in agriculture and animal husbandry, by improved storage techniques, and by improved methods of processing. The world population-food imbalance demands the maximization of our food supply that science and technology can effect. These advances have not been without hazards to man, the pollution of the environment with many different kinds of chemicals, and the addition to food of substances that may or may not be totally safe. These developments have contributed to the greater need for laws to regulate the safety of the food supply.

Chapter 4

Food Laws and the Regulation of the Food Supply

The story of adulterated food is an old one; the history of legislation to regulate adulteration and provide people with wholesome food is equally old. Two well-known examples from biblical history are the restrictions on eating pork and meat from animals killed other than by prescribed slaughter. Bread and wine were adulterated in ancient Greece and Rome. A Sanskrit law of 300 B.C. imposed fines on any who sold adulterated grains or oils. Chinese classics of the second century B.C. relate that there were government officials responsible for preventing the manufacture of adulterated food. During the Middle Ages, as commerce expanded and the manufacture of some food was transferred from home to shop, the fraudulent practice of including cheaper materials in foods increased. Spices were in great demand; they were often highly diluted. The first English food law was the Assize of Bread proclaimed by King John in 1202. It prohibited the adulteration of bread with such ingredients as ground peas or beans. In 1266, legislation was passed in England to protect the purchaser against short weight in bread and the sale of unsound meat. In general, these early attempts at control were ineffectual. Cheating became more sophisticated and more common during the sixteenth, seventeenth, and eighteenth centuries. In the nineteenth century, the enormity of the problem came to light as the science of analytical chemistry and the microscope provided tools for detecting and measuring adulteration.

It was in England that the problem was first publicized and action taken. In 1820, a German chemist and pharmacist living in London, Frederick C. Accum, published *A Treatise on Adulteration of Food, and Culinary Poisons.* This work was published in the United States in the same year by a pirate publisher. At midcentury, Dr. Arthur H. Hassell conducted investigations for the *Lancet,* a British medical journal, revealing that scarcely any common foodstuff was free from adulteration. Aroused public opinion forced the passage of legislation to control food adulteration. The first efforts were weak, but in 1875 Parliament passed a law that, with subsequent amendments, remained the basic British food law for many years. By the end of the century, most European countries had general food statutes.

LEGISLATION IN THE UNITED STATES

In the United States, the first law on record was passed in 1784 by Massachusetts; it penalized the seller of diseased, corrupted, or unwholesome provisions. In 1850, a pure food and drink law was passed in California. General interest in food and drug laws did not develop until after the Civil War; however, during the relatively short time since, a voluminous history of food legislation in the United States has been accumulated. Only federal legislation will be discussed here. At first, the federal food laws were enacted to provide revenue, to prevent the importation of unwholesome and adulteratd food, and to protect domestic agriculture. Later, the main purposes of federal legislation became the protection of the consumer from fraud and the protection of the public health. A brief history of the various enactments of the federal government follows.

History of Legislation

The first federal food law was the Tea Act of 1883; it prohibited the importation of spurious and adulterated teas. This tea act was repealed by a tea act of 1897, which also prohibited the importation of adulterated and spurious teas; but it also provided for the establishment of a body of tea experts who would each year—on or before February 15—establish minimum standards of quality for imported teas and for the inspection of all teas entering United States ports.

In 1886, the original Oleomargarine Act was passed. It imposed taxes on, regulated the manufacture and sale of, and controlled the importation of oleomargarine. The tax was not repealed until 1950, at which time the Food, Drug, and Cosmetic Act was amended to regulate the sale of colored margarine and the serving of colored margarine in public eating places "whether the margarine originates from an interstate source or from the state in which sold."

In 1890, an act to prohibit the importation of adulterated food and drink was enacted.

The Meat Inspection Act of 1890 provided for the inspection of salted pork and bacon and live animals intended for export. It was legislation in response to embargos and complaints on the quality of the meat imported from the United States by European countries. The act authorized the inspection and quarantine of imported animals.

The Cattle Inspection Act of 1891 authorized the inspection of all cattle intended for export; voluntary inspection of animals before and after slaughter if they were to be shipped in interstate commerce; the tagging of inspected meats to inform consumers of the inspection; and the nonmandatory inspection of carcasses to be sent to canning and processing plants.

In 1896, the Filled Cheese Act was passed. This legislation defined cheese and imposed a tax upon and regulated the manufacture, sale, importation, and export of "filled cheese." This product is manufactured from milk or skim milk with added butter, animal fats, vegetable oils, or a combination of these ingredients in imitation of cheese. A filled cream cheese was being sold in 1970 as "imitation" cream cheese.

In 1902, the Renovated or Process Butter Act defined renovated or process butter and adulterated butter. Further, it imposed a tax upon them and decreed that they could not be prepared from filthy or decomposed materials. Legislation enacted the same year prohibited the false branding of food and dairy products as to place of origin. Appropriations were also made for establishing pure food standards and to characterize adulterants.

In 1906, the first Food and Drugs Act was passed; it will be discussed briefly later in this chapter. In the same year, the Meat Inspection Act was passed for the purpose of "preventing the use in interstate or foreign commerce of meat and meat food products which are unsound, unhealthful, unwholesome, or otherwise unfit for human food." This act made mandatory the inspection, examination, and certification as "Inspected and Passed" of all carcasses or parts thereof, of meat, and of meat products destined for interstate or foreign commerce. The law provided for the establishment of an inspection service for the examination and certification of the wholesomeness of animals, carcasses, or parts thereof, and of meats and meat products; and for the development of a sanitary code for slaughterhouses and meat-packing and -processing plants. Further, the law decreed that no meat product could contain dyes, chemicals, preservatives, or ingredients that might render it injurious to health. Cattle, sheep, swine, and goats were covered in the law. The Imported-Meat Act of 1913 extended the provisions of the law to imported meat and meat products. The Horse-Meat Act of 1919 requires the conspicuous labeling of meat and meat products from horses as "Horse-meat" and "Horse-meat products."

The Wholesome Meat Act of December, 1967, applied the provisions of the Meat Inspection Act to meat and meat food products in intrastate commerce. It placed under inspection the 25 per cent of all meat sold and the 15 per cent of all slaughter that had previously been uninspected. States were given two years, with the extension of one year possible, to establish inspection programs "at least equal" to federal inspection. The law made federal inspection mandatory in the absence of satisfactory state inspection. Only three states—California, Florida, and Maryland—met the December, 1969, deadline. As of early 1971, thirty-five states had their meat inspection programs certified as being "equal to" federal inspection. In North Dakota, inspection was brought under the federal system in June, 1970. In early 1971, fourteen states—Colorado, Hawaii, Indiana, Kentucky, Louisiana, Massachusetts, Minnesota, Montana, New Hampshire, North Carolina, Ohio, Oregon, Texas, and West Virginia—were placed under federal inspection.

An act of 1910 was concerned with the adulteration and misbranding of insecticides and fungicides. The 1954 amendment to the Federal Food, Drug, and Cosmetic Act required regulation of the residues of chemical pesticides on raw agricultural products.

In 1923, the Filled Milk Act to prohibit the shipment in interstate commerce of filled milk was passed. It defined filled milk as milk, skim milk, or cream in any form to which any fat or oil other than milk fat was introduced. The law exempted certain proprietary foods designed for feeding infants and children.

In 1923, by an act of Congress, butter was defined.

The Import Milk Act of 1927 contained provisions to ensure that all milk and cream imported into the United States came from healthy cows, was handled in sanitary establishments, and was handled under sanitary conditions; it restricted the importation of milk by requiring that the shipper hold a valid permit from the Secretary of Agriculture.

The McNary-Mapes Amendment of the Food and Drug Law of 1906 was enacted in 1930. It authorized the Secretary of Agriculture to promulgate for canned foods—except meats—definitions and standards of identity and reasonable standards of quality, condition, and/or fill of container, when in his best judgment they would promote honesty and fair dealing in the interest of the consumer. It required that substandard foods be conspicuously labeled substandard in quality. The first food standards issued were for canned whole tomatoes, tomato puree, and tomato paste; they were not issued until July, 1939.

In 1934, an amendment to the Food and Drug Law of 1906 provided for the inspection of seafoods on the request of packers. This amendment remained in force when the Food, Drug, and Cosmetic Act of 1938 replaced the 1906 law. In 1958, this responsibility was transferred to the Bureau of Commercial Fisheries of the United States Department of the Interior. In 1969, the shellfish sanitation program came under the aegis of the Food and Drug Administration. In October, 1970, the Bureau of Commercial Fisheries was abolished. Inspection of fishery products and the promulgation of grade standards passed to the National Marine Fisheries Service of the National Oceanic and Atmospheric Administration of the United States Department of Commerce. Pressure for mandatory inspection of fish and fish products was mounting early in the 1970's. The discovery of mercury in canned tuna and frozen swordfish alerted both the public and officialdom to the need to assure the wholesomeness of fish and fish products.

In 1938, the new Federal Food, Drug, and Cosmetic Act was passed; it is discussed subsequently in this chapter. It has been amended several times. Three amendments of special interest are the Miller Pesticide Chemicals Act of 1954, the Food Additives Amendment of 1958, and the Color Additive Amendments of 1960. They, too, are discussed subsequently.

In 1957, the Poultry Products Inspection Act was passed. It established mandatory inspection of poultry and poultry products in foreign and interstate commerce and became effective January 1, 1959. The Wholesome Poultry Products Act of 1968 requires state inspection "at least equal" to federal inspection of poultry and poultry products in intrastate commerce. The states were given two years—until August, 1970—with a possible extension of one year, to take the steps necessary for compliance. Federal inspection would then become mandatory in the absence of state inspection programs certified as equal to federal inspection. As of early 1971, five states—California, Missouri, New Mexico, South Carolina, and Washington—had received "equal to" certification; thirty-two states were given until August, 1971, to develop their programs; and thirteen states were put under federal inspection—Arkansas, Colorado, Georgia, Idaho, Maine, Michigan, Minnesota, Montana, North Dakota, Oregon, South Dakota, Utah, and West Virginia.

The Fair Packaging and Labeling Act became law on November 3, 1966. It did not repeal, invalidate, or supersede the Food, Drug, and Cosmetic Act of 1938. It superseded any and all state and local laws that were less stringent or had different information requirements for the labeling of the net contents of the package of any consumer commodity. It became effective on July 1, 1967. The act carried a provision for the postponement for one year of the effective date of the act with respect to any class or type of consumer commodity should the postponement be in the public interest. Provisions of the act are discussed subsequently.

In 1969, the Food and Drug Administration took over the administration of some units of the Public Health Service established for the sanitary control of milk, shellfish, and food service in public places and for interstate travel sanitation.

In December, 1970, the Egg Products Inspection Law was enacted. It requires that plants processing eggs for interstate, intrastate, and foreign commerce operate under mandatory, continuous inspection of the United States Department of Agriculture. Further, it regulates the disposition of such "restricted eggs" as checks, dirties, and incubator rejects. It became effective for eggs broken for egg products in July, 1971, and for packaged shell eggs in July, 1972.

Thus ends a brief history of federal legislation relating specifically to food; however, legislation is an on-going process and it can be expected that new laws and amendments to old laws will be forthcoming in the 1970's. The enactment of each piece of legislation in the interest of the consumer came as a result of the dedicated efforts of one or more persons and was often helped by the occurrence of some fortuitous, though perhaps tragic, circumstance—the publication of Upton Sinclair's *The Jungle,* the sulfanilamide tragedy of the 1930's, and the thalidomide tragedy of the 1960's. Because these laws ran counter to the interests of the industries and because of industry's powerful lobbies, they were often years in the making and were not infrequently weak and watered-down versions of the laws proposed by those who held the public interest and the public health their concerns. Ralph Nader characterized the Fair Packaging and Labeling Act "the most deceptive package of all." Even so, the laws have often been better than the administration of them. The publication in 1970 of James S. Turner's *The Chemical Feast* cast serious doubts on the integrity of the Food and Drug Administration and suggested that it failed to protect the public interest in the promulgation of food standards and in the approval of food additives. For opinions on the quality of law enforcement the reader is urged to consult the references suggested at the end of this chapter.

In October, 1970, by executive order, the General Services Administration was instructed to establish a Consumer Product Information Coordinating Center for the purpose of collecting and disseminating such product information gathered by governmental agencies through research, development, and procurement as would be useful to consumers.

In February, 1971, an Office of Consumer Affairs in the Executive Office of the President was established by executive order. Mrs. Virginia H. Knauer was named director of the agency, which replaced the President's Committee on Consumer Interests. The agency's functions are the following: to receive consumer complaints; to channel complaints to the agency that has the power to take corrective action; to represent the consumer in an advisory capacity with federal agencies; to determine the nature of consumer problems; to participate in consumer education programs; to participate in programs for improving consumer goods and services; and to assist in the dissemination of consumer product information.

THE WILEY FOOD AND DRUGS ACT OF 1906

During the post-Civil War period, chemists of the Department of Agriculture became interested in the problem of adulterated and misbranded fertilizers, feedstuffs, and foods. In 1869, Dr. Thomas Antisell pointed out the extensive adulteration of fertilizers and feedstuffs. In 1879, Dr. Peter Collier presented evidence of adulteration in butter, oleomargarine, alcoholic beverages, and coffee. In 1879, Congressman Hendrick B. Wright of

Pennsylvania introduced the first bill to secure comprehensive protection from adulterated and misbranded foods. Nearly two hundred measures were introduced before that date and the passage of the Wiley Act in 1906.

In 1883, Dr. Harvey W. Wiley became Chief Chemist of the Chemical Division of the Department of Agriculture. Under his direction, methods of detecting adulteration and determining the nature of adulterations progressed. *Bulletin 13, Food and Food Adulterants* appeared in eight parts between 1887 and 1893. The various parts reported findings on dairy products; spices and condiments; lard and lard adulterations; baking powders; tea, coffee, and cocoa products; canned vegetables; and alcoholic beverages. This bulletin was a technical reference for chemists engaged in food-control work. To arouse public interest in the problem of food adulteration, another bulletin entitled *A Popular Treatise on the Extent and Character of Food Adulterations* was published in 1890. This bulletin pointed out that fraud extended to almost every article of food and that, although many of the adulterations were not injurious to health but were only economic cheats, some adulterations were poisonous. The need for protection beyond what state laws could provide was indicated. The ultimate passage of a federal law was a triumph for Dr. Wiley, who had dedicated himself to that purpose. It was an act "For preventing the manufacture, sale, or transportation of adulterated or misbranded or poisonous or deleterious foods, drugs, medicines, and liquors, and for regulating traffic therein, and for other purposes."

The Wiley Food and Drugs Act of 1906 became effective on January 1, 1907. It defined food as "all articles used for food, drink, confectionery or condiments by man, or other animals, whether simple, mixed, or compound." Briefly, the provisions of the law were as follows:

1.   The import, export, and interstate traffic of adulterated or misbranded foods and drugs were prohibited.

2.   The Secretaries of the Treasury, of Agriculture, and of Commerce and Labor were empowered to make rules and regulations for carrying out the law.

3.   Food and drug examinations were to be carried out by the Bureau of Chemistry of the Department of Agriculture.

4.   Violations of the law were punishable by fine, imprisonment, or both. Suspected food could be seized.

5.   A food was deemed adulterated:
   a.   if any substance had been mixed or packed with it to reduce or injuriously affect its quality or strength;
   b.   if any other substance had been substituted wholly or in part for the article supposedly being sold;
   c.   if any valuable constituent of the article had been wholly or in part abstracted;

    d. if it had been treated in such way as to conceal damage or inferiority;

    e. if any poisonous or deleterious substance had been added;

    f. if it consisted in whole or in part of filthy, decomposed, or putrid vegetable or animal substance; if it contained any portion of an animal unfit for food, whether manufactured or not, or if it was the product of a diseased animal or one that had died other than by slaughter.

6. A food was deemed misbranded:

    a. if it was an imitation or was offered for sale under the distinctive name of another article;

    b. if it was labeled or branded so as to deceive or mislead the purchaser;

    c. if a correct statement of contents in terms of weight or measure did not appear on a packaged item;

    d. if the package or label bore any statement, design, or device regarding ingredients or added substances that was false or misleading. However, mixtures sold under *their own distinctive names* were required to bear on the label only the name of the food and the place of manufacture. Imitations, blends, and compounds were required to be identified as such on the label.

Enforcement of the 1906 law was difficult. There were no definitions or standards for foods that had the force of law; foods sold under their own distinctive brand names were free from the law; fines for violation were so small that payment was not a serious penalty; it was necessary to prove intent to deceive; and false and misleading information could be placed on circulars distributed separately. The law was amended several times, and numerous rules and regulations for the enforcement of the law were in effect by 1930. However, before the last amendment to the law was enacted in 1934, a new law had been introduced in the Senate.

A separate law-enforcement agency was established in 1927 in the United States Department of Agriculture. It was first known as the Food, Drug, and Insecticide Administration. In 1930, it became the Food and Drug Administration but continued as a division of the United States Department of Agriculture until 1940, when it was transferred to the Federal Security Agency, which became the United States Department of Health, Education, and Welfare in 1953.

FOOD, DRUG, AND COSMETIC ACT OF 1938, AND AMENDMENTS

The new law was prepared by officials of the Food and Drug Administration and staff members of the Solicitor's Office of the United States Department of Agriculture. It was designed to correct the shortcomings of the old law. It has been called the Tugwell Bill because it was sponsored by the then Secretary of Agriculture, Rexford G. Tugwell; it is better known as the Copeland Bill because it was introduced in the Senate by Senator Royal S. Copeland on June 6, 1933. The bill was reintroduced four times before a law acceptable to Congress was signed by the President on June 25, 1938, to become effective on January 1, 1939.

The Federal Food, Drug, and Cosmetic Act is an act "To prohibit the movement in interstate commerce of adulterated and misbranded food, drugs, devices, and cosmetics, and for other purposes." The provisions of the law and the subsequent amendments are summarized briefly and somewhat aribtrarily under these headings: general provisions; definitions; adulterated food; misbranded food; label and labeling regulations; standards; and amendments.

General Provisions

First and most important, underlying the law was the determination to protect the public health; second, there was the determination to protect the consumer from the fradulent practices of unscrupulous enterprisers. To accomplish these ends, the law deems a food adulterated if it has been prepared, packed, or held under insanitary conditions whereby it may become contaminated with filth or rendered injurious to health, or if the container may render the product injurious to health. The law and its subsequent amendments prohibit the presence in food of poisonous, deleterious, and unsafe substances—except for some substances, such as pesticide chemicals on raw agricultural products, for which tolerances are established by regulations. Adulteration and misbranding are specifically and precisely defined. A distinction between label and labeling is made. The law imposes stringent label requirements. Penalties for violations are greater than under the old law, and the power of injunction is given the administering body. To facilitate the administration of the law, the law provided for the promulgation of reasonable standards and definitions of identity, reasonable standards of quality, and/or reasonable standards of fill of container that would have the force of law.

Definitions

For purposes of administering the law and its amendments, hundreds of terms have been clearly defined—especially in the standards and definitions of identity promulgated under the law. Some important definitions are included here: some are quoted exactly; a few are simplified.

1. "*Food* means (a) articles used for food or drink for man or other animals, (b) chewing gum, and (c) articles used for components of any such article."

2. *Label* means a display of written, printed, or graphic matter upon the immediate container of any article, and also on the outside container or wrapper (if there is one), or a display that is easily legible through the outside container or wrapper. The term *immediate container* does not include package liners.

3. "*Labeling* means all labels and other written, printed, or graphic matter (a) upon any article or any of its containers or wrappers, or (b) accompanying such article."

4. "The term *raw agricultural commodity* means any food in its raw or natural state, including all fruits that are washed, colored, or otherwise treated in their unpeeled natural form prior to marketing."

5. "*Pesticide chemical* means any substance which, alone, in chemical combination, or in formulation with one or more other substances, is an 'economic poison' within the meaning of the Federal Insecticide, Fungicide, and Rodenticide Act as now in force or as hereafter amended, and which is used in the production, storage, or transportation of raw agricultural commodities."

6. "*Food additive* means any substance the intended use of which results or may reasonably be expected to result, directly or indirectly, in its becoming a component or otherwise affecting the characteristics of any food (including any substance intended for use in producing, manufacturing, packing, processing, preparing, treating, packaging, transporting, or holding food; and including any source of radiation intended for any such use), if such substance is not generally recognized, among experts qualified by scientific training and experience to evaluate its safety, as having been adequately shown through scientific procedures (or, in the case of a substance used in food prior to January 1, 1958, through either scientific procedures or experience based on common use in food) to be safe under the conditions of its intended use"; except that such terms do not include color additives, pesticide chemicals, and some substances granted prior sanction pursuant to earlier legislation.

7. "*Safe* has reference to the health of man and animals."

8. "*Safety* means there is no convincing evidence which establishes with reasonable certainty that no harm will come from the intended use of the food additive or color additive."

9. "*Color additive* means a material which:
    a. is a dye, pigment, or other substance made by a process of synthesis or similar artifice, or extracted, isolated, or otherwise derived, with or without intermediate or final change of identity, from a vegetable, animal, mineral, or other source, and
    b. when added or applied to a food, drug, or cosmetic, or to the human body or any part thereof, is capable (alone or through reaction with other substance) of imparting color thereto; except that such term does not include any material which the Secretary

of the Department of Health, Education and Welfare, by regulation, determines is used (or intended to be used) solely for a purpose or purposes other than coloring."

10.   "The term *color* includes black, white, and intermediate grays."

Adulterated Food

A food is deemed adulterated when any of the following is true.

1.   It bears or contains any poisonous or deleterious substance that may render it injurious to health; if the substance is not an added one, the food is not considered adulterated if the quantity present is not considered injurious to health.

2.   It bears or contains any added poisonous or added deleterious substance that is unsafe.

3.   It bears or contains a food additive or color additive that is deemed unsafe or that is used contrary to regulations.

4.   It is a raw agricultural product and contains the residue of a chemical in excess of established tolerance or an unauthorized pesticide.

5.   It consists in whole or in part of any filthy, putrid, or decomposed substance or is otherwise unfit for food.

6.   It has been prepared, packed, or held under insanitary conditions whereby it may have become contaminated with filth or rendered injurious to health.

7.   It is, in whole or in part, the product of a diseased animal or of an animal that died otherwise than by slaughter.

8.   The container is composed, in whole or in part, of any poisonous or deleterious substance that might render the contents injurious to health.

9.   It has been intentionally subjected to radiation, except such as is deemed safe.

10.   If any valuable constituent has been omitted in whole or in part, or abstracted, or if any substance has been substituted wholly or in part therefor.

11.   If damage or inferiority has been concealed in any way.

12.   If any substance has been added or mixed or packed with it to increase its bulk or weight, or to reduce its quality or strength, or to make it appear better or of greater value than it is.

Among the seizures, during 1970-1971, of foods considered adulterated were the following: (1) contaminated by salmonella, staphylococcus, or *Esterichia coli*—frozen whole eggs, sodium caseinate (used in food manufacture), frozen breaded shrimp, frozen cooked shrimp, frozen hash-brown potatoes, pecan pieces, walnut meats, frozen meat, and shrimp patties; (2) held and/or prepared under insanitary conditions, contaminated by insects and/or rodents—chili con carne, cheese, cornmeal and grits, chilies, fruitcake, rice, macaroni and noodles, shelled pecans, cashews and peanuts, flour, frozen onion rings, frozen shrimp, pickled banana peppers, nonfat dry milk, whole pepper, dry beans, popcorn, Idaho potatoes, and mixed nuts; (3) contained decomposed or partly decomposed food material—canned peas, butter, canned mushrooms, canned sweet potatoes, frozen perch fillets, frozen rock-lobster tails, tomato paste, frozen egg products, and frozen shrimp, crabmeat, lobster tails, and frog legs; (4) contained pesticide chemicals or unsafe food additives—lettuce, Feta cheese, Romano cheese.

In March, 1972, the Food and Drug Administration made public the levels for natural contaminants or unavoidable defects in food that present no health hazard. The levels—most of which were defined in the 1930's—recognize that it is not possible to grow, harvest, and process some crops totally free of natural defects. Some classes of food for which defect levels have been established include chocolate and cocoa; coffee beans; fish, shellfish, and seafood; flours; assorted canned fruits; spices; dried prunes and raisins; nuts; some canned and frozen vegetables; and tomato products. The natural defects recognized as unavoidable include molds, the eggs and larvae of some insects, certain insects and insect parts, rodent hairs, as well as other defects peculiar to and natural to certain foods.

Misbranded Food

A food is considered misbranded when any of the following is true.

1. If labeling is false or misleading in any particular.
2. If it is offered for sale under the name of another food.
3. If it is an imitation of another food, unless its label bears—in type of uniform size and prominence—the word *imitation* and, immediately thereafter, the name of the food imitated, for example, "Imitation Vanilla."
4. If its container is so made, formed, or filled as to be misleading.
5. If it appears in package form without a label carrying (a) the name and place of business of the manufacturer, packer, or distributor and (b) an accurate statement of the quantity of the contents in terms of weight, measure, or numerical count.
6. If labels and labeling do not present required information prominently and in terms that can be read and understood easily.
7. If a food for which the definition and standard of identity has been prescribed does not conform to this definition and standard, and the label does not bear the name of the food as specified and the common names of the optional ingredients as required.
8. If it is a food for which standards of quality and fill of container have been established, and it falls below such standards, and the label does not bear a statement of substandard quality or fill.

9.   When the label of a food fabricated from two or more ingredients does not name the ingredients in order of predominance by weight—except that spices, flavorings, and colorings other than those sold in a pure state may be designated as spices, flavorings, and colorings without each being named.

10.   If it contains any artificial flavoring, artificial coloring, or chemical preservative, unless it is so labeled. Exemptions include cheese, butter, and ice cream, these are not required to bear a statement of the use of artificial color.

11.   If it purports to be or is represented to be for special dietary uses, unless its label bears information concerning the vitamin, mineral, and other dietary properties necessary to inform purchasers fully of its value for such uses.

12.   If it is a color additive, unless its packaging and labeling conform to the packaging and labeling requirements applicable to it.

Among seizures of foods considered misbranded in 1970–1971 were strawberry preserves, canned pineapple, canned green beans, and salad dressings that did not conform to the definitions and standards of identity therefor; short-weight packages of creamy honey; cod misbranded as haddock, and flounder and Greenland turbot misbranded as sole and halibut; and diet cola drinks that failed to declare the sugar content. There were many seizures of items not in conformity with the Fair Packaging and Labeling Act.

Label and Labeling Regulations

General regulations for the enforcement of prohibitions of misbranding are numerous. Some are of special interest to consumers. Information required on all labels includes the following:

1.   The common or usual name of undefined products; the legal name of defined products, which consists of the common or usual name plus any additional statement required by the standard.

2.   The accurate statement of quantity in terms of weight, measure, or count. The statement of quantity of contents is exclusive of wrappers and other material packed with food. If a product is liquid, the statement must be in terms of the largest applicable unit of the U.S. gallon, quart, pint, or fluid ounce, that is, one quart, not two pints or thirty-two ounces. When volume exceeds one unit and is less than the next, contents must be expressed in terms of the larger unit and a fraction thereof, for example, one quart, one pint; but not three pints nor forty-eight ounces. If a product is solid, semisolid, viscous, or a mixture of solid and edible liquid, contents must be expressed by weight in terms of the avoirdupois pound and ounce. Pickles are an exception to this. Contents must be expressed in the largest applicable unit: one pound, not sixteen ounces. When

weight exceeds one unit and is less than two units, weight is expressed in terms of the larger unit, that is, one and a half pounds or one pound, eight ounces.

The Fair Packaging and Labeling Act requires that net contents on commodities containing less than four pounds or one gallon be expressed in avoirdupois or fluid ounces, respectively, in order to facilitate value comparisons, in addition to expression in the largest whole units of pounds, pints, or quarts.

3. The name and place of business of the manufacturer, packer, or distributor. If the food is not manufactured by the company whose name appears on the label, the name must be qualified by a statement that discloses the connection such company has as "Manufactured for _____ and Packed by _____," "Distributed by _____," "Packed by _____." For example, a can of soup may carry any of these statements: "Made by Supreme Soup Company," "Made for Supreme Soup Company and packed by Goode Soup Company," "Distributed by Blue Sky Wholesale Distributors." The products of food manufacturers are often sold under different labels but the label must define the situation; however, the manufacturer's name need not be revealed. However, as a result of the contaminated soup episodes of the summer of 1971, legislation was proposed early in 1972 that would require the manufacturer's name on labels.

Label information required under certain conditions includes the following:

4. Label statement of all ingredients including water in order of predominance for all undefined food products. This order of stating ingredients does not apply to water used for processing where the consumer can distinguish between the packing medium and the product, such as water present in a can of peas. Legislation was proposed early in 1972 that would require the naming of all ingredients in defined foods. Spices, flavorings, and coloring may be designated on the label as "spices," "flavorings," and "coloring" without the designation of each by name.

5. Declaration of optional ingredients present in defined foods if the standard of identity requires such declaration.

6. Statement of any dietary properties claimed for foods promoted for special dietary uses.

7. Declaration of use of artificial color and flavorings, and of chemical preservatives.

8. Statement of substandard quality or fill of container for any product that fails to meet established standards.

9. Description of a product as "imitation" if it fails to conform to the promulgated definition and standard of identity.

Prominence of Required Statements. Food products are considered misbranded if required information is not prominently displayed in terms that can be easily read and understood. Regulations for administering this requirement of the law were established. Prominence and conspicuousness of labeling are deemed lacking when

1.   Reqired information is not present on the part or panel of the label that is presented or displayed under customary conditions of purchase.

2.   Required information fails to appear on two or more parts or panels of the label, each of which has sufficient space therefor, and each of which is designed so as to be the part or panel displayed under ordinary conditions of purchase.

3.   There is insufficient label space for the presentation of required information.

4.   Required information is presented without sufficient background contrast, is obscured by designs or vignettes, is crowded with other printed or graphic matter, or is presented in a style or size of type that makes reading difficult.

Failure of food packages to conform to requirements for prominence of labeling was a factor that favored the enactment of the Fair Packaging and Labeling Act of 1966.

Standards

A law that prohibits adulteration and misbranding of food requires standards and regulations that provide the frame of reference for judgment of adulteration and misbranding. The aforementioned seizures would not have been possible without them. Dr. Wiley and his supporters were not unaware of this fact. They hoped to obtain, subsequent to the enactment of the 1906 law, authority for the Secretary of Agriculture to promulgate standards of purity in accordance with which judgments of adulteration could be made. However, only two acts to this end were accomplished under the old law: an act to define butter was passed in 1923, and a law to establish the standard of quality, condition, and fill of container for canned goods was enacted in 1930. During those years, many definitions and standards for food products were developed and adopted for the use of officials enforcing the Food and Drug Act. They did not have the force of law however. The 1938 Act empowered the Secretary to promulgate regulations "fixing and establishing for any food, under its common or usual name so far as practicable, a reasonable definition and standard of identity, a reasonable standard of quality, and/or reasonable standards of fill of container," when in his judgment such action would promote honesty and fair dealing in the interest of consumers. The latter two standards apply only to canned foods; the first, to a great number of foods including alimentary pastes, bakery products, cereal flours and related products, chocolate and cocoa products, cheeses and cheese products, dressings for foods, fruit preserves and jellies, some canned fruits and fruit juices and fruit juice concentrates, some canned shellfish and tuna, egg products, margarine, frozen desserts, canned vegetables and vegetable products, and some processed meat food and poultry food products. Most of these definitions were established by the Food and Drug Administration. Butter and skim milk are defined by special acts of the Congress; meat and poultry food products, by the appropriate division of the United States Department of Agriculture. Frequent reference is made to the specifics of definitions and standards of identity for some foods in the chapters concerned with food buying.

Definitions and Standards of Identity.   Definitions and standards of identity are detailed definitions and prescriptions for foods and food products, i.e., foods composed of two or more foods. They establish the standards that permit judgment of adulteration and misbranding. They also, by the preciseness of definition, establish minimum quality standards for those foods for which they have been promulgated, although they are not standards for grading for quality. For example, a standard that establishes the minimum milk-fat content of ice cream not only permits detection of adulteration, but it also establishes the minimum quality in as much as the quality of ice creams is to no small extent determined by fat content.

Definitions and standards are often years in the making and they are frequently modified as technological developments, consumer wants, and industry interests deem change desirable. For example, some modifications of older definitions permit the canning of some fruits in slightly sweetened water, the addition of butter to some canned vegetables, and the use of flavor enhancers in food products. All interested parties—consumers, industry, and law enforcement officials—may participate in the formulation of the definition and standard of identity for a food, which may explain why they are often long in the making; however, according to Turner (17) the standards and definitions per se and the labeling requirements for them have favored industry over the consumer.

In general, definitions and standards of identity are lengthy and technical. Some specific requirements of some definitions for some commonly consumed foods are given here; and although it will be gross oversimplification, a summary of the kinds of requirements that definitions and standards establish follows:

1.   In raisin bread and raisin rolls or raisin buns, not less than 50 parts by weight of seeded or seedless raisins are used per 100 parts by weight of flour.

2.   Baking chocolate contains not less than 50 per cent and not more than 58 per cent by weight of cacao fat.

3. Fruit jellies, jams, and preserves are made from mixtures composed of 45 parts by weight of the fruit constituent and 55 parts by weight of sugar.

4. Tomato catsup can be prepared from one or a combination of the following: the liquid obtained from tomatoes of red or reddish varieties, the liquid obtained from the residue left after preparing such tomatoes for canning, or the liquid obtained from the residue from partial extraction of tomatoes. The concentrated juices can be processed only by heat to prevent spoilage; the use of chemical preservatives is prohibited. The label must state that juices prepared from residues were used in production.

5. Cream cheese can contain no less than 35 per cent of milk fat and no more than 55 per cent of moisture.

6. Canned tomatoes are mature tomatoes of red or reddish varieties that are peeled and cored and to which one or more optional ingredients may be added. These are named.

7. Margarine must contain no less than 80 per cent of fat.

8. Cream must contain no less than 18 per cent of milk fat.

9. Canned tuna is the food prepared from the flesh of an enumerated list of fish species. Only loins and other striated muscle of the fish may be processed. Packing media include oils and water. Only the species *Thunnus germo* (albacore) can be described as white tuna; it must not be darker than a prescribed Munsell value. Grated tuna consists of a mixture of pieces of uniform size that pass through a half-inch mesh screen, but the particles are discrete and do not form a paste.

10. If the milk used in making cheddar cheese is not pasteurized, the cheese made from it must be cured at a temperature of not less than 35°F for not less than sixty days.

11. Pasteurized process cheese spread must be spreadable at 70°F; during pasteurization is must have been heated for not less than thirty seconds at a temperature of not less than 150°F.

12. Mayonnaise can contain not less than 65 per cent by weight of edible oil.

13. Peanut butter can contain no more than 10 per cent by weight of seasoning and stabilizing ingredients; the fat content of the finished food cannot exceed 55 per cent. Incidentally, although the standard for this food was proposed in 1959, it was not until 1970 that it was finally established; and then, only by a court ruling.

14. Canned green beans must be a food prepared from succulent pods of the green bean plant. The pods may be prepared whole, or cut lengthwise, or cut transversely; in the latter instance, they are called *cuts*. "The food is sealed in a container and so processed by heat as to prevent spoilage."

15. Bread must be prepared by the baking of a kneaded, yeast-leavened dough made from flour moistened with water or other specified liquid ingredients or a combination thereof.

From the examples presented, a summary can be prepared of the kinds and standard (except for so-called incidental additives); if it fails to con-
Standards and definitions of identity may:

1. Establish the minimum content—also the maximum content sometimes—of one or more components of a food.

2. Establish the permissible ingredient content of a food.

3. Establish the minimum quantity of one or more ingredients in a food.

4. Name the ingredients that may be optionally included in the preparation of a food.

5. Require label statement of the use of some permissible and some optional ingredients.

6. Identify the species of plant or animal that may be used.

7. Define the meaning of terms descriptive of color and form, that is, *white, grated, cuts,* and many others.

8. Describe the product that can be processed as in canning.

9. Define packing media for many foods, such as water, syrups, juices, or oils.

10. Describe processing requirements, for example, "sealed in a container and so processed by heat as to prevent spoilage."

11. Prescribe essentials in production, such as that bread must be yeast leavened and baked.

12. Require label statement of the use of many food additives with explanation for use.

Foods for which the definitions and standards of identity have been promulgated are not required to bear label statements of their ingredient content in order of predominance; however, a label statement of the inclusion of some permissible and some optional ingredients may be required. There are also exceptions; for example, the requirements for margarine are such that a listing of ingredients in order of predominance occurs. A survey of some defined foods available in the supermarket discloses that some do carry label statements of their ingredient content. Mandatory listing in order of predominance for defined and standardized foods may be legislated in the 1970's. There exists strong opposition to the exemptions these foods enjoy. This opposition is in the interest of public health: some persons may be allergic to substances not listed; others are advised against consumption of such substances as monosodium glutamate because of health reasons. Opposition also occurs because industry has used food standardization as a means of avoiding the listing of substances that might affect consumption, such as caffeine in cola drinks.

A food does not conform to the definition and standard of identity if it contains an ingredient for which there is no provision in the definition and standard (except for co-called incidental additives); if it fails to contain a required ingredient; or if the quantity of any ingredient or component fails to conform to the prescribed limitations. A food that does not conform to the definition must be labeled "imitation."

Imitation pasteurized process cheese spread may lack the required 20 per cent milk fat; imitation ice cream (Mellorine) contains a fat other than milk fat. Consumers think *imitation* implies substitute, ersatz, not genuine, or counterfeit. For this reason, it is desirable that another term be coined for foods that do not meet definitions and standards of identity. At present, *imitation* can be understood only within the context of the law.

To illustrate, two definitions are given: the definition and standard of identity for nonfat dry milk, a single food, and for canned fruit cocktail, a mixture of foods. The definition for nonfat dry milk is quoted from the Skim Milk Act of 1956. It is easily read. It leaves the reader in no doubt as to the precise nature of nonfat dry milk.

> Nonfat dry milk is the product resulting from the removal of fat and water from milk, and contains the lactose, milk proteins, and milk minerals in the same relative proportions as in the fresh milk from which made. It contains not over 5 per centum by weight of moisture. The fat content is not over 1½ per centum by weight unless otherwise indicated. The term milk, when used herein, means sweet milk of cows.

The definition and standard of identity for canned fruit cocktail is also easy to read. It illustrates well the specificity of definitions and standards of identity. It also has implicit in it an explanation for product differences in the definition of minimum and maximum content of the different fruits. The definition and standard of identity for canned fruit cocktail is reprinted from the unofficial copy of the regulations that were originally published in the Federal Register.

> *Canned fruit cocktail, canned cocktail fruits, canned fruits for cocktail; identity; label statement of optional ingredients.* (a) Canned fruit cocktail, canned cocktail fruits, canned fruits for cocktail, is the food prepared from the mixture of fruit ingredients prescribed in paragraph (b) of this section, in the forms and proportions therein prescribed, and one of the optional packing media specified in paragraph (c) of this section. It is sealed in a container and is so processed by heat as to prevent spoilage.
>
> (b) The fruit ingredients referred to in paragraph (a) of this section, the forms of each, and the percent by weight of each in the mixture of drained fruit from the finished canned fruit cocktail are as follows:
>
> (1) Peaches of any yellow variety, which are pitted, peeled, and diced, not less than 30 percent and not more than 50 percent;
>
> (2) Pears of any variety, which are peeled, cored, and diced, not less than 25 percent and not more than 45 percent;
>
> (3) Whole grapes of any seedless variety, not less than 6 percent and not more than 20 percent;

(4) Pineapples of any variety, which are peeled, cored, and cut into sectors or into dice, not less than 6 percent and not more than 16 percent; and

(5) One of the following optional cherry ingredients, each of which is stemmed, pitted, and cut into approximate halves, not less than 2 percent and not more than 6 percent;

(i) Cherries of any light, sweet variety;

(ii) Cherries artificially colored red; or

(iii) Cherries artificially colored red and artificially flavored.

Each such fruit ingredient is prepared from mature fruit which is fresh canned. Notwithstanding the preceding provisions of this paragraph, each 4½ ounces avoirdupois of the finished canned fruit cocktail and each fraction thereof greater than 2 ounces avoirdupois contain not less than 2 sectors or 3 dice of pineapple and not less than 1 approximate half of the optional cherry ingredient.

(c) The optional packing media referred to in paragraph (a) of this section are as follows:

(1) Water.

(2) Fruit juice.

(3) Light sirup.

(4) Heavy sirup.

(5) Extra heavy sirup.

(6) Light fruit juice sirup.

(7) Heavy fruit juice sirup.

(8) Extra heavy fruit juice sirup.

Each of packing media (3), (4), and (5) is prepared with water as its liquid ingredient, and each of packing media (6), (7), and (8) is prepared with fruit juice as its liquid ingredient. Except as provided in paragraph (d) (6) of this section, each of packing media (3) to (8), inclusive, is prepared with any one of the following saccharine ingredients: sugar; or any combination of sugar and dextrose in which the weight of the solids of the dextrose used is not more than one-half the weight of the solids of the sugar used; or any combination of sugar and corn sirup in which the weight of the solids of the corn sirup used is not more than one-third the weight of the solids of the sugar used; or any combination of sugar, dextrose, and corn sirup in which the weight of the solids of the dextrose used multiplied by 2, added to the weight of the solids of the corn sirup used multiplied by 3, is not more than the weight of the solids of the sugar used. The respective densities of packing media (3) to (8), inclusive, as measured on the Brix hydrometer 15 days or more after the fruit cocktail is canned are within the range prescribed for each in the following list:

Number of packing medium:	Brix measurement
(3) and (6)	14° or more but less than 18°
(4) and (7)	18° or more but less than 22°
(5) and (8)	22° or more but not more than 35°

(d) For the purposes of this section:

(1) The term "water" means, in addition to water, both the liquid drained from any fruit ingredient previously canned in water as its sole packing medium and any mixture of water and fruit juice, including the liquid drained from any fruit ingredient previously canned in such mixture.

(2) The term "fruit juice" means the fresh or canned, expressed juice or juices of one or more of the mature fruits named in paragraph (b) of this section including the liquid drained from any fruit ingredient previously canned in such juice or juices as its sole packing medium, to which no water has been added, directly or indirectly. Fruit juice may be strained or filtered.

(3) The term "sugar" means refined sucrose or invert sugar sirup. The term "invert sugar sirup" means an aqueous sirup of inverted or partly inverted, refined or partly refined sucrose, the solids of which contain not more than 0.3 per cent by weight of ash and which is colorless, odorless and flavorless except for sweetness.

(4) The term "dextrose" means the hydrated or anhydrous, refined monosaccharide obtained from hydrolized starch.

(5) The term "corn sirup" means an aqueous solution obtained by the incomplete hydrolysis of corn starch and includes dried corn sirup; the solids of corn sirup and dried corn sirup contain not less than 58 per cent by weight of reducing sugars.

(6) When the optional packing medium is prepared with fruit juice and invert sugar sirup or corn sirup other than dried sirup, it shall be considered to be light sirup, heavy sirup, or an extra heavy sirup as the case may be, and not a light fruit juice sirup, heavy fruit juice sirup, or an extra heavy fruit juice sirup.

(7) The term "light sirup," "heavy sirup," or "extra heavy sirup" includes a sirup which conforms in all other respects to the provisions of this section, in the preparation of which there is used the liquid drained from any fruit ingredient previously canned in a packing medium consisting wholly of the liquid and saccharine ingredients of a light sirup, heavy sirup, or extra heavy sirup.

(8) Except as provided in subparagraph (6) of this paragraph, the term "light fruit juice sirup," heavy fruit juice sirup," or "extra heavy fruit juice sirup" includes a sirup which conforms in all other respects to the provisions of this section, in the preparation of which there is used the liquid drained from any fruit ingredients previously canned in a packing medium consisting wholly of the liquid and saccharine ingredients of light fruit juice sirup, heavy fruit juice sirup, or extra heavy fruit juice sirup.

(e) (1) The optional ingredients specified in paragraphs (b) (5) (ii) and (iii) and (c) (1) to (8) of this section, inclusive, are hereby designated as optional ingredients which, when used, shall be named on the label by the name whereby each is so specified.

(2) Such names shall immediately and conspicuously, without intervening written, printed or graphic matter, precede or follow the name "fruit cocktail," "cocktail fruits," or "fruits for cocktail" wherever it appears on the label so conspicuously as to be easily seen under customary conditions of purchase.

In its report of June, 1966, the National Commission on Food Marketing recommended that the Food and Drug Administration establish standards of identity for all foods for which standards are practicable. Not only are these standards essential for the administration of the Food, Drug, and Cosmetic Act of 1938; they also protect the consumer in the marketplace because they regulate what her dollars buy. The standards are also effective in protecting the honest producer of food products from the dishonest and unscrupulous one. Consumer groups and consumer advocates will be pressing for more and revised and better definitions and standards of identity in the 1970's.

Standards of Quality. For a limited number of canned fruits and vegetables, standards of quality have been prescribed. These standards preclude the marketing of tough green beans, hard peas, and stringy peaches. They do not grade foods as Fancy, Choice, or Good. They define in terms of flavor, color, size, and condition the quality level below which a food cannot be sold unless it is labeled to inform the customer that it is below standard quality. For example, if tomatoes in a pack are poor in color, they must be conspicuously labeled, "Below Standard in Quality." The type of inferiority is usually mentioned, for example, "Below Standard in Quality—Poor Color." Regulations require that the statement of substandard quality be placed on the can where it can be easily seen, that it be printed in two lines, and that it be enclosed within lines forming a rectangle the size of which is scaled to can size.

Standards of quality have been established for these canned fruits: apricots, cherries, fruit cocktail, peaches, pears, pineapple, and pineapple juice; and for these canned vegetables: green and wax beans, corn, peas, and tomatoes. These standards of quality become the U.S. Standard or U.S. Grade C for those foods for which they have been established.

The quality standards for canned fruit cocktail are quoted below.

(1) Not more than 20 per cent by weight of the units in the container of peach or pear, or of pineapple if the units therof are diced, are more than ¾ inch in greatest edge dimension, or pass through the meshes of a sieve designated as 5/16 inch in Table I of "Standard Specifications for Sieves" pubilshed March 1, 1940, in L. C. 584 of the National Bureau of Standards, U.S. Department of Commerce. If the units of pineapple are in the form of sectors, not more than 20 per cent of such sectors in the container fail to conform to the following dimensions: The length of the outside arc is not more than ¾ inch but is more than ⅜ inch; the thickness is not more than ½ inch but is more than 5/16 inch; the length (measured along the radius from the inside arc to the outside arc) is not more than 1¼ inches but is more than ¾ inch.

(2) Not more than 10 percent of the grapes in a container containing ten grapes or more, and not more than one grape in a container containing less than ten grapes, is cracked to the extent of being severed into two parts or is crushed to the extent that their normal shape is destroyed.

(3) Not more than 10 per cent of the grapes in a container containing ten grapes or more, and not more than one grape in a container containing less than ten grapes, has the cap stem attached.

(4) There is present in the finished canned fruit cocktail not more than one square inch of pear peel per each one pound of drained weight of units of pear plus the weight of a proportion of the packing medium which is the same proportion as the drained weight of the units of pear bears to the drained weight of the entire contents of the can. . . .

(5) There is present in the finished canned fruit cocktail not more than one square inch of peach peel per each one pound of drained weight of units of peach plus the weight of a proportion of the packing medium which is the same proportion as the drained weight of units of peach bears to the drained weight of the entire contents of the can. . . .

(6) Not more than 15 per cent of the units of cherry ingredient; and not more than 20 per cent of the units of peach, pear, or grape, in the container is blemished with scab, hail injury, scar tissue or other abnormality.

(7) If the cherry ingredient is artificially colored, the color of not more than 15 per cent of the units thereof in a container containing more than six units, and of not more than one unit in a container containing six or less, is other than evenly distributed in the unit or other than uniform with the color of the other units of the cherry ingredient.

Standards of Fill of Container.   Standards of fill of container have been established for some canned foods. Standard of fill of container is defined as the maximum quantity that can be sealed and processed in a can without crushing or breaking any ingredient or as a percentage of the total capacity of the container as determined under specified conditions. For example, the standard of fill of container for canned tomatoes is a fill not less than 90 per cent of the total capacity of the container. Cans filled to a lesser extent must be conspicuously labeled, "Below Standard in Fill," in type of specified kind and size, and the statement must be enclosed within lines forming a bold border around it. Standards of fill have been established for only a limited list of canned products. Changes in standards of fill are under study as a result of change in filling practices in the canning industry. Hopefully, more and better standards of fill will be realized in the 1970's. A provision of the Fair Packaging and Labeling Act would prevent the nonfunctional slack fill of packages of consumer commodities of all kinds.

Amendments to the Food, Drug, and Cosmetic Act

Three amendments to the Food, Drug, and Cosmetic Act of 1938 are of supreme importance to consumers because they were enacted in the interest of public health. They are the Pesticide Chemicals Act of 1954, the Food Additives Amendment of 1958, and the Color Additive Amendments of 1960. When the 1938 law was written, it was believed that its provisions relating to the presence of poisonous and deleterious substances in food were sufficient. Although the law deemed a food adulterated if it contained any poisonous or deleterious substance that might render it injurious to health, it permitted this exception. It exempted from declaration as adulterated those foods containing added poisonous or deleterious substances when their use was unavoidable in production of good manufacturing practice so long as the quantities present did not exceed tolerance levels established by the Secretary of Agriculture. Subsequent developments in agricultural practices and food technology pointed to three inadequacies in the law. First, the administering body, the Food and Drug Administration, was forced to prove the poisonous and deleterious nature of substances added to food. Second, gathering proof of the poisonous and deleterious nature of substances required extensive research that was costly in time and money. The Food and Drug Administration had neither the funds, the facilities, nor the personnel to carry out the research necessitated by the ever-increasing use of pesticides in agriculture and additives by the food industries. Third, public health was endangered by the continued use of additives suspected of being poisonous or deleterious until such time as convincing proof could stay the use of a substance by condemning food as adulterated. All three amendments to the law place the burden of proof of safety on the manufacturers of pesticides and additives. The Food and Drug Administration issues regulations governing the use of these added substances after proof of safety has been submitted. The regulations are specific in regard to intended uses and to the quantities that may be employed for the respective uses permitted.

The Pesticide Chemicals Act of 1954.   Specifically, the Pesticide Chemicals Act prohibits the marketing in interstate commerce of any raw agricultural product if it bears the residue of a pesticide chemical unless (1) the pesticide chemical is safe, (2) the residue is within the tolerance established as safe, or (3) the pesticide has been officially exempted from tolerance limitations. Pesticide use has received much attention as man has become concerned over his pollution of his environment. The United States Department of Agriculture in 1970 canceled many uses of a number of pesticides on food and feed crops. Researches are in the direction of the development of and the recommended use of biological, environmental, and other nonchemical means of control.

The Food Additives Amendment of 1958.   The Food Additives Amendment decrees that no new additive be used in or on food (1) until proof of safety for intended use has been submitted to the Food and Drug Administration; (2) until the Food and Drug Administration has issued a regulation prescribing the additive's use; and (3) unless it is used in conformity with the regulation. In no circumstance can an additive be deemed safe if it is found to induce cancer in man or animal; this is the Delaney anti-

cancer clause that created the "cranberry incident" in 1959 and the cycla-
mate disaster of 1969. No additive the use of which would promote
deception of the consumer is legal. The act covers both intentional and
incidental additives, such as those that may arise during processing and
from packaging materials. The regulation that establishes the safety of an
additive specifies its uses and limits the quantities that may be used. The
law became effective immediately for substances not in use as of January
1, 1958. It exempted "any substance used in accordance with a sanction or
approval granted prior to the enactment" of the law. Substances of this ilk
were not legally considered additives, though in actuality they were additions to food, that is, additives. It further exempted substances in use prior
to January 1, 1958 when these were generally recognized as safe (GRAS)
"among experts qualified by scientific training and experience to evaluate
safety," because they had "been adequately shown through scientific procedures . . . to be safe under the conditions of intended use" and when
safety could be shown by "experience based on common use in food."
The original list of 182 GRAS items expanded to some 600. The test of
time proved some not safe: unlimited use of vitamin D; safrole, the extract
of sassafras, for years the chief flavoring constituent of root beer; folic
acid; brominated vegetable oils; and the cyclamates. Following the removal of the cyclamates from the GRAS list on October 18, 1969, the Food
and Drug Administration undertook a full-scale review of all GRAS substances, all substances granted prior sanction, and all additives considered
safe. New dimensions have been added to the concept of safety—those of
teratogenic and mutagenic effects. The teratogenic effects noted in researches on cyclamates influenced their ultimate ban. Legislation was proposed in 1970 that would extend the Delaney clause to ban the use of any
additive found to cause mutations or defects in human or animal embryos.

In December, 1970, the Food and Drug Administration published in the
Federal Register specific criteria for classifying foods and food substances
as GRAS or as regulated food additives. Because it is not possible to ascer-
tain that any substance is absolutely safe, these criteria proposed that
"safe" be understood to connote that the Food and Drug Administration,
after reviewing all available evidence, concludes that there exists no significant risk of harm from the use of a substance as intended. The criteria
established that GRAS status must be based on scientific data derived
from credible toxicological testing or on reasoned judgment founded on
experience with common food use. When published, the new GRAS list
will include five categories of substances: (1) substances of natural biological origin that have been modified by processes proposed for introduction
into commercial use after January 1, 1958; (2) substances that have had a
significant alteration of composition by breeding or selection; (3) distil-
lates, isolates, extracts, concentrates of extracts, or reaction products of
foods considered as GRAS; (4) substances not of biological origin, includ-

ing those for which evidence is offered that they are identical with a GRAS counterpart of natural origin; and (5) substances of natural biological origin intended for consumption for other than their nutrient properties. Substances that will require regulations for use as food additives are of two categories: those for which there is no history of safe use under proposed conditions of use and those for which total intake limitations must be imposed to assure safety. Saccharin is a substance in the latter category; a regulation proposing limitations in its use was published in 1971.

Additive use is more extravagant in the United States than in some other countries. The British banned cyclamates as of January 1, 1970, and some European countries have restricted the use of sodium nitrite. Early in 1971, the food industry advised the Food and Drug Administration that they reserve the right to add chemicals and other substances to foods without advising the government—a statement that could make null and void considerable legislation.

The Color Additive Amendment of 1960. This act established the same rules and regulations for coloring substances as the 1958 amendment did for food additives, even to the inclusion of the Delaney anticancer clause. A food is deemed adulterated if it does not conform to the stipulations of these amendments. According to the act, a color additive is deemed unsafe unless (1) there is in effect a regulation that prescribes conditions for its use; (2) it is used in conformity with the regulation; (3) it comes from a batch certified as safe; (4) the color additive and its use are exempted. Until these amendments were enacted only coal-tar colors had to be certified as "harmless and suitable for use." Under the present law, all colors must be safe as used and limits can be set on the amounts of color used. The food colorings used by the homemaker are safe, but she must use them judiciously. Industry is prohibited from adding color to a food to make it appear better than it is. It is legal, however, to add color to some varieties of oranges; but they must be stamped "Color Added" or with another similar phrase to inform the consumer. The addition of artificial color to a food must be stated on the label unless the food is exempted.

THE FAIR PACKAGING AND LABELING ACT

The Fair Packaging and Labeling Act is also known as the Hart Act. Five years elapsed between the time Senator Philip Hart opened hearings in June, 1961 to investigate the packaging and labeling of products sold in the supermarket and the passage of the act by the Senate in June, 1966. The Act was passed by the House of Representatives in October, 1966; was signed by President Johnson in November, 1966; and became effective

July 1, 1967. The act carried a provision for postponement of effective date for one year for any class or type of consumer commodity should such postponement be in the public interest.

The declared purpose of the law is to prevent the use of unfair or deceptive methods of packaging or labeling of commodities distributed in interstate and foreign commerce. It is the intent of the law that packages and labels shall accurately inform consumers as to the quantity of contents and shall enable them to make value comparisons of the many products available in the supermarket. The number of products on the shelves of supermarkets had exploded from about one thousand five hundred at the end of World War II to approximately ten thousand in 1970. The package became the product salesman and it did not always tell the whole truth and nothing but the truth. Consumer complaints about packaging and labeling, as brought out in the hearings, include the following:

1. Comparison shopping was difficult because net weight of contents was not in even units of weight but in fractions, such as $13\frac{3}{8}$ ounces.

2. Required information was not prominently displayed.

3. Meaningless adjectives qualified quantity, such as "giant quart," and small, medium, large, and family-size packages. Often the family-size package in one brand was no larger than the medium-size package in another brand, and the cost of the contents did not always decrease as the size of the package increased.

4. Some packages and labels were deceptive in that a bargain was implied where none existed; for example, a product might be labeled "seven cents off." The consumer queries, "Seven cents off of what?" Often the product was priced no lower than the same product without the cents-off label. "Economy-size" packages were often no less expensive than the product in a smaller package.

5. Packages were often slack filled.

6. The pictures on packages were frequently deceptive.

7. The suggested number of servings was often deceptive.

8. The shape and dimensions of a package frequently deceived as to quantity, and the amount of packaging materials included "to protect" the contents of packages was excessive.

The Fair Packaging and Labeling Act went beyond the requirements of the Food, Drug, and Cosmetic Act by enlarging the concept of labeling and packaging. In essence, it demands that the required information be easy to find and easy to read and that the required information be usable, as in making price comparisons. Further, the act recognizes that labeling and packaging can deceive. The law concerns itself with consumer commodities. Consumer commodities include food, drugs, devices, and cosmetics—as these are defined in the Food, Drug, and Cosmetic Act—and expendable commodities used for personal care and household services.

The Federal Trade Commission enforces the law as it affects commodities other than food, drugs, devices, and cosmetics; the Food and Drug Administration as it affects food, drugs, devices, and cosmetics. The Department of Commerce is responsible for obtaining industry agreements that would reduce the number of package sizes in which commodities are packaged.

The law is short, the regulations are long. The law

1. Demands specific rules and regulations on the labeling of consumer commodities.
2. Asks for the control of nonfunctional slack fill of packages.
3. Provides for the control of cents-off and price promotions.
4. Provides for a way of reducing the number of packages in which consumer commodities are packaged.

Regulations for the administration of the new law were first published in March, 1967. Revised final regulations were published in September, 1967, with an announcement that they would take effect without a public hearing. They became effective for all new packages, new label designs, and labels being reordered as of January 1, 1968, and for all packages in interstate commerce as of July 1, 1968. This date was extended by one year to permit the use of old labels. To facilitate compliance with the regulations for the packaging and the labeling of food, the requirements of the Food, Drug, and Cosmetic Act and the Fair Packaging and Labeling Act were incorporated into a single set of regulations. Definitions and interpretations of some terms of the Food, Drug, and Cosmetic Act were modified.

Definitions

1. *Labeling* includes all written, printed, or graphic matter accompanying an article at any time while such article is in interstate commerce or held for sale after shipment or delivery in interstate commerce.

2. *Label* means any display of written, printed, or graphic matter on the immediate container of any article, or any such matter affixed to any consumer commodity or affixed to or appearing upon a package containing any consumer commodity.

3. *Principal display panel* of a food package means that part of a label that is most likely to be shown or examined under customary conditions of display for retail sale. This panel must be large enough to accommodate all the mandatory label information clearly and conspicuously. Whenever a package has more than one principal display panel, the required information must be duplicated on each principal display panel.

4. The term *area of principal display panel* means the area of the side or surface that bears the principal display panel. In the case of a rectangular package where one entire side can be the principal-display-panel

side, the area is the product of the height times the width of that side. In the case of a cylindrical or nearly cylindrical container, 40 per cent of the product of the height of the container times its circumference is the area of the principal display panel. In the case of any otherwise shaped container, 40 per cent of the total surface is the area of the principal display panel. The purpose of these definitions is to establish the type size for declaration of net contents, i.e., to make them readable.

5. The term *chemical preservative* means any chemical that, when added to food, tends to prevent or retard deterioration thereof, but does not include common salt, sugars, vinegars, spices or oils thereof, substances added to food by direct exposure to wood smoke, or chemicals applied for their insecticidal or herbicidal properties.

6. The term *artificial coloring* means coloring that contains a manufactured dye or pigment or one extracted from plant or other material in which the dye or pigment occurred naturally.

7. The term *artificial flavoring* means a flavoring containing a manufactured aromatic substance.

8. A *random package* is one of a lot of packages of a commodity with varying weights, or no fixed weight patterns, like fresh fruits and vegetables and meats. The weight of random packages is expressed in pounds and decimal fractions of the pound carried out to not more than two decimal places. The label of the package must note the cost per pound or per the specified number of pounds and the cost of the contents of the package.

Regulations

Some regulations for the enforcement of the Fair Packaging and Labeling Act have been edited and shortened. They follow.

1. The principal display panel of a food in package form shall bear a statement of the identify of the commodity. It must be identified in the common or usual name of the food. If there is no common name, appropriately descriptive terms or a commonly understood fanciful name may be used. If a food is marketed in various optional forms—such as whole, diced, sliced, and so on—the particular form shall be a prominent written part of the statement of identity, unless depicted by vignette or unless visible through the container, for example, "Small Whole Beets."

2. The identifying statement must be presented in bold type and in lines generally parallel to the base of the package as it is displayed.

3. The label of a packaged food must bear the name and place of business of the manufacturer, packer, or distributor. If the name is not that of the manufacturer, then a statement must clarify the role of the company named.

4.   The principal display panel of a packaged food must bear an accurate statement of the net quantity of contents in weight, measure, or numerical count. This statement must appear without any qualifying terms that may exaggerate, such as "big pint." It must be spaced within the bottom 30 per cent of the area of the principal display panel as a distinct item and separated from any other label information and in lines generally parallel to the base of the package. It must appear in easily legible bold-face type, and in a type size established in relation to the area of the principal display panel of the package. Five minimum type sizes to be used on packages from five square inches or less to more than four hundred square inches are specified. The statement must be in terms of fluid measure for liquids. The statement must be in avoirdupois pounds and ounces for food that is solid, semisolid, or viscous, or a mixture of solid and liquid. Exempted are random packages.

5.   The net contents declaration is one of food contents only; it cannot include the weight of any packaging material.

6.   A dual declaration of net contents is required for packages containing less than four pounds but at least one pound; or less than one gallon but at least one pint. The more prominent declaration must be in total avoirdupois ounces or fluid ounces; the second declaration is placed within parentheses to set it apart, for example, "24 ounces (1½ pounds)" or "24 fluid ounces (1½ pints)."

7.   If the label of a food package represents the contents in terms of the number of servings, it must describe the size of the serving in terms of weight, or of liquid or dry measure, or in other commonly understood terms of measurement, such as tablespoonfuls or cupfuls.

8.   The ingredients of a packaged food must be listed by their common names in order of decreasing predominance in adequate type size without crowding. The entire ingredient listing must appear on a single panel of the label. In cases where a single expensive ingredient is promoted as significant to the value of the food, declaration of the percentage of the expensive ingredient is required: i.e., a blend of "cottonseed oil and olive oil" in which there was 80 per cent of cottonseed oil would bear a statement of the 20 per cent of olive oil. This regulation does not apply to standardized and defined products.

9.   A statement of the use of artificial coloring, artificial flavoring, or chemical preservative must be present on the food or its container or its wrapper in such a way that the statement is likely to be read by the ordinary person under customary conditions of the purchase and use of the food. Exempted from the required statement of the use of artificial color are butter, ice cream, and cheddar cheese.

There were seizures of packages not in compliance with the Fair Packaging and Labeling Law in 1970 and in 1971, but it is quite likely that the majority of packages the consumer will buy in the 1970's will be in compliance. Some packages are exempted from compliance. Individual serving-size packages of foods containing less than one-half ounce or less than one-half fluid ounce, like the packages of sugar, coffee whitener, catsup, and mustard supplied in restaurants and individually wrapped pieces of candy of less than one-half ounce net weight, are exempted from declaration of weight. Random packages; soft drink bottles; ice cream, milk, cream, and other fluid dairy products in standard one-half pint, pint, one-half gallon, and gallon containers; white flour in conventional packages; and margarine in one-pound rectangular packages are some foods exempt from the regulation that statement of net contents must be spaced within the bottom 30 per cent of the principal display panel. And exemptions from the requirement of dual listing of net contents include ice cream and frozen desserts, flour in two-pound packages, and single-strength and less than single-strength fruit juice beverages, imitation juice beverages, and drinking water in glass and plastic containers.

The Food and Drug Administration and the Federal Trade Commission proposed regulations to govern the use of cents-off and reduced price promotions in 1970. The finalized regulations became effective in January 1972. They are in essence as follows.

1.   A cents-off or other reduced-price promotion of a consumer commodity is prohibited unless that commodity has been sold thirty days prior to the offer within the geographic trade area at an ordinary and customary price—a price considered the regular price.

2.   The exact amount of the price reduction must be clearly and conspicuously set forth. After June 15, 1972, packages must be marked, "Price Marked Is ——— Cents Off the Regular Price."

3.   The frequency of promotions is limited to three per year with a lapse of at least thirty days between each promotion. The maximum total period of time for any promotion is limited to six months per year.

4.   Reduced-price promotions of newly introduced consumer commodities and commodities newly introduced into a geographic area are not subject to the above (1 through 3) limitations but are subject to these "introductory offer" limitations. Labeling must identify the offering as introductory; it must suggest the postintroduction price; and the offer cannot exceed six months in duration.

5.   The package of a food or commodity promoted as the "economy size," "thrifty pack," "bargain size," or by other qualifying term that implies reduced price is required to have an established ordinary and customary price for the regular- and other-size containers. The price per unit of weight, measure, or count of the economy size must be at least 5 per cent less than the regular price per unit of weight, measure, or count of the least expensive retail size of the same consumer commodity. Only one package of a line can be labeled the "economy" package.

6.   Such offers as "two-for-one," "one-cent sale," and other half-price

promotions must be bona fide, that is, based on the regular price of thirty days prior to the promotion. The duration of and number of such promotions permitted per year are limited.

By early 1971, the Bureau of Standards of the United States Department of Commerce could report that a number of industries had voluntarily agreed to limit the number of sizes of packages in which different commodities were packaged. Further, the fractional ounce was fast disappearing. For example, the cereal industry agreed to package in whole ounces only and reduced the number of packages from thirty-three to eighteen. Other commodities packaged in fewer numbers of packages by 1971 were cheese, crackers and cookies, instant coffee and tea, teabags, peanut butter, salad oil, nonfat dry milk, and instant potatoes.

Regulations that prohibit nonfunctional slack-fill will likely be promulgated in the 1970's. Forecasts are that such regulations as these on labeling may also be forthcoming: complete information on the nutritional content of processed foods; a two-level contents statement—net and drained weights; percentages of ingredients in processed foods; and a statement of change in weight of a package that may result from a change in design.

DEPARTMENTS OF THE FEDERAL GOVERNMENT CONCERNED WITH FOOD STANDARDS AND FOOD LAWS AND THE ADMINISTRATION THEREOF

The Department of Health, Education, and Welfare

A unit within the Department of Health, Education, and Welfare is the Public Health Service. The Food and Drug Administration is a subunit of the Public Health Service.

The Food and Drug Administration. In 1940, the Food and Drug Administration was removed from the Department of Agriculture to the Federal Security Agency. In 1953, that agency became the Department of Health, Education, and Welfare wherein the Food and Drug Administration was included in the Consumer Protection and Environmental Health Service of the Public Health Service. In 1970, the Food and Drug Administration became a separate entity reporting directly to the Assistant Secretary for Health and Scientific Affairs. Within it, the Bureau of Foods bears the responsibility for the administration of these laws: the Tea Importation Act, the Filled Milk Act, the Import Milk Act, the Federal Food, Drug, and Cosmetic Act and amendments, and the Fair Packaging and Labeling Act. The laws have a dual purpose: to protect the public health by ensuring the wholesomeness and safety of food and to protect the consumer from fraud by preventing adulteration and misbranding.

For administrative purposes, the United States is divided into ten regions in which there are seventeen Food and Drug Administration offices equipped with laboratories and manned with chemists and inspectors. In addition, there are ten regional offices of the Department of Health, Education, and Welfare.

In the administration of the laws, the Food and Drug Administration uses every means to inform industries of the requirements of the laws so that they may comply with them. When there is violation of the law, three procedures are possible: seizure of food that violates the law; criminal prosecution of the person or firm responsible for violation of the law; and finally, injunction proceedings to keep more of the offending food from getting into interstate commerce. Seized products may be destroyed or otherwise disposed of; or they may be reconditioned, that is, brought into compliance with the law. Criminal prosecution of a firm or person for violation of the law can lead to fine or imprisonment or both, the severity of the penalty being established by proof of intent to defraud or mislead. Some activities of the Food and Drug Administration that are of interest to consumers are these.

1.   It promulgates definitions and standards of identity for food products.

2.   For some canned foods, it has promulgated definitions and standards of identity, reasonable standards of quality, and reasonable standards of fill of container. Other definitions and standards are in process.

3.   Six times yearly it tests the diet of a nineteen-year-old man for such contaminants as radio-nuclides, pesticide residues, salmonellae, and such poisonous elements as mercury to affirm the safety of the national food supply.

4.   It formulates the regulations essential to the administration of laws, for example, regulations for the safe use of food additives and color additives.

5.   In cooperation with the United States Department of Agriculture, it issues regulations for the safe use of chemical pesticides on raw agricultural products.

6.   It inspects factories and warehouses to determine the prevailing sanitary conditions and practices.

7.   It inspects, examines, and tests foods to determine that they satisfy the requirements of the law.

8.   During natural disasters, such as hurricanes and floods, it assists state and local officials in examining and supervising the distribution of food and drugs to prevent the use of polluted materials.

9.   It acts to discover the causes of outbreaks of food poisoning.

10.   It inspects imported foods to determine that they comply with domestic standards.

Legislation leaves no doubt as to the mission of the Food and Drug Administration. The report, made public in August, 1969, of a seven-member panel of Food and Drug Administration officials named to assess the organization, concluded that the Food and Drug Administration, as it was then constituted, could not protect the consumer from bad food. The 1969 Ralph Nader Summer Study of the Food and Drug Administration culminated in the scathing report entitled *The Chemical Feast*. Since that time the Food and Drug Administration has been reorganized and it has been given more ample funds. The 1970's will see its obligations expand rather than decrease.

The United States Department of Agriculture

The Department of Agriculture engages in manifold activities. It is not within the purview of this text to discuss them fully. All of the department's activities are of consequence to the consumer. Of most immediate interest, it engages directly and indirectly, through grants, in research leading to improved methods of food production; to improved breeds of animals and improved varieties of food plants; to improved control of and eradication of plant and animal diseases and pests; and to improved methods of harvesting, processing, and distributing agricultural products. It administers the meat, poultry, and egg inspection acts. The department promulgates standards for grading food products according to quality; it promulgates definitions and standards of identity for foods that contain meat or poultry. It approves the formulas for, the labels for, and the packaging of processed meat food and poultry food products. Four divisions of the Consumer and Marketing Service are responsible for the services of most interest to consumers: the Livestock Division, the Poultry Division, the Fruit and Vegetable Division, and the Dairy Division.

Inspection of Food. Inspection of food assures the consumer of the wholesomeness and the purity of food that the law exacts. The Meat Inspection Act of 1906 made mandatory the inspection of meat and meat products destined for interstate and export commerce. The Wholesome Meat Act of 1967 applied provisions of the 1906 law to meat and meat food products in intrastate commerce. Federal inspection is mandatory in any state that has no satisfactory inspection system. In 1971, fifteen states were under federal inspection.

The inspection process begins with live animals, continues through slaughter and processing, includes the inspection of the plant and the machinery and all the ingredients used in the production of processed meat food products, and assures that products for which standards and definitions of identity exist conform to them.

The mark of inspection reading, "U.S. Inspected and Passed," or the abbreviated form thereof, appears directly on meat or meat food products or on the labels thereof. The mark on carcasses, primal cuts, and meat food products in animal casings, beef tongues, beef hearts, and smoked meats not in casings appears within a circle in abbreviated form—"U.S. INSP'D & P'S'D"—and includes the number of the establishment where processing and inspection occurred (Figure 4–1 left). The mark of inspection on cooked, cured, and processed meat food products carries a full statement of inspection and the number of the plant where the processing and inspection occurred (Figure 4–1 right). Only purple ink is approved for marking carcasses and cuts derived therefrom. Any approved color, excepting green, can be used for marking other meat products so long as there is acceptable contrast with the color of the product.

The Poultry Products Inspection Act of 1957 as amended made inspection mandatory for ready-to-cook poultry and poultry food products in interstate and foreign commerce. The Wholesome Poultry Products Act of 1968 requires inspection of poultry in intrastate commerce and makes federal inspection mandatory in any state without an inspection program at least equal to the federal program. Inspection regulations require that each bird be individually examined and that processing occur in a sanitary manner in approved, properly equipped establishments. The same inspection symbol is used on all inspected poultry and poultry food products (see Figure 4–2). The Poultry Division of the Consumer and Marketing Service administers the law.

The Egg Products Inspection Act of 1970 requires continuous, mandatory inspection of egg processing plants. The Poultry Division administers the law.

The effectiveness of the inspection programs of the Department of Agriculture was questioned in the summer of 1971 because of the contamination of chicken-vegetable soup processed by the Campbell Soup Company with the botulinum toxin. The department is responsible for the inspection during processing of foods that contain certain proportions of meat and poultry.

FIGURE 4–1.   Meat inspection marks. Left, the mark applied directly to carcass and cuts. Right, the mark appearing on labels on processed meat food products. (*United States Department of Agriculture photographs.*)

FIGURE 4–2.   Poultry inspection mark appearing on ready-to-cook poultry and processed poultry food products. (*United States Department of Agriculture photograph.*)

It is quite probable that legislation in the 1970's will attempt to improve the quality of the food inspection programs. It has been proposed that a separate agency be established and made responsible for this function.

Standards for Grading Food for Quality.   Sorting or classifying food according to quality requires objective standards for evaluation. The Agricultural Marketing Act of 1946 enabled the United States Department of Agriculture to establish the Agricultural Marketing Service (since 1965, the Consumer and Marketing Service) to define standards for foods not already covered by laws and regulations. Proposed standards for grading for quality are developed in consultation with trade groups; they are used tentatively until such time as they are proved practicable, when they become official permissive standards for grading. They are frequently revised to reflect changes in production, use, and marketing practices. There are three types of grade standards: wholesale grades, grades for food for processing, and consumer grades. There are wholesome grades for items in all classes of foods; they apply to large-scale shipments; they allow certain percentages of tolerance for undergrade specimens; and they apply to quality at the time of grading in general. The food grading services are often operated with the cooperation of state departments of agriculture; they are voluntary and the users pay a fee to cover costs. The percentage of the supply officially graded varies with products and ranges from none to 80 per cent for beef. Officially graded food products carry the U.S. grade shield at the option of the packer or distributor. Supermarkets buy by grade: information on grade may be available to the consumer who asks, for example, about the lettuce or the green beans. The number of grades stocked by supermarkets may be only one as for beef or two as for butter and eggs.

Consumer grades have been established for some foods. They are designed to apply to the small units of food we buy; they permit less tolerance for undergrade specimens than wholesale grades. There are consumer grades for six kinds of meat: beef, veal, calf, lamb, yearling mutton, and mutton; for six kinds of poultry, including chicken and turkey; for butter;

for eggs; for cheddar and Swiss cheese; for nonfat dry milk; for fruit jellies and jams; for peanut butter; for some canned fruits and vegetables; for some frozen fruits and vegetables; for some fresh vegetables; and for some other food products. We do not find all these products grade-labeled in the supermarket; however, more grade-labeled food products could readily be made available to the consumer. Consumer advocates are pressing for mandatory grade-labeling of the foods for which it is feasible. The food industries, the advertising agencies, and the mass media are strongly opposed to mandatory grade-labeling because it makes the brand image worthless.

There is no one system for designation of grade. In general, consumer grades, except for meats, are preceded by the letters *U.S.*; are enclosed within the outline of a shield (the precise shape of the shield differs for different products) and are designated by letters: AA, A, B, C, and D. For some foods there may be two grades only; for others, there may be several. For example, butter grades are U.S. Grade AA, U.S. Grade A, and U.S. Grade B. Consumer grades for potatoes are only U.S. Grade A and U.S. Grade B. However, potatoes are often sold at retail according to wholesale grades of which there are four: U.S. Fancy, U.S. No. 1, U.S. Commercial, and U.S. No. 2. Meat grades are designated by words; instead of *U.S.*, *USDA* appears with the grade designation, for example, USDA Choice. Numbers and numbers modified by adjectives are used for wholesale grades in general. The top grade of one commodity may be the U.S. No. 1 grade; but the top grade of another may be designated as U.S. Fancy or Extra No. 1, in which case the U.S. No. 1 grade is second to the best.

The attributes of foods that determine quality differ with different products; the standard used for grading butter could not be used for grading eggs. Attributes that consumers prize are flavor, color, and texture. Official graders consider such other factors as appearance, freedom from defects, size of units, degree of maturity, and so on. Grading systems permit the scoring of foods on a point system. For example, frozen peas are scored on color, defects, and tenderness and maturity; the maximum points that may be assigned to each factor are 20, 40, and 40, respectively. For purposes of illustration, grade designations for frozen peas are reprinted in part from the *United States Standards for Frozen Peas* as issued on May 28, 1959.

PRODUCT DESCRIPTION AND GRADES

Product Description

"Frozen peas" means the frozen product prepared from the clean, sound, succulent seed of the common garden pea (Pisum sativum) by shelling, washing, blanching, sorting, proper draining, and is frozen in accordance with good commercial practice and maintained at temperatures necessary for the preservation of the product.

Grades of Frozen Peas

(a) "U.S. Grade A" (or a "U.S. Fancy") is the quality of frozen peas that possess similar varietal characteristics; that possess a good flavor; that possess a good color; that are practically free from defects; that are tender; and for those factors which are rated in accordance with the scoring system outlined in this subpart the total score is not less than 90 points: *Provided,* That the frozen peas may possess a reasonably good color, scoring not less than 17 points and may be only reasonably free from defects with respect to pieces of peas if the total score is not less than 90 points.

(b) "U.S. Grade B" (or "U.S. Extra Standard") is the quality of frozen peas that possess similar varietal characteristics; that possess a fairly good flavor; that possess a reasonably good color; that are reasonably free from defects; that are reasonably tender; and for those factors which are rated in accordance with the scoring system outlined in this subpart the total score is not less than 80 points: *Provided,* That the frozen peas may possess a fairly good color and may be fairly free from defects with respect to pieces of peas if the total score is not less than 80 points.

(c) "U.S. Grade C" (or "U.S. Standard") is the quality of frozen peas that possess similar varietal characteristics; that possess a fairly good flavor; that possess a fairly good color; that are fairly free from defects; that are fairly tender; and that for those factors which are scored in accordance with the scoring system outlined in this subpart the total score is not less than 70 points: *Provided,* That the frozen peas may fail to meet the requirements of this paragraph for defects with respect to pieces of peas if the total score is not less than 70 points.

(d) "Substandard" is the quality of frozen peas that fail to meet the requirements of U.S. Grade C.

Summary of Scoring System

Factor	Points Maximum	Grade A	Grade B	Grade C	SStd.
Color	20	18–20	16–17**	14–15**	0–13*
Defects	40	36–40	32–35**	28–31**	0–27**
Tenderness and maturity	40	36–40	32–35*	28–31*	0–27*
Total Score Minimum	—	90	80	70	—

* Limiting rule, sample units that score in this classification may not be of higher grade.

** Partial limiting rule, sample units that score in this classification may be of next grade above.

SCORING FACTORS

COLOR—Grade A—bright, practically uniform, good, green color for variety, appearance not more than slightly affected by presence of peas that vary markedly; $\frac{1}{2}\%$, by count, may be blond or cream colored or peas that seriously detract. Grade B—reasonably bright, reasonably uniform green color for variety, appearance not materially affected by peas that vary markedly; $1\frac{1}{2}\%$ by count, may be blond or cream colored or peas that seriously detract. Grade C—fairly uniform green color for variety, may be dull but not off color, appearance not seriously affected by peas that vary markedly; 2% by count, may be blond or cream colored or peas that seriously detract.

TENDERNESS AND MATURITY—As determined by brine flotation test with skins removed and the tenderness of the cooked product.

Grade A—No more than 10% sink in a 13% salt solution and are tender after cooking. Grade B—no more than 12% sink in a 15% salt solution and

Summary of Maximum Allowances for Defects

	Grade Classification				
Kind of Defect	*Grade A*	*Grade B*		*Grade C*	
		When present as single group	Combination of any 2	When present as single group	Combination of any 2
Harmless extraneous vegetable material (For each 30 ozs.)	$\frac{1}{4}$ sq. in. or 1 piece of any size	$\frac{1}{2}$ sq. in. or 1 piece of any size	$\frac{1}{4}$ sq. in. or 1 piece of any size	1 sq. in. or 1 piece of any size	$\frac{1}{2}$ sq. in. or 1 piece of any size
Group 1 Flat material Pea pods, leaves, etc.	or	or		or	
Group 2 Spherical material Night shade, thistle buds, etc.	1 unit or	2 units or	1 unit	3 units or	2 units
Group 3 Cylindrical material Stems, etc.	1 piece or pieces not exceeding $\frac{1}{2}$ in. aggregate	1 piece or pieces not exceeding 1 in. aggregate	1 piece or pieces not exceeding $\frac{1}{2}$ in. aggregate	1 piece or pieces not exceeding 2 in. aggregate	1 piece or pieces not exceeding 1 in. aggregate
Pieces of peas	7%* by count	10%* by count		15%* by count	
Blemished peas	2% by count	4% by count		6% by count	
Seriously blemished peas	which includes $\frac{1}{2}\%$ by count	which includes 1% by count		which includes 3% by count	

* Limiting rule does not apply.

are reasonably tender after cooking. Grade C—no more than 16% sink in a 16% salt solution and are fairly tender after cooking.

DEFECTS—Harmless material, pieces of peas, blemished and seriously blemished peas, and other defects which affect appearance or eating quality.

Grade A—practically free; Grade B—reasonably free; Grade C—fairly free.

Official standards for grading are long and detailed documents. Many definitions are included in standards, as are methods for determining objectively measurable characteristics. Standards for grading foods are available free from the appropriate division of the United States Department of Agriculture.

When packers, processors, and distributors do their own grading of foods and when they use the grade designations of official standards, the products must conform to the grades given or the products are considered misbranded. Further, no *U.S.* or *USDA* may appear as part of the grade designation and grade cannot appear within the outline of a shield. There will be further discussion of food quality in succeeding chapters.

Department of Commerce

Through its National Bureau of Standards this department defines standards of weights and measures that are official at all levels. Among its definitions are those of the approximate weights in avoirdupois ounces per cup of some foods the homemaker uses, such as flour, sugar, and nonfat dry milk. Under the authority of the Fair Packaging and Labeling Act, this agency has achieved some success in the reduction of the number of packages of different size in which consumer commodities are packaged.

In October, 1970, the fish inspection and standards promulgation functions of the abolished Bureau of Commercial Fisheries of the United States Department of Interior were transferred to the National Marine Fisheries Service of the National Oceanic and Atmospheric Administration of the United States Department of Commerce.

The Federal Trade Commission

The role of the Federal Trade Commission is to maintain a freely competitive environment in commerce and to restrain monopoly. It is enabled by several laws that resulted from the growth of big business during this century. It must prevent unfair and deceptive acts and practices in commerce, it must prevent false and misleading advertising, and it must deter unfair pricing practices. It acts through cease-and-desist orders and by instigation of civil penalty suits against violators of its orders. Both the Nader Report issued in January, 1969, and the report of an investigation under the auspices of the American Bar Association revealed that consumer protection by the agency was ineffectual and that it tended to favor trade interests.

The Federal Trade Commission shares in the administration of the Fair Packaging and Labeling Act. It participated in the formulation of the regulation of cents-off and price-reduction promotions.

It proposed a Trade Regulation Rule in late 1969 to regulate retail food store advertising and marketing practices because a report of food chain selling practices in Washington, D.C., and in San Francisco had revealed that not all advertised items were available at advertised prices in all stores of chains. The rule requires that advertised specials be sold at the advertised price or less and that the advertised items be available in amounts sufficient to meet reasonably anticipated demand. It permits the use of such specific disclaimers as "available only in stores with delicatessen departments"; but it bans the use of such general disclaimers as "not all items available in all stores." The rule became effective in July, 1971.

In 1969, the Federal Trade Commission issued a statement of policy for coupons to put an end to coupons of short expiration date and to put a stop to limitations or conditions written only in very fine print. Also in 1969, it promulgated regulations on games of chance in the food-retailing and gasoline industries.

Reorganization within the Federal Trade Commission in 1970 gave rise to the Bureau of Consumer Protection. The bureau investigates and provides guidance and counseling to business, consumers, and government officials; it endeavors to secure voluntary compliance with the law in matters involving deceptive and unfair practices; and it is empowered to litigate and secure compliance. Further, it is responsible for establishing consumer education programs to alert the public to unfair trade practices.

In 1971, the Federal Trade Commission adopted a resolution that would require advertisers, on demand, to document advertising statements regarding a product's performance, safety, comparative price, quality, or effectiveness. Much information so derived would be made public, thereby assisting consumers in decision-making. Failure to validate statements to the satisfaction of the commission would lead to charges of false advertising against a company. It can be anticipated that false advertising about food products will be uncovered.

Finally, in late 1970 and in 1971, the Federal Trade Commission began to look seriously at and to question the nutritional claims made in the advertising of some food companies.

THE CODEX ALIMENTARIUS

The signing of an International Cheese Convention by eight countries in 1953 led to a Conference on Food Standards under the joint auspices of the Food and Agriculture Organization and the World Health Organization in October, 1962. The Conference recommended the establishment of the Codex Alimentarius Commission, which first convened in Rome in 1963 at the headquarters of the Food and Agriculture Organization of the United Nations. Representatives of thirty nations and sixteen international organizations were present. The purpose of the meeting was to set up a body of definitions to be called the "Codex Alimentarius." The Commission set up a plan of work that divided the tasks among committees international in composition. Because of differences in concepts of what a given food should be, difficulties will always be encountered in establishing standards. Standards will be minimum but they will be rational standards for quality, chemical composition, permitted additives, and limits for bacterial contamination in the world's food commodities.

SUGGESTED REFERENCES

1. *The Almanac of Canning, Freezing, Preservation Industries.* Westminister, Maryland: E. E. Judge, 1970.

2. Anderson, Oscar E., *The Health of a Nation, Harvey W. Wiley and the Fight for Pure Food.* Chicago: University of Chicago Press, 1958.

3. Bishop, James E., Jr., and Henry W. Hubbard, *Let the Seller Beware.* Washington, D.C.: National Press, Inc., 1969.

4. *Consumers All—The Yearbook of Agriculture 1965.* Washington, D.C.: United States Department of Agriculture, 1965.

5. Cox, Edward D., R. C. Fellmeth, and J. E. Schulz, *Nader's Raiders.* New York: Grove Press, Inc., 1970 (paperback). First published in 1969 as "The Nader Report" on the Federal Trade Commission by Richard W. Baron Publishing Company, Inc.

6. *Fair Packaging and Labeling Act with Explanation.* Chicago: Commerce Clearing House, Inc., 1966.

7. *Federal Food, Drug, and Cosmetic Act with Amendments.* Washington, D.C.: U.S. Government Printing Office, 1970.

8. Gunderson, F., H. Gunderson, and E. R. Ferguson, Jr., *Food Standards and Definitions in the United States—A Guidebook.* New York: Academic Press, 1963.

9. Kallet, A., and F. J. Schlink, *100,000,000 Guinea Pigs.* New York: Grosset & Dunlap, 1933.

10. Lamb, Ruth deForest, *American Chamber of Horrors—The Truth About Food and Drugs.* New York: Farrar & Rinehart, Inc., 1936.

11. Magnuson, W. G., and J. Carper, *The Dark Side of the Market Place —The Plight of the American Consumer.* New York: Prentice-Hall, 1968.

12. Mowbray, A. Q., *The Thumb on the Scale or the Supermarket Shell Game.* New York: J. B. Lippincott Co., 1967.

13. Neal, Harry Edwards, *The Protectors—The Study of the Food and Drug Administration.* New York: Julian Messner 1968.

14. *Protecting Our Food Supply—The Yearbook of Agriculture 1966.* Washington D.C.: United States Department of Agriculture, 1966.

15. Sanford, David, *Hot War on the Consumer.* New York: Pitman Publishing Company, 1969.

16. Sinclair, Upton, *The Jungle.* New York: The New American Library of World Literature, 1960. Originally published by Doubleday, Page, & Co., 1905.

17. Turner, James S., *The Chemical Feast.* New York: Grossman Publishers, 1970 (paperback).

18. Wiley, H. W., *Foods and Their Adulteration,* 3rd ed. Philadelphia: P. Blakiston's Son and Co., 1917.

19. ———, *The History of a Crime Against the Food Law.* Washington, D.C.: Harvey M. Wiley, 1929.

20. ———, *Wiley's Autobiography.* Indianapolis, Indiana: Bobbs-Merrill Co., 1930.

Chapter 5
Purchasing Food—
Some General Precepts

Estimated food-at-home costs—United States average for a family of four persons were about $1,600, $2,050, and $2,500 respectively for low-, moderate-, and higher-cost budgets as of March, 1971 (5). Weekly expenditures would be about $30, $40, and $50 respectively. Each person consumes about 1,450 pounds of food per year; for a family of four, this means about three tons of food. If the weight of packaging, cans, and bottles is not forgotten, this weight would greatly exceed three tons. From this, it can be deduced that the buying of food for a family of four is a burden both weightwise and moneywise; and one not to be taken lightly. During the 1960's, the retail price index for food at home rose from 100.6 in 1960 to 127.7 in 1970 (see Figure 5–1). However, the rise from 1960 to 1965 was only 7 points; from 1960 through 1968, about 15 points; the remaining 12-point rise came in the two years of 1969 and 1970. A 5-point rise during 1966 and a 7.5 rise, particularly an almost 13-point rise for meats, in 1969 provoked consumer boycotts of supermarkets in 1966 and 1969.

The reference base for the calculation of the Consumer Price Index and the retail food price indexes was changed from the 1957–59 years to the 1967 year in 1971. According to the 1967 reference base, the cost of all food increased 3 per cent; of food at home, 2.4 per cent; and of food away from home, 5.2 per cent in 1971. Predictions in early 1972 were that during 1972, prices for food at home would rise 4 per cent.

Shopping for food has become increasingly time-consuming and challenging. The 1960's produced some legislation in the housewife's favor (see Chapter 4) and more is promised for the 1970's, namely, more quality grade labeling for processed foods, the open dating of perishable food products, unit pricing, the naming of all ingredients in processed foods, and a statement of the nutrient content in the labeling of many foods.

120

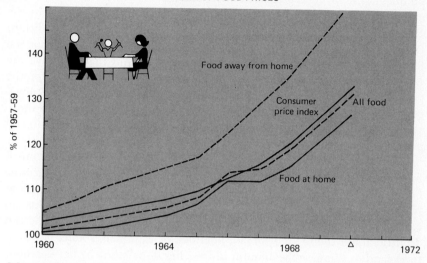

INDEX OF FOOD PRICES

Food away from home

Consumer
price index

All food

Food at home

% of 1957-59

140

130

120

110

100

1960   1964   1968   1972

BLS data, urban wage earners and clerical workers.   △ 7- month average.

FIGURE 5–1.   Index of food prices. (*United States Department of Agriculture photograph.*)

The 1960's also produced a gold mine of information on how to shop for food and an impressive number of gadgets for easy calculation of the unit cost of food and nonfood items. In this chapter, we shall organize and summarize some of this wealth of information, to establish some general principles; in the six chapters that follow, we shall present specific information about foods in different food classes.

The food dollar is a "stretchable" one in the sense that it can buy more or less food depending upon what it is spent for; that is, it can buy two pounds of hamburger on special or one-half pound of lamb chops; six pounds of bananas or one dozen oranges; six pounds of fresh carrots or one and a half pounds of frozen, precooked spinach soufflé; almost one gallon of fresh, fluid whole milk in a one-gallon plastic container or two gallons of reconstituted nonfat dry milk. These choices are available for several reasons. First, we have a somewhat competitive economy and different kinds of food stores in which to shop. Secondly, we have an efficient agriculture, highly developed systems of food transport, and a technology that provides great varieties of foods that are widely distributed. Thirdly, our food supply is quality sorted to some extent. And, finally, our food is subjected technologically to a variety of treatments. The net result is the multiplicity of choices that makes it possible to buy much or little food for the dollar.

Although many variables influence spending for food and some housewives neither need to nor desire to practice thrift in food purchases, many families want to maximize their food dollars, that is, have them buy as much food of the kinds they favor as possible. Shopping for food in the 1970's demands that the housewife prepare for the shopping expedition; that she know what the marketplace offers; that she read labels; that she have the desire and ability to make comparisons; and that she have the wisdom to make choices that match her goals. Knowledge is hers for the asking and taking. She acquires skills and abilities as she gains in knowledge and experience. The desire to make comparisons is a matter of motivation—as are the acquisition of knowledge and skills, the definition of goals, and the decisions ultimately made.

The homemaker's decisions in at least six ways determine how much food her dollars buy. This sentence might well read: six factors determine how much food the dollar buys. Although it is a true statement, it fails to place the burden of responsibility on the housewife in situations she can control. She is more or less helpless in the face of economic laws: she can do little about the price of bread, potatoes, or eggs. She is able, however, to expand or decrease the amount of food her dollars buy by her decisions on (1) where to shop, (2) when to shop, (3) what to buy, (4) how to buy it, (5) how much to take advantage of abundant supply and sales, and (6) whether or not to buy services rendered in the preparation of foods, that is, convenience.

Influence of Decision on Where to Shop

We saw in Chapter 2 that there are different types of food stores. Some are discount food stores that feature low prices. Some are large supermarkets located in shopping centers. Some are convenience stores conveniently located. Others are specialty stores. Some are independently owned and operated; others are units of giant chains. Some sell everything a consumer might conceivably need and want; others specialize in a specific class of foods, such as meats, fish, fresh produce, dairy products, or baked goods. Price advantages are to be found if the consumer seeks them; but she will have to comparison-shop, that is, do her own research. Table 5–1 shows the difference in the costs of some selected foods priced the same day in a supermarket, a discount supermarket, and a convenience store. So that identical items can be compared, nationally known brands of staples and a few other widely available foods are included in the list.

The difference in the costs of the items purchased in the discount supermarket and the supermarket was not startling; one cent or five cents here and there on an item. However, the difference in the total costs of like items in the convenience store and in the two supermarkets was more than one third. In Table 5–2, the minimum costs of a selection of items as priced in three different supermarkets are presented. Similarities and dif-

TABLE 5-1. *Cost of Selected Items as Purchased in Different Types of Food Stores*

Items	Quantity	Chain Super-market	Discount Super-market	Conveni-ence Store
Brown Sugar	1-lb. box	$0.22+	$0.21	$0.31
Catsup, Heinz	16-oz. bottle	0.31	0.29	0.43
Corn Flakes, Kellogg's	8 oz.	0.25	0.23	0.35
Cream Cheese	3 oz.	0.16	0.15	0.25
Hamburger	1 lb.	0.69	0.64	1.03[1]
Frankfurters, Oscar Mayer	1 lb.	0.89	0.88	1.05
Maxwell House Instant Coffee	2 oz.	0.55	0.55	0.75
Jello	1 box	0.12+	0.12	0.15
Parkay Margarine	1 lb.	0.39	0.36	0.49
Tide	3 lbs., 1 oz.	0.93	0.88	1.15
Scott Toilet Tissue	2 rolls	0.39	0.36	0.46
Campbell's Tomato Soup	1 can	0.14+	0.13	0.19
Tuna, Chicken-of-the-Sea, light chunk	1 can	0.43	0.37	0.59
Totals		$5.47+	$5.17	$7.20

[1] Frozen.

ferences in the costs of items can be noted. One of these chains appeared to have a higher pricing formula than the other two. Because all prices recorded are the minimums for the selected items, it can be assumed that differences in quality would not be great.

A study of food prices in two typical supermarkets in a shopping area serving middle-income families in Greensboro, North Carolina has been reported (14). There was some variation between stores in the average monthly cost of a weekly market basket. The average cost for a three-month period was virtually the same. However, had the consumer patronized both stores and purchased to her advantage in both, she would have reduced the cost of the market basket by about 10 per cent. Bivens (2) studied the minimum cost of fifteen items in the stores of several chains in the Milwaukee metropolitan area over a twelve-month period. He reported a consistency in the pricing policy of the chains. He also reported that the chains ranked from high to low in the total cost of the fifteen selected items. The average difference between the total cost of the fifteen items in the high-pricing chain and the low-pricing chain was about 12 per cent. A study of food prices in the four major cities of Ohio—Cleveland, Cincinnati, Columbus, and Toledo (16)—revealed that there were statistically significant differences in the cost of a market basket of foods as

TABLE 5–2. *Cost of a Market Basket of Items as Purchased in Three Supermarkets at Minimum Cost*

Items	Super-market A[1]	Super-market B[2]	Super-market C[2]
Bacon, 1 lb.	$.64	$.65	$.39
Bananas, 1 lb.	.15	.13	.11
Bread, 20-oz. loaf	.26½	.25	.27½
Carrots, 1 lb.	.19	.19½	.19½
Cheese, cheddar, mild, 1 lb.	.98	1.09	.89
Corn, cream-style, No. 303 can	.19½	.22	.20
Flour, general purpose, 5 lbs.	.65	.59	.59
Margarine, 1 lb.	.22	.22	.20
Milk, nonfat dry (to make 8 quarts)	1.19	1.09	1.09
Orange juice, frozen concentrate, six pack	.99	.99	1.09
Peanut butter, smooth, 12-oz. jar	.39	.38	.45
Peas, frozen, 10 oz.	.25	.25	.25
Pudding mix, 1 box	.13½	.14½	.15
Tomatoes, canned, No. 303 can	.19½	.22	.20
Totals	$6.44	$6.42	$6.08

[1]Supermarket A—regional chain.
[2]Supermarkets B and C—national chains.

these were purchased in different types of stores. The cost of the market basket was lowest in the discount food store. The cost of the market basket increased in this order: national chain, local chain, regional chain, and affiliated independent. The cost of the market basket was highest in the market that had the biggest share of the market. A study was reported by Kammer and Shawhan (13) of chain supermarkets, chain discount stores, chain convenience stores, and independent stores in Cincinnati, Ohio. Prices in high- and low-income areas were similar but there was price difference by type of store. In order of increasing cost by store type they were chain discount market, chain supermarket, independent store, and, finally, chain convenience store.

Although comparison shopping may disclose only small cost differences for individual items, it must be remembered that numberwise many purchases are made in food stores. Differences in cents, or even fractions of a cent, add up to significant sums and would thereby expand or decrease the quantities of food that dollars buy. Savings of 10 per cent can add up to significant sums when thought of in terms of annual spending. As supermarkets adapt their operations more and more to the wants of their particular clientele, differences may become greater. The housewife can choose—though she may not—to shop where pricing is to her advantage.

INFLUENCE OF DECISION ON WHEN TO SHOP

The study (14) of food prices in two supermarkets in Greensboro, North Carolina disclosed that if a family had purchased five pounds of beef chuck on each Friday that it was specialed, the bill would have been $39.30. If the same quantity of beef chuck had been bought each Tuesday, the price would have been $62.30 or $23.00 more. In general, foods and food products are specialed for weekend selling. However, some markets also have beginning-of-the-week specials to attract customers into the store on the days business is slow. Sunday specials are featured in supermarkets where they are permitted to be open on Sundays. Supermarkets that give stamps may feature specials and double-stamp days early in the week.

To call attention to the day of shopping as a factor that influences the cost of food is in actuality calling attention to a factor to be discussed subsequently, the factor of sales and specials.

INFLUENCE OF DECISION ON WHAT TO BUY

It is a fact that some foods in food classes cost more than other foods— one does not expect all automobiles, houses, or sweaters to cost the same, and we cannot expect all meats, fruits, vegetables, or cheeses to be alike in cost. Lamb chops cost more than pork chops; porterhouse steak, more than hamburger; shrimp, more than codfish; duckling, more than chicken; asparagus, more than beets; Belgian endive, more than head lettuce; fresh strawberries more than bananas; frozen raspberries, more than frozen strawberries; and so on. Within food classes there are high-cost, moderate-cost, and low-cost items. The more expensive are our choices, the less food we get per dollar spent. Tables 5–3, 5–4, and 5–5 have been especially designed to show this. Table 5–3 shows the differing costs for like numbers of servings of meat; the dollar bought less meat in Plan A than in Plan B. Meats are among the foods that should be compared on a cost-per-serving basis. Table 5–4 shows the difference in cost of like numbers of servings of vegetables. Similarly, Table 5–5 shows the difference in cost of similar quantities of dairy foods and nondairy products.

Food classes are the following: meats (*meats* is usually understood to include poultry and fish); fruits and vegetables; dairy products; eggs; grain products, including flour, cereals, breads, and baked goods; fats and oils; sugars and sweets, including syrups and jams and jellies; and beans, peas, and nuts, including peanut butter. In these classes the greatest spread in

TABLE 5-3.   *Two Plans for Selecting Meats*[1]

Plan A

Selected Items	Quantities Lbs.	Number of Portions	Cost
Sirloin steak, choice grade, bone in	2	4	$2.70
Loin lamb chops, choice grade	2	4	3.74
Chicken, broiler	3	4	1.20
Loin pork chops, medium thick	1⅓	4	1.37
Shrimp, frozen breaded	1¼	4	2.00
Ham, canned	2¼	8	2.60
Totals		28	$13.61

Plan B

Selected Items	Quantities Lbs.	Number of Portions	Cost
Hamburger	2	8	$1.32
Smoked picnic, bone in	3½	8	1.89
Chicken, broiler	3	4	1.20
Ocean perch, frozen	1	4	.71
Frankfurters	⅘	4	.65
Totals		28	$5.77

[1]Estimated Retail Food Prices by Cities, February, 1971, United States Department of Labor. United States average prices.

cost is in meat; the next, in fruits and vegetables. The cost and difficulties of production; the cost of harvesting; the supply and perishability; the cost of transportation; the cost of handling; and the cost of any essential processing are among factors that explain differing costs of foods within the same class.

Decisions on what to buy, that is, to serve in our meals, are not easy when so much is available so much of the time. In parts of the United States we can buy fresh strawberries, melons, and tomatoes when the ground is snow covered. The decision to serve baked apples or pumpkin pie instead of strawberry shortcake, or cole slaw instead of tomato salad, may be critical, even distasteful. To decide to buy hamburger instead of sirloin steak, a leg of lamb, or shrimp is not easy either. But our choices among available foods must be tailored to our resources; our meals are composed from what we can buy. However, there are ways to buy foods in all classes so that the dollars buy more or less of them.

TABLE 5–4.   *Two Plans for Selecting Vegetables*

Plan A

Selected Items	Number of Portions	Cost
Canned corn, 1 No. 303 can	4	$.21
Carrots, fresh, 4⁄5 lb. @ 2 lb./35¢	4	.12
Lettuce, 2⁄3 lb. @ 29¢ each	4	.20
Peas, frozen, 12 oz. @ 69¢/2 lb.	4	.25
Tomatoes, canned, 2⁄3 No. 2½ can @ 33¢ each	4	.22
Totals	20	$1.00[1]

Plan B

Selected Items	Number of Portions	Cost
Asparagus, 1½ lb. @ 69¢	4	$.69
Chilled corn, 4 ears @ 69¢/10 ears	4	.28
Japanese vegetables, frozen, 12 oz. @ 49¢/10 oz.	4	.59
Lettuce, Bibb, 4 small heads @ 39¢/4 heads	4	.39
Tomatoes, @ 49¢/lb.	4	.49
Totals	20	$2.44[2]

[1]Discount supermarket prices.
[2]Supermarket prices.

INFLUENCE OF DECISION ON HOW TO BUY

The homemaker who delegates the shopping responsibility may learn very quickly that *how you buy* makes a difference in how much food a dollar buys. Her shopping list may read: peas, pears, peaches, orange juice, and bread. Her emissary may select precisely the items on her list, but may purchase frozen peas in butter sauce, six fresh pears, a small can of Grade A peaches, a carton of reconstituted orange juice, and a premium-priced loaf of bread. However, the homemaker had in mind and would herself have bought a can of peas and large cans of peaches and pears of medium quality, a can of frozen orange juice concentrate, and a chain-brand loaf of bread. The state or form (whether a food is fresh or processed in some way), the quality of an item (whether the best or less than the best), and the size and kind of package purchased influence the cost of food and determine, therefore, how much food the dollar buys.

Table 5–5.   *Two Plans for Selecting Dairy Foods and Nondairy Foods*

Plan A

Selected Items	Quantities	Cost[1]
Milk, homogenized vitamin D @ 65¢/ half gal.	4 half-gal.	$2.60
Milk, low fat @ 65¢/half gal.	4 half-gal.	2.60
Half and half @ 47¢/pt.	1 pint	.47
Whipping cream @ 52¢/half pt.	½ pint	.52
Cheddar cheese, sharp @ 89¢/half lb.	½ lb.	.89
Cottage cheese	1 lb.	.47
Ice cream	½ gallon	1.49
Total cost		$9.04

Plan B

Selected Items	Quantities	Cost[2]
Milk, homogenized vitamin D @ $1.03/ gal.	2 gal.	$2.06
Milk, nonfat dry @ $2.75/4 lb.	1¾ lb.	1.10
Coffee whitener	1 pint	.29
Topping mix	1 pkg.	.29
Process American cheese @ $1.99/3 lb.	½ lb.	.37
Cottage cheese	1 lb.	.39
Ice milk @ 59¢/half gal.	½ gallon	.59
Total cost		$5.09

[1]Supermarket prices.
[2]Discount supermarket prices.

The Influence of State or Form

We use the terms *state* or *form* to indicate that a food is fresh or in its natural condition, or that it has been modified in some way by processing. Each year developments in processing modify our foods more and more. Sometimes the price advantage lies with fresh, unmodified food and sometimes with food processed in some way. Some examples follow. Frozen orange juice concentrate, frozen peas, and frozen lima beans are nearly always less expensive than their fresh counterparts. But fresh potatoes are less expensive than many of the dehydrated and frozen products. Reconstituted nonfat dry milk costs one third to one half as much as fresh, fluid skim milk. Reconstituted evaporated milk costs slightly less than fresh, fluid whole milk. Some cheese products are less expensive than natural cheeses of the same kind. Coffee brewed from ground coffee beans costs more than coffee made from an instant product. Minute-rice costs more per serving than milled rice. Mixes for gravies, sauces, and seasonings are expensive in terms of their component ingredients. Some processed foods are preserved foods like canned and frozen fish, meats, fruits, and vegetables; others are convenience products like the following: presliced cheeses and luncheon meats, pregrated cheeses, ready-made cheese and sour cream dips, preshaped and breaded meat patties and cutlets, mixed and seasoned meat loaves, prepared and rolled pastry, individual portions of instant hot cereals, iced-tea mixes, ready-to-bake pancake batter, and so on. The purchase of convenience plus food will be subsequently discussed. But it is important to recognize that some foods are purchased in convenient forms. A little of do-it-yourself can reduce the cost of some food items. To maximize food dollars it is necessary to compare the costs of fresh forms with canned, frozen, and dehydrated forms and of the instants and ready-mades with do-it-yourself equivalents. For example, a graham cracker pie shell weighing six ounces can cost 39 cents, whereas a pound of graham cracker crumbs may cost only 29 cents; and a serving of instant oatmeal to make in the bowl costs about five cents, while a serving of instant oatmeal to be prepared on the range costs about half as much.

Table 5–6 shows the cost of ready-rolled pastry plus the price paid for the aluminum foil pie pan in contrast to the cost of pastry prepared from

TABLE 5–6.   *The Cost of Pastry Purchased Ready-Rolled, as a Mix, and Home-Prepared*

Items	Market Unit and Cost	Cost per Five-Ounce Shell
Ready-rolled pastry shells:		
Brand A—2 shells	\$.29/11 oz.	\$.13[1]
Brand B—2 shells	.38/10 oz.	.19[1]
Brand B—5 shells	.99/25 oz.	.20[1]
Pastry made with mix:		
Brand A—10 oz. mix plus 2 oz. water	.25/12 oz.	.104
Brand B—11 oz. mix plus 2 oz. water	.28/13 oz.	.107
Brand C—9½ oz. mix plus 2 oz. water	.28/11½ oz.	.120
Pastry made from scratch:		
Flour (8.2 oz.) @ cost of 5¢[2]		
Shortening (6.6 oz.) @ cost of 9¢[2]		
Water (2.8 oz.)		
Total	.14/15.4 oz.	.045

[1]Retail cost of aluminum foil pie pans was 59 cents for six, or ten cents each; however, because the pans are considered packaging, their cost was not deducted.

[2]Nonspecial costs: flour, 5 lbs./60 cents; shortening, 3 lbs./99 cents.

scratch. In most households, the aluminum foil pans are expendable: their cost is a packaging cost.

Influence of Quality

Grading food for quality was discussed in Chapter 4; it will be discussed further in the six chapters that follow. Much of our food supply is quality-sorted even though not identified by grade because it is graded for distribution at the wholesale level. Price differentials between markets may be the result of differences in the quality of foods sold. Presumably, we can by inquiry in the supermarket learn something of the quality of the foods available for purchase.

Bivens (2) priced fifteen items at minimum and maximum cost each month for one year. The fifteen items were white bread, peanut butter (creamy style), grape jelly, all-purpose flour, corn flakes, regular-grind coffee, dry milk, evaporated milk, pancake syrup, vanilla ice cream, frozen corn, frozen peas, frozen orange-juice concentrate, and margarine. He described the difference between the total minimum and the total maximum cost as a gross measure of the premium paid for quality, brand, and/or store preference. This premium difference ranged from $1.27 to $2.81 over the twelve-month period. In percentage, it was from 23 to 46.5 per cent more; however, it was approximately 40 per cent more in all but two months of the period. The percentage increase in the total cost of the fifteen items bought at maximum cost was from about 30 per cent to about 87 per cent over the period of twelve months; the percentage cost of the fifteen items at minimum cost ranged from 53 per cent to 77 per cent of the total paid at maximum cost.

Top quality foods are the best of their kind, and the supply is limited. In general, they are priced higher than products of lesser quality: U.S. Grade AA eggs cost more than U.S. Grade B eggs; U.S. Grade AA butter costs more than U.S. Grade A butter; U.S. Grade A canned peaches cost more than U.S. Grade C canned peaches; USDA Choice beef costs more than USDA Standard beef; and U.S. Fancy potatoes cost more than U.S. No. 1 potatoes. It is possible to buy ungraded products that, if graded by the expert, would be of best quality at a lower cost than of products that might score poorly if graded. This situation confuses consumers. Perhaps it explains reliance on brand names. Price is a guide to quality though not an infallible one.

Most foods of less than the best grade are satisfactory for most uses. Occasionally the use to be made of a food makes it desirable, but not essential, that the best of its kind be purchased; for example, top quality eggs for poaching, top grade butter for eating on hot breads, and top quality fruits for eating out of hand. It would be a satisfaction to purchase a porterhouse steak of Choice grade for charcoal grilling, but a tenderized chuck steak could be equally tasty. Few housewives find it necessary or important, or even possible, to purchase only top quality products. The fact is that the supply is short and the price long.

There is also so-called quality merchandise among prefabricated foods, such as cakes, breads, frozen dinners, frozen fruit pies, canned soups, salad dressings, sausage products, and ice creams. Shoppers think of certain brands as superior and expensive. Superiority may be real or imagined. Palatability factors, such as flavor and texture, are involved in these judgments which are subjective in nature. Consumers have their own standards; these differ from person to person, family to family, and region to region. If there were fifteen brands of chocolate chip cookies available in a market area, it is quite probable that a few might actually be superior to to others because of the quality of the basic materials from which they were made and the care taken during manufacturing; but it is also quite likely that personal preferences would account for the deemed superiority of one or more brands over others. Nationally known brands and store brands are often comparable in quality, if not the same product, but some consumers prefer the former. Certainly preferences among brands of all kinds of prefabricated foods will determine how much food the dollar buys.

It is possible that in the 1970's, the Fair Packaging and Labeling Act will be amended to require that processors' names appear on all processed foods. Such legislation would mean that store-brands would lose their anonymity of source and, possibly, their price advantage.

Influence of Size and Kind of Package Purchased

In general, the larger the container of a food, the lower is the cost per unit of the food (see Table 5-7). A quart of homogenized whole milk costs more when purchased in a quart container than when purchased in a half-gallon or a gallon container. An ounce of corn flakes costs less if purchased in a twelve-ounce box than if purchased in an eight-ounce box; a serving of frozen peas, less when purchased in a two-pound bag than in a ten-ounce box; a serving of tomato juice, less when purchased in a No. 3 cylinder can than in a six-pack of individual portions; and a pound of coffee, less when purchased in a three-pound can. Innumerable foods can be bought in a variety of sizes and packages whether the container be bag, bottle, or box. This multiplicity of packages permits consumers who differ in their respective needs to purchase the needed or desired quantity of a given commodity.

It would be misleading not to point out that family size, storage facilities personal food likes, and the storage qualities of a food must be considered when one is purchasing items available in packages of different sizes. What would be economy for one homemaker might be extravagance

TABLE 5–7.   *Package Size and Unit Costs*

	Cost of Market Unit	Unit Cost (Cents)
Corn Flakes[1]		
Package of 18 ounces	$.47	2.6 per oz.
Package of 12 ounces	.35	3.0 per oz.
Package of 8 ounces	.25	3.1 per oz.
One-ounce package	.19/3	6.3 per oz.
Fruit Cocktail[1]		
No. 2½ can (28 ounces)	$.53	30 per pound
No. 303 can	.35	35 per pound
No. 8 Z can	.43/2	43 per pound
Single-serving container		
(4½ oz. ea.)	.67/4	60 per pound
Peanut Butter (Smooth)[2]		
2½-pound jar	$1.19	47.60 per pound[3]
2-pound jar	.89	44.50 per pound
1-pound jar	.59	59.00 per pound
12-ounce jar	.49	65.30 per pound
8-ounce jar	.35	70.00 per pound

[1]National brand.
[2]Store Brand.
[3]An example of the biggest not being the cheapest.

for another. The purchase of a ten-ounce jar of instant coffee for a family of two is probably not wise because of the instability of instant coffee; but the purchase of a five-pound sack of sugar instead of the more expensive one-pound pack would be sensible. Many staples have a long storage life; thus, given ample storage facilities, the average housewife can buy some food items in packages economical in size. In addition to looking at the size of the package, the consumer might well look at the container per se. Some commodities are packed in usable containers like tumblers and containers for refrigerator storage of food; others, in unusually shaped bottles and jars that suggest the nature of the contents; some packages contain premiums. The consumer pays for the container and the premium. If she wants it, fine; if she does not, it is wise to compare the cost of the commodity in the unusual container with the cost of the more simply packaged commodity and buy accordingly.

Contemporary packaging trends are in the direction of "convenience packaging." Perhaps the wide acceptance of the tea bag explains it. At any rate, more and more packages consist of a number of small, measured units of the commodity—nonfat dry milk, salt, raisins, cookies, crackers, cereals, tomato and fruit juices, and single-serving foods are some. Comparison of the cost of the commodity in the convenient package with the cost of the commodity purchased in a standard package will disclose the cost of the packaging. For example, one quart of reconstituted nonfat dry milk costs approximately fourteen cents if prepared from solids measured from a fourteen-quart package; eighteen cents if prepared from a three-quart package of premeasured solids. The so-called variety packs of cereals are an example of the greater cost of a commodity because of packaging style. Good packaging protects contents from staling. This may be an important factor in the purchase of such items as cookies and crackers when these are used over an extended time period. The cost of packaging may offset losses that could occur because of staling.

Another convenient pack is the aerosol container. In general, the commodity so packaged costs more than it does when more simply packaged. However, the degree of aeration possible extends contents to a large volume, for example, seven ounces of whipping cream to a volume of one quart. Hand-whipped, the volume of one-half pint of whipping cream is one pint.

Consumers can save small sums by giving attention to the size and kind of packages they purchase. And, because we buy so many items year after year, small savings add up to large ones.

Influence of Supply, Sales, and Specials

Other decisions that influence the returns in food for dollars spent are those relevant to the purchase of foods in plentiful supply and to the purchase of sale items and "specials." Skill in recognizing food bargains can influence the total expenditure for food. For the food shopper, there are two kinds of bargains: those produced in nature and those that are man-made.

To take advantage of a bargain, it is essential to be able to recognize the bargain situation. For this reason, the sophisticated shopper reads the food news and the advertising of local food markets in her newspaper meticulously. Intelligent use of this information rests on her knowledge of food costs—that is, what she has been paying for a pound, box, can, bunch, bag, or bottle of the different foods she buys. By being aware of current costs, the consumer is able to identify loss leaders, special sales items, and promotion goods that are "good buys"; and she recognizes when prices reflect changing supplies.

The seasons produce bargains; these bargains vary in different regions of the country because the crops and the time of harvest differ. At harvest time there is abundant supply. Then, the vegetables and fruits peculiar to a region are superior in quality and low in cost. Dollars buy large quantities or, conversely, large quantities can be purchased for fewer dollars than at other times. It is the time to eat them in abundance, even preserve them for later consumption by canning or freezing.

A downward trend in the cost of a commodity usually points to an increasing supply; an upward trend, to a diminishing supply. It is good common sense to eat a lot of eggs, green beans, apples, cranberries, tomatoes, oranges, asparagus, squash, pineapple, or grapefruit when they are plentiful and low in cost, and to use them less frequently when they are scarce and relatively expensive. For this reason, meal plans reflect the seasons, especially when families seek to obtain as much food as possible—of the kinds they like—for their dollars. Perhaps further clarification regarding meals and the seasons is indicated. Contemporary methods of food preservation and food transportation make all kinds of food available at all times of the year. New peas and fresh strawberry shortcake for Christmas dinner are possible. Roast stuffed turkey, mashed squash, and pumpkin pie can be served on the Fourth of July. Even so, we still associate new peas and strawberries with late spring or early summer and turkey, squash, and pumpkin pie with autumn. Meals tend to reflect the seasons because at certain seasons certain foods are plentiful, but also because of associations.

Sales, loss leaders, promotions, and coupons provide many bargains. A loss leader is an article sold for less than its regular price, often below cost, for the purpose of bringing in customers. Sometimes it is coffee; another week it may be chicken pot pies, hamburger, frying chickens, shortening, and so on. Every week some of these special bargains are to be had if one is able to recognize them. Sometimes they are such bargains that the number of units a consumer may purchase is limited.

In addition to these finds, special sales of canned goods, frozen foods, meat and meat products, mixes, and other commodities offer the alert consumer other opportunities to get extra dividends with the food dollar. In the "battle of the brands," special promotions by one company give it a temporary advantage over others and the consumer a bargain.

The use of coupons is a contemporary practice in bidding for business. These are offered by markets and by food companies. When food markets issue the coupons, it is possible to purchase items at marked reductions from the usual price; however, the purchase of a specified number of dollars' worth of groceries is sometimes prerequisite to redemption of the coupon at the stated price. For example, it may be possible to buy one pound of butter for half the retail price if one purchases a total of $5 worth of groceries. A common practice among food processors is to print coupons in magazines and newspapers. These coupons are redeemable at all, or nearly all, food markets at the saving indicated on the face of the coupon. Their use may reduce the cost of an item by as much as 16 per cent; for example, a coupon may be worth seven cents toward the purchase of a brand-name margarine that sells for forty-three cents. Further, food processors distribute their coupons by mail; these too are redeemable at almost all food markets.

No discussion of loss leaders, sales, and promotion stunts is complete unless the following points are made: first, advertised items are not always specially priced. Second, special promotions of what appear to be specially priced items may be for packages reduced in size. What is more, the item may actually cost more per unit than the regular package. Last, it is not uncommon to discover that items are sale priced in multiples, such as five for the dollar wherein the cost of the unit, be it can or box, is no different from the regular price. All of these facts emphasize the importance of knowing prices and of comparison shopping.

No one would expect the homemaker to go to every market in her community to take advantage of the special bargains of the week, although a few do just that. If she will just take advantage of those in the market(s) she patronizes regularly, she will be cents ahead each week and dollars ahead each year.

Carman (4) concluded that between private brands, store specials, and manufacturers' deals, the careful shopper seems able to achieve a lower grocery bill for packaged goods by shopping at one or two well-managed and aggressive markets. He states that the consumer reduces the average price paid by good timing rather than through extensive store research or store switching.

Influence of Purchased Convenience

Convenience foods are legion. Some are new—such as ready-to-eat chocolate pudding, toaster pizzas, self-basting turkeys, spoon-and-serve whipped topping, frozen asparagus in Hollandaise sauce, frozen potato knishes, and canned Newburg sauce, to mention but a few. Others are more familiar—baking powder, bread, butter, canned soups, canned pork and beans, catsup, Jello, canned vegetables, and cake flour. Some convenience products, such as baking powder, spices, herbs, vanilla, and cake flour, have been available so long that we have ceased to think of them as convenience products. Almost every item the homemaker in the United States puts in her market basket today is a convenience food product because one or more steps in its preparation for use have been completed for her. Any discussion of convenience foods must explicitly define them.

For purposes of this discussion, convenience foods will be those that were generally unavailable before World War II and that have service added to the basic ingredients to reduce the amount of preparation required in the home kitchen: instants like instant coffee and instant mashed potatoes; mixes, the assortment of which is almost unlimited in the 1970's, from biscuits to pineapple up-side-down cake; precooked canned dishes like roast beef hash and Hollandaise sauce; precooked and frozen dishes like meat-stuffed ravioli and dinners; ready-for-use items like pastry shells and ready-sliced cold cuts; so-called fast foods, that is, ready-to-eat foods like Kentucky fried chicken; and so on *ad infinitum*. In addition to built-in maid service, foods have built-in chef service in the 1970's. Three aspects of convenience foods will be discussed: the amount of added service, the cost of added service, and palatability.

The Amount of Added Service in Convenience Foods.   Convenience foods are classed as finished foods and as semiprepared foods. Finished foods are ready for eating immediately or after heating (like canned soups, frozen precooked dinners, and ready-to-bake biscuits) or after thawing (like frozen pastries and frozen fruits). Semiprepared foods include mixes; they have some service yet to be performed. In general, finished foods have more service added to ingredients than is added to the semiprepared foods. Within each category there will always be differences in the amount of service added because some dishes are more time-consuming to prepare than others, for example, frozen prebaked cake and bottled French dressing. The more service added to ingredients, the less time the homemaker must supply. When she makes homemade dishes, she spends time actively in measuring, mixing, and manipulating ingredients; in trimming, slicing, or dicing; peeling and squeezing; dusting or crumbing and browning; whipping; washing tools and equipment; and so on. Additional time is required for cooking or chilling her homemade dishes. The cooking period may require full attention, as for stirring or turning, or it may not. The total time used in food preparation consists of active time and inactive time when attention can be directed elsewhere. The use of mixes reduces active time by eliminating nearly all measuring time and some mixing time. Ready-to-use products like canned pie fillings reduce active time. Total time is reduced as active time diminishes. Studies have been reported that measure the reductions in time use.

Figure 5–2 shows graphically diminishing time use in the preparation of angel food cake, devil's food cake, yellow cake, and pies. Mixes save from 66 to 80 per cent of active time and from 25 to nearly 50 per cent of total time. Although the thawing time for the frozen ready-baked devil's food cake was longer than the total time for the homemade cake, the time used required no energy or attention. Woolsey and Tinklin (19) found that active time was 30, 19, and 10 minutes for brownies made from basic ingredients, mix, and refrigerated dough, respectively. Total time was approximately 105, 94, and 89 minutes; the differences were not as marked as one might anticipate.

Studies of the time saved in buying convenient dishes containing meat, fish, poultry, and cheese have been made (9). Table 5–8 shows active and total time invested in preparing some homemade dishes and in using

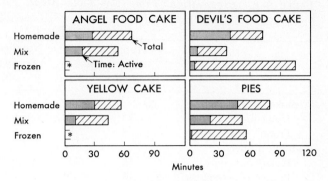

*Not studied in frozen form

FIGURE 5–2.   Preparation times, including active and total time, for angel food, devil's food, and yellow cakes and pies. (*United States Department of Agriculture photograph.*)

similar convenience products. Active time ranges from about one minute for uncooked ham to fifty-four minutes for chicken chow mein. More than one half of the homemade dishes researched required more than twenty-five minutes of active time. Total time for some main dishes of meals may be very long when meat must be thawed before cooking or when the cooking period is long, as for preparing a pot roast. Weiss (18) found that the time required to prepare the three meals of a day decreased from 5.5 hours to 3.1 hours to 1.6 hours as the dishes of meals were homemade, partially prepared, and ready-to-serve, respectively.

Mixes differ in the amount of time-saving they offer homemakers. Cake mixes and others composed of many ingredients that must be carefully measured have more service introduced than mixes composed of a few ingredients that do not require accurate measurement like salad dressing seasonings, mixes for sauces and gravies, and the cream frosting mixes. The more time saved, the more we would predict great demand; however, demand is modified by the cost of the convenience introduced and the palatability of the product.

The level of convenience a product offers differs for homemakers who differ in experience, skill, and interest in cookery. Each consumer must evaluate each product in terms of the convenience it means to her. The level of convenience in a product may be little and the cost of it may be excessive, but it may be highly valued by some homemakers. The salad dressing mix may be an example. It does not save much time or energy and the convenience is pretty expensive, yet the product makes a tasty dressing. Many homemakers think they lack the skill to select the proper seasonings to make equally tasty dressings. Further, many homemakers feel that it is less expensive to purchase the mixes than to stock various

TABLE 5–8. *Preparation Time for Some Meat, Fish, Poultry, and Cheese Dishes*

	Approximate Time (min.)		Number of Servings Prepared
	Active	Total	
Fried codfish sticks			
Home-prepared	22	38	6
Frozen ready-to-heat	4	19	6
Haddock dinners			
Home-prepared	36	202[1]	4
Frozen ready-to-heat	5	30	3
Shrimp creole			
Home-prepared	59	96	6
Frozen ready-to-heat	3	25	3
Ham			
Uncooked	3	175	27
Precooked	2	165	27
Fried chicken, batter dipped			
Home cooked	18	48	7
Frozen prefried	16	34	4
Chicken chow mein			
Home cooked	55	194	4
Canned	2	12	3
Frozen	3	27	4
Spaghetti with cheese in tomato sauce			
Home cooked	25	86	6
Canned	2	12	2

Source: Gilpin, G. L., et al., *Meat, Fish, Poultry and Cheese: Home Preparation Time, Yield, and Composition of Various Market Forms*, Home Economics Research Report No. 30, Human Nutrition Research Division, Agricultural Research Service, United States Department of Agriculture, Washington, D.C., August, 1965.
[1]Includes time for thawing frozen haddock.

herbs and spices they might use only from time to time. The purchase of a cinnamon-sugar mixture is often justified on the same basis, although the cost of the mixture is excessive when compared with the cost of the component ingredients purchased separately. In the final analysis, the value of the convenience built into the food is personal.

The Cost of Convenience. The service added to ingredients may cost much or little; in some instances the convenient product costs less than the home-prepared product. Except during certain seasons of the year and in limited areas of the United States, orange juice prepared from frozen orange juice concentrate costs less than freshly squeezed orange juice; frozen and canned peas and lima beans cost less than fresh ones; and instant coffee costs less than home-brewed coffee.

In her study, Weiss (18) found that meals prepared from fully prepared foods cost approximately 36 per cent more and meals prepared from partially prepared foods cost about 18 per cent more than the same meals entirely home prepared.

Asp, Noble, and Clark (1) found that using commercial mixes for baked goods increased costs as follows: for yellow cake, 20 per cent; for baking-powder biscuits and cookies, 50 per cent; and for pie pastry, 75 per cent.

Woolsey and Tinklin (19) found that brownies prepared from an incomplete mix and from a refrigerated dough cost about 14 per cent more than the homemade product. Frozen and bakery products cost 100 per cent and 50 per cent more, respectively, than the homemade product.

Extensive study of the cost of convenience has been made under the supervision of the Marketing Economics Division, Economic Research Service, United States Department of Agriculture (10). It was found that almost three fourths of the 128 convenience forms studied were more expensive than the homemade counterparts.

TABLE 5–9. *Average Cost per Serving of Selected Homemade and Convenience Main Dishes and Dinners*

Items	Cost (Cents)	Items	Cost (Cents)
Spanish rice		Meat loaf dinner	
Homemade	3.9	Home cooked	38.9
Canned	6.0	Frozen	60.8
Package combination	6.8	Beef dinner	
Pizza		Home cooked	31.9
Homemade	21.1	Frozen	60.6
Chilled	29.8	Chicken dinner	
Frozen	43.1	Home cooked	24
Package combination	25.7	Frozen	58.6
Beef patties (2 oz.)		Turkey dinner	
Home prepared	8.7	Home cooked	24.8
Canned	12.9	Frozen	65.2
Frozen	22.0		

Source: Harp, H. H., and Dunham, D. F., *Comparative Costs to Consumers of Convenience Foods and Home-Prepared Foods.* Marketing Research Report No. 609, Economic Research Service, Marketing Economics Division, United States Department of Agriculture, Washington, D.C., June, 1963.

TABLE 5–10.   *Average Cost per Serving of Selected Homemade and Convenience Baked Products*

Items	Cost (Cents)	Items	Cost (Cents)
Yeast rolls (1.3 oz.)		Pancakes (5.3 oz.)	
Homemade	1.6	Homemade	5.3
Complete mix	2.1	Incomplete mix	5.6
Frozen	2.2	Complete mix	6.6
Brown-and-serve	4.0	Frozen	14.5
Ready-to-serve	5.0	Biscuits (1.4 oz.)	
		Homemade	1.6
		Complete mix	1.6
Cherry pie (4.5 oz.)		Refrigerated	1.9
Homemade	6.7	Frozen	5.3
Complete mix	7.3	White frosting (0.52 oz.)	
Frozen	10.1	Homemade	0.6
Ready-to-serve	13.6	Mix	1.5
		Egg white assigned 60% cost of egg	
Devil's food cake (1.7 oz.)		Brownies (0.7 oz.)	
Homemade	3.6	Homemade	3.0
Incomplete mix	2.5	Incomplete mix	2.8
Frozen	8.2	Frozen	4.0
Ready-to-serve	6.2	Ready-to-serve	4.2

Source: Harp, H. H., and Dunham, D. F., *Comparative Costs to Consumers of Convenience Foods and Home-Prepared Foods.* Marketing Research Report No. 609, Economic Research Service, Marketing Economics Division, United States Department of Agriculture, Washington, D.C., June, 1963.

The cost of the convenience of canned and frozen vegetables varies with product, season, and probably region of the country. In the last-mentioned study (10), it was found that canned and frozen peas, lima beans, spinach, and cut corn were less expensive than the fresh forms. However, canned carrots; frozen asparagus, corn on the cob, and broccoli spears; and canned and frozen green beans and Brussels sprouts were all more expensive than their fresh counterparts. Processing reduces perishability and also the bulk and weight of vegetables. Items that sell in large volume, such as peas and corn, cost less than low-volume vegetables such as asparagus.

The cost of the convenience of several processed fruits was studied (10). All processed orange and lemon juice products (with the exception of lemon juice in plastic, lemon-shaped containers) were less expensive than their fresh counterparts. Frozen pie cherries, peaches, pineapple, grapefruit sections, and red raspberries cost more than the same fruits canned.

Cost comparisons of fresh and processed fruits are best made seasonally and regionally. Probably frozen strawberries are less expensive than fresh strawberries most of the year in most regions of the United States.

The cost per serving of selected homemade and convenience main dishes of meals as determined in this study are given in Table 5–9. Nearly all the dishes studied cost more in the convenience form when the ingredient content of the homemade products was adjusted to the content of the commercially prepared or frozen products. The cost of some of the items was increased as much as 150 per cent.

In this study, forty-five commercial products were studied and all but eight of these were more expensive than homemade counterparts. Table 5–10 shows the average cost per serving of selected homemade and convenience baked products. Only commercial mixes for yellow cake, devil's food cake, brownies, and chocolate frosting were less expensive than homemade products. Ingredients of the mixes, ready-prepared items, and home-prepared items are rarely identical.

During the decade between the two United States Department of Agriculture studies of household food consumption, there was 33 per cent increased spending for thirty-two convenience foods (see Figure 5–3). Spending increased for fresh and commercial fruit juices, frozen and powdered fruit ades and punches, frozen potato products, instant coffee, and bakery products other than bread (3). Total spending for convenience food was highly correlated with income.

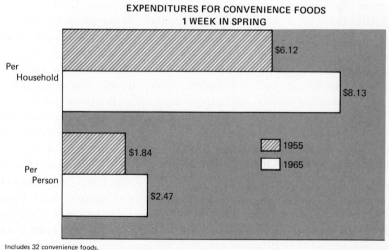

FIGURE 5–3. Expenditures for convenience foods. (*United States Department of Agriculture photograph.*)

Peterkin and Cromwell (16) reported on the costs of home-prepared and on ready-cooked, frozen dinners (TV dinners) of the same composition. Convenient beef dinners cost about 25 per cent more; fried chicken dinners, about 100 per cent more; and meat loaf dinners and turkey dinners about 60 per cent more than the home-prepared counterparts. They reported differences in the costs of similar convenience main dishes; differences were partly accounted for by differences in the content of meat. For beef pot pies, chicken pot pies, and chicken chow mein, the convenience of the ready-made dishes increased costs from 20 to 150 per cent. They found that ready-to-eat brownies and sugar cookies cost about the same as the homemade kinds. However, they found that ready-to-serve apple pie and pound cake and toaster-ready waffles were from two to three times as costly as homemade counterparts.

The Palatability of Convenience Foods.   Judgments of the palatability, or eating qualities, of convenience foods are personal and they will be influenced by past experiences with food. Persons accustomed to home-prepared food of good quality are quite uncharitable in their evaluations of precooked, frozen dinners, ready-to-bake apple pie, and instant coffee. On the other hand, persons long accustomed to eating precooked, frozen dinners; precooked, frozen fish sticks; bakery cakes; and instant coffee may judge them as good as homemade counterparts. The tastiness of home-cooked food depends on the skill and experience of the cook. There have always been some superior cooks and there have been poor cooks. The same is true in the 1970's. The frame of reference for judgment explains the many and diverse judgments on different convenience foods.

Quality evaluations of convenience products by panels of experts have been made. These experts judge food products in accordance with defined standards of quality. Food products are scored on the basis of such attributes as tenderness, proper texture, good aroma and flavor, the absence of off-flavors, the proper taste, the proper color, the absence of defects, the presence of foreign matter, and others. In such evaluations, potato products prepared from fresh potatoes, fresh vegetables, fresh fruits, and home-prepared dinners have been favored (10, 11, 12). Baked products prepared from mixes may be more tender than homemade counterparts and may be judged equal in flavor; bakery products may be less tender and have less flavor (10, 15). When frozen baked cakes were judged, only one was rated very good, six were rated good, and the remaining samples were judged fair or so inconsistent in quality that they could not be rated (7). Frozen ready-to-bake apple, blueberry, and cherry pies were judged after baking in accordance with established standards for fruit pies. In general, the fillings were scant in fruit and long on filler, the nonfruit part of the filling. The pies were variable in quality with only one exception. Some noted defects of the pies were lack of flavor or flavor not characteristic of the fruit in the pie; off-flavors in the crust; the presence of cores, skins, seeds, and blemished fruits; and gummy or runny fillings (8). When homemade chocolate cream pie was compared with chocolate cream pie prepared from a dry cream-pie mix, the homemade chocolate cream pie was judged superior in palatability (6). Further, it was noted that there was not much difference between the pie mix and the homemade pie in terms of cost or preparation time.

The Consumer and Convenience. It is desirable to consider the meal manager's gains and losses when convenience foods are purchased. First, she can prepare elaborate dishes using convenience items like soups, sauce and gravy mixes, frozen and canned meats, poultry, and seafoods. Meals of several courses can be composed entirely of semiprepared and ready-prepared foods. Menu planning and meal preparation are easy. Exotic meals that would be difficult and time-consuming to prepare are possible, a source of satisfaction. The purchase of convenience foods is the purchase of skill in cookery. Secondly, the purchase of convenience foods is the purchase of time and energy: time and energy spent in shopping; in cleaning and trimming fruits and vegetables; in cooking; in washing bowls, pots and pans, and tools used in food preparation; and in all the other tasks that cooking entails. For the homemaker who is a wage earner, for the homemaker with many family responsibilities, or for the homemaker with community responsibilities, this gain in time is of inestimable value. She may devote this time to leisure activities or to other duties. A third gain is freedom from doing these tasks if the homemaker dislikes cooking. Some persons like to cook; others do not. Those who like to cook do not find the small tasks it entails distasteful; those who do not like to cook find them odious. A last possible gain is greater satisfaction in the fulfillment of the meal responsibility. When the manager of meals has little skill and little time, these convenience products make it possible for her to offer more variety and perhaps food of better quality than she would otherwise find possible. In fact, some of the frozen prepared foods are so difficult and time-consuming to prepare in the home kitchen that few homemakers would ever serve them; and some of the mixes give products superior to those that inexperienced cooks can produce. It is easy to argue that the availability of convenience items has provided families with tastier meals.

It is also possible to argue that mass-produced food does not taste as good as home-cooked food and that there is a possible loss of enjoyment of food attendant on the use of convenience foods. In all honesty, one must admit that not all home-cooked food is equally good and that not all convenience foods are equally tasty. However, there is little doubt that the family possessing a good cook—whether mother, father, son, or daughter —loses out when ready-made foods replace home-cooked ones. This afore-mentioned loss in eating pleasure may be accompanied by another—a lost opportunity to be creative. Few have the native talent to create works in music, literature, or the visual arts; however, few could fail to be artists in the kitchen. It is a rare person who does not gain satisfaction from being creative—a fact recognized by the producers of convenience foods, who have printed ideas *ad infinitum* for creative uses of their biscuit mixes, roll mixes, stews, baked beans, pudding mixes, juice concentrates, soup mixes, and canned soups. We live during a time when fabrics and clothing are factory produced, yet many women weave, and many more sew. It is quite realistic to believe that many women and men will continue to prepare food in the home, either because they like to be creative with food or because they like the results, or for both reasons. A last possible loss attendant on the generous use of convenience foods is in dollars and cents that the family could spend in other ways. Convenience does not come without cost. How much a consumer spends for convenience depends on what convenience items she purchases and how extensively she purchases them. She certainly should never evaluate her time by the difference in cost between homemade pie and frozen pie, frozen dinners and home-prepared meals, canned stew and home-prepared stew. It may be that in managing meals it is of economic importance to the family to buy basic ingredients and provide the service of preparation for the table.

The availability in the marketplace of convenience foods forces the meal manager to evaluate and to make decisions. We pay for the service added to ingredients when we buy convenience products; in general, the more convenience introduced, the more we pay. Actually, the consumer can, for herself, estimate the cost of the service introduced into the products she buys.

The difference in the cost of the home-produced item and the cost of the convenience product is the cost of convenience; it may be expressed as the percentage of cost for convenience or as the percentage increase in cost for convenience. The steps in determining the cost of the homemade product and the convenience product are given in Table 5–11. The same kinds of ingredients should be used, insofar as possible, in estimating costs. To compare the cost of a homemade cake prepared with butter and four eggs with the cost of a cake prepared from a mix in which the fat is a hydrogenated shortening and only two eggs are used is to ignore the real difference between them—the ingredients, not the price. In many areas of the country it will cost more to make a lemon meringue pie from basic ingredients than from a mix; the same would be true for a lemon chiffon pie. When like is not compared with like, the cost of convenience cannot be measured. However, nothing in this statement alters the fact that the mix for lemon pie filling provides an inexpensive and convenient product.

The cost of convenience tends to diminish for a given product as more consumers buy it and as the industry improves methods of production.

TABLE 5–11.   *The Cost of Convenience of Plain Cake Mix*[1]
The cost of making plain cake from a recipe

Ingredients	Measure of Ingredients	Weight of Ingredients	Cost of Ingredients
Cake flour	2 cups	180 gms.	$0.105
Sugar	1⅓ cups	264 gms.	0.075
Shortening	½ cup	93 gms.	0.070
Milk (nonfat dry)	1 cup	246 gms.	0.040
Eggs	2	118 gms.	0.065
Baking powder, salt	2 tsp., 1 tsp.	10 gms.	0.005
Vanilla	1 tsp.	4 gms.	0.005
Totals		915 gms.	$0.365

The cost of making plain cake from a mix

Ingredients	Measure of Ingredients	Weight of Ingredients	Cost of Ingredients
Mix (1 lb., 2½ oz.)		524 gms.	$0.45
Water	1⅓ cups	325 gms.	—
Eggs	2	118 gms.	0.065
Totals		967 gms.	$0.515

The percentages of cost for *food* and for *convenience* are:

		Weight	Cost
a. Weight and cost of recipe product	a.	915 gms.	$0.365
b. Weight and cost of convenience product	b.	967 gms.	0.515
c. Cost of like weight of recipe product	c.	967 gms.	0.386
d. Cost of convenience: b minus c	d.		0.129 (.13)
e. Percentage of cost of convenience product for service: d/b times 100	e.	30%	
f. Percentage of cost of convenience product for ingredients: 100 minus e	f.	70%	
g. Percentage increase in cost for convenience: d/c times 100	g.	43%	

[1]Cost as of February, 1972.

Brownie mixes and ready-to-bake frozen pies are examples of products with diminishing convenience costs. Because the situation is ever changing, it is desirable to reevaluate products from time to time. Convenience built into foods must be paid for; no thinking person would believe otherwise. The more convenience purchased, the larger must be the budget for food. Conversely, to control or limit the dollars spent for food, limit the purchase of convenience along with food.

An observation relative to the ingredients of some convenience foods, especially the heat-and-eat main dishes, warrants some discussion because this, too, affects spending for food for meals. For example, an eight-ounce chicken pot pie is composed approximately as follows: crust and gravy, six ounces; chicken, one and one-eighth ounces; and vegetables, less than one ounce. If the average portion of meat is three ounces of cooked meat and the average portion of a vegetable is two and one-half ounces, then the chicken pot pie, savory as it may be, provides neither a serving of meat nor a serving of a vegetable. The planner of meals ought to know this and plan her meal around the pot pie accordingly. Certainly it should include one or more servings of vegetables and a food containing a significant quantity of protein. For example, the menu might include, in addition to the pot pie, green beans, a cottage cheese salad, and fruit for dessert. The purchase of the pot pie is in reality rather expensive spending for what amounts to bread and gravy. If a nutritionally good meal is planned around such a choice, the expenditure can be excessive for some budgets.

December, 1971, the Food and Drug Administration proposed voluntary guidelines for the nutritional content of precooked, frozen convenient dinners. The guidelines were based on the recommendations of the Committee on Food Standards and Fortifications Policy of the National Academy of Sciences. The proposal requires that such dinners contain at least these three components: meat, fish, poultry, or cheese protein; potatoes, rice, or other cereal-based dish; and a vegetable, such as peas, corn, carrots, or other. It further requests that dinners contain a minimum of 340 calories, 15 grams of protein, and certain specified minimum levels of vitamin A, thiamine, riboflavin, niacin, iron, and iodine. Labeling regulations are such that precooked, frozen dinners that meet the standards could be voluntarily so labeled. The regulations were in process March, 1972.

It is doubtful that anyone would propose that the American homemaker return to her kitchen to prepare all the food for the family's meals. On the other hand, it is suggested that the homemaker scrutinize rather carefully the items she buys from these points of view: the measure of convenience she is purchasing, the price she is paying for the convenience, and ingredient composition. The last will determine nutritive value and further influence spending for food.

Summary. In this chapter general food-buying precepts have been discussed. It has been proposed that the homemaker's decisions on (1) where to shop, (2) when to shop, (3) what to buy, (4) how to buy it, (5) how much to take advantage of abundant supply, sales, and specials, and

(6) whether or not to buy services rendered in the preparation of foods determine how much food her dollars buy.

SOME GENERAL PRECEPTS FOR SHOPPERS FOR FOOD

1. Plan for the shopping expedition for conservation in the uses of time and money.

2. Do your own shopping, shop alone, and don't shop when you are hungry.

3. Shop as infrequently as storage facilities permit to conserve in the uses of time and money.

4. Prepare a shopping list; however, be flexible about it. Change your mind when it is practical to do so. Use the advertisements from your market(s) and your newspaper in preparing your list. Dovetail meal-planning with the preparation of the shopping list.

5. Allow yourself ample time for shopping and take as much time as required to compare prices and products and seek the information you need.

6. Avoid the impulse purchase of luxuries and table delicacies that you do not need and that you know your plan for spending will not accommodate.

7. Know the prices of the items you regularly buy. The list will not be excessively long because we tend to buy the same items week after week.

8. Compare prices in the markets available to you. Shop at the market that provides the kinds of commodities that you want to buy at the prices you want to pay. Shop at more than one market if it is practicable.

9. Comparison-shop. Compare the costs of servings of meats and fruits and vegetables; compare the costs of different brands of the same products; compare the unit costs of packages different in size; compare the costs of items of different quality; and compare the costs of different products packaged differently.

10. Buy and try different brands.

11. Take advantage of sales, specials, and promotions, including coupons.

12. Buy foods in plentiful supply.

13. Shop on weekend days unless your market has equally good pricing advantages for the early days of the week.

14. Check the weights of newly packaged items, sale items, and multiple-priced items; price increases may be concealed here.

15. Buy the largest package consistent with your need for a product.

16. Buy grade labeled commodities when you can, but select the quality matched to the intended use.

17.   Unless your plan for spending is generous, be cautious in the purchase of ready-to-eat foods. At least attempt to discover if the cost of the convenience is worth it to you.

REFERENCES CITED

1.   Asp, E., I. Noble, and F. Clark, "Pilot Study of Money and Time Spent in Preparing Baked Products from Individual and Premixed Ingredients," *Journal of Home Economics* 49:717 (1957).

2.   Bivens, Gordon E., "An Exploration of Food Price Competition in a Local Market," *Journal of Consumer Affairs* 2:61 (1968).

3.   ————, "Household Use of Convenience Foods," *Family Economics Review,* Consumer and Food Economics Research Division, United States Department of Agriculture, Washington, D.C. (December 1967), p. 6.

4.   Carman, James M., "Some Insights into Reasonable Grocery Shopping Strategies," *Journal of Marketing* 33:69 (1969).

5.   "Cost of Food at Home," *Family Economics Review,* Consumer and Food Economics Research Division, United States Department of Agriculture, Washington, D.C. (March 1971), p. 34.

6.   "For Eaters—Taste Tests of Cream Pies," *Consumer Reports,* 35:175 (1970).

7.   "Frozen Cakes," *Consumer Reports* 35:55 (1970).

8.   "Frozen Pies," *Consumer Reports* 34:568 (1969).

9.   Gilpin, G. L., et al., *Meat, Fish, Poultry, and Cheese: Home Preparation Time, Yield, and Composition of Various Market Forms,* Home Economics Research Report No. 30, Human Nutrition Research Division, Agricultural Research Service, United States Department of Agriculture, Washington, D.C. (August 1965).

10.   Harp, H. H., and D. F. Dunham, *Comparative Cost to Consumers of Convenience Foods and Home-Prepared Foods,* Marketing Research Report No. 609, Economic Research Service, Marketing Economics Division, United States Department of Agriculture, Washington, D.C. (June 1963).

11.   "How Good Are Dehydrated Potatoes?" *Consumer Reports* 28:384 (1963).

12.   "Instant Potatoes," *Consumer Reports* 36:435 (1971).

13.   Kammer, J. B., and G. L. Shawhan, "Comparison of Food Prices in High- and Low-Income Areas," *Journal of Home Economics* 62:56 (1970).

14.   Lifquist, R. "Variations in Food Prices in One Shopping Area," *Family Economics Review,* Consumer and Food Economics Research Division, United States Department of Agriculture, Washington, D.C. (June 1965), p. 13.

15. Matthews, R. H., et al., *Baked Products: Consumer Quality, Composition, Yield, and Preparation Time of Various Market Forms,* Home Economics Research Report No. 22, Agricultural Research Service, United States Department of Agriculture, Washington, D.C. (1963).
16. Peterkin, Betty, and Cynthia Cromwell, "Convenience and the Cost of Food," *Family Economics Review,* Consumer and Food Economics Research Division, United States Department of Agriculture, Washington, D.C. (June 1971), p. 9.
17. Simonds, Lois A., "Variations in Food Costs in Major Ohio Cities," *Journal of Consumer Affairs* 3:52 (1969).
18. Weiss, G. S., "Time and Money Costs of Meals Using Home and Pre-Kitchen-Prepared Foods," *Journal of Home Economics* 46:98 (1954).
19. Woolsey, M. E., and G. L. Tinklin, "Brownies: Comparison of Various Market Forms, Preparation, Time, Yield, Cost, and Quality," *Journal of the American Dietetic Association* 49:128 (1966).

SUGGESTED REFERENCES

1. Ferguson, Mike and Marilyn, *Champagne Living on a Beer Budget.* New York: G. P. Putnam's Sons, 1968.
2. Margolius, Sidney, *How to Make the Most of Your Money.* New York: Hawthorn Books, Inc., 1969.
3. ———, *The Great American Food Hoax.* New York: Walker and Company, 1971.
4. Scaduto, Anthony, *Getting the Most for Your Money.* New York: David McKay Company, Inc., 1970.
5. *Your Money's Worth in Foods,* Home and Garden Bulletin No. 183, Consumer and Food Economics Research Division, United States Department of Agriculture, Washington, D.C. (1970).

Chapter 6

Purchasing Food—Meat, Poultry, and Fish

Americans in the United States like meat. The estimated per capita consumption of the civilian population was in 1970: in carcass weight, 113.4 pounds of beef, 65.8 pounds of pork, and 6.3 pounds of lamb and veal; in ready-to-cook weight, 42.2 pounds of chicken and 8.3 pounds of turkey; and in edible weight, 11.3 pounds of fish (8). It adds up to an amazing total of 247.3 pounds. The 113.4 pounds of beef were 61 per cent of the red meat total. We ate more of all of these in 1970 than in 1969, excepting veal, lamb, and turkey, of which we eat relatively small quantities. The data for 1970 show increased consumption from the 1957–1959 average as follows: 28.9 pounds of red meat, 14.7 pounds of chicken, 2.3 pounds of turkey, and 0.8 pounds of fish. The big gain was in beef consumption: 31.3 pounds—one third more than in 1960 (see Figures 6–1 and 6–2). The retail value of the total domestic consumption of fresh, cured, canned, and frozen meat, fish, and poultry was, in 1970, about $35 billion.

Consumers spent $17.8 billion for fresh and cured meat, fish, and poultry; $9.3 billion for fresh beef, pork, veal, and lamb; and almost $7 billion for beef alone in grocery stores and supermarkets in 1970 (10).

To translate all these data into family spending and purchasing, we shall refer to the data from the United States Department of Agriculture household food consumption study (4). According to this study, the average household used 15.08 pounds of meat, poultry, and fish with a money value of $9.47 during the week of the survey (Spring 1965). The quantity purchased was 13.78 pounds with a money value of $8.73. The average household consisted of 3.29 persons; per-person consumption was 4.58 pounds of meat, fish, and poultry with a money value of $2.88. However, it must be noted that the quantities bought, the money value of the quantities bought, and the cost per pound of the quantities bought per house-

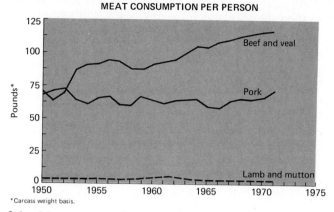

FIGURE 6–1. Meat consumption per person. (*United States Department of Agriculture photograph.*)

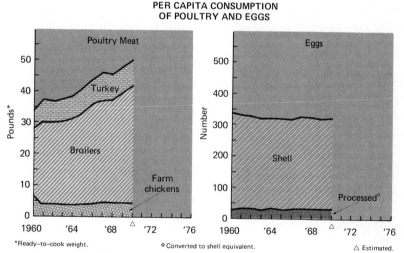

FIGURE 6–2. Per capita consumption of poultry and eggs. (*United States Department of Agriculture photograph.*)

hold per week varied with income (Table 6–1). In all fairness, it must be pointed out that these are averages that obscure different practices of individual families; that quantities are slightly greater currently; and that the money value of the quantities used would be greater currently. Nonetheless, these data point to a quite obvious truth, namely, that the extent of the money resource determines both quantitatively and qualitatively the meat-purchasing practices of families. Housewives tend to spend about one third of their food dollars for meat, poultry, and fish. Frequently, this occurs at the expense of good nutrition when not enough dollars are available to buy all of the foods essential for good nutrition. Meat, because it pleases, is bought instead of milk and fruits and vegetables. The meal manager's most difficult decisions and the ones that require the most knowledge and skill in planning meals and in buying food are her choices of meat. In general, *meat* means poultry and fish as well as red meat.

The meal manager requires a certain number of servings of meat for each meal in which she serves it. She may choose and then pay the cost or she may decide the cost and choose accordingly, for the number of servings purchased for any given number of dollars is determined by the kind, the cut, and the quality of the purchased items. A dollar buys more servings of chicken than duckling, of pork chops than lamb chops, of stew than steak, of cod than shrimp, and of USDA Standard beef than of USDA Choice beef. The costs per serving of some selected kinds and cuts of meat, poultry, and fish are given in Table 6–2.

To discuss the various factors that affect the cost of meat items purchased and to provide the meal manager with a frame of reference for choice-making, it is necessary to define or standardize the serving. The estimated cost of a defined serving then becomes the frame of reference for decision-making.

TABLE 6–1. *Quantity of Meat Bought, Money Value of Meat Bought, and Money Value per Pound of Meat Bought per Urban Household, Spring 1965, According to Income*[1]

Money Income After Taxes in 1964	Pounds of Meat, Fish, and Poultry Bought per House-hold per Week	Money Value of Meat, Fish, and Poultry Bought per Household per Week	Average Money Value per Pound
All households	$14.28	$9.27[2]	$.65[2]
$3,000–$3,999	12.86	7.21	.56
$5,000–$5,999	15.31	9.69	.63
$7,000–$7,999	16.65	11.20	.67
$10,000–$14,999	16.80	12.34	.73
$15,000 and over	19.13	15.44	.80

[1]Adapted from Table 3, page 58, of *Food Consumption of Households in the United States, Spring 1965* (3).

[2]The Retail Food Price Index was in 1965 (1957–1959 = 100) for meats, 106.8; for poultry, 90; for fish, 110.6. In 1970, it was for meats, 133.8; for poultry, 96.4; for fish, 143.7.

TABLE 6–2. *Estimated Per-Serving Costs of Selected Kinds and Cuts of Meat, Poultry, and Fish*

Kind	Cost per Pound[1]	Approximate Number of Servings per pound[2]	Cost per Serving
Beef			
Chuck blade cut	$.78	2	$.39
Chuck arm cut	.89	3	.30
Hamburger	.66	4	.165
Stew, boneless	.99[3]	4	.25
Round cut, boneless	1.28	4	.32
Sirloin steak	1.32	2	.66
Rib roast, bone in	1.12	2	.56
Rump roast, boneless	1.27	3	.42
Pork			
Boston butt, bone in	.59[3]	2½	.236
Chops	1.03	2½	.41
Loin roast, end cut	.75	2	.375
Ham, smoked, bone in	.74	3	.25
Smoked picnic, bone in	.54	2½	.216
Lamb			
Leg roast	.99[3]	2½	.40
Loin chops	1.88	2	.94
Shoulder, bone in	.89[3]	2½	.356
Veal			
Cutlet, boneless	2.25	4	.56
Chops	2.49[3]	2½	1.00
Poultry			
Broiler-fryer chicken	.40	1⅓	.30
Turkey	.54	1½	.36
Duckling	.69[3]	1⅓	.518
Rock Cornish game hen	.89[3]	1	.89
Fish and Shellfish			
Cod fillet, frozen	.78[3]	4	.20
Haddock fillet, frozen	.93	4	.23
Ocean perch fillet, frozen	.69	3⅓	.21
Lobster tails, frozen	5.32[3]	3	1.77
Shrimp, frozen shelled and deveined	2.40[3]	4	.60

[1]United States average prices (February 1971) except as marked otherwise.

[2]Minimum yield per pound in general. Yields can be greater because of trimming practices, quality, and age.

[3]Regional, nonspecial price.

THE SIZE OF MEAT PORTIONS

The size of a serving of meat, poultry, or fish varies with families and for different family members. However, it is possible to think and plan in terms of standardized servings, then serve them at such ratios as four individual servings from three standardized servings or three individual servings from four standardized servings. Some meat portions are larger than the standardized serving; they are large chops and steaks served as individual portions, lobster tails, small whole fish (such as brook trout), Rock Cornish game hens, and others.

When the budget for food is conservative, the size of a serving may be smaller than the standardized portion. In meal planning, something less expensive is added to compensate, perhaps dumplings or pastry; or the meat may be combined with potatoes, noodles, or vegetables.

The average, or standardized, serving is three ounces of cooked lean meat. This quantity of cooked lean meat will be derived from four to four and one-half ounces of fat-free and bone-free uncooked lean meat so long as cooking losses are no greater than 25 to 33 per cent. Cooking losses of meat vary with the temperature of cooking, the length of the cooking period, the degree of doneness to which cooked, and the manner of cooking. Losses are of water and drippings. Low-temperature cooking for the shortest suitable period of time minimizes losses. The amount of meat that must be purchased to yield this four or more ounces of fat-free and bone-free lean meat is determined by the amount of fat and bone present in a cut and the size and shape of a cut; that is, the larger the cut, the smaller the percentage of loss, and the greater the surface area, the greater the loss. Very young birds have a higher ratio of bone to lean than mature birds, i.e., a stewing hen serves out more portions per pound than an eight-week-old fryer. Fish serve out one or more portions per pound depending on the degree of bone and skin removal. Fully boned and skinned fish fillets, gently and quickly cooked, can yield four servings per pound, but may yield only three. Perhaps it should be noted that many persons will think that three ounces of cooked lean meat make a stingy portion.

Some items and cuts that may yield about four average portions per pound are hamburger, ground beef, lamb patties, ham patties, minute or cube steaks, liver, beef and pork tenderloins, fully boned and skinned fish fillets, center-cut ham slices, flank steak, trimmed cuts from the beef round, stew meat, and shelled and deveined frozen shrimp. Of these, liver, well-trimmed stew meat, and ground beef can be expanded to give five servings to the pound, depending, of course, on how and with what they are combined. So-called muscle boning, which simply means separating the muscles of such large cuts as the chuck and the round to fabricate steaks and roasts—which we prefer—produces lean cuts that may yield up to four servings per pound. When about one fourth, one half, and three fourths of cuts are waste, they yield approximately, three, two, and one servings per pound, respectively. Items that may yield three portions per pound are rib veal and pork chops; boned cuts from the shoulder of beef, pork, veal, and lamb; whole or half ham; boned beef rump roast; shrimp in the shell; and chicken breasts and boned poultry roasts. Cuts that may be expected to yield two or two to three servings per pound include chicken legs (that is, the drumstick plus thigh), drumsticks, and thighs; lamb chops and lamb legs; porterhouse and sirloin steaks; bone-in rib roasts; bone-in shoulder roasts and steaks of beef; unboned lamb and pork shoulder roasts; possibly pork and veal loin chops; and picnic shoulder. Cuts that serve only one or one to two servings per pound include spare ribs, lamb shanks, short ribs of beef, duckling, and Rock Cornish game hen.

It is quite difficult to state precisely the number of servings a pound of meat, poultry, or fish will yield; tables often suggest yields in a range of one to two, two to three, three to four, and four to five. The range allows for variations in cuts and in the trimming practices of different super-markets. Cuts from meat-type hogs and meat-type steers contain less fat than cuts from old-type animals, and it would be anticipated that they would provide close to the upper limit in numbers of servings per pound according to cut. See-through prepackaging of meats permits the buyer to assess the amount of waste, at least to some degree. The label on the package states the weight of the contents. With these bits of information, the consumer can, by examination of the packages in a display, select an approximate quantity for the desired number of servings.

Cuts of Meat

Animal carcasses are cut into primal or wholesale cuts, which are, in turn, cut into retail cuts. Retail cuts differ in cost per pound and preferred methods of cooking as they differ in the wholesale cut of origin. Skill in identifying the wholesale cut of origin of a retail cut is of value to the meal manager. Both bone shapes and muscle structure provide clues to identifying the part of the carcass from which a cut is derived. Beef, veal, pork, and lamb carcasses are similar in bone and muscle structure; they are cut differently into primal cuts, but the retail cuts are very similar though they vary in size. Figures 6–3, 6–4, 6–5, and 6–6 show the bone structure of beef, veal, pork, and lamb carcasses and how they are cut into wholesale cuts.

Figure 6–7 shows retail cuts and carcass origin. The beef carcass is used in the illustration, but the veal, pork, or lamb carcass would have been equally satisfactory. Preferred retail cuts for all kinds of meat are rib cuts, loin cuts, sirloin cuts, and cuts from the round. This preference is explain-

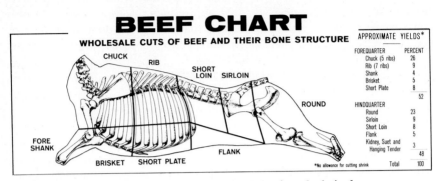

FIGURE 6–3. Beef chart—wholesale cuts of beef and their bone structure. (*Courtesy of the National Live Stock and Meat Board.*)

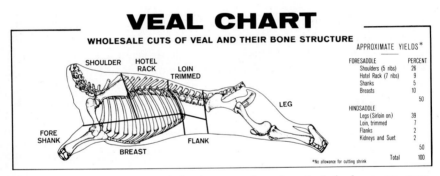

FIGURE 6–4. Veal chart—wholesale cuts of veal and their bone structure. (*Courtesy of the National Live Stock and Meat Board.*)

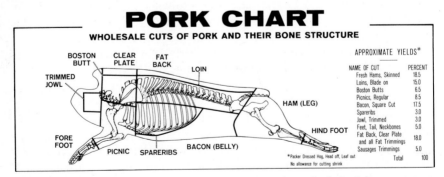

FIGURE 6–5. Pork chart—wholesale cuts of pork and their bone structure. (*Courtesy of the National Live Stock and Meat Board.*)

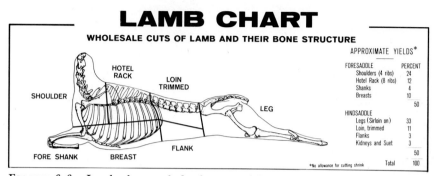

FIGURE 6–6.   Lamb chart—wholesale cuts of lamb and their bone structure. (*Courtesy of the National Live Stock and Meat Board.*)

able by meat muscle structure and inherent tenderness with the possible exception of the beef round. Unless boned, these cuts are readily identified by the shapes of bone segments present in them; in the absence of bones, they are identifiable by muscle structure. Figure 6–8 shows how bone shapes reveal the carcass origin of cuts. Rib bones and T-bones identify roasts, chops, and steaks that are preferred and also expensive. Small circles of bone identify foreleg and round. The blade bone and the irregular shapes from the hip bone identify shoulder and sirloin cuts.

Figure 6–7 also shows the basic muscle structure of the different cuts.

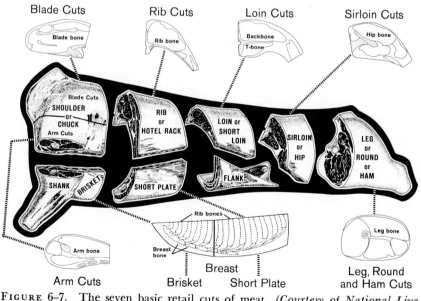

FIGURE 6–7.   The seven basic retail cuts of meat. (*Courtesy of National Live Stock and Meat Board.*)

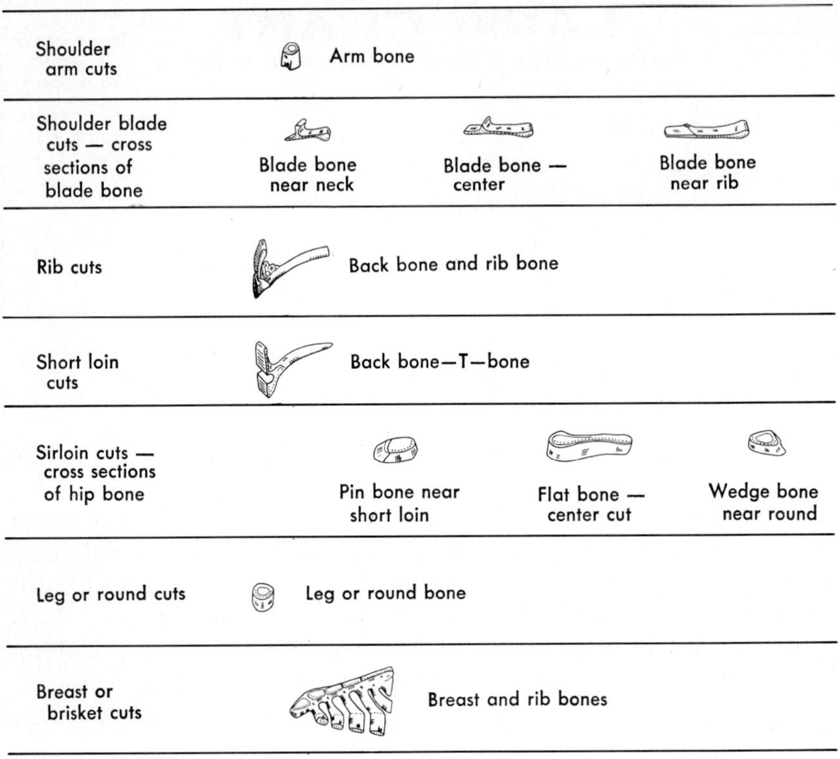

Shoulder arm cuts	Arm bone		

Shoulder blade cuts — cross sections of blade bone	Blade bone near neck	Blade bone — center	Blade bone near rib

Rib cuts	Back bone and rib bone

Short loin cuts	Back bone—T—bone

Sirloin cuts — cross sections of hip bone	Pin bone near short loin	Flat bone — center cut	Wedge bone near round

Leg or round cuts	Leg or round bone

Breast or brisket cuts	Breast and rib bones

FIGURE 6–8.   Bones identify seven groups of retail cuts. (*Courtesy of National Live Stock and Meat Board.*)

Rib cuts, loin cuts, and sirloin cuts are composed of two muscles principally: the *longissimus dorsi*, which is called rib eye, loin eye, and top sirloin depending on location, and the tenderloin muscle. The round is composed of four muscles. However, it is sometimes cut so that only three muscles are present. Other parts are composed of several muscles that vary in size.

Beef Cuts

Figure 6–9 shows retail cuts of beef and where they originate. Beef cuts are described as tender and less tender. An animal has muscles of locomotion and muscles that support; the latter are tender, the former are less tender. The supporting muscles lie along the animal's back; the muscles of locomotion are in the legs, shoulders, and neck. In general, tender cuts are cut from the rib, short loin, and sirloin; less tender cuts are derived from all other carcass parts (see Figure 6–3). There are limited exceptions

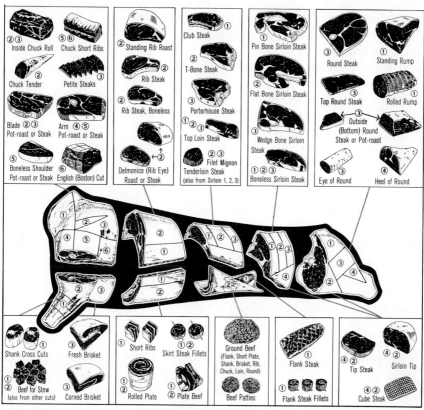

NATIONAL LIVE STOCK AND MEAT BOARD

FIGURE 6–9. Retail cuts of beef and where they come from. (*Courtesy of National Live Stock and Meat Board.*)

to the statement; some cuts from top-quality carcasses are tender that are less tender when from low-quality carcasses. Tender cuts of meat can be cooked by dry heat methods: roasting, broiling, pan-broiling, and pan-frying. Less tender cuts of meat are made tender by moist heat methods of cooking: braising and stewing. Consumer preference is for tender cuts: rib roast and rib steaks; club, T-bone, and porterhouse steaks; and sirloin steaks. The yield of a side of beef in these cuts is approximately 26 per cent. Unless they are boned, cuts from the rib section are identifiable by the curved rib bone and the presence of the large rib-eye muscle. Steaks cut from the short loin are identifiable by the T-shaped bone that derives from the backbone—although if a steak is thin, no bone may be present— and the loin eye opposed by a smaller muscle, the tenderloin, which varies in size depending on the origin of the steak (see Figure 6–9). The tenderloin muscle is a long tapering muscle that extends along the backbone through the short loin and into the sirloin with the thickest part in porter-house steaks. The tenderloin muscle is the tenderest in the entire carcass. It is sometimes stripped from the loin and it may be cut into steaks or sold as a roast. It is the most expensive beef cut. Unless they are boned, sirloin steaks contain bone pieces of irregular shape that are derived from the hipbone. The shape of the hipbone varies in the different steaks. Those cut nearest the short loin contain the tip of the hipbone; they are pin-bone steaks. The next steaks contain the widest section of the hipbone; they are flat-bone or spoon-bone sirloin steaks. The next steaks contain a round or oval bone; those cut nearest the round contain a wedge-shaped bone. Refer to Figure 6–3 for concepts of the bony structure of these steaks. The best sirloin steaks are the pin-bone and flat-bone steaks because of their neat muscle structure. Figure 6–10 shows photographs of steaks from the short loin. The general appearance of the sirloin steaks cut from the part nearest the round is not as favorable as is the appearance of steaks cut nearest the short loin. Boning and muscle-boning of the sirloin gives meaty cuts with a variety of names that confuse the consumer.

Traditional cuts from the chuck that are readily identifiable are the blade and arm steaks and roasts (Figure 6–11). The seventh-rib cut, the cut

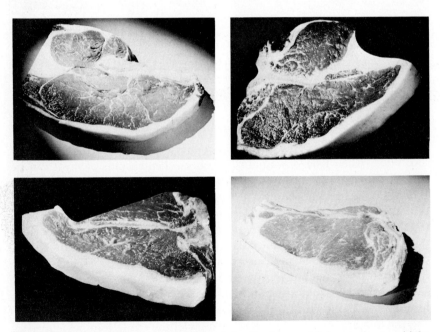

FIGURE 6–10. Unboned steaks. Top left, flat bone sirloin steak; top right, porterhouse steak; bottom left, T-bone steak; bottom right, club steak. (*United States Department of Agriculture photographs.*)

FIGURE 6–11. [OPPOSITE] Unboned cuts from the chuck and the round. Top —arm cut. Center—cut from the round. Bottom—blade cut. (*United States Department of Agriculture photographs.*)

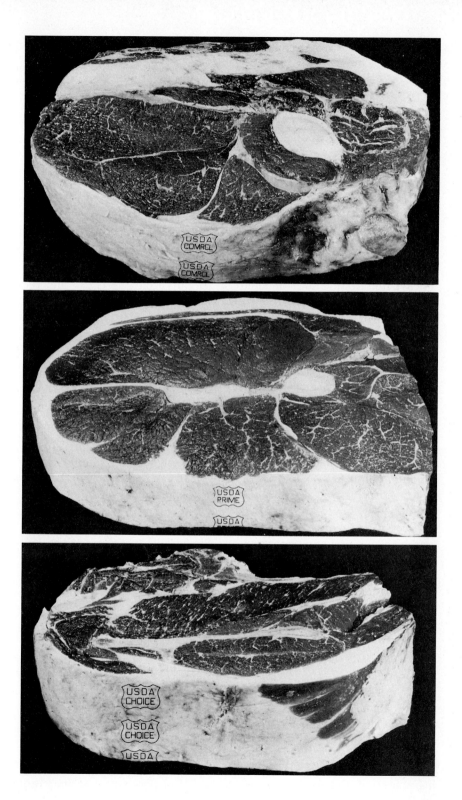

adjacent to the rib section, is considered the best because it contains part of the rib eye. Boning and muscle-boning of the chuck produce roasts and steaks bearing such names as petite steak and flatiron roast. The State of New York requires that standard names of cuts appear on retail labels.

The beef round is sliced to give round steaks and is cut into heel-of-beef cuts and rump cuts. The round is sometimes cut into top round, bottom round, and eye-of-round sections that are sliced for steaks or cut into large pieces for pot roasts or roasting. Top round, also called inside round, is the most tender part of the round. Cuts from the round are quite free of fat. The only bone that may be present is the thighbone, which is recognized as a small circle of bone with a center of marrow. Cuts from the round provide three to four standard portions when the bone-free cuts are bought and cooking time is not excessive. Traditional cuts from the chuck and the round are shown in Figure 6–11. Cuts from the chuck and the round are less tender cuts unless they come from high-quality carcasses; generally, they are cooked by moist heat. The list of tender cuts is extended by blade cuts and top round if the grade of beef is USDA Prime; by top round only if the grade is USDA Choice.

The remaining wholesale cuts provide hamburger, stew meat, short ribs, flank steak, and brisket of beef. Grinding beef to make hamburger is a means of tenderizing less tender cuts. The federal standard for hamburger requires that it contain no more than 30 per cent of beef fat, no meat by-products, and no extender. Ground beef may contain as much as 30 per cent beef fat, but will generally contain from 20 to 25 per cent. Ground beef is priced higher than hamburger. In some markets ground chuck, ground round, and ground sirloin are available; in general, they are priced differently, but always higher than hamburger. Ground meat is perishable: it should be carefully stored, and if frozen, it should be used within a three-month period. "Beef patties" are prepared from chopped fresh or frozen beef and may contain added fat and water, seasonings, and binder or extender. "Fabricated steaks" are prepared from beef or veal or combinations thereof. The meat is comminuted and shaped. The product cannot contain more than 30 per cent fat, nor can it contain added water or binder or extender. The fabricated steak is labeled in various ways to reveal its comminuted nature—"Beef Steak, Chopped, Shaped, Frozen," "Minute Steak, Formed, Wafer Sliced, Frozen," "Beef Steak, Veal Added, Chopped and Shaped."

Pork Cuts

Although all pork cuts are tender, only roasts are cooked by dry heat. However, thin chops can safely be pan-fried or pan-broiled. The possible presence of *trichinae* in pork makes it desirable that all pork cuts be cooked well done; for small cuts, this implies moist heat methods of cooking to prevent drying. There is not the variety of pork cuts that there is of

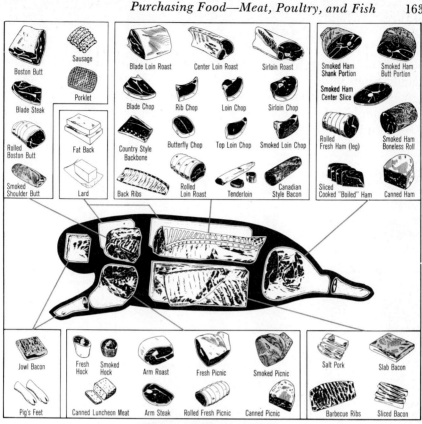

NATIONAL LIVE STOCK AND MEAT BOARD

FIGURE 6–12.   Retail cuts of pork and where they come from. (*Courtesy of the National Live Stock and Meat Board.*)

beef cuts. The large loin (see Figure 6–12) is cut into chops and roasts. Roasts are center cut, blade or rib end, and sirloin loin. Chops from the loin are rib, loin, and butterfly. Rib chops are identified by the slightly curved rib bone and the presence of the rib-eye muscle outside of the curve. Loin chops are identified by the T-bone and the presence of the tenderloin and rib-eye muscles on the two sides of the T-bone. These resemble T-bone and porterhouse steaks, but they are smaller, of course. Butterfly chops are boneless; they are composed of a thick section of the rib-eye muscle partially cut through and opened out and flattened. The fore part of the carcass provides the picnic shoulder and the Boston butt. The Boston butt is cut into what may be called shoulder chops or blade steaks, or it may be boned or left unboned as Boston butt roast. When smoked, the cut is identified as smoked butt. The picnic shoulder is cut into arm steaks or chops and pig hocks; when boned or unboned and smoked it is identified as picnic shoulder. Fresh ham cuts into pork steaks identified by a small circle of bone and boned or unboned roasts. Smoked ham is similarly cut into ham slices and butt or shank ham portions.

Veal Cuts

Veal cuts resemble beef cuts but are smaller. As with beef and pork, the shoulder cuts into blade and arm roasts and steaks; the rib into rib chops or rib roast; and the loin into loin chops or sirloin steaks. The veal round cuts into round steak, sometimes called veal cutlet, and into leg or round roasts (see Figure 6–13).

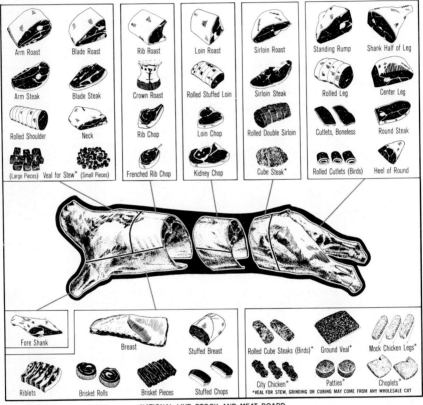

NATIONAL LIVE STOCK AND MEAT BOARD

FIGURE 6–13.   Retail cuts of veal and where they come from. (*Courtesy of the National Live Stock and Meat Board.*)

Lamb Cuts

All lamb cuts are tender. The carcass is small so that cuts appear to be miniatures of beef cuts. As heretofore, the various wholesale cuts are cut into both roasts and chops. Some commonly seen lamb cuts are derived as follows: the shoulder cuts into blade and arm chops or boned or unboned shoulder roast (see Figure 6–14). The rack cuts into rib chops or rib roast.

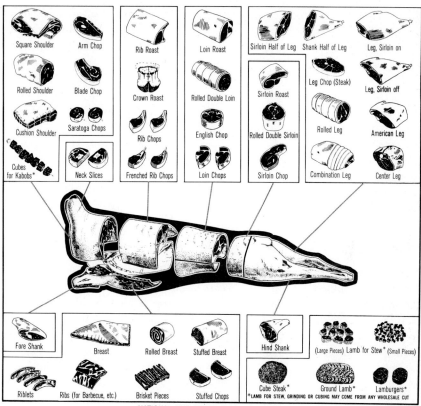

FIGURE 6–14. Retail cuts of lamb and where they come from. (*Courtesy of the National Live Stock and Meat Board.*)

The loin cuts into loin chops. The leg is a roast; it may be semiboned (American-style), or unboned (French-style). Half legs are available in some markets as sirloin and shank halves. Sometimes lamb legs are cut into slices—leg chops or steaks. Lamb shanks are the forelegs.

Summary. Different cuts of meat from the same species have similar nutrient value and comparable flavor; they may differ in tenderness and other palatability factors. For all kinds of meat, the cuts from the rib and loin sections are the most highly prized; they are also the most expensive to purchase. The lamb leg is a premium cut; it is expensive to purchase. Ham and fresh ham and the veal cutlet and the veal leg roast are excellent cuts; the pork cuts are fairly expensive; the veal cuts, very expensive. Shoulder cuts of all kinds of meat are moderately priced; when properly cooked, they make fine eating. The other parts of carcasses are the less favored parts; in general, they are cut into stew or chop-suey meat, or ground finely to coarsely for hamburger, meat loaf, patties, chili meat, or sausage. Though not necessarily cheap, their cost per serving is less than that of other cuts.

It is possible to identify the part of the carcass from which a cut originates by the shape of the bone or bones present. In the absence of bone, the most highly prized cuts are identifiable by the presence of the rib-eye, or loin-eye, muscle and the tenderloin muscle. The tenderloin of beef and the eye of the round can be confused. Top and bottom round can be identified in the absence of bone; however, the carcass origin of some boneless beef cuts may be difficult to identify. It is important to know from what part of the carcass a beef cut has been derived in order to know how to cook it.

Poultry Cuts

Chickens and turkeys are cut into parts, prepared as boneless roasts, and prepared as boneless thigh and breast fillets. All have been defined by the United States Department of Agriculture for poultry products in interstate commerce. *Poultry product* means any ready-to-cook poultry or poultry food product. *Ready-to-cook poultry* means any dressed poultry from which the protruding pinfeathers, vestigial feathers, head, shanks, oil gland, and all viscera have been removed, with or without giblets; it is ready to cook without need of further processing. The term *giblets* means the liver from which the bile sac has been removed, the heart from which the pericardial sac has been removed, and the gizzard from which the lining and contents have been removed. *Dressed poultry* means poultry from which feathers and blood have been removed. Any packages labeled as follows will contain poultry parts as specified.

1. *Breasts, breasts with ribs, wishbones* are breast pieces separated from the carcass as the names imply. The breast may be cut into two nearly equal parts along the breastbone. No neck skin can be included in any of these.

2. *Legs* include thigh and drumstick, whether disjointed or not. Legs separated into parts that are packaged and sold separately become *thighs* and *drumsticks*. No back skin can be included on legs and thighs.

3. *Wings* must include the entire wing with skin and muscle intact, but the wing tip may be removed.

4. *Backs* include the pelvic bones and all the vertebrae posterior to the shoulder joint. The meat may not be removed from pelvic bones. But *stripped backs* will have the meat removed from the pelvic bones.

5. *Necks*, with or without neck skin, are separated from the carcass at the shoulder joint.

6. *Halves* are the nearly equal parts derived by the full-length split of

the back and the breast of the carcass. *Quarters* are halves cut crosswise at almost right angles to the backbone.

7.   *Poultry roast* (or *roll*, or *bar*, or *log*) is prepared from the meat of young poultry of A Quality with respect to fleshing and fat covering. *A Quality* means the top quality designation in the United States standards for ready-to-cook poultry and parts. The meat is trimmed of tendons, cartilage, large blood vessels, blood clots, blemishes, discoloration, and other undesirable parts. Seventy-five per cent or more of the outer surface must be covered with skin either attached or used as a wrap. Slices of the cooked roast should separate into no more than three parts. Label statement must reveal the combination of light and dark meat if they are present in other than natural proportions. Dark meat has long been considered fatter and less tender than white meat, but more flavorful. Young poultry is marketed at such an early age that these differences have practically ceased to exist.

8.   *Boneless breast* and *boneless thigh* (also called *breast fillet* and *thigh fillet*) are deboned parts that must meet the A Quality requirements for ready-to-cook poultry parts.

Excepting the poultry roast and the breast and thigh fillets, all of these cuts are abundantly available fresh or frozen and prepackaged in the supermarket. For birds at eight to ten weeks of age, the breast is about 33 per cent of its ready-to-cook weight; the two legs, about 33 per cent; and the bony parts, about 34 per cent (7). However, averages published by the National Broiler Council are these: legs with thighs, about 30 per cent; breast with ribs, about 30 per cent; remaining parts, 37 per cent; cutting losses, 3 per cent. When properly priced, the parts are equally as good buys as the whole chicken. Proper pricing means that breasts are priced about 40 per cent more; thighs, about 33 per cent more; drumsticks, about 25 per cent more; and legs, about 30 per cent more than whole fryers. Obviously, the bony parts—wings, backs, and necks—should cost less per pound than the whole fryer (11). At all ages, males weigh more than females; this is also true for each part, or cut. When available, parts from male fryers provide more generous portions than parts from female fryers.

Fryers weigh from two and a half to four pounds of ready-to-cook weight, depending on age and sex. They are usually about nine weeks of age. The yield in cooked meat at this age is about 40 per cent and the yield in skin is about 9 per cent: that is, approximately half of the purchased weight is edible (5).

The Quality of Meat, Poultry, and Fish

Quality in meat, poultry, and fish has for the consumer two connotations: wholesomeness and palatability. If one of these connotations has first place, it is probably wholesomeness.

Wholesomeness as an Aspect of Quality

Wholesomeness as an aspect of quality means fit and safe for eating. It means that all meat and meat food products—animal, poultry, and fish— derive from healthy animals; and that slaughter, all processing, all transport, and all storage take place under sanitary conditions; and that all products are free from disease-producing microorganisms and filth of any kind. Federal inspection for wholesomeness is mandatory for all meat and poultry and for processed meat and poultry food products destined for interstate and foreign commerce. The Wholesome Meat Act of 1967 and the Wholesome Poultry Products Act of 1968 required that the states provide inspection equal to federal inspection for products destined for intrastate commerce. In the absence of state inspection programs equal to federal inspection, federal inspection became mandatory. See Chapter 4.

Inspection begins with live animals and continues through slaughter and processing. Animals and animal parts considered unfit for food are condemned and removed from food channels. High standards of sanitation are enforced in slaughtering and processing plants.

The investigation of and the evaluation of supermarket hamburger and ground beef products reported in August of 1971 (2) disclosed high bacterial counts and high coliform counts that suggested poor sanitary and storage practices in the supermarket. Although retailers of meat come under the provisions of the meat inspection acts, they are not routinely inspected. Rigid, routine inspections at the retail level are important and essential for assurance of the wholesomeness of the meat purchased by the consumer.

Processed meat and poultry food products are made according to approved formulas. The meat or poultry ingredient is reinspected to make certain that it is wholesome. All ingredients and additives used in production are inspected for wholesomeness. Inspection continues through each step in production to packaging and labeling. It is mandatory that ingredients be named in order from the one present in greatest amount to the one present in least amount. Although this labeling is informative to a degree, it does not inform as to the quantity of meat or poultry present in a product.

All federally inspected products are identified by appropriate inspection marks (see Figure 6–15). In addition to the statement of inspection, the number assigned to the processing plant is included within the inspection mark. The inspection mark for meats is stamped in purple ink on all wholesale cuts; it may or may not be trimmed from retail cuts. The purple ink is a safe color in accordance with requirements of the Food, Drug, and Cosmetic Act. On fresh and uncooked frozen poultry and poultry parts, the inspection mark appears on the overwrap, on an insert within the package, or on the wing tip of the ready-to-cook bird. It may stand alone

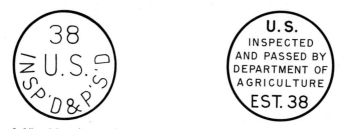

FIGURE 6–15.   Meat inspection marks. Left, the mark on carcass and cuts. Right, the mark on processed meat food products. (*United States Department of Agriculture photographs.*)

or be combined with the grade shield within a shield (Figures 6–16 and 6–19). The inspection mark on processed meat and poultry food products, such as frozen dinners, chili con carne, and chicken pies, is printed on the box, can, or wrapper.

The wholesomeness of fish food products is assured only by the provisions of the Food, Drug, and Cosmetic Act; that is, there is no mandatory inspection of fish and fish food products during processing as there is for meat and poultry. There is need for such inspection and legislation to require it will be forthcoming in the 1970's. As of October, 1970, the inspection of fishery products and the promulgation of grade standards for fishery products have been a function of the National Marine Fisheries Service of the National Oceanic and Atmospheric Administration of the United States Department of Commerce. This transfer from the Department of the Interior resulted in changes in the inspection mark.

To prevent the transmission of disease through shellfish, a shellfish sanitation program is administered jointly by the coastal shellfish producing states, the Food and Drug Administration, and the shellfish industry. Water quality is monitored and, when indicated, areas are closed to the taking of shellfish. Both oysters and clams live and breed in estuarine water that can become polluted. In 1971, oysters were found to contain cadmium in amounts greater than now considered safe. Shellfish shippers

FIGURE 6–16.   Poultry inspection mark. (*United States Department of Agriculture photograph.*)

are certified and each package of shellfish should bear the certificate number of the shipper.

Although consumers confuse inspection and grade marks, they understand the purpose of inspection and they believe that food products are inspected for wholesomeness (3).

Palatability as an Aspect of Quality

Most consumers, except beginners perhaps, have a concept for the assessment of quality in meats, including fish and poultry. This concept includes freshness as it can be judged by color and smell; appropriate color; minimum quantities of fat and bone, except as a cut demands the presence of a distinctive bone of good size; muscle composition of a few well-shaped pieces; the potential for easy and neat carving; and a no-drip package. Consumers can be observed in the supermarket making judgments; packages of meat that fail in assessment are passed over. Of course, meat must eat well, that is, be tender, juicy, and of good flavor.

The intrinsic factors that affect the qualities of tenderness, juiciness, and flavor are known; hence, standards for the quality grading of uncooked meat, poultry, and fish can be established. They are the work of the appropriate divisions of the United States Department of Agriculture for meats and poultry and of the National Marine Fisheries Service of the United States Department of Commerce. Formerly, the Bureau of Commercial Fisheries of the United States Department of the Interior defined standards for grading fishery products. Products graded in accordance with established standards bear the appropriate grade marks. Standards have been developed for grading beef; veal and calf; lamb, yearling mutton, and mutton; chickens and turkeys; and for a variety of frozen fish fillets and steaks. In the calendar year 1970, 13.9 billion pounds of beef (65 per cent of the total) and 476 million pounds of veal, calf, lamb, and mutton (43 per cent of the total) were graded for quality. In the fiscal year 1970, 1.4 billion pounds of turkey (96 per cent) and 5,461 million pounds of chicken (74 per cent) were graded for quality.

Grading for Quality

Factors considered in grading for quality are cutability, conformation, and quality. *Cutability* refers to the amount of usable meat in a carcass. High cutability implies thick muscling and minimum fat covering. There are cutability grades for beef, pork, and lamb. *Conformation* refers to shape or body build. Good conformation implies thick fleshing of desired parts—shoulders, ribs, loins, and rounds in animals and broad, thick breasts and plump legs in poultry. *Quality* refers to the characteristics associated with tenderness, juiciness, and flavor of lean meat; they are maturity, the amount and distribution of fat, and the color, firmness, and texture of the lean. As animals and birds age, bones lose redness and become dense and white, lean darkens and becomes coarse in texture, and fat may change in color and accumulate in excessive quantities. Meat from mature animals and birds is less tender and drier than that from younger ones. Fat is deposited as an external covering of the body, within the abdominal cavity, and between and within muscles. Fat intermingled with lean within a muscle is termed *marbling*. The presence of fat in meat protects it against drying during cooking; hence it affects juiciness. Further, good flavor is associated with the presence of fat. The color, firmness, and texture of the lean affect quality. Lean of good quality is of the proper color for its kind, firm, and fine of grain.

Grading Beef for Quality. There are two kinds of USDA grades for beef: yield grades and palatability, or quality, grades. Yield grades were adopted in 1965. They are expressions of the percentage yields of boneless, closely trimmed retail cuts from the high-value parts of the carcass—round, loin, rib, and chuck—that is, the cutability of a carcass. Carcasses of the same quality grade can differ in yield grade. There are five yield grades from USDA Yield Grade I through USDA Yield Grade 5. Differences in the yields of trimmed cuts are from 82 per cent to about 64 per cent for carcasses of like weight from USDA Yield Grade 1 to USDA Yield Grade 5. Yield grades are based on the size of the ribeye muscle, the external and internal fat, and carcass weight. The ribeye diminishes in area and the quantity of fat increases as the grade moves from a lower to a higher number, a fact that explains the different appearance of like cuts of the same quality grade (see Figure 6–17). The meat-type steer—a product of breeding and feeding management—produces a thickly muscled carcass of minimum fat content that rates high in cutability, i.e., a yield grade of low number.

Palatability grades describe beef as USDA Prime, USDA Choice, and so on. The palatability grade is based on a composite evaluation of the conformation of the carcass and the palatability-indicating characteristics of the lean. Conformation refers to the thickness of muscling and to the overall degree of thickness and fullness of the carcass and its various parts. Conformation is an assessment of the ratio of lean to bone. Superior conformation in an animal means meatiness; by contrast, poor conformation implies more boniness than meatiness. Palatability-indicating characteristics include the marbling, firmness, texture, and color of the lean. Marbling and firmness are assessed in a cut surface in relation to the apparent maturity of the animal from which the carcass derived. Maturity is assessed by an evaluation of the size, shape, and ossification of the bones and cartilages and the color and texture of the lean flesh. Lean flesh darkens and coarsens in texture with advancing maturity and bones lose porosity and

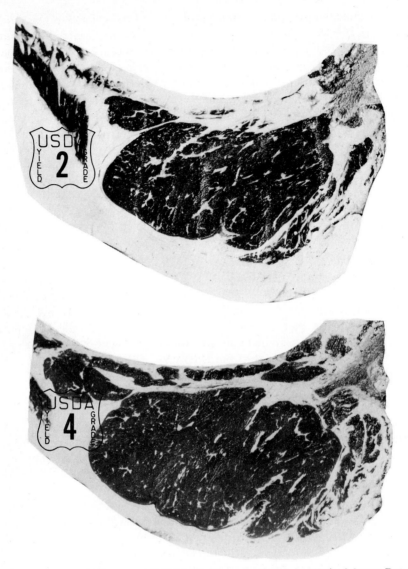

FIGURE 6–17.   Rib roasts of USDA Yield grades 2 and 4. (*United States Department of Agriculture photographs.*)

pinkness and become dense, flinty, and white. The relationship between marbling, maturity, and quality in establishing a quality grade is such that the requisite amount of marbling increases with advancing maturity.

There are eight quality grades for beef from the best to the poorest. They are Prime, Choice, Good, Standard, Commercial, Utility, Cutter, and Canner. When federally graded, the grade name is preceded by *USDA* and the whole enclosed within a shield (Figure 6–18). The grade mark is

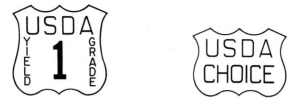

FIGURE 6–18.   USDA yield grade and quality grade symbols. *(United States Department of Agriculture photographs.)*

imprinted with a roller stamp in purple ink the full length of the carcass and across the shoulders. Most retail cuts from graded carcasses will carry one or more or part of one of these marks. Beef production by grade was in 1969: USDA Prime, 4 per cent; USDA Choice, 56 per cent; USDA Good, 17 per cent; USDA Standard and USDA Commercial, 8 per cent; and USDA Utility, Canner, and Cutter, 15 per cent. Of the top five grades, only the USDA Commercial grade is applied to mature carcasses. Very little of Prime beef reaches the supermarket; this quality is purchased by the restaurant trade. The lower three grades are seldom sold as retail cuts but are used instead in making hamburger and meat food products. USDA Choice is the grade most abundantly available. However, not all similar cuts of USDA Choice beef are alike because there is a wide spread between top and bottom Choice, a fact that causes consumer dissatisfaction with the grading system. As already pointed out, there are five yield grades for beef, meaning five differences in the size of the rib-eye muscle. Further, animals of all sex conditions can be graded Choice. Range in maturity is possible. Range in conformation is from "moderately thick muscled with moderately thick and full loins and ribs and moderately plump rounds" to "heavily muscled with moderately thick loins and ribs and plump and bulging rounds." Finally, the lean differs in degree of marbling; in color from light red to medium to dark red; and in texture from slightly soft to firm; and cuts differ in meatiness.

Supermarkets may stock only Choice beef or they may carry one or more lower qualities. Prices of cuts should vary with quality. In a large meat department or in a so-called meat market, it is quite possible to find identical cuts of different grades at different prices. Grade differences could demand different cooking methods. Properly cooked, both grades should be tasty; however, the cut with more marbling might have more flavor and be juicier.

Consumers Union (6) made a study of beef specials in twenty-four supermarkets in two cities—Baltimore and Washington, D.C. Between December, 1969 and February, 1970, chuck roasts were specialed in all stores; rib roasts in twenty-one; sirloin steak in eighteen; and round roast in twelve. The beef specials were marked down an average of 20 per cent: the chuck and rib roasts, 18 per cent; the sirloin steak, 24 per cent; and the round roast, 33 per cent. The beef specials differed in eating quality; the cost per pound rarely correlated with the quality rank.

The consumer who can buy only ungraded beef should look for lean of fine grain, creamy-white fat, and some marbling if she wants a cut of Choice quality. Good and Standard beef have lean of bright color and fine grain, bones that are red and spongy appearing, no marbling, and a thin external fat layer. Commercial and Utility beef have lean of dark red color and coarse texture, bones that are white and dense, and a variable fat content that is yellowish instead of creamy.

Quality in Veal and Calf.   Veal and calf are two classifications of young bovine animals. Genuine *veal* comes from animals not more than three months of age that have been milk fed only. *Calf* derives from animals three to eight months of age that have been given feeds other than milk. Typical veal has lean of grayish pink color and smooth, velvety texture; the fat is soft and pliable. Calf has lean of grayish red color; the fat is harder and flaky. In the trade *veal* means all young animals up to one year of age. In some states, it is permitted to describe as *baby beef* animals slaughtered when under fifteen months of age. Little veal and calf are graded for retail trade. Official USDA grades include Prime, Choice, Good, Standard, and lower grades. The better-quality carcasses have better conformation and are fatter; they are more juicy and flavorful than carcasses of the lower grades. Except for cuts from very young veal, veal and calf chops, steaks, and cutlets are traditionally cooked by moist heat methods to develop juiciness and flavor. Large cuts can be oven roasted. Per-capita consumption of veal by Americans in the United States is only about three pounds per year. Veal and calf cuts are much more expensive than beef and pork cuts, which may explain the greater than 50 per cent reduction in consumption since 1957–1959.

Quality in Pork.   Pork is not graded for quality. During the 1960's, much progress was made in the production of meat-type hogs. These animals weigh about two hundred pounds at five to six months of age, they have larger muscles and longer sides as well as 57 per cent less fat than old-type hogs. The USDA standards for grading slaughter swine, feeder pigs, and pork carcasses were revised in 1968 to reflect this. Pork carcasses are judged of either acceptable or unacceptable quality on the basis of firmness of fat and lean and color of lean. Pork carcasses adjudged unacceptable are graded U.S. Utility. Carcasses of acceptable quality are graded from U.S. No. 1 to U.S. No. 4 on the basis of yield in the four lean cuts: hams, loins, picnics, and Boston butts. The range in yield of these cuts is from 53 per cent and over to less than 47 per cent for the four grades from U.S. No. 1 to U.S. No. 4. It was estimated that about 75 per cent of barrows and gilts slaughtered in 1968 were of yield grades No. 2

and No. 3 and that only 2 per cent were U.S. Utility grade. Yield grade is based on the degree of fatness and the degree of muscling. Six degrees of muscling from very thick to very thin are recognized. Because there are no consumer grades for pork, the meal manager grades her own. Like the expert, she should look for thick muscles and thin fat.

Fine pork has gravy-pink lean that is fine in grain and firm of texture. There is some marbling of the lean. The fat is white and the bones are spongy and pinkish, a sign of immaturity. The lean of cuts from older animals is darker in color and coarse in texture. Pork should be tender, juicy, and flavorful.

Quality in Lamb, Yearling Mutton, and Mutton.   Americans in the United States ate only 3.4 pounds of lamb and mutton per capita in 1970, one pound less than in 1957–1959. Classifications of sheep are lamb, yearling mutton, and mutton. Lamb may be baby lamb, spring lamb, and lamb. *Baby lamb* refers to animals from six to eight weeks of age. *Spring lamb* or *genuine spring lamb* comes from new-crop lambs slaughtered during the period beginning in March and terminating the week containing the first Monday in October. Thereafter and until fourteen months of age, the product is *lamb*. *Yearling mutton* and *mutton* are derived from animals one to two years of age, the distinction between the two being fixed by the degree of ossification of the foreshanks. Lamb carcasses have slightly wide and moderately flat rib bones, break joints on the front shanks, and bright, red lean of fine texture. The yearling mutton carcass has either break joints or "spool" joints on the front shanks, moderately wide and flat rib bones, and slightly dark lean of slightly coarse texture. Very little mutton is eaten in the United States.

USDA grades for lamb and yearling mutton are Prime, Choice, Good, Utility, and Cull; there is no Prime grade for mutton but the other grades apply. Some quality-graded lamb can be purchased in the supermarket. There are five yield grades for lamb; they are also applicable to yearling mutton and mutton. Like the beef yield grades, they separate carcasses of the same quality grade according to yields of the premium cuts: chops and legs. Lamb chops and legs are high-priced; lamb shanks, lamb neck slices, and lamb breasts are less expensive. Lamb shoulder cuts are intermediate in cost. Lamb is tender and can be cooked by dry heat; yearling mutton and mutton should be cooked by moist heat.

Grading Poultry for Quality.   Modern poultry is the outcome of cross-breeding, scientific feeding, and controlled environmental conditions. Per capita consumption per year rose from 27.5 pounds in 1957–1959 to 42.2 pounds in 1970. "Chicken every Sunday" is no longer only for the affluent.

Poultry means chickens, turkeys, ducks, guineas, and geese; but only chickens, turkeys, and ducks will be described. All are marketed young—

broiler and fryer chickens at eight to nine weeks of age and twenty-pound tom turkeys at five months of age—and mature. Young poultry is tender and the meat is juicy; but it may lack the flavor of mature poultry. Poultry is usually labeled to reveal age because age dictates the method of cooking.

The classes of young and mature chickens, turkeys, and ducks are described.

1. A *Rock Cornish game hen* or *Cornish game hen* is a young immature chicken bred from a Cornish chicken or the progeny of a Cornish chicken crossed with another breed of chicken. It should weigh no more than two pounds ready-to-cook weight and is usually five or six weeks of age.

2. A *broiler* or *fryer* is a young chicken, of either sex, usually nine to twelve weeks old. It has tender meat; soft, pliable, smooth-textured skin; and flexible breastbone cartilage.

3. A *roaster* is a young chicken, of either sex, usually between three and five months of age. It has tender meat, smooth-textured skin; and breastbone cartilage that may be somewhat less flexible than that of a broiler or fryer.

4. A *capon* is a surgically unsexed male chicken, usually less than eight months old. It has tender meat and soft, pliable, smooth-textured skin.

5. A *stag* is a male chicken, usually less than ten months of age. It has somewhat toughened and dark flesh, coarse skin, and a somewhat hardened breastbone cartilage.

6. A *hen* or *stewing chicken* or *fowl* is a mature female chicken, more than ten months old. The flesh is less tender than that of a roaster, and the breastbone tip is nonflexible.

7. A *cock* or *rooster* is a mature male chicken with toughened and darkened flesh, coarse skin, and a hardened breastbone tip.

In labeling practices, the first four of these classes may be described as "young chicken" and the last three, as "mature chicken" or "old chicken."

Descriptions of turkey classes follow.

1. A *fryer-roaster turkey* is a young, immature turkey of either sex, usually less than sixteen weeks old. It has tender flesh; soft, pliable, smooth-textured skin; and a flexible breastbone cartilage.

2. A *young hen turkey* is a young female turkey five to seven months old. It has tender flesh; smooth-textured, soft, and pliable skin; and a somewhat flexible breastbone cartilage.

3. A *young tom turkey* is a young male turkey with the same characteristics as a young hen turkey.

4. A *yearling hen turkey* is a fully matured female turkey, usually under fifteen months old. The flesh is reasonably tender, and the skin is reasonably smooth-textured.

5. A *yearling tom turkey* is a fully matured male turkey with the same characteristics as the yearling hen turkey.

6. A *mature turkey* or *old turkey* is a bird of either sex, older than fifteen months. It has toughened flesh and coarse skin.

For labeling purposes, the designation of sex name is optional and the first three classes may be grouped and designated as "young turkeys."

The consumption of ducks has increased in recent years, so it may be practical to define the various classes of ducks.

1. A *broiler duckling* or *fryer duckling* is a bird of either sex, less than eight weeks old, with tender flesh, a soft bill, and a soft windpipe.

2. A *roaster duckling* is a young bird of either sex, usually less than sixteen weeks old. The flesh is tender; although the bill and the windpipe are a little hardened, they are easily dented.

3. A *mature duck* or *old duck* is a bird of either sex over six months of age with toughened flesh and hardened bill and windpipe.

Grading of poultry for quality is voluntary and only poultry that has been federally inspected for wholesomeness can be graded. The inspection mark and the grade mark may be combined as in Figure 6–19; the class name is included, e.g., "frying chicken." Consumer grades have been established for ready-to-cook birds and parts. There are three grades: U.S. Grade A, U.S. Grade B, and U.S. Grade C. The factors considered in grading are conformation, fleshing (meatiness), the amount of fat, and the presence or absence of such defects as bruised flesh, torn or discolored skin,

FIGURE 6–19. Combination grade and inspection symbol for poultry showing class of bird. *(United States Department of Agriculture photograph.)*

and broken or disjointed bones. U.S. Grade A birds have a well-developed covering of flesh, considering the kind, class, and part. The breast is rounded and the drumstick, thigh, and wing are moderately fleshed (see Figures 6–20 and 6–21). U.S. Grade B birds are described as having a substantial covering of flesh on the breast and sufficient flesh on the drumstick, thigh, and wing to prevent a thin appearance. U.S. Grade C birds

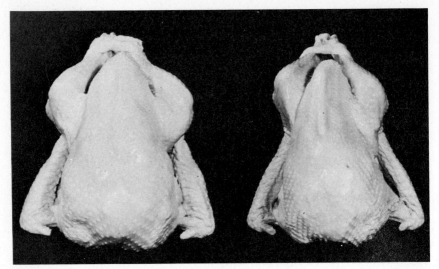

FIGURE 6–20.   U.S. Grade A and U.S. Grade B turkeys. (*United States Department of Agriculture photographs.*)

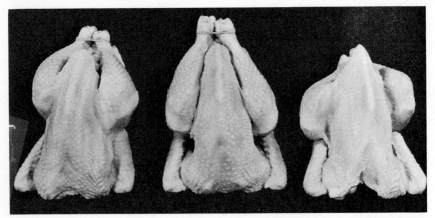

FIGURE 6–21.   Ready-to-cook chickens of U.S. Grade A, U.S. Grade B, and U.S. Grade C qualities. (*United States Department of Agriculture photographs.*)

are those that do not meet the requirements for either U.S. Grade A or U.S. Grade B. Poultry roasts and fillets can be prepared only from top-quality poultry; they can be graded U.S. Grade A. In general, only U.S. Grade A poultry products are grade labeled; products of lesser quality are sold unlabeled. "Breastiness" and good fleshing on the legs are marks of quality. Not much mature poultry is available in the supermarket. In general, mature poultry is cooked by moist heat, i.e., stewing or braising.

For some dishes, such as chicken salad, chicken pie, and creamed chicken, older birds are preferred because of their better developed flavor. The price paid for the cheap, tender chicken of the 1960's was the loss of old-fashioned chicken flavor.

The darkening of the bones and the flesh near them in chickens that have been frozen and thawed before cooking is not a factor of quality. This phenomenon occurs only in young chickens; when chickens become twelve to sixteen weeks old, the degree of the darkening diminishes. The darkening is the outcome of the effect of heat on the hemoglobin of the red blood cells that have migrated from spongy bone marrow during thawing. The more quickly thawing is effected, the less darkening occurs. Microwave cooking from the frozen state practically eliminates darkening (9).

Fish Products. Graded fish products include the following frozen fillets: cod, haddock, ocean perch, sole, and flounder; the following frozen steaks: halibut and salmon; and raw headless shrimp and scallops. With the exception of shrimp, for which three grades have been established, there are two grades and the substandard classification. Grades are U.S. Grade A, U.S. Grade B, and U.S. Grade C, where relevant. In grading, products are examined in the frozen, thawed, and cooked states. They are evaluated on the basis of flavor and odor, the appearance of the flesh, the size of pieces, the absence of defects, and the character of the cooked flesh. Grade is assigned on the basis of points scored in each category.

Standards for grading have been established for the following further-processed frozen products: raw breaded fish portions, raw breaded fish sticks, fried fish portions, fried fish sticks, fried scallops, and raw breaded regular and lightly breaded shrimp. Standards provide for two grades (U.S. Grade A and U.S. Grade B) and the substandard classification. Grades define the minimum fish content: for raw breaded fish portions not less than 75 per cent; for raw breaded fish sticks not less than 72 per cent; for fried fish portions not less than 65 per cent; and for fried fish sticks not less than 60 per cent by weight. Fish portions must weigh more than one and one-half ounces; fish sticks weigh less than one and one-half ounces; and both must be at least three-eighths inches thick. Frozen fried scallops contain a minimum of 60 per cent scallop meat. Frozen regular breaded raw shrimp contain not less than 50 per cent and lightly breaded raw shrimp not less than 65 per cent of shrimp material. Quality is determined by examination of the product in both frozen and cooked states and is evaluated by flavor and odor and such characteristics as the texture of coating and flesh, defects of coating and flesh, and the size and shape of the pieces. Scoring is on the basis of points assigned for certain quality attributes; grading is done on the basis of the score. Grade A products would be uniform in the size of the pieces, free from blemishes and defects, and of good flavor. Grade B products, though of good flavor, would not be as uniform in the size of the pieces and would not be as free of blemishes as Grade A. The grade most widely distributed is Grade A. Whether fresh or frozen, fish is perishable; hence, frozen products mistreated in transit or during storage will be less than the stated grade quality. Cost comparisons reveal that the further-processed products are more expensive than frozen raw fillets and steaks. They are convenience products; part of their cost is the cost of the added service.

Summary.   Quality means wholesomeness and palatability. Inspection for wholesomeness of meat and poultry in interstate and intrastate commerce is mandatory; inspection of imported meat is mandatory. Inspection of fish for wholesomeness is voluntary, and inspected products will be so labeled. Standards for evaluating quality in different kinds of meat and different kinds of poultry have been established. Standards for grading some fish products have been established. Grading for quality is voluntary and the service is paid for by the processor. Cost varies with quality, with the best being the most expensive most of the time. Proper cooking is essential for optimum palatability of all meat, poultry, and fish, even the best.

Miscellaneous Information About Meats

In this section we shall discuss: buying meat for the freezer, cured meats, sausages, kosher meats, tenderizing meats, meat extenders and meat analogs, meat food products, poultry food products, and shellfish. At the end of the chapter are guides to buying meat, poultry, fish and shellfish; a section on how to store meat; and guides to meat cookery.

Buying Meat for the Freezer

Though consumers purchase frozen poultry, they prefer to buy fresh red meats, especially beef, and freeze them in the home freezer or to buy them for the freezer and have them quick frozen by provisioners who provide the requisite services. A consumer must make several decisions when buying meat for the freezer. The first of these would be to consider the advantages and disadvantages of the practice, which would not be the same for all consumers. Here are some possible advantages.

1.   A ready supply of meat that makes weekly shopping for meats unnecessary.

2.   A supply of meat of constant quality: if it were excellent, this would be a boon; if only fair, it might become a disadvantage.

3.   A supply of meat at, perhaps, less than the retail cost of comparable cuts. The consumer must calculate this.

These disadvantages might be listed.

1. The immediate investment of a rather large sum of money for the meat supply for several months.

2. An assortment of cuts that may or may not be those customarily eaten. No one should buy a side of beef without knowing that the percentage of tender roasts and steaks is only about 20 per cent of gross weight. That would be about sixty pounds from a side of three hundred pounds gross weight of medium yield grade. There would be about eighty pounds of less tender roasts and steaks and about the same weight of stew meat and hamburger plus a few pounds of brisket.

3. The need to think ahead and properly thaw meat for cooking. Although meat may be cooked from the frozen state, much of what is in the freezer will need browning and special treatment because it is less tender.

4. The determination of whether or not it will be economically feasible to make this purchase. This means comparing the cost of the freezer meat against the cost of the same assortment of cuts bought at retail. This must be done in the local market area because market conditions vary in the different regions of the United States. The ready availability of beef specials in nearly all market areas complicates these calculations, as does the variability of the cost of meat in relation to the supply at different seasons.

Having made the decision to purchase meat for the freezer, it would next be necessary to select an honest and reliable dealer who could provide wholesome meat of the desired quality and the required services: cutting, packaging, and quick freezing; and if pork is purchased for freezing, curing service for bacon, hams, and other cuts that will not be used fresh, and service for sausage-making. Third would be the choice of how much and what to buy: carcass, side, forequarter or hindquarter, wholesale cuts, or even special retail cuts. The purchase of a carcass would be the equivalent of the purchase of two sides of beef. What this entails has already been discussed. The forequarter contains the rib section for tender roasts and the chuck, which is meaty but yields less tender cuts. The hindquarter yields tender steaks, the rump, and the less tender round. The forequarter yields more meat than the hindquarter. Wholesale cuts, when these can be purchased, include the round, the chuck, the rib, and the trimmed loin. The price per pound would be the highest for the loin and the least for the forequarter. In descending order of price per pound, they would rank something like this: loin, rib, hindquarter and round, carcass, and, lastly, forequarter. Retail cuts at special prices, to be frozen in the home freezer, offer opportunities for good buys. Family preference as well as the extent of the money resource would be factors that would influence the decision on which part and how much to buy.

The consumer must choose the quality to purchase. The yield grade is important for beef as well as the quality grade. Because the price per pound will vary according to the quality and yield grades, it is important to know for a certainty the grades purchased; the consumer should ask to see the USDA grade marks. The yield of beef carcasses varies according to the yield grade from about 80 per cent for Yield Grade No. 1 to about 64 per cent for Yield Grade No. 5. Though pork is not graded extensively, graded carcasses can be ordered. Grades are U.S. No. 1 through U.S. No. 4. Differences are in the yield of the major lean cuts: ham, loin, Boston butt, and picnic shoulder. Buy USDA Prime or USDA Choice lamb for the freezer. Both pork and lamb carcasses are from young animals, and the quality is less variable than in beef.

It is vitally important that all meat for the freezer be properly wrapped in moisture- and vapor-proof wraps to avoid freezer burn. Steaks, chops, and meat patties should be separated by waxed freezer paper to prevent their sticking together. There are time limits for satisfactory storage; therefore, all packages should be dated so that they can be used in proper sequence. Though thawed meat can be refrozen, it does lose in quality.

Cured Meats

The curing of meat began as a means of preservation; it continues in use because curing processes effect desired color and flavor changes in cured products. Modern curing methods are quick. They do not always produce products that can be stored without refrigeration. A constant in the curing process is the application of the curing salts; in addition, products may or may not be heat processed, with or without smoking. Cured meats include salt pork, bacon, ham, picnic shoulder, smoked pork cuts, Canadian-style bacon, dried beef, corned beef, and some sausage products.

The main ingredients of the curing mixture are sodium chloride, sodium or potassium nitrate and nitrite, and sugar; in addition the mixture may contain ascorbic or citric acid and other substances that enhance color development and various phosphates that favor moisture retention. The curing mixture may be applied dry to the meat as in the making of salt pork and Smithfield and Italian-style hams. Curing takes place when the salts are dissolved by meat juices and then penetrate the meat. The dry curing mix may be applied to the meat, and the meat may then be covered with a solution of the mixture called the *pickle,* as in curing bacon. Or cuts may be immersed in the pickle or the pickle may be injected, as in curing hams. The pink color of cured meats is produced by the action of sodium nitrite on meat pigments and subsequent heating. The safety of the nitrite is suspect; it is under study. At sometime during the 1970's its safety will be established or limitations on its use will be forthcoming.

In the preparation of hams the curing solution is pumped into the ham, which is then rolled in brine, hung to drain briefly, and then smoked.

Smoked or *cook-before-eating hams* are heated to an internal temperature of 140°F, a temperature high enough to destroy *trichinae*. *Fully cooked hams* are heated to an internal temperature of 150°F. Such hams can be safely eaten without further heating; however, palatability is improved if they are heated to 130°F before eating. If it has been prepared under federal inspection, a product labeled "ham" has, during the smoking process, been shrunk back in weight to its original fresh weight. Hams weighing more than original fresh weight must be labeled "ham, water added" if they contain up to 10 per cent added moisture, "imitation ham" if they contain more than 10 per cent added moisture. Hams are prepared only from the hind quarter of the carcass; the products prepared from the fore quarter must be designated as "smoked picnic shoulder," "smoked Boston butt," "smoked pork cuts," or other names that clearly inform that they are not ham. Forequarter cuts are priced lower than ham. Ham halves are labeled "butt half" and "shank half"; hams from which center slices are removed should be labeled "butt end" or "butt portion" and "shank end" or "shank portion" to inform the consumer that the center part of the ham has been removed. The butt part has a higher ratio of lean to bone than the shank part and is often priced higher. Boneless hams from which skin and almost all fat have been removed have been widely accepted because of their convenience and ease of serving.

Ham and other cured pork cuts are canned. Not all canned products have been smoked, but labels must inform as to whether the product within the can has been smoked or not. Although fully cooked, not all canned hams have been processed to the degree that they can be stored at room temperature. Those that are labeled "Perishable—Keep under Refrigeration" must be stored like fresh meat in the refrigerator. Fully processed canned hams are nonperishable and may be shelf stored. It is important to read the label to know exactly what the product is. When the meat product is put into cans, it may have an increase of up to 8 per cent over curing weight; dry gelatin is put into the can to combine with the juices as they cook out during heat processing. For this reason, a product may be labeled "Fully Cooked Ham with Natural Juices, Gelatin Added." The product in the can is ham by definition but it is only part or parts of a ham, excepting in the largest cans, which may contain a whole ham. The product in the can is bone free but not fat free; it is frequently a disappointment to the consumer, who finds that it does not slice out to give pleasing looking servings. The nonperishable hams have less flavor than the perishable ones; neither has the palatability qualities of uncanned ham. A Consumers Union study revealed that there was little difference in the cost per pound of edible weight between canned and uncanned hams; however, because of the greater water content of the canned hams, the cost per pound of protein was considerably less for uncanned ham than for canned hams (1).

Dry-cured and *aged hams* are produced in some regions of the United States, for example, Virginia, Kentucky, Georgia, and Tennessee. These so-called country-style hams undergo dry curing, slow smoking, and long drying. The surface of the ham is frequently rubbed with black pepper before smoking; such hams have a characteristic flavor and a firm texture, moisture loss having reduced the ham to about 85 per cent of fresh weight during aging. They must be fully cooked before eating. They are priced much higher than the usual ham available in the supermarket. *Prosciutto hams* are given long, dry cures and smoked; those prepared under federal inspection can be safely eaten without cooking.

Top-quality hams range in weight from eight to eighteen pounds, but much larger ones can be purchased. Lighter-weight hams are priced higher than heavier hams. Center-cut slices from hams are priced higher than the whole ham or the remaining parts. The product called *boiled ham* is cured and cooked, but not smoked.

Canadian-style bacon is the cured boned loin; it costs more per pound than ham. It contains very little fat. It yields four to five average servings per pound; as an accompaniment to eggs it will provide about eight portions.

In the preparation of *bacon*, hog bellies are trimmed into blocks; the odd-shaped pieces become bacon ends. Pieces are cured and smoked and then pressed into uniform blocks for slicing. Thin-sliced bacon averages thirty slices per pound and regular-sliced averages twenty-four slices per pound. Slab bacon that is sliced at home is the same product, though it is less perishable than the presliced bacon. Packaged, presliced bacon is perishable and quickly becomes rancid because it is fast cured; it would be desirable that packaged bacon carry the date of packaging. Bacon should be kept refrigerated and though it can be frozen, freezing is not recommended because the product loses quality. The similar beef cut similarly cured is called *breakfast beef*; it would be misbranding to label it "bacon."

Corned beef is prepared by the curing of brisket, plate, and rump cuts from fairly high-grade beef carcasses in pickle. All cuts contain added moisture: brisket, 20 per cent more than uncured weight; others, 10 per cent. When bought directly from the cure, corned beef must be fully cooked. *Pastrami* is prepared from the same beef cuts; it is dry cured, rubbed with spices and black pepper, smoked, and cooked. It may be eaten without further cooking. *Chipped* or *dried, sliced beef* is prepared by the curing and drying of cuts from the rounds of low-grade carcasses.

Sausages

There are many varieties of sausages. They are frequently named for their place of origin; for example, the frankfurter originated in Frankfurt, Germany, and bologna, in Bologna, Italy. The many sausages differ in the kind or kinds of meat used in manufacture; in the fineness of the grind of the meat(s); in the kinds and combinations of seasonings and spices used; and in the kinds of and extent of processing. On the basis of the kind and extent of processing, sausages may be grouped into three classes: (1) fresh sausages and smoked sausages that must be cooked before eating; (2) smoked, cooked; cooked, smoked; and cooked sausages; and (3) semidry and dry sausages. Further, sausages differ in size and shape from the small breakfast links to large rings and loaves. Meats used in the making of sausage include pork, beef, veal, mutton, lamb, goat, chicken, and turkey; but most sausages are made from combinations of beef, pork, and veal. A regulation of 1971 of the United States Department of Agriculture permits the labeling of goat meat as *chevon*. Meat cuts used include pork shoulders; beef chuck, brisket, and flank; and trimmings of all kinds. The use of such meat by-products as heart meat, tongue meat, and tripe is permitted unless prohibited by state law. A long list of seasonings is used in sausage-making; it would include anise, allspice, caraway, cardamom, chives, cloves, coriander, dill, garlic, ginger, mustard, nutmeg, onion, black and white and red pepper, thyme, and others. A particular seasoning may be peculiar to a particular sausage. It is permitted that some sausages contain such binders and extenders as cereal, vegetable starch, and nonfat dry milk to the extent of 3.5 per cent or isolated soy protein to 2 per cent of the finished product. It is required that labels bear a list of the ingredients in a sausage in decreasing order of predominance, excepting seasonings.

Fresh sausages that must be cooked before eating are available, in this age of convenience foods, partially cooked by parboiling. The fresh sausage mostly widely eaten is fresh pork sausage. It is seasoned with salt, sage, pepper, and sugar. It may be purchased in links, rolls, bars, patties, and in bulk. That in interstate commerce may contain no more than 3 per cent added water and no more than 50 per cent fat as derived from the meat pieces used, i.e., fat may not be added in sausage-making. Pork sausage labeled as "country style" or "farm style" cannot contain binder or extender. A product labeled as "sausage," "breakfast sausage," or "fresh sausage" contains pork, but in addition it may contain beef and/or other permitted meat by-products. *Bockwurst* is a fresh sausage prepared from pork and veal and seasoned with chives, cloves, lemon, mace, sage, and white pepper. It is traditionally eaten at Easter time. *Bratwurst* as sold in the United States is made from beef, pork, and veal. It is seasoned with coriander, ginger, mustard, and lemon. Fresh *Thuringer* is similarly composed but is seasoned with caraway, celery seed, coriander, ginger, and mace. Pork sausage, breakfast sausage, and Thuringer are available smoked; they must be cooked before eating.

Smoked, cooked sausages are smoked after cooking; cooked, smoked sausages are cooked after smoking; and cooked sausages are exactly that. Smoked, cooked sausages are prepared from cured meats or the sausage mixture is cured during sausage-making. In the preparation of smoked, cooked sausages, the sausage mixture is shaped by being stuffed into casings and then linked; the product is given either a light or heavy smoke; finally, the product is cooked. They may be eaten without further cooking, but their flavor is enhanced by heating. Some of the better-known sausages in this group are bologna, the second of all sausage favorites; brotwurst; frankfurters, the first of all sausage favorites; knackwurst; and mettwurst. *Bologna* is made of finely cut cured beef and pork. It is usually seasoned with cloves, coriander, garlic, and ginger, though allspice, caraway, mace, nutmeg, and pepper may be included. *Brotwurst* is made of cured pork and veal or beef. It is seasoned with coriander, ginger, mustard, and lemon juice and rind. It is shaped into fat links about four inches long. *Frankfurters* are made exclusively from beef or from combinations of beef, pork, mutton, lamb, veal, goat, and poultry. Any frankfurter that contains more than 15 per cent of poultry meat must be labeled "Hot Dog with Chicken Added" or some similar distinguishing name. Frankfurters can be "all meat" or they can contain 3.5 per cent of nonfat dry milk and/ or cereal as a binding agent. They can contain no more than 10 per cent of added water; any products that exceed limits in the use of water or binder must be labeled "imitation frankfurter." They can contain no more than 30 per cent fat. In the making of frankfurters, the meats are ground, curing salts and spices are added, water is added as mixing and grinding continue, and the mixture is stuffed into natural or artificial casings. The product is smoked for one to three hours, then cooked, and finally, if the product is the skinless type, the artificial casings are removed. The commonly used spices include pepper, nutmeg, mace, cinnamon, mustard, coriander, sage, and garlic. Brand differences may be differences in spicing formulas. *Knackwurst* resembles the frankfurter but contains more garlic. This sausage is served with sauerkraut and German potato salad. *Mettwurst* is prepared with cured beef and pork. It is usually spiced with allspice, coriander, ginger, and mustard. *Smokies* are made of coarsely ground beef and pork; they are similar to frankfurters but are more heavily smoked.

Liver sausage is a cooked sausage that can be made from a variety of meats and meat by-products; it must contain not less than 30 per cent of liver computed on the weight of the fresh liver. It is seasoned with onions, coriander, ginger, marjoram, and mustard. *Braunschweiger* is smoked liver sausage; that is, it is a sausage that is smoked after cooking. So-called *luncheon meats* are cooked sausages. They are available in infinite variety. The meat components, seasonings, and fineness of grind differ for the different kinds.

Since 1969, cooked sausage products in interstate commerce have been limited in fat content to 30 per cent in the finished product. Partially de-fatted pork tissue or partially defatted beef tissue may make up to 15 per cent of the meat component. They may contain up to 15 per cent of poultry products without a change in the name of the product; when more than 15 per cent is present, poultry must appear in the product name. Labeled as "all meat," they are made only from muscle meat and contain no extenders. Labeled as "all beef," they can contain only meat from beef animals.

Dry and *semidry sausages* are also known as summer sausage. The low moisture content and salt content are preservative; hence, they are less perishable than the sausages previously described. In the preparation of the dry sausages, the meats are ground and mixed with the curing ingredients and spices; the mixture is stuffed into casings; the sausages are then dried. The dry, or hard, sausages have moisture content reduced more than 20 per cent; the semidry, less than 20 per cent. Cervelats and salamis are the two most familiar groups of dry sausage products. Generally, the *cervelats* are semidry, though they may be dry; they are mildly seasoned and they are smoked. Generally, the salamis are dry, though they may be semidry; they are highly seasoned and may or may not be smoked. Types of cervelat differ according to the country of origin in the ratio of beef to pork, seasonings, and the degree of smoking. American cervelat is called *summer sausage*; it is usually made of all beef, is soft and mild in flavor, and is smoked. Swedish cervelat is made of coarsely ground beef and sometimes pork; it is seasoned with thyme, is salty, and is heavily smoked. The *salamis* originated in Europe, most of them in Italy, where the warm climate favored the abundant use of salt, spices, and drying as a means of meat preservation. The salamis differ in texture and spicing according to their place of origin. Italian salamis are seasoned with garlic and hot pepper. Cooked salami is a class of salami; it includes beer salami, cotto salami, and kosher salami. They are softer than the dry salamis, from which they differ mainly in that they are only briefly cured, cooked, and only briefly dried or not dried at all. Kosher salami is an all-beef product made under rabbinical supervision. *Chorizos* is a Spanish-type dry sausage made of pork and seasoned with red pepper and allspice. *Pepperoni* is an Italian dry sausage much used in making pizza. There are two types. The hot kind is made of beef and pork with chili peppers. The sweet pepperoni is usually made of all pork and mildly seasoned. Seasonings used in both types include allspice, anise, garlic, and peppers of different kinds. *Lebanon bologna* is a semidry sausage. Its place of origin was Lebanon, Pennsylvania. It is usually an all-beef product, heavily smoked, and seasoned with cloves, coriander, garlic, and ginger.

Hamburger and Ground Beef

About one half of the beef consumed in the United States is eaten in ground forms. Some of these are defined in the regulations promulgated for the administration of the Wholesome Meat Act. *Hamburger* is chopped fresh and/or frozen beef with or without added beef fat as such and/or seasoning. Fat content cannot exceed 30 per cent; and the product cannot contain added water or extenders or binders. *Ground beef* or *chopped beef* consists of chopped fresh and/or frozen beef with or without seasoning and without added beef fat, water, or extenders or binders. Fat content cannot exceed 30 per cent. *Ground chuck, ground round,* and *ground sirloin* are prepared by the grinding of those cuts; they are not defined and they have fat contents of about 10 to 20 per cent, 10 per cent, and 20 per cent, respectively. *Beef patties* are defined: they consist of chopped fresh and/or frozen beef with or without added beef fat, seasonings, extenders, partially defatted beef tissue, and water. *Prefabricated steaks* are defined. They may be composed of beef, veal, or combinations thereof as beef and veal or veal and beef. They cannot contain more than 30 per cent fat, added water, or binder or extender. Seasonings or flavorings permitted in these products include MSG, sweetener, hydrolyzed plant protein, and selected flavor-protecting additives. The earlier-mentioned study by the Consumers Union (2) suggested that the consumer got the best product by buying a cut of beef and having it ground to order in the supermarket or by grinding it in the home kitchen.

Kosher Meats

Kosher meats and kosher further-processed meat food products are those that are clean and fit for food according to the Jewish dietary laws, which require that animals be ritually slain and that their blood be ritually drawn. All processing must be under orthodox rabbinical supervision, and only kosher ingredients and kosher equipment can be used. Equipment can be cleaned only with kosher agents—those of vegetable or synthetic origin. Three symbols mark food as kosher. The letter *K* marks food approved by the supervisory service of the Joseph Jacobs Organization of New York City. The letters *VH* are authorized by the Vaad Harabonium in Massachusetts. The U emblem is that of the Union of Orthodox Jewish Congregations of America; it is registered in the United States patent office. A variety of kosher products is manufactured by four hundred or more companies for the million or so families that purchase kosher food. Many non-Jewish consumers purchase kosher food, perhaps for the reason that they think it superior in quality and wholesomeness.

Tenderizing Meats

Only approximately one quarter of the cuts from a beef carcass are inherently tender. Moist heat methods of cooking tenderize less tender cuts; however, these methods are time-consuming, and they effect texture changes that many persons do not favor. Grinding or other mechanical treatment of less tender cuts makes it possible to treat the products like tender cuts; for example, hamburgers and fabricated steaks can be broiled and cube steaks can be pan-fried. In addition to these methods of tenderizing, enzymatic treatment tenderizes.

Tenderizing by enzyme action comes about in three ways. First, enzymes within the tissues of the animal carcass will modify tissues chemically and physically to effect tenderizing. Considerable tenderizing occurs during the movement of fresh meat from packer to use by the consumer, a period of from six to ten days. Ribs and loins of beef of high quality and lamb and mutton are aged both to increase tenderness and to develop flavor. Two methods of aging are in use. In *dry aging,* beef is held at temperatures from 34°F to 38°F for two to six weeks. Only beef with a well-developed layer of external fat that protects against spoilage and dehydration is so aged. Humidity in the aging room is controlled to achieve the desired effect, either mold development to produce a gamey flavor or minimum dehydration. This method of aging is expensive; hence, cuts are priced accordingly. *Fast-aged* beef is held at about 70°F for two days at high humidity levels; ultraviolet light is used to control spoilage. Dry-aged beef goes to the restaurant trade; fast-aged, into retail trade. Pork is not aged because rancidity develops in the fat. Veal has too little external fat to permit aging.

Secondly, proteolytic enzymes can be applied to or injected into cuts commercially. In the home kitchen, a salt mixture containing the enzymes can be sprinkled over the surface of a cut. Piercing with a fork permits the enzyme to penetrate the meat. The enzyme is active between 130°F and 160°F and is inactivated as temperature rises during cooking. Enzyme treatment permits the use of dry heat methods of cooking for less tender cuts. Cuts treated commercially with enzymes must bear labels stating this fact.

Lastly, a solution of a tenderizing enzyme is injected into animals before slaughter; hence, the enzyme will be present in all parts of the muscles. This commercial process is patented. Beef cuts so prepared are higher priced than untreated cuts of comparable grade, but are less expensive than tender cuts from top-quality carcasses.

Meat Extenders and Meat Analogs

Modern technology has produced protein-rich extenders for meat in meat food products; it has also produced meat analogs—sometimes described as simulated meats, synthetic meats, and imitation meats—that look, taste, and smell like the meats they simulate. In general, the soybean is the protein source. Three products are utilized: soy flour or grits, soy concentrates, and soy isolates with protein contents of 40 to 55, 60 to 70, and 90 or more per cent protein, respectively. For use as meat products, the soy products are textured either by extrusion or spinning. Extruded products are less expensive than spun products; in general, extruded products are used as extenders. For the manufacture of the analogs, the spun products are variously treated to form fibers that can be compacted to simulate the structure and texture of meats. The soy protein hydrates at a ratio of one part to three parts of water, so that the percentage of protein in the simulated product is comparable to that of fresh meat. Vitamins, minerals, fats, and amino acids can be added to produce products comparable in composition to meat. The addition of colorants and flavor substances provides the appearance and flavor and aroma characteristic of the different kinds of meat. Products that resemble beef, ham, bacon, chicken, and turkey prepared in various styles are available. Arguments in favor of the analogs are

1. Nutritional composition can be engineered, that is, fat and cholesterol can be modified or eliminated and nutrients needed to improve the quality of the national diet can be added.
2. Quality is constant because products are made by formula.
3. They are convenient because they are ready to heat and eat.
4. Cost could be less than that of fresh meat cuts.

Meat analogs are not expected to make major gains in use in the 1970's. Consumption is by institutions, food faddists, and persons who avoid meats for religious reasons.

Soy protein products will probably increase in use as extenders in the 1970's. At moderate usage levels, the extenders do not change the flavor of a meat food product as, for example, meat loaves, sausages, or chili. The soy protein product absorbs the juices and fat that cook out of meat, thereby reducing cooking losses and resulting in juicier products. The use of extenders is limited to small percentages in products for which there are definitions and standards of identity. However, foods eaten away from home can contain higher percentages of extender because they are not regulated by the same labeling requirements as food sold at retail. For example, hamburger sold at retail does not contain extender, but hamburgers eaten at a drive-in can contain extender. Modifications of current definitions and standards of identity would permit greater use of extender. In 1971, the United States Department of Agriculture permitted certain soy extenders to be used as part of the protein requirement in the school lunch program. There is opposition to the use of extenders because many consumers would be unaware of the presence of the vegetable protein in products even though its presence was noted in the label.

In December 1970, a petition was filed that proposed the establishment of a definition and a standard of identity for a class of foods to be known as *textured protein products* prepared from vegetable protein and other ingredients. The 1970 proposal would establish the nutrient content of the textured protein products on the basis of the nutrient content of representative protein foods as listed in the United States Department of Agriculture Handbook, No. 8, "Composition of Foods." Optional ingredients would include other edible proteins, amino acids, minerals, vitamins, edible fats and oils, natural and artificial flavors and colors, and such permitted additives as would serve a purpose in production. The textured protein products would be named by the physical form, e.g., "chunks" or "slices," and would be characterized as "flavored like _____" or "_____-like flavor" or "with a flavor like _____." For example, a product that simulated chicken would have *chicken* appearing in the above blanks. Labeling requirements would make mandatory a listing of all ingredients in descending order of predominance, including the name of the textured protein. The promulgation of a definition and standard of identity for textured protein foods will definitely come in the 1970's.

FISH AND SHELLFISH

Americans buy more fresh than frozen fish and shellfish; but they buy more that is canned than fresh. Per-capita consumption was 10.5 pounds in 1957–1959 and only 11.3 pounds in 1970. The problem of the mercury pollution of fish will quite likely affect fish consumption in the 1970's. The pollution of estuarine waters with sewage has decreased the take of oysters and other shellfish.

Fresh Fish

Fresh fish can be purchased in any of the following styles, depending on the kind: whole as it comes from the water; drawn—entrails removed; dressed or pan-dressed—scales, entrails, and usually the head, tail, and fins removed; steaks—cross-section slices cut five-eighths to one inch thick from dressed fish; chunks—crosswise sections of large dressed fish; and fillets—the sides of fish cut lengthwise away from the backbone with or without removal of the skin. The signs of freshness in fish are readily recognizable: fresh whole fish should have bulging eyes, reddish-pink gills free of slime, iridescent skin, firm flesh, and a fresh, clean odor. Dressed fish, chunks, steaks, and fillets should exhibit these characteristics when relevant and in addition should exhibit a fresh-cut appearance without evidence of browning or drying. The pollution of lakes and rivers has reduced the supply of freshwater fish. Proper chilling of ocean catches and shipment by air favor the availability of fresh ocean fish in large urban markets.

Frozen Fish

Many species of fish are available frozen; in addition, frozen ready-to-cook breaded products and frozen precooked products can be purchased.

Some products are graded and bear the proper inspection seal. In 1971, the Food and Drug Administration recommended that swordfish no longer be consumed because of mercury contamination. Standards of identity are in process for frozen breaded fish portions and frozen breaded fish sticks; it is probable that they will be finalized in the 1970's.

Canned Fish

Approximately one half of the fish consumed in the United States is canned. Tuna, salmon, and sardines are the kinds most frequently purchased. Canned tuna has been defined and a standard of fill of container has been established. The definition and standard of identity for canned tuna name the species of fish that may be canned and labeled as tuna; specify that only loins and other striated muscles free of skin, scales, bones, gills, blood clots, and viscera may be used; define what shall be in the can when the style of pack is labeled as "solid pack," "chunks," "flakes," or "grated tuna"; establish the color of tuna as white, light, dark, and blended, on the basis of Munsell values; name the packing media and optional ingredients; and specify that the name of a pack shall be formed by combining the designation of the form of the pack with the color of the pack, for example, "Solid-Pack White Tuna." The style of pack makes little difference in the weight of the contents of cans except that the solid-pack cans contain a little more than the other styles. Several species of tuna are canned, but of these only the Albacore is white. Cans of tuna vary widely in cost; the species and the color of the fish and the style of the pack affect cost. Solid-pack white tuna costs more than grated dark or blended tuna. The intended use would dictate the kind of pack to be purchased. Meat from fish commonly known as bonito or bonita (*Sarda chilensis*) and "yellowtail" (*Seriola dorsalis*) may not be labeled as "tuna," but must be labeled as "bonito" or "bonita" or "yellowtail." They are less expensive than tuna. Quantities of canned tuna were withdrawn from the market because of mercury contamination in the winter of 1970.

Work on establishing a standard of identity and fill of container for salmon was in process (1972). Six species of salmon are canned. The species differ in color, texture, and flavor. The higher-priced products are deeper in color and have a higher oil content. In descending order of price, they are red or sockeye salmon, chinook or king salmon, medium red or silver-side or coho salmon, pink salmon, and chum or keta salmon. This is also a list in descending order of color from orange-red to pale pink. The king or chinook is considered the best. The less expensive salmon is a good choice for making salmon loaf and casserole dishes.

Sardines are small fish of different species of the herring family. A standard of identity for sardines is scheduled and may be forthcoming in the 1970's. Maine sardines are immature Atlantic herring (*Clupea harengus*).

The State of Maine promulgated, in 1958, standards for grades and fill of container for "Canned Maine Sardines in Oil." Canned Maine sardines may be Fancy, Extra Standard, Standard, or Substandard in quality. Grade is established by the scoring of odor, taste, texture, and freedom from defects (workmanship). The heads must always be removed, but tails must be removed only if the number of fish in a can is fewer than eight.

Sardines are imported from several countries, especially the Scandinavian ones. The European pilchard (*Sardinia pilchardus* or *Clupea pilchardus*) and brisling or sprat (*Clupea sprattus*) are commonly packed in oil and labeled as sardines. The terms *brisling sardines* and *sild sardines* are permissible in labeling small brisling and herring, respectively. All imported foods are inspected for wholesomeness and for conformity with other requirements of United States food laws.

Anchovies have been adopted widely by an affluent society; they are often present in Greek salad, Caesar's salad, and Green Goddess dressing. They are fish of the family *Engraulidae*; no other small fish, though they may resemble anchovies, can be labeled as anchovies. The product in cans is the fillets, which are packed in oil either flat or rolled around a caper after preservation by salting or pickling. Anchovy paste contains comminuted anchovies; other ingredients present must be named on the label.

Caviar, a product better known in the 1970's than it was in the 1950's, is sturgeon roe prepared by a special process. It is imported from Russia and Iran. It is gray to black in color, and the size of the eggs ranges from tiny to larger. Caviar prepared from other fish varieties must be identified by the name of the fish of origin. Red caviar is prepared from salmon roe. The best Russian caviar is very expensive.

Shellfish

Shellfish are of two types: mollusks and crustaceans. The mollusks are bivalves; they have hard, hinged shells. Oysters, clams, and scallops are mollusks. The crustaceans have segmented shells and include shrimp, lobsters, and crabs. The distribution of fresh shellfish is somewhat limited, but all can be purchased frozen or canned in most markets. In general, they are priced higher per portion than fish and many cuts of meat. The best liked are shrimp, lobster, and crab.

Fresh shrimp may be purchased in a few metropolitan markets; canned and frozen, in most supermarkets; and freeze-dried, in some markets. Headless shrimp are block-frozen and individually quick-frozen. Frozen shrimp are available in the shell, deshelled and deveined, and cooked or uncooked. The best and most convenient of these is the deshelled and deveined, uncooked product. In addition, breaded cooked and ready-to-cook breaded shrimp, stuffed shrimp, cocktail shrimp with sauce, and numerous other convenience dishes are available frozen. Although shrimp are found in all the coastal waters of the United States from Maine to Alaska, the United States imports about half of the quantity consumed from more than sixty countries. Shrimp from around the world differ in color, size, and shape. The color range is from greenish-gray to brownish-red, but regardless of color in the raw, all cooked shrimp have the same pinkish color. They also have about the same flavor. The term *green shrimp* refers to all or any uncooked shrimp. Shrimp vary in size from tiny ones no larger than a dime, which may number as many as 300 per pound, to jumbos that number 10 to 15 per pound. In the supermarket they are sold by size: small—about 60 per pound; medium—40 to 50 per pound; large—about 20 per pound. They are priced accordingly. They are some-times available in mixed sizes and pieces labeled "salad shrimp." Shape-wise, some shrimp are pencil slim and others are plump. Shrimp are sized for canning; small, medium, and large sizes can be found, though not always in the same market. Fill of container has been established for shrimp canned in nontransparent containers. Travel outside of the United States has introduced Americans to the prawn, to scampi, and to the lan-goustine. All are members of the same crustacean family but they are not shrimp, though they do resemble them.

There are two kinds of lobsters: the true lobster and the spiny or rock lobster. The true lobster (family *Homaridae*) is taken from North Atlantic waters, has claws, and is superior in flavor to the spiny lobster. The rock or spiny lobster (family *Palinuridae*) is a sea crayfish, of which only the tail provides meat. There are several kinds marketed: those from Cuba, Florida, and the Bahamas have a smooth, brownish-green shell with white spots; those from South Africa, Australia, and New Zealand, a rough shell with color varying from maroon to brown; those from Southern California and Mexico, a smooth yellow-green shell. The meat is white. Tails vary from small to large; frequently the small ones are more tender than the very large ones. If purchased fresh, either type of lobster should be alive and remain so until cooked by being dropped into boiling water. In many areas, lobster can be purchased only canned or frozen.

There is little fresh crab available except in coastal areas. Canned crab meat, precooked and frozen crab meat, and precooked and frozen crab dishes are widely available. Crab meat is derived from four varieties of crabs: the blue crab, the New England rock crab, the Pacific or Dungeness crab, and the king crab of Alaska. Both body meat and claw meat are used. The body meat of the blue crab is white, that of the claws, brownish. The meat of the New England crab is brownish. The Pacific crab has reddish claw meat and white body meat. The meat of the king crab is white with a red external surface; in general, only the claw meat is used. Soft-shelled crabs are blue crabs taken after the hard shell has been discarded and the new one is still soft. Crab meat is fairly expensive.

Oysters are bivalves. They are graded and sold by size. On the east coast,

Standards are small; Selects, medium; Extra Selects, large; and Counts, extra large. Pacific oysters are similarly graded but are called by size: Small, Medium, Large, and Extra Large. However, the number of oysters per gallon is greater for Atlantic oysters than for Pacific oysters of the same size designation; that is, Selects or medium run 210 to 300 oysters per gallon, whereas Medium Pacific oysters run 64 to 96 per gallon.

Definitions and standards of identity have been promulgated for canned oysters and shucked raw oysters. Fill of container has been established for canned oysters. The standards for shucked raw oysters define conditions for controlling water content; they also establish size by defining the number of oysters per gallon—that is, Extra Selects are of such a size that one gallon contains more than 160 oysters but not more than 210 oysters. In the original package or can there should be no more than 10 per cent liquid by weight. Oysters should be creamy white, and the liquid should be clear. There has long been a taboo on the eating of fresh oysters during the months May through August. There are two explanations for the taboo. One is that these months are the breeding season and the oysters are less succulent. The other is that oysters, and other shellfish, eaten during these months can cause food poisoning. During these months a food abundantly available to the shellfish is an organism called *Gonyaulax catanella*; this organism though harmless to the oyster is toxic for man.

Scallops, like oysters, are derived from bivalves. A scallop is part of the muscle used in the opening and closing of the shell. Scallops come in two sizes: the large white cubes from sea scallops and the smaller pinkish cubes from bay scallops. The smaller ones are more expensive and a greater delicacy than the larger ones. They are marketed ready-to-cook and precooked and frozen.

Several species of clams are eaten. They are not abundantly available fresh but can be purchased canned, frozen raw, and frozen fried. Pacific Coast clams are butter, littleneck, pismo, and razor clams. Atlantic Coast clams are hard, soft, and surf clams. The hard-shell clams are called *quahog* in New England.

MEAT FOOD PRODUCTS AND POULTRY FOOD PRODUCTS

Meat and poultry food products include cooked meats, sausages, ready-made dishes, and such ready-for-cooking items as breaded chops and steaks. The variety is great and is ever increasing. The products are available fresh, precooked and frozen, precooked, frozen, dehydrated, and canned.

If we are to decide rationally about purchasing ready-mades, it is helpful to know the extent to which their production is regulated. For products that move in interstate commerce, the following kinds of regulations exist. First, the meat and poultry component and all other ingredients must have been inspected for wholesomeness. Second, definitions and standards of identity establish the composition of some meat and poultry food products; they establish minimum meat content and name the other ingredients that may or must be present in a product. Third, all processors are required to register complete formulas for the products they make with the Consumer and Marketing Service of the United States Department of Agriculture. These formulas and the labels for the finished products must be approved. Last, for all undefined products there must be a truthful label and a listing of ingredients in decreasing order of predominance from the one present in greatest weight to the one present in least amount. For products moving only in intrastate commerce, inspection equal to federal inspection is mandatory. However, states differ in standards for products and the labeling thereof. Probably, a large proportion of meat and poultry food products move in interstate commerce.

Defined Meat Food Products

Definitions and standards of identity or composition require that meat food products contain meat in accordance with the following stipulations.

1. A product marked "all beef" or "all pork" can contain no meat other than the kind named. *Meat* means only muscle tissue with natural amounts of fat. An *all meat* product contains no extenders, such as cereal or nonfat dry milk.

2. Chili con carne with beans—not less than 25 per cent meat computed on the weight of the fresh meat. Of this amount 25 per cent can be head meat, cheek meat, and heart meat exclusive of the heart cap when so designated on the label.

3. Chili con carne—not less than 40 per cent meat computed on the weight of the fresh meat. Of this, 25 per cent may be as in 2. The product may contain not more than 8 per cent, individually or collectively, of cereal, soy flour, soy protein concentrate, isolated soy protein, or nonfat dry milk.

4. Hash—not less than 35 per cent meat computed on the weight of the cooked and trimmed meat. Five per cent of the meat ingredient may be as in 2 for corned beef hash, but not in beef hash.

5. Meat stews—not less than 25 per cent meat of the kind named on the label, computed on the weight of the fresh meat.

6. Spaghetti with meat balls and sauce, spaghetti with meat and sauce —not less than 12 per cent meat computed on fresh weight. The meat balls may be prepared with not more than 12 per cent, collectively or individually, cereal, nonfat dry milk, or soy protein product.

7. Spaghetti sauce with meat—not less than 6 per cent meat computed on fresh weight.

8. Lima beans with ham in sauce, beans with ham in sauce, beans with bacon in sauce—not less than 12 per cent ham or cooked bacon.

9. Chow mein vegetables with meat, chop suey vegetables with meat —not less than 12 per cent meat based on fresh weight prior to inclusion with other ingredients.

10. Beans with frankfurters in sauce, sauerkraut with weiners and juice, and similar products—not less than 20 per cent frankfurters based on cooked weight prior to inclusion with beans or sauerkraut.

11. Beef with gravy and gravy with beef—at least 50 per cent meat for the former, 35 per cent meat for the latter on the cooked basis; the beef shall not contain more than 30 per cent trimmable fat.

12. Meat pies—not less than 25 per cent meat on the basis of fresh uncooked meat.

13. Pizza with meat—15 per cent meat.

14. Pizza with sausage—12 per cent cooked sausage or 10 per cent dry sausage.

15. Liver sausage and other liver products—not less than 30 per cent liver computed on the fresh basis.

16. Ham spread, tongue spread, and similar products—not less than 50 per cent of the meat ingredient computed on the weight of the fresh meat. Ham spread can contain no more than 35 per cent fat.

17. Potted meat food product and deviled meat food product—shall contain no extenders and water only to replace that lost during processing.

18. Beef Stroganoff—45 per cent fresh uncooked beef or 30 per cent cooked beef, and at least 10 per cent sour cream.

19. Breaded chops, steaks, cutlets—breading not to exceed 30 per cent of finished weight.

20. Frozen dinners—not less than 25 per cent cooked meat or meat food product exclusive of appetizer, bread, and dessert.

21. Lasagna with meat sauce—at least 12 per cent meat.

22. Veal birds—at least 60 per cent meat, not more than 40 per cent stuffing.

23. Veal *cordon bleu*—60 per cent veal, 5 per cent ham and Swiss, Gruyère, or Mozzarella cheese.

Defined Poultry Food Products

Poultry food product means any food consisting of any edible part or parts of poultry in combination with other ingredients. Some definitions and regulations have been promulgated that establish the quantities of poultry in poultry food products, the ratio of light to dark meat in them, the inclusion of skin and fat in them, and labeling requirements. These are summarized here.

1.   The natural proportions of skin on the whole boneless carcass are for chicken, 20 per cent raw and 25 per cent cooked; for turkeys, 15 per cent raw and 20 per cent cooked.

2.   Uses of the terms *light* and *dark meat* must conform to the following specifications:

	Per Cent Light Meat	Per Cent Dark Meat
Natural proportions	50–65	50–35
Light meat	100	0
Dark meat	0	100
Light and dark meat	51–65	49–35
Dark and light meat	35–49	65–51
Mostly white meat	66 or more	34 or less
Mostly dark meat	34 or less	66 or more

3.   Products containing light and dark chicken or turkey meat in other than natural proportions must clearly and conspicuously state the type(s) of meat in use in conjunction with the name of the food, e.g., "Boned Turkey (Dark Meat)."

4.   Cooked poultry meat used in making poultry food products must have a solids content of 34 per cent; if it does not, the percentage of poultry meat required in a product must be increased in relation to the deficiency.

5.   Canned, boned poultry contains light and dark meats, fats, and skin in natural proportions according to kind. Canned and boned solid-pack products must contain a minimum of 95 per cent of poultry meat, including skin and fat. Canned poultry with broth must contain at least 80 per cent poultry meat, skin, and fat. The percentage of poultry meat may decrease to 50 per cent if statement is made of the percentage of broth.

6.   Frozen poultry pies must contain not less than 14 per cent of cooked, deboned poultry of the kind indicated on the label, or one and one-eighth ounces per eight-ounce pie. Note that this is less than one half of an average serving of meat.

7.   Frozen poultry dinners must contain not less than two ounces or 18 per cent of cooked, deboned poultry meat of the kind indicated on the label.

8.   Poultry burgers must consist of 100 per cent poultry meat of the kind indicated on the label. Skin and fat cannot be present in excess of natural proportions. Products containing binders or fillers must be labeled "patties" and identified as to kind, i.e., "chicken patties."

9.   The percentages of poultry in poultry dishes are calculated on an

as-serve basis; definitions are of the minimums of cooked, deboned poultry meat of the kind named on the label. Percentages of poultry meat are

(a) Poultry soups must contain not less than 2 per cent.

(b) Chop suey with poultry must contain not less than 2 per cent, but poultry chop suey and poultry chow mein must contain not less than 4 per cent.

(c) Poultry tamales and dumplings or noodles with poultry must contain not less than 6 per cent; poultry stew, not less than 12 per cent; and poultry with noodles or dumplings, 15 per cent.

(d) Creamed poultry, poultry cacciatore, poultry fricassee, and poultry à la king must all contain not less than 20 per cent.

(e) Sliced poultry with gravy must contain not less than 35 per cent poultry meat.

10. Cooked poultry roasts must have been heated to an internal temperature of 160°F.

The list of defined ready-made dishes is short; a list of available ready-made dishes would be long. The consumer must buy them and try them if she is to know their ingredient composition. However, before she buys, she can rule out some of the available products by estimating cost per portion, in accordance with the number of servings suggested on the label. For example, if lobster Newburg will cost her ninety-eight cents per serving and her daily meat allowance is forty cents per person, then frozen precooked lobster Newburg is a ready-made she need not buy and try. On the other hand, if frozen prepared chicken à la king costs only forty cents per serving, she may wish to buy and try it. If she finds the quantity of chicken skimpy, she may not buy again but make her own instead, using canned chicken and a canned soup for the sauce. All ready-made meat products are convenience foods; consumers evaluate them differently because each consumer has her own particular frame of reference for judgment.

SOME GUIDES TO BUYING MEAT, POULTRY, AND FISH AND SHELLFISH

The average meal manager spends from one fourth to one third of her food dollars for meat, poultry, and fish and shellfish products, fresh, cured, canned, and frozen. Further, the average meal manager likes to maximize the dollars she spends for these products. A bad buy ends in waste and dissatisfaction. There is no other class of food purchases that requires as much knowledge or provides as much profit from experience as the purchase of meats. Supermarkets differ in the quality of the meats stocked, in trimming and boning practices, in pricing policy, in the names given retail cuts, and in packaging techniques. Further, there is evidence (6) that the weights recorded on meat packages are not always the true weights. The meal manager should research her market resources and patronize the store or stores that are honest and that provide her the quality she wants at the price she can pay.

1.   Because all meat and poultry must be inspected, the consumer expects to buy only wholesome products. Never buy a torn or damaged package. If any just-purchased product, fresh or frozen, has an offensive odor or is discolored, molded, or slimy when opened in the home kitchen, return it at once to the market where it was purchased.

2.   Buy graded products whenever possible. Remember that less than the best is still wholesome food; properly prepared it can be more tasty than a high-quality product poorly prepared.

3.   Learn how to identify the carcass origin of retail cuts. Many fanciful names that reveal little information are in use to describe meat cuts. For example, "Sarasota Steak" might be eye-of-round steak, sirloin tip, or a steak fabricated from a special grind of beef.

4.   Buy cuts according to intended use: less tender cuts for pot roasts, USDA Choice standing rib roast for roast beef, blade steak or round steak for Swiss steak, a sirloin steak for broiling, and so on. If two grades of beef are available in the market, choose from among them according to intended use.

5.   From among prepackaged meats with transparent wraps, choose those with a good ratio of lean to bone and fat. Note that shoppers do just this in the supermarket.

6.   Buy the quantity wanted for the intended use; too much for one meal and not enough for another may be wasteful.

7.   Read the food ads in your newspaper and buy "specials." But choose selectively. They may reflect abundant supply, as of frying chickens, or they may be loss leaders to bring customers into the supermarket. To take advantage of bargains, know the current price of the items you regularly buy, for example, the price of hamburger or sirloin steak.

8.   To match a purchase to your plan of spending for food, estimate the cost per serving. Know your average daily allowance for meat. Know how to overspend it to widen your choices, but don't overspend recklessly. See Chapter 13.

9.   Properly priced, chicken wings and backs are good buys. You can have a pot of soup and enough chicken meat for a casserole, a salad, or sandwiches.

10.   Buy the largest roast, or cut of ham, or bird that your budget permits and that you can serve out satisfactorily. Dripping and moisture losses are less and the number of servings per pound average out better from large cuts than from small ones.

11.   Large birds have a more favorable ratio of lean to bone than small ones.

12.   In general arm cuts have a better ratio of lean to bone than blade cuts, but the latter are more tender.

13.   The butt portion of a ham has a better lean to bone ratio than the shank portion; the latter should be priced lower.

14.   Compare the prices of whole and cut-up chickens, you can usually save pennies by cutting up whole birds.

15.   Ready-stuffed turkeys are more expensive than the unstuffed ones.

16.   Read the statement of weights on packages of luncheon meats, sausages, frankfurters, and specialty items; they are frequently smaller than the eight ounces or one pound that you think you are buying.

17.   White tuna is more expensive than darker tuna; solid-pack tuna is more expensive than chunk or grated tuna; pink salmon is less expensive than red salmon. Buy according to intended use; the less expensive kinds are satisfactory for casserole dishes.

18.   The best of the sirloin steaks are the pin-bone and the flat-bone cuts.

19.   Properly priced, chicken parts are as good buys as whole chickens. Proper pricing means that breasts cost about 40 per cent more; drumsticks, 25 per cent more; and thighs, 33 per cent more per pound than whole chickens.

20.   Estimate and evaluate the cost of the convenience in ready-to-heat meat, poultry, and fish dishes. Consider also the time required to heat the dish to have it safe for eating. Carefully check on the quantity of meat in these dishes; it may be far less than an average meat portion. It is quite possible to broil, pan-broil, or pan-fry something for a meal in less time, at a lower cost, and with more nutrition than some ready-to-heat-and-eat dishes require in resources and offer in protein.

How to Store Meat

Assuredly, you purchased wholesome meat. Keep it that way by proper handling and storage—clean to avoid contamination and cold to retard spoilage and protect quality.

1.   Transport fresh, cured, and frozen meat, poultry, and fish and shellfish from the store as rapidly as possible.

2.   Wash your hands thoroughly before and after touching or handling any unwrapped products.

3.   Use only clean gadgets in the handling of meats. Put them only into clean containers. Thoroughly wash the containers after each use. Thoroughly clean all surfaces on which raw meat or poultry have been placed.

4.   The temperature in the refrigerator should be 35°F to 40°F; in the freezer 0°F or less. Place meat in the coldest part of a refrigerator that is not uniformly cold throughout.

5.   Prepackaged fresh meat, chilled poultry, and fresh fish and shellfish may be held for one or two days in the transparent wrap, but be certain that the package is leakproof to avoid contaminating other foods. Use poultry and fish and seafood within two days. Loosely rewrap meat to be held longer than two days to permit moving air to dry the surface slightly and deter the growth of spoilage organisms. Any of these products purchased wrapped in butcher paper should be unwrapped and placed on a plate or tray and lightly covered with film or foil. Chops, steaks, and roasts may be held up to five days; but stew meat, ground meats, and variety meats are best used within two days.

6.   Cured meats, such as bacon, ham, and frankfurters, may be refrigerator-stored for up to one week. Ready-cooked products may be stored in the original wraps. Modern cures are nonpreservative; cured meats of the 1970's are perishable.

7.   Trim and cut into meal- or portion-sized pieces meat, poultry, fish and shellfish to be frozen for storage. Wrap tightly in moisture- and vapor-proof packaging material, foil, or film. Freeze at one time no more than two pounds per cubic foot of freezer space.

8.   The storage life of frozen fresh meats is eight to twelve months for beef and lamb roasts and beef steaks; four to eight months for pork, veal, and calf roasts; three to four months for lamb, pork, and veal chops and variety meats; two to three months for ground meats and stew meats; one to two months for pork sausage; and two to three months for cooked meats. Cured meats do not freeze well because rancidity develops quickly. Freeze them only in an emergency and then use them within one month. The storage life for frozen poultry is twelve months for chicken and turkey; six months for ducks and geese; six months for cooked poultry dishes; and four months for fried chicken. The storage life for frozen fish and seafood is four to six months only; for cooked products, only two or three months. The storage life of all of these is less if the temperature within the freezer is higher than 0°F.

9.   Tightly wrap or store in covered containers all cooked meat, poultry, and fish and shellfish and refrigerate them promptly. Separate poultry and stuffing and store them in different containers. Use them within two days. To extend their storage life, tightly wrap and freeze them. Storage life will be two to three months. Reheat frozen casseroles, stews, and other meat-containing dishes without thawing them.

10.   Frozen meat may be cooked with or without thawing but unthawed meat requires one and one third to one and one half times longer to cook than thawed meat. Thaw frozen meat in its wrappings in the refrigerator and cook it as soon as possible after thawing. Thawed meat is as perishable as fresh meat. Thawed meat and poultry may be refrozen if they are still

icy cold and refrigerator storage was limited to one or two days. Both products will lose in palatability however.

11. Frozen poultry may be cooked with or without thawing, but commercially frozen stuffed poultry should be cooked without thawing. Frozen poultry may be thawed in any of three ways. The preferred method is to thaw it in the refrigerator in its original wrapper until it is pliable. A large bird may require up to three days for thawing. Or thaw it in cold water in its watertight wrapper for more rapid thawing. Or thaw it in a cool place; but leave it in the original wrapper and place it in a double paper bag or wrap it with newspaper or place it in a corrugated paper bag to keep its surface cool.

12. Leftover broth and gravy should be refrigerated immediately and reheated to a full rolling boil before eating.

13. The average freezer will keep food frozen for two days in the time of a blackout or a power failure. Partially thawed food can be safely refrozen.

GUIDES TO MEAT COOKERY

Cook properly what you have purchased for maximum eating satisfaction and for full returns on the investment made. Two factors govern the successful cooking of meat, poultry, and fish and shellfish—temperature and time. With some exceptions, temperatures should be low to moderate. The cooking time should be no longer than that required to reach the desired degree of doneness. The qualities desired in cooked meat are tenderness, the proper texture, juiciness, and good flavor and aroma. Tenderness is inherent in some cuts of meat, young poultry, and fish and shellfish; in other cuts of meat and mature poultry it is achieved by slow cooking in moist heat. Naturally tender cuts of meat, young poultry, and fish and shellfish can be toughened by improper cooking. Juiciness is inherent and it is protected by fat and the prevention of moisture loss by evaporation. The temperature and the length of cooking time control this loss. Flavor and aroma develop during cooking; browning is an aid to this. In general, meat cuts cooked by dry heat are preferred over cuts cooked by moist heat.

1. Match the cooking method to the cut of meat and to the age of the poultry.

2. Cook by dry heat methods only tender cuts of beef, young poultry, lamb chops and roasts, veal and pork roasts, ham, hamburger, lamb and ham patties, and fish. Dry heat methods include broiling and pan-broiling; pan-frying; rotisserie cooking; and roasting and baking.

3. Cook by moist heat less tender cuts of beef, mature poultry, small veal and pork cuts, and all stew meat. Moist heat methods include brais-

ing, stewing, cooking sealed within aluminum foil, and cooking in the pressure cooker. However, you can use meat tenderizer on some less tender cuts, such as blade and arm steaks of beef, to permit the use of dry heat.

4. Thin pork chops can be pan-fried. Thicker chops can be baked. Brown well and cover tightly to braise small pork and veal cuts. Always thoroughly cook throughout all pork cuts and fresh pork sausages.

5. To minimize losses, cook bacon in the oven.

6. Also, cook fresh pork sausages and patties in the oven; or place them in a cold fry pan with one-quarter to one-half cup cold water, cover and let steam for ten minutes, remove cover and brown.

7. To limit roasting time to a minimum, use a meat thermometer and cook roasts to the desired degree of doneness: 170°F for well-done beef, pork, lamb, and veal; 160°F for medium beef and lamb; and 140°F for rare beef. The temperature rises a few degrees after a roast is removed from the oven. Make certain that the thermometer registers accurately and that it is inserted correctly.

8. Roasts carve more neatly if they are removed from the oven and held for some fifteen minutes or so before carving.

9. Pan-frying and pan-broiling differ only in that the accumulating fat is removed from the pan in pan-broiling.

10. For maximum flavor, brown well all cuts to be braised, including stew meats, Swiss steak, and pot roasts, as well as meat to be cooked in a pressure cooker.

11. Wrapping a cut or a bird in aluminum foil is to cook by moist heat. The usual oven temperature for cooking meats is 300°F or 325°F. Foil-wrapped cuts may be cooked at 200°F for a very long time. Foil-wrapped turkeys may be roasted at 400°F. The foil is removed during the last part of the cooking period to permit browning.

12. Fish and young poultry may be cooked at higher than the usual temperature of 300°F because the cooking period is short. Frequently, the fish or poultry is protected by a cover of crumbs or vegetables. Young poultry prepared this way is called *oven-fried*. Always cook poultry thoroughly.

13. In cooking ground meat, handle it as little as possible to avoid compacting the meat, thereby making it dense and hard. Broil or pan-broil hamburgers that contain no pork medium-well-done to keep them juicy.

14. Roast poultry to a temperature of 180°F to 185°F and be sure that the stuffing has reached a temperature of 165°F. Some persons roast a bird breast side up; others, breast side down. Never stuff a bird until just before it goes into the oven.

15. Cook fish and shellfish gently and briefly. Fish becomes an opaque white when done.

16. Follow directions and always thoroughly heat frozen entrees containing meat, poultry, or fish.

References Cited

1. "Canned Hams," *Consumer Reports* 35:581 (1970).
2. "A Close Look at Hamburger," *Consumer Reports* 36:478 (1971).
3. *Consumer's Knowledge and Use of Government Grades for Selected Food Items,* Marketing Research Report No. 876, Economic Research Service, United States Department of Agriculture, Washington, D.C. (1970), p. iv.
4. *Food Consumption of Households in the United States, Spring 1965,* Consumer and Food Economics Research Division, United States Department of Agriculture, Washington, D.C. (1968), p. 9.
5. Jacobson, M., et al., "Yields from Meat-Type Chickens of Five Ages," *Journal of the American Dietetic Association* 54:308 (1969).
6. "Meats on Sale," *Consumer Reports* 35:472 (1970).
7. Moran, E. T., Jr., and H. L. Orr, "A Characterization of the Broiler as a Function of Sex and Age; Live Performance, Processing, Grade and Cooking Yields," *Food Technology* 23:1077 (1970).
8. "Per Capita Food Consumption," *National Food Situation,* Economic Research Service, United States Department of Agriculture, Washington, D.C. (February 1971), p. 12.
9. Stadelman, W. J., "Thawing Time Before Cooking Critical in Reducing Chicken Bone Darkening," *Quick Frozen Food* 32:63 (1970).
10. "Twenty-Fourth Annual Consumer Expenditure Study: 1970 Highlights," *Supermarketing* (September 1971), p. 38.
11. *Your Money's Worth in Foods,* Home and Garden Bulletin No. 183, Consumer and Food Research Division, United States Department of Agriculture, Washington, D.C. (1970).

Chapter 7
Purchasing Food—Cheeses

Though cheese is a dairy product and as such might have been discussed in the next chapter, cheeses have become of sufficient interest to consumers in the United States to warrant devoting a chapter to them. Travel at home and abroad has introduced us to new varieties and to different cheese dishes. Our ever-growing preoccupation with gourmet cooking and ethnic and sophisticated cookbooks has fed this interest in cheeses. Wine and cheese tastings have become popular as have such dishes as Swiss fondue and quiche Lorraine. Research and technology are producing low-fat cheeses of acceptable flavor for the calorie conscious. Few foods are as versatile as are cheeses. They are suitable for any meal or snack of the day and for any part of a meal. Few foods come in such plenteous variety, few are suitable in so many combinations, and few lend themselves to so many culinary purposes. This chapter will be informative about how to purchase cheeses, but it will also be informative about cheeses per se: their production; the characteristics of varieties, their similarities and differences; and how and with what to serve them. A dictionary of the better-known and widely available cheeses appears at the end of the chapter.

Historically, cheese is an ancient food. Cheese-making probably developed with agriculture and herding, though legend credits the discovery of cheese to an Arab trader who filled a pouch made of a sheep's stomach with milk in preparation for a desert journey. At the end of his day's journey, the pouch contained the curds and whey, both food and drink, produced as the result of the coagulation of the milk by the rennin of the sheep's stomach. In actuality, cheese-making is preservation of a food by dehydration. It is believed that the art of cheese-making was brought from Asia to Europe. Cheese was made in many parts of the Roman Empire, and the Romans adopted the art and took it to those countries that they conquered, including Switzerland and England. The Pilgrims carried cheese with them to America, and the Dutch and English brought both the herds and the art of cheese-making with them. Until the mid-nineteenth century, cheese was farm- or home-made. The first factory for the commercial production of cheese was built in 1851 near Rome, New York. Commercial cheese-making began in Wisconsin in the same decade; the first Wisconsin cheese factory was built in 1864 in Sheboygan County. What was an art became science and technology. The leading cheese-making state is Wisconsin, which makes about one half of the national output; New York and Minnesota are the next largest cheese-producing states. In 1969, the total cheese production was nearly one million tons; it was sold at retail for $1.4 billion. In 1970, annual per-capita cheese consumption was 11.5 pounds in contrast to 8.3 pounds in 1960.

Because cheeses were farm made and cheese-making a folk art, there are many varieties different in size, shape, color, finish, hardness, texture, and flavor and aroma. According to Axler (1) there are 1,200 named cheeses of the world, 500 distinct varieties, and 200 very fine cheeses. New ones are introduced each year. The United States Department of Agriculture in its handbook on cheese varieties (6) names 800 and describes 400 varieties, but suggests that there are only 18 distinct kinds of cheeses. Some varieties are similar; for example, the many blue-veined cheeses are similar, yet different in texture and piquancy of flavor, and have different names, such as the Gorgonzola of Italy, the English Stilton, and the French Roquefort; yet no two are the same. Although the cheese-making process is simple, namely, the production and treatment of the curd of milk, there may be many steps in the process and there are many variables that characterize the final product. Some of these are the kind, age, composition, condition, and treatment of the milk; the mode of curd formation; the treatment of the curd—how heated, how cut, how drained, and whether stirred or not; the ripening of the curd; the kinds of ripening agents; the temperature of ripening; the length of the period of ripening; and even the kinds and quantities of microorganisms in the air during cheese-making and ripening. Some or all of these differ from place to place and account for subtle differences in cheese varieties and in the same varieties made in different places, for example, New York cheddar cheese is different from Wisconsin cheddar cheese and French Camembert differs from domestic Camembert.

Because it will be difficult to discuss cheese-making and cheese varieties without naming varieties, it is desirable to discuss their naming briefly. The names of varieties are variously derived; many stem from place names, where the variety originated, such as Camembert, Cheddar, and Cheshire; where the variety was first marketed, such as Limburger, Edam, and Stilton; from the monastries and monks who made them like Trappist, Münster (Meunster), and Port du Salut (Port Salut). Other cheeses have been named from a special ingredient, such as sage cheese, though as presently made it no longer has fresh sage as an ingredient; pepato with added pepper; and Friesian clove; or from the shape of the cheese, such as brick, pineapple, and hand cheeses; or from a special characteristic like the blue veining of Danish blue. A few varieties were named for saints, such as St. Claude and St. Paulin, or persons directly or indirectly connected with their development like Liederkranz, which got its name from the name of the choral society to which its originator belonged. Because most cheeses are of European origin, many variety names are European. However, many varieties made worldwide bear original names regardless of place of manufacture, for example, Swiss cheese made in Wisconsin is called Swiss cheese.

THE CHEESE-MAKING PROCESS

During the past century, the making of cheese has passed from a folk art with its attendant uncertainties and failures, as well as great successes, to a highly scientific technology with its attendant efficiency and lack of failures and, possibly, great successes. Mass-produced cheeses are frequently described as mediocre by the turophile, but in all justice it should be mentioned that not all farm-made cheeses were great and some were truly bad.

Whether home-made or factory-made, cheeses are batch-made in vats or kettles; continuous cheese-making remains a development for the future. The steps in the process are the preparation of the milk; curd formation; the treatment of the curd to compact it and remove the whey; the preparation for ripening of a cheese to be ripened or the preparation of a fresh cheese for market; the ripening of all ripened cheeses; and, finally, perhaps aging. The preparation of the milk includes such steps as the blending of milks of different milkings; the blending of milks of different kinds, such as cow's milk with goat's milk; skimming milk; adding cream or skim milk to milk; acidification; heating; pasteurization; and homogenization. The fat content of a cheese is regulated here. At the proper time, starter and/or extract of rennin or milk-clotting enzymes are added. Starters are cultures of harmless bacteria of single or multiple strains. They effect formation of lactic acid and flavor components. The acid causes coagulation of the milk proteins. Curd formation is slower when only starter is used and the curd is soft; the addition of rennin extract or of milk-clotting enzymes hastens curd formation and the curd is "meatier." The curd for cheeses to be subsequently ripened is formed with starter and a milk-clotting ingredient. When the curd has properly formed, it is cut, heated, manipulated, salted, drained, and pressed, according to cheese variety. The final moisture content, the density, and, to a degree, the body and texture of the finished cheese are established in these steps. Fresh, un-ripened cheeses are prepared for market when the curd has been properly

TABLE 7-1. *Cheese-Making Techniques and the Resultant Cheeses*

Techniques	Cheese Characteristics	Typical Varieties
Acid-coagulated curd	Tender and soft	Cottage cheese, cream cheese, Neufchâtel cheese
Curd cut and matted	Compact and firm	Cheddar and Swiss cheeses
Curd cut but not matted	Somewhat open texture	Colby, Edam, Gouda cheeses
Curd worked when hot	Plastic	Provolone, Mozzarella cheeses
Ripened throughout by bacteria with eye formation	Small to large eyes	Colby, Edam, Gouda cheeses
Ripened on surface by bacteria mainly	Soft, smooth, waxy body and mild to strong in flavor	Brick, Port du Salut, Bel Paese, Limburger, Münster, Liederkranz
Ripened throughout by molds	Blue veins, piquant flavor	Roquefort, Danablu
Ripened on surface by molds	Edible crust, soft and creamy interior, pungent flavor	Camembert, Brie, Livarot

209

treated for kind; for example, creamed cottage cheese has the creaming mixture introduced (see Table 7–1).

However, for most cheese varieties a period of ripening, or curing, follows. It is the period during which the already introduced ripening agents, bacteria or molds or both, effect the changes that produce the desired flavor and aroma, the desired body and texture, and the appropriate appearance, including the proper color. The period of ripening may be just days, as for Camembert cheese, or several months, as for cheddar cheese. The temperature and humidity for ripening, or curing, differ for different cheese varieties and for the same variety made in different places; for example, in the United States, cheddar cheese is cured at a temperature of 32°F to 45°F, whereas in Canada and England the temperature is 60°F and the relative humidity, 90 per cent. A cheese not properly ripened is characterized as *green* or *young*; it lacks flavor and aroma and may have a texture described as *tough* or *rubbery*.

Some hard cheeses are permitted to age. This aging is a postripening period during which flavor and texture may be further improved. *Aging* means holding in storage under proper conditions and it is expensive; hence, aged cheeses are expensive and they are gourmet items purchasable only in specialty shops. A situation confusing for the consumer exists because identity standards for some cheese varieties require that they be made from pasteurized milk or "aged for sixty days." In this instance, *aging* means only that sixty days elapsed from the time of production to the time of packaging and releasing for sale. The cheeses available in most supermarkets are not truly aged; in fact, they may be quite green in the sense that they are not fully ripened.

Unripened Cheeses

Fresh or unripened cheeses include the several styles of cottage cheese; cream cheese; Neufchâtel cheese as made in the United States: Quesco Blanco; the Italian Mozzarella alternatively called Scamorza; and ricotta cheeses. All of these are mild and delicate in flavor and aroma.

Ripened Cheeses

The great majority of cheese varieties are cured, or ripened, or permitted to mature, so that microorganisms and enzymes can effect the fermentations and changes in milk fat and milk protein that result in the desired flavor and aroma, texture, and appearance peculiar to a cheese variety. The change agents, which include bacteria, molds, and possibly yeasts, may be introduced via the milk (when it is used unpasteurized), into the milk, into the curd during cheese-making, by application to the surface of the green cheese by spraying or smearing, from the environment, or a combination of these. When cheeses are made from pasteurized milk, pure cultures of organisms are introduced; because these cultures do not carry the variety of organisms nor carry them in the proportions of raw milk, the domestic varieties may differ in flavor from imported varieties of the same name. The ripening process proceeds in rooms where temperature and humidity are controlled or in caves. The environment may be warm and humid or cool and dry; the time for ripening is long or short accordingly. The surface of a ripening cheese may be protected or the so-called naked cheese may rest on rush mats, hay, straw, baskets, or treated shelves. Ripening changes can occur throughout a cheese, as with cheddar cheese; from the surface to the interior, as with soft varieties like Camembert and Liederkranz; and both in the interior and from the external surface as with Bel Paese, brick, and Port du Salut. Moisture content or the softness of the cheese determines the mode of ripening. Because soft cheeses are perishable, they are kept small and/or thin; they are quickly ripened from the surface. The firmer cheeses are less perishable; they can be permitted to ripen slowly and in the interior.

The period of ripening is a most important one in the production of a fine cheese; at the same time, mishaps during this period can produce bad cheeses, such as Swiss cheese without eyes, gassy eyes or holes in a variety where none should be present, bad flavors, and a bitter taste. Unless pasteurized, a cheese continues to ripen in transit, in storage, and in the refrigerator.

CLASSIFYING CHEESE VARIETIES

No completely satisfactory method of classifying cheese varieties has yet been devised. The most commonly encountered system is the one that classifies by texture, that is, as soft, semisoft, hard, and very hard, or cheeses for grating. The disadvantage of the system is the varying degree of hardness of different samples of the same variety and of quite similar varieties. Another system classifies them by mode of ripening, as unripened, or fresh cheeses, and as cheeses ripened by bacteria, by molds, by surface organisms, or by combinations of these. Such a system groups together quite unsimilar cheeses. Another system of classification groups cheeses by country of origin, as French, Swiss, Danish, Italian, and so on. Axler contends that the cheeses of a country can be characterized—for example, the French cheeses as brilliant, the German as robust, the English as solid, and the Scandinavian as earthy (1). Marquis and Haskell (4) classify cheeses by similarities in flavor and suggest such classes as fresh country cheeses, bland and buttery cheeses, the Swisses, the Parmesans, the cheddars, flavor-relatives of cheddar, blue-veined cheeses, strong cheeses, spiced and flavored cheeses, and others. In the dictionary of cheeses that appears at the end of this chapter some cheeses are briefly described in alphabetical order. We shall endeavor here to identify some groups of cheese varieties, more especially the ones that consumers in the United States favor.

Fresh Cheeses

Interest in weight control and low-fat diets led to an annual per-capita consumption of about five pounds of cottage cheese in 1970. In late 1970, identity standards were proposed by the Food and Drug Administration for creamed cottage cheese of four levels of fat content: ½ per cent, 1 per cent, 2 per cent, and 4 per cent. For all excepting the 4-per-cent cheese, moisture content would be slightly in excess of 80 per cent. The product would be labeled to reveal the content of milk fat. Until these standards are adopted, creamed cottage cheese contains no less than 4 per cent of milk fat. Creaming mixtures, as they are defined, can contain cream, milk, skim milk, or a combination of them; any of several milk derivatives; salt; certain flavor substances; a culture of lactic acid and flavor-producing bacteria; certain food acids; and stabilizers. The creaming mixture may be either a sweet or a sour cream mixture. Cottage cheese looks better and tastes better when creamed. Curd styles of cottage cheese are several, and the names describing them are bewildering. Large-curd cottage cheese is sometimes labeled "California-style," also "popcorn cheese." Small-curd cottage cheese is also called "country-style" or "farm-style." Further, there are a flaked-curd style and a whipped cream style, which is a smooth, homogeneous mixture. Some other names for cottage cheese or cheeses similar to cottage cheese are Dutch cheese, Schmierkäse, pot cheese, farmer's cheese, New York or country cheese, Pennsylvania cheese, and Amish cup cheese. Actually, these vary some in flavor, texture, and moisture content, and Amish cup cheese and Schmierkäse are briefly ripened.

Fresh ricotta cheese resembles cottage cheese but is smoother and sweeter. It is prepared from whey, which contains coagulable lactalbumin, derived in the making of such cheeses as cheddar and Swiss cheese, combined with either whole or skim milk. Dry ricotta cheese is similarly made but is cured or dried to produce a gratable cheese for culinary purposes. Other unripened whey cheeses include the Scandinavian Mysöst, Gjetöst, and Primöst made by the condensation of the whey derived from the making of different cheese varieties.

Cream cheese and Neufchâtel cheese differ in that the former by definition must contain not less than 33 per cent milk fat and not more than 55 per cent moisture; the latter, not less than 20 per cent milk fat and not more than 65 per cent moisture.

Cheddar Cheese and Related Varieties

In the United States, cheese means cheddar cheese. It is sometimes called "American," "English," "Yankee," "dairy," "store," and "rat-trap" cheese. Its name derives from the village of Cheddar in Somersetshire, England, where it was originally made. Its flavor varies from mild to sharp, depending on the length of the ripening period and on whether or not it has been aged post ripening. Periods of ripening that result in mild, medium, and sharp flavors are approximately one to three months, four to seven months, and eight to twelve months, respectively, with five months considered the minimum to produce a cheese of good quality. However, the temperature and humidity of the ripening environment determine the speed at which the many reactions that effect ripening occur; when these are low, ripening requires longer than when these are higher. Cheddar cheese ages well to produce full aroma and a waxy texture; it may be aged up to two years.

Cheddar cheese may be artificially colored with the dye annatto; hence, color may range from creamy white to deep orange. Regional color preferences are such that cheddar cheese made in New England is very light or creamy white; in the West and the Midwest, medium light; and in the South, deep orange. Federal definition establishes the maximum allowable moisture content as 39 per cent and minimum fat as 32 per cent or 50 per cent of total solids. In the United States much cheddar is made from pasteurized milk. Marquis and Haskell (4) state that New York, Vermont, and Canadian cheddar cheeses are made from unpasteurized milk and they rate them superior in quality. However, in *Cheese Varieties and Descriptions* (6), it is stated that pasteurizing the milk improves the quality of cheddar cheese.

Cheese varieties similar to cheddar include English Cheshire and Gloucester, Welsh Caerphilly, granular or stirred-curd cheese, Colby, Monterey, pineapple, and coon cheeses. Colby is a modified cheddar cheese that originated in Vermont; it is softer, has more holes, and is milder than cheddar. Monterey, or Jack, cheese is also a modified cheddar; it originated in California. In the production of both of these cheeses, the cheddaring step is eliminated. Modifications in curd treatment result in cheeses different in moisture content, body and texture, and flavor and aroma.

Cheese Varieties with Eyes

Swiss cheese or Emmenthal (Emmenthaler) was originally made in the Emmenthal Valley in the Canton of Bern and its name is so derived. It is one of the most difficult of all kinds to make. Proprionic-acid-forming bacteria are primarily responsible for the eye formation and the flavor of Swiss cheese. Swiss cheese is made in many countries and bears different names; but none exactly duplicates the flavor and texture of Emmenthal from Switzerland. It is a creamy white, hard cheese of mild, sweet, and nutlike flavor; it has large, shiny eyes.

Other cheeses with eyes include Gruyère, fontina, Edam, Gouda, and Samsoe. These cheeses are smaller and have smaller eyes than Swiss cheese. Edam and Gouda are of Dutch origin and quite similar. Edam cheeses are small; they are identified by a red-colored surface if imported, or a red, waxed surface if domestic in origin. Gouda cheese is richer in fat than Edam and the cheeses are larger, although a "baby Gouda" is available on the market. It may be coated with red wax. Gruyère is Swiss in origin but much is made in France. Samsoe is the Danish and fontina, an Italian version of this cheese type.

Blue-Veined Cheeses

In the making of blue-veined cheeses the curds are innoculated with the mold spores of *Penicillium roqueforti* prepared from bread crumbs. Then, when the cheeses are ready for curing, they are pierced or spiked to permit passage of the air essential for spore development into the interior of the cheese. The blue veins are the growing mycelia of the mold spores. They are richly productive of the enzymes that modify milk fat and protein, giving rise to the many compounds that give these cheeses their unique flavor. In addition to the mold, bacteria inside the cheese, and yeast and bacteria on the surface of the cheeses contribute to flavor development.

The big three of the blue-veined cheeses are Roquefort, Stilton, and Gorgonzola; others are French blue, Danish blue (Danablu), and domestic blue. The blue-veined cheeses differ in texture: the Danish are soft and buttery, Roquefort is firm and crumbly, and Stilton is of a pebbly consistency. Further, they differ in appearance, with the veins ranging from blue as in Roquefort to green as in Gorgonzola to blue-green as in Stilton. The body of the cheese may be white or slightly yellow. They differ in flavor from mellow to piquant. The turophile can distinguish one from the other. Roquefort cheese is made from ewe's milk set with lamb rennet, and the cheeses are cured in limestone caves in the area of the village of Roquefort in southern France. Only cheeses made in this area may be labeled "Roquefort." Other blue-veined French cheeses are "French bleu." We import more Danish blue than any other blue-veined cheese and more Gorgonzola than Roquefort. Domestic blue cheeses are considered good but not distinguished (4).

Cheeses Surface-Ripened by Molds

Cheeses surface-ripened by mold include Brie and Camembert of French origin and Crema Danica, a Danish cheese. The latter is more delicate in flavor than the other two. The ripening of these cheeses takes place from the surface inward and is by mold growth on the surface and also by bacteria and probably yeasts that grow on the surface. The cheeses are small and their thickness is only an inch or so. The interior of the cheeses may range from waxy to an almost fluid consistency, depending on how well ripened they are, and should definitely be soft and creamy yellow. The moldy crust is eaten; it is white to off-white for American Camembert, golden for French Camembert, yellow to reddish for Brie, and pure white for Crema Danica.

Cheeses Surface-Ripened by Bacteria

The group of cheeses surface-ripened by bacteria, and probably yeasts also, is extensive; some varieties are Bel Paese, Münster, brick, Limburger, St. Paulin, Liederkranz, Port du Salut, and Livarot. All of these varieties are obtainable, either domestic or imported, in the supermarket, but the ones preferred are brick, Münster, Liederkranz, and Limburger. These varieties are characterized by a smooth, soft, waxy body. They contain more moisture than other ripened cheeses. The flavor ranges from the mild of Münster to the fullsome of Limburger. In the making of these varieties, the green cheeses are sprayed or smeared with the ripening organism *Brevibacterium linens*; they are then placed on wooden shelves impregnated with the organism. The ultimate flavor of the cheese variety is determined by the number of days the cheese remains on the shelf before being removed to the curing room.

Grana Cheeses

Grana describes a group of Italian cheeses so named because of their grainy texture when fully ripened. They are hard cheeses, as a result of ripening periods of one to two years, and are for grating; however, when young they may be used as table cheeses. Outside of Italy, and sometimes in Italy, they are known as *Parmesan*. There are two main types of grana cheeses: Grana Lombardo made north of the Po River and Grana Reggiano made south of the Po. There are subvarieties of these, all named for their place of origin. They differ mainly in the season of the year when they are made and in the details of the production process. They are large cheeses, the interior of which is yellow and the surface black from having been rubbed with a mixture of burnt umber, lamp black, and dextrin dispersed in oil. They vary in flavor from mild to sharp. The finest are Parmigiano and Reggiano. They are imported into the United States under the name "Parmesan" and "Parmesan Reggiano." They are also made domestically as well as in Argentina and in Uruguay, but none are considered as fine as the Italian varieties.

Romano cheese is another grana variety that may be eaten as a table cheese but when long-cured becomes a grating cheese. It is saltier and sharper in flavor than Parmesan.

The pregrated and prepackaged containers of the grana cheeses are compounded from different cheese varieties. The label describes what is in the container. The turophile holds them in low repute and prefers to grate Parmesan cheese immediately before use.

Pasta Filata Varieties

Pasta filata varieties include the already-mentioned Mozzarella (or Scamorza) and pizza cheeses, which are unripened, and the ripened Caciocavallo and Provolone. The former are soft and moist; the latter, firm. Pasta filata varieties are Italian cheeses characterized by the treatment of the curd following whey removal. The curd is immersed in hot water or whey and worked, stretched, and molded while plastic. The curd is truly tough and elastic.

Caciocavallo and Provolone are similarly made, and similar in flavor; however, the former contains less fat and is usually not smoked. Each variety is molded into distinctive shapes. Caciocavallo is spindle-shaped and one weighs four to five pounds. Provolone cheeses are made in different sizes and shapes and each bears a distinguishing name. The style called *Provolone* is pear-shaped and weighs between nine and fourteen pounds in the United States. Small styles are spherical. Sausage-shaped Provolone cheeses may range from small to very large—two hundred pounds or more. Most Provolone cheeses are smoked. For table use, the cheeses are cured up to four months; when cured longer, they are suitable for grating.

Spiced and Flavored Cheeses

Opinion differs on the merits of flavoring and spicing cheeses. The turophile suggests that a truly good cheese is rarely improved by such procedures and that its flavor should be savored unaltered. The probable original reasons for spicing and flavoring, pickling, and smoking cheeses were to preserve; to mask bad flavor in a poor cheese; to introduce flavor into a poor and tasteless cheese; and finally, perhaps, to relieve the monotony of meals. Seasonings include such herbs and spices as cloves, caraway, cumin, black pepper, red pepper and paprika, sage, and clover as in sapsago cheese; port or sherry wines; brandy; onions, garlic, chives, pimentos, olives, pickles, sausage bits, and so on. Münster with caraway; cheddar with port wine; Liptauer cheese with hot red pepper, paprika, capers, anchovy paste, and other assorted seasoners; cream cheese with bacon bits; and cream cheese with olives are but a few of the great variety to be found in the supermarket. Whatever the reason for spicing or flavoring a cheese, the products are sometimes quite tasty, though they may not taste much like a good cheese—which is all to the good if one doesn't like cheese.

STANDARDS FOR CHEESE

Standards have been established for the grading of cheddar and Swiss cheeses. The top grade for cheddar cheese is Grade AA; others are U.S. Grades A, B, and C. The top grade for Swiss cheese is Grade A; others are U.S. Grades B, C, and D. Only small quantities of grade-labeled cheese appear on the retail market. Products prepared under the supervision of the United States Department of Agriculture may bear the USDA inspection shield. Figure 7-1 shows the "Quality Approved" seal that may

FIGURE 7-1. The "Quality Approved" symbol that may appear on cottage cheese and process cheese products. (*United States Department of Agriculture photograph.*)

appear on cartons of cottage cheese and on processed cheese products. Definitions and standards of identity have been promulgated for a long list of cheeses. They regulate such aspects of cheese production as the treatment of milk, the kinds of additives permitted, the minimum period of aging, the maximum moisture and minimum fat content of the finished cheeses, and so on.

CHEESE PRODUCTS

American preference is for cheeses with mild flavors and smooth consistencies, an unnatural combination in cheese-making. To achieve the desired textures and flavors, the following cheese products are manufactured: pasteurized process cheese, pasteurized blended cheese, pasteurized process cheese food, pasteurized process cheese spread, cold-pack cheese, cold-pack cheese food, cream cheese with other foods, and pasteurized Neufchâtel cheese spread with other foods. Definitions and standards of identity have been promulgated for all of these. They limit the extent to which cheese may be replaced by other ingredients and define maximum moisture content, minimum butterfat content, and minimum cheese content. Further, they define the ratio of cheeses when two or more varieties are incorporated into products, name cheese varieties that may not be cheese components, name the ingredients other than cheese that may be added, and require detailed labeling. Any products that do not meet established standards must be labeled "imitation."

A pasteurized process cheese is prepared by the comminuting and mixing of one or more cheeses of the same variety or of two or more varieties, and, with the aid of an emulsifier, the heating of the mixture to form a homogeneous mass. Heating is for not less than thirty seconds at a temperature of not less than 150°F. Certain cheeses are exempted from use; they are cottage cheese, cream cheese, Neufchâtel cheese, and some others. The weight of each variety of cheese in a pasteurized process cheese made from two cheese varieties is not less than 25 per cent of the total weight of both, except that the weight of the blue-veined cheeses is not less than 10 per cent and the weight of Limburger not less than 5 per cent of the total weight of both. The weight of each variety in a pasteurized process cheese composed from three or more varieties is not less than 15 per cent of the weight of all, except that the weight of blue-veined cheeses is not less than 5 per cent and the weight of Limburger not less than 3 per cent of the total weight of all. Pasteurized process cheese may be smoked; or cheeses from which it is made may have been smoked before comminuting and mixing; or it may contain substances prepared by condensing or precipitating wood smoke.

The emulsifying agents permitted by the identity standards include assorted phosphate, citrate, and tartrate salts of sodium, potassium, and calcium. Optional ingredients include acidifying agents like vinegar and acetic, lactic, and citric acids; cream; water; salt; artificial coloring; certain mold inhibitors if the pasteurized process cheese is in the form of slices or cuts in consumer-size packages; and spices and flavorings, other than any that singly or in combination with other ingredients simulate the flavor of a cheese of any age or variety. If a pasteurized process cheese has been smoked or contains an ingredient that simulates the flavor of smoking or contains added spice or flavoring or mold-inhibiting ingredients, a statement to that effect must be made on the label. Similarly, the cheese ingredients of a process cheese must be named on the label in order of predominance whenever two or more varieties are compounded, with two exceptions. First, a pasteurized process cheese made from Swiss and Gruyère cheeses in which the Gruyère variety is not less than 25 per cent of the weight of both may be called "Pasteurized Process Gruyère Cheese." And secondly, a pasteurized process cheese compounded from cheddar cheese, Colby cheese, washed curd cheese, or granular cheese, or from a mixture of two or more of these, may be designated as "Pasteurized Process American Cheese." When these same varieties, singly or in a mixture of two or more, are combined with other varieties of cheeses, the product may be designated as "American Cheese." It becomes quite obvious that though cheddar cheese may be called "American," a product called "American Cheese" is not going to be true cheddar cheese.

Standards permit the addition of properly prepared cooked, canned, or dried fruits and vegetables, and properly prepared cooked or canned meat to pasteurized process cheese. Such additions are accompanied by slight modifications of water and fat content. Any fruit, vegetable, or meat ingredient of a process cheese must be named in the labeling.

Pasteurized process cheeses in the supermarket include American, Swiss, Gruyère, brick, Limburger, and Münster. The moisture content of a pasteurized process cheese made from only one variety of cheese is no more than 1 per cent greater than the maximum moisture content prescribed by the definition and standard of identity, if there be one, for the variety; but in no case is it more than 43 per cent with these exceptions: it is no more than 40 per cent for Colby cheese; 44 per cent for Swiss cheese and Gruyère cheese; and 51 per cent for Limburger cheese. Similarly, the fat content of the solids of a pasteurized process cheese made from a single variety of cheese is not less than the minimum prescribed by the definition and standard of identity for that cheese, if there be one; but in no case is it less than 47 per cent, with the exceptions of 43 and 45 per cent for pasteurized process Swiss and Gruyère cheeses, respectively.

The moisture content of a pasteurized process cheese made from two or more varieties is not more than 1 per cent greater than the arithmetical average of the maximum moisture contents prescribed by the definitions and standards of identity, if there be any, for the varieties used; but in no case is the moisture more than 43 per cent, except that a pasteurized process cheese made of a combination of cheddar, Colby, and washed curd cheeses is no more than 40 per cent, and a combination of Swiss and Gruyère cheeses is no more than 44 per cent. Similarly, the fat content of solids is not less than the arithmetical average of the minimum fat contents prescribed by the definitions and standards of identity, if there be any, for the varieties of cheese used; but in no case is it less than 47 per cent, excepting that for a mixture of Swiss and Gruyère cheeses it is not less than 45 per cent.

In summary, pasteurized process cheeses differ little in composition from the cheeses from which they are made; hence, they have approximately the same nutrient content. They are often less expensive than the same natural varieties, especially the well-ripened ones. Because they have been pasteurized, flavor is not subsequently changed. For some culinary purposes, they are superior to natural cheeses. When heated, they do not curdle or form a tough, rubbery mass; they melt to a smooth and homogeneous viscous mass because of added emulsifiers.

Pasteurized process cheese food is the food prepared by comminuting and mixing, with the aid of heat, of one or more optional cheese ingredients with certain optional dairy ingredients into a homogeneous plastic mass. The addition of dairy products to the mix reduces the quantity of cheese and in turn alters the moisture and fat content of the final product. Some prohibited cheese ingredients are cream cheese, Neufchâtel cheese, cottage cheese, skim-milk cheese, hard grating cheeses, and semisoft part skim-milk cheese. The weight of each variety of cheese in a cheese food made with two varieties of cheese is not less than 25 per cent of the total weight of both, except that the weight of the blue-veined cheeses or Limburger cheese is not less than 10 per cent. The weight of each variety of cheese in a cheese food made with three or more varieties is not less than 15 per cent of the total weight of all, except that the weight of the blue-veined cheeses and Limburger cheese is not less than 5 per cent. However, these limits do not apply to the quantities of cheddar, Colby, washed curd, and granular cheeses in mixtures that are designated as "American Cheese." Cheese must constitute 51 per cent of the weight of the cheese food. Optional dairy ingredients include cream, milk, skim milk, cheese whey, or condensates of these, and skim-milk cheese. Maximum water content of cheese food is 44 per cent and minimum fat content is 23 per cent. Other optional ingredients include emulsifying agents, acidifying agents, water, artificial color, spices or flavorings, and a mold inhibitor for consumer-size packages of slices and cuts. The product may derive smoke flavor as heretofore described, and it may contain fruits, vegetables, and meats as heretofore described. The label must bear the names of the cheese varieties in the product and the names of all optional ingredients used. Pasteurization is for not less than thirty seconds at a temperature not less than 150°F.

Pasteurized process cheese foods are snack foods and specialty cheese products. Figured in terms of the cheese component, costs may seem excessive. These foods do, however, provide cheese products of desired texture and consistency with mild to sharp flavors.

An identity standard has been established for grated American cheese food. The optional cheese ingredients include cheddar, Colby, washed curd, and granular cheeses; optional dairy ingredients are nonfat dry milk and dried whey.

Pasteurized process cheese spread is the food prepared by the comminuting and mixing, with the aid of heat, of such cheese ingredients, such dairy ingredients, and such other ingredients as the standard permits into a homogeneous plastic mass that is spreadable at 70°F. Permitted or optional cheese ingredients are the same as for making pasteurized process cheese food.

Moisture content is more than 44 per cent but not more than 60 per cent; fat content is not less than 20 per cent. Because of the higher moisture content, such water-binding agents as vegetable gums and gelatin are permitted ingredients. Other optional ingredients are the same as for pasteurized process cheese food; in addition a sweetening agent is allowed. The weight of the cheese component must constitute not less than 51 per cent of the weight of the finished product. Quantity stipulations when more than one variety of cheese is used are the same as for cheese foods. The label of a pasteurized cheese spread must bear the common or usual names of all optional ingredients used, except that the vegetable gums need not be named but may be designated as "vegetable gum." The product must be pasteurized at not less than 150°F for not less than thirty seconds. This product is sometimes heated—that is, melted—to make a cheese sauce; it is also suitable for the grilled-cheese sandwich, as is pasteurized process cheese. Pasteurized process cheese spreads are packaged for the retail trade in loaves weighing from eight ounces to two pounds and in glass jars and plastic containers. There is some difference in cost, depending on the style and the brand name. Imitation cheese spreads are available in some markets; they do not conform to established standards of moisture or fat content, or they include ingredients other than those permitted for cheese spreads.

Pasteurized cheese spread is a food that conforms to the definition and standard of identity for pasteurized process cheese spread except that no emulsifying agents are used. These products may contain fruits, vegetables, and meats.

Cream cheese with other foods is a food product prepared from cream cheese; other ingredients, such as fruits, vegetables, meats, relishes, and pickles are added. Allowable water content is 60 per cent; fat content may not be less than 27 per cent. The product may or may not be heat-processed. The label must bear a list of ingredients and statement of the use of a color additive.

Pasteurized Neufchâtel cheese spread with other foods is a product prepared from Neufchâtel cheese. It may contain such other ingredients as fruits, vegetables, meats, and pickles; water-binding agents; dairy ingredients; artificial coloring. It must be heat-processed. Moisture content cannot exceed 65 per cent; fat content cannot be less than 20 per cent.

Both the cream cheese and the Neufchâtel cheese products are available in a wide variety of packages and flavor combinations. It is far less costly to make your own.

Cold-pack cheese, club cheese, or *crock cheese* is a product similar to pasteurized process cheese, except that it is not heat-processed. All cheeses included must have been made from pasteurized milk or held for at least sixty days at a temperature not less than 35°F before being comminuted.

Cold-pack cheese food is similar to pasteurized process cheese food except that it has not been heat-processed. Stipulations regarding milk are the same as for cold-pack cheese. This product may have added fruits, vegetables, or meats.

In summary, the variety of products made from cheese seems infinite. Definitions and standards regulate precisely what they can and cannot be. In general, the consumer will find the following information on labels of cheese products: names of cheeses; names of added dairy ingredients; names of acidifying agents; names of emulsifying and water-binding agents; names of added foods; statement of use of flavors and spices, artificial color, sweetening agents, salt and water. Frequently, statements of percentage of moisture and fat content appear on the label.

Identity standards for *grated cheeses* were promulgated in 1970. They are defined as the food prepared by the grinding, grating, shredding, or otherwise comminuting of cheese of one variety or a mixture of two or more varieties. Optional cheese varieties are those for which definitions and standards of identity have been promulgated, excepting cream cheese, Neufchâtel cheese, cottage cheese, cook cheese, and skim-milk cheese. Each cheese used must be present at the level of not less than 2 per cent by weight of the finished food. The product is prepared by the removal of water from the cheese ingredients. The name of the food if it is made from one only variety is "grated _____ cheese," the blank being filled with the name of the cheese, such as Parmesan or Romano. When the only cheese ingredients are Romano or Parmesan cheeses, each being present at a level of not less than 25 per cent by weight of the finished food, the product is labeled with these two names in the order of predominance by weight as either "Grated Parmesan and Romano Cheese" or "Grated Romano and Parmesan Cheese." The varietal designation "Reggiano" may be used for Parmesan. The label of the grated cheese made from a mixture of varieties—not including Romano and Parmesan cheeses—with each variety used being present at a level of not less than 25 per cent of the weight of the finished food, bears the names of the varieties in descending order of predominance. The label of a product made with a mixture of cheese varieties in which one or more of the varieties is present at a level of not less than 25 per cent—not including Parmesan or Romano cheeses—of the weight of the finished food and in which one or more other varieties are present at a level of not less than 2 per cent, but in the aggregate not more than 10 per cent, bears the names of the cheese varieties present at not less than 25 per cent in order of predominance, accompanied by "with Other Grated Cheeses." This latter phrase may be in letters half as high as the names of the cheeses present in the label. For example, a label might read "Grated Swiss Cheese with Other Grated Cheeses." The varietal label "American Cheese" may be used for a mixture of two or more of the varieties cheddar, Colby, granular, and washed curd cheeses. In summary, the labeling of a packaged grated cheese names the varieties of cheeses of which it is composed with the exception that 10 per cent may be present that is not named.

Quite new cheese products include spray-dried American or cheddar cheese for use in pizza, dips, and by the food industries in the manufacture of mixes and easy-to-prepare dishes for consumers. Further, an assignment of dehydrated products, including the blue-veined cheeses, is in use by the food industries for food dressings, mixes, dips, and so on. Freeze-dried cottage cheese for campers and institutional feeding is available.

QUALITY IN CHEESES

It would be encouraging to the consumer to be able to state that twentieth-century science and technology have eliminated cheeses of poor quality; unfortunately this is not true. Cheeses of mediocre, even poor, quality are to be found in the supermarket and in specialty cheese shops. Quality in cheese varieties means the aroma, flavor, texture and body, and appearance proper to a variety. For unripened cheeses, this means a fresh, clean smell like that of fresh milk or cream; a delicate flavor and a taste that ranges from sweet to slightly acid; tender, soft curds or body; and a snowy to creamy white color. For ripened cheeses quality means freedom from noncharacteristic odors and flavors that may be described as stale, barny, moldy, yeasty, surfury, ammoniacal, bitter, rancid, sour, flat, or weedy. Further, quality means the right body and texture—that is, softness, butteriness, or firmness—and also freedom from such defects as pastiness, crumbliness, gas holes, rubberiness, mealiness, and compactness, unless one of these is an attribute of the variety. Quality is reflected in color: white, creamy white, pale yellow, or other, depending on the variety. Finally, quality means the development of the flavor and aroma unique to a variety.

The ultimate quality of a cheese is established in a number of quite obvious ways: the place where it was produced; the quality of the milk used; the sanitary conditions in the place of production; the knowledge, skill, and care used in the production of the cheese, including the ripening period; the extent of the period of ripening; the conditions of storage after ripening; and finally, the packaging of the cheese for sale. Except for the rare exceptions of graded cheddar and Swiss cheeses, there is no guarantee of quality, whether a cheese is imported or domestic in origin. Those with expertise suggest that some varieties are superior when imported from the country of origin, like Swiss cheese made in Switzerland; but they agree that many domestic varieties are excellent, such as cream and Neufchâtel cheeses and Herkimer County cheddar—actually true English cheddar cheese cannot be imported into the United States, though its near relatives can. Unfortunately, quality varies for a given variety from time to time; for example, Brie, Camembert, and Liederkranz cheeses are better at some times than at others, depending on how ripe they are at the time of purchase. It is probably desirable to reiterate that a cheese variety made in different places is not always the same cheese, for example, Italian versus domestic Parmesan. Lastly, it might be noted that quality judgments are going to be personal and based on experience—many persons will disqualify a Limburger without tasting.

How to Buy Cheese

The cheese-purchasing decisions of the consumer, like most other decisions, will be based on wants: prime eating enjoyment, good nutrition, low-calorie input, avoidance of milk fat, economy, and probably others. If one's goal is the enjoyment of fine cheeses and the satisfaction of being well informed on cheese varieties, one must research the resources of the marketplace and experiment with the different available products. In the early 1970's, most supermarkets were stocking at least fifty kinds of cheeses, with the large supermarkets stocking two or three times as many. Specialty shops stock equal or greater numbers of varieties. The turophile suggests that, whenever possible, cheeses be examined for defects and signs of negligent care and poor storage practices and that they be sampled before purchase; this latter is possible only in the specialty cheese shop. Prepackaged cheeses have to be taken on faith or purchased as the result of previous experience.

Cheeses, except the cream cheeses, are excellent sources of high-quality protein. They are good alternates for meat. However, most cheeses, excepting cottage cheese and the whey cheeses, contain milk fat in varying amounts, depending on the richness of the milk from which they were prepared. In general, the commonly known and widely consumed varieties range from 25 to 33 per cent fat. In the 1970's, many persons are shunning animal fats because of their implication in the etiology of coronary disease and fats in general because of calorie content.

Researchers at the Dairy Products Laboratory of the Eastern Utilization Research and Development Division of the United States Department of Agriculture have developed a new cheese that they named *EUDA*, for the division, and that is only 6 per cent fat, is ripened, and is of good flavor. Researchers at the University of Minnesota and at Iowa State University have made cheddar, Colby, brick, Port du Salut, and Swiss cheeses of good flavor containing about half to two thirds the usual fat content of these varieties (8). One problem in making low-fat cheeses is that many of the compounds that give flavor to the ripened cheese derive from the milk fat. Homogenization of the milk, because it increases the surface area of the fat particles of the milk, has been a factor leading to the successful production of low-fat cheeses. Filled Mozzarella and cheddar cheeses, in which the milk fat is replaced by unsaturated fat acids, are being produced.

The dollar can be manipulated to buy more or less cheese; it can also purchase cheese in place of expensive meat, to provide meat-alternate dishes like the ubiquitous macaroni and cheese. To discuss economy first, there is some saving in buying chunks or slabs of cheese rather than cheese of the same variety and quality that is presliced, precut into serving pieces, cubed, or grated; in buying the less well-ripened rather than the fully ripened cheese; and in buying the lower rather than the higher quality cheese when it is available—for example, cheddar cheese of less than the best in quality is often specialed in the supermarket. Also, pasteurized process cheese products are less expensive than thir natural counterparts; and the plain cheeses and products without added ingredients are less expensive than those to which such ingredients as fruits, vegetables, nuts, meat, herbs, and spirits have been added. As it has been suggested elsewhere, these latter products are frequently concocted from inferior cheeses. In general, imported varieties are more expensive than domestic counterparts of the same quality. Some cheese varieties are expensive to buy because they are perishable, require great skill in the making, or are scarce in supply. The dollar will certainly not buy as much Roquefort cheese or French Camembert as it will domestic blue cheese. As usual, it is what one chooses to buy that determines how much food one gets for the dollar.

The use of cheese as an alternate for meat is an old-time practice, probably Welsh rabbit was a dish concocted by the housewife to fill the void of the hunter's empty bag. The Swiss fondue, the Jewish blintz, the grilled-cheese sandwich, the Mexican cheese enchilada, the Italian pasta with grated cheese, and the bread-and-cheese meal of the peasants of many lands are all good dishes, yet were and often are economy measures. And the cottage cheese salad for lunch is less expensive than a roast beef sandwich—and several times as rich in protein. And cheese for snacks can be significantly less expensive than such other items as cold meats, smoked oysters, seafood, and so on.

SOME GUIDES FOR THE BUYER OF CHEESES

1. Learn to recognize quality in the cheese varieties that you buy.
2. Read the label on natural cheeses to learn as much about the cheese as labels reveal: place of production, by whom marketed, variety, degree of flavor development (as mellow or sharp), length of period of ripening, and so on, when some or all of these are given. Liederkranz and some other perishable cheeses may bear a so-called pull date, that is, a date after which they are not to be sold.
3. Read carefully the labels on cheese products: the pasteurized process cheese foods, the spreads, and the cold-pack or club cheeses. Labels reveal

the ingredients of these products and sometimes the moisture and fat contents.

4. Select between natural and process cheeses with intended use in mind. You will save money by using the less expensive process cheese for sandwiches and cooking. Further, the process cheese melts to a smooth consistency, which the natural cheese rarely does.

5. Make your own spreads and dips.

How to Store Cheeses

Properly packaged cheeses can be satisfactorily stored for shorter or longer periods of time—depending on kind—in the refrigerator or in another cool place. The unripened cheeses are perishable and these should be consumed soon after purchase. The firm and ripened cheeses, like cheddar and Swiss, keep for extended periods of time, and the blue-veined varieties also store well; but the soft varieties surface-ripened by mold store only briefly without losing quality. During the storage period such changes as drying, mold development, flavor loss and/or flavor modification, and modification of body and texture can occur. To protect them against changes, all cheeses should be wrapped in foil or plastic film if they cannot be kept in the original wrapper, or placed in glass or plastic containers. It is sometimes as important to prevent a cheese's contamination of other foods, like butter, as it is to protect the cheese itself. Much prepackaged cheese is protected against mold development by the presence of mold inhibitors. However, mold development on a cheese is of little consequence; it can be scraped off or cut away and the underlying cheese will probably be unaffected. If large pieces of cheese are to be stored long, one can seal the cut surface by dipping it in hot paraffin. Though freezing as a means of preservation is not completely satisfactory because freezing alters the body and texture of the cheese, making it mealy and crumbly, some firm and semisoft varieties can be frozen. They are brick, cheddar, Edam and Gouda, Camembert, Mozzarella, Münster, Port du Salut, and Provolone (5). To this list Kosikowski adds cottage cheese (3). For freezing, the cheese should be packaged in moisture-vapor-proof wrap or left securely wrapped in the original packaging. Pieces should be no larger than one pound. Storage life is up to six months. The cheese should be thawed in the refrigerator and used as soon as possible. If the texture is so modified that the cheese is not suitable for eating as such, the cheese can be made into cheese dressings, dips, or used for culinary purposes.

How to Serve Cheese

All cheeses are considered to have their best flavor and texture when served at "room temperature," which of course can range from 60°F to

80°F. Axler suggests 56°F (1). The time out of the refrigerator before serving will vary for different varieties and should be long enough for flavor and aroma and body and consistency to become right. This will be longer for firm than for soft or semisoft cheeses. Following are some suggestions for serving cheeses.

1. In arranging a cheese board:
    a. Put only cheeses on it, that is, no garnishes and no breads or crackers.
    b. Keep a reasonable distance between each variety.
    c. Do not precut; have a knife or a server for each variety.
2. In general, serve breads and crackers on the side. Conventional choices are rye bread or pumpernickel with Swiss, German, or Dutch cheeses; French bread with French cheeses; and Italian bread with Italian cheeses. Plain and unsalted or lightly salted crackers are good with most cheeses. Melba toast, Norwegian flatbread, and sesame wafers are all good, as are the many crisp concoctions of the food industries.
3. Serve sweet butter with strong and rather salty or lean and dry cheeses like Gorgonzola or aged cheddar. English or Dijon mustard and gherkins or celery are good with cheddar-type cheeses. Thin onion slices are good with Liederkranz.
4. There are many excellent fruit and cheese combinations: apples or pears with the blue-veined cheeses; Tokay grapes with brick cheese; apples, pears, and tart plums with Camembert cheese; tart apples or melon slices with cheddar cheese; apples, orange sections, or pineapple spears with Edam or Gouda; pears with Provolone; and apples or grapes with Swiss (2). Wason suggests also: peaches with Gorgonzola, honeydew melon with Edam or Samsoe, and oranges with Roquefort (7).
5. Individual appointments for serving cheeses include an individual plate of dessert or salad size and individual knives; also an individual fork when fruits are served that require a fork for eating, such as melon slices or juicy peaches (that is, when the fruits are not finger foods).
6. Cheeses with or without fruits are excellent dessert courses and are becoming more and more a custom in the United States. The cheese dessert can follow almost any main course, especially light ones, but it would be inappropriate with Chinese or Japanese meals and Indian curries, probably because cheese is not a food native to the diets of those countries. A cheese course may precede the sweet dessert in meals served according to the European tradition.
7. Almost any beverage is suitable with cheese: coffee, tea, milk, beer, wines, and liqueurs. At the moment, cheese and wine tasting is popular in the United States, as is the serving of a wine with a dessert of cheeses. For great lore on the subject, consult some of the books listed at the end of this chapter, especially the one by André Simon, an internationally respected

authority on cheese and wine. A simple rule suggests that light, dry white wines be served with cheese of delicate flavor, that full-bodied red wines be served with cheeses of stout character, and that cheeses in the middle range be served with correspondingly middle-range wines (7).

DICTIONARY OF CHEESES

Asiago—Italian in origin. A hard grating cheese. Yellow in color. Sharp in flavor.

American—See cheddar. Term used to identify a group of cheeses somewhat like cheddar: Colby, washed curd, stirred, or granular cheeses. Also Monterey. It applies to a pasteurized process cheese compounded from two or more of the above named near-relatives of cheddar cheese.

Appenzell (or *Appenzeller*)—Swiss in origin. More flavorful than Emmenthal and Gruyère. Wrinkled brown rind; small holes; pale yellow, deeper in color near rind.

Baker's cheese—A skim-milk cheese much like cottage cheese but softer, finer grained, more moist, and more acid. Used in making cheesecake and pastries. When creamed, it is eaten like cottage cheese.

Baronet cheese—Brand name of a cheese that is bland and buttery; has flavor not unlike Münster with an overtone of cheddar.

Beer cheese (*bierkäse*)—German in origin. Resembles brick cheese; American-made variety is milder in flavor than the German.

Bel Paese—Trade name of a fine Italian cheese. Italian import bears map of Italy and picture of a priest on the label of its chipboard box; the Wisconsin product, the map of the Western Hemisphere. An uncooked, ripened cheese. Soft, creamy yellow interior, slightly gray surface; flavor is mild to moderately robust. Many similar cheeses are made, the group is referred to as *butter cheese*.

Bleu (*Fromage bleu*)—French name for blue-veined cheeses made in France.

Blue (*blue-veined*) *cheese*—Made in Canada, Argentina, Denmark, Sweden, and United States. Semisoft; firm to crumbly texture; white interior with blue-green veining of mold; flavor peculiar to the cheese and for different varieties mild to sharp.

Brick cheese—Domestic in origin. Not as strong as Limburger in flavor, but salty and medium to moderately sharp in flavor. Semisoft to medium firm in texture, containing many holes. Creamy yellow.

Brie—French in origin. Very perishable. Soft; interior fluid when very ripe. Interior, creamy yellow; edible crust, white flecked with brown. Mild to pungent flavor. Similar to Camembert.

Camembert—French in origin. Soft; interior fluid when fully ripe. Creamy interior with thin edible crust. Medium to pungent flavor. Continues to ripen after packaging. Similar to Brie.

Caciocavallo—Italian in origin. Plastic-curd cheese. Resembles Provolone but less fat and usually not smoked. Firm in texture, white with tan-colored surface.

Cheddar—English in origin. Creamy white to orange in color. Semihard; firm to crumbly in texture and mild to sharp in flavor, depending on aging time.

Cheddar, English—Barred from importation into the United States.

Colby cheese—Domestic in origin. Cheddar-type cheese, but softer, more open (has more holes), milder in flavor; color ranges from creamy white to yellow-orange.

Coon—Cheddar cheese cured by special patented method. High-quality cheese cured at high temperature and high humidity. Green mold grows on surface to aid in flavor development. When fully developed, cheese is dipped in hot paraffin; heat causes green mold to turn black. Crumbly; sharp but mellow flavor.

Cream cheese—Domestic in origin. Soft, smooth cheese eaten fresh. Snow white and very mild in flavor.

Crema Danica—Danish in origin, a new variety, and imported only. Interior pale yellow; surface white; flavor delicate. Sold in a square chipboard box containing two foil-wrapper bar-shaped sticks.

Danablu—Danish blue-veined cheese. Soft, buttery texture; strong and rich in flavor; creamy white in color with rich blue veining.

Edam—Dutch in origin. Semisoft to hard; firmer than Gouda; cannonball shape with red wax rind; yellow; has small eyes; mild, nutty flavor. Made from partially skimmed milk. May be smoked.

Emmenthal (Emmenthaler)—Swiss cheese. No cheese similarly made has quite the same character. Semihard; firm in texture with very large, shiny eyes; ivory in color. Sweet, nutlike flavor. Swiss cheese imported from Switzerland bears "Switzerland" printed in red repeatedly on surface of cheese.

Esrom—Danish Port du Salut.

Feta—Greek in origin. Originally made from ewe's or goat's milk. Curd is heavily salted and preserved in brine. Snowy white in color; somewhat firm in texture.

Fontina—Italian in origin. Resembles Swiss Gruyère. Small eyes; semisoft to hard; yellow in color; delicate, nutty flavor.

Gjetöst—Norwegian in origin; imported only. Whey cheese made from whey from goat's milk or mixture of whey from goat's and cow's milk. Golden brown in color; firm in consistency; sweetish in taste.

Gold-N-Rich—Brand name for a bland and buttery cheese of fine flavor. Rather like Bel Paese with a touch of cheddar.

Gorgonzola—Italian blue-veined cheese. Creamy yellow with pale green veins. Softer and milder of flavor than Roquefort cheese.

Gouda—Dutch in origin. Similar to Edam, but softer because of higher fat content. "Baby Gouda" resembles Edam. Wheels are orange or red waxed. Firm, waxy body, small eyes, mild flavor. Sometimes flavored with caraway seeds.

Grana—A group of Italian cheeses that are granular in texture, hard, sharp in flavor, and suitable for grating. See Parmesan.

Gruyère—Swiss in origin; made also in nearby France. Made much as Swiss cheese is made. Small eyes; ivory to pale yellow in color with a wrinkled brown rind; mild and sweet in flavor. The pasteurized process product lacks the true flavor of the cheese.

Herkimer—Cheddar cheese made in Herkimer County, New York. Creamy white in color: dry and crumbly in texture; and sharp in flavor. Limited in availability.

Kuminöst—Swedish in origin. Mild, white cheese; studded with caraway seeds that give it a slightly sour taste.

Liederkranz—Domestic in origin. Made only by the Borden Company in Ohio. Similar to but milder in flavor than Limburger. Creamy white in interior; rusty orange surface; soft and smooth in texture. It is eaten in its entirety. When purchased it may not be fully ripe; it ripens in the refrigerator. Dated with date for withdrawal from sale.

Limburger—Belgian in origin. Semisoft; creamy white with reddish-yellow surface; very strong in flavor and aroma.

Liptauer—Hungarian in origin. Pickled cheese seasoned with a number of condiments: paprika, capers, chives, garlic, onions, and so on.

Mel-o-pure—Trade name of a domestic cheese. Cream-colored; firm in texture; mild in flavor, reminiscent of cheddar cheese and Bel Paese.

Monterey (or *Jack*)—Domestic in origin. Cheddar-type cheese first made in California. Mild in flavor.

Mozzarella—Italian in origin. Generally eaten with little or no ripening. White plastic-curd cheese; mild in flavor. Melts to a creamy smoothness and becomes somewhat elastic when heated. The Food and Drug Administration has prepared one identity standard for Mozzarella cheese and Scamorza cheese; one for part-skim Mozzarella cheese and part-skim Scamorza cheese; and one for low-moisture part-skim Mozzarella cheese and low-moisture part-skim Scamorza cheese. These three differ in moisture and fat contents, with the part-skim cheeses containing not less than 30 per cent milk fat calculated on the basis of the solids content.

Münster (*Muenster*)—German in origin. Resembles brick cheese but is less well ripened and milder in flavor. Semisoft; interior contains many holes; creamy white with red-orange surface that results from smearing with annatto.

Neufchâtel (*Neuchâtel*)—French in origin. Domestic Neufchâtel is unripened. White; soft and smooth in texture; very mild in flavor. Resembles cream cheese; has a lower fat content.

Parmesan—Italian in origin. Imported kind is best, bears "Parmigiano-Reggiano" stenciled on rind. A very hard cheese for grating.

Pineapple—Domestic in origin. Name derived from shape and diagonal markings on surface (which cause it to resemble a pineapple). A cheddar-type cheese.

Mysöst—Norwegian in origin. Whey cheese, brown in color, firm in consistency, sweet tasting.

Oka—Canadian Port du Salut.

Pizza cheese—According to Kosikowski (3), pizza cheese is similar to low-moisture Mozzarella cheese.

Port du Salut (Port Salut)—French in origin, originally a monastery cheese. Flavor ranges from mild to robust, reminiscent of Limburger cheese. Semisoft and buttery; creamy yellow interior with rusty surface.

Primöst—Norwegian in origin. Whey cheese; unripened; semisoft; caramel colored; mild and sweet in flavor. Also called *Mysöst*.

Provolone—Italian in origin. Ripened and smoked cheese of the plastic-curd type; semihard; compact and flaky in texture. Yellow interior; golden beige surface. Made in a variety of shapes: bowl, pear, and sausage. Mellow to sharp, salty, and smoky in flavor.

Ricotta—Italian in origin. Originally a whey cheese, now made from milk and whey. Like cottage cheese when fresh; bland and semisweet in flavor. Dried to make a cheese for grating.

Romano—Italian in origin. A hard table cheese after some curing; after long curing, a very hard cheese for grating. Salty, sharp, and piquant in flavor. Yellowish interior; greenish black surface.

Roquefort—Made only in France and only in the Roquefort area. Made from milk of special breed of sheep and cured in the caves of Roquefort. White with blue-green veins; semisoft to hard; sometimes crumbly. Distinctive sharp, peppery, and piquant in flavor.

Sage cheese—Domestic in origin. Cheddar-type cheese flavored with extract of sage and given a mottled green effect by the introduction of finely cut green corn. Originally seasoned with sage.

Samsoe—Danish version of Swiss cheese. Small eyes; a flavor more like Edam than Swiss cheese.

Sapsago—Swiss in origin and imported only. A very hard cheese for grating. Pale green in color because of presence of added powdered, dry clover leaves. Sharp and herblike in flavor.

Scamorza (Scamorze)—Italian in origin. Soft, mild, plastic-curd cheese to be eaten fresh. See Mozzarella cheese.

Stilton—English blue-veined cheese. (A fine cheese.) Off-white to amber at rind and much marbled with blue-green veining. Wrinkled, brown melonlike rind. Flavor combines the flavor of cheddar with the flavor of blue-veined varieties, but is milder than either Roquefort or Gorgonzola.

Swiss cheese—See Emmenthal. Characterized by large, shiny eyes; the more eyes the sharper the flavor. Ivory to yellow in color; semihard; sweet and nutlike in flavor. The most difficult of all cheeses to make, and much imitated, but no imitation is exactly like Emmenthal.

REFERENCES CITED

1. Axler, Bruce H., *The Cheese Handbook*. New York: Hastings House, 1968.
2. *Cheese in Family Meals*, Home and Garden Bulletin No. 112, United States Department of Agriculture, Washington, D.C. (1966).
3. Kosikowski, Frank V., *Cheese and Fermented Milk Foods*. Ithaca, New York: Frank V. Kosikowski, 1966.
4. Marquis, Vivienne and Patricia Haskell, *The Cheese Book*. New York: Simon & Schuster, 1965.
5. Meister, H. E. and J. L. Brogdon, "Versatility, Inc., with Milk and Our Other Dairy Foods" in *Food for Us All—Yearbook of Agriculture 1969*. Washington, D.C.: United States Department of Agriculture, 1969, p. 156.
6. Sanders, G.P., *Cheese Varieties and Descriptions*, Agriculture Handbook No. 54, United States Department of Agriculture, Washington, D.C. (1953).
7. Wason, Elizabeth, *A Salute to Cheese*. New York: Hawthorn Books, Inc., 1966.
8. Webb, Byron H., "A New Low-Fat Cheese," in *Science for Better Living—The Yearbook of Agriculture, 1968*. Washington, D.C.: The United States Department of Agriculture, 1968, pp. 289–293.

SUGGESTED REFERENCES

1. Brown, Bob, *The Complete Book of Cheese*. New York: Random House, 1955.
2. McCully, Helen, *Nobody Ever Tells You These Things About Food and Drink*. New York: Holt, Rinehart, and Winston, 1967.
3. Simon, André, *Cheeses of the World*. London: Faber and Faber, 1956.

Chapter 8

Purchasing Food—Dairy Products, Nondairy Products, and Eggs

Per-capita consumption of milk, cream, butter, and eggs declined during the decade of the 1960's; of cheese and nondairy products increased; and of ice cream remained relatively constant with minor fluctuations (5). According to the United States Department of Agriculture study of Food Consumption of Households in the United States, Spring, 1965 (2), the average household consumption of milk was just under ten quarts per week; approximately nine quarts of the quantity were fresh fluid milk; the remainder, either canned milk or nonfat dairy milk. The money value of this milk was estimated at $2.24; it represented an expenditure of 8 per cent of the food dollar. Actually, the quantity of fresh and processed milk consumed per household increased with income and did not reach the average until income exceeded $5,000 (after taxes) per year. The consumption of canned milk decreased as income increased; the consumption of nonfat dry milk as such decreased; but the consumption of mixtures containing nonfat dry milk like diet beverages and malted milk drinks increased with income. Cream, ice cream, and egg consumption increased with income. The average household consumption of eggs was 1.7 dozen per week. Butter consumption reached the all-time low of approximately five pounds per capita in 1970; margarine consumption was more than twice this: eleven pounds per capita. Other changes during the decade were increased consumption of low-fat dairy products, such as skimmed and low-fat milk and half-and-half cream, and increased consumption of nondairy toppings and coffee whiteners.

Most of the dollars spent for this group of foods are spent for milk for drinking and for use in cooking. Milk can be purchased as the fresh fluid product or as a product processed by canning or by dehydration. The fresh fluid product may be whole, low-fat, skimmed, filled, or imitation;

TABLE 8–1. *The Cost of One Quart of Selected Fluid Milk Products as Purchased in Containers of Different Sizes from Different Market Sources*[1]

Item	Market Source	Cost	Market Unit	Cost per Quart
Homogenized vitamin D milk	House delivery	$.75	half gal.	$.375
Homogenized vitamin D milk	House delivery	.41	qt.	.41
Homogenized vitamin D milk	Vending machine	.50	half gal.	.25
Homogenized vitamin D milk	Supermarket	1.09	gal.	.272
Homogenized vitamin D milk	Supermarket	.65	half gal.	.325
Homogenized vitamin D milk	Supermarket	.35	qt.	.35
Homogenized vitamin D milk	Discount supermarket	1.03	gal.	.26
Homogenized vitamin D milk	Discount supermarket	.59	half gal.	.30
Homogenized vitamin D milk	Convenience store	.67	half gal.	.335
Homogenized vitamin D milk	Convenience store	.39	qt.	.39
Low-fat milk	House delivery	.75	half gal.	.375
Low-fat milk	Supermarket	.65	half gal.	.325
Low-fat milk	Supermarket	.35	qt.	.35
Low-fat milk	Discount supermarket	.59	half gal.	.30
Low-fat milk	Convenience store	.67	half gal.	.335
Golden Guernsey milk	Supermarket	.71	half gal.	.355
Golden Guernsey milk	Supermarket	.38	qt.	.38
Fortified buttermilk	Supermarket	.35	qt.	.35
Fortified buttermilk	Discount supermarket	.29	qt.	.29
Chocolate low-fat milk	House delivery	.45	qt.	.45
Chocolate low-fat milk	Supermarket	.39	qt.	.39
Chocolate low-fat milk	Discount supermarket	.35	qt.	.35
Chocolate low-fat milk	Convenience store	.41	qt.	.41

[1]Prices as of Winter 1971 in Florida.

234

cost varies accordingly. The product can be delivered to the home, or it can be bought at a supermarket or other grocery store, at a dairy store, or at some other special retail outlet, for example, from a vending machine at the gas station. Cost varies accordingly. Though the purchase of this group of products does not use a large proportion of the food dollar, knowledge about both products and market resources assists the consumer in maximizing food dollars. Table 8–1 shows how the cost of a quart of milk can vary, according to the product purchased, the size of the container purchased, and the place it is purchased if all were available at one time in one place. Information about and definitions of the different dairy and nondairy products follow. Extensive interstate commerce in dairy products makes all definitions important to consumers.

DAIRY PRODUCTS

Dairy products that will be discussed include whole milk, skim milk, low-fat milks, acidified and cultured milk products, flavored milk products, fortified milk products, filled milk, imitation milk, whipping cream, coffee cream, half-and-half cream, cultured cream products, frozen desserts, and butter.

Fluid Milk

The *Grade "A" Pasteurized Milk Ordinance—1965 Recommendations of the United States Public Health Service* defined milk and certain milk products and established standards for Grade A pasteurized milk and milk products (3). These standards have been adopted by many states, counties, and cities; others have established their own standards. Where the ordinance has been adopted, *milk* is defined as the lacteal secretion, practically free of colostrum, obtained by the complete milking of one or more cows; it contains not less than 3.25 per cent of milk fat and not less than 8.25 per cent of solids not fat. *Milk products* are defined as the different products, such as skim milk, cultured buttermilk, and evaporated milk, that result from altering milk in some way through processing. Further, where the ordinance has been adopted, only Grade A pasteurized milk and milk products may be sold to the final consumer, to grocery stores, and to public eating places; but in an emergency, "ungraded" products may be sold as authorized by the local health authority. *Grade A raw milk for pasteurization* must meet the following standards: it must have been cooled immediately following milking to 50°F or less and maintained thereat until processed; individual producer milk cannot exceed 100,000 bacteria per milliliter prior to commingling with other producer milk; the count of commingled milk cannot exceed 300,000 bacteria per milliliter; and there can be no detectable antibiotic residue. *Grade A pasteurized milk and milk products* must be cooled immediately after pasteurization to 45°F or less and held thereat; bacterial and coliform limits are 20,000 and 10 respectively, except that cultured products are exempt from bacterial limits. *Pasteurization* means heat processing every particle of milk or of a milk product to at least 145°F and holding it continuously at or above this temperature for at least thirty minutes, or heat processing it to at least 161°F and holding it continuously at or above this temperature for at least fifteen seconds. Milk with a higher fat content than whole milk and products to which sugar is added must be processed for the same lengths of time but the temperature must be five degrees higher.

The composition of fluid whole milk is often regulated by state laws that set minimum standards for milk fat and solids nonfat. For *whole milk* the minimum fat content ranges between 3.0 and 3.8 per cent with the usual minimum being 3.5 per cent. The minimum nonfat solids content ranges between 8.0 and 8.5 per cent. *Skim milk* has the milk fat content reduced to less than 0.5 per cent but it contains not less than 8.0 per cent nonfat milk solids. Skim milk is marketed unaltered; it is also fortified with vitamins A and D (so that these are present in the same quantities as in vitamin D whole milk) and with added nonfat dry milk solids to give it a 10 per cent content of solids nonfat. This addition of nonfat dry milk improves the body and the appearance of skim milk and it makes the product more generally acceptable than unaltered skim milk. *Low-fat* milk has a content of milk fat between 0.5 and 2 per cent. *Two per cent* milk has a fat content of 2 per cent and usually a solids nonfat content of 10 per cent.

Whole milk that forms a cream layer has been largely displaced by homogenized milk that does not. *Homogenized milk* has been mechanically treated to break fat globules into minute particles and disperse them throughout the milk. Homogenization follows pasteurization. Homogenized milk has a softer curd, more body, and a richer flavor than unhomogenized milk.

Acidified milk and milk products are obtained by the addition of food grade acids to pasteurized cream, half and half, milk, skim milk, and low-fat milk so that the resulting acidity is not less than 0.2 per cent expressed as lactic acid. *Cultured buttermilk* is pasteurized skim milk or low-fat milk that has been soured by lactic acid producing bacteria or other similar culture. Cultured buttermilk may contain butter flakes. *Cultured milk* is pasteurized whole milk that has been soured by lactic-acid-producing bacteria or other similar culture. *Yogurt* is a cultured milk product. It is prepared from either whole or skim milk. It comes in many flavors and with added fruits. Its consumption has increased during the decade of the 1960's. It is an expensive form of milk and as a dessert it is more expensive than ice cream or ice milk. It derives no special nutrient benefit from the fermentation process. Yogurt is used in cooking; it sometimes replaces sour cream, thus reducing the calorie content and the fat content of dishes.

Milk that has the flavor of chocolate is available as whole milk, low-fat milk, or skim milk; it is flavored with either chocolate or cocoa. The whole milk product flavored with chocolate is labeled "chocolate milk"; when flavored with cocoa, "chocolate-flavored milk." The low-fat products are similarly labeled as "chocolate low-fat milk" and "chocolate-flavored low-fat milk." The skim-milk products are designated as "chocolate drink" and "chocolate-flavored drink." All are sweetened, and additives that stabilize or prevent the settling of the chocolate ingredient are used. Milk products of varying fat content may be flavored with such flavors as maple, strawberry, coffee, and others: they are labeled "flavored milk," "flavored low-fat milk," and "flavored drink," accordingly. *Fortified milk products* have added vitamin and mineral content. *Vitamin D milk* has the vitamin D content increased to 400 USP units per quart. Fortified skim milk generally contains 2,000 IU of added vitamin A and 400 USP units of added vitamin D. Milk for special dietary uses is available with the added vitamins thiamin, niacin, and riboflavin and the added minerals iron and/or iodine. *Reconstituted* and *recombined* milk and milk products are those that result from the recombining of milk constituents with potable water. Skim milk distributed at retail is frequently a reconstituted product prepared from nonfat dry solids and unpolluted water.

Filled milk is milk in which milk fat has been replaced by vegetable fat. It has been manufactured since 1916. It has been prohibited in interstate commerce since 1923, when the dairy people, to protect their own interests, prevailed upon Congress to enact the Filled Milk Act on the grounds that filled milk was an adulterated product. Filled milk has long been in use by the armed forces at overseas bases because of its superior keeping qualities; and its use has been required at overseas bases since 1967. Some states prohibit the product in intrastate commerce; in New York it must be labeled "melloream" and in California, "imitation milk." Some confusion exists as to what filled milk is. It is prepared from skim milk and vegetable fat or from recombined skim milk and vegetable fat plus such additives as are required to give a good product and are, of course, permitted. The vegetable fat of the first filled milks was coconut oil because it was cheap; hence, it permitted the sale of the product on the basis of price competition with whole milk. Currently, the product is prepared with vegetable fats such as soybean and corn oils, which have a more favorable ratio of unsaturated fat acids to saturated fat acids. Filled milk, where it is in the marketplace, is probably a good buy; but the label ought to be read for information as to the kind of fat present, also the presence or absence of vitamins A and D. Of course, filled milk should be priced competitively with whole milk. Possibly, modification of federal and state laws in the 1970's will permit this product to be sold more widely.

Imitation milk is a nondairy product. Like the coffee whiteners, the whipped toppings, and margarine, it simulates and it is a substitute for a dairy product. Unfortunately, the first imitation-milk products were not true substitutes; they lacked the nutrients of milk in proper proportions. Milk is important in the diet of persons of all ages. An imitation that is not a true substitute poses problems that the failure of coffee whiteners and toppings to simulate creams truly does not; in fact, in addition to their low cost, a merit of these products is that they lack the fat of cream, which means that they lack the calories of cream. In May, 1968, the Food and Drug Administration proposed standards of identity and standards of quality for imitation milks and creams; the proposed standards would have established nutrient contents like those of the natural products. In May, 1970, the proposals were withdrawn for imitation milks on the grounds that the quantities of these products then being produced were so negligible as not to warrant the promulgation of the proposals. Perhaps, the idea for nondairy milk, produced other than for those allergic to milk, was born too soon. Properly composed to provide the nutrients of milk, especially the protein and the calcium, nondairy milk could be tailored for the low-cholesterol diet and other special dietary uses. When produced, it has been compounded from vegetable fat, soybean protein, sodium caseinate, corn syrup solids, flavoring agents, stabilizers, emulsifiers, and water. To avoid confusing the consumer it has been recommended that the filled and imitation products be packaged differently from milk, that *milk* not appear in the name of the imitation products, and that they not be sold alongside the dairy products in the dairy section in the supermarket (6).

Cream

A number of creams have been defined; in order of increasing milk-fat content they are half and half, coffee cream, light whipping cream, and heavy whipping cream. Homogenized whole milk has replaced cream in use as a coffee lightener to some extent. *Half-and-half*, which is a mixture of milk and cream of 10.5 per cent milk-fat content has to such an extent replaced coffee cream in use that the latter is unavailable in some grocery stores. *Coffee cream*, or *light cream*, or *table cream*, contains not less than 18 per cent milk fat. *Light whipping cream* has a milk-fat content of not less than 30 per cent; *heavy whipping cream*, not less than 36 per cent. All are available sterilized and aseptically packaged for longer storage life. Both coffee cream and whipping cream are available in aerosol containers. The former is less expensive than the latter. The volume to which each of these is whipped as it is expelled from the aerosol can is greater than the volume of the product whipped in the home kitchen. It is not possible to whip light cream in the home kitchen without the use of a special additive. The product purchased in the aerosol container is more expensive than the same product purchased unwhipped. Both half-and-half and whipping cream are occasional supermarket specials. The convenience of the ready-whipped products cannot be argued; and neither can the flavor of whipped fresh cream.

Sour cream is prepared from light cream. Pasteurized and homogenized cream is innoculated with a starter of organisms that produce the body, the flavor and aroma, and the acidity characteristic of the soured cream. Filled cream is also soured, but it may lack the flavor of real cultured sour cream. When available, it is less expensive than sour cream and would be suitable for all the culinary uses made of sour cream. *Sour half-and-half* is prepared from half-and-half cream. Sour cream and sour half-and-half can be used interchangeably for most culinary purposes except in baking, where the difference in fat content might affect the quality of the results. These products are spray-dried and are the product used in dry mixes for sour-cream sauce. When heated, sour cream will curdle quickly. It should be added near the end of the cooking period and used only over gentle heat. Sour cream thins when acid is added, as in salad dressing, but it rethickens on chilling. Sour cream can be whipped (it will thin momentarily and then thicken), but it will not form as stiff a foam as whipping cream.

Concentrated Milk Products

Fluid milk and milk products are concentrated by the removal of water; these concentrated products are evaporated milk, sweetened condensed milk, concentrated milk, nonfat dry milk, dried whole milk, and dried buttermilk. *Evaporated milk* is sterilized homogenized milk that has been reduced in volume by about 60 per cent loss of water. When aseptically canned, this product undergoes less flavor change and color modification than does the canned and sterilized product. When diluted with an equal volume of water, evaporated milk equals whole milk in composition. Vitamin D has been added to it in such a quantity that the vitamin D content is not less than 400 USP units per quart of diluted milk. Evaporated milk is now packaged in easy-open cans and contains an added stabilizer that retards fat separation. It costs about two thirds as much as fresh whole milk. Private-label brands are less expensive than national brands. Evaporated skim milk is also available. *Sweetened condensed milk* contains added sweetener; it has been condensed by the removal of about 50 per cent of the water content of whole milk. The content of milk fat is not less than 8.5 per cent; of sugar, about 44 per cent. The product is used mainly in cookery; it has some qualities that make it useful in the preparation of desserts and candies. *Concentrated milk* is prepared from pasteurized milk; the removal of water reduces volume to about one third. The product is not sterilized and does not contain added sugar. It must be preserved by freezing or refrigeration. The product has good flavor.

Both whole and skim milk can be dehydrated to a content of not more than 5 per cent of water. Dried whole milk is used mainly in infant feeding, but it can be reconstituted and used as fresh fluid milk. To prevent the development of rancidity, dried whole milk is packed in an inert gas and hermetically sealed in containers. Once the container is open, rancidity develops unless the milk is refrigerated. Its cost is not much different from that of fresh whole milk. Nonfat dry milk is inexpensive; when reconstituted it costs from one half to two thirds less than fluid whole milk or fluid fortified skim milk. It can be reconstituted and used like any fluid milk product. It can be used in the dry form for baking.

Because some persons do not like the flavor of skim milk, reconstituted nonfat dry milk is often blended quart for quart with whole fluid milk to produce a milk with good flavor at reduced cost. (The meal manager should be reminded that skim milks are lacking in fat and vitamin A unless fortified with the latter.) When calorie allowances permit, one ounce of margarine or butter will come very close to providing the vitamin A value of one quart of whole milk. If calorie allowances do not permit the butter or margarine, vitamin A can be derived from green and yellow vegetables and yellow fruits. In 1968, the definition and standard of identity for nonfat dry milk was amended to permit fortification with vitamins A and D: the consumer should buy the fortified kind. Grades for nonfat dry milk have been established; the only quality of instant nonfat dry milk is U.S. Extra Grade (Figure 8–1). There are two grades, U.S. Extra and U.S. Standard, for regular nonfat dry milk. The cost of nonfat dry milk in the supermarket differs with package size, whether premeasured or not, and brand. A supermarket's own brand will cost less than the nationally advertised brands (see Table 8–2). Nonfat dry milk is used extensively

FIGURE 8–1. Grademark for instant nonfat dry milk. (*United States Department of Agriculture photograph.*)

TABLE 8–2.   *Cost per Quart of Nonfat Dry Milk as It Varies with Purchase of Different Brands and Different Packages*

Items	Market Unit	Cost of Market Unit	Cost per. Quart
Brand A—not premeasured	20 qt.	$2.75	$.138
—not premeasured	14 qt.	1.99	.142
—not premeasured	8 qt.	1.25	.156
—not premeasured	3 qt.	.53	.180[1]
Brand A—premeasured for quarts	10 qt.	1.67	.167
—premeasured for quarts	5 qt.	.87	.174
Brand B—premeasured for half-gallons	10 half gal.	2.67	.135[2]
—premeasured for quarts	10 qt.	1.45	.145
Brand C—premeasured for quarts	8 qt.	1.33	.166
Brand D—premeasured for quarts	8 qt.	1.19	.150
—premeasured for quarts	4 qt.	.63	.160

[1]Most expensive.

[2]Least expensive, store brand

by the food industries in the preparation of meat products, breads and pastries, prepared mixes, ice cream mixes, and so on. Dried buttermilk is also extensively used by the food industries. *Malted milk* is prepared from whole milk and the liquid derived from the mash of ground barley malt and wheat flour. It contains not less than 7.5 per cent milk fat and not more than 3.5 per cent moisture. Mixes for chocolate-malted-milk drinks contain the malted milk and chocolate, cocoa, sugar, and nonfat dry milk. Mixes for diet drinks and instant breakfasts include nonfat dry milk, flavor substances, and other ingredients. Both dried cream and dried whey are extensively used by the food industries. Even a casual reading of the labels of food products reveals their presence.

At a given time and in a given place, milk and milk products differ in cost depending on treatment, fat content, size of container, and source from which purchased (see Table 8–1). Consumers find it advantageous to comparison-shop for milk as well as for other foods. Milk costs less per unit when purchased in gallon and half-gallon containers than in quart or half-pint containers. Generally, whole milk costs more than skim milk. Fluid skim milk costs more than nonfat dry milk reconstituted by the consumer. Home-delivered milk costs more than milk purchased at the supermarket, and milk purchased from a dairy store or other special outlet costs less than milk purchased at the supermarket. The cost of fluid milk products varies in cities and regions within the United States, i.e., the cost of one half-gallon of vitamin D milk at the grocery store was in February,

1971, sixty-eight cents in Atlanta, Georgia, and forty-eight cents in Milwaukee, Wisconsin (1).

Frozen Desserts

Frozen desserts include ice cream, frozen custard or French ice cream, ice milk, and sherbets and ices. All are made by the freezing while stirring of the ingredient mix from which each is prepared. Stirring effects the introduction of air and increases the volume of the mix 100 per cent or more. Increase in volume is called *overrun*; the extent of the overrun is controlled by the regulation of the solids content and/or the weight of the finished product. All mixes must be pasteurized, and all can be homogenized. The list of milk products that can be used in the mix is very long; it includes cream, dried cream, butter, milk, concentrated milk, evaporated milk, sweetened condensed milk, nonfat dry milk, and others. In addition to milk ingredients, the mix may contain some or all of the following: sweetening agents; eggs; natural and/or artificial flavoring agents; characterizing ingredients, such as fruits, fruit purees, fruit juices, and nuts; artificial color; and emulsifying and stabilizing agents. The content of stabilizing agent is limited to 0.5 per cent by federal definitions. Ice cream, French ice cream, ice milk, fruit sherbets, and water ices have been defined. The regulations of the states may be more stringent than federal regulations.

Ice cream has a minimum milk-fat content and total milk solids content of 10 and 20 per cent, respectively, of the weight of the finished product; exemptions permit the weight of milk fat and total milk solids to be only 8 and 16 per cent for ice creams in which chocolate, nuts, confections, and certain fruits are ingredients. Ice cream has not less than 1.6 pounds of total solids per gallon and weighs not less than 4.5 pounds per gallon. The only labeling requirement is that of characterizing ingredients, that is, the particular flavorings and food ingredients that characterize an ice cream. If an ice cream contains no artificial flavor, it takes the name(s) of the characterizing flavor(s), for example, "Vanilla Ice Cream." But, if an ice cream is flavored by both natural and artificial flavors and the natural one predominates, it is labeled as "flavored," that is, "Vanilla-Flavored Ice Cream." When an artificial flavor predominates or is the sole characterizing agent, the ice cream is described as "artificial" or "artificially flavored" ice cream, for example, "Artificially Flavored Vanilla Ice Cream." These labeling requirements apply to all frozen desserts. Optimum fat content imparts good body and flavor to ice cream. Available commercial ice creams differ in quality.

Frozen custard or *French ice cream* or *French custard ice cream* is ice cream in which the weight of egg-yolk solids is not less than 1.4 per cent the weight of the finished product. This product is priced higher than ice cream. *Ice milk* is less rich and less caloric than ice cream. Milk fat is not less than 2 per cent and not more than 7 per cent; total milk solids are not less than 11 per cent of the finished weight. The weight of total solids can be no less than 1.3 pounds per gallon; the weight per gallon is 4.5 pounds. The natural and artificial characterizing ingredients must be named on the labels. Label statement of use of artificial color is mandatory. Ice milk is available in hard- and soft-frozen forms.

Fruit sherbets contain not less than 1 per cent and not more than 2 per cent milk fat and not less than 2 per cent and not more than 5 per cent milk solids in the finished product. Fruit sherbets must weigh no less than 6 pounds per gallon. The characterizing ingredients of sherbet include fruits and fruit juices. The quantity of the fruit component must be 2 per cent in the case of citrus fruits, 6 per cent in the case of berries, and 10 per cent in the case of other fruits of the finished weight of the sherbet. Label statement of characterizing ingredients and use of artificial color is mandatory. *Water ices* contain no milk products, but in other respects are like fruit sherbets.

Mellorine is a product made with vegetable fat instead of milk fat; it is sold as imitation ice cream in some states.

Frozen desserts, especially ice creams available in the supermarket and dairy stores, differ in quality from products that just satisfy minimal requirements to products that are rich in milk fat, eggs, sugar, and other food ingredients. They differ in cost accordingly. The products of lower quality are lower priced; they are also correspondingly lower in calories. Frozen desserts can also differ in cost because of differences in the characterizing agents. Plain vanilla ice cream costs less to manufacture than an ice cream that contains nuts and fruits.

Butter

Butter consumption has trended downward in recent years, partly because butter has remained more expensive than margarines, and also because the margarines have improved in aroma and texture. Further, butter consumption has declined because of the implication of its saturated fatty acids in cardiovascular disease.

By definition, butter contains not less than 80 per cent milk fat. It is churned from pasteurized specially cultured sweet or sour cream of about 33 per cent milk fat content. The churned product is salted and worked to the legal moisture content. It is usually artificially colored; however, no statement of use of artificial color is required in labeling. The quality of butter depends mainly on the quality of the cream churned. Standards for grading butter for quality have been developed. See Figure 8–2 for the grade symbols. It will be noted that the quality grade is "when graded." Milk fat is subject to the rapid development of rancidity; hence, graded

FIGURE 8–2. Grade symbols for graded butter. (*United States Department of Agriculture photograph.*)

butter purchased at retail is frequently less than the indicated quality, a fact that has contributed to the consumption of less butter and more margarine. Butter quality is judged mainly on flavor and aroma but also on body, texture, color, and salt. Grades are U.S. Grade AA or U.S. 93 Score, U.S. Grade A or U.S. 92 Score, and U.S. Grade B or U.S. 90 Score. *Score* refers to the number of points a product could score out of 100. U.S. Grade AA butter is made from fresh cream; it has a delicate and pleasing flavor and aroma and smooth and creamy texture. Grade A butter is made from fresh cream; its flavor is good and it is only slightly lower in quality than U.S. Grade AA butter. U.S. Grade B butter is made from sour cream. Its flavor is like old-time country butter and it is preferred by some consumers though other consumers might describe it as having poor flavor.

Reprocessed butter is prepared from low-grade butter worked with fresh milk to remove some of the objectionable flavor substances and rectify other faults. *Danish butter* is manufactured from pasteurized cream innoculated with a mixture of organisms that produce flavors resembling old-style butter churned from soured cream. *Sweet butter* is unsalted butter. Salt acts as a preservative in butter; sweet butter is more perishable than salted butter and is usually priced higher. *Whipped butter* is butter into which air or an inert gas has been introduced. Whipped butter develops rancidity more rapidly than unwhipped butter. Its appeal is its ease of spreading and lower calorie content volume for volume. Garlic butter, honey butter, and maple butter are mixtures of butter and the named ingredients. Whipped butter and flavored butters are more expensive than butter weight for weight.

Packaging practices can modify the cost of butter of the same grade; for example, one pound blocks may cost less than one pound packaged in four four-ounce units. Ungraded butter wrapped in parchment but without further packaging is frequently specialed and may be a good buy. The best policy in buying butter is to buy and try. In supermarkets where there is rapid turnover of products, an ungraded product may be superior in quality to a graded product that moves slowly.

NONDAIRY PRODUCTS

Nondairy products simulate—that is, are substitutes for—dairy products. The ones that will be described here are the coffee creamers, toppings, and margarines. Imitation or nondairy milk was described earlier in this chapter, see page 238. The ingredients of these products include vegetable fat, vegetable protein, sodium caseinate, sweeteners, artificial flavors, artificial color, various additives (including preservatives, gums, emulsifiers, and stabilizers), and perhaps such vitamins as vitamin A and riboflavin. Though sodium caseinate is a milk derivative, it is considered a chemical rather than a milk ingredient. Nondairy products can be designed to have special dietary properties and they have fairly good storage life, two facts that explain their ready acceptance.

Coffee Whiteners

Coffee whiteners, or coffee creamers, or coffee lighteners can simulate either coffee cream or half-and-half, or they can contain less fat than either. They can be purchased as liquid, frozen liquid, or spray-dried coffee whitener. They are bland in flavor and almost odor free. All have good storage life when compared with fresh cream; and the powdered whiteners, of which there are several brands, are shelf storable. It should be noted, however, that they do not store indefinitely without loss of flavor and, with the flavor gone, taste becomes more apparent and may become unacceptable. Purchase of the economy-size package may not be warranted for the small family. The list of ingredients in one such product marketed in 1971 was as follows: "water, hydrogenated palm kernel oil, sodium caseinate, sugar, di-potassium phosphate, propylene glycol monostearate, polysorbate 60, stearoyl-lactylate, salt, artificial flavor and color." It is an imposing list of "goodies."

Nondairy Toppings

Nondairy toppings are available as dry mixes, as liquid mix ready for whipping, in pressurized containers, and frozen ready-whipped in plastic containers. The dry mixes are the most versatile. The mix can be added to water, milk, coffee, or chocolate milk; or spices can be added to the dry mix to produce flavorful toppings. The liquid mix would be whipped in the same manner as whipping cream. The product in the aerosol container whips to good volume as it is propelled from the container. The ready-whipped topping can be spooned from the container and immediately placed on food. The products may differ in the stability of the foam. Advantages of the nondairy toppings over whipping cream are lower fat content, lower cost per serving, and greater convenience. For all that, the lover of good food prefers whipping cream.

Margarine

Even though the fats and oils used in the production of margarine may be churned in milk or milk products and even though small quantities of butter can by definition be present in margarine, we shall consider the margarines of the marketplace to be nondairy products produced to resemble butter, a dairy product. An identity standard has been promulgated for margarine. It recognizes *margarine* and *oleomargarine* as synonymous and makes mandatory the full listing of all ingredients in decreasing order of predominance. The product has the same fat content as butter: no less than 80 per cent. The fat component may be of plant and/or animal origin, but is generally of plant origin. Oils in use in margarine manufacture include soybean oil, corn oil, safflower oil, coconut oil, cottonseed oil, neutral lard, oleo oil (the fraction of beef fat fluid at room temperature), and oleo stock (beef fat rendered at low temperature). However, 70 per cent of the oil used in margarine production is soybean oil. The oils may be partially hydrogenated. The kinds and combinations of oils used vary from time to time relative to costs. Margarine is prepared by thorough mixing of the fat component with a pasteurized and cultured milk component, or with water, or with a mixture of finely ground soybeans and water when the fat component is a vegetable fat or oil. Permitted ingredients include flavor substances that give it the flavor of butter, artificial coloring, butter, salt, and additives such as emulsifiers, an antispattering agent, and preservatives. When vitamin A is added—and it is almost universally—margarine contains not less than fifteen thousand units per pound, a content that makes it equal in vitamin A value to the yearly average for butter. The production of soft, easy-spread margarines with favorable polyunsaturated to saturated fatty acid ratios improved consumer acceptance of the product. Imitation margarines with half the fat content required by the definition have half the calorie content of regular margarines. Whipped margarine, like whipped butter, has fewer calories per equal volume than regular margarine.

Margarines are available at widely differing costs, with the most expensive ones being twice as costly as the least expensive ones. The kind of oil or oils, the treatment of the product, the packaging of the product, and the brand name account for cost differences. Store brands are less expensive than name brands. They are also frequent specials. Careful reading of information in the labeling reveals differences in composition. Freezing to extend storage life is practical.

Eggs

Until very recently, eggs were one of the few foods that the housewife purchased little altered by technology, about 90 per cent of production being consumed as shell eggs (Figure 6–2). The percentage not used as shell eggs was used by the food industries as fluid, frozen, or dehydrated products. It is now possible for the consumer to purchase omelet mixtures ready for the fry pan. She can also buy seasoning mixtures for omelets; but in this instance, she must provide the eggs. Instant scrambled eggs, frozen fried eggs, canned eggnog, and many other convenient egg foods are being market tested. Precooked and frozen scrambled eggs with sausage are one combination of ready-to-eat breakfasts marketed.

In most retail markets, the consumer can purchase shell eggs by grade and size—and sometimes by shell color. Although white eggs are preferred to brown eggs in some areas and brown to white in other areas, the color of the shell per se in no way affects the quality, the flavor, or the nutrient value of the egg. The shell color is determined by the breed of chicken. In areas where white eggs are preferred to brown eggs, they command a higher price; conversely, brown eggs may cost more in areas where they are preferred.

The grading and classing of eggs is sorting them according to quality and weight. Egg quality is determined by four primary factors: the clarity and thickness of the white, the condition of the yolk, the condition and size of the air cell, and the texture and condition of the shell. The usual method of grading eggs is by candling, that is, inspection of the interior of the unbroken egg under bright light in a darkened place. In large operations, eggs are candled en masse on conveyers that move over multiple lights. Consumer grades for shell eggs are U.S. Grade AA, U.S. Grade A, U.S. Grade B, and U.S. Grade C; however, the latter two grades are not often found in the supermarket as such (Figure 8–3). Tolerances permit small percentages of the lower grades and also eggs described as "Check" in cartons; for example, a carton of eggs of U.S. AA Grade is permitted to contain two eggs of A grade and two eggs of B, C, or Check quality. In

FIGURE 8–3. Grademark for graded eggs. (*United States Department of Agriculture photograph.*)

fact, each carton of Grade A and Grade B eggs is required to contain only eight eggs of those qualities respectively; the remaining four may be of lesser quality, as above.

Eggs begin to lose quality immediately after laying, and deterioration is rapid unless delayed by refrigeration. Eggs that bear the USDA grade symbol must have been graded in a room wherein the temperature range was from 40°F to 70°F and held thereafter at not less than 60°F. Only eggs of "current production,"—that is, those held under refrigeration no longer than thirty days—are identified with consumer grade-marks. Changes that occur in eggs as they deteriorate are several: the air cell enlarges, the firm

TABLE 8-3. *Summary of United States Standards for Quality of Individual Shell Eggs*[1]

| Quality Factor | Specifications for each quality factor | | | |
	AA Quality	A Quality	B Quality	C Quality
Shell	Clean; unbroken; practically normal.	Clean; unbroken; practically normal.	Clean to very slightly stained; may be slightly abnormal.	Clean to moderately stained; unbroken; may be abnormal.
Air cell	1/8 inch or less in depth; practically regular.	3/16 inch or less in depth; practically regular.	3/8 inch or less in depth; may be free or bubbly.	May be over 3/8 inch in depth; may be free or bubbly.
White	Clear; firm.	Clear; may be reasonably firm.	Clear; may be slightly weak.	May be weak and watery; small blood clots or spots may be present.
Yolk	Outline slightly defined; practically free from defects.	Outline may be fairly well defined; practically free from defects.	Outline may be well defined; may be slightly enlarged and flattened; may show definite but not serious defects.	Outline may be plainly visible; may be enlarged and flattened; may show clearly visible germ development but no blood; may show other serious defects.

[1]Source: *Regulations Governing the Grading of Shell Eggs and United States Standards, Grades, and Weight Classes for Shell Eggs*; Poultry Division, Consumer and Marketing Service, United States Department of Agriculture, Washington, D.C., July, 1969.

white thins, and the yolk increases in water content, thereby stretching the membrane that surrounds it. Candling reveals these changes. As the firm white thins, the yolk becomes mobile and visible; the presence of blood spots in the white is detectable. Table 8–3 summarizes the grade specifications for each grade. Note that shells may not be broken and that only Grade B and Grade C eggs may have stained shells. Eggs with coarse-textured shells score lower than eggs with fine-textured shells. Because eggs can deteriorate post grading, it is required that each carton be marked with either the grading date, the expiration date, or a combination of grading and expiration date either on the carton or on the tape used to seal the carton. The grading date may be expressed as the month and day or the number of the month and day (for example, 5-19 for May 19), or as the consecutive day of the year (for example, 129 for May 19). If the expiration date is used, it is stated as month and day or the number of the month and day preceded by the letters *EXP* or a statement such as, "Not to Be Sold After." The expiration date is no more than fourteen days later than the date of grading.

A second set of grade symbols may be found on graded eggs available in the supermarket. In 1959, a program for the production and marketing of quality-controlled eggs was initiated by the United States Department of Agriculture and the industry. Eggs produced under this program are Grade AA, or Fresh Fancy Quality, and Grade A, and they are further identified by the statement, "Produced and Marketed Under Federal-State Quality Control Program," which accompanies the grade symbol (Figure 8–4). To control the quality of Fresh Fancy Quality eggs, it is required that they be gathered twice or three times daily, that they be promptly cooled to a temperature of 60°F or less, and that they be held at 60°F or less and at a relative humidity of approximately 70 per cent. The quality of the eggs is determined by measurement of the height of the thick white and observation of the yolk, which must be well-rounded and quite uni-

FIGURE 8–4. Grade symbol for Fresh Fancy Quality eggs. (*United States Department of Agriculture photograph.*)

FIGURE 8–5. Measuring the thickness of the thick white of eggs. (*United States Department of Agriculture photograph.*)

form in color (Figure 8–5). The quality of the white is expressed in *Haugh units,* a numerical value derived from the weight of the egg expressed in ounces and the height of the white as measured by a micrometer. Because various factors determine the thickness of egg white, eggs from different flocks are graded separately. A flock consists of birds within sixty days of age. A flock remains on the program only so long as a biweekly sample of eggs scores not less than the designated number of Haugh units and meets

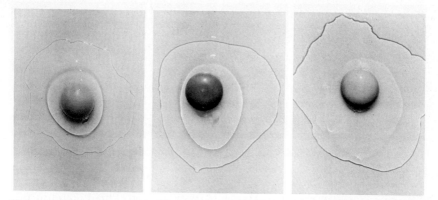

FIGURE 8–6. Appearance of broken-out eggs. From left to right, U.S. AA Grade, U.S. A Grade, and U.S. Grade B qualities. (*United States Department of Agriculture photographs.*)

other stipulations. For Fresh Fancy Quality eggs, the sample must average not less than 84 Haugh units and not more than one egg in a sample of ten can have a Haugh value of less than 60 Haugh units. For U.S. A Grade quality, the sample must average not less than 62 Haugh units and no more than two eggs in a sample of ten can have a Haugh value of less than 60 Haugh units. Cartons of Fresh Fancy Quality eggs are required to be marked with an expiration date that is ten days from the date of packing. Packing must occur within six days of testing.

The broken-out egg quickly reveals its quality (Figure 8–6). The broken-out U.S. Grade AA egg does not spread much (it covers a small area); the white is thick and stands firmly around the yolk; the yolk appears rounded. The broken-out U.S. Grade A egg spreads some; the white does not cling as firmly around the yolk; the yolk is flattened somewhat. The broken-out U.S. Grade B egg spreads widely; the yolk is flattened. The changes are not necessarily accompanied by flavor change. Eggs with bad flavor are rarely purchased. Grade B eggs do not give a good appearance when poached or fried; but they are satisfactory for other egg dishes and for cooking.

Of practical concern to the consumer is information regarding the pricing of eggs in relation to size. Eggs are classified by weight per dozen as Jumbo, Extra Large, Large, Medium, Small, and Peewee. Of these classes, Extra Large, Large, and Medium are commonly available in the supermarket. Crossbreeding of chickens and scientific feeding of laying hens have increased not only egg production but the size of eggs as well. Small eggs were not uncommon a few years ago; they are rarely seen today. And eggs of Jumbo size may often be found in large supermarkets. Class and weight per dozen eggs are Jumbo, thirty ounces; Extra Large, twenty-seven ounces; Large, twenty-four ounces; Medium, twenty-one ounces; Small, eighteen ounces; and Peewee, fifteen ounces (see Figure 8–7). The weight

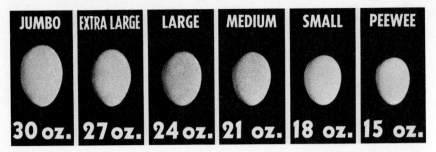

FIGURE 8–7. Weight classes for eggs. (*United States Department of Agriculture photograph.*)

difference between each two classes is three ounces. This difference provides a basis for selection among classes. Because Extra Large, Large, and Medium are the sizes most frequently available, only comparative prices among them will be discussed. Extra Large eggs weigh three ounces more and Medium eggs three ounces less than Large eggs, that is, one-eighth or about 12 per cent more or less. Accordingly, the price differential should be about 12 per cent for equal weights of eggs. Thus if Large eggs are priced at sixty-four cents, Extra Large at seventy-two cents, and Medium at fifty-six cents, there is no difference in cost and any selection buys as much egg as any other. Actually, pricing is rarely so precise; in practice, the smaller size may be overpriced and the larger size underpriced. A rule of thumb suggests that if the difference is less than seven cents between one size and the next smaller size, buy the larger size (4). Obviously, price comparisons must be made within the same quality grades. The consumer may decide that the smallest absolute investment is her goal; in this instance, she would purchase the smallest available size. Differences of three or six ounces divided among twelve units are not very significant. It is said that recipes assume the use of Medium eggs. Some recently developed recipes express egg requirements in measure.

Purchased eggs should be refrigerated immediately in the carton in which they were purchased. Commercially, eggs may be dipped in or sprayed with colorless mineral oil as an aid to the conservation of quality. Oiling retards the losses of water and carbon dioxide and delays the chemical and physical changes that accompany staling. Eggs are packed in cartons with the large end uppermost to prevent mechanical damage to the egg.

Nearly every state has some sort of egg law. The federal standards frequently form the basis for these laws. In many states, eggs are federal-state graded. In some states only graded eggs can be sold.

In December, 1970, the Egg Products Inspection Act was passed; it became effective July 15, 1971. It requires that all eggs broken for commercial purposes be pasteurized and that the breaking process be carried out under continuous inspection.

Summary. The variety in dairy products and in nondairy products increases with time; eggs remain simply eggs, but the decade of the 1970's may see the production of imitation eggs. Variety, quality differences, packaging styles, and different market resources make it possible for consumers to be selective. We can comparison-shop, buy and try, then decide how to spend dollars for the products we want and/or can buy. Dollars can buy greater or lesser quantities of dairy products, of nondairy products, and of eggs—our decisions determine whether we get the lesser or the greater quantities. The following guides suggest how to maximize the dollars for these products.

BUYING GUIDES

Milk

1. Research your market area for a dairy store or other special markets that sell dairy products at prices lower than supermarkets. Milk processing is so regulated and standardized and packaging so tight that you can assume products are safe.

2. Avoid home delivery if at all possible because the cost for this service is high. The United States average price was sixty-seven cents for one half-gallon of vitamin D milk delivered versus fifty-eight cents for the same product bought at the grocery store in February, 1971.

3. Buy the largest container of fluid milk that you can use and store; the cost per unit should decrease as the container size increases.

4. Look for filled milk. If available and if priced right, it will be a good buy. Read the label to discover the kind of fat substituted for milk fat. It ought not to be coconut oil, but rather soybean or corn oil.

5. Look for nondairy milk, but don't buy it unless its composition simulates that of milk.

6. If you buy nonfat dry milk for reconstituting for drinking, comparison-shop your markets for the best product at the lowest cost. Private-label products are less expensive than national brands. All instant nonfat dry milk products are of the same grade.

7. Use as much nonfat dry milk as you can. It is your most-for-the-dollar milk. Buy it in the largest container practical for your use. You will spend more when you buy the package with measured-out units that reconstitute to one quart.

8. Use evaporated milk for an inexpensive, rich milk in cooking.

9. Use nonfat dry milk and evaporated milk for whipping whenever suitable. Many recipes have been especially developed for such intended use.

10. Use the topping mixes instead of whipping cream; they are less expensive in dollars and calories.

11.   Whipping cream is sometimes specialed; buy and freeze it if you prefer it for desserts and toppings.

12.   Use nondairy products in coffee; they are somewhat less expensive and may be lower in calories than dairy counterparts.

13.   Make your own chocolate milk and other milk beverages, including diet drinks and "instant breakfast" mixes.

Butter

1.   The pound-block of butter is often less expensive than butter packed in four-ounce sticks.

2.   You can freeze butter to preserve quality.

3.   Even when graded, the quality of butter is not always as good as the consumer expects. Frequently, an ungraded product of local origin will be very good. Try what the market offers.

4.   Whipped butter is expensive and deteriorates rapidly. Flavored butters like garlic butter are expensive. Compare the cost ounce for ounce of the flavored and unflavored products. Make your own.

5.   Unsalted butter is more expensive than salted butter and keeps less well.

6.   Buy margarine instead of butter; it is much less expensive. Or use a combination of butter and margarine in cooking if you prefer the butter flavor. Butter flavoring is available for culinary uses.

Eggs

1.   Buy eggs only from a refrigerated cabinet.

2.   For frying or poaching, U.S. Grade A or U.S. Grade AA eggs give the best appearance. U.S. Grade B eggs would be suitable for other uses.

3.   Buy the size of egg that gives the best bargain.

4.   Before buying omelet mixtures, calculate the cost. The convenience of the mixture is pretty expensive.

5.   Color of shell is not a factor of quality.

6.   Refrigerate eggs in the cartons in which they were purchased.

7.   Per pound, frozen whole eggs equal ten whole Large eggs and dried whole eggs equal thirty-two eggs.

8.   Two and one-half tablespoons of dried whole egg plus two and one-half tablespoons of water are equivalent to one egg.

REFERENCES CITED

1.   *Estimated Retail Food Prices by Cities*, United States Department of Labor, Washington, D.C. (February 1971).

2. *Food Consumption of Households in the United States, Spring, 1965,* Consumer and Food Economics Research Division, United States Department of Agriculture, Washington, D.C. (1968), p. 203.

3. *Grade "A" Pasteurized Milk Ordinance—1965 Recommendations of the United States Public Health Service,* Public Health Service Publication No. 229, United States Department of Health, Education, and Welfare, Washington, D.C. (1965).

4. Handy, A. Elizabeth, "Eggs—Nature's Prepackaged Masterpiece of Nutrition" in *Food for Us All—Yearbook of Agriculture 1969,* United States Department of Agriculture, Washington, D.C., 1969.

5. "Per Capita Food Consumption," *National Food Situation,* Economic Research Service, United States Department of Agriculture, Washington, D.C. (February 1971), p. 12.

6. "Substitute Milk," *Consumer Reports* 34:8 (January 1969).

Chapter 9
Purchasing Food—Fruits

Models and patterns for planning nutritionally adequate meals suggest a minimum of four servings of fruits and/or vegetables per day. Food preference studies of men in the armed forces (5) suggested that fruits have high preference; vegetables, low. The *Gallup Survey—The National Poll of Patron Preferences, Prejudices, and Trends* (2) found that 63 per cent of those surveyed would select fresh fruit cocktail as an appetizer, 47 per cent would select a grapefruit half, 42 per cent would choose apple pie for dessert, and 19 per cent of women would choose fresh fruit for dessert. During this century, per-capita consumption of fruit trended upward until in the mid-1940's; since then it has slowly trended downward, a direction sustained in the 1960's. Per-capita consumption of the civilian population was a total of some 130 pounds (retail weight) in both 1970 and 1971 in contrast to 142 pounds in 1960, and 150 pounds in 1950 (see Figures 9–1 and 9–2). The food consumption survey made in spring of 1965 (1) found per-household fruit consumption per week to be 8.2 pounds fresh and about 4 pounds processed, that is, as canned fruits, canned and frozen juices, fresh juice, and dried fruit. The money value of this quantity of fruit was about $2.10, an expenditure of about 7 per cent of the dollar spent for food at home. About 57 per cent of this expenditure was for fresh fruit, with apples and bananas the choices for which most money was spent. However, as might be anticipated, the quantity of fruit consumed was less than the household average when income was below $5,000 (after taxes) per household per year; thereafter the quantities of fresh and processed fruits, excepting dried ones, increased with income.

Fruits in all forms are abundantly available, the fresh in great variety the year round; but they are sometimes costly enough so that the food

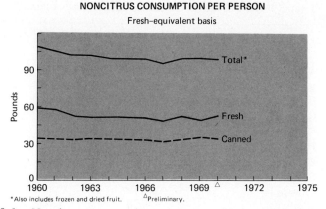

FIGURE 9–1. Noncitrus consumption per person. (*United States Department of Agriculture photograph.*)

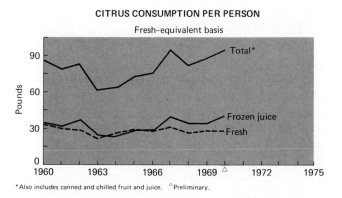

FIGURE 9–2. Citrus consumption per person. (*United States Department of Agriculture photograph.*)

dollar is used to buy meat, potatoes, and milk instead, the rationale being that the latter are necessary and the former, luxuries. It is true that some fresh fruits, some frozen fruits, and some canned items are costly. To decide what to buy, it is necessary to compare them on the basis of cost per serving: the different ones available fresh, fresh with the same kinds canned or frozen, and the canned with the same kind frozen. For example, a serving of bananas costs less than one of strawberries even when the latter are in season; a serving of canned or frozen orange juice, less than fresh-squeezed orange juice; and canned pineapple, less than frozen. When it is necessary to maximize the dollar, the consumer ought actually to estimate per-serving costs and then buy accordingly, that is to say, one eats what the purse will bear (Table 9–1).

TABLE 9-1.   *Per-Serving Cost of Some Fresh Fruits*[1]

Items	Market Unit and Cost	Per-Serving Cost[2]
Apples, Delicious	69¢/8	$0.086
Bananas	12¢/lb.	0.040
Cantaloupe	59¢/each	0.300
Grapefruit	25¢/2	0.063
Grapes	79¢/lb.	0.200
Honeydew melon	79¢/each	0.133
Oranges	99¢/12	0.085
Pears	39¢/lb.	0.200
Pineapple	39¢/each	0.100
Rhubarb	39¢/lb.	0.100
Strawberries	39¢/pint	0.130
Watermelon	69¢/¼ melon	0.170

[1]All prices as of Spring, 1971 when most of these would be out of season. All prices are supermarket prices.

[2]Average servings.

Fruit portions are not as standardized as are some other food portions. Canned fruit portions weigh about four ounces, including the weight of juices; frozen fruit portions weigh about three ounces because of the smaller quantity of juices. Fresh fruit portions vary with kind: a portion of grapes may weigh three ounces, but a portion of melon may weigh much more. The size of fresh fruit portions is judged by the eye; for example, a melon will cut four, six, or eight portions. When of small to medium size, apples, bananas, oranges, peaches, and pears serve out as portions. Unless whole fruits or pieces are very large, the No. 303 can and the No. 2½ can will yield four and six or seven portions, respectively, of canned fruit. There is, perhaps, more variation in the actual size of fruit portions than other food portions.

FRESH FRUITS

Because of developments in agriculture (that is, fruit production; increased knowledge of how to harvest, package, and store fruits; technological developments; and rapid systems of transport) we enjoy a great variety of fresh fruits throughout the year regardless of our region of residence—strawberries in December and plums and watermelons in March. Fresh fruits are at their best when ripe; after reaching the peak of ripeness they are highly perishable and deteriorate quickly. Quick cooling after harvesting, proper packaging, storage at appropriate temperatures in transit and in warehouses, control of humidity, and control of the carbon dioxide-oxygen ratio in the storage atmosphere and in packaging are means of protecting quality and retarding spoilage in fresh fruits. Maintenance of the proper degree of humidity keeps fruits from drying; the right carbon dioxide-oxygen ratio retards ripening and spoilage by yeasts and molds. Ethylene gas is sometimes used to hasten ripening and color development of products, such as bananas and tomatoes, harvested in the unripe state. Ethylene gas effects destruction of chlorophyll and stimulates the development of red pigments. Their perishability makes fresh fruits high margin items; we often find the processed ones less expensive than the same ones fresh except at harvest time.

The perishability of fresh fruits precludes the use of consumer grades for fresh fruits; there are, however, commercial grades for most of the fresh fruits that consumers purchase in any quantity. For about half of them the top grade is U.S. Fancy followed by U.S. No. 1, U.S. No. 2, or other grade; for the remainder, the top grade is U.S. No. 1 followed by U.S. No. 2 and so on. Exceptions include the apple and the pear. For the apple, the top grade is U.S. Extra Fancy followed by U.S. Fancy; for winter pears, the top grade is U.S. Extra No. 1 followed by U.S. No. 1. Trading at wholesale is by grade; wholesale containers are often grade labeled. It becomes possible therefore to discover the quality of a fruit when it was packaged for shipment by inquiry in the produce department. Many fresh fruits, especially winter pears, nectarines, and table grapes are the U.S. Fancy quality or the U.S. No. 1 quality. Further, bags of apples, grapefruit, and oranges labeled with wholesale grade are sometimes sold in the supermarket.

We do our own quality grading of fresh fruits at the supermarket. Such factors as aroma, color, condition of stem end or blossom end, appearance, and feel of skin are clues to degree of ripeness. The degree of ripeness, the size and shape of fruits, and freedom from blemishes, defects, and spoilage are guides to quality. The intended use and the kind of fruit determine the quality that should be purchased. Some fruits to be eaten fresh, such as melons, strawberries, and pineapples, ought to be of the best quality; others, such as apples and plums to be stewed, can be of lower quality.

The selection of fresh fruits and their subsequent proper management require some knowledge, or are favored by some knowledge. Fruits mature, that is, they develop the full size and the character unique for each species and variety; then they ripen. Ripening is a relatively short period during which enzymes effect some or all of the following changes: decrease in tartness, decrease in starchiness, increase in sweetness, decrease in astringency, softening, color modification, and development of flavor and aroma. Ripening changes do not occur in fruits harvested when immature. Fruits fall into two groups with regard to the ripening period. One group includes those that are harvested when mature but not ripe and that ripen during storage, for example, apples, bananas, and pears. The second group includes those fruits that must be both mature and ripe at harvest, such as oranges, grapes, and strawberries. This latter group may develop color and some aroma if harvested unripe, but they will not become sweeter (the orange and melon, for example). In general, this is the more perishable group; once fruits in this group have reached a peak in development, they require proper treatment and storage. Even so, they deteriorate rapidly by becoming overripe because the enzymes that effected ripening continue to effect chemical changes. Overripe fruits are characterized by wateriness, extreme softness, fiberiness, and modified flavor that may range from insipid to distasteful. An overripe melon exemplifies these changes: it becomes mushy and very juicy; the seeds are free from the pulp; and the flavor is not pleasant.

Information of special interest about frequently, and not so frequently, purchased fruits follows.

Apples

The apple is more widely grown than any other fruit. Apple production has become an exact and complex science, with the result that apples are bigger, better in shape, and more free from defects than heretofore. Though there are several hundred named apple varieties, there are only twenty-four popular commercial varieties. These are grown in some thirty-four of the states; but the main producers are Washington, New York, Michigan, Virginia, California, and Pennsylvania. Low-temperature and controlled-atmosphere storage have extended the apple season from late summer into June, even July. However, the longer the period of storage, the shorter will be the poststorage life of the apple; and the higher the ambient temperature, the more rapid its deterioration. Apples are better and they keep better at some times of the year than at others.

Apple varieties differ in shape from globular to oblate; in external color, which may be red, green, yellow, russet, or a combination of these; in flesh color, which may be creamy or snow white; in size; in flavor from sweet to sour with or without bitterness or astringency; in fullness of aroma; in flesh characteristics; in seasonal availability; and in suitability for different uses.

Summer varieties of apples come onto the market in all regions of the United States. Although these are less anticipated than formerly, they are still welcomed. They are perishable, they are tart, and they make good sauce and pies. Summer varieties include the Astrachan, the Fenton, the Gravenstein, and the Yellow Transparent. The latter is good eaten fresh when it is ripe.

Among the fall and winter varieties, the apple produced and consumed in greatest quantity is the Delicious; the second is the McIntosh. The apple, like the banana and the pear, ripens post harvest; however, it must be mature at harvesting. It contains starch that is converted to sugar during ripening, increasing the sweatness of the apple; further, texture is modified. A mature but unripened apple can be hard and sour. After purchase, apples should be kept in a cool place, and that means the refrigerator in most homes in the 1970's, though for eating out of hand, an apple may have more flavor if brought to room temperature before eating. The apple is an excellent choice of fruit to serve with many different cheese varieties.

In general, choices among apple varieties are limited in supermarkets. When available, good varieties for eating out of hand are Cortland, Red Delicious, Golden Delicious, Grimes Golden, Jonathan, McIntosh, Stayman, and Winesap. Good varieties for pie and apple sauce are Baldwin, Gravenstein, Rhode Island Greening, Grimes Golden, Jonathan, McIntosh, Northern Spy, Winesap, and Yellow Newton. Varieties good for baking because they retain their shape are Northern Spy, Rhode Island Greening, Rome Beauty, Winesap, and York Imperial. All-purpose varieties include Grimes Golden, Jonathan, Golden Delicious, McIntosh, Stayman, and Winesap. Two varieties with long storage life are the Yellow Newton and the Winesap, these are of good quality in late winter and spring.

Most apples are marketed by grade. Many consumer packages show the variety, the grade, and the size. Frequently, when apples are displayed unpackaged, a nearby sign provides this information. The U.S. grades in descending order are U.S. Extra Fancy, U.S. Fancy, U.S. No. 1, U.S. Utility, and combinations of these grades as Combination U.S. Extra Fancy and U.S. Fancy. U.S. grades require that each closed container of U.S. graded apples show the numerical count or minimum diameter. A bushel of apples weighs about fifty pounds and the number of apples per bushel ranges from 48 to 232 but nothing smaller than 175 apples per bushel is marketed fresh. Extra Large apples have a count of 48, 56, 64, and 72; Large, 80, 88, and 100; Medium, 113, 125, and 138; Small, 150, 163, and 175 per bushel. A pound of apples would have a count of from 1 to 3 to 4, depending on size. Apples marketed in bags run in diameter ranges, such as $2\frac{1}{4}$ to $2\frac{3}{4}$ inches; or $2\frac{1}{2}$ to 3 inches. Apple sizes are usually based on these standards: small are less than $2\frac{1}{2}$ inches in diameter; medium, $2\frac{1}{2}$ to 3; large, over 3 inches in diameter.

When purchasing apples, buy a variety suited to the intended use whenever possible. Select fruit that is firm, of proper color for variety, and free of such defects as will affect the eating quality and/or the yield of usable fruit.

Avocadoes

The avocado is available throughout the year. Those from California—Calavo—are heaviest in supply from January to July and from Florida—Flavocado—from August to January. Because there are two species of avocado and many commercial varieties; those on the market differ in shape, size, color, thickness of skin, and thickness of pulp. In general the avocado is pear-shaped though it may be almost as round as an orange. The skin may be thick or thin; smooth or pebbled; and though usually some shade of green, the skin of the avocado may be purple to black. The avocado ripens after harvest. Left at room temperature the flesh softens and becomes yellow in color. It has a delicate, nutty flavor that is enhanced by salt and/or acid, such as lemon or lime juice or vinegar. An avocado is ready for eating when it feels soft under gentle pressure. It is a tropical fruit and does not like the cold; keep it under only mild refrigeration. The avocado may be peeled and then sliced or cubed and used in salads or fruit cups. It is also cut in half and eaten with a spoon, or the peeled half may be filled with a seafood or chicken salad. Quacamole is a dish prepared by the mashing and seasoning of the pulp.

Citrus Fruits

Though much of the crop of citrus fruits is processed, the fresh fruits are available throughout the year. Supply, quality, and cost vary from time to time; the quality is best and the cost most reasonable when the supply is best. Citrus fruits are tree ripened; their storage life is limited; their quality varies inversely with the length of the storage period.

Six species of citrus fruits provide the citrus fruits we eat and use. The species produced in greatest quantity is the sweet orange, *Citrus sinensis.* There are numerous varieties of sweet oranges; they are available almost throughout the year; they vary in price from season to season. They differ in size, color and thickness of skin, the presence or absence of seeds, and flavor. A second species is the Mandarin orange, *Citrus reticulata.* This group includes tangerines, Satsumas, and Temple and King oranges. These are yellow to deep orange in color and are oblate in shape, that is, flattened at the poles. They are easily peeled and sectioned. The third orange species is *Citrus aurantium,* the Seville or bitter orange. This group provides the rootstock on which commercial varieties are budded. The fruits of the species are not eaten but are used in making marmalade and in the production of orange juice concentrates. Species names will appear subsequently when the definitions for orange juice and orange juice concentrates are discussed. *Citrus paradisi* includes the many varieties of grapefruit; the remaining two species are lemons and limes.

Citrus-growing areas are California, Arizona, New Mexico, Texas,

Florida, and also Mississippi and Louisiana. Oranges are produced in the Gulf States—Florida, Mississippi, and Louisiana; in the western states of California, Arizona, and New Mexico; and in Texas. Oranges grown in the Gulf States are generally thin-skinned, juicy, and more often a light-orange color than are western oranges, which are thicker skinned, less juicy, and deeper in color due to environmental conditions. The oranges from Texas resemble those from both the East and the West. The Valencia is the most important commercial orange variety. It is thin-skinned, juicy, of well-colored flesh, and contains some seeds. The season of the western Valencia is from April through October; it is excellent for slicing as well as juicing. The season for the Florida Valencia is February through May and through June if stored. The Valencia is slow in maturing and is present on the tree when it blooms for the next crop. Fruit may "regreen" at the stem end with the flush of spring growth. This green in no way affects the quality of the orange. Oranges are required by state regulations to be well matured before being harvested and shipped out of the state. Maturity is measured by a test of sugar, acid, and solids content. The Washington Navel is the next most important orange variety. It is principally a California orange, though it is produced in the other orange-growing areas. It has thicker and more pebbled skin than the Valencia variety; it is truly orange in color; it has a characterizing mark at the blossom end that is the aborted ovary; it is seedless. This variety peels and sections easily and is suited for slicing, salads, fruit cups, and so on. California navels are shipped from November through May; the Florida variety from October through January.

There are other Florida orange varieties, the season for them extends from October through May. Juice varieties include the almost seedless early Hamlin; the seedy Parson Brown; the seedy Pineapple orange; the Homosassa; and various unnamed seedling oranges. Of these the Pineapple has the best flavor. The new Murcott Honey orange is for eating out of hand; it is sweet, is almost seedless, and has the taste of honey. These Florida oranges may have artificially colored rinds to give them a richer orange color.

There are several varieties of the species *Citrus reticulata*, or Mandarin orange. Tangerines, of which there are several varieties, are the best known of this species. They are associated with Christmas, though they are available from November to March. They are small, from two to almost three inches in diameter; are flattened at top and bottom; have a loose skin that is deep orange in color; have orange-colored flesh; and are sweet and juicy. The Temple orange is larger than the tangerine; it is less vivid in color than the tangerine; it has a pebbled skin and a fine flavor and aroma. It is best in December. The King orange resembles the Temple orange, but it is lighter in color, has an astringent taste, and is not as good as the Temple orange. The Satsuma orange is like the tangerine, though usually larger; it matures earlier than the tangerine. The Calamondin belongs to this species. It is of no commercial value, but makes excellent marmalade. It looks like a very small tangerine.

About half of the grapefruit crop is eaten fresh. Fresh grapefruit are marketed in all months, with the largest supplies available from January through May and the smallest quantities from June through September. The Florida season begins with September and ends in July. Florida is the big producer of grapefruit and Florida-derived varieties have been introduced around the world. The California season begins in October and continues through the year, with the desert valleys providing fruit from October through June and the other areas from June into September. Texas and Arizona produce grapefruit from October through June. The main varieties of grapefruit are the seedy Duncan and its related kinds and the Marsh Seedless and its related kinds. The former is the progenitor of all other varieties. There are seedy varieties similar to the Duncan, but differences are so slight that varietal names have been dropped and they are known as Duncan or Florida Common. Characteristics of this variety and its related types are a smooth yellow rind about one-fourth inch thick; thirty to fifty seeds per fruit; range in shape from spherical to oblate; medium to large in size, or from a diameter of three and one-half to five inches; twelve to fourteen segments per fruit; and finally, a truly excellent flavor. The Marsh Seedless variety originated as a seedling from the Duncan. It is similar to the Duncan in shape; has a smooth, light yellow rind; is medium to large in size; has three to eight seeds per fruit or may be seedless; is juicy and well flavored. The first pink variety was the Foster; it was a bud sport discovered early in the century; it is seedy. Deriving from the Marsh Seedless as a bud sport is the Thompson, or Pink Marsh; it is pink-fleshed and seedless. The Ruby is a red-fleshed variety that originated from the Thompson as a bud sport. It has a crimson flush on the rind; membranes as well as flesh are pigmented, but not the juice. Burgundy Red is a bud mutation of the Marsh; it has a thick rind, reddish flesh, and a few seeds. The Ruby originated in Texas, the others in Florida. The pink and pale varieties do not differ in flavor but the seedy varieties have more flavor than the seedless. The blossom half of the grapefruit is sweeter than the stem half (3).

The use of fresh lemons and limes has trended downward because of the availability of processed products. Virtually all lemons come from California and Arizona, whereas most limes come from Florida. Lemon picking is continuous throughout the year as the lemon tree has the unique ability of fruiting, budding, and flowering simultaneously. The lemon is picked green and cured in storage to the yellow-ripe condition. Storage life is long, being up to four months, so that a supply of lemons going to market can be regulated to demand. The Perrine lemon is a cross between lemon and lime. It was thought at one time that it might enable Florida to compete with California in lemon production; however, a severe winter killed the trees and the industry did not recover.

Limes are available most of the year but the peak season is from June to September. The commercial lime is the Persian or Tahiti lime. Permitted to mature it becomes as large as the lemon and, like all citrus fruits, changes from green to yellow or orange if left on the tree long enough; but it is marketed in the smaller, bright-green stage. The Key lime, also called Mexican or West Indian lime, is small and pale yellow, and of superior flavor. It has little commercial value because it is perishable after harvest.

The kumquat is a citrus fruit, a sort of elongated tiny orange. When eaten fresh or preserved, the entire fruit is eaten. It is more likely to be eaten preserved or made into marmalade.

The ugli fruit is a citrus variety, recently available in the supermarket. It is imported from Jamaica. The fruit is uninspired looking but the flesh is delicious and has a combined flavor of orange, grapefruit, and tangerine.

The karambola is appearing in the supermarket of the 1970's. It grows in Florida. It looks like a crenelated lemon and is the size of the lemon. Slices of the fruit appear star-shaped.

Crosses within the family of citrus fruits are easily accomplished; many are of interest though of no commercial value. The only one of commercial value is the tangelo, a cross between the tangerine and the grapefruit. There are four varieties of the tangelo; they differ principally in shape and color. The fruit looks like an orange but has the tang of grapefruit and is juicy, easy to peel, and delicious. It is available from November through February with November the peak month.

There are U.S. grades for grapefruit, oranges, lemons, limes, and tangerines; and for tangelos from Florida. The top grade for all, except lemons and limes, is U.S. Fancy. U.S. No. 1 is the top grade for limes and lemons, but the next to the best grade for the other varieties. Some citrus fruits are grade-labeled for the retail market.

In general, these citrus fruits are sized for shipment according to the number packed into the shipping carton; the larger the number the smaller the fruits within. Oranges, grapefruit, and tangerines are also packed in perforated, polyethylene bags and open-mesh bags for shipping. Hydrocooled fruit treated with fungicide before shipping, and packaged in perforated polyethylene bags has excellent keeping quality. Labels must bear statement of the use of fungicide and, where relevant, the use of artificial color on oranges.

After purchase, citrus fruits should be refrigerated. Lemons and limes store better if not put into the hydrator.

Grapes

There are two types of grapes, the European and the American. The European-type grape does not slip out of its skin; but its seeds are easily removed. The American-type grape slips out of its skin and the seeds are held within the pulp. The American-type grapes are grown in the East, whereas the European-type grapes are grown in California. The season of the former is much shorter than that of the latter.

Most of the table grapes we find in food stores are of the European type. The different varieties mature one after the other; the season begins in June and lasts until the next spring. Table grapes are plump, firm-fleshed, sweet, and delicate in flavor. They are sprayed during production with gibberellins to produce fruit of good size. The varieties differ in color to give us white, red, and purple grapes. The Perlette and the Thompson Seedless, the most popular of all the varieties, are two white varieties, that is, greenish-yellow, that are seedless. The Thompson Seedless comes a bit later and has a longer season than the Perlette. It is oval in shape, whereas the Perlette is round. Other white grapes include the White Muscat and the Almeria and Calmeria, which are called "lady-finger" grapes. These latter are elongated large grapes that grow in loose bunches. The White Muscat is not important commercially though it is found in fancy fruit markets. Red varieties include the Tokay, or Flame Tokay; the Emperor; the Red Malaga; and the Cardinal. The Tokay and the Red Emperor are popular varieties; the Tokay matures earlier and has a thinner skin than the Red Emperor. The latter stores extremely well so it is available into the spring. The Red Malaga is a seeded, pink to reddish-purple grape of medium size and thin skin. The Cardinal is a cross between the Red Tokay and the Ribier. The Cardinal is an early red, it is large and round, and of a cherry-red to reddish-purple color when ripe. The Ribier is a large, round blue-black grape that is on the market during the summer. It is mildly astringent.

Grapes must reach certain standards of maturity before they can be harvested and shipped out-of-state. In buying grapes one should look for maximum color for the variety, for plumpness, and for green, pliable stems. Grapes are quite perishable and will shrink and shatter as they age.

The season for American-type grapes is short. The Concord is the best known. It is blue-black and has a silvery bloom. The Delaware is a small pink variety and the Niagara is a large white variety. These varieties are good table grapes. The Catawba is a large purplish-red grape used more for juice and wine than as a table grape.

Melons

Both the available melon varieties and the season of availability of melons have increased during the past decade. *Muskmelon* is the general name for all types of melons except the watermelon. The species is *Cucumis melo* and the two important botanical varieties are *reticulatis*, to which the cantaloupe belongs, and *inodorous* to which the Casaba, Crenshaw, Honeydew, Honeyball, and Persian melons belong. The watermelon is a member of the same gourd family but it is of another botanical variety, *Citrullus vulgaris*. The cantaloupe and the watermelon are grown widely in the United States but the other melon varieties are grown in California, Arizona, and Texas because of favorable environmental conditions. Melons are imported from Mexico and other Latin American countries. Bright and sunny weather prior to harvest is essential if melons are to develop the sweetness that must be present at maturity. Most melons soften at the blossom end as they ripen; they pass from a firm to a softer state that may be felt under slight pressure; some, but not all, develop in aroma. And most will be mature but not ripe at picking. Even the best of melons as brought from the supermarket are improved by a few days of storage at room temperature. During this period there is flavor development and softening of the flesh. Though available for many months of the year, most of these varieties are better during the months of July through October.

There are many varieties of cantaloupes, they have been bred for disease resistance and suitability to different environmental conditions. They differ in size and shape, the thickness and texture of the flesh, the external characteristics of the rind, and delicacy of flavor. Cantaloupes are round to oval in shape, and they are more or less ribbed by longitudinal furrows. The surface is coarsely netted in gray over a ground color that is grayish or yellowish when the melon is ripe. The ripe melon has the full aroma characteristic of the cantaloupe. The flesh is salmon-orange in color. There is a sunken, calloused scar at the stem end that indicates that the melon was mature when picked. Cantaloupes are harvested at these stages of maturity: "full slip," or hard ripe, when the stem separates from the melon under slight pressure leaving a clean stem-scar but the melon is still firm and yellow-green; "choice," or "showing good color," when the melons are full slip and yellowish; and "full ripe." Melons sent to distant markets are picked full slip. Choice and ripe melons are only distributed locally. The full-slip melon is not ripe but it is mature; it will not become sweeter but flavor will develop and softening will occur. Cantaloupes with the stem attached were immature at picking and will be poor in quality. Full-slip melons should not be refrigerated until they soften and are aromatic. Overripe melons are soft, watery, and poor in flavor.

The *Casaba melon* is nearly round but may be pointed at the stem end; the rind is furrowed lengthwise of the melon; and when ripe, the rind is yellow and the flesh creamy white. The melon has no aroma. The flesh is juicy and sweet. The *Crenshaw melon* is pear-shaped; rounded at the blossom end, and pointed at the stem end. The rind is smooth and free of netting and furrows; it is gold and green in color. The flesh is salmon-colored, thick, juicy and sweet, and of excellent flavor. The melon has some aroma when ripe. The *Honeyball melon* is small, round, slightly netted, and green-white to pale yellow in color. The flesh is greenish-white. It is aromatic when ripe. The *Honeydew melon* is oval in shape; the rind is smooth; when ripe, the rind feels velvety to the touch and is creamy white to creamy yellow in color. It is only slightly aromatic. The flesh is pale green, thick, sweet, and juicy. Flavor is improved if the melon is served at room temperature and is doused with lemon or lime juice. The *Persian melon* resembles the cantaloupe but is much larger. It is round, the rind is netted and green or bronze-green in color. The ripe melon is aromatic. The flesh is orange in color, thick, sweet and juicy, and of fine flavor.

Watermelons have been bred for different purposes and there are many varieties. They differ in size, shape, and color of rind and flesh. Plugging of the watermelon to determine quality has been discontinued; instead, the melons are cut into halves, quarters, and smaller pieces so that quality may be visually determined. In general, the flesh should be red and the seeds black or dark brown. White seeds indicate that the fruit was immature when picked. It is difficult to judge the quality of an uncut melon. Qualities to look for are a symmetrical shape, a bloom on the surface that gives a velvety appearance, and a yellowish rather than white underside. When the peel is scratched, it comes off a ripe melon readily.

Pears

The main pear variety is the Bartlett; it is in season from July, when it is shipped from California, into November, when Washington and Oregon are the main shipping states. The Bartlett is picked green but mature; as it ripens, it becomes a light yellow. Fall and winter pear varieties are Anjou, Bosc, Comice, and Winter Nelis. The growing states are Washington and Oregon and the season is from November to May. The Anjou variety is not as elongated as the Bartlett; it is rounder at the blossom end. It is not as yellow as the Bartlett when ripe; it remains a pale green. It has a slight astringency. The Bosc pear is more elongated at the stem end than other varieties. When western grown, it is brownish as the result of russeting. It is a sweet pear of delicate flavor. The Comice is a plump pear, rounded at the blossom end with a short, thick neck; its full name is *Doyenne du Comice*; it is a best variety and does not ship well. It is used principally in gift packages for which each fruit can be carefully wrapped and put into special containers to permit shipment without bruising. The skin is often blushed-over a pale yellowish-green. The flesh of this variety is fine in texture, juicy, and aromatic. Pears deteriorate rapidly and should be eaten soon after they reach the proper degree of ripeness.

Pineapples

The pineapple, a native of South America, is a composite fruit made up of from one hundred to two hundred berrylike fruitlets fused on a core that is a continuation of the stem that bears it. Fruits vary in height from five to ten inches and in weight accordingly. Though available fresh all the year, pineapples are in best supply from March through June. They are imported from Hawaii, Puerto Rico, Mexico, Costa Rica, Bermuda, and the Bahamas. A high proportion of the crop is processed.

The pineapple does not sweeten or ripen after picking; ideally it would be harvested when ripe. However, the fully ripe fruit is extremely perishable. Those marketed fresh are picked before full ripeness at the stage called "mature green." After such harvest, the shell changes color, the fruit softens, and the acid content may decrease or increase, depending on handling practices. Well-selected pineapples held at room temperature for two or three days undergo the described changes and may develop some in aroma. They are extremely perishable and should be eaten when all the signs point to ripeness. The fruit is sweeter at the stem end than at the crown, a reason for serving longitudinal rather than horizontal slices or for cubing and mixing the parts of the fruit. There are two important commercial varieties. The Red Spanish is small and named for its red-yellow color; its flesh is pale yellow; the leaves of the crown are serrated. It ships well. The Smooth Cayenne has crown leaves that are smooth along the edge. It is dark green until it changes to yellow-orange; its flesh is yellow, soft, and juicy. It is a fruit of better eating qualities than the Red Spanish.

Tropical and Subtropical Fruits

There is a significant number of tropical and subtropical fruits available in the supermarket of the 1970's that were generally unknown just a few years ago. Consumers have been introduced to these fruits as they have traveled from region to region within the United States and to other countries. They are commercially produced in California and Florida and sometimes Texas; they are also imported from Mexico, other Latin American countries, and the Caribbean islands and elsewhere. They tend to be perishable and are especially packaged for shipment by air freight in general. *Figs* are highly perishable and are little sold fresh. They are small, seedy fruits eaten in their entirety. Color varies with variety from yellow-green to almost black. A taste for them has to be acquired. The *guava* is known to most persons as a kind of jelly; exotic, but not flavorful. It is eaten as a fresh fruit where it is grown. The fruit is small and seedy like the fresh fig. One variety is yellow, another reddish. The *lychee*, once known only to travelers in the Orient, is being produced in Florida. It is also called the *lychee nut*. The fruit is small but spherical in shape. It contains a large seed and is covered with a thin, brown coat or shell. Between seed and shell is a thin layer of yellow-green flesh that is sweet and juicy but not particularly flavorful.

The *kiwi* is imported from New Zealand. It is also called the *Chinese gooseberry*. It is about the size of a lemon and has a brown and fibery skin and green flesh with tiny black seeds. The flavor is reminiscent of melons. The fruits keep well in the refrigerator and should be ripened at room temperature before being served by itself or in combination with other fruits in salads. The *mango* is a tropical fruit. It is grown in Florida, where the season is from June to mid-August. It is imported from Mexico, Puerto Rico, and the West Indies. The fruit is round to oval in shape and it has a smooth skin. The ground color is green, often blushed with red; it becomes yellow as the fruit ripens. Picked at the proper stage, the fruit ripens post harvest. The varieties differ in size from small to those that weigh as much as a pound. The flesh is yellow-orange in color, juicy, and with a flavor that is like the blended flavors of peach, pear, and pineapple. The fruit contains a large flat seed to which the flesh clings. It is a superb dessert fruit.

The *nectarine* is a fuzzless peach; it is not a cross but a mutation from a peach. Neither is it something new, but is a fruit that was known two hundred years ago. It is grown in California. The many varieties of nectarines mature in succession to give a season that extends from June to October, but the peak of the season is July and August. It is mature but not ripe at harvest. The skin is smooth and usually of an orange-yellow ground color touched with red. The flesh may be white, yellow, or orange. The flesh is somewhat firmer and less juicy than that of a peach of the same degree of ripeness.

The *papaya* is not a melon, though it resembles melons, but the fruit of a herbaceous plant. It varies in size from small to very large; it has a thick flesh, and contains many seeds. The flesh ranges in color from yellow to a salmon-orange. It is a delicious fruit, but because it ships poorly, it is best eaten where it is grown. Those available in food stores in northern areas may be of poor eating quality. The *persimmon* available in the supermarket is an autumn fruit in season from October through December. Persimmons are grown in California. The fruit is about the size of a small to medium-sized peach and is oval-shaped; it has a smooth and glossy orange to orange-red skin. The pulp is jellylike, sweet, and of delicate flavor. The commercial variety is seedless. It is eaten out of hand or is cut into halves and eaten with a spoon.

Processed Fruits

Fruits are preserved—that is, processed—by canning, freezing, and drying and dehydration. Per-capita consumption in 1970 was of more canned than frozen fruits, of more canned than frozen juices, and of larger quantities of frozen than of dehydrated products (4). (See Figures 9–1 and 9–2.)

Canned Fruits

Because the contents of the metal can are not visible to the buyer, certain provisions were written into the Food, Drug, and Cosmetic Act of 1938. This act empowered the Food and Drug Administration to promulgate definitions and standards of identity, standards of reasonable quality, and standards of fill of container for canned fruits and vegetables. Since 1938, identity standards have been established for applesauce; apricots; berries including blueberries, black and red raspberries, strawberries, and some others; cherries, both sweet and sour; figs; fruit cocktail; grapefruit; seedless grapes; peaches; pears; pineapple; plums; and prunes. These identity standards descriptively specify the fruit content, the packing media, and the permitted optional ingredients other than fruit and packing media; they define the sweetness of the packing media as determined by Brix measurement; and finally they state that the food is to be sealed in a container and so processed by heat as to prevent spoilage. See Chapter 4 for the identity standard for canned fruit cocktail. The original standards for eight of these have been amended to permit packing in slightly sweetened water, these packs are sweeter than water packs but are not as sweet as fruits packed in light syrup.

Reasonable standards of quality have been prepared for apricots, cherries, fruit cocktail, grapefruit, peaches, pears, and pineapple. The standards for canned grapefruit are recent: they became effective in March, 1970. Quality standards define in terms of flavor, color, size, and condition the level of quality below which a canned product cannot be sold unless it is labeled to inform the consumer that it is below standard quality. These standards are amended or revised from time to time as consumer wants and horticultural developments make change desirable. For example, it was proposed in May, 1970 that the standard of quality for canned apricot halves be amended to delete the minimum weight requirement for apricot halves and quarters. The rationale for this proposal was that consumers have ceased to regard size as an indicator of quality, and that consumers buy smaller cans of apricots. Smaller apricot units provide for a better fill.

Standards of fill of container have been established for applesauce, apricots, cherries, fruit cocktail, grapefruit, peaches, pears, and crushed pineapple. The standards for canned grapefruit are recent, having become effective in March, 1970. In general, the standard of fill of container is the maximum quantity of the fruit ingredient that can be sealed in the container and processed by heat without the crushing or breaking of the fruit. For canned fruit cocktail, the fill is such that the total weight of the drained fruit is not less than 65 per cent of the water capacity of the container as prescribed; for grapefruit and crushed pineapple plus packing medium, it is not less than 90 per cent of the total capacity of the container.

Canned fruits are not extensively grade-labeled in the United States. The Report of the National Commission on Food Marketing recommended mandatory grade-labeling of all foods where such grading would be feasible. Canned fruits and vegetables are a category of foods for which grade-labeling is both feasible and desirable. Permissive grades have been established for many different fruits and juices. Canned fruits are scored on these factors when relevant; color, uniformity of size and symmetry, absence of defects, and character. Character refers to maturity, texture, and tenderness. For different fruits, the different factors are assigned a number of points. The grade of a product is determined by the number of points scored; for example, canned pears would be graded U.S. Grade A, B, or C if they scored not less than 90, 80, or 70 points respectively. Grades for canned fruits are U.S. Grade A or U.S. Fancy, U.S. Grade B or U.S. Choice, and U.S. Grade C or U.S. Standard. There are some exceptions; for example, there is no U.S. Grade B for applesauce or sour cherries. U.S. Grade A products are of excellent quality; they have good color; the pieces are uniform in size and shape; they are virtually free from defects; and they have ripened to the right degree and are tender. U.S. Grade B or U.S. Choice grade is of good quality, and much canned fruit is of this grade; the product may be described as having the desired characteristics to a "reasonable" extent. The color and size, and symmetry of the pieces will be less uniform; there may be a few defects; and the fruit may be slightly less tender than Grade A products. U.S. Grade C canned fruits are of fairly good quality: they are fairly uniform in color and size and symmetry of pieces, fairly free of defects, and fairly tender. All of these grades must have good flavor and aroma, possess similar varietal characteristics, and have been processed under continuous inspection. Continuous inspection assures compliance with the requirements that all ingredients be wholesome and that all steps in processing be carried out under defined sanitary conditions. In the 1970's, consumer interest groups are pressing for mandatory grade-labeling of canned fruits and vegetables.

Fruits are packed in different styles, such as whole, halves, slices, chunks, and peeled versus unpeeled. Price sometimes differs, with the broken slices, chunks, and unpeeled being priced lower than full slices, full halves, and peeled products. The meal manager buys and tries these products when the budget is conservative and it is desirable to maximize dollars. Further, canned fruits are sweetened to different degrees. In decreasing order of sweetness they are packed in heavy, medium, and light syrups, in slightly sweetened water, and in water. They vary in cost accordingly and the actual amount of sugar is not significantly greater in the packs in heavy than in light syrups. Fruits are packed in cans of different sizes; the cost per serving should be less in the No. 2½ can than in the No. 303, and less in the No. 303 than in the small eight-ounce can. Packaged individual servings are convenient, but their cost may sometimes preclude their purchase.

Table 9–2 shows how the cost of a unit of canned peaches can vary with the kind of purchase made, especially with the size of the can bought and the brand of the product purchased. Table 9–3 points out that the cost per unit of the commonly eaten canned fruits can be fairly similar—applesauce, peaches, and plums; of those listed only the sweet cherries are truly high-priced.

TABLE 9–2.   *Cost per Pound of Canned Peaches as Cost Differs with the Kind, Quality, and Size of Can Purchased*

	Market Unit and Cost	Cost per Pound[1]
Yellow Cling Peach Halves		
Brand A—in heavy syrup	$.41/No. 2–½	$.23
Brand A—in heavy syrup	.31/No. 303	.31
Brand A—in heavy syrup	.39/2 No. 8Z	.39
Brand B—in heavy syrup	.29/No. 2–½	.16
Brand B—in heavy syrup	.27/No. 303	.27
Brand B—in heavy syrup	.37/2 No. 8Z	.37
Brand C—in heavy syrup	.39/No. 2–½	.22
Brand D—in light syrup	.33/No. 2–½	.20
Brand D—in light syrup	.25/No. 303	.25
Brand E—in slightly sweetened water	.28/No. 303	.28
Brand F—a low-calorie water pack	.25/No. 303	.25
Freestone Peaches		
Brand A—halves in heavy syrup	.29/No. 2–½	.16
Brand B—halves in heavy syrup	.51/No. 2–½	.30
Brand C—halves in heavy syrup	.45/No. 2–½	.26
Brand D—chunks in heavy syrup	.39/No. 2–½	.22

[1]One pound would come close to providing four servings. Figures are based on a weight of twenty-eight ounces per No. 2–½ can, sixteen ounces per No. 303 can, and eight ounces per 8Z can.

TABLE 9-3.   *Cost per Pound of Selected Canned Fruits*

Items	Market Unit and Cost	Cost per Pound[2]
Applesauce	$.45/1 lb. 3 oz.[1]	$.205
Apricots	.33/No.2-1/2 can[1]	.190
Cherries, sweet black	.59/No. 303 can	.590
Fruit Cocktail	.49/No. 2-1/2 can[1]	.28
Peach halves, yellow cling	.33/No. 2-1/2 can[1]	.190
Pears	.43/No. 2-1/2 can[1]	.245
Pineapple slices	.37/No. 2-1/2 can[1]	.21
Plums	.33/No. 2-1/2 can[1]	.190

[1]Store brand.
[2]Based on weight of twenty-eight ounces per No. 2-1/2 can.

The consumer can learn something of the contents of a can of fruit by reading the label. It is mandatory that packers (1) label any product substandard in quality or in fill of container if standards for these have been promulgated; (2) describe the pack as whole, halves, slices, chunks, diced, grated, peeled, and so forth; (3) state the type or variety of fruit, for example, cling or freestone peaches, Bartlett pears; (4) indicate the sweetness of syrups as light, heavy, or extra heavy; and (5) label packs processed without sugar or in slightly sweetened water. All canned fruits must be labeled in conformity with the Fair Packaging and Labeling Act; of particular importance to the consumer is a statement of the size of serving when a statement of the number of servings is given on a label.

Frozen Fruits

A variety of frozen fruits and juice concentrates is available. Some fruits have superior palatability when frozen (pineapple, strawberries, and orange juice), others are superior when canned (peaches, pears, and plums). With the exceptions of strawberries and orange juice concentrate, frozen products tend to be priced higher than canned counterparts. The reasons would seem to be these: first, only foods of superior quality are frozen, whereas less than the best can be canned satisfactorily; second, frozen foods require special handling and equipment in transport and storage, whereas canned foods do not; and finally, frozen foods remain perishable, whereas canned foods are not subject to change under normal conditions of storage. In time, however, canned fruits can lose flavor, and color may fade. Actually, some fruits have a more acceptable texture when canned than when they are frozen—peaches, for example.

In addition to conventional freezing, fruits are preserved by dehydro-freezing, freeze-drying, and cryogenic freezing. In dehydrofreezing, there is partial removal of water followed by freezing. Large volumes of fruits, and vegetables are processed by this technique for manufacturing—for example, the fruits for pies. In freeze-drying, the product is frozen first and then the water is removed. Again, these fruits are used mainly by the food industries. Cryogenic freezing occurs at extremely low temperatures, i.e., below — 300°F. There is little crystal formation; rupture of cells is infrequent; products retain good texture and structure. Avocadoes, bananas, papayas, pineapples, and melons are satisfactorily frozen by this method.

There are no definitions and standards of identity for frozen fruits and no standards of quality. However, work is in progress on standards of identity for and fill of container for frozen strawberries; they should be finalized in the 1970's.

There are, however, standards for grading almost all of the products that are available frozen: citrus juice concentrates, including lemonade and limeade; apricots; several kinds of berries, including blueberries, strawberries, and red raspberries; cherries; grapefruit sections; melon balls; pineapple; and rhubarb. It is possible to buy graded frozen fruits and frozen juice concentrates in the supermarket, probably because frozen products tend to be top quality. Standards for quality grades include U.S. Grade A or U.S. Fancy, U.S. Grade B or U.S. Choice, and U.S. Grade C or U.S. Standard; but for some frozen fruits and juice concentrates there are only two grades, U.S. Grade A and U.S. Grade C, as for example, for frozen red, tart pitted cherries. Most fruits can be held six months to one year in a freezer that maintains a constant temperature of 0°F or lower.

Chilled Fruits

Convenient chilled fruits are found in the dairy case in many supermarkets. They are packed in glass jars. They include grapefruit sections, orange and grapefruit sections, pineapple, peaches, and mixed fruits. They are processed by a hot-pack method in which pasteurized juice is poured over the fresh fruit. If refrigerated, the product will keep for six months. In a cold-pack method, fresh juice is poured over the fruit and a preservative is added. If refrigerated, the product will keep for fourteen days. By noting weight of contents and calculating that a portion of fruits varies between three and four ounces depending on the quantity of syrup, one can estimate the cost per serving and to decide whether this particular product is more or less expensive than another form of the fruit, and if it fits the food budget. These fruits are used for salads and fruit cups especially.

Dried Fruits and Dehydrated Fruit Products

Preservation of fruits by sun-drying is old in time. Sun-dried fruits include raisins, figs, apricots, peaches, and pears. To deter spoilage and to prevent loss of color, fruits are subjected to the fumes of burning sulfur or are treated by being dipped in a solution of a sulfur compound. Dehydration is artificial drying under conditions of controlled heat and humidity. Apples, blueberries, sour cherries, prunes, and bananas are some fruits that are artificially dried. Dried fruits have a somewhat different flavor than those preserved by canning or freezing and from their fresh counterparts. Standards for grading dried fruits have been developed. Quality grades are the same as for other processed fruits: U.S. Grade A or Fancy, U.S. Grade B or Choice, and U.S. Grade C or Standard. Dried fruits, especially prunes and apricots, are size-graded. Small fruits are priced lower than larger fruits.

Improved packaging of dried fruits in film bags and plastic-coated boxes has resulted in fruits of better quality and longer shelf life. Dried fruits, such as apricots, prunes, and raisins, do lose quality if long held in kitchen storage.

Juice concentrates have been processed by dehydration. Fruit purees are mat and foam spray-dried; juices are spray-dried. The products are powders. Spray-dried orange juice becomes instant orange juice. Freeze-dried fruit crystals for instant juices will be products of the 1970's.

Per-Serving Costs of Fruits

Per-serving costs for selected fresh fruits were presented in Table 9–1. The per-pound cost of canned peaches was explored in Table 9–2. Table 9–3 shows the costs for selected canned fruits. The meal manager has to match her choices to her plan for spending for food. It should be noted, however, that costs are not the same at all seasons of the year, nor are they the same in all regions of the United States at the same time. It is important for a meal manager to make her own comparisons, not once, but from time to time.

FRUIT BEVERAGES

The supermarket stocks a variety of products described euphemistically as "fruit beverages and punches." There is great diversity among them in concentration, composition, and processing method. They are ready to drink, that is, single strength, like apple juice. They are concentrated and must be diluted for drinking like orange juice concentrate. And they are available as powders. In composition, they range from "all juice," like apple juice, to "no juice," like *Kool-Aid*. In between the extremes in composition are products that contain some natural ingredients and some synthetic ingredients that provide color and flavor. Further, there are differences in the composition of natural fruit juices. Juices can be diluted to become ades, drinks, nectars, and punches. There are as yet no standards and no definitions that establish a diluted juice as one or the other, though the Food and Drug Administration proposed some in 1964.

Truly fresh juices are of limited availability because of perishability. Some juices available in bottles and cartons in the supermarket have been pasteurized to enhance keeping quality; they must, however, be kept refrigerated because they have not been processed long enough for sterilization. Flavor is modified by pasteurization. Canned juices have been heated long enough to destroy spoilage organisms; canning also modifies flavor. Freezing the juice concentrate and the proper dehydration of a juice produce products that have good flavor when reconstituted.

Citrus Fruit Beverages

The standards of identity for orange juice and orange juice products include standards for canned, frozen, and pasteurized orange juices; canned and frozen orange juice concentrate; orange juice from concentrate; and for the following, which are for further manufacturing; orange juice and concentrated orange juice with preservative, and concentrated orange juice for manufacturing.

Orange juice is defined as the unfermented juice of mature oranges of the species *Citrus sinensis*. In bottles or cartons, it is available in some markets where it would be called fresh orange juice. This juice, when it is available, is expensive. It is also expensive to prepare at home in many regions of the country. *Frozen orange juice* is unfermented orange juice that has been frozen. *Pasteurized orange juice* is orange juice to which the following may be added: 10 per cent by volume, but no more, of juice from mature oranges of the species *Citrus reticulata*, orange pulp and orange oil, and a sweetening agent. This juice is heat-treated to destroy viable microorganisms and to reduce enzyme activity that modifies flavor. It may be preserved by either freezing or refrigeration. This product is available in many supermarkets. *Canned orange juice* may be the same combination of ingredients as pasteurized orange juice; it is sealed in containers and so processed by heat as to prevent spoilage. *Orange juice from concentrate* is prepared by the mixing of potable water with prepared orange juice concentrate. To this mixture may be added orange juice, exclusive of canned orange juice, orange pulp and orange oil, and a sweetener. It may be heated to reduce enzyme activity and the number of viable microorganisms. This product is available in the supermarket; it will be in the refrigerator cabinet.

Both canned and frozen orange juice concentrate are defined. We buy far more of the frozen than of the canned concentrate. *Orange juice concentrates* are prepared by the removal of water from the unfermented juice of mature oranges of the species *Citrus sinensis* to which may have been added any or all of the following: 10 per cent by volume before concentration of unfermented juice from *Citrus reticulata*, or hybrids, and 5 per cent by volume of juice from unfermented *Citrus aurantium*, orange oil, orange pulp, orange essence, orange juice concentrate, and a sweetener. Any of the ingredients used may have been heat-treated. The diluted concentrate must have 11.8 per cent of orange solids; the dilution ratio cannot be less than three plus one—that is, three volumes of water plus one of concentrate must produce orange juice. The concentrate may be frozen or sealed in containers and so processed by heat as to prevent spoilage. The wide range of possible ingredients and of the level of heat treatments of ingredients probably account for the cost and palatability differences among different brands of frozen orange juice concentrates.

There are standards for the quality grading of canned orange juice, all single strength ready-to-drink grapefruit juices, canned blended grapefruit and orange juices, canned tangerine juice, and frozen concentrated orange juice. Quality standards for canned orange juice based on scores for color, flavor, and defects are three: U.S. Grade A, U.S. Grade C, and Substandard. Quality grades for grapefruit juice apply to all single strength ready-to-drink grapefruit juices including canned grapefruit juice, "chilled" grapefruit juice, and grapefruit juice prepared from the concentrate regardless of the processing technique. There are three grades based on scores for color, flavor, and defects: U.S. Grade A, U.S. Grade B, and Substandard. Blended orange and grapefruit juices will contain from 50 to 75 per cent of orange juice depending on the color of the orange juice, being the higher percentage when the color is light. Grades are U.S. Grade A, U.S. Grade C, and Substandard.

Diluted orange juice beverages are available. The Food and Drug Administration proposed standards for diluted juice drinks in 1964. In March 1972, the Food and Drug Administration proposed standards for diluted orange juice drinks. According to the proposed standards, orange juice products would be labeled as follows and would be diluted as defined: "orange juice blend drink," 75 to 90 per cent orange juice; "orange juice drink," 35 to 70 per cent orange juice; "orange drink," 10 to 35 per cent orange juice; and "orange-flavored drink," less than 8 per cent orange juice. The standards require statement on the label of the percentage of orange juice in each product; also that six fluid ounces of the finished beverage contain sixty milligrams of vitamin C. It is expected that the standards will become effective in 1972.

Beverages and products from which to prepare beverages that simulate orange juice and grapefruit juice are sold under trade names. The synthetic product is available as a frozen or canned concentrate and as a dry

TABLE 9–4. *Per-Serving Cost and Vitamin C Content of Four-Ounce Servings of Some Citrus Juices and Citrus-Flavored Beverages*

Items	Market Unit and Cost	Volume of Product	Cost per 4-Ounce Serving (Cents)	Vitamin C per 4-Ounce Serving (Mgms.)
Orange juice, fresh squeezed	59¢/dozen	1 qt.	7.4	62[1]
Orange juice, pasteurized	39¢/qt.	1 qt.	4.9	62[1]
Orange juice, canned	39¢/No. 3 Cyl.	46 oz.	3.4	50[1]
Orange juice from concentrate	99¢/6 cans	24 oz. ea.	2.75	60[1]
Orange juice from concentrate	77¢/3 cans	24 oz. ea.	4.3	60[1]
Orange Plus—frozen concentrate for imitation orange juice[2]	48¢/can	1–½ qt.	4.0	72
Tang—synthetic mix[2]	99¢/18 oz.	4 qt.	3.0	81
Start—synthetic mix[2]	25¢/can	1 qt.	3.0	81
Orange Nip— frozen concentrate for orange drink[2]	29¢/can	24 oz.	5.0	15
Instant Replay—mix for orange drink[2]	35¢	1–½ qt.	3.0	15
Brand A Orange Drink[2]	33¢/No. 3 Cyl.	46 oz.	2.9	20
Brand B Orange Drink[2]	31¢/qt.	1 qt.	4.0	20

[1]Values from *Nutritive Value of Foods*, Home and Garden Bulletin No. 72, Consumer and Food Economics Research Division, United States Department of Agriculture, Washington, D.C. (1970).
[2]Sugar plus some natural and some synthetic ingredients.

mix. The advantages of the synthetics are in the lower cost and the relatively constant level of the vitamin C content; the disadvantage is the limited nutrient content of the product as compared with the natural fruit product. Products that blend natural fruit ingredients with synthetic ingredients are numerous. All of these products must bear a label that lists ingredients and bears a statement of the quantity of vitamin C that a portion of a stated size will supply when the product is labeled "vitamin C enriched."

The cost per four-ounce portion of some different orange juice products, of some products that contain both natural and synthetic ingredients, and of some synthetics are given in Table 9–4. Estimates of the vitamin C contents of the different products are included. Juices and reconstituted concentrates lose little of their vitamin C content so long as they are kept refrigerated and are used soon after preparation.

Grapefruit juice is available pasteurized and canned; blended orange and grapefruit juice is canned; and frozen blended orange and grapefruit juice and grapefruit juice concentrates are available. Although the cost per serving of these may be slightly less than that of orange products, the bitter taste of them precludes their use by some consumers who find the bitter taste distasteful. Canned tangerine juice and frozen concentrated tangerine juice are available; the vitamin C content is less than that of orange and grapefruit juices.

Canned and bottled lemon and lime juices are less expensive than juice from fresh fruits in some regions of the United States during some seasons of the year. The products are more expensive when marketed in plastic squeeze containers that resemble their respective fruits than when packaged in cans or bottles. Frozen concentrates for lemonade and limeade are available. There are identity standards for lemonade and colored lemonade. The latter may be colored naturally by the addition of a colored fruit juice, such as grape juice, or it may be artificially colored.

Finally, except for the peak of the harvest season, citrus juice products are less expensive than fresh fruit counterparts.

Other Fruit Juices and Fruit Juice Beverages

Other fruits from which juices or beverages are prepared include apple, apricot, cranberry, grape, papaya, pineapple, and prune. Identity standards have been promulgated only for pineapple juice and prune juice. Only for apple juice are there standards for quality grading. Grades for apple juice are three: U.S. Grade A, U.S. Grade C, and Substandard. Canned apple juice is defined as the unfermented liquid prepared from the first-pressing juice of sound, fresh apples. It is prepared without concentration, without dilution, and without the addition of sweetening agents. It is processed by heat, to assure preservation of the product, in hermetically sealed containers. The use of an antioxidant is permitted. Frozen apple juice concentrate and frozen grape juice concentrate are available.

Some interesting new juice products of the 1960's were blended juice beverages, such as apple-cranberry juice and cranberry-grape juice. The meal manager with a limited budget for food may wish to compare the cost of some of these combination juices with other juices; some are fairly expensive.

Another development of the 1960's was the packaging of juices in six-packs of single servings. The single servings—though very convenient— are more expensive than the same product purchased in a container larger in size.

Dry mixes for making fruit-flavored beverages are widely available and widely consumed. Labels must name ingredients in decreasing order of predominance. The label reveals the extent to which ingredients are wholly synthetic and the extent to which natural fruit ingredients are included. These dry mixes are available in a variety of flavors. However, the dry mixes deserve some study. Comparison of the ingredient content of those with and without sugar reveals little if any difference except for added sugar. A bit of simple arithmetic then discloses the high cost of the sugar in the presweetened kinds. For example, as priced in the winter of 1971, presweetened Brand A cost twenty-five cents for two quarts; Brand A, sweetened by the consumer, sixteen and one-half cents for two quarts including the cost of one cup of added sugar; and Brand B, sweetened by the consumer, cost eleven cents for two quarts, including the cost of the added sugar. Unsweetened Brand A cost ten cents and unsweetened Brand B, five cents. The cost of the sugar in presweetened Brand A becomes fifteen cents for one cup of sugar when the United States average cost for five pounds of sugar was sixty-seven cents, that is 6.7 cents per cup of sugar. The cost of the sugar in the presweetened product was more than twice the market cost of sugar.

To maximize the dollars spent for beverages, concentrates, and powdered mixes, compare products for quality, ingredient content, and cost. Do read labels.

Summary. Fruits are available to the meal manager in great variety, both as fresh products and as processed products. There are no consumer grades for fresh fruits, though there are commercial grades for many fresh fruits. The consumer must learn to grade fresh fruits herself. There are grade standards for some processed fruits; however, not much that is available in the supermarket is graded. The fact that little that is available is graded means that the consumer can at different times buy products of quite different quality. For this reason many consumers rely on brand names as clues to quality. Fresh fruits differ in cost per serving depending on kind, region of residence, and season. The processed product is often far less expensive than the fresh counterpart, such as frozen strawberries and orange juice prepared from frozen orange juice concentrate, canned pears, and canned applesauce. Frozen fruits are generally more expensive than canned fruits, as, for example, pineapple. The cost per serving of canned fruits is determined by the quality of the product, the size of the can purchased, the style of the pack, the brand (that is, whether national brand or private label), and even where it is purchased. To some extent, the same is true of frozen fruits. Decisions on what to buy are made by the meal manager on the basis of resources, family preferences, and experience. Knowledge and skill in the marketplace are great assets.

GUIDES TO BUYING FRESH FRUITS AND. FRUIT PRODUCTS

1.   In general, do not buy overripe, soft, bruised, or moldy fruits.

2.   Some blemishes, especially those on peels and rinds that are discarded, although they influence grade, do not necessarily affect the quality of the fruits; for example, the bronzing of citrus fruits does not affect their quality.

3.   Select fruits the peels or skins of which have the proper texture, have a proper color, and are unbroken. Any damage to peels or rinds leads to deterioration or rotting.

4.   Buy citrus fruits and pineapples that feel heavy in relation to size; they will be juicy.

5.   Select fruits with good color and aroma. These will be guides to ripeness; for example, strawberries should have good color and a rich aroma.

6.   Some melons have no aroma that is perceivable until cut. Although melons do not become sweeter after picking, they do soften and some develop in aroma.

7.   Bananas, pears, avocadoes, and apples are some fruits that ripen post harvest. They are safely purchased while unripe.

8.   Both at the supermarket and at home, handle fruits gently; bruising hastens spoilage.

9.   If more than one variety is available, buy according to the intended use, for example, apples.

10.   When size is a factor of cost, buy according to use and remember that the biggest is not always the best.

11.   Buy by weight rather than count or measure when it is possible to do so.

12.   When more than one quality of fruit is available, buy according to use, e.g., top quality for freezing.

13.   Buy bananas when yellow with green tips. When speckled, they are at their prime. Refrigerate them with caution; though they may lose quality, they will be suitable for such uses as making banana cake or bread.

14.   Read labels on beverage and drink containers and on mixes for punches, ades, and drinks. Except for sugar, products may be wholly synthetic or they may contain small quantities only of natural ingredients.

15.   When buying canned fruits, try several different brands. The most expensive may not be the best for flavor. Packs composed of pieces irregular in shape ought to be low in cost and may be quite flavorful.

16.   Frozen fruits have good flavor but may have poor texture.

REFERENCES CITED

1.   *Food Consumption of Households in the United States Spring, 1965,* Consumer and Food Economics Research Division, United States Department of Agriculture, Washington, D.C. (1968), p. 12.

2.   *Gallup Survey—The National Poll of Patron Preferences, Prejudices, and Trends,* Vol. 1, Food Service Magazine, Madison, Wisconsin (1967).

3.   Miller, Erston V., and James I. Munger, *Good Fruits and How to Know Them.* Pittsburgh: Boxwood Press, 1967.

4.   "Per Capita Food Consumption," *National Food Situation,* Economic Research Service, United States Department of Agriculture, Washington, D.C. (February, 1971), p. 12.

5.   Peryam, D. R., et al., *Food Preferences of Men in the U.S. Armed Forces,* Department of the Army, Quartermaster Research and Engineering Command, Quartermaster and Container Institute for Armed Forces, Chicago (1960).

Chapter 10

Purchasing Food— Vegetables

Models and patterns for use in planning nutritionally adequate meals suggest a minimum of four servings of fruits and/or vegetables per day. Of all foods that we eat, vegetables are the least liked, except for potatoes, that is. And only a few of a goodly assortment of vegetables are generally accepted. Food preference studies of men in the armed forces (6) revealed that preferred vegetables were cut corn, corn on the cob, green string beans, sliced fresh tomatoes, and green peas. The *Gallup Survey—The National Poll of Patron Preferences, Prejudices, and Trends* (3) disclosed that first vegetable preferences were, in descending order, green beans, asparagus, corn and tomatoes in the same position, french fried onion rings, broccoli, lima beans, peas, carrots, cauliflower, and spinach. But the percentages of persons who would select these vegetables were small, ranging from 20 per cent for green beans to 5 per cent for spinach. Potato preferences were in descending order of preference, baked, mashed, and french fried; au gratin and boiled potatoes scored so low as not to be significant. Liked vegetable salads were cabbage salads, head lettuce salad, chopped green vegetable salad, and tomato-and-lettuce salad. The patron preference for soup, however, was vegetable soup. In 1970, civilian per-capita consumption of potatoes and sweet potatoes was about 123 pounds and of other vegetables about 100 pounds fresh, 50 pounds canned, and 9 pounds frozen (4) (Figures 10–1 and 10–2). The same advances in knowledge, science, and technology that provide abundance and variety in fresh fruits all the year also provide abundance and variety in fresh vegetables all the year. Fresh vegetables are so prepared and packaged for distribution in the supermarket as to be almost as convenient as the canned and frozen ones. Different varieties of fresh beans and peas are shelled; corn on the cob is husked; greens are trimmed and washed; root vegetables are

284

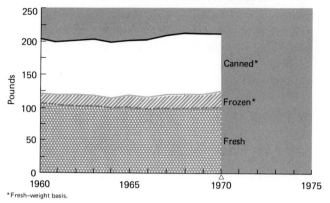

FIGURE 10–2. Per capita consumption of potatoes. (*United States Department of Agriculture photograph.*)

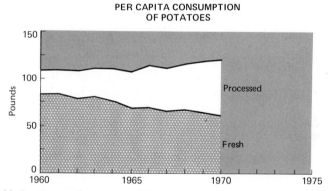

FIGURE 10–2. Per capita consumption of potatoes. (*United States Department of Agriculture photograph.*)

topped; broccoli and cauliflower are trimmed; and so on. The most the cook has to do is casual trimming and rinsing. If an acceptable serving is two and a half to three ounces of drained cooked weight, then many of the fresh vegetables as we buy them serve out at least four servings to the pound because the percentage of waste rarely exceeds one third of the purchased weight. Only the hard squashes, asparagus, and unpodded beans and peas have a high percentage of waste. Fresh green beans, shelled beans and peas, topped carrots, and some others may provide as many as five to six servings per pound of fresh weight. This means that what appears to be a high cost per pound for a fresh vegetable actually may be reasonable. Further, this fact emphasizes the importance of comparing costs on the portion basis.

According to the 1965 study of household food consumption (2), 19 per cent of the dollar spent for food eaten at home was spent for fruits and vegetables, including potatoes and sweet potatoes. The average household purchased a little more than five pounds of potatoes and sweet potatoes and about twenty-five pounds of fruits and vegetables per week. Per-capita consumption per day was about four ounces of potatoes and sweet potatoes and slightly more than a pound of fruits and vegetables, including juices. The quantities of fresh vegetables, of frozen vegetables and fruits, and of fruit and vegetable juices purchased increased as income increased to $15,000 and over per year.

The quantity of vegetables that the dollar purchases is established by choices among them; the form purchased, that is, whether fresh, frozen, or canned or ready-prepared; the size of the package purchased; the brand purchased if canned or frozen; and the market patronized. Some vegetable choices are always more costly than others, for example, broccoli and brussels sprouts cost more per portion than cabbage. However, if one excludes the more exotic ones like fresh mushrooms and artichokes, there is not the wide range in cost per portion of vegetables that there is in cost per serving of fruits. The season of the year and the region of residence are factors to be considered when one is comparing the cost of fresh vegetables with the cost of a canned or frozen product. It is probably safe to state that frozen and canned peas and immature lima beans will always cost less than fresh peas and fresh lima beans; but canned or frozen carrots may cost more than fresh carrots (see Table 10–1). The frozen peas in a two-pound bag will generally cost less per ounce than those in a ten-ounce carton. Private-label canned and frozen products generally cost less per can or carton of like size than national brands. Finally, there is some difference among supermarkets in the pricing of both private-label and name-brand canned and frozen products. Research of the resources of the local market can disclose to the consumer where the best bargains are to be found. Frozen and canned products are purchased for their convenience, and the frozen, ready-prepared gourmet vegetables are purchased for the built-in chef service.

THE SIZE OF VEGETABLE PORTIONS

Vegetable portions are not large. As income permits, we like larger and larger meat portions, also large fruit portions; but vegetable portions rarely get larger and larger. The average serving of a vegetable—except potatoes—is from two and one half to three ounces of drained cooked weight, perhaps the lower limit when the budget is conservative and the upper limit for preferred vegetables when the budget is generous. Most

TABLE 10–1. *Per-serving Cost of Selected Vegetables, Fresh and Frozen*[1]

	Fresh		Frozen	
	Market Unit and Cost	Cost per Serving[2]	Market Unit and Cost	Cost per Serving[2]
Asparagus	69¢/1–½ lb.	$.190	59¢/8 oz.	$.30
Beans, green	33¢/lb.	.060	53¢/1–½ lb.	.066
Broccoli	39¢/1–½ lb.	.080	33¢/10 oz.	.110
Cabbage	10¢/lb.	.025	—	—
Carrots	35¢/2 lb.	.040	45¢/1–½ lb.	.060
Cauliflower	33¢/1–⅓ lb.	.055	33¢/10 oz.	.110
Corn	69¢/10 ears	.070	53¢/4 ears	.130
Mushrooms	59¢/6 oz.	.200	59¢/6 oz.	.200
Peas	39¢/lb.	.200	49¢/1–½ lb.	.066
Spinach	49¢/10 oz.	.200	20¢/10 oz.	.08
Squash, butternut	49¢/lb.	.140	43¢/14 oz.	.14
Tomatoes	49¢/lb.	.125	—	—
Turnips	19¢/lb.	.057	—	—
Yellow summer squash	29¢/lb.	.075	25¢/10 oz.	.09

[1]Priced in the same supermarket on the same day.

[2]Estimated according to *Family Food Buying, A Guide for Calculating Amounts to Buy and Comparing Costs,* Home Economics Research Report No. 37, Agricultural Research Service, United States Department of Agriculture, Washington, D.C. (1970).

persons are quite satisfied with about a one-half cup portion. Potato portions are larger, from three to four ounces depending on preference, and they may be much larger when whole baked or boiled potatoes are served; also when the food budget is conservative. Salads of mixed greens, of mixed salad vegetables, of head lettuce, and of cabbage weigh two and one half to four ounces per serving without dressings. The No. 303 can and the No. 2 vacuum can provide four average servings of canned vegetables; the eight-ounce can, two servings. Ten-ounce and nine-ounce cartons of frozen vegetables provide from three to four servings. The large bags of individually quick-frozen (IQF) vegetables provide about six servings per pound. Commercial methods of trimming and packaging fresh vegetables for distribution so reduce waste that many serve out four to six portions per pound.

FRESH VEGETABLES

Although nearly all vegetables, from asparagus to zucchini, can be purchased fresh all the year, consumption of fresh vegetables declined during the 1960's and consumption of processed ones increased. Canned vegetables preseasoned with butter, mushrooms, or bacon; frozen vegetables preseasoned in numerous ways and prepared in sauces in boil-in-bag pouches; and frozen gourmet vegetable casseroles in suitable-for-the-table containers have preempted some of the fresh vegetable market. Advances in canning and freezing technology have improved the color, flavor, and texture of processed vegetables; but it is their convenience that has given them their favorable position.

The selection of fresh vegetables of quality is easier than the selection of fresh fruits. With few exceptions, such as the tomato, there is no concern with a proper degree of ripeness, immaturity rather than maturity being preferable in vegetables. Garden freshness is important and few fresh vegetables store well except as modern technology has effected rapid cooling and special packaging. Fresh vegetables of good quality will be crisp-appearing, of good color, and free of brown areas that point to spoilage or maturity. As with fruits, the first and the last to appear in a season may be quite expensive and may be of lower quality than those available at the peak of the season. Some fresh vegetables will cost more per serving than others, regardless of season; for example, fresh carrots and onions are never as expensive as are fresh asparagus and spinach. Cooked fresh vegetables have a fine flavor and a firm, near-crisp texture that canned and frozen vegetables lack. Consumers do not agree on the merits of frozen over canned vegetables and vice versa.

There are consumer grades for a number of fresh vegetables; they are U.S. Grade A and U.S. Grade B in general. There is, however, a third grade (U.S. Grade AA) for celery stalks. Some of the vegetables for which these grade standards have been defined are broccoli, brussels sprouts, carrots, husked corn-on-the-cob, potatoes, spinach, and turnips. Graded produce may sometimes be found in the supermarket. There are commercial grade standards for practically all fresh vegetables. In general, the top quality is U.S. No. 1 followed by U.S. No. 2; for some, the top grade is U.S. Fancy followed by the two grades U.S. No. 1 and U.S. No. 2. Grade differences may account for the different pricing of vegetables in different supermarkets. The abundant supply of fresh vegetables the year around in the supermarkets of the 1970's makes it desirable to describe a few of them.

Artichokes

The artichoke is included simply because national affluence and the trend toward gourmet dining has made it a more popular vegetable in the early 1970's than it was in the early 1960's. It is the unopened flower bud of a thistlelike perennial. More of it is inedible than edible. The edible parts are the small tender part at the base of the leaflike scales that cover the bud; the young flowers within the bud; and the base on which they are borne. Never buy artichokes unless they are heavy, compact, plump, and of a good green color. Artichoke hearts are available frozen, canned, and pickled.

Greens for Salads

There are four types of lettuce and a varied assortment of greens available for salads. These, too, are more abundantly available in the 1970's than they were in the 1960's. The lettuce types include crisphead, butterhead, cos or romaine, and leaf lettuce. Commercially produced salad greens include curled-leaved endive, escarole, Belgian or French endive, watercress, spinach, and Chinese cabbage. All greens for salads should always be young, tender, crisp, and dry. Less tender parts of heads can be cooked and served as a green vegetable. Prepared mixtures of salad greens and salad vegetables are widely available for the restaurant trade; they are also available in some supermarkets.

Lettuce.   The best-known and best-liked lettuce is crisphead, or iceberg lettuce, or head lettuce, as it is more commonly known. Sizes of heads vary, with preference for those of medium size. Heads are trimmed and prepackaged for distribution; there is little, if any, waste when they are of good quality. A one-pound head will provide five or more servings and as many as sixteen lettuce cups or lettuce underliners for fruit or other salads. Boston and Bibb lettuce are of the butterhead type. Heads of Boston lettuce are smaller and softer, and the leaves are smoother and greener than the leaves of iceberg lettuce. Heads of Bibb lettuce are small and loosely formed. Leaves are very tender, bright green, and delicate in flavor. A salad may be composed from a single head of Bibb lettuce, or a head may be large enough for several salads. Leaf lettuce is more delicate and perishable than iceberg lettuce; the leaves of commercial leaf lettuce are large and branch from a stalk. Much so-called garden lettuce is leaf lettuce, of which there are many varieties. Cos or romaine forms a long slender head. The leaves are large, coarse-textured, and strong-flavored. The leaves may be light to dark green, depending on the variety. Small heads may be served whole as a salad.

Chicory, Endive, and Escarole.   Chicory, endive, and escarole are variants of the same vegetable species. *Curled-leaved endive,* or chicory, as it is sometimes called, is a spreading plant. The leaves are narrow, irregularly shaped, ragged and curly, deep green unless bleached, and somewhat bitter. The center leaves may be bleached to a pale greenish-yellow. *Escarole* has broader, less ragged-appearing leaves that are less bitter.

Belgian or *French endive*, also called chicory and witloof, forms solid, spindle-shaped heads of yellow-tipped white leaves, which are bitter. This green is highly prized by the gourmet. It is sometimes cooked.

Onions

Dry onions are of two types: the mild-flavored, or sweet Bermuda and Spanish onions, and the strong-flavored globe onions. The *Bermuda onion* is a flat onion two to five inches in diameter with a thin white, yellow, or red skin. The *Spanish onion* is globular in shape, it is sometimes very large, and it has a white or yellowish-brown skin. We prefer the Bermuda and the Spanish onions on hamburgers, hotdogs, and salads—in fact, whenever we eat the onion raw. *Globe onions* are smaller than the Spanish onion, globular in shape, and white, red, or yellow in color. Globe onions are used in cooking.

Green onions and *scallions* are any onion variety pulled before maturity; they have a white part and, continuous with it, tubular green leaves. They are used in their entirety as long as the green parts remain unspoiled. *Chives* are mini green onions. They are available frozen and freeze-dried. They are also pot-grown in the kitchen. *Garlic* is a cluster of easily separated parts called cloves. The cluster of parts is surrounded by a white onion-type skin. It is available as a dehydrated powder and in garlic salt. *Shallots* resemble garlic in that the shallot is a cluster of cloves; shallots are purplish-brown in color. They are much milder in flavor than garlic. They are available freeze-dried. *Leeks* look like giant green onions. They have a short, thick white part and flat green leaves. They are always cooked as a vegetable and preferably only the white part is used, though opinion differs on this. They are more mild in flavor than onions. They are more widely available in the early 1970's than they were in the early 1960's.

Potatoes

Potato consumption in the United States decreased during this century well into the 1950's, when the advent of processed potato products reversed the trend. The consumption of fresh potatoes has continued to decline but this decline has been offset by increased consumption of processed products (see Figure 10–2). In 1965, 32 per cent of the dollar spent for potatoes was spent for processed products (1). By early 1970 about half of potato consumption was of fresh potatoes and about half of potatoes processed in some form: canned, dehydrated, frozen, and the ubiquitous potato chip.

Fresh potato quality has been improved in recent decades by the development of disease- and pest-resistant varieties, improved cultural methods, improved technology at harvest, controlled storage conditions, and better packaging. Potatoes are classified as round and long, and as red, white, and russet. However, with respect to shape, newer varieties are neither long nor round but intermediate, being oblong and thick, as is the Kennebec. Round white varieties include the Katahdin, Sebago, Chippewa, and the Irish cobbler; round red varieties include the Red Pontiac and Triumph; a long white variety is the White Rose; a long russet is the Burbank Russet. On the basis of cooking properties, potatoes are of two types: nonwaxy, or mealy, potatoes of high specific gravity, and waxy potatoes of low specific gravity. Some potato varieties have characteristics of both types; they are all-purpose potatoes, such as the Kennebec and the Irish cobbler. Mealy potatoes are preferred for baking and mashing; waxy potatoes that remain firm and hold their shape for boiling, potato salad, and a variety of potato dishes wherein the pieces are to remain discrete and unbroken. Russet varieties are mealy potatoes; the red varieties are waxy potatoes. The Idaho potato is a russet variety. So-called new potatoes are waxy. In general, *new* refers to immature potatoes marketed in late winter and early spring. They vary in shape and color; they are sometimes artificially colored red.

Some potatoes are sold by varietal name; unlabeled varieties are difficult to identify though the types are readily identifiable. The fact that fresh potatoes are less used but are used for special reasons and purposes makes it desirable that they be selected more knowingly than heretofore. Some information on varieties is included for that reason. The Russet Burbank is long and cylindrical or slightly flattened; the skin is russeted and heavily netted; it has many shallow eyes; its flesh is white. It is described as an Idaho potato regardless of where it is grown. It is a fine baker but is also a good all-purpose potato. It is the best-selling potato; the second is the Katahdin, a round type. Its tubers are large, short, and elliptical to round and medium thick; its skin is smooth; its eyes are few. It is an especially good potato for boiling, though it will darken. The Kennebec is a newer variety and is the best all-purpose potato to date. It is oblong and medium thick with shallow eyes; the skin is smooth and of a creamy buff color. The Red Pontiac is large, oblong to round, and blunt at the end; its skin is smooth and red; its eyes are few and fairly deep. The White Rose is large, long, elliptical, and flattened; its skin is smooth and of fawn color; its eyes are few and shallow. The Chippewa is elliptical to oblong; its skin is nearly white; its eyes are shallow. It is good for boiling and does not darken after cooking. The Irish cobbler is round; its skin is smooth.

There are four commercial grades for potatoes: U.S. Fancy, U.S. No. 1,

U.S. Commercial, and U.S. No. 2. Potatoes of the top three grades differ principally in requirements for size, freedom from damage caused by dirt or other foreign matter, and tolerance for defects. Some potatoes packaged for consumers are graded in accordance with commercial grades. U.S. No. 1 is the lowest grade the average consumer would wish to buy. In this grade the smallest potato allowed is one and seven-eighths inches in diameter.

Potatoes graded in accordance with consumer grades are available in some markets. There are two consumer grades: U.S. Grade A and U.S. Grade B. The use of letters for the consumer grades makes it possible to distinguish between potatoes graded according to commercial and consumer standards. The two consumer grades are subdivided into four subclassifications on the basis of size: U.S. Small, U.S. Medium, U.S. Medium to Large, and U.S. Large. For round varieties the diameter is one and a half to two and a quarter, two and a quarter to three, two and a quarter to four, and three to four inches, respectively, for U.S. Small, U.S. Medium, U.S. Medium to Large, and U.S. Large potatoes. For the long varieties, weights are four to ten ounces, four to sixteen ounces, and ten to sixteen ounces, respectively, for U.S. Medium, U.S. Medium to Large, and U.S. Large varieties. Tolerance for undersized and oversized potatoes is allowed. Grade A potatoes must be fairly well shaped; fairly clean; free from freezing injury, black-heart, late blight, sot rot; free from damage caused by sunburn, second growth, growth cracks, hollow heart, internal discoloration, cuts, shriveling, sprouting, scab, wireworm, and mechanical injury. Grade B potatoes have the same characteristics as Grade A potatoes; however, the tolerance for defects is 20 per cent instead of an allowed 5 per cent for U.S. Grade A potatoes.

Potatoes that show a green color have been sunburned during harvest or storage. They have a bitter taste that makes them unpalatable. Paring and trimming losses differ with the quality and size of potatoes; the range is from about 10 to 40 per cent, with 20 per cent as an overall average loss (5). Smaller potatoes have greater paring losses but if priced right provide more food for dollars spent than larger potatoes.

Processed Potato Products. Potatoes are processed by canning, dehydration, explosion puffing, dehydrofreezing, and freezing; altogether some fifty different forms are available. Among canned products are small whole potatoes, sliced potatoes, German potato salad, and shoestring potatoes. Dehydration of the potato resulted in instant mashed potatoes and the cut-up forms for hash brown, au gratin, and scalloped potatoes and other dishes. There are two types of instant potatoes for mashing: potato flakes and potato granules. In the production of potato flakes, potatoes are cooked and mashed, then spread onto a heated, revolving drum. The thin sheet of dehydrated potato is scraped from the drum and broken into flakes. Potato granules are intact, individual potato cells; the prepared mash is dried in a fluidized bed dryer with warm air being blown through the porous bed. Assorted frozen potato products and frozen potato dishes are to be found in the supermarket; their production exceeded two billion pounds in 1969. The frozen french fried potato is, of course, the most widely consumed. New products are introduced and old ones depart if the consumer does not find them acceptable.

Squashes

Squashes are members of the gourd family, which includes muskmelons, watermelons, cucumbers, and pumpkins. They vary in size and in internal and external color. The many varieties of squash can be grouped into two groups: hard-shelled varieties and soft-shelled varieties. Hard-shelled varieties may be small or large. They are harvested mature; they have a fairly thick rind and a definite seed cavity in which the seeds are hard and inedible. The soft-shelled squashes are immature when harvested; there is no seed cavity and the seeds are edible.

Only about 25 per cent of the hard-shelled type is sold fresh; the remainder of the crop is frozen. The best known of the hard-shelled squashes are the Hubbard and the golden delicious. They are pear-shaped, large, and heavy. The rind is hard, and the flesh is thick and golden yellow. These are usually sold by the piece and by weight. The next best known is the green acorn squash. These are small, furrowed, round to oval in shape, and thinly fleshed. The butternut squash is bell- or gourd-shaped with a smooth, thin, beige rind that is easily peeled. Its flesh is orange and it has a smooth, fine texture. It has a delicate flavor and is a favorite among the hard-shelled squashes. The buttercup squash is turban-shaped, flat at the stem end and rounded at the blossom end. The flesh is bright orange, creamy in texture, and flavorsome. Hard-shelled squashes provide two to three servings per pound.

Soft-shelled squashes are very thin-skinned; they are eaten in their entirety except for very small areas that are trimmed away at the blossom and stem ends. Yellow varieties are the *yellow straightneck* and *yellow crookneck*. Both have creamy white flesh. The *zucchini* or Italian varieties are green; the flesh is white. *Cocozelle* is also green and striped. The *scallop*, or *pattypan*, is disk-shaped with a scalloped edge; it is very pale green. All soft-shelled squashes are best when young and tender; the skin should be easily pierced by the fingernail. Depending on the method of cooking, they provide three to four servings per pound; because of their high water content, they shrink during cooking. They are probably less well liked than the hard-shelled varieties.

CANNED VEGETABLES AND CANNED VEGETABLE PRODUCTS

Canned vegetables are preferred over frozen vegetables by many consumers, perhaps only those over thirty. Improved varieties, improved technology, and rules and regulations favor good quality in canned products. Standards of identity have been promulgated for nearly all canned vegetables. Reasonable standards of quality have been defined for green and wax beans, corn, peas, and tomatoes; that is, for the preferred vegetables. Standard of fill of container has been established for corn, peas, mushrooms, and tomatoes; however, all containers must be as full as is practicable under good commercial practice. The proportion of each vegetable in a mixture of canned vegetables is not defined, but label declaration in order of predominance is mandatory, e.g., "peas and carrots" or "carrots and peas." In the canning of vegetables, the use of additives is permitted to protect color, flavor, and texture; further, the use of various ingredients is permitted to make the products more tasty. Some permitted additives and ingredients are salt, sugar, and spices; seasonings like onions and garlic; monosodium glutamate and other flavor enhancers; calcium salts to modify texture; citric acid and vinegar to modify taste; hydrolyzed vegetable protein; and vitamin C. In general, label statement of their use is mandatory. Vegetables packed whole, such as beets, carrots, potatoes, and green beans, tend to be more expensive than the different cut, sliced, and diced styles. The French-cut and julienne-cut styles are lengthwise cuts; these tend to be more expensive than other cut styles.

Permissive grades have been described for many canned vegetables. The grades are U.S. Grade A or U.S. Fancy, U.S. Grade B or U.S. Extra Standard, U.S. Grade C or U.S. Standard, and Substandard (for samples that fail to meet the requirements for U.S. Grade C). The grade is determined by the number of points scored out of a possible one hundred. Products are scored for color, clarity of liquor, tenderness and maturity, uniformity of unit size, freedom from defects, and sometimes flavor. U.S. Grade A products uniformly possess desirable qualities and are practically free from defects. U.S. Grade B products are reasonably good in all respects; U.S. Grade C, fairly good. A high proportion of canned vegetables is U.S. Grade B. Although not a factor of grade, recommended minimum drained weights are frequently suggested in the standards. A goal of consumer interest groups is the mandatory grade-labeling of canned vegetables.

Canned vegetables of top quality may cost as much as the same vegetables frozen. However, the range in cost of canned vegetables is wide; the least expensive may cost half as much as the most expensive. On this basis, it can be stated that canned vegetables are less expensive than frozen ones and often less expensive than fresh ones. Canned vegetables store conveniently and are less perishable than frozen products.

Vacuum-packed vegetables are those packed into the can with no, or a minimum quantity of, packing medium. The can is exhausted and sealed by a vacuum-sealing machine. After sealing, the cans are heat-processed in the same way as ordinary packs. The can used for vacuum packs is the squat No. 2. The net weight of this can is about twelve ounces; the drained weight of the contents will be about the same as the drained weight of the No. 303 can, the net weight of which is one pound. Both the squat No. 2 and the No. 303 cans provide about four average servings of a vegetable; the No. 8Z Tall, two average servings. These three container sizes are the ones in widest use for vegetable packs; however, the No. 300, the No. 1 Picnic, the No. 3 Squat, the No. 2, and the No. 2½, as well as others are used but, in general, only for certain specific products, for example, the No. 3 Squat for sweet potatoes.

In accordance with provisions of the Fair Packaging and Labeling Act, recommended consumer can sizes have been proposed for canned foods in metal containers. These proposed standards were submitted to the National Bureau of Standards in March, 1970 by the National Canners Association after discussion within the industry and with representatives of the National Bureau of Standards. The standards were for products by category, that is, for fruits except pineapple; for ripe olives; for juices, drinks, and nectars; and for pie fruits and fillings. The categories for vegetables and vegetable products were vegetables, dry beans, asparagus, tomatoes and tomato products, mushrooms, pimientos, and soups. The number of sizes per category was reduced from the then-current practice. Their acceptance will be forthcoming in the 1970's.

Tomato Products

Four concentrated tomato products and catsup are worth being informed about. The concentrated products are concentrated tomato juice, tomato puree or tomato pulp, tomato paste, and tomato sauce. There are U.S. quality grade standards for all and identity standards for all except tomato sauce. *Concentrated tomato juice* is the food prepared from the juice obtained from mature red or reddish tomato varieties. It is strained to exclude skins, seeds, and other coarse or hard substances and is concentrated. It contains not less than 20 per cent but not more than 24 per cent of natural tomato solids. When canned, it is processed by heat to prevent spoilage. Diluted with three volumes of water, the product is tomato juice. The remaining products may be prepared from one, a combination of two, or all of the following: the liquid obtained from mature red or reddish tomatoes; the liquid obtained from the residue from preparing tomatoes for canning, consisting of peelings and cores with or without tomato pieces; the liquid obtained from the residue from partial extraction of tomatoes. Labeling must identify the tomato ingredient(s) used in the preparation of all of these. The liquid is obtained by straining so as to exclude skins, seeds, and other coarse or hard substances. It is then concentrated and seasoned as permitted. *Tomato paste* contains not less than 24 per cent of salt-free tomato solids; it may contain salt, spice, flavoring, and baking soda; it is so processed by heat as to prevent spoilage. Tomato paste may contain as much as 39 per cent of tomato solids. Its concentration may be described as "extra heavy," "heavy," "medium," or "light." *Tomato puree*, or *pulp*, contains not less than 8 per cent but less than 24 per cent salt-free tomato solids. It may be seasoned with salt. The product is sometimes labeled "heavy," "medium," or "light" on the basis of concentration. These products can be quality-graded on the basis of color and freedom from defects. U.S. Grade A would be the best product. *Tomato sauce* contains from 9.5 to 15.2 per cent of salt-free tomato solids. Added ingredients include salt, spices, vinegar, sweetener, onion, garlic, and other vegetable flavoring ingredients, such as herbs. Brand differences among all three of these products may be ascribable to the concentration of tomato solids and to the kinds of flavoring ingredients. Concentrated tomato juice, tomato paste, or tomato puree would be the basic ingredient from which to prepare a tomato sauce for spaghetti or pizza. *Catsup* is prepared from the tomato ingredients named above, concentrated, seasoned with salt, vinegar, spices or flavorings or both, onions or garlic or both, and sweetened. When sealed in a container it is processed by heat to prevent spoilage; any use of preservatives is deemed adulteration. The solids content ranges from not less than 25 per cent to not more than 33 per cent, depending on grade.

Dry Beans and Peas

Though beans are a naturally dried vegetable, the fact that the commonly eaten varieties are available canned keeps them in use in an age of instants when, if it were necessary to prepare them from scratch, they would probably cease to be eaten, at least in the United States. These canned beans are fully cooked, ready to eat, or ready for use in casseroles, stews, soups, chili, and salads. The standards of identity for miscellaneous vegetables include identity standards for shelled beans, lima or butter beans, black-eye beans or black-eye peas, and field peas. There are U.S. quality grade standards for canned dried beans of the following types: white beans, lima beans, black-eye beans or black-eye peas, red beans, and beans or "peas" of other types. They are usually packed in three styles: in tomato sauce with pork, or meat, or a pork or meat product; in sweet sauce with pork, or meat, or a pork or meat product; and in brine. Canned and available on the supermarket shelf are black beans; garbanzo beans, or "chick peas," frequently an ingredient in three-bean salad; navy beans;

Great Northern beans; kidney beans, pink and red beans; pinto beans; and lima beans. Kidney beans, pink and red beans, and pinto beans are the ones used in making chili. They, too, are present in three-bean salad.

The pea bean is available precooked and dehydrated; the product makes instant baked beans a possibility. A dehydrated bean powder prepared from cooked beans is available for bean soups and bean dips.

Olives

Olives, like mushrooms and artichokes, have lost status as a luxury food. Domestically, they are produced in California, and they are imported from Spain, Portugal, Italy, and Greece. The olive is a fruit rather than a vegetable. It contains a bitter principle. It is straw-colored when ripe but turns jet-black if left on the tree; oil is removed at the jet-black stage. To produce the Spanish style or green olive, olives are harvested when straw-colored, treated with lye to remove the bitter principle, then allowed to undergo lactic acid fermentation. They may be bottled without pitting or may be pitted and stuffed with such items as pimientos, pickled onions, almonds, or anchovies. They are sized and bottled in brine. The ripe black olive is harvested when straw-colored and undergoes lactic acid fermentation; it is treated with lye and exposed to the air between lye treatments for the development of the black color. Green and ripe olives are packed according to size, which may range from Small with about 135 per pound to Super Colossal with 32 or less per pound. Green ripe olives receive no lactic acid fermentation and during the lye treatment are not exposed to the air so that they retain their natural color. So-called Italian or Greek olives, or olives given a dry, salt cure, are harvested when black. They are treated with salt for partial removal of the bitter principle. The salting removes moisture and gives the olive its wrinkled appearance. It retains some of the bitter principle, which gives it a bitterish taste. These olives are bottled without brine, in brine, or in oil, and with or without garlic.

FROZEN VEGETABLES

Nearly four billion pounds of vegetables were frozen in 1969; of this pack we purchased some $737.8 millions worth in the supermarket. The vegetables packed were, in descending order of quantities, potato products—more than two billion pounds—peas, green and wax beans, cut corn, broccoli, and spinach; those packed in the least quantities were collards, mustard greens, and succotash. The development of varieties especially for freezing; quick-freezing at the site of harvest; and improvements in freezing technology have all resulted in an ever-increasing variety of frozen vegetables of improved quality and of frozen vegetable dishes. In technology, fluidized freezing has resulted in the individually quick-frozen (IQF) vegetables that do not stick together; and cryogenic freezing has extended the list of frozen vegetables to include tomatoes, onions, green peppers, and mushrooms. The list of frozen vegetable dishes is long; though they come and go, some are here to stay, such as spinach soufflé and the boil-in-bag combinations like creamed peas and potatoes. They are convenience dishes in which the quantity of vegetable may be small; and it may have been purchased at a high price. To illustrate, an eight-ounce package of "Green Peas with Cream Sauce (Sauce in Concentrated Form) with Selected Seasonings" cost 35 cents in 1971. The package contained 6.6 ounces of peas, which could have been bought for from 14 to 16.5 cents, depending on whether they were purchased in a ten-ounce or a two-pound package. One concludes that the remaining 20 odd cents of the purchase price was for the sauce ingredients and the service. The listed ingredients of the sauce were "margarine, nonfat dry milk, modified food starch, wheat flour, cream, sugar, salt, MSG, and onion powder." One tablespoon of butter was to be added to the milk or water used in the preparation of the product. Similar analyses of other vegetable dishes reveal that the cost of the convenience is a high proportion of the cost of the product. Further, it has been demonstrated that consumers in the United States don't really like so-called vegetable dishes (see Chapter 14).

There are no standards or definitions of identity for frozen vegetables, though work is in progress on standards of identity and quality for frozen peas and green beans. Standards for grading have been defined for many frozen vegetables. They are graded on the basis of color, freedom from defects, and character. The number of grades differs with different vegetables: for some, such as peas, there are three possible grades and the Substandard classification; for others, such as broccoli, there are only two grades and the Substandard classification. Grades are designated as U.S. Grade A or U.S. Fancy, U.S. Grade B or U.S. Extra Standard, and U.S. Grade C or U.S. Standard. Any product failing to meet the requirements of the lowest defined grade would be classed as Substandard and would have to be so labeled. Quality-graded frozen vegetables are available in supermarkets. As for all foods preserved by freezing, vegetables must be stored at 0°F or lower. Storage life is up to eight months.

The frozen vegetable may cost more per serving than the same vegetable canned; it will frequently cost less than the fresh counterpart. Private-label frozen vegetables generally cost less per serving than national brands. Frozen vegetables are sometimes specialed to give the consumer good buys. The cost per portion varies with the size of the package purchased and the style of processing of the product, e.g., French-cut green beans versus green bean cuts. Finally, frozen prepared vegetable dishes, those with built-in chef service, cost more than the same vegetables purchased without this convenience.

The Per-Serving Cost of Vegetables

The year-around availability of practically all vegetables fresh means that the per-serving cost varies with the season; the per-serving cost remains fairly constant for canned and frozen vegetables. The latter vary in cost depending on the quality purchased, the size of the unit purchased, the amount of added convenience, and the supermarket where they are purchased. In Table 10-1, the costs per serving of some fresh vegetables are presented. The costs are as of early spring, 1971, when all would be out of season except in areas of production: they would have originated from truck farms across the country from California to Florida. The cost per serving ranges from about three cents to about twenty cents. In the same table, the per-serving costs of the same vegetables purchased frozen are given. It can be seen that the cost of the frozen vegetable may exceed or be less than that of the fresh counterpart.

In Table 10-2, the costs per portion of some frozen ready-prepared vegetable dishes are given. In general, the ready-prepared dish exceeds both

Table 10-2. *Per-Serving Cost of Some Frozen Ready-made Vegetable Dishes*

	Market Unit and Cost	*Cost per 3-Ounce Serving*[1]
Broccoli with Hollandaise sauce	45¢/10 oz.	$.135
Cauliflower in cheese sauce	49¢/10 oz.	.147
Corn in butter sauce	39¢/10 oz.	.117
Creamed spinach	45¢/9 oz.	.150
Green beans with almonds	45¢/9 oz.	.150
Green beans in butter sauce	39¢/9 oz.	.130
Japanese vegetables	49¢/10 oz.	.147
Mixed vegetables with onion sauce	45¢/8 oz.	.180
Peas and onions	45¢/10 oz.	.135
Carrots in butter sauce	39¢/10 oz.	.117
Parisian vegetables	49¢/10 oz.	.147
Spanish vegetables	49¢/10 oz.	.147
Deviled spinach	47¢/12 oz.	.120

[1] It is possible that some housewives would serve out these dishes as four portions; however, it is more than likely that the majority would serve only three portions from them.

TABLE 10-3.   *Per-Serving Cost of Selected Canned Vegetables*

	Name Brand		Store Brand[1]	
	Market Unit and Cost	Cost per Serving[2]	Market Unit and Cost	Cost per Serving[2]
Beans, green cuts	No. 303/29¢	$.075	6 No. 303/$1	$.040
Beans, green whole	No. 303/29¢	.075	No. 303/25¢	.062
Beets, cuts	No. 303/31¢	.080	6 No. 303/$1	.040
Beets, medium whole	No. 303/35¢	.090	6 No. 303/$1	.040
Corn, cream style	No. 303/29¢	.075	No. 303/20¢	.050
Mixed vegetables	No. 303/25¢	.062	No. 303/20¢	.050
Peas, medium-sized	No. 303/29¢	.075	No. 303/20¢	.050
Spinach	No. 303/25¢	.062	No. 303/20¢	.050
Sweet potatoes	No. 303/37¢	.092	No. 303/20¢	.050
Tomatoes, whole	No. 2-1/2/41¢	.070	No. 2-1/2/33¢	.055
Tomatoes, stewed	No. 303/33¢	.082	No. 303/25¢	.062

[1]National chain store brand.

[2]Estimated on the basis of four servings per No. 303 can and six per No. 2-1/2 can.

the fresh and the frozen vegetable in cost. In Table 10-3, the costs per serving of name brands and store brands of some canned vegetables are given. Differences in the serving costs of canned vegetables are not great; there is some difference in per-serving costs according to the brand purchased, however. The dollar can very definitely purchase more or less of vegetable servings. And, it is of interest that the preferred vegetables are not the most expensive by any means.

Summary.   Vegetables are available in great variety fresh and processed by canning, dehydration, and freezing. Fresh vegetables differ in cost per portion. Depending on the season and the region of residence, the fresh product may cost more than the processed one and frozen products may exceed canned ones in cost. The cost per serving of canned products is established by the quality purchased, the size of the can purchased, the style of the pack, the brand, and the market wherein they are purchased. The same may be said for frozen products. The addition of the gourmet touch to frozen vegetables adds to the cost. Both frozen and canned vegetables are frequent supermarket specials. Decisions on what to buy must be made by the meal manager on the bases of resources and personal preferences.

GUIDES TO BUYING FRESH VEGETABLES

1.   Except for tomatoes, winter squash, potatoes, and a few others, immaturity is preferred in vegetables. This is true of peas, beans, corn, cu-

cumbers, radishes, soft-shelled squashes, carrots, asparagus, broccoli, and so forth. Learn to recognize the signs of maturity. Among them are (a) a dry or dull appearance in contrast to a shiny appearance, as in pea pods and soft-shelled squashes; (b) a dull or yellowish green in contrast to a bright green, as in asparagus and green beans; (c) thickening and coarsening in the texture of the skin, as in green beans and pea pods; (d) browning.

2. Select vegetables of good color.

3. Buy only fresh, crisp-looking vegetables.

4. Avoid buying vegetables showing brown areas—signs of either decay or maturity.

5. Select vegetables that are free of defects that must be pared away unless they are priced advantageously.

6. Unless vegetables washed for packaging have been dried well, they soon rot. Look for areas of decay in packaged greens, beans, peas, lettuce, radishes, spinach, and others.

7. Look for brown areas of spoilage on vegetables that are kept moist on vegetable counters, such as lettuce, radishes, and so forth.

8. Be flexible: if the vegetable you intended to purchase is of inferior quality, buy one of better quality.

9. Even though canned and frozen vegetables are convenient, buy fresh vegetables occasionally for their good flavor and texture, which canning and freezing so frequently modify. Buy them when they are in season locally; they have the best flavor and are the least costly then.

10. Compare the cost of fresh, canned, and frozen products on the cost-per-serving basis. Match your choice to your food budget.

11. Tomatoes are picked underripe. Let them ripen at room temperature, but not in direct sunlight. If you wrap them individually and keep them in a cool, dark place, they will develop in color but not in flavor.

REFERENCES CITED

1. "Changing Patterns of Potato Consumption," *Family Economics Review*, Consumer and Food Economics Research Division, United States Department of Agriculture, Washington, D.C. (June 1968), p. 7.

2. *Food Consumption of Households in the United States, Spring, 1965*, Consumer and Food Economics Research Division, United States Department of Agriculture, Washington, D.C. (1968), p. 2.

3. *Gallup Survey—The National Poll of Patron Preferences, Prejudices, and Trends*, Volumes 1 and 2, Food Service Magazine, Madison, Wisconsin (1967, 1969).

4. "Per Capita Food Consumption," *National Food Situation*, Research Service, United States Department of Agriculture, Washington, D.C. (February 1971), p. 12.

5. Pecot, R. K. and B. K. Watt, *Food Yields—Summarized by Different Stages of Preparation,* Agricultural Handbook No. 102, Agricultural Research Service, United States Department of Agriculture, Washington, D.C. (June 1956).
6. Peryam, David R. et al., *Food Preferences of Men in the U.S. Armed Forces,* Department of the Army, Quartermaster Research and Engineering Command, and Container Institute for Armed Forces, Chicago (1960).

Chapter 11

Purchasing Food— Grain Food Products and Miscellaneous Food Products

For all the food products discussed thus far we spend about two thirds of the food dollar. We spend nearly one third (32 per cent) of the dollar for an assortment of food classes: grain products, including bread, bakery products, cereals, and flour; shortening and oils; salad dressings; sugars, jams and jellies, and syrups; beverages; baking supplies; and assorted others, such as condiments. As elsewhere, the choices made and the manner of buying items determine how much of these products the dollar buys. For example, the cereals of variety packs cost more per ounce than the same cereals purchased in larger packages; a glass of raspberry jelly more than apple jelly; rolls more than bread; olive oil more than corn oil; and so on. Selective buying from among these products is possible because of the great variety of similar or nearly similar products, the many brands available, quality differences, and kinds of packaging.

Some of the foods of these classes have been defined and standardized. This means that the basic ingredients are named, sometimes the ratio of ingredients is defined, and the permitted and optional ingredients are named. This situation suggests that products within these classes, such as bread and salad dressing, for example, may actually be similar except for differences in such palatability factors as flavor and texture, and perhaps in packaging.

GRAIN PRODUCTS

During the decade between the 1955 and 1965 studies of household food consumption made by the United States Department of Agriculture, the consumption of flour and cereals decreased from 5.87 to 4.69 pounds per household per week and the consumption of bakery products, including

303

bread, increased from 6.7 to 7.63 pounds per household per week (3). According to the study, the consumption of bakery items increased with income; it reached the average when income was about $5,000 per year (after taxes), and continued to rise thereafter. On the other hand, the consumption of cereals and flour reached the maximum at an income of about $4,000 per year (after taxes) and continued to decline thereafter. All of which says that there is less and less baking in the household. Per-person consumption per day was three and one-half slices of bread, two and one-quarter ounces of other bakery products, and three ounces of flour and other cereal products (1). These data are averages, obviously: many persons consumed more and many others less. About 12 per cent, or one eighth, of the food dollar was spent on these grain products; it is an expenditure of only a third as much as we spend for meat, poultry, fish, and eggs (3).

Bakery Products

A variety of ready-made breads, rolls, cakes, pies, pastries, waffles, pancakes, cookies, crackers, snack items, and so on *ad infinitum* is available. Some products are fresh baked; others are prebaked and frozen; and some are canned. Further, many items are available in different degrees of preparation from dry mix to ready-to-bake. New products are introduced daily; continual surveillance of the marketplace is essential if one is to be aware of all that is there for the taking. There are products for the gourmet and products for the masses. The returns for a dollar spent depend on the selections made, that is, store-label enriched bread at twenty-two cents per pound versus Mrs. O'Brien's Irish Bread at fifty-nine cents per pound; frozen all-butter devil's food cake at about ninety-four cents per pound versus store-label devil's food cake at about fifty-one cents per pound; or fig newton's at forty-five cents per pound versus chocolate dreams at fifty-five cents for ten ounces. At least two factors determine what products the consumer purchases: income and preferences.

Definitions and standards of identity have been promulgated for some breads and rolls, standards are in progress for frozen cherry pies, and all products must bear a list of ingredients in decreasing order of predominance.

Definitions and standards of identity have been promulgated for five kinds of bread: bread and rolls or buns, or white bread and white rolls or white buns; enriched bread and rolls or buns; milk bread and rolls or buns; raisin bread and rolls or buns; and whole wheat, graham, and entire wheat bread and rolls or buns. Much bread crosses state lines; hence, these definitions are of consequence to consumers. The definitions specify the ingredients that must be used and name the optional ingredients that may be used in the manufacture of the breads; the definitions establish the solids content of bread at 62 per cent; and they require label statements of the use of chemicals to retard spoilage. *White bread* must contain flour, water or other specified liquid ingredients, yeast, and salt. The following are optional ingredients: shortening; milk; buttermilk, whey, milk proteins; eggs; sugar, syrup, or molasses; flours such as corn flour, potato flour, and soy flour; and various ingredients peculiar to the commercial production of bread. The quantities of some ingredients are limited according to the amount of flour used. The standards for white bread apply also to French, Italian, and Vienna breads.

The standards for enriched bread, milk bread, raisin bread, and whole wheat bread must conform to those for white bread, with certain exceptions. *Enriched bread* must be enriched according to standards of the Food and Drug Administration with the following nutrients: thiamine, riboflavin, niacin, and iron. The labels on enriched bread must state the percentages of minimum daily requirements, or other standards, for these nutrients as established by the Food and Drug Administration that can be obtained from a specified quantity of bread—usually one-half pound. More than half the states require the enrichment of white bread and flour; in other states, many commercial bakeries voluntarily enrich their products. A large proportion of commercial white bread is enriched. It is important for good nutrition that the white bread purchased be enriched.

Milk bread must contain not less than 8.2 parts of milk solids from whole milk per 100 parts of flour. *Raisin bread* and rolls or buns must contain 50 parts by weight of raisins per 100 parts of flour. *Whole wheat, graham,* or *entire wheat bread* must be made entirely from whole wheat flour. When a mixture of whole wheat and white flour is used in breadmaking, the bread is called *wheat* or *wheaten bread.* All rolls or buns and raisin bread may contain added wheat gluten to the extent of 4 parts per 100 parts of flour. The following are some nonstandardized breads: rye bread, pumpernickel bread, potato bread, gluten bread, cracked wheat bread, and wheaten bread. Most rye breads are made with a light rye flour in combination with wheat flour. Pumpernickel rye bread is made with a dark rye flour and the dough is made sour by special fermentation with acid-producing bacteria. Sour dough white bread is also made.

Low calorie, "slenderizing," and diet breads differ little in calorie content from other breads; the omission of fat from a formula alters the calorie value of a slice of bread little because the quantity of fat in bread is small. Weight for weight, breads are quite similar in calorie content. Small, thin slices have fewer calories per slice because they weigh less than thicker slices. Differences in the textures of breads cause some small slices to have the same calorie content as some larger slices. Much commercial bread is soft and light; it has the texture that bakers find is preferred. Breads of the "home baked" type are more compact.

Breads vary in nutrient content as they vary in ingredient composition.

The percentage of nonfat dry milk varies in bread formulas from 4 to more than 10 per cent. Milk adds calcium and protein and improves the quality of bread proteins. Eggs, wheat germ, and soy flour also add nutrients to bread. Enriched bread is comparable to whole wheat bread in nutrient content. Proposed new levels of enrichment of enriched flour and enriched self-rising flour, enriched bread and enriched rolls, and enriched farina would give the enriched products a nutrient content superior to whole wheat products in the nutrients of enrichment. The addition of the amino acid lysine to bread is probably not warranted in the United States so long as mixed diets containing meats, milk, and eggs are generously consumed.

The greatest differences among breads are in texture and flavor. Some of the premium-priced breads have qualities more like those of home-baked breads than lower-priced breads. The kinds of flour, the quantity of milk, and the assortment of other ingredients used modify flavor and sometimes texture. Methods of wrapping bread to keep it sanitary keep the crust soft.

It is possible to simulate yeast breads in texture and volume using chemical leaveners in place of yeast. Although the first such breads produced lacked the aroma of yeast-leavened bread, it is now possible to add substances producing this special aroma.

Dinner rolls or buns in great variety may be purchased in a variety of stages of preparation: mix, ready-to-bake, partially baked brown-and-serve, frozen ready-baked, and ready-baked. Some are priced higher than others. Store brands tend to cost less than national brands. Bread is less expensive than rolls, but rolls are very well liked. Breakfast rolls and breads, English muffins, coffee cakes, and cakes are also available in great variety and in store brands and name brands. Store-bought cookies too are available in diverse kinds and in different brands. The outcome is that all bakery products can be purchased at quite different costs. In Table 11–1, the costs per pound for a variety of products are presented. It will be observed that the most costly may be twice as expensive as the least costly. Again, the dollar can buy more or less.

All bakery products are convenience foods: the cost of the basic ingredients may be much or little. Pastry for pie is a simple mixture of ingredients; the cost of the convenience for pastry bought in different stages of preparation appeared in Chapter 5 as Table 5–6. Products differ in palatability, that is, how good they taste. Many persons do not like the pies, cakes, cookies, and so on that can be purchased ready for heating or eating. No doubt some are better than others; but then, some home-prepared items are better than others.

For all baked goods, including bread, rolls, pies, cookies, waffles, pancakes, and so on, the careful and conservative shopper must compare dif-

TABLE 11–1.   *Cost per Pound of Selected Breads, Rolls, and Baked Goods*

Items	Cost as Purchased	Cost per Pound
Bread, balloon loaf, white enriched	39¢/20 oz.	$.32
Bread, store brand, white enriched	55¢/2 20-oz. loaves	.22
Bread, store brand, white enriched	33¢/lb. loaf	.33
Bread, mini loaves, store brand, white enriched	39¢/1 lb. (3)	.39
Bread, Brand A, white enriched	41¢/1 lb.	.41
Bread, Brand B, sour dough, frozen	69¢/1 lb.	.69
Rolls, brown-and-serve, Brand A	25¢/10 oz. (12)	.40
Rolls, brown-and-serve, seeded, Brand A	27¢/10 oz. (9)	.43
Rolls, brown-and-serve, Brand B	41¢/8 oz. (12)	.82
Rolls, brown-and-serve, seeded, Brand B	41¢/7 oz. (9)	.94
Breakfast sweet rolls, store brand	49¢/12 oz.	.65
Breakfast sweet rolls, bakery	60¢/1 lb. (6)	.60
Breakfast sweet rolls, Brand A	89¢/12 oz.	1.19
Coffee cake, store brand	79¢/1 lb.	.79
Coffee cake, fruit ring, Brand A	69¢/10 oz.	1.10
Coffee cake, cinnamon, Brand A	89¢/12–½ oz.	1.14
Hamburger buns, store brand	27¢/11 oz. (8)	.39
Hamburger buns, Brand A	33¢/10 oz. (8)	.53
Hamburger buns, seeded, Brand B	63¢/1 lb. (12)	.63
English muffins, store brand	35¢/14 oz. (6)	.40
English muffins, Brand A	37¢/7–½ oz. (4)	.79
English muffins, Brand B, frozen	29¢/8 oz. (4)	.58
Cinnamon loaf, Brand A	49¢/1 lb.	.49
Cinnamon loaf, Brand B	59¢/1 lb.	.59
Cake, frosted, store brand	45¢/12 oz.	.60
Cake, frosted, Brand A	83¢/14 oz.	.95
Cake, frosted, Brand B	89¢/1 lb.	.89
Cake, frosted, Brand C	89¢/17 oz.	.84
Cookies, cream-filled, Brand A	55¢/10 oz.	.88
Cookies, cream-filled, Brand B	53¢/14–½ oz.	.59
Cookies, cream-filled, Brand C	73¢/26 oz.	.45

ferent and similar products on the basis of cost per unit of weight. The cost of the convenience ought to be estimated too. It may take time, but it is possible to find products that match the food budget, the planned use of time, and personal preferences. Many of these baked products are easy to make and quick to mix up with the equipment and ingredients available in the 1970's.

Breakfast Cereals

Ready-prepared cereals cost more per portion than cook-before-serving cereals. Ready-sweetened cereals cost more than the unsweetened kinds. Seasoned and/or fruited cereals cost more than the plain product. Per unit of weight, the cereal in a large box costs less than the cereal in a small box

TABLE 11–2.   *Cost per Pound of Some Selected Ready-to-Eat Breakfast Cereals and of Two Cook-Before-Eating Cereals*

Items	Market Unit and Cost	Cost per Pound
Flake cereals		
Corn flakes	35¢/12 oz.	$.47
Oat flakes	55¢/12 oz.	.74
Rice flakes	49¢/10 oz.	.78
Total Corn Flakes[1]	45¢/7 oz.	1.03
Total Wheat Flakes[1]	65¢/12 oz.	.87
Corn cereals		
Brand A—corn flakes	35¢/12 oz.	.47
Brand A—sugar-frosted flakes (corn)	41¢/10 oz.	.66
Brand A—Sugar Pops (corn)	45¢/9 oz.	.80
Brand B—Corn Chex	45¢/12 oz.	.60
Brand B—Sugar Chex (corn)	43¢/7 oz.	.96
Brand C—Corn Puffs (fruit flavor)	45¢/8 oz.	.90
Wheat cereals		
Wheaties	47¢/10 oz.	.75
Wheat Chex	47¢/15 oz.	.50
Shredded wheat (biscuits)	35¢/10 oz.	.56
Shredded wheat (spoon size)	39¢/12 oz.	.52
Frosted Mini Wheats	43¢/10 oz.	.69
Sugar Smacks	59¢/14 oz.	.67
Puffed wheat	29¢/3 oz.	1.60
Mixed-grain cereals		
Product 19	47¢/8 oz.	.94
Cheerios	37¢/7 oz.	.88
Special K	43¢/7 oz.	.96
Apple Jacks	43¢/7 oz.	.96
Fruit Loops	41¢/7 oz.	.94
Team	49¢/13 oz.	.60
Crunch Berries	57¢/11 oz.	.83
Variety packs		
Brand A	55¢/10 oz.	.88
Brand B	43¢/7–¾ oz.	.88
Cook-before-eating cereals		
Oatmeal	39¢/18 oz.	.35
Wheat	35¢/14 oz.	.40

[1]Plus nine vitamins and iron.

or a variety pack. The per-pound costs of some cereal flakes, of some corn cereals, of some wheat cereals, of some mixed-grain cereals, of two variety packs, and of two cook-before-eating cereals are given in Table 11–2. The range is from $0.50 to $1.60 per pound for the ready-to-eat cereals. In general, an ounce of these cereals provides an average serving. Some of the products were enriched with more nutrients than others, and nutrients were present in greater quantities in some than in others. The labeling on some cereal boxes pointed out that the milk added to the cereal was rich in nutrients. Both wheat and oat cereals of the cook-before-eating kind were less expensive than the ready-to-eat products.

Breakfast cereals are not defined or standardized; nearly all ready-to-eat breakfast cereals are enriched with vitamins and minerals; some, with added protein. Labeling requirements make mandatory the naming of all ingredients in a cereal and the stating of the quantities of added vitamins and minerals as the percentages of the daily minimum requirements supplied by a specified quantity. Generally, breakfast cereals are eaten with milk, from which the dish derives nutrients. The cereal industries have been criticized for making much of the nutrient value of cereals without always being fair about the role of milk in making them nutritious.

Breakfast cereals that require cooking are instant, quick-cooking, and regular. Precooked cereals are also available: the cereal is emptied into the cereal bowl, boiling water is poured over the cereal, and it is ready for eating. The cost of this convenience for oatmeal doubles the cost of the cereal. Many of the cook-before-eating cereals are enriched.

Flour

According to the household food consumption study made in 1965, the average household consumption of flour was less than one pound per week and of flour mixes less than one-half pound per week. The money value of this quantity of flour would be insignificant. Name-brand products cost more than private-label and locally milled flours. Flours are milled from hard and soft wheats, and flours differ in strength, that is, the degree to which they develop gluten. All-purpose flour is versatile in use. It is blended so as to be suitable for making yeast breads, which require gluten development, and also for making cakes and pastry. Cake flour is preferred for cakes unless the recipes have been developed to permit the use of general-purpose flour. Instant flour is so processed that it is supposed to blend without lumping in either hot or cold liquid. Regular flours lump when blended with hot liquid. Opinion is not universal on the merits of instantized flour. Self-rising flour contains a leavening agent; when it is used, no baking powder or soda is added in the making of a product. Whole wheat flour, rye flour, cornmeal, and even oatmeal are used in bread-making but almost always with some white flour because none of the former are gluten formers. There is a resurgence of interest in bread-making in the United States, not so much for reasons of economy but as a hobby, for good nutrition, and for the delicious aroma and flavor that the commercial products so often lack. The already-mentioned surveys of housewives made in 1970 disclosed that some families were making bread and other bakery products from basic ingredients to cut down on food spending.

Alimentary Pastes or Pasta

The alimentary pastes, or pasta, are dry wheat-dough products that require cooking; familiar ones are spaghetti and macaroni. There are more of these products in the supermarket of the 1970's than there were in the early 1960's. Except for noodles, which contain egg, all the various forms and shapes are made from the same basic dough, have the same texture, are similarly lacking in flavor, and could be used interchangeably were it not that certain dishes traditionally require the use of certain shapes—lasagna, for example, requires the broad noodle, crinkled on the edges. Shape classes are four: cord-shaped like some spaghetti, vermicelli, twists, and fusilli; tube-shaped like macaroni, some spaghetti, ziti, and manicotti; ribbon-shaped like noodles; and the odd-shaped kinds like shells, bows, rote (wheel-shaped), and ever so many others.

Definitions and standards of identity have been promulgated for some products in this class. Macaroni products are prepared by the drying of formed units of dough made from semolina, durum flour, farina, flour, or any combination of two or more of these with water, and with or without one or more of the permitted optional ingredients. Noodle products are prepared from the same flours and any of several forms of egg (i.e., fresh, frozen, or dried), with or without water, and with or without certain optional ingredients. The definitions and standards of identity, in addition to prescribing ingredient composition, establish the solids content and the level of enrichment for fortified products, and require label statement of the use of certain optional ingredients. The optional ingredient disodium phosphate, which is added to hasten cooking, must be named on the label. An identity standard was in process (1971) for macaroni products with improved protein quality. The quantity of protein would be not less than 20 per cent of the finished product; the protein quality would be not less than 95 per cent of that of casein. The best pasta products are made from semolina or durum flour: they hold shapes well during cooking and they retain the firmness characteristic of pasta. The products are packaged in packages of assorted sizes; per unit of weight, the cost of the product should decrease with an increase in the package size.

Convenience foods that contain one of the pasta are numerous: canned and frozen ready-to-heat-and-eat dishes; delicatessen salads and ready-to-eat dishes; and the pasta packaged with a ready-made sauce or mix for a sauce.

Miscellaneous Cereals

Rice, barley, buckwheat, and bulgur are cereals in this miscellaneous cereal group. Rice is more commonly used than the others. Rice is white, that is, polished or highly milled, and brown or unpolished. The latter retains some bran and the germ of the kernel; it has a higher nutritive value than polished rice (it is also more subject to spoilage). Both white and brown rice may be purchased in regular form and as instant products. Enriched rice is polished rice that has added nutrients. Parboiled rice has been steeped in hot water, drained, steamed, and dried before milling. Parboiling or steeping effects the transfer of nutrients from the bran coat to the rice kernel; such rice has more nutrient value than polished rice. Converted rice is parboiled rice. Instant or minute rice has been precooked and dehydrated. Wild rice is not rice, but the seed of a grass that grows in marshes and the shallow water of lakes in Minnesota and Canada. It is a scarce commodity and is very expensive. It can be purchased mixed with white rice.

Rice kernels are typed as long grain, medium grain, and short grain. The kernels of long-grain rice are thin; those of short-grain rice, plump; and of medium-grain, in between. Generally, two types can be bought in most supermarkets. The price per pound may differ. All types are packaged in different quantities; per unit of weight, the rice in the larger packages should cost less. Perhaps, it should be said again that differences in cost because of differences in package size are not always great. For example, rice of the same brand name and kernel size might be priced: one pound—twenty-three cents; two pounds—forty-three cents; and three pounds—sixty-three cents. If one pound were always purchased, the cost of two pounds would be forty-six cents and of three pounds, sixty-nine cents—savings of only three and six cents, respectively. However, when these savings are calculated on a percentage basis of the price paid, they become 7 and 9.5 per cent, respectively, and thereby gain in stature.

Rice is packaged with various assortments of herbs and spices. The assortments are characterized as accompaniments for different dishes. These products are expensive; for example, when eight ounces of long-grain rice could be purchased for eleven and a half cents, the seasoned products were generally priced at twenty-five to forty-two cents per eight ounces. The cost of the convenience of instant rice is expensive too: approximately forty-six cents for the equivalent of one pound of long-grain rice costing twenty-three cents. Rice is rarely washed before use. Cook

polished rice in one and a half to two volumes of water; the yield will be
the combined volume of rice and water, that is, three cups of cooked rice
from one cup of dry rice as a rule.

Barley, granular buckwheat, and bulgur are cereals used similarly to rice
for the preparation of dishes that are to be served with meat or that include meat. Barley is a familiar ingredient in soups. It is used whole and
cooked with seasonings and meats in the making of dishes sometimes
called *pilaf* or *pilau*. Roasted buckwheat is ground to different degrees of
fineness to form meal; it is sometimes called *kasha*. Bulgur is whole wheat
that has been precooked, dried, and ground to different degrees of fineness.
Both buckwheat and bulgur are also cooked with seasonings to prepare
pilaf. An affluent society has adopted these dishes, which are traditional in
the Middle East.

SWEETENERS FOR FOOD

Sugar consumption increased slightly during the decade of the 1960's; it
was about two pounds per capita per week in 1970 (8). This was total consumption and included sugar used by the food industries. Average household use according to the 1965 study of food consumption was just under
two pounds per week; however, the amount was slightly greater in the
income range of $3,000 to $9,000 (after taxes), from which it might be inferred that there was more home preparation of food requiring the use of
sugar within this income range. The usual household uses white sugar,
brown sugar, and confectioners sugar. The latter is often labeled "Confectioners Ten-X Powdered Sugar." Brown sugar may be light or dark in
color, it is a "moist" sugar that may dry and harden unless packaged or
stored so as to be airtight. Should brown sugar become hard and dry, it
can be pulverized in a blender or it can be softened enough by heat in a
slow oven to become measurable. It measures out slightly more than two
cups to the pound (two cups per pound is the approximate measure of
white sugar). It is available in a granulated form. Be sure to read and follow the information on the package about the use of granulated brown
sugar when substituting it for white or brown sugar, because it measures
out about three cups to the pound. Confectioners sugar is finely pulverized white sugar; cornstarch may be present to prevent caking. Confectioners sugar measures about four cups to the pound. A granulated form
is available.

Corn syrups, cane syrups including molasses, maple syrup, sorghum
syrup, and honey are some other sweeteners for food. Molasses syrups used
in cooking are light to dark in color and mild to strong in flavor. Molasses
syrups for the table are light in color and mild in flavor. Corn syrups are
light or dark in color, are used in cooking and also for the table; and are
less sweet than sugar syrups and also less expensive. Sorghum syrup, de-

rived from sorghum cane, has a special flavor highly prized in regions within the Midwest and the South. Pure maple syrup is a standardized product containing not more than 35 per cent water, and it must weigh eleven pounds per gallon. It is the most expensive of the syrups. Maple syrup is blended with sugar syrup for table use; a blend must be properly labeled. Imitation maple syrup is artificially flavored sugar syrup or blended syrup.

Standards for grading maple syrup and honey have been formulated; U.S. Fancy is the top grade for both. Syrups for table use—that is, on hot breads, pancakes, waffles, and so on—are prepared by the blending of two or more of the aforementioned syrups. Other ingredients that may be present in these syrups are butter, artificial flavoring, artificial coloring, stabilizers, and preservatives. A label statement of all ingredients is mandatory, and the syrups of the blend must be listed in decreasing order of predominance. A variety of fruit-flavored syrups, made with fruit juices and sugar syrups, are products of the 1960's. Again, study labels for information as to ingredient composition. Identity standards for table syrups were proposed in October, 1970; they are in progress (1972).

The available variety of table syrups priced over a wide range in costs suggests the wisdom of reading labels to discover composition. Certainly, any syrup with a first listing of corn syrup should cost less than one with a first listing of maple syrup. The cost of a syrup will be determined by the kind of syrup or the blend of syrups. The size of the container and the kind of container will also be factors in cost; the unusual come-to-the-table-container may add to the cost of the syrup.

Honey is available as comb honey, as extracted-from-the-comb honey, and in a finely crystallized form called *honey spread*. Comb honey is limited in availability and expensive. The flavor and color of honey depend on the flower source. Clover honey is mild in flavor; buckwheat honey is strong in flavor.

Interest in so-called natural foods, organic foods (produced without the use of chemical fertilizers or pesticides), and vegetarian diets escalated in the late 1960's and early 1970's. This interest produced great interest in breads composed of many and diverse ingredients; in brown rice and other unmilled or slightly milled cereals; many kinds of dry beans and peas; many kinds of such seeds as sesame seeds and sunflower seeds; and in molasses and honey. Stores established for the sale of natural foods and so-called health foods became ubiquitous in the early 1970's.

BEVERAGES

According to the study made by the United States Department of Agriculture in 1965, 10 per cent of the dollar spent for food consumed at home was spent for beverages (excluding milk). This was 2 per cent more than was spent for beverages in 1955. During the decade between the two studies, the consumption of coffee increased from thirty-eight to forty-eight cups, of soft drinks from five to nine cups, and of fruit ades and punches from one to thirteen cups per household per week (7). In 1969, we spent in grocery stores as much for soft drinks as for coffee, both ground and instant; about half as much for instant coffee as for ground beans; half as much for tea as for instant coffee; and some more than half as much for instant tea and iced-tea mixes as for loose tea and tea bags. In all, it was some $3,593,360,000 (9). In the United States, we consume about one half of the world's coffee supply.

Coffee

Coffee consumption, on the green bean basis, declined slightly during the 1960's; it was about 13.6 pounds per capita for the year 1971. High retail prices, declining consumption among teen-agers and young adults, high extraction rates for instant coffee, and increasing cup yields per pound of roasted coffee all contributed to the decline in consumption (on a green bean basis).

Coffee for brewing is derived from the fruits of different species of evergreen trees of the genus *Coffea*. Each fruit, or coffee berry, contains two seeds, or beans, covered by a parchmentlike membrane. These are embedded within the pulp of the fruit. The first step in processing the coffee berry for market is the removal of the pulp; the beans then undergo a fermentation process essential for flavor development. Following fermentation, the beans are cured; lastly, the covering membrane is removed. The beans are green at this stage, when they are shipped from the producing area. Most of the beans imported into the United States come from South America, especially Brazil. The green beans differ in flavor potential, and different brands of coffee differ in the basic blends of beans. The green beans must be roasted for the development of flavor and aroma. During roasting, *caffeol*, a mixture of essential oils, develops from the fat in the bean. These oils are volatile, explaining the aroma of coffee; they are also soluble in water, explaining the flavor of coffee. Further, other flavor components develop and the bean changes in color from green to different shades of brown, depending on the length of the roasting period. Roasting may be light, medium, dark, or almost black. The time required for the right amount of roasting differs with different varieties of coffee beans. For this reason, blends for the best coffees are not compounded until after roasting; however, most processors blend before roasting. After roasting, the beans are generally ground and the product is vacuum-packed in cans. Once the vacuum-packed can of ground coffee is opened, the coffee is perishable and should be kept in a cool place. Unground beans may be purchased—many persons prefer to grind their own for a more flavorful brew.

Beans are ground to different degrees of fineness for the different methods of brewing coffee: a coarse, or regular, grind for percolated coffee; fine, for drip coffee; and very fine for espresso coffee. The finer the grind, the more readily are the solubles removed from the coffee: the flavor components, the caffeine, and the tannins. Caffeine is the stimulating principle and the tannins are bitter. The quality of a brewed coffee and of an instant coffee (which is also brewed coffee) is established not only by the blend of beans and the kind of roast, but also by proper brewing. Proper brewing means the proper grind for the kind of coffee maker being used, the proper amount of ground coffee for the strength of brew desired, regulation of the length of time the water is in contact with the ground coffee, temperature control, and the use of clean equipment. The higher the temperature of brewing above 200°F and the longer the period of brewing, the less flavorful and more bitter is the brew. A coarse grind is indicated for methods of brewing when there is repeated or continuous contact of the water with the ground coffee as in percolation. A finer degree of grind is indicated for methods wherein there is only one-time contact between water and the ground coffee, as in the drip method of brewing. The strength of coffee is regulated by the amount of coffee used, not by long periods of extraction, which result in greater extraction of bitter substances. Tannins are increasingly soluble and the volatiles escape more readily as the temperature approaches the boiling point; that is, boiling during extraction results in a bitter and nonflavorful brew. Coffee oils accumulate in a rinsed-only coffee maker: they become rancid and contribute undesirable flavor components to the brew.

Instant coffee was not an instant success. Though it had been around since early in the century and had been served to the armed forces during two world wars, domestic consumption of the product did not reach 20 per cent of the beverage consumed until the 1960's. In 1970, about 16 per cent of the coffee beans roasted in the United States were processed to prepare instant coffee (2). As practiced, this processing results in about twice the volume of the beverage that is produced in the home brewing of ground beans (6). Instant coffees are the dehydrated beverage and the different instants are produced by different methods of brewing and dehydrating, especially the latter. Consumers Union (5, 6) has reported the results of two coffee tastings. In each tasting, instants were compared with brewed coffee in graduated strengths from weak to strong. In the first tasting, a freeze-dried product was preferred at the medium strength; at the strong strength, freshly brewed coffee was preferred and the freeze-dried instant was second. In the second tasting, 45 different instant coffees (33 regular and 12 freeze-dried) prepared in three strengths were compared with each other and with three freshly brewed coffees, likewise prepared in three strengths. The weaker-strength brew was preferred; all coffees were about equally well liked; and differences among the brands of instant coffee were insig-

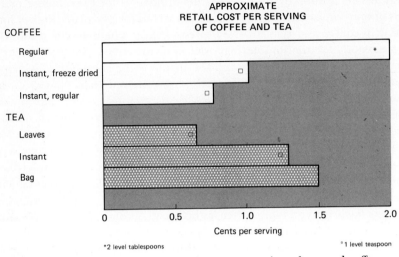

FIGURE 11-1.   Approximate retail cost per serving of tea and coffee.

nificant, that is, the freeze-dried products were not found to be superior to the regular instant coffees. However, there were products that rated above average. Different persons have different preferences, and some experimentation with brands and at different strengths seems indicated. The instants have a lower caffeine content than freshly brewed coffee because more brewed coffee is prepared from a measure or weight of ground coffee, i.e., there is a higher extraction rate. Freshly brewed coffee costs almost twice as much per serving as coffee prepared with a freeze-dried instant. Coffee prepared from the freeze-dried instant costs more than coffee prepared from a regular instant (see Figure 11-1). Coffee is a frequent supermarket special; in general, purchase at the discounted price is dependent on other purchases that total a specified minimum. During the 1960's this minimum was $5, but in the 1970's it has become $7 in some supermarkets.

Decaffeinated coffee is prepared by a special treatment that removes the caffeine from the green beans. This coffee is more expensive than regular coffee.

Chicory root is dried, roasted, and ground and added to coffee to produce a flavor especially liked in Louisiana and by many persons in other places. Chicory was considered an adulterant of coffee at one time.

Teas

There are many kinds of teas, but all derive from the same shrub, *Camellia sinensis*. The main domestic supply is imported from Ceylon, India, Indonesia, and Africa, with small quantities coming from Taiwan,

Japan, and Argentina. About 40 per cent comes from Ceylon. The quality of teas imported into the United States is regulated by standards established annually by tea tasters under the authority granted the Food and Drug Administration by the Tea Import Act of 1897.

Tea consumption in the United States increased during the 1960's from 0.61 pounds to 0.73 pounds per capita, an increase of about 20 per cent. During the decade, the use of tea bags, instant tea, and tea mixes increased, whereas the use of loose tea declined. Tea bags accounted for about one half of the tea consumption in 1969. An estimated two thirds of the tea consumption is in the form of iced tea, for which the instant product is ideal. Instant-tea consumption was close to 40 per cent of the tea consumption in 1969, whereas for coffee the instant has not yet exceeded 20 per cent of the total coffee consumption (4).

Some teas are named for the place of origin, e.g., Darjeeling, Assam, Ceylon, Formosan, and so on. Brands of tea are blends of leaves with different qualities. Teas are typed, according to the method of treating the leaves, as black or green. Almost all tea (96 to 97 per cent) consumed in the United States is black tea. The same kind of leaf is used for producing both types, but not in the same locale. If leaves are fermented and then dried, the tea is black tea; if the leaves are dried without fermentation, the tea is green tea. The steps in the production of black teas include withering, rolling, fermenting, and drying. Withered and rolled leaves may be put through a machine that crushes, cuts, and curls them prior to fermentation and drying. Teas so treated are described as "broken teas." Breaking the tea leaves intensifies the flavor of the brew and makes a stronger and darker brew than leaf grades. Broken teas are preferred in the United States.

Teas are graded according to the size and the wholeness of leaves at the end of processing and not on any inherent palatability qualities. The latter are evaluated in cup tests by tea tasters. To establish tea grades, the finished teas are passed through sieves. Leaf grades are orange pekoe, pekoe, pekoe souchong, and souchong. Broken teas are broken orange pekoe, broken pekoe, orange fannings, and pekoe fannings. Broken orange pekoe is the most expensive tea. Available loose tea is generally a mixture of pekoe and orange pekoe. Teas are perishable; shelf life for loose tea and tea bags is not more than six months.

Tea leaves contain flavor oils, tannins, and caffeine. All are extracted into the beverage during brewing, that is, the infusion of the tea leaves. The amount of tannins extracted into the beverage is regulated by the temperature of brewing and the length of time the leaves are in contact with the water. The addition of milk to tea effects the coagulation of the tannins with the milk proteins and reduces astringency and bitterness. The addition of lemon to tea modifies the tannins and lightens the color of the brew. The flavor and aroma of teas are delicate when compared to those of coffee. Flowers and spices are sometimes added to teas to give them more or a different flavor and aroma. Lapsang souchong is a tea with a special flavor that is highly prized by connoisseurs.

Instant teas are brewed tea that is dehydrated by spray-drying. One pound of instant tea is equivalent to three pounds of loose tea. Some instant products contain additives to protect flavor and aroma. Iced-tea mixtures contain sweeteners, lemon or other flavorings, and additives to stabilize and prserve the products.

Per serving, tea brewed from loose tea costs less than half as much as tea brewed with tea bags. Tea prepared from instant products costs slightly less than tea brewed from tea bags (see Figure 11–1). Iced-tea prepared from a mix containing sugar costs about four times as much as that prepared from instant tea. Instant tea like instant coffee has a short shelf life; it should be stored in a cool place. A ready-to-drink tea beverage has been marketed in the No. 3 Cylinder can and in a six-pack; it is the most expensive of all of the convenience tea products and it is primarily a purchase of water.

FATS AND OILS

Fats are solid at room temperatures; oils are liquid. Fats include butter and margarine (which have already been discussed) and lard and shortenings. All are used in cookery; butter and margarine are table spreads. Butter and olive oil are the most expensive of the fats and oils. The other oils, such as corn oil, cottonseed oil, and peanut oil, are comparable to each other in cost. Lard may be less expensive than the man-made shortenings.

Lard is 100 per cent fat. It is rendered from the fatty tissue of swine. The method of processing determines its texture, color, flavor, and cost. Steam-rendered lard that has been deodorized and decolorized is sold as *bland lard.* It provides an excellent all-purpose shortening for culinary purposes and is especially good for making pastries because of its shortening power. Lard in combination with butter or margarine is excellent for sautéeing and browning food. The best bland lard will cost less than the most expensive shortenings, except when the latter are offered as specials. Per-capita consumption of lard has trended downward since World War II; consumption of manufactured shortenings has trended upward (8).

Shortenings, as the term is generally used, refers to the manufactured fats prepared from vegetable oils, animal fats, or combinations of vegetable oils and animal fats. They are 100 per cent fat. The oils and/or fats from which they are manufactured are hydrogenated to produce plastic fats of the desired degree of hardness; they are decolorized and deodorized. Some shortenings are whipped or aerated to make them creamy and to increase plasticity and whiteness. Mono- and di-glycerides are added to some shortenings to improve baking qualities, especially for cake-making. Most shortenings will have added antioxidants to prolong shelf life. The products are priced higher in one-pound than in three-pound cans. Retailer brands are less expensive than national brands. All-purpose shortenings are priced lower than shortenings created for special purposes. Shortenings are frequent supermarket specials.

Oil consumption has trended upward since 1950 (8). Oils are 100 per cent fat. Oils for food are expressed from corn, cottonseeds, peanuts, soybeans and olives. Oils are fluid at room temperatures, but may solidify at refrigeration temperatures. Salad oils are treated to prevent this solidification or crystallization—a treatment called *winterizing. Virgin* olive oil is the first oil pressed from olives under light pressure. A blend of olive and other oils must bear label statement of the blending of oils. Preference for olive oil for cooking and for French dressing is regional and ethnic in origin. The high temperature at which oils smoke makes them excellent for frying. Further, the fact that an oil is fluid makes it an easy-to-use ingredient in cookery and baking. Oils are packaged in containers that range in size from four ounces to one gallon. The oil is less expensive in the larger containers.

Dressings for foods are foods in which fat is an important constituent. Definitions and standards of identity have been promulgated for mayonnaise, French dressing, and salad dressing.

Mayonnaise contains not less than 65 per cent vegetable oil by weight, egg yolk, and certain acidifying ingredients. It may be seasoned or flavored with one or more of the following: salt, certain sweetening agents, mustard, paprika, and other spices—excepting turmeric and saffron; monosodium glutamate; and other suitable food seasonings or flavorings, so long as they do not impart a yellow color simulating the color of egg yolk. If citric acid is one of the acidifying agents, a statement of its use must appear on the label. Mayonnaise is more expensive than salad dressing. Few homemakers prepare mayonnaise.

French dressing contains acidifying ingredients and not less than 35 per cent vegetable oil by weight. The dressing may be seasoned or flavored with one or more of the following: salt; certain sweeteners; mustard, paprika, and other spices or spice oils or spice extracts; monosodium glutamate; and certain tomato products and sherry wine. Certain emulsifying ingredients are also permitted. Whenever citric acid and an emulsifying agent are ingredients, they must be named on the label. Commercial French dressings are more expensive than home-produced French dressings. Unlike mayonnaise, French dressings are easily made at home. Mixes that provide the proper seasonings and flavorings are available; however, they are expensive.

Salad dressing is another product much less frequently prepared in the home than formerly. Salad dressing must contain not less than 30 per cent oil by weight. In addition, the following may be used: salt; certain sweeteners; spices, except those which would impart a color simulating egg yolk; monosodium glutamate; egg yolk; acidifying ingredients; seasonings; certain emulsifying agents; and a cooked or partly cooked starchy paste. Inclusion of citric acid and emulsifying agents must be mentioned on the label. There has been great increase in the kinds and varieties of salad dressings marketed in recent years. Many are tasty but relatively expensive. Consumers who wish to maximize their dollars should compare them for cost and ingredient composition. Many can be easily, quickly, and inexpensively prepared in the home kitchen.

Low-calorie salad dressings do not conform to the definitions for French dressing or salad dressings. The Food and Drug Administration has ruled that none shall contain more than 15 calories per serving. The actual calorie content of a sampling of the products in the supermarket (Winter, 1971) ranged from three to approximately ten calories per teaspoon of the product for Italian dressing and Thousand Island dressing, respectively. All products bore label statements of their calorie content and the percentages of oil, carbohydrate, and protein. The percentage of oil was from 2.5 per cent in an Italian dressing to 15 per cent in a Thousand Island dressing. The ban of the use of cyclamates has made the use of sugar in salad dressings necessary—the products are more caloric than formerly. It is a good idea to read labels for information.

FRUIT BUTTERS, FRUIT JELLIES, AND FRUIT PRESERVES OR JAMS

Identity standards have been promulgated for fruit butters, fruit jellies, fruit preserves or jams, and artificially sweetened fruit jellies and fruit preserves and jams. Certain stipulations are true for the composition and labeling of all of these products. All may be composed from one fruit or a combination of two, three, four, or five fruits. In any combination of two or more fruit ingredients, the weight of each can be no less than one fifth of the combined weight, except that the weight of pineapple in preserves and jams may be less. A product made from a single fruit is labeled by that name. A product made from two or more fruits can be labeled "Mixed Fruit" or it can be labeled by the names of the fruits in order of predominance by weight, such as "Apple-Strawberry Jelly"; however, in the former instance, the naming of fruits in the listing of ingredients in order of predominance is mandatory. That is, the consumer can know from what fruits the mixed fruit jam or jelly was prepared.

Fruit butters are prepared from fruit purees prepared by the sieving of cooked fruits. The product must be composed from five parts by weight of fruit puree and two parts by weight of sugar or other sweetening agent. Concentration by heat is to no less than 43 per cent soluble solids content. *Fruit jellies* are made from fruit juices. The ratio of fruit juice to sugar or other sweetener is 45 parts to 55 parts by weight. Concentration by heat is to a soluble solids content of not less than 65 per cent. *Fruit jams* and *preserves* are composed from forty-five parts by weight of fruit and fifty-five parts by weight of sugar or other sweetener. Concentration by heat is to a soluble solids content of not less than 65 to 68 per cent, depending on the fruit components. Jams are prepared from crushed fruits; preserves contain whole small fruits or large pieces of large fruits.

The costs of these products differ, jellies being more expensive than the others, and fruit butters being the least expensive. Costs differ according to the fruit ingredient. Raspberry, blackberry, and strawberry products are, in general, more expensive than apple, grape, or plum products. Products made from single fruits are more expensive than those prepared from mixtures of fruits. Again, the size of the container is a factor in the cost.

Summary. A third of the food dollar is spent to purchase a variety of food items. Nearly all of these items can be bought without or with differing degrees of built-in convenience, in packages of assorted sizes, in both retailer and national brands, and in truly great varieties of flavors and kinds. The consumer's buying policy should be to buy and try. Comparison-shopping separates the expensive from the less expensive. Do read labels.

REFERENCES CITED

1. Clark, Faith, "A Scorecard on How We Americans Are Eating," in *Food For Us All—The Yearbook of Agriculture 1969.* Washington, D.C.: United States Department of Agriculture, 1969.
2. "Coffee, Cocoa, and Tea Situation," *National Food Situation,* Economic Research Service, United States Department of Agriculture, Washington, D.C. (February 1971), p. 19.
3. *Food Consumption of Households in the United States, Spring, 1965,* Consumer and Food Economics Research Division, United States Department of Agriculture, Washington, D.C. (1968), p. 203.
4. Gray, Frederick D., "Tea Situation: Trends and Prospects," *National Food Situation,* Economic Research Service, United States Department of Agriculture, Washington, D.C. (November 1970), p. 26.
5. "How Good Is Freeze Dried Coffee," *Consumer Reports* 34:434 (1969).
6. "Instant Coffees," *Consumer Reports* 36:32 (1971).
7. Moses, W. R., and M. F. Tennant, "Beverages: Milk, Coffee, Tea,

Juices, Chocolate," in *Food For Us All—Yearbook of Agriculture, 1969*. Washington, D.C.: United States Department of Agriculture, 1969.

8. "Per Capita Food Consumption," *National Food Situation*, Economic Research Service, United States Department of Agriculture, Washington, D.C. (February 1971), p. 12.

9. "Twenty-Third Annual Consumer Expenditure Study," *Supermarketing* 25:27 (1969).

Chapter 12

Meal Management Goals— Good Nutrition

Four goals for meals, family or personal, have been established. The first goal is good nutrition; other satisfactions that meals are to provide and other goals to be achieved must be added to this one. High regard for scientific facts, although one may not fully understand them; the universal desire for the normal growth of children; and the abundant health that enough of the right food confers are values that underlie this goal. Because these values may be in conflict with others, some persons fail to consume an adequate diet even though the right foods may be abundantly available.

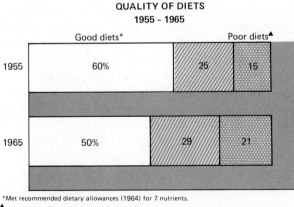

FIGURE 12–1. Quality of diets, 1955–1965. (*United States Department of Agriculture photograph.*)

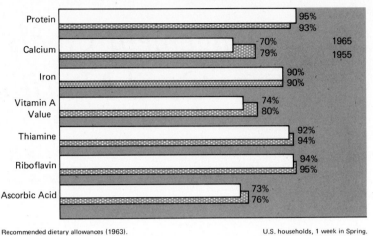

DIETS MEETING ALLOWANCES FOR NUTRIENTS
1955 AND 1965

Recommended dietary allowances (1963).   U.S. households, 1 week in Spring.

FIGURE 12–2.   Diets meeting allowances for nutrients, 1955 and 1965. (*United States Department of Agriculture photograph.*)

The 1960's were a decade of rising incomes and abundant food supplies. During the decade, the percentage of disposable personal income spent for food declined. Surprisingly, the 1965 household food consumption survey of the United States Department of Agriculture revealed that household diets of 1965 were not as good as the diets of 1955 (see Figure 12–1). In 1955, 60 per cent of household diets were considered good versus 50 per cent in 1965. In 1955, 15 per cent of households had diets considered poor versus 21 per cent in 1965. *Good Diets* were defined as those that met the Recommended Dietary Allowances (RDA) of the Food and Nutrition Board–National Research Council for seven nutrients—protein, calcium, iron, vitamin A value, thiamine, riboflavin, and ascorbic acid (vitamin C). *Poor diets* provided less than two thirds of the recommended allowances for one or more of the seven nutrients. In Department of Agriculture surveys, two thirds of the allowance for a nutrient is considered a level below which diets could become nutritionally inadequate in time (2). In both 1955 and 1965, calcium, vitamin A value, and vitamin C were the nutrients most often below allowances; in 1965, the percentages meeting allowances were less than in 1955 (see Figure 12–2).

Although there were good and poor diets at all income levels, there was a correlation between income and diet quality: quality improved as income increased (see Figure 12–3).

In addition to evaluating household diets, the survey evaluated the diets of household members. The latter evaluation is based on records of

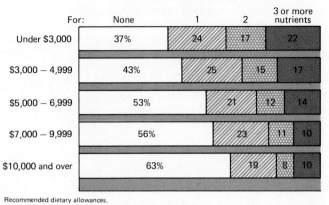

**INCOME
AND DIETS BELOW ALLOWANCES**

For:	None	1	2	3 or more nutrients
Under $3,000	37%	24	17	22
$3,000 – 4,999	43%	25	15	17
$5,000 – 6,999	53%	21	12	14
$7,000 – 9,999	56%	23	11	10
$10,000 and over	63%	19	8	10

Recommended dietary allowances.
Nationwide Household Food Consumption Survey, Spring 1965.

FIGURE 12–3. Income and diets below allowances. (*United States Department of Agriculture photograph.*)

food as eaten; the former, on records of food as brought into the home. From the data on actual food eaten, the nutritive value of the average diet of twenty-two different sex-age groups was calculated. For most of the sex-age groups, diets were almost as good as or better than the RDA for calories, protein, vitamin A value, thiamine, riboflavin, and ascorbic acid. The average calorie input was about as recommended for males but was about 10 per cent below for females. Protein consumption exceeded the RDA for all age groups. Diets were 30 per cent or more below the allowances for calcium and iron for some of the sex-age groups (3) (see Figures 12–4 and 12–5). The diets of males were superior to those of females in both calcium and iron, though the males in some age groups received less than the recommended allowances. The Food and Nutrition Board indicates that the recommended dietary allowances for iron are not expected to be met through ordinary food products by all sex-age groups. Per one thousand calories of food, a normal United States diet provides about 6 milligrams of iron at present levels of iron fortification of bread, flour, and cereals. On that basis and considering calorie allowances, the 1968 recommended dietary allowances for iron cannot be met by normal diets for these sex-age groups: children under three, boys twelve to fourteen, and females under fifty-five. Actually, diets provide from about 5 to 6.6 milligrams of iron per one thousand calories (6). Figure 12–6 discloses that the diets of women of practically all ages need some improvement. The diets of males in some age groups need improvement. It should be recalled that these data are averages of the different sex-age groups; within groups there would be individuals whose diets were less good than the averages.

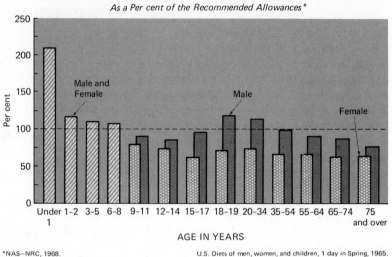

FIGURE 12–4.   Calcium from one day's diet, as a percent of the Recommended Allowances. (*United States Department of Agriculture photograph.*)

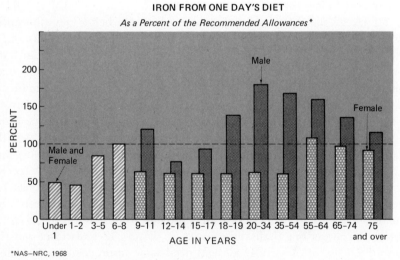

FIGURE 12–5.   Iron from one day's diet, as a percent of the Recommended Allowances. (*United States Department of Agriculture photograph.*)

NUTRIENTS LESS THAN THE RECOMMENDED DIETARY ALLOWANCES[▲]

Sex—Age (years)	Protein	Calcium	Iron	Vitamin A Value	Thiamine	Ribo-flavin	Ascorbic Acid
Male and Female:							
under 1							
1-2			• • • •				
3-5			• • • •				
6-8			• •				
Male:							
9-11		•					
12-14		• •	• • •		•		
15-17		•	•				
18-19							
20-34							
35-54		•					
55-64		• •					
65-74		• •					
75 & over		• • •		•		• •	•
Female:							
9-11		• • •	• • • •		•		
12-14		• • •	• • • •	•	•		
15-17		• • • •	• • • •		• •		
18-19		• • •	• • • •	•	•		
20-34		• • •	• • • •		•	•	
35-54		• • • •	• • • •		•	• •	
55-64		• • • •			•	• •	
65-74		• • • •	•		• •	• •	
75 & over		• • • •	•	• •	• •		• • •

*-1 through 10%	**-11 through 20%	***-21 through 29%	****-30% or more

▲ NAS — NRC, 1968
U.S. Diets of men, women, and children, 1 day in Spring, 1965

FIGURE 12–6. Nutrients less than the Recommended Dietary Allowances. (*United States Department of Agriculture photograph.*)

There were changes in eating habits during the decade that explain some of the loss in nutrient value of the diets of 1965. The consumption of beef, poultry, and peanut butter in the meat group of foods increased. The consumption of eggs, of milk and milk products, of fruits and vegetables, and of breads and cereals declined. The consumption increased of such snack foods as potato chips, crackers, cookies, doughnuts, frozen desserts, candy, ades, punches, and soft drinks (1). See Figures 12–7, 12–8, and 12–9 for consumption changes in the milk, meat, and bread and cereal groups of foods. Paralleling changes in the kinds of food eaten were changes in the patterning of meals. More meals were eaten away from home, more snacks were eaten, and more meals were missed. The content of meals broke with tradition, and sandwiches, hotdogs, hamburgers, pizza, potato chips, soup, soft drinks, and pastries and confections became fare for any time of the day or night. Although all of this is true, it is not true for all. There remain many families who eat three meals daily and many homemakers who try to serve meals that meet nutrient needs.

To be able to plan nutritionally good meals does not require depth of knowledge about nutrition, nor does it require that people eat food they do not like because it may be good for them. Yet all persons can make

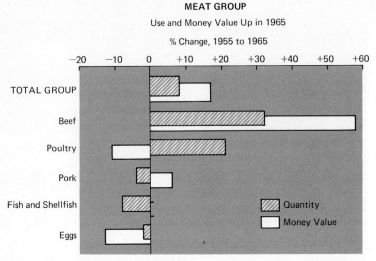

FIGURE 12–7.   Meat group. Use and money value up in 1965. (*United States Department of Agriculture photograph.*)

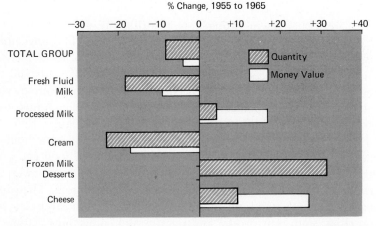

FIGURE 12–8.   Milk group. Use and money value down in 1965. (*United States Department of Agriculture photograph.*)

better decisions about the food they eat and the meals they plan when they know some facts about food and nutrition. It is these facts that provide the bench mark for making decisions. An elementary presentation of these facts follows.

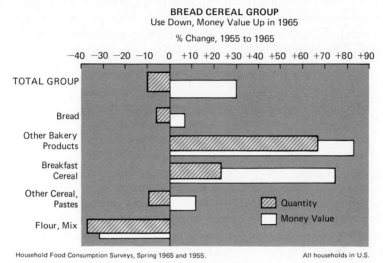

FIGURE 12–9.   Bread cereal group. Use down, money value up in 1965. (*United States Department of Agriculture photograph.*)

NUTRIENT NEEDS

Nutrients include oxidizable substances; amino acids, that is, proteins; one or two fat acids; various mineral elements; assorted vitamins; and water. These different nutrients have different functions: the oxidizable substances are sources of energy; other nutrients are the structural materials from which the various tissues are fabricated and maintained; some nutrients function directly or indirectly in the biochemical reactions the sum total of which is life.

With the exception of energy, the living body has but limited capacity for the storage of nutrients. Hence, there is a daily need for most nutrients throughout the life span. All persons need the same nutrients, but not in the same quantities. Growing children and pregnant women need more of some nutrients than normal adults; large persons need more of some nutrients than small persons; active persons need more of some nutrients than inactive persons; persons suffering from some chronic diseases may require more of some nutrients than healthy persons; and persons recovering from such stresses as disease and surgery require more of some nutrients than normal, healthy persons. Individual differences in the efficiency of utilization of nutrients explain further differences in individual nutrient needs.

It is not necessary that a person know his individual nutrient needs nor the exact distribution of nutrients in all foods to select a good diet. All essential nutrients are provided by a diet composed of meats and legumes, milk and dairy products, eggs, fruits and vegetables, and cereals and products made from them when eaten in sufficient quantities. This means that the meal manager can think of nutrient needs in terms of pork chops, milk, cheese, potatoes, green beans, bread, margarine, and so on in Western countries; or in terms of rice, fish, bean curd, vegetables, and fruit in Oriental countries.

Before discussing the planning of nutritionally good meals per se it is desirable to discuss some of the specific nutrients, their respective functions in nutrition, and standards for assessing the nutritive quality of diets.

Calories

Calorie is the word used to express the energy value of foods. Energy is made available as foods are burned or oxidized in the body. Energy makes possible the work or activity in which an individual engages; at the same time it supports such vital activities as respiration and the work of the heart; and it maintains a degree of tone in all muscles. The energy spent to support vital activities is known as the basal metabolism and is for each person a relatively constant daily requirement. The calories spent in work or activity may vary somewhat from day to day. Heat is a byproduct of energy transformations in the body. Some of this heat is used to maintain the constant temperature of the body, but much of it is lost to the environment.

Three nutrients are oxidizable: carbohydrates, fats, and proteins. Carbohydrates and proteins are equivalent in calorie value—that is, they both yield four calories per gram; fats are richer, yielding nine calories per gram. Foods differ in calorie value because they differ in content of these three nutrients and water. Water has no calorie value; therefore foods that contain much water, such as lettuce, spinach, tomatoes, and many other vegetables, are low in calories. Foods of the same water content vary in calorie value according to their fat content: those containing much fat are richer in calories than those containing little fat. Foods of high fat and carbohydrate content, like cakes and pastries, are rich in calories.

Individuals differ in their calorie needs according to their age, their size, and the amount of activity in which they engage. Large, nonobese adults need more calories than small adults of the same age and activity level; older adults need fewer calories than young adults; and physically active individuals need more calories than sedentary individuals. By adjusting food intake to maintain desirable weight levels, adults satisfy their respective calorie needs.

Children require sufficient calories to permit them to grow normally and develop to the limits of their inherited potential for growth.

Calories are one of the nutrients the living body is able to store. Regardless of the nature of the food eaten, excess calories are converted by the

TABLE 12–1. *Desirable Weights*[1]
Weight in Pounds According to Frame (in Indoor Clothing)

Men of ages 25 and over

HEIGHT (with Shoes on) 1-Inch Heels Feet Inches		SMALL FRAME	MEDIUM FRAME	LARGE FRAME
5	2	112–120	118–129	126–141
5	3	115–123	121–133	129–144
5	4	118–126	124–136	132–148
5	5	121–129	127–139	135–152
5	6	124–133	130–143	138–156
5	7	128–137	134–147	142–161
5	8	132–141	138–152	147–166
5	9	136–145	142–156	151–170
5	10	140–150	146–160	155–174
5	11	144–154	150–165	159–179
6	0	148–158	154–170	164–184
6	1	152–162	158–175	168–189
6	2	156–167	162–180	173–194
6	3	160–171	167–185	178–199
6	4	164–175	172–190	182–204

Women of ages 25 and over

HEIGHT (with Shoes on) 2-Inch Heels Feet Inches		SMALL FRAME	MEDIUM FRAME	LARGE FRAME
4	10	92– 98	96–107	104–119
4	11	94–101	98–110	106–122
5	0	96–104	101–113	109–125
5	1	99–107	104–116	112–128
5	2	102–110	107–119	115–131
5	3	105–113	110–122	118–134
5	4	108–116	113–126	121–138
5	5	111–119	116–130	125–142
5	6	114–123	120–135	129–146
5	7	118–127	124–139	133–150
5	8	122–131	128–143	137–154
5	9	126–135	132–147	141–158
5	10	130–140	136–151	145–163
5	11	134–144	140–155	149–168
6	0	138–148	144–159	153–173

Courtesy of the Metropolitan Life Insurance Company.
[1]For girls between 18 and 25, subtract 1 pound for each year under 25.

body to fat and stored. The storage of fat leads to increases in body weight. Hence, one can control body weight by limiting the intake of calories to the output. One can lose weight by eating fewer calories than the body needs, thereby forcing the body to burn stored fat for calories. Adults should attain desirable weight by age twenty-five and maintain it thereafter. *Desirable weight* is the right weight for body build; it is the weight at which the body is neither too fat nor too lean, but right in relation to height, bone structure, and muscle development (see Table 12–1).

It is desirable that the calories of the diet be selected from a wide variety of foods so that all essential nutrients are provided. An appropriate selection of foods includes fruits, vegetables, meats, eggs, dairy products, and cereal products. Excessive consumption of cookies, rich pastries, candies, carbonated beverages, popcorn, and similar foods that are predominantly composed of carbohydrates should be avoided if the customary allowance of calories is to carry with it the other nutrients needed for adequate nutrition.

In general, the nutritive value of diets diminishes as the calorie content decreases. Diets of low calorie content must be carefully selected if they are to provide all the essential nutrients.

Proteins

The proteins in foods provide the amino acids listed among essential nutrients. More than twenty different amino acids have been found in food and tissue proteins. Proteins differ in their specific amino acid composition and in the quantities of the different amino acids present. Most protein-containing foods contain several different proteins. Only plants and some microorganisms can synthesize amino acids from the elements of which they are composed: carbon, hydrogen, oxygen, and nitrogen. Man and animals must ingest amino acids by consuming foods containing proteins. During digestion the proteins are decomposed to amino acids; these are absorbed, then recombined within various tissues to produce the proteins unique to different tissues.

Man must derive eight amino acids preformed; these are the dietary-essential amino acids. The other essential amino acids can be fabricated from absorbed amino acids and other compounds that arise as substances are metabolized (utilized) within tissue cells. These are the dietary-dispensable amino acids. During growth, additional amino acids may be dietary essential because they cannot be produced in sufficient quantities to meet the demands of growth.

Amino acids are utilized in the building and rebuilding of body tissues and for the production of numerous biological substances, including some hormones, digestive enzymes, mucous secretions, and so on.

Proteins are essential in the diet of persons of all ages. They are especially important during periods when new tissues are being formed: growth, pregnancy, wound healing, and recovery from illness and hunger. The human organism cannot store amino acids; all those essential for protein fabrication must be present simultaneously. Amino acids not used as such are stripped of nitrogen; the nitrogen is excreted; and the residue of the molecule is oxidized or converted to fat and stored as potential energy. The human organism does not store much protein either. The inability to store amino acids and protein explains the daily dietary need for protein.

Because food proteins differ in composition, some are of better nutritional value than others. Proteins that supply the assortment of amino acids that approximates amino acid needs are said to be of high nutritional value. The proteins of meats, milk, eggs, young leaves, some tubers, and the soybean are of excellent to good nutritional value. Food proteins that provide an assortment of amino acids lacking in one or more amino acids are considered of less nutritive value. Cereal proteins tend to be deficient in the amino acid lysine, whereas pulses, or legumes, are deficient in a different amino acid though they may be relatively rich in lysine. The combinations of food that have evolved, such as milk with cereals, bits of meat or fish with cereals, vegetable combinations with cereals, and legumes with cereals have all effected mixtures of proteins of better nutritive value than those of some of the individual foods of the mixtures. Diets composed of a variety of foods like those eaten in the industrially developed countries provide abundantly for human amino acid needs. Diets that include only one or more foods containing protein, like those eaten in some of the developing countries, often do not meet the human need for amino acids.

Foods differ in the amounts of protein they contain. Meats, cheeses, legumes, and peanuts contain the most, about 25 per cent. Cereals, the staples of world diets, contain from 8 to 10 per cent. Fruits and vegetables contain only 1 to 4 per cent. All foods except fats, sugars, syrups, and starches contain some protein. The amount of protein per serving of food varies. Meats including fish and poultry provide about twenty grams per average portion. Cottage cheese has about fifteen grams if creamed; about nineteen grams if not creamed. Fruits and vegetables, on the other hand, with few exceptions, supply no more than a gram or two of protein per serving. Breads and cereals provide two to four grams per serving; an egg, an ounce of cheese, a glass of milk, an ounce of nuts or peanut butter will supply six to eight grams of protein. Table 12–2 presents average protein values of commonly consumed foods. This table provides a valuable tool for planning and evaluating meals with reference to protein content.

The protein requirements of individuals differ according to age, size, and condition. Normal adults need 0.9 grams of protein per kilo (2.2 pounds) of desirable body weight per day. Weight in excess of desirable

TABLE 12–2.   *Values for a Quick Method of Estimating Protein Content of Meals*

Foods	Standard Portion	Grams of Protein
Meat, fish, poultry (lean, some fat)	3 oz. cooked (4 oz. raw)	21
Peanuts, shelled	3 oz.	21
Cottage cheese, creamed	½ cup (¼ lb.)	15
Baked beans	1 cup cooked	15
Milk	1 8-oz. glass	8
Cheddar cheese	1 oz.	7
Egg	1	6
Frankfurter (10 per lb.)	1	6
Luncheon meats	1 oz.	4
New peas and lima beans	½ cup (2½ oz.)	4
Peanut butter	1 tbsp. (½ oz.)	4
Milk puddings	½ cup	4
Cake	1/12 9-in. cake	4
Cooked wheat or oat cereal	1 oz. uncooked	3
Ice cream	⅙ qt.	3
Bacon	2 strips	3
Cooked rice or corn cereal	1 oz. uncooked	2
Ready-to-eat cereals	1 oz.	2
Bread, biscuit, roll	1 (1 oz.)	2
Vegetables (not legumes)	½ cup (2½ oz.)	1
Fruits	½ cup or medium in size	1
Cookies	1 (2-in.)	1
Crackers	4 (2-in.)	1

weight is body fat; protein is not required for its maintenance and repair. For this reason, protein allowances are based on desirable weights. For women this allowance is increased by ten grams daily during pregnancy and by twenty grams daily during the period of lactation.

Allowances for protein during growth begin with 3.2 grams per kilo of weight during infancy and diminish to 1.2 grams per kilo of weight during adolescence. Allowances per unit of weight decrease as the rate of growth decreases. However, total protein allowances increase throughout the period of growth, then level off to adult allowances based on desirable adult weight. The model to be discussed later in this chapter is designed to assure the meeting of protein needs in meal planning.

In the economy of the body, energy needs take priority over the need for protein. For this reason, unless an individual has a reserve of calories in the form of body fat, the protein of food eaten is burned for energy. Enough food to provide the required calories must be available to non-obese persons if protein is to be spared for tissue maintenance and growth.

Experimental evidence indicates that distributing protein foods among the three meals of the day favors effective utilization of the protein in foods. Breakfast is a better meal when it includes milk, an egg, peanut butter, or meat along with toast and jam.

Minerals

Some mineral elements are essential in human nutrition; however, all but four are needed in such minute amounts that it is customary to consider that all are adequately supplied if these four are—iron, iodine, calcium, and phosphorus.

Iron.   The iron present in the living body is found in numerous compounds in all tissues, but it is found mainly in the hemoglobin of red blood cells, where it functions in the transport of oxygen from the lungs to the tissues and in the transport of carbon dioxide from the tissues to the lungs.

Iron is unlike all other nutrients in that it is excreted from the body only in exceedingly minute amounts; little is lost except as blood is lost. For this reason adult males can be maintained for long periods of time on diets that contain only small amounts of iron.

The need for iron in the diet is great during growth because blood volume increases with increases in body size. The female from menarche to menopause needs dietary iron to replace that lost during menstruation and to supply the iron requirement of pregnancy. The recommended allowance of eighteen milligrams of iron per day for girls and women is almost impossible of achievement through diet, iron supplementation of diet being indicated. The proposed iron fortification of some staple foods and the enrichment of flour, bread, and some cereals at higher than current levels would favor improved iron nutrition of girls and women and also of young children and boys aged thirteen to sixteen. Food chemists of the Agricultural Research Service of the United States Department of Agriculture were testing (1970) a process for the fortification of whole milk at the level of ten milligrams per quart, a level that would, on the basis of milk consumption, bring diets low in iron up to acceptable levels (7).

Iron is distributed widely in minute amounts in foods. Meats, eggs, vegetables (especially the leafy ones), legumes, and cereal grains are sources of this element. The iron lost from cereals in processing and milling is restored when bread and white flour, cornmeal, breakfast cereals, and rice are enriched. Iron occurs naturally in some drinking waters. Because iron can be stored in the liver, the liver of a well-nourished animal is a rich source of this nutrient. For this reason, it is recommended that liver be eaten weekly by children and pregnant women. The administration of iron in the form of a ferrous salt, which is readily assimilable, is frequently recommended in the treatment of anemia due to iron deficiency.

Iodine.   Iodine is essential for the synthesis of the thyroid hormones. Without this element, the thyroid gland enlarges in an effort to compensate for function failure, and goiter results. The thyroid hormones have important metabolic functions. Hormone deficiency is manifested in children by failure to develop physically and mentally, and in adults by a low basal metabolism and other physical and physiological changes.

Because a little iodine is lost from the body each day, there is a continuous dietary need for iodine throughout life. The normal need for iodine is increased during adolescence and pregnancy.

Iodine is not present in the soil and water in all parts of the United States, particularly the Great Lakes region and westward. Goiter is endemic in the areas where it is lacking.

The iodine in the diet is obtained from sea foods, foods produced where iodine occurs in the soil, foods produced through use of iodine-enriched rations in animal feeding, and from iodized salt. Iodized salt should be used routinely in the states of the Great Lakes region and westward to the Pacific Coast. Iodine is a constituent of crude, unrefined salt. During the refining of salt, the iodine is lost. Iodized salt is merely salt to which the iodine has been returned. Beginning June, 1973 a Food and Drug Administration regulation will require that the label of table salt carry a statement to the effect that the salt does or does not supply iodine. The nutritional need for iodine is satisfied when iodized salt is used.

Calcium and Phosphorus.   The bones and teeth contain 99 per cent of the calcium and 70 per cent of the phosphorus of the body. These elements make these tissues rigid; hence, they are essential for developing and maintaining them. Phosphorus is an important element in soft tissues, as well as in hard ones.

Milk and foods prepared from milk are the major sources of calcium in diets of persons living in the United States. Some other foods contain small quantities of calcium; a thousand calories of a mixed diet free of milk and milk products provides only about 0.2 gram of calcium. The adult allowance for calcium is 0.8 gram, and the allowances for children and teen-agers range between 0.7 and 1.4 grams. It is difficult to meet the need for this nutrient without consuming some milk or milk products unless calorie allowances are great. Calcium allowances are met by the consumption of milk as follows: children to age nine, two to three eight-ounce glasses; children nine to twelve, three to four eight-ounce glasses; adolescents, one quart; adults, one pint; pregnant women, one quart; and lactating women, one and one half quarts. Although some positive statement about the inclusion of milk and/or alternatives in meals have been made, in all fairness it should be pointed out that the abundant use of nonfat dry milk solids and whey solids in many prefabricated foods means that many foods will carry the nutrients of milk. For example, breads and frankfurters may have 3.5 per cent of nonfat dry milk solids.

Unlike calcium, phosphorus is widely distributed in foods. It occurs in substantial amounts in the protein-rich foods. It is generally agreed that any diet adequate in protein and calcium will be adequate in phosphorus; there is no need to plan specifically for the inclusion of phosphorus in the diet.

Satisfactory utilization of calcium and phosphorus depends on an adequate supply of vitamin D. Lack of vitamin D predisposes the infant to rickets even in the presence of an ample supply of calcium and phosphorus.

Vitamins

Vitamins are organic compounds essential to health and well-being. They function in the many biochemical reactions that take place in the living organism; they are required in only minute quantities.

Man and other animals have limited capacities for the synthesis of vitamins; therefore, they are dependent on plants and microorganisms for these nutrients. Man derives his supply of vitamins largely from plants and other animals.

Although a large number of vitamins are essential in human nutrition, it is necessary to discuss only six, for it is commonly agreed that in a well-constituted diet containing these six, the others are provided.

Vitamins are divided into two groups on the basis of solubility: those that are fat-soluble and those that are water-soluble. The property of water solubility is taken into account in the cooking of some foods.

Vitamin D. Attention was focused on vitamin D in the brief discussion of calcium and phosphorus. Vitamin D is fat-soluble. Although its actual functions are little understood, vitamin D increases utilization and retention of calcium and phosphorus.

Vitamin D is present in small quantities in milk and eggs and in larger quantities in fish oils, especially liver oils. Vitamin D may be administered to infants or children in the form of cod liver or other fish oils. Fluid, nonfat dry, and canned milks are fortified with sufficient vitamin D to meet the need for this vitamin, 400 USP units per quart.

Animals, including man, have the capacity to synthesize an inactive form of this vitamin; such a form is called a *provitamin*. The provitamin of vitamin D is made biologically active by the exposure of some part of the body to ultraviolet light, which converts the inactive form to the true vitamin. Adults and children not given a source of this vitamin derive some vitamin D in this way.

A lack of vitamin D is manifested by rickets in children and a similar condition of poorly calcified bones called *osteomalacia* in adults. Because the role of Vitamin D was recognized as early as World War I, few cases of severe or crippling rickets have been seen in American children in recent years.

Vitamin D consumed in excessive amounts induces a toxic condition characterized by bone dissolution and hypercalcemia. A form of rickets has been observed in children receiving excessive amounts of vitamin D. The fortification of food other than milk and infant formula products with vitamin D is probably not indicated.

Vitamin A. Vitamin A, like vitamin D, is fat-soluble and occurs in inactive forms. The provitamins of vitamin A are synthesized by plants; animals, including man, convert these forms to the active vitamin. The provitamins are yellowish pigments; their presence is evident in yellow fruits and vegetables, such as carrots and peaches. They also occur abundantly in the green parts of plants and in lesser quantities in other fruits and vegetables where their yellowish color is obscured. Foods that contain the provitamin have vitamin A value.

One precise function of this vitamin has been elucidated, that is, as component of the visual pigments of the rods and cones of the retina. These pigments respond to light intensities and trigger the excitations that result in visual sensations. Vitamin A deficiency results in poor vision in dim light, i.e., night blindness. The vitamin has other functions; they have not been specifically defined but are inferred by reference to the deficiency state. Vitamin A is essential for normal growth, normal reproduction, and maintenance of the integrity of various body tissues. The tissues of the eye are especially sensitive to the lack of this vitamin with blindness a common result of the deficiency. Vitamin A deficiency is one of the two most common nutritional deficiency diseases in the world today (5).

Vitamin A consumed in excessive amounts via large doses of the pure vitamin produces a toxic state known as hypervitaminosis A.

Although it is possible for the animal body to store this vitamin in times of plenty against periods of want, it is desirable that the diet include some of the vitamin each day. Green vegetables and yellow fruits and vegetables, milk, cream, butter and fortified margarine, egg yolk, and liver are the best sources of the provitamin of vitamin A and true vitamin A. Margarine, when fortified, has vitamin A added in a quantity approximating the yearly average content of butter. The more intense the color in green and yellow vegetables, the greater is the content of provitamin A and its vitamin A value. Spinach, broccoli, and sweet potatoes are richer sources than are head lettuce, cabbage, and rutabagas. The quantity of this vitamin in one serving of a dark green or deep yellow vegetable or fruit, in the other fruits and vegetables eaten, and in the milk, eggs, and butter or margarine of the diet will meet normal needs for the vitamin.

Provitamin A and true vitamin A are relatively stable in foods that are properly refrigerated. Because they are fat-soluble rather than water-soluble, they are not lost when cooking waters are discarded.

Vitamin C—Ascorbic Acid.   Vitamin C was first known as the anti-scurvy vitamin because of the discovery, about two hundred years ago, that an unknown substance in lemons and other fresh fruits and vegetables prevented scurvy. Sailors and all who went on long sea voyages were susceptible to this disease, which often resulted in death.

The function of the vitamin has been identified: it is essential at a specific point in the formulation of collagen, a protein abundantly present in many tissues. The lack of the vitamin is manifested in a group of physical changes caused by the failure to maintain normal collagen. Scurvy is rarely seen today; however, it sometimes occurs in infants, small children, and elderly persons as a result of consuming restricted diets.

Vitamin C is water-soluble and readily oxidizable; it is subject to losses in the processes to which food is subjected in marketing and processing. Except for tomatoes, citrus juices, and other acid fruits, foods lose some of their vitamin C during storage, cooking, and canning. Losses are extensive during extended periods of cold storage and during long periods of cooking or of holding food at high temperatures in the presence of oxygen. The discarding of cooking waters results in the loss of any of the vitamin that has been dissolved in it.

This vitamin can be conserved in foods if they are protected from air and kept chilled, cooked in the shortest possible time, and not cut up into numerous small pieces from which the vitamin can be lost through solution or oxidation. Vegetables and fruits are the dietary sources of this vitamin for persons living in the United States. All are not equally good sources. The good sources include oranges and orange juice, grapefruit and grapefruit juice, some synthetic citrus drinks, cantaloupe, fresh strawberries, broccoli, and brussels sprouts. Fair sources include tangerines, lemons, fresh and cooked greens, cabbage, cauliflower, tomatoes, and potatoes. The daily allowance for vitamin C will be met if meals include one serving of a good source plus some of the fair sources.

Thiamine.   Thiamine is a water-soluble vitamin and one of the three factors in the B-complex, which will be discussed here. Thiamine like the other B-vitamins is a component in one or more of the enzymes essential in oxidizing food. Lack of this vitamin first affects certain nerves; subsequently both voluntary and involuntary muscles are affected. Beriberi, a disease prevalent where white rice is the staple of the diet, can be prevented by the administration of thiamine.

Thiamine occurs in minute amounts in a wide variety of foods. Seeds, including cereal grains, legumes, and nuts, are fair sources of this vitamin. In the refining of cereal grains, as when rice and wheat are milled, this nutrient and others are lost. To replace these losses, white flour, white bread, cornmeal, breakfast cereals, and white rice are often enriched with thiamine and other nutrients. Pork and the livers of all animals are relatively rich sources of thiamine.

Because of its role in oxidizing food, thiamine allowances are related to energy requirements. Except when calorie intake is restricted in order to lose weight, a varied diet—including whole grain or enriched cereals and bread—will satisfy the thiamine requirements. It may be necessary to supplement the diet with this vitamin when calorie intake is restricted.

Because thiamine is water-soluble, it is lost from foods when cooking waters are discarded. It is also lost when foods are subjected to high temperatures and cooked for extensive periods of time.

Riboflavin. Riboflavin, a second factor of the B-complex, is a component in several enzymes essential in biochemical reactions. A lack of riboflavin affects several tissues: the skin, the tongue, the mucous membranes of the mouth, and nerves.

Riboflavin is widely distributed in foods: milk is rich in it, and meat and eggs are relatively good sources. Any diet providing sufficient milk and protein will provide ample riboflavin. Enriched bread, white flour, cornmeal, breakfast cereals, and rice are enriched with this vitamin. Riboflavin is relatively stable to cooking procedures.

Niacin. Niacin is the third factor of the B-complex to be discussed. It is one of the vitamins that can be synthesized in the human body if a sufficient supply of the raw material from which it is constructed is available. A specific amino acid, *tryptophan*, is one essential. About sixty milligrams of tryptophan are equivalent to one milligram of niacin. The nutritive need for niacin is supplied both by the vitamin itself and by proteins that provide tryptophan. Meat, milk, eggs, legumes, and nuts are suppliers of tryptophan. The diets of people in the United States contain much meat; hence, they are good in protein and in niacin-equivalent value.

Lack of this vitamin results in the disease called *pellagra*; it is endemic in some countries where corn is the staple of the diet. It was prevalent for a number of years in the southern states of the United States. The disease is characterized by skin lesions, lesions of the mouth and the digestive tract, and certain nervous symptoms.

Niacin is widely distributed in foods, but occurs only in minute amounts, except in meats and fish. Meats, milk, and eggs are good sources of tryptophan; they are indirect sources of the vitamin. Diets that supply the normal need for calcium, protein, and other nutrients meet dietary needs for niacin. Enriched bread, flour, breakfast cereals, cornmeal, pasta, and rice are enriched with niacin.

DIETARY STANDARDS

Until 1972, two sets of dietary standards were in use: the *Minimum Daily Requirements of Specific Nutrients* (MDR) established by the Food and Drug Administration in 1941; and the *Recommended Dietary Allowances* (RDA) of the Food and Nutrition Board, National Academy of Sciences—National Research Council. The Minimum Daily Requirements were established for purposes of administering the Food, Drug, and Cosmetic Act of 1938. The MDR provided a standard for the labeling of dietary supplements, foods for special dietary uses, and enriched and fortified foods. The amounts of certain vitamins and minerals present in those products had to be expressed on labels as percentages of the minimum daily requirements that would be supplied by a specified quantity of the product consumed during the period of one day. However, human nutrient requirements are individual and unknown. Hence, as early as 1966, the Food and Drug Administration proposed that the Recommended Dietary Allowances replace the Minimum Daily Requirements in use; however, not until 1972 did the Recommended Dietary Allowances replace them in use.

The seventh revision (1968) of the *Recommended Dietary Allowances* as abridged is presented in Table 12–3. Allowances for calories and nine nutrients are given in quantitative units for twenty-six population groups according to age, sex, and condition. The allowances are established on the basis of research studies and represent the consensus of those qualified to make judgments. The allowances are designed for the maintenance of good nutrition for practically all healthy persons in the United States; they are intended to cover individual variations among most normal persons. Allowance levels are greater than minimum requirements except for calories. With the exception of iron, they can be attained with a variety of common foods. They provide a tool for estimating the nutrient adequacy of the diets of population groups when diets are evaluated by dietary surveys. Further, the RDA provide a frame of reference for estimating the food needs of population groups and for designing models for planning meals and for food plans. Finally, as a result of the discon-

TABLE 12–3. *Recommended Daily Dietary Allowances[a]—Seventh Revised Edition, 1968, Abridged.[1] (Designed for the Maintenance of good nutrition of practically all healthy people in the USA)*

	Age[b] (Years) From up to	Weight (Lbs.)	Height (In.)	Calories	Protein	Vitamin A Activity (IU)	Vitamin D (IU)	Ascorbic Acid (mg.)	Niacin (mg. equiv.)[c]	Riboflavin (mg.)	Thiamine (mg.)	Calcium (g.)	Iron (mg.)
Infants	0–1/6	9	22	kg. × 120	kg. × 2.2[d]	1,500	400	35	5	0.4	0.2	0.4	6
	1/6–1/2	15	25	kg. × 110	kg. × 2.0[d]	1,500	400	35	7	0.5	0.4	0.5	10
	1/2–1	20	28	kg. × 100	kg. × 1.8[d]	1,500	400	35	8	0.6	0.5	0.6	15
Children	1–2	26	32	1,100	25	2,000	400	40	8	0.6	0.6	0.7	15
	2–3	31	36	1,250	25	2,000	400	40	8	0.7	0.6	0.8	15
	3–4	35	39	1,400	30	2,500	400	40	9	0.8	0.7	0.8	10
	4–6	42	43	1,600	30	2,500	400	40	11	0.9	0.8	0.8	10
	6–8	51	48	2,000	35	3,500	400	40	13	1.1	1.0	0.9	10
	8–10	62	52	2,200	40	3,500	400	40	15	1.2	1.1	1.0	10
Males	10–12	77	55	2,500	45	4,500	400	40	17	1.3	1.3	1.2	10
	12–14	95	59	2,700	50	5,000	400	45	18	1.4	1.4	1.4	18
	14–18	130	67	3,000	60	5,000	400	55	20	1.5	1.5	1.4	18
	18–22	147	69	2,800	60	5,000	400	60	18	1.6	1.4	0.8	10
	22–35	154	69	2,800	65	5,000	—	60	18	1.7	1.4	0.8	10
	35–55	154	68	2,600	65	5,000	—	60	17	1.7	1.3	0.8	10
	55–75+	154	67	2,400	65	5,000	—	60	14	1.7	1.2	0.8	10

Females												
10–12	77	56	2,250	50	4,500	400	40	15	1.3	1.1	1.2	18
12–14	97	61	2,300	50	5,000	400	45	15	1.4	1.2	1.3	18
14–16	114	62	2,400	55	5,000	400	50	16	1.4	1.2	1.3	18
16–18	119	63	2,300	55	5,000	400	50	15	1.5	1.2	1.3	18
18–22	128	64	2,000	55	5,000	400	55	13	1.5	1.0	0.8	18
22–35	128	64	2,000	55	5,000	—	55	13	1.5	1.0	0.8	18
35–55	128	63	1,850	55	5,000	—	55	13	1.5	1.0	0.8	18
55–75+	128	62	1,700	55	5,000	400	55	13	1.5	1.0	0.8	10
Pregnancy			+200	65	6,000	400	60	15	1.8	+0.1	+0.4	18
Lactation			+1,000	75	8,000	400	60	20	2.0	+0.5	+0.5	18

[1]Abridged from *Recommended Dietary Allowances*, Seventh Revised Edition. Publication 1694, Food and Nutrition Board, National Research Council, National Academy of Sciences, Washington, D.C., 1968.

[a]The allowance levels are intended to cover individual variations among most normal persons as they live in the United States under usual environmental stresses. The recommended allowances can be attained with a variety of common foods, providing other nutrients for which human requirements have been less well defined.

[b]Entries on lines for age range 22–35 years represent the reference man and woman at age 22. All other entries represent allowances for the midpoint of the specified age range.

[c]Niacin equivalents include dietary sources of the vitamin itself plus 1 mg. equivalent for each 60 mg. of dietary tryptophan.

[d]Assumed protein equivalent to human milk. For proteins not 100 per cent utilized, factors should be increased proportionately.

343

Table 12–4. *A Model for Use in Planning Meals*

Food Groups	Foods Included	Suggested Servings per Day
Meat group	All kinds of meat, poultry, and fish; meat analogs; eggs; cheeses; peanut butter; all kinds of dry beans and peas; nuts	Two or more
Milk group	Whole milk, low-fat milk, skim milk, buttermilk, canned milk products, dried milk products, cheeses, ice cream, ice milk, all foods prepared using milk as an ingredient	Children to age 9, 2 to 3 cups; children 9 to 12, 3 to 4 cups; adolescents, 1 quart; adults, 1 pint
Fruit and vegetable group	Fruits and vegetables including potatoes and sweet potatoes	Four or more servings with one good source of vitamin C. Every other day one dark green or deep yellow vegetable
Bread and cereal group	Breads, rolls, pastries, cookies, breakfast cereals, rice, macaroni, spaghetti, noodles, crackers	Four or more servings
Fats and sweets group	Sugars, syrups, ice cream toppings, jams, jellies, confections, butter and margarine, lard and shortenings, salad dressings	None required, but add to make foods pleasing and meals acceptable as calories permit

tinuance in the use of the Minimum Daily Requirements, the Recommended Dietary Allowances became the standard for the labeling of dietary supplements, foods for special dietary uses, and enriched and fortified foods. Because allowances for nutrients are greater than were the minimum daily requirements, the percentages of nutrients provided by a specified quantity of a food, such as bread, become lower. For example, eight ounces of an enriched bread that would provide 55 per cent of the minimum adult male requirement for thiamine would provide only about 45 per cent of the recommended dietary allowance for thiamine. It is not likely that percentage changes will confuse consumers unduly because the percentages per se have not been significant to consumers.

Some summary statements about nutrients and food that may be useful in planning meals follow.

1.   In general, nutrient needs can be met through food.

2.   No one food contains all the nutrients; but all foods, except some that are highly refined, contain several nutrients: oxidizable substances; proteins, that is, amino acids; one or more vitamins; and one or more mineral nutrients.

3.   Some foods are especially rich in one or more nutrients: milk in protein, calcium, riboflavin, and vitamin A value; meats in protein and the B-vitamins; citrus fruits in vitamin C; leafy vegetables in vitamin A value; and so on.

4.   Some foods are miserly in their nutrient content; for example, sugars and some fats provide only calories. Cereals and some roots and tubers contain only small quantities of protein, minerals, and vitamins; they must be eaten in prodigious quantities to supply nutrient allowances.

5.   To meet the nutrient allowances for vitamins A and C, it is necessary to introduce specific foods into meals: fresh fruits and vegetables for vitamin C; deep yellow and dark green vegetables, milk fat, enriched margarine, and eggs for vitamin A value and true vitamin A.

6.   For Americans in the United States, milk and/or foods prepared from milk are essential to meet the nutrient allowance for calcium.

7.   If attention is directed to the inclusion of foods for protein, calcium, and vitamins A and C, the remaining nutrient needs will be provided except for iron. However, when calories are restricted, this does not always hold true.

8.   Protein can be satisfactorily supplied by mixtures of legumes or cereals combined with small quantities of milk, meats, fish, and eggs.

PLANNING FOR GOOD NUTRITION

To bridge the gap between quantitative expressions of nutrient allowances and meals planned to meet them, patterns or models for use in planning meals have been designed. Although they have been given different names, such as "Food for Fitness," "Basic Seven," "Basic Four," and "Guide to Good Eating," all used in the United States have been essentially the same. Foods commonly eaten in the United States are classified into five classes or groups: meat group, milk group, fruit and vegetable group, bread and cereal group, and the fats and sweets group. Patterns recommend numbers of servings in each group and provide information about how to select within groups. Table 12–4 is a model for planning nutritionally adequate meals. It is not the only model that would provide good nutrition; some persons in the United States and many peoples of the world eat quite different combinations of foods yet derive nutritionally good diets.

TABLE 12–5.   *The Nutrient Content of Foods Selected According to a Model for Use in Planning Meals*[1]

Group	Selected Items	Quantities	Calories	Protein (gms.)	Calcium (mg.)	Iron (mg.)	Vitamin A (IU)	Thiamine (mg.)	Riboflavin (mg.)	Niacin (mg.)	Vitamin C (mg.)
Meat	Beef, cooked	3 oz.	245	23	10	2.9	30	0.04	0.18	3.50	—
	Egg	1	80	6	27	1.1	590	0.05	0.15	—	—
Milk	Milk, skim[2]	1	180	18	592	0.2	1,000	0.18	0.88	0.40	—
Fruit	Orange juice	4 oz.	60	1	12	0.1	275	0.11	0.01	0.50	60
Vegetable	Carrots	½ cup	23	1	24	0.5	7,610	0.04	0.04	0.35	5
	Potatoes	1 small	80	2	7	0.6	—	0.11	0.04	1.40	20
	Pear	1 medium	100	1	13	0.5	30	0.04	0.07	0.20	7
Bread	Bread[3]	3 slices	210	6	63	1.8	—	0.18	0.15	1.80	—
Cereal	Corn flakes[3]	1 oz.	100	2	4	0.4	—	0.11	0.02	0.50	—
	Totals		1,078	60	752	8.1	9,535	0.86	1.54	8.65	92
	Allowances:[4] women[5]		2,000	55	800	18.0	5,000	1.00	1.50	13.00	55

[1]Values from *Nutritive Value of Foods*, Home and Garden Bulletin No. 72, Revised August, 1970, Consumer and Food Economics Research Division, Agricultural Research Service, United States Department of Agriculture (4).
[2]Fortified.
[3]Enriched.
[4]*Recommended Daily Dietary Allowances*, Revised 1968 (Abridged).
[5]Age 18–35 years; weight 128 pounds; "light" physical activity.

Although the model presented is self-explanatory, each group will be briefly described and discussed. The *meat group* includes all kinds of meat, fish, and poultry; simulated meats; eggs; all legumes including beans, peas, lentils, chick peas, peanuts, and special foods made from the soybean; nuts, though these are of little importance in the United States; cheeses, especially cottage cheese; and milk. Peanut butter is an important food in the group because of its wide acceptance and consumption in large quantities by children and adolescents. One ounce (two tablespoons) of peanut butter contains as much protein as one ounce of cooked lean meat. Cottage cheese has become an important food in this group because of its low calorie content. The one-half cup portion of creamed cottage cheese has about 75 per cent as much protein as a portion of lean meat.

The important nutritional contribution of this group to the diet is protein. However, the foods of this group supply calories, minerals, and vitamins as well. In general, diets abundant in proteins derived from a mixture of foods are abundant in other nutrients.

The plan specifies that two or more servings of foods in this group be included in meals each day. Two foods selected from the group will not be equal in protein content—that is, one egg is one third as rich in protein as a serving of meat. However, one average serving of meat plus one other selection, such as one egg or one ounce of cheese, will suffice to meet the recommended allowances for all or nearly all persons, so long as all the other foods required by the model are eaten. That means that the proper quantities of milk must be ingested. As noted earlier, our diets are rich in protein but frequently poor in calcium.

Sandwiches made with one ounce of meat, fish, or poultry, or with one egg, one ounce of cheese, or one ounce of peanut butter will contain about eleven grams of protein; each would be an alternative for half a serving of meat. One-half cup of cottage cheese equals three fourths of a serving of meat. One cup of baked beans, served with one frankfurter, is equal to a portion of meat. Two ounces of spaghetti plus two ounces of meat will also provide the protein equivalent of a portion of meat. Mixed dishes are only as rich in protein as they are rich in foods containing protein. The favorites, such as tuna and noodles, macaroni and cheese, and spaghetti with meat sauce, will provide per serving from about 66 to 100 per cent as much protein as a serving of meat—twenty-one grams. Homemakers who are attempting to control spending for food, to cope with limited food likes, and to plan reducing diets will find it advantageous to estimate the quantity of protein in the meals they plan.

The *milk group* includes milk and foods made from milk (except butter). Foods made from milk include those the homemaker buys, such as cheeses and ice cream, and those she makes, such as creamed dishes, milk puddings and pie fillings, and custards. This group's unique nutrient contributions to the diet are calcium and riboflavin. Food consumption habits in the United States are such that it is difficult to meet the nutrient needs for calcium without the use of milk in one form or another. However, this group also adds protein, calories, vitamin A value if whole milk or fortified milk has been used, and other minerals and vitamins. Skimmed milk has about one half the calorie value of whole milk, but unless fortified has no vitamin A value. The specified minimum quantities of milk to be consumed daily are adults, one pint; children under nine, two to three cups; children nine to twelve, three to four cups; adolescents and pregnant women, one quart; lactating women, one and a half quarts.

Alternatives for milk include ice cream and cheeses, except cottage cheese and cream cheese. These latter cheeses are relatively poor in calcium, because it is lost into whey during the cheese-making process. The calcium content of one eight-ounce glass of milk may vary, but a value of 290 milligrams can be established for purposes of comparison. Here are equivalents for one eight-ounce glass of milk: one and one-third ounces of such cheeses as cheddar, Colby, Swiss, and brick, whether the natural or the process kind; one and two-thirds ounces of cheddar cheese foods and spreads; about three fourths of a pound of cottage cheese; and almost one pint of ice cream or ice milk. Meals selected from a variety of foods, but free of milk or alternatives for milk except as it occurs in bread, provide approximately 200 milligrams of calcium per 1,000 calories. Milk consumption can be adjusted to calorie intake—the more calories of food consumed in a mixed diet, the less milk need be consumed to meet the allowance for calcium. The fewer calories consumed, the more milk must be consumed to meet the allowance for calcium. Because calorie allowances for adults are not large, it is quite probable that most adults need to consume the recommended quantities of milk or alternatives.

The model suggests at least four servings daily from the *fruit* and *vegetable group*. The plan specifies that one serving be a good source of vitamin C, such as orange, grapefruit, fresh strawberries, cantaloupe, broccoli, or brussels sprouts. This serving good in vitamin C plus the three remaining servings of fruits and/or vegetables supply the nutrient need for this vitamin much, if not all, of the time.

A second specific recommendation for selections in this group is that a deep yellow or dark green vegetable be served at least every other day to add vitamin A value to the diet. The older "Basic Seven" pattern suggested a daily serving of a green or yellow fruit or vegetable. This seems a preferable suggestion; it does not necessitate discriminating between deep yellow and yellow, and dark green and green. Neither does it necessitate recalling whether or not one was served yesterday or planning to include these vegetables on alternate days. Vitamin A is a nutrient that is stored in the liver. This store acts as a reserve that can be drawn upon when the diet is not currently meeting needs for the vitamin.

Including four servings of fruits and/or vegetables in the three meals of the day, or even two meals of the day, is not difficult. Some families will eat twice this number; others, less. The present trend away from eating cakes, pies, and puddings makes fruits an obvious choice for dessert. Fruits satisfy the desire for something sweet but are low in calories.

A serving of vegetables is approximately two and one-half ounces of drained, cooked vegetable. Salads vary considerably in weight, but those served with the main course will contain between two and three ounces of salad ingredients. Salad dressings add to this weight. Fruit portions tend to be larger, weighing four or more ounces, depending on the quantity of waste and the amount of juice in canned and frozen fruits.

Vegetables and fruits are included in the model because they introduce minerals and vitamins into the diet. A few vegetables, like potatoes and corn, have relatively high calorie value, but some vegetables and fruits are very low in calorie value; hence, in relation to calorie content, they are rich in nutrients. Furthermore, fruits and vegetables are valuable in meal planning because they introduce color, texture, and interesting flavors; these attributes make meals pleasing.

The *bread* and *cereal group* includes breakfast cereals, breads and baked goods, rice, noodles, macaroni, spaghetti, and all the other foods that derive from cereal grains. Cereals and flours tend to be highly milled; to restore nutrient losses that occur as a result of milling they are enriched or fortified. Whole-grain or enriched cereals and further-processed cereal foods contribute calories, calcium, iron, thiamine, riboflavin, and niacin; when eaten in sufficient quantity, they become significant sources of protein. The adolescent who eats a bowl of cereal and two pieces of toast for breakfast, two sandwiches at lunch, and three rolls at dinner derives almost as much protein from them as from one portion of meat.

A portion of bread is one slice, one roll, one muffin, one biscuit, one doughnut, or one pancake. A cereal portion usually weighs one ounce as it comes from a box, but cooked cereals weigh more as served because of the water absorbed during cooking. Noodle, spaghetti, macaroni, and rice portions often weigh more than one ounce, depending on their use. The model suggests four or more servings daily of the whole-grain or enriched kinds. Children, adolescents, and men often want much more than this; women, less.

The *fats* and *sweets group* includes sugar, syrups, ice cream toppings, jams and jellies, and confections; and butter, margarine, shortenings, and salad dressings. This group of foods is not essential to the nutritionally adequate diet, but fats and sugars make foods and meals more pleasing. These foods add calorie value to meals; they are important when meals must be high in calories. Margarine and butter add vitamin A value to the diet.

TABLE 12-6. *The Total Nutrient Content of Foods Selected According to a Model for Planning Meals Plus Foods Added in Meal Planning*[1]

Selected Foods	Quantities	Calories	Protein (gms.)	Calcium (mgs.)	Iron (mgs.)	Vitamin A (IU)	Thiamine (mgs.)	Riboflavin (mgs.)	Niacin (mgs.)	Vitamin C (mgs.)
Table fat	1 oz.	200	—	6	—	940	—	—	—	—
Gravy[2]	4 tbsp.	32	—	—	—	—	—	—	—	—
Cream of mushroom soup[3]	1 cup	135	2	41	0.5	70	0.02	0.12	0.70	—
Lettuce	2 oz.	10	—	34	0.7	950	0.03	0.04	0.20	9
Tomato	½ of 3 in. tomato	20	1	12	0.4	820	0.05	0.03	0.60	21
French dressing	½ oz.	65	—	—	—	—	—	—	—	—
Apple pie	1/7 of 9 in. pie	360	3	11	0.4	40	0.03	0.03	0.50	1
Ice milk	½ cup	100	3	102	—	140	0.04	0.14	0.50	—
Totals		922	9	206	2.0	2,920	0.17	0.36	2.50	31
Totals of "model"[4]		1,078	60	752	8.1	9,535	0.86	1.54	8.65	92
Grand total		2,000[5]	69	958	10.1	12,455	1.03	1.90	11.15	123
Allowances		2,000	55	800	18	5,000	1.00	1.50	13.00	55

[1]Values from *Nutritive Value of Foods*, Home and Garden Bulletin No. 72, Revised August, 1970 (4).
[2]Made with 1 tbsp. fat and 1 tbsp. flour per cup liquid.
[3]Diluted with water.
[4]See Table 12-5.
[5]Approximate only; the calorie content of dishes varies because composition varies from time to time, e.g., pot roast and gravy, apple pie.

The manner in which foods are combined into meals is personal. Though it is desirable to introduce one or more foods containing protein into each meal, foods can be combined in any way that persons find pleasing. Some like sandwiches for breakfast and bacon and eggs for the evening meal; others want bacon and eggs for breakfast and sandwiches at noon. Perhaps our diets would improve if those who plan meals forgot traditional meal patterns. More persons might eat a good breakfast if it were other than cereal and/or toast. A grilled-cheese sandwich, pie à la mode, Sloppy Joes, hamburgers, a bowl of bean soup, or even pizza might be more enticing as the first meal of the day. And a peasant meal of porridge and bread might be a soothing meal at the end of a difficult and stressful day. The availability of ready-to-eat and of heat-and-eat foods makes it easy for the meal manager to experiment and to offer different combinations within the meals of the day and on the different days of the week.

The nutrient content of an assortment of foods selected as the model prescribes is presented in Table 12–5. For comparisons, the recommended dietary allowances for women aged eighteen to thirty-five, weighing 128 pounds, and of "light" activity are given. It will be noted that the nutrient content is high, whereas calorie content is low. Selections made according to the model provide for all nutrient needs except calories, iron, and niacin. Actually niacin is amply provided because it will be further provided by tryptophan derived from the food proteins of meat, milk, and egg. When meals are planned around this core of foods, other foods must be added to bring the calorie level up to the standard, to make foods more pleasing, and to make meals acceptable. Suggested menus are these.

Breakfast		*Lunch*
Orange Juice		Cream of Mushroom Soup
Corn Flakes	Milk	Egg Sandwich
Toast		Milk
Milk		Pear

Dinner
Pot Roast of Beef with Gravy
Potatoes   Carrots
Tomato and Lettuce Salad with French Dressing
Apple Pie à la Mode
Coffee

Table 12–6 shows the total nutrient content of these meals—the foods selected according to the model plus the foods added in planning meals. It will be noted that iron remains the only nutrient below the recommended allowances. As noted earlier, it is not expected that the allowances for iron will be met for women from eighteen to thirty-five when calories allowances are this ungenerous.

Summary.   The first goal of meal management is good nutrition. In the decade between 1955 and 1965, when incomes were rising, the food supply was generous, and, presumably, we were an informed nation about nutrition, the diets of households declined in nutritive value from 60 per cent good in 1955 to 50 per cent good in 1965. There were good and poor diets at all levels of income, indicating that a given level of income per se does not assure good nutrition. Individual diets were generally satisfactory in most nutrients; however, iron and calcium were more than 30 per cent below the recommended allowances for females of all ages and iron below the recommended allowances for young children. During the 1960's the consumption of meat, snack foods, and beverages increased; the consumption of milk and milk products and of fruits and vegetables declined. These changes in consumption patterns are reflected in the changed nutrient value of diets. To improve our meals nutritionally, it is quite possible that more education is required; it is also probable that we must care more about good nutrition, both collectively and individually.

REFERENCES CITED

1. "Changing Food Consumption in the United States," *Family Economics Review*, Consumer and Food Economics Research Division, United States Department of Agriculture, Washington, D.C. (September 1967).

2. *Dietary Levels of Households in the United States, Spring, 1965*, Agricultural Research Service, United States Department of Agriculture, Washington, D.C. (1968).

3. *Food Intake and Nutritive Value of Diets of Men, Women, and Children in the United States Spring, 1965*, A Preliminary Report, ARS 16–18, Agricultural Research Service, United States Department of Agriculture, Washington, D.C. (1969).

4. *Nutritive Value of Foods*, Home and Garden Bulletin No. 72, Consumer and Food Economics Division, Agricultural Research Service, United States Department of Agriculture, Washington, D.C. (1970).

5. *Present Knowledge of Nutrition*, Third Edition, The Nutrition Foundation, New York (1967), p. 53.

6. *Recommended Dietary Allowances, Seventh Edition 1968*, A Report of the Food and Nutrition Board, National Research Council, Publication 1694, National Academy of Sciences, Washington, D.C. (1968), p. 58.

7. *Toward the New*, Agricultural Information Bulletin No. 341, Agriculture Research Service, United States Department of Agriculture, Washington, D.C. (1970), p. 6.

Chapter 13

Meal Management Goals—
Planned Spending

Americans spent 16 per cent of disposable personal income for food in 1971 in contrast to 20 per cent in 1960. This percentage has been declining with minor fluctuations since 1947, when it was 25.7 per cent. Figure 13–1 shows change as it occurred in the 1960's. The percentage of personal disposable income spent for food at home was 16.2 per cent in 1960, 13.2 in 1970, and 12.7 in 1971. In 1970, consumers in the United States spent about $94 billion for food eaten at home or carried out of the home (7).

During the decade of the 1960's, per-capita spending for food increased

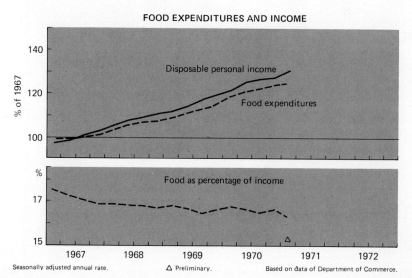

FOOD EXPENDITURES AND INCOME

FIGURE 13–1. Food expenditures and income. (*United States Department of Agriculture photograph*)

353

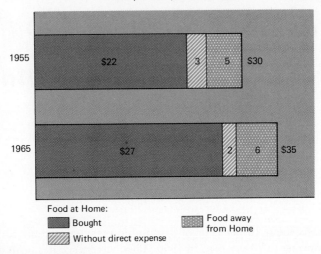

FIGURE 13–2. Food of U.S. families. Value per week, 1955 and 1965. (*United States Department of Agriculture photograph.*)

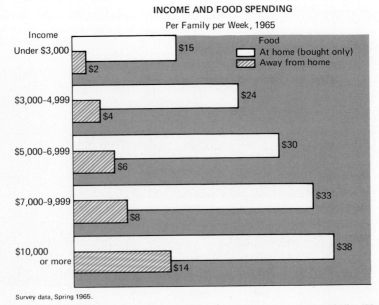

FIGURE 13–3. Income and food spending per family per week, 1965. (*United States Department of Agriculture photograph.*)

as the food price index for food at home rose from 100.6 in 1960 to 127.7 in 1970; and for food away from home, from 105.5 to 155.4. Figure 13–2 shows the values of one week's food in 1955 and 1965 as they were established by household food consumption surveys of the United States Department of Agriculture. The value increase of $5, or 16 per cent, in 1965 occurred during a period when the index rose from 94.4 to 107.2 for food at home and from 91.8 to 117.8 for food away from home. The average percentage expenditure for food eaten away from home scarcely changed from 1955 to 1965.

Figure 13–3 shows that food spending per family increased with income. The percentages spent for food away from home increased with income from about 12 per cent at the lowest income level to about 27 per cent at the upper income level. These data seem to provide indirect evidence that spending for food is planned—i.e., matched to the money resource—and that most meals are eaten at home or carried out of the home; that is, the proportion spent for food at home far exceeds that spent for food away from home.

Figure 13–4 shows that there were some changes in food consumption during the decade 1955–1965. There was consumption of more meat and bakery products and consumption of less foods in other food groups. Figure 13–5 shows consumption changes and money-value changes in the meat group. A precise look at changes in consumption practices during the 1960's is summarized in Table 13–1.

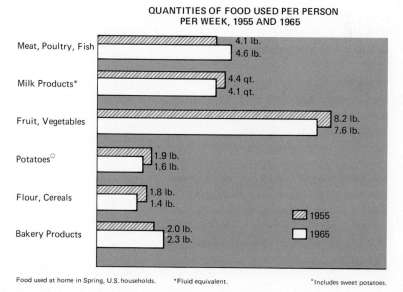

FIGURE 13–4. Quantities of food used per person per week, 1955 and 1965. (*United States Department of Agriculture photograph.*)

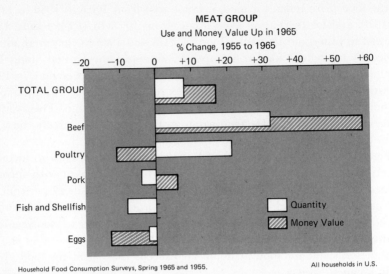

FIGURE 13–5.   Meat group. Use and money value up in 1965. (*United States Department of Agriculture photograph.*)

TABLE 13–1.   *Per Capita Civilian Consumption of Major Food Commodities[1] (Primary Distribution Weights)*

	Pounds	
	1957–1959 Average	*1970*
Meat (carcass weight)	156.6	185.5
Beef (carcass weight)	82.1	113.4
Poultry (ready-to-cook weight)	33.5	50.5
Eggs (number)	356.0	315.0
Cheese	7.9	11.4
Fluid milk and cream	337.0	261.0
Fats and oils	45.3	53.1
Butter	8.2	5.2
Margarine	8.9	11.0
Fruits, fresh	95.5	79.4
Fruits, processed	47.8	51.1
Vegetables, fresh	104.1	98.7
Vegetables, processed	49.9	58.8
Potatoes and sweet potatoes	115.2	123.7
Wheat flour and cereals	122.8	113.9
Sugar	96.1	102.2

[1]Adapted from Table 5, "Civilian per Capita Consumption of Major Food Commodities," *National Food Situation*, February, 1971, p. 12.

Table 13–1 and Figures 13–4 and 13–5 tells us these things: we like meats; we are partial to convenience foods; as we eat more of what we like, we may eat less of such foods as milk, fruits, and vegetables, to the detriment of our diet. Figures 12–1 and 12–2, presented in the previous chapter, called attention to a loss in the nutritive quality of household diets in the decade 1955 to 1965, and to the correlation of diet quality with income, though there will always be both good and poor diets at all levels of income.

It becomes clear that the goal of planned spending for food (i.e., budgeting for food), will not be easily attained. The goal of good nutrition, the character of food preferences, and available income do not all work together; there must be accommodation. In this chapter, we assume that the goal of good nutrition is a constant. We will explore ways of achieving it at different levels of spending for food. Admittedly, there may have to be some compromise in food preferences. The following will be considered: factors that affect the food needs of families thus affecting the budget for food; factors that influence how families purchase food needs; food plans; establishing a food budget; and living on a food budget.

FACTORS THAT AFFECT THE FOOD NEEDS OF FAMILIES

Many families are concerned about how much they spend for food. Some wish to know if they are overspending; others wish to know if they are underspending—questions that imply the existence of a norm. Actually there is a norm; however, it is not one of dollars but one of nutrient or food needs. The composition of the family and the general health of family members establish precise food needs. The food needs come first: foods are bought as circumstances dictate and as personal preferences prescribe. They can be purchased within wide extremes in cost.

In the preceding chapter, we saw that individuals differed in their nutrient allowances as they differed in age, sex, size, and activity. Further, women have increased nutrient allowances when pregnant and lactating. It costs more to feed some persons than others because their nutrient needs —that is, their food needs—are greater. For example, it costs more to feed a man than a woman of the same age unless the woman is pregnant or lactating, when it costs more to feed her than him; it costs more to feed boys than girls after they reach the age of twelve; and it costs more to feed a six-year-old than a three-year-old. Family food needs are the composite of the food needs of family members. Families similarly composed have the same food needs, although they might make different expenditures for food. Dissimilar families have different total food needs. Quantitative differences in the food needs of families result in different required expenditures for food (see Figure 13–6). Obviously, family size is a factor in es-

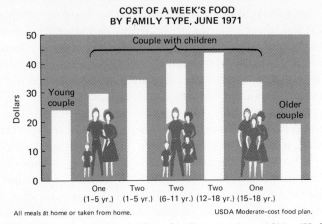

FIGURE 13–6.   Cost of a week's food by family type, June 1971. (*United States Department of Agriculture photograph.*)

tablishing food needs; it will be a factor in establishing the food budget. In general, larger families spend more for food than smaller families, but the per-capita expenditure is smaller. For farm families, it was $320, $244, and $200 per person per year for families of two, four, and six persons, respectively, according to a study made in 1961; the total expenditure of the six-member farm family was $1,203 in contrast to $640 by the two-member family (4).

Qualitative differences in food needs also affect spending for food. Families in which one or more persons are allergic to common foods, are diabetic, or have other dietary problems require larger expenditures for food than similar families without dietary problems. Allergies to such common foods as milk, wheat, corn, or eggs necessitate the purchase of especially processed foods that are expensive to buy. Special foods for diabetics and even some weight-reduction diets are also expensive to buy. Significant determinants of the budget for food are the quantity and the kinds of food it must buy.

FACTORS THAT INFLUENCE HOW FAMILIES PURCHASE FOOD NEEDS

Theoretically, all similar families, because they have the same food requirements, would spend the same sum for food—that is, they have the same food budget. Actually, this rarely happens. Similar quantities of an assortment of nutrients can be purchased at widely differing costs because the foods purchased to provide these nutrients may be very different. The bag of groceries that one homemaker takes home from the supermarket may hold sirloin steak, fresh broccoli, Belgian endive, a honeydew melon, a frozen ready-to-eat cake, and a dozen oranges; that of another home-maker may hold hamburger, frozen spinach, head lettuce, two pounds of apples, a cake mix, and a can of frozen orange juice concentrate. The nutrient content of the two bags of food would be quite similar, but the cost would be quite different. It is what she chooses to buy to fulfill family food needs that determine how much the meal manager spends. Her deci-sions are influenced by the following: family income; her ability to choose the foods that she can afford to buy; her knowledge of the marketplace; her shopping skills and abilities; the extent of her time resource and her willingness to use time for shopping and meal preparation; family food preferences; the region of residence in the United States; and, finally, family goals and values.

Income is a powerful factor in determining how much can be spent for food. Although there are exceptions, it is generally true that as incomes increase, families spend more total dollars for food and more per capita. The average value of food purchased per person per week according to the household food consumption survey of 1965 was as follows (6).

Income	*Food at Home*	*Food Away from Home*
Less than $3,000	$5.87	$ .70
$3,000–$4,999	7.05	1.17
$5,000–$6,999	8.30	1.67
$7,000–$9,999	9.29	2.31
$10,000 and over	10.57	3.89

As income rises families use more milk and milk products; more meat fish, and poultry; more bakery goods; more fruits and vegetables; and more soups and mixtures of all kinds; they use less flour and cereal, eggs, and sugar and sweets (5). Further, as noted in Chapter 2, the higher-income shopper buys above the average such items as frozen entrees, frozen fruits and vegetables, frozen cakes and pastries, the less common fruits and vegetables, specialty cheeses, and so on. Income permits us to carry home the bag of groceries containing sirloin steak, fresh peas and strawberries out of season locally, a premium-priced loaf of bread, and a frozen pre-pared cheese cake. Income also suggests that the bag of groceries contain hamburger, canned or frozen peas, canned peaches, a store-brand loaf of bread, and that dessert be a simple one made at home. High-income fam-ilies, those with $10,000 or more, do not all spend alike for food, however; some spend more conservatively than others. According to the 1965 survey, about 40 per cent of the high-income families used food valued below the cost of the liberal plan; about 20 per cent, below the moderate-cost plan (8). Food plans will be discussed subsequently.

Because the marketplace offers a vast assortment of foods with and without built-in service, the nutritionally good diet can be purchased within extremes in cost. A very important skill of the meal manager is that of being able to choose the foods that match her money resource for food. The section on food plans that follows—pages 362 through 394—explores and discusses decision-making in relation to planned spending for food.

Knowledge of the marketplace and shopping skills and abilities are prerequisites to decision-making in accordance with a spending plan, that is, controlling the expenditure for food. The intent of Chapters 5 through 11 was to provide knowledge that would lead to the development of skills and abilities useful in the marketplace. Although twentieth-century agriculture and technology have made shopping for food a delight, they have also made it complex. No longer is the purchase of even such staples as bread and milk easy. Both are available in such variety and at such varying costs that they cannot be purchased without some positive thinking. One needs to know how the available products are alike; how they are different; when the purchase price buys food and when it pays for the costs of a brand name and the costs of built-in service; and much more. According to the 1965 survey, low-income households received a greater nutritional return for their food dollars than higher-income households. The reason for this was that some of the less expensive foods that they used in larger quantities, such as nonfat dry milk and cereals, have a high nutrient content in relation to cost (2).

There are time and energy costs in meal management. The less time the meal manager has to give or is willing to give to shopping and meal preparation, the more dollars she must spend for foods with built-in service. During the decade of 1960–1970, the number of wives in the labor force increased from three to four in ten; half of the married mothers of schoolage children worked in 1970. The fact of the housewife's employment outside the home supports the demand for and the ability to pay for convenience foods. According to the 1965 household food consumption survey, spending for convenience foods was 33 per cent greater per household in 1965 than in 1955. These data were derived from an analysis of spending for thirty-two items. The list of items included many mixes, canned and frozen fruit and vegetable products, bakery products, ready-to-eat cereals, instant coffee, processed potato products, puddings and pie fillings, icings, and canned soups and soup mixes. It also included such items as hamburgers, frankfurters, luncheon meats, frozen desserts, and potato chips—items that we have ceased to think of as convenience foods. The average expenditure for convenience foods was about 30 per cent of the total sum spent for food used at home in 1965 versus 27 per cent in 1955. Obviously, convenience foods are here to stay. However, meal managers can pick and

choose among convenience foods. The cost of the convenience in ready-
fried chicken is probably no less than 50 per cent of its total cost in contrast to 30 per cent for plain cake mix. The decision of the meal manager
to purchase the ready-fried chicken may be conditioned by the time and
energy costs of meal preparation.

Family food likes and dislikes affect food spending. If family members
insist on eating bacon-and-egg breakfasts, will eat only steaks and chops
for dinner, prefer only fresh fruits and vegetables and will never eat cereal
breakfasts, macaroni and cheese, chop suey, or meat loaf for dinner, or
canned and frozen fruits and vegetables, then food preferences influence
very significantly the expenditure for food.

In the United States, place of residence is a factor in establishing the
size of the grocery bill (see Figure 13–7). According to the food consumption survey of 1965, food at home costs most in the Northeast and least in
the South. Further there are differences within regions. In its budgets, the
Bureau of Labor Statistics gives estimates for food for cities within a region and in metropolitan areas and they are not the same. For example, in
the 1970 budgets for a four-person family, annual food costs of the intermediate budget were estimated to be $2,513 for St. Louis, Missouri and
$2,222 for Green Bay, Wisconsin in the North Central region. The costs of
the food plans to be discussed subsequently differ from region to region.

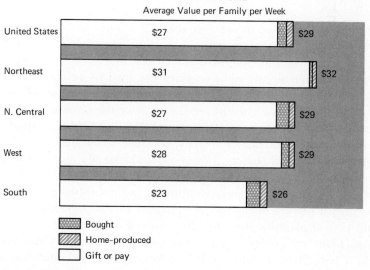

FOOD AT HOME

Average Value per Family per Week

Bought
Home–produced
Gift or pay

Survey data, Spring 1965.

FIGURE 13–7.   Food at home. Average value per family per week. (*United
States Department of Agriculture photograph.*)

Lastly, very similar families may have very different goals for tomorrow and quite different value systems that influence spending patterns. Goals for the ownership of a home, or a new and larger home in a better neighborhood, or a second home in the mountains, or an organ, or any of the vast array of things an affluent society wants may cause some families to spend conservatively for food. Although thrift for the sake of thrift is no longer a value in our culture, limitation of spending for one want in order to satisfy another is practiced. Families that place a high value on education, on such cultural experiences as travel in foreign countries, and on the ownership of original works of art, first editions, or antique cars may spend far less on food than other families with similar resources. On the other hand, families that enjoy good food and wines may, and can easily, spend extravagantly to buy their food wants. The money they spend for food buys them the pleasures and satisfactions that other families derive in other ways.

In summary, family food needs can be purchased within wide extremes in cost because the bags of groceries that supply these needs may contain quite different food items. What the bags contain is unique even for similar families because many forces act and interact to influence the meal manager's choices when she plans her meals and her shopping, and when she is shopping. Different ways of buying food needs may be described as food plans. Food plans have been developed for buying food needs at different levels of spending.

FOOD PLANS

Food plans have been in use since the 1920's. They have been revised as new knowledge of nutrition required their modification; as the food consumption practices of the population changed; and as the economic status of the population improved. The plans are used by teachers, extension workers, social agencies, and others who work with families. The plans presented and discussed herein are the work of the Consumer and Food Economics Research Division, Agricultural Research Service, United States Department of Agriculture. The plans take into account the 1968 revision of the *Recommended Dietary Allowances* and changed food consumption practices as these were revealed in the 1965 household food consumption survey. The costs of the plans are estimated and published quarterly. The plans permit the use of the model presented in the previous chapter for the purpose of planning nutritionally adequate meals.

Food plans are guides to the purchase of food needs. There are five plans: a basic low-cost plan, a second low-cost plan adapted for southeastern food habits, a moderate-cost plan, a liberal-cost plan, and an economy plan. The plans suggest weekly quantities of food to be purchased in

TABLE 13-2. *Basic Low-Cost Family Food Plan*

Weekly Quantities of Food[1] for Each Member of Family

Sex-Age Group	Milk, Cheese, Ice Cream[2] Qt.	Meat, Poultry, Fish[3] Lb. Oz.	Eggs No.	Dry Beans, Peas, Nuts Lb. Oz.	Flour, Cereals, Baked Goods[4] Lb. Oz.	Citrus Fruit, Tomatoes Lb. Oz.	Dark Green and Deep Yellow Vegetables Lb. Oz.	Potatoes Lb. Oz.	Other Vegetables and Fruits Lb. Oz.	Fats, Oils Lb. Oz.	Sugars, Sweets Lb. Oz.
Children:											
7 months to 1 year	5½	1 0	5	0 0	0 12	1 8	0 2	0 8	1 0	0 1	0 2
1–3 years	5½	1 4	5	0 1	1 4	1 8	0 4	0 12	2 4	0 4	0 4
4–6 years	5½	1 8	5	0 2	2 0	1 12	0 4	1 4	3 4	0 6	0 6
7–9 years	5½	2 0	6	0 4	2 4	2 0	0 8	2 0	4 4	0 8	0 10
10–12 years	6½	2 4	6	0 6	3 0	2 4	0 8	2 8	5 0	0 8	0 12
Girls:											
13–15 years	7	2 8	6	0 4	3 0	2 4	0 12	2 8	5 0	0 10	0 12
16–19 years	7	2 8	6	0 4	2 12	2 4	0 12	2 4	4 12	0 6	0 10
Boys:											
13–15 years	7	2 8	6	0 6	4 4	2 8	0 12	3 4	5 4	0 12	0 12
16–19 years	7	3 4	6	0 8	5 4	2 8	0 12	4 12	5 8	0 14	0 14
Women:											
20–34 years	3½	2 8	5	0 4	2 8	2 0	0 12	2 0	5 0	0 6	0 10
35–54 years	3½	2 8	5	0 4	2 8	2 0	0 12	1 8	4 8	0 4	0 10
55–74 years	3½	2 8	5	0 4	2 4	2 0	0 12	1 4	3 8	0 4	0 6
75 years and over	3½	2 8	5	0 4	2 0	2 0	0 12	1 4	3 0	0 4	0 6
Pregnant	7	2 8	7	0 4	2 8	3 8	1 8	2 0	5 0	0 6	0 8
Nursing	10	3 4	7	0 4	3 0	4 8	1 8	3 4	5 8	0 8	0 10
Men:											
20–34 years	3½	3 12	6	0 6	4 4	2 4	0 12	3 4	5 8	0 12	1 0
35–54 years	3½	3 8	6	0 6	3 12	2 4	0 12	3 0	5 0	0 10	0 12
55–74 years	3½	3 4	6	0 4	3 8	2 4	0 12	2 8	4 12	0 10	0 10
75 years and over	3½	3 4	6	0 4	3 4	2 0	0 12	2 4	4 8	0 8	0 10

Source: *Family Food Budgeting for Good Meals and Good Nutrition,* Home and Garden Bulletin No. 94, Consumer and Food Economics Research Division, Agricultural Research Service, United States Department of Agriculture, Washington, D.C., p. 7.

[1]Food as purchased or brought into the kitchen from garden or farm.
[2]Fluid whole or its calcium equivalent in cheese, evaporated milk, dry milk, ice cream.
[3]Bacon and salt pork should not exceed ⅓ pound for each 5 pounds of meat group.
[4]Weight in terms of flour and cereal. Count 1½ pounds bread as 1 pound flour.

TABLE 13–3. *Second Low-Cost Family Food Plan* [Especially adapted for southeastern food habits]

Sex-Age Group	Milk, Cheese, Ice Cream² Qt.	Meat, Poultry, Fish³ Lb. Oz.	Eggs No.	Dry Beans, Peas, Nuts Lb. Oz.	Flour, Cereals, Baked Goods⁴ Lb. Oz.	Citrus Fruit, Tomatoes Lb. Oz.	Dark Green and Deep Yellow Vegetables Lb. Oz.	Potatoes Lb. Oz.	Other Vegetables and Fruits Lb. Oz.	Fats, Oils Lb. Oz.	Sugars, Sweets Lb. Oz.
							Weekly Quantities of Food¹ for Each Member of Family				
Children:											
7 months to 1 year	5½	0 12	5	0 0	0 12	1 8	0 2	0 8	1 0	0 1	0 1
1–3 years	5½	1 0	5	0 1	1 8	1 8	0 4	0 8	2 0	0 4	0 4
4–6 years	5½	1 4	5	0 2	2 4	1 8	0 4	0 8	3 0	0 8	0 6
7–9 years	5	1 12	6	0 6	2 12	1 12	0 8	1 8	4 0	0 10	0 10
10–12 years	6	2 0	6	0 8	3 8	2 0	0 8	2 0	4 12	0 10	0 12
Girls:											
13–15 years	7	2 0	6	0 6	3 8	2 4	0 12	2 0	4 12	0 12	0 12
16–19 years	7	2 0	6	0 6	3 4	2 4	0 12	1 12	4 8	0 8	0 10
Boys:											
13–15 years	6½	2 0	6	0 8	4 12	2 4	0 12	2 12	5 0	0 14	0 12
16–19 years	6½	2 12	6	0 10	5 12	2 4	0 12	4 4	5 4	1 0	0 14
Women:											
20–34 years	3½	2 0	5	0 6	3 0	1 12	0 12	1 0	4 12	0 8	0 10
35–54 years	3½	2 0	5	0 6	3 0	1 12	0 12	1 0	4 4	0 6	0 10
55–74 years	3½	2 0	5	0 4	2 8	1 12	0 12	1 0	3 0	0 6	0 6
75 years and over	3½	2 0	5	0 4	2 4	1 12	0 12	1 0	2 12	0 6	0 8
Pregnant	7	2 4	7	0 4	3 0	3 4	1 8	1 0	4 12	0 8	0 8
Nursing	10	2 12	7	0 6	3 8	4 8	1 8	2 4	5 4	0 12	0 8
Men:											
20–34 years	3	3 4	6	0 8	4 12	2 0	0 12	2 12	5 4	0 14	1 0
35–54 years	3	3 0	6	0 8	4 4	2 0	0 12	2 8	4 12	0 12	0 12
55–74 years	3	2 12	6	0 6	4 0	2 0	0 12	2 0	4 4	0 12	0 10
75 years and over	3	2 12	6	0 6	3 8	2 0	0 12	2 0	4 0	0 10	0 10

Source: *Family Food Budgeting for Good Meals and Good Nutrition*, Home and Garden Bulletin No. 94, Consumer and Food Economics Research Division, Agricultural Research Service, United States Department of Agriculture, Washington, D.C., p. 8.

¹Food as purchased or brought into the kitchen from garden or farm.
²Fluid whole or its calcium equivalent in cheese, evaporated milk, dry milk, ice cream.
³Bacon and salt pork should not exceed ⅓ pound for each 5 pounds of meat group.
⁴Weight in terms of flour and cereal. Count 1½ pounds bread as 1 pound flour.

TABLE 13–4. *Moderate-Cost Family Food Plan*

					Weekly Quantities of Food[1] for Each Member of Family						
Sex-Age Group	Milk, Cheese, Ice Cream[2] Qt.	Meat, Poultry, Fish[3] Lb. Oz.	Eggs No.	Dry Beans, Peas, Nuts Lb. Oz.	Flour, Cereals, Baked Goods[4] Lb. Oz.	Citrus Fruit, Tomatoes Lb. Oz.	Dark Green and Deep Yellow Vegetables Lb. Oz.	Potatoes Lb. Oz.	Other Vegetables and Fruits Lb. Oz.	Fats, Oils Lb. Oz.	Sugars, Sweets Lb. Oz.
Children:											
7 months to 1 year	6	1 4	6	0 0	0 12	1 8	0 2	0 8	1 8	0 1	0 2
1–3 years	6	1 12	6	0 1	1 0	1 8	0 4	0 12	2 12	0 4	0 4
4–6 years	6	2 4	6	0 1	1 12	2 0	0 4	1 0	4 0	0 6	0 10
7–9 years	6	3 0	7	0 2	2 0	2 4	0 8	1 12	4 12	0 10	0 14
10–12 years	6½	4 0	7	0 4	2 12	2 8	0 12	2 4	5 8	0 10	0 14
Girls:											
13–15 years	7	4 8	7	0 2	2 12	2 8	0 12	2 4	5 12	0 12	0 14
16–19 years	7	4 4	7	0 2	2 8	2 8	0 12	2 0	5 8	0 10	0 12
Boys:											
13–15 years	7	4 12	7	0 4	4 0	2 12	0 12	3 0	6 0	0 14	1 0
16–19 years	7	5 8	7	0 6	5 0	3 0	0 12	4 4	6 4	1 2	1 2
Women:											
20–34 years	3½	4 4	6	0 2	2 4	2 8	0 12	1 8	5 12	0 8	0 14
35–54 years	3½	4 4	6	0 2	2 0	2 8	0 12	1 4	5 4	0 8	0 12
55–74 years	3½	4 4	6	0 2	1 12	2 4	0 12	1 4	4 4	0 6	0 8
75 years and over	3½	3 12	6	0 2	1 12	2 4	0 12	1 0	3 12	0 6	0 8
Pregnant	7	4 4	7	0 2	2 4	3 8	1 8	1 8	5 12	0 8	0 12
Nursing	10	5 0	7	0 2	2 12	5 0	1 8	2 12	6 4	0 12	0 12
Men:											
20–34 years	3½	5 8	7	0 4	4 0	2 12	0 12	3 0	6 8	1 0	1 4
35–54 years	3½	5 4	7	0 4	3 8	2 12	0 12	2 8	5 12	0 14	1 0
55–74 years	3½	5 0	7	0 2	3 4	2 12	0 12	2 4	5 8	0 12	0 14
75 years and over	3½	5 0	7	0 2	2 12	2 8	0 12	2 0	5 4	0 10	0 12

Source: *Family Food Budgeting for Good Meals and Good Nutrition,* Home and Garden Bulletin No. 94, Consumer and Food Economics Research Division, Agricultural Research Service, United States Department of Agriculture, Washington, D.C., p. 9.

[1]Food as purchased or brought into the kitchen from garden or farm.
[2]Fluid whole or its calcium equivalent in cheese, evaporated milk, dry milk, ice cream.
[3]Bacon and salt pork should not exceed ⅓ pound for each 5 pounds of meat group.
[4]Weight in terms of flour and cereal. Count 1½ pounds bread as 1 pound flour.

TABLE 13-5. *Liberal Family Food Plan*

Sex-Age Group	Milk, Cheese, Ice Cream[2] Qt.	Meat, Poultry, Fish[3] Lb. Oz.	Eggs No.	Dry Beans, Peas, Nuts Lb. Oz.	Flour, Cereals, Baked Goods[4] Lb. Oz.	Citrus Fruit, Tomatoes Lb. Oz.	Dark Green and Deep Yellow Vegetables Lb. Oz.	Potatoes Lb. Oz.	Other Vegetables and Fruits Lb. Oz.	Fats, Oils Lb. Oz.	Sugars, Sweets Lb. Oz.
Children:											
7 months to 1 year	6	1 4	7	0 0	0 12	1 12	0 2	0 8	1 8	0 2	0 2
1–3 years	6	2 4	7	0 1	1 0	1 12	0 4	0 12	2 12	0 4	0 4
4–6 years	6	3 0	7	0 1	1 8	2 4	0 8	0 12	4 8	0 8	0 12
7–9 years	6	3 12	7	0 2	1 12	2 12	0 8	1 8	5 4	0 10	1 0
10–12 years	6½	4 12	7	0 4	2 12	3 0	0 12	2 4	6 0	0 10	1 0
Girls:											
13–15 years	7	5 8	7	0 2	2 8	3 0	0 12	2 4	6 0	0 12	1 2
16–19 years	7	5 4	7	0 2	2 4	3 0	0 12	1 12	5 12	0 10	1 0
Boys:											
13–15 years	7	5 8	7	0 4	4 0	3 4	0 12	3 0	6 8	0 14	1 4
16–19 years	7	6 4	7	0 6	5 0	3 8	0 12	4 4	7 4	1 4	1 2
Women:											
20–34 years	4	4 12	6	0 1	2 0	3 0	0 12	1 4	6 4	0 8	1 2
35–54 years	4	4 12	6	0 1	1 12	3 0	0 12	1 0	6 0	0 8	1 0
55–74 years	4	4 12	6	0 1	1 8	3 0	0 12	1 0	4 8	0 6	0 12
75 years and over	4	4 4	6	0 1	1 8	3 0	0 12	0 12	4 0	0 6	0 10
Pregnant	7	4 12	7	0 1	2 0	4 8	1 8	1 4	6 4	0 8	1 0
Nursing	10	5 12	7	0 2	2 12	5 8	1 8	2 8	6 4	0 12	1 2
Men:											
20–34 years	4	6 0	7	0 4	3 12	3 0	0 12	2 12	7 12	1 0	1 8
35–54 years	4	5 8	7	0 4	3 8	3 0	0 12	2 4	6 8	0 14	1 4
55–74 years	4	5 4	7	0 2	3 4	3 0	0 12	2 0	6 0	0 12	1 2
75 years and over	4	5 4	7	0 2	2 12	2 12	0 12	1 12	5 12	0 10	1 0

Weekly Quantities of Food[1] for Each Member of Family

Source: *Family Food Budgeting for Good Meals and Good Nutrition*, Home and Garden Bulletin No. 94, Consumer and Food Economics Research Division, Agricultural Research Service, United States Department of Agriculture, Washington, D.C., p. 10.

[1]Food as purchased or brought into the kitchen from garden or farm.
[2]Fluid whole or its calcium equivalent in cheese, evaporated milk, dry milk, ice cream.
[3]Bacon and salt pork should not exceed ⅓ pound for each 5 pounds of meat group.
[4]Weight in terms of flour and cereal. Count 1½ pounds bread as 1 pound flour.

TABLE 13-6. *Economy Family Food Plan*
[Least expensive of any of the food plans: Designed for temporary use when funds are limited]

Sex-Age Group	Milk, Cheese, Ice Cream² Qt.	Meat, Poultry, Fish³ Lb. Oz.	Eggs No.	Dry Beans, Peas, Nuts Lb. Oz.	Flour, Cereals, Baked Goods⁴ Lb. Oz.	Citrus Fruit, Tomatoes Lb. Oz.	Dark Green and Deep Yellow Vegetables Lb. Oz.	Potatoes Lb. Oz.	Other Vegetables and Fruits Lb. Oz.	Fats, Oils Lb. Oz.	Sugars, Sweets Lb. Oz.
Children:											
7 months to 1 year	5½	0 8	4	0 0	0 12	1 0	0 4	0 8	1 0	0 1	0 1
1–3 years	5	0 12	4	0 1	1 8	1 0	0 4	1 0	2 0	0 4	0 4
4–6 years	5	1 0	4	0 4	2 4	1 4	0 4	1 8	2 0	0 6	0 6
7–9 years	5	1 8	5	0 6	2 8	1 8	0 8	2 4	3 0	0 10	0 10
10–12 years	6	1 12	5	0 8	3 4	1 12	0 8	2 12	3 4	0 10	0 12
Girls:											
13–15 years	6½	2 0	5	0 8	3 4	1 12	0 12	3 0	3 8	0 12	0 10
16–19 years	6½	2 0	5	0 8	3 0	1 12	0 12	2 12	3 4	0 8	0 10
Boys:											
13–15 years	6	2 0	5	0 10	4 8	2 0	0 12	3 4	3 8	0 14	0 12
16–19 years	6	2 8	5	0 12	5 8	2 0	0 12	4 12	3 8	1 0	0 14
Women:											
20–34 years	3	1 4	4	0 4	3 0	1 12	0 12	3 0	3 0	0 8	0 12
35–54 years	3	1 4	4	0 4	3 0	1 12	0 12	2 12	2 12	0 6	0 12
55–74 years	3	1 4	4	0 4	2 8	1 12	0 12	2 8	2 8	0 6	0 6
75 years and over	3	1 4	4	0 4	2 4	1 12	0 12	2 4	2 4	0 6	0 6
Pregnant	7	2 0	7	0 4	2 8	3 0	1 8	2 8	4 0	0 6	0 8
Nursing	10	2 0	6	0 4	3 4	4 0	1 8	3 12	4 8	0 10	0 12
Men:											
20–34 years	3	2 0	5	0 10	4 12	1 12	0 12	4 4	3 8	0 14	1 2
35–54 years	3	2 0	5	0 10	4 4	1 12	0 12	3 8	3 0	0 12	0 14
55–74 years	3	2 0	5	0 6	4 0	1 12	0 12	3 0	2 12	0 12	0 12
75 years and over	3	2 0	5	0 6	3 8	1 12	0 12	2 12	2 8	0 10	0 12

Source: *Family Food Budgeting for Good Meals and Good Nutrition*, Home and Garden Bulletin No. 94, Consumer and Food Economics Research Division, Agricultural Research Service, United States Department of Agriculture, Washington, D.C., p. 6.

¹Food as purchased or brought into the kitchen from garden or farm. ²Fluid whole or its calcium equivalent in cheese, evaporated milk, dry milk, ice cream. ³Bacon and salt pork should not exceed ⅓ pound for each 5 pounds of meat group. ⁴Weight in terms of flour and cereal. Count 1½ pounds bread as 1 pound flour.

eleven food groups for nineteen sex-age groups (see Tables 13–2 through 13–6).

The suggested weekly quantities of food differ from plan to plan as the level of spending changes. The plans provide sufficient food so that all meals can be eaten at home or carried out of the home. The published estimates of the costs of the plans assume that all food is purchased and that purchase prices are similar to average prices paid by urban families.

The plans differ in cost about as follows:

1. The economy plan costs about 20 to 25 per cent less than the basic low-cost plan. It can be one third less.
2. The moderate-cost plan costs about 30 per cent more than the basic low-cost plan.
3. The liberal-cost plan costs about 50 per cent more than the basic low-cost plan and about 20 per cent more than the moderate-cost plan.
4. The second low-cost plan costs only slightly less than the basic low-cost plan.

The costs of the plans change from time to time in response to the economy, in response to changes in the food supply, and, probably, in response to developments in food technology. The costs differ from region to region within the United States and within regions as well. Published estimated costs are United States average costs; except once each year, in March, regional costs are published in *Family Economics Review*. Published estimates are weekly and monthly costs for persons in twenty sex-age groups; for two-member young families; for two-member older families; for four-member families with preschool children; and for four-member families with school-age children (see Figure 13–6). The costs of the plans for families that differ from these in composition are established by the totaling of the costs as estimated for each family member according to sex and age. Because estimated costs assume that all meals are eaten at home or carried out of the home, adjustments can be made for each person eating meals away from home. Five per cent is deducted from the individual's estimated weekly cost for each meal eaten away from home. For example, if a child has five lunches at school, 25 per cent would be deducted from the estimated cost for him. Published costs are for individuals in four-person families. For families different in size, these adjustments are made: for family of one, add 20 per cent; for family of two, add 10 per cent; for family of three, add 5 per cent; for family of five, subtract 5 per cent; for family of six or more, subtract 10 per cent.

The food plans suggest quantities of food to buy in the following eleven food groups: milk and milk products; meat, poultry, and fish; eggs; dry beans, peas, and nuts; flour, cereals, and baked goods; citrus fruit and tomatoes; dark green and deep yellow vegetables; potatoes; other vegetables and fruits; fats and oils; and sugars and sweets. Quantities suggested are of food as brought into the kitchen and include some waste. The quantities of milk and milk products suggested are in terms of milk (calcium) equivalents. Equivalents for one quart of milk are six ounces of such cheeses as cheddar and cheddar types, Swiss cheese, and pasteurized process cheeses; two and a half pounds of creamed cottage cheese; and one and two thirds quarts of ice cream or ice milk. Quanties of flour, cereals, and baked goods are in terms of flour-cereal equivalents; one and a half pounds of baked goods are equivalent to one pound of flour.

Though the market baskets of the plans are similarly composed, they do differ. The quantitative differences are illustrated in Table 13–7, which presents the suggested weekly quantities of food according to all five plans for a family of four composed as follows: parents, twenty to thirty-four years of age; one child, four to six years of age; and one child, ten to twelve years of age. As the cost of the plan diminishes, the suggested quantities of food in each of the following groups decrease: milk, cheese, and ice cream; meat, poultry, and fish; eggs; citrus fruits and tomatoes; other fruits and vegetables; and sugars and sweets. At the same time, the suggested quantities of foods in these groups increase: dry beans, peas, and nuts; flour, cereals, and baked goods; and potatoes. The most striking difference in the plans, or market baskets, is in the suggested quantities for the meat group. Income permitting, families spend about one third of their food dollars for meat. For this reason, a plan that severely restricts meat consumption is neither popular with most families nor of practical use for some families.

In addition to quantitative differences, there are qualitative differences in the market baskets of the food plans. Differences are in the kinds and cuts of meat purchased; in fruit and vegetable choices; in the kinds of and amounts of convenience foods purchased; in the quality of the foods bought; and in the variety of the foods purchased. There is no apparent provision in the food plans for such purchases as of catsup, coffee, or baking supplies. The published costs of the plans do provide for some such purchases. However, published costs do not provide for such nonfood purchases as detergents, cigarettes, paper goods, and so on. Nonfood spending is about 25 per cent of supermarket spending. Nonfood purchases should not be considered part of the food budget.

The cost of the low-cost plan can be calculated and the costs of the other plans derived from it if one does the appropriate percentage calculations. In fact, the costs of any of the plans can be calculated. One can make such a calculation by estimating the costs of the quantities of foods required by the plan selected in accordance with the plan and adding for miscellaneous items and state taxes. Such a calculation appears later in the chapter for the economy plan.

TABLE 13–7.   *Weekly Quantities of and Cost of Food for a Family of Four[1] According to All Plans*

Food Groups	Liberal-Cost Plan	Moderate-Cost Plan	Basic Low-Cost Plan	Second Low-Cost Plan	Economy Plan
			Quantities		
Milk, cheese, ice cream (qt.)	20½	19½	19	18	17
Meat, poultry, fish (lb.)	18½	16	10	8½	6
Eggs (number)	27	26	22	22	18
Dry beans, peas, nuts (lb.)	5/8	11/16	1⅛	1½	1⅝
Flour, cereals, baked goods (lb.)	10	10¾	11¾	13½	13¼
Citrus fruit, tomatoes (lb.)	11¼	9¾	8¼	7¼	6½
Dark green and deep yellow vegetables (lb.)	2¾	2½	2¼	2¼	2¼
Potatoes (lb.)	7	8¼	9	6¼	11½
Other vegetables and fruits (lb.)	24½	21¾	18¾	17¾	11¾
Fats, oils (lb.)	2⅝	2½	2	2½	2⅜
Sugars, sweets (lb.)	4⅜	3⅝	2¾	2¾	3
Cost per week (U.S. average)	$45.70	$37.70	$29.50	$24.60[2]	$23.60[3]

Source: Table developed from Tables 13–2 through 13–6 in this chapter. Costs from *Family Economics Review*, March, 1971. Costs are United States average except as indicated.

[1] Family: parents 20–34 years, child 4–6 years, child 10–12 years.

[2] South only.

[3] Estimated as 20 per cent less than the low-cost plan.

THE BASIC LOW-COST PLAN

The low-cost plan is for conservative spending for food. Its use is not peculiar to, nor specific for, any demographic group. The percentages of urban families surveyed in 1965 that used food valued below the cost of the moderate-cost plan were 59 per cent, 39 per cent, and 21 per cent for families with incomes under $3,000, $5,000 to $6,999, and $10,000 and over, respectively. Though the suggested weekly quantities of food of the low-cost plan can provide for good nutrition, the 1965 survey revealed that only 30 per cent of the families with food valued at the cost of the low-cost plan had good diets and that 60 per cent had diets that were fair or better (8). The meal manager who uses the low-cost plan needs knowledge about the marketplace and what it offers, skill in decision-making in the marketplace, skill in menu planning, skill and ability in the kitchen because she will have to prepare at home much of the food for family meals, and the time and energy to do the planning, shopping, and preparation of meals. Limitation in the use of the money resource inevitably demands greater use of other resources.

To make choices that yield generous returns for dollars, the meal manager must know, first of all, what a dollar can buy—that is, much or little, depending on her decisions. She should be familiar with the information in previous chapters. Second, she ought to know the number of servings obtainable from the different market units that she buys. Some cans and frozen packs give this information on the label, but the homemaker must be able to estimate the number of servings different cuts of meat and different fresh fruits and vegetables yield, because many of her decisions must be made on the basis of cost per portion. For example, spareribs and hamburger may have the same unit cost; but hamburger will yield four portions to the pound, whereas spareribs will yield two portions at most, perhaps only one. If fresh spinach and fresh carrots sell for the same unit cost, the purchase of carrots will yield more food for the same money— carrots yield twice as much servings per pound as spinach. Third, the consumer should know the current costs of the items she purchases: a ten-pound bag of flour, a pound of coffee, a sack of potatoes, and so on. Knowing the costs of what she buys helps her find the bargains, which in turn help stretch her dollars. Fourth, she needs to know when foods are in abundant supply and when they are scarce. When pork, grapefruit, squash, cranberries, apples, or any other food item is in good supply, it is less expensive than at other times and less expensive than some other similar food items. Buying foods that are in good supply generally yields good returns for dollars spent. Fifth, she must read labels. From labels, she discovers how similar or how different products are. For example, two brands of margarine may have identical listings of ingredients and the same vitamin A value; but one may cost 50 per cent more than the other for some obscure reason. From labels, she can also learn of what ingredients products are composed. She can discover that a lemon cream pie contains neither lemon nor cream. Sixth, she must compare prices, i.e., the cost per unit of this and that flour, this and that loaf of bread, this and that brand of nonfat dry milk, this and that kind of breakfast cereal, and so on. Seventh, she should know which convenience foods she can buy and which ones she should not purchase. When much convenience is purchased, spending for food is no longer conservative. In general, buying pan-ready omelet mixes, thaw-and-eat cakes, and ready-prepared puddings is not consistent with a low-cost plan for spending for food. On the other hand, frozen orange juice concentrate and instant coffee are good buys. Eighth, the meal manager is wise to read avidly the food ads of her supermarket, from week to week. With her knowledge of food prices and her familiarity with her own buying practices she can discover specials and bargains that give her good returns for her dollars. Finally, she must know how to spend her food dollar so as to achieve good nutrition. Unfortunately, the low-cost plan does not permit the spending of as much of the food dollar for meats, fish, and poultry as families prefer. The suggested division of the food dollar to buy foods of the low-cost plan is here presented (3).

Milk, cheese, ice cream	18 per cent
Meat, poultry, fish	24 per cent
Flour, cereals, baked goods	16 per cent
Fruits and vegetables	24 per cent
All other groups	18 per cent
Total	100 per cent

The 1965 survey noted that families spending at about the estimated cost of the low-cost plan spent about 33 per cent of the dollar for the meat group. They spent less than the desirable percentages for milk, cheese, and ice cream and for fruits and vegetables; they spent about the same percentages for all other food groups. As would be anticipated, the diets were most often below allowances in calcium, vitamin A value, and vitamin C (3).

Because decisions relating to the purchase of meat are the most critical ones made by the meal manager attempting to feed her family on a conservative budget for food, guides to assist her are proposed. To illustrate, let us assume that a homemaker's budget for food is $27.00 weekly and that her family is composed of four, including herself. The low-cost plan assumes the purchase of meat for one meal daily—it does not allow for the purchase of much more than that unless the skilled shopper can manipulate her dollars to buy more. Therefore, our homemaker must purchase twenty-eight servings of meat, fish, or poultry for $6.75—one fourth of her budget. The average cost of a serving would be $0.24. This sum is her average daily allowance per serving. This does not mean that she buys nothing that costs more per serving, but it does mean that when one choice exceeds the average in cost another must be less than the average in cost. Her guide to choosing cuts of meat, kinds of fish, and poultry is the estimated cost per serving. If, in her best judgment, a roast of beef will serve two portions per pound and if the beef roast costs $0.99 per pound, then one serving costs $0.50. If she chooses the roast, she will have spent the "meat money" for two meals on one meal. On the other hand, if boneless beef stew is priced at $0.99 per pound, it will provide four servings for each pound purchased; one serving costs approximately $0.25. The latter would be a suitable choice; the former quite impractical because the economy of scale operates with roasts as in other situations. Practically, a roast that would serve out two portions to the pound should weigh four or more pounds. The purchase of the four-pound roast would spend over half of the week's meat budget for eight portions, or meat for two days. To compensate, choices for five days of meals would have to be ultraconservatively made and such alternatives for meat as beans (the poor man's meat) and cereal would certainly be indicated. Choice of the above beef roast would not be consistent with the budget. However, chuck roasts of beef are frequent specials; they are not always out of bounds for the low-cost plan. The experienced manager watches for and waits for meat specials that fit her plan for spending.

If a meal manager can balance inexpensive choices against expensive ones, she can select for one day in a week something that costs twice her daily allowance; if she cannot, she fares best if she makes choices that are only one third to two thirds more expensive than her calculated average cost per serving. To be more explicit, some guides to choice-making for meats when the budget is conservative follow.

1. Determine what one fourth of the food budget is in dollars and cents.

2. Calculate the allowable average cost of a serving.

3. Make any choice that costs twice the allowable average only with extreme caution; balance with at least three choices costing less than the average daily allowance.

4. Limit choices that exceed the allowable average cost by two thirds to two weekly and balance with four choices costing less than the allowable average.

5. Limit choices that exceed the allowable average cost by one third to three weekly and balance with at least three choices less than the average in cost.

TABLE 13-8. *Three Plans for Selecting Meat, Poultry, and Fish in Accordance with Guides to Decision-Making When the Basic Low-Cost Plan Is Used*[1,2]

Plan 1			Plan 2			Plan 3		
Choices	Cost per Pound	Cost per Serving	Choices	Cost per Pound	Cost per Serving	Choices	Cost per Pound	Cost per Serving
Pork chops	1.03	.35	Chicken, fryer	.40	.30	Chuck roast, special	.72*	.36
Hamburger	.69	.17	Hamburger	.69	.17	Chuck roast, special	.72*	.36
Haddock fillet	.96	.24	Ocean perch	.71	.18	Lamb patties	.99	.25
Liver, beef	.67	.17	Liver, beef	.69	.17	Tuna (can)	.53	.13
Chicken, fryer	.40	.30	Beef stew	.99	.25	Chicken, fryer	.40	.30
Picnic shoulder	.54	.27	Sirloin steak, special	1.08*	.54	Frankfurters	.80	.16
Picnic shoulder	.54	.27	Frankfurters	.80	.16	Hamburger	.69	.17
Total		$1.77	Total		$1.77			$1.73

[1]Estimated cost of the low-cost plan for a family of four: $29.50 per week. One-fourth of budget for meat is about $7.35. Average daily allowance per serving is about $.26. Cost of seven servings is about $1.80.

[2]All prices, except those marked (*), are United States average prices from *Estimated Retail Food Prices by Cities—February, 1971*, Bureau of Labor Statistics, United States Department of Labor Washington, D.C.

Meat choices for the homemaker with a conservative budget for food are not drastically limited if she becomes skillful in balancing expensive and inexpensive choices and if she shops for specials. To illustrate, Table 13–8 presents three plans for selecting meat. Actual costs vary so much from time to time, region to region, and market to market, however, that these plans cannot be taken as literal selection guides.

Earlier, it was suggested that families spend one fourth of the food budget for fruits and vegetables. The model for nutritive adequacy suggests a minimum of four servings per person per day. For a family of four this would mean 16 servings daily, or 112 weekly. If the homemaker has a weekly budget of $28, she could spend $7—or approximately $1.00 daily for fruits and vegetables. The average cost per serving would be approximately $0.06; the cost for four servings, $0.25. If fresh peas yield two portions to the pound and cost $0.39 per pound, they cost $0.20 per serving. Obviously, fresh peas would not be a practical choice for the budget. However, if frozen peas cost $0.20 for four servings, one serving costs $0.05; frozen peas would be a practical choice for the budget. The cost of a serving is the homemaker's decision-making guide. As with meal selections, more expensive choices are balanced by less expensive ones: broccoli at $0.08 by potatoes at $0.02 and canned peas at $0.07 by carrots at $0.03.

To summarize, some guides to selecting fruits and vegetables in accordance with the low-cost food plan are presented.

1.   Determine what one fourth of the weekly food budget is in dollars and cents.

2.   Calculate the daily allowance for fruits and vegetables.

3.   Calculate the average cost per serving.

4.   Generally, one serving of potatoes and a serving of citrus juice will use about one third of the daily budget for fruits and vegetables.

5.   Select the two remaining fruits and/or vegetables, using the average allowance as a guide and balancing a more expensive choice with a less expensive one.

6.   Be cautious in borrowing from tomorrow's budget for today's fruits and vegetables.

Choices in other food groups would be about as anticipated. In the dairy group choices would be some nonfat dry milk, some dry buttermilk, some canned milk, and fresh fluid milk in the largest container practical; process cheeses; and ice creams and ice milks that are priced low. Margarines that are priced low; butter when specialed; and retailer brands of shortenings, peanut butter, jams and jellies, and coffee products would be choices consistent with the plan. Cereal purchased would be the less expensive kinds packaged in the largest package practical for a given family. Baked goods would be store-brand breads, rolls, doughnuts, and so on. Purchased cookies would be the less expensive kinds. Convenience foods purchased would be limited to some baked goods, cake mixes, simple dessert mixes like gelatine desserts and milk puddings; soups; the least expensive salad dressings; canned precooked and baked beans; and others that the meal manager finds offer good returns for the money invested.

The following general observations can be made about the foods in the low-cost market basket. All would be wholesome. Choices within the meat and fruit and vegetable classes might range from quite inexpensive good buys to moderately priced items. Many items would be of average or better quality, but there would not be many premium-quality foods. Many items would be store brands. There would be relatively few ready-made dishes.

MEAL PLANNING FOR THE BASIC LOW-COST FOOD PLAN

If meals are to be eaten, they must prove satisfying to those for whom they are planned. Translating groceries into meals demands use of the arts of menu planning, as well as knowledge of nutrition. The latter has already been discussed, the former will be discussed in Chapter 14. Good nutrition and satisfying meals are meal management goals regardless of budget. However, the more limited the food budget, the more we rely on the arts of menu planning and good cooking to achieve them. To illustrate, if the homemaker serves a thick steak or rib roast of beef, it will be tender, juicy, and flavorful unless she badly mistreats it during cooking. Furthermore, she can safely serve potatoes and almost any vegetable because attention is focused on the meat—the rest of the meal is subordinate. On the other hand, if the homemaker serves beef liver, she must not only know how to cook it properly but she must also succeed in cooking it so that it will be tender, juicy, and flavorful. Further, it is desirable that she serve with it a vegetable compatible with the flavor of liver—not every vegetable will do. Carrots, onions, and spinach are vegetables that are generally liked; cauliflower, eggplant, and celery are some that are not well liked when served with liver. Furthermore, portions of meat are average or smaller than average portions when the budget is conservative. Hence, the other items of a meal are of greater consequence than when the budget permits serving larger than average portions of meat. The methods of preparing potatoes and vegetables, the salads or relishes, bread, and dessert ought to be selected to complement one another, rather than in willy-nilly fashion.

Cookery tends to be "lean" rather than "rich." Recipes should be selected that require only moderate quantities of fat, sugar, eggs, and so forth. In the interest of economy, nonessential ingredients like chopped almonds, pimientos, green peppers, mushrooms, bamboo shoots, and wine are omitted. Judicious substitutes, such as cocoa for chocolate, evaporated

Menus for One Week of Low-Cost Meals

	Breakfast	Lunch or Supper	Dinner
Saturday	Orange Juice[3] Hot Cereal Milk Raisin Toast Jam Coffee Milk[1]	Egg Sandwiches Carrot and Celery Sticks Lemon Pudding[4] Cookies Milk	Spaghetti with Meat Balls Hard Rolls[6] Carrot and Celery Sticks Oranges Apples Coffee Milk
Sunday	Grapefruit Halves French Toast Syrup Coffee Milk	Grilled Cheese Sandwiches Brownies Bananas Milk	Fried Chicken Mashed Potatoes Peas[3] Hot Biscuits Ice Milk Coffee Milk
Monday	Orange Juice[3] Poached Eggs on Toast Toast Jam Coffee Milk	Soup[5] Peanut Butter Sandwiches Celery Sticks Pickles Plums[2] Milk	Pot Roast of Beef Browned Potatoes Onions Carrots Bread Cake[5] Coffee Milk
Tuesday	Orange Juice[3] Ready-to-Eat Cereal Milk Toast Peanut Butter Coffee Milk	Baked Beans[2] Cole Slaw Bread Brownies Milk	Cold Sliced Beef Hashed Brown Potatoes Green Beans[2] Bread Cake à la Mode Coffee Milk
Wednesday	Orange Juice[3] Hot Cereal Milk Cinnamon Toast Coffee Milk	Creamed Eggs on Toast Celery Sticks Cake Milk	Barbecued Frankfurters Scalloped Potatoes Squash Cabbage Salad Bread Apricots[2] Cookies Coffee Milk
Thursday	Orange Juice[3] Ready-to-Eat Cereal Milk Toast Jam Coffee Milk	Corn Chowder[7] Cheese Sandwiches Cookies[6]	Liver with Bacon Potatoes Spinach[2] Carrot and Celery Sticks Bread Apple Pie Coffee Milk
Friday	Orange Juice[3] Soft-Boiled Eggs Toast Jam Coffee Milk	Spanish Rice[7] Lettuce-Apple Salad Bread Baked Custard Milk	Fried Ocean Perch[2] Baked Potatoes Buttered Beets[2] Hot Rolls[6] Fruit Cup Cookies Coffee Milk

[1]Milk should be served to adults twice daily, to children at all meals. Servings should be reduced in size if a significant quantity of milk has been used in cooking. [2]Canned. [3]Frozen product. [4]Instant. [5]Mix. [6]Ready-to-eat. [7]Home-prepared.

milk for cream, bouillon cubes for bouillon, margarine for butter, tomato juice for tomato soup or tomatoes, can be made. Cooking with canned soup and soup mixes, cream cheese, mayonnaise, potato chips, and other convenience products is not compatible with the budget. However, well-prepared simple dishes are often more delicious than those more expensively and elaborately concocted.

Perhaps it should be reiterated that making right decisions is critical, that wise shopping is imperative, and that meal planning and preparation are more time-consuming when the plan for spending is conservative than when it is more generous. Nevertheless low-cost meals can be pleasing and satisfying; in fact, they may be superior to more expensive meals carelessly planned and prepared. Menus for one week of low-cost meals are presented. The only item that might seem inconsistent with a low-cost plan is the pot roast of beef; it would, of course, have to have been a supermarket special.

A SECOND LOW-COST PLAN

The basic low-cost plan has been adapted to the food habits and preferences of the indigenous population of the southeastern states. Table 13–9 shows the difference in the market baskets of the two plans as these are estimated for the same family of four persons—parents aged twenty to

TABLE 13–9.   *Differences in the Quantities of Food Provided by the Two Low-Cost Plans*

| | Quantities | | |
Food Class	Basic Low-Cost Plan	Low-Cost Plan for Southeastern States	Differences
Milk, cheese, ice cream (qt.)	19	18	1 less
Meat, poultry, fish (lb.)	10	8½	1½ less
Eggs	22	22	0
Beans, peas, nuts (lb.)	1⅛	1½	⅜ more
Flour, cereals, baked goods (lb.)	11¾	13½	1¾ more
Citrus fruit, tomatoes (lb.)	8¼	7¼	1 less
Dark green and deep yellow vegetables (lb.)	2¼	2¼	0
Potatoes (lb.)	9	6¼	2¾ less
Other fruits, vegetables (lb.)	18¾	17¾	1 less
Fats, oils (lb.)	2	2½	½ more
Sugars, sweets (lb.)	2¾	2¾	0

Source: Tables 13–2 and 13–3.

TABLE 13–10.   *Weekly Quantities of Food for the Same Family According to the Moderate-Cost and Basic Low-Cost Plans and Differences Between Plans*

Food Class	Quantities		
	Moderate-Cost Plan	Plan Low-Cost	Differences
Milk, cheese, ice cream (qt.)	19½	19	½ more
Meat, poultry, fish (lb.)	16	10	5 more
Eggs	26	22	4 more
Beans, peas, nuts (lb.)	11/16	1⅛	7/16 less
Flour, cereals, baked goods (lb.)	10¾	11¾	1 less
Citrus fruits, tomatoes (lb.)	9¾	8¼	1½ more
Dark green and deep yellow vegetables (lb.)	2½	2¼	¼ more
Potatoes (lb.)	8¼	9	¾ less
Other fruits, vegetables (lb.)	21¾	18¾	3 more
Fats, oils (lb.)	2½	2	½ more
Sugar, sweets (lb.)	3⅝	2¾	⅞ more

Source: Tables 13–2 and 13–4.

thirty-four years, child aged ten to twelve years, and child aged four to six years. The market basket of the plan adapted to southeastern states has some more flour and cereal products and some less meat and dairy products in it—that is, provision is made for hominy grits, rice, cornbread, and hot biscuits, as these are eaten in this region. The adapted plan costs just slightly less than the basic low-cost plan: $26.40 versus $27.50 for a family of four living in the South in December, 1970.

THE MODERATE-COST PLAN

Suggested quantities in the eleven food groups for the moderate-cost plan are given in Table 13–4. In the United States this plan is generally more acceptable than the low-cost plan. Differences in the quantities of food suggested by the two plans for the same family appear in Table 13–10. When it is realized that the small quantities added would be eaten by four persons over a period of seven days, it becomes clear that the market baskets of the two plans differ significantly only in the quantities of meat therein. Different buying practices and different selections made within the different food groups partially explain the greater cost of the moderate-cost plan.

The cost of the moderate-cost plan is approximately one third more than the cost of the basic low-cost plan. A family that would spend $27 on the low-cost plan would spend approximately $36 on the moderate-cost plan. Part of the additional $9 would be spent for additional meat, but it might also be used for more expensive cuts of meat and more expensive foods in other classes. Exactly how this additional $8 to $9 would be spent would be the meal manager's decision. She might use it almost exclusively for convenience; her food selections might not differ from those of the low-cost plan. On the other hand, she might use the extra dollars to purchase butter, coffee cream, whipping cream, expensive vegetables and salad fruits, and other delicacies of the table.

Although food choices do not have to be made as carefully when the plan is moderate-cost, it is very easy to exceed the budget unless spending guides are carefully followed. As with the low-cost plan, guides are based on the fraction of the dollar that can safely be used for purchasing meats and fruits and vegetables. One third of the food dollar can be spent for meats; one fourth for fruits and vegetables. For example, if the housewife plans to spend $36 to feed her family of four, she can safely spend $12 for meats and $9 for fruits and vegetables. With these allowances she can buy some chef's service, as in the purchase of precooked dinners and sauced vegetables, but definitely not without limit. Should there be compelling reasons, such as special dietary needs, or should she choose to do so for her own reasons, she could spend fewer dollars for meats and fruits and vegetables and still purchase the nutritionally adequate diet. But she would probably not use less than one fourth of her dollars for meat and one fifth for fruits and vegetables.

With the sum she can spend for meat, she will want to buy at least twenty-eight servings, perhaps more. To be specific, let us suggest ten more —a total of thirty-eight servings. This means that the allowable average cost of a serving would be $0.24 ($9.00 for thirty-eight servings) when she uses one fourth of her budget ($36.00) for meat, and $0.31 ($12.00 for thirty-eight servings) when she uses one third. Her selections can exceed the allowed average as suggested in the low-cost spending guide, with this modification—she need not be as cautious in making choices costing twice the daily allowance. Guides for spending for meat can be summarized as follows:

1. Decide how much of the budget will be spent for meats.
2. Decide how many portions of meat to purchase.
3. Determine the allowable average cost of a serving of meat.
4. Balance any choices that cost twice the allowable average with three that cost less than the average.
5. Balance any choice that costs two thirds more than the allowable average with two choices that cost less.
6. Balance any choice that costs one third more than the allowed average with one that costs less.

Decisions on fruits and vegetables should begin with the number of portions to be purchased. If, for example, ten extra portions of fruit are desired, then the total purchased would be the 112 required for four persons by the model for planning meals plus ten, totaling approximately 122 weekly. If one fourth of the budget ($36.00) is to be spent for fruits and vegetables, the average cost of a serving would be about $0.07 ($9.00 for 122 servings), if one fifth is spent, $0.06 ($7.00 for 122 servings). The budget is not yet large enough for unrestricted choice; frozen fruits, and fruits and vegetables out of season must still be selected judiciously. Many vegetables, however, can be purchased fresh or frozen.

When purchasing convenience, such as the frozen precooked dinner, the meal manager should recognize that the cost of the dinner is for meat, for vegetables, and for the built-in service. If she knows her average daily meat and vegetable allowances, she can quickly estimate the cost of the convenience of the frozen dinner. For example, $0.31 for meat and $0.12 to $0.14 for two servings of vegetables, as suggested, adds up to $0.43 to $0.45. If the frozen dinner costs $0.65, the cost of convenience is about $0.20, which may be more than her budget will allow. On the other hand, if the frozen dinner costs only $0.49, the cost of convenience may be permissible providing one frozen dinner per person is ample. The moderate-cost plan does not permit the extensive purchase of convenience, of the better cuts of meat, and of the more expensive foods in the different groups.

Some moderate-cost meals would be very different from low-cost meals;

TABLE 13–11. *Quantities of Food for the Same Family According to the Liberal-Cost and Moderate-Cost Plans and Differences Between Plans*

	Quantities		
Food Class	*Liberal-Cost Plan*	*Moderate-Cost Plan*	*Differences*
Milk (qt.)	20½	19½	1 more
Meat, poultry, fish (lb.)	18½	16	2½ more
Eggs	27	26	1 more
Beans, peas, nuts (lb.)	⅝	11/16	1/16 less
Flour, cereals, baked goods (lb.)	10	10¾	¾ less
Citrus fruits, tomatoes (lb.)	11¼	9¾	1½ more
Dark green and deep yellow vegetables (lb.)	2¾	2½	¼ more
Potatoes (lb.)	7	8¼	1¼ less
Other fruits, vegetables (lb.)	24½	21¾	2¾ more
Fats, oils (lb.)	2⅝	2½	⅛ more
Sugars, sweets (lb.)	4⅜	3⅝	¾ more

Source: Tables 13–4 and 13–5.

Menus for One Week of Moderate-Cost Meals

	Breakfast	Lunch or Supper	Dinner
Saturday	Orange Juice[3] Bacon Scrambled Eggs Toast Jam Coffee Milk[1]	Spaghetti and Meat Balls[2] Carrot and Celery Sticks Bread Butter Apples Milk	Corned Beef Potatoes Cabbage Carrots Rolls Brownies[5] Coffee Milk
Sunday	Grapefruit Halves French Toast Syrup Coffee Milk	Corned Beef Sandwiches Fresh Pears Milk	Roast Pork with Dressing Squash[3] Peas[3] Celery Sticks Olives Rolls Ice Milk Brownies Coffee Milk
Monday	Orange Juice[3] Cereal Milk Toast Peanut Butter Coffee Milk	Chicken Pot Pies[6] Cole Slaw Milk	Sliced Cold Roast Pork Baked Potatoes Broccoli[3] Grapefruit-Apple Salad Bread Butter Cake[6] Coffee Milk
Tuesday	Grapefruit Halves Poached Eggs on Toast Toast Jam Coffee Milk	Soup[5] Cold Meat Sandwiches Bananas Cookies Milk	Swiss Steak Mashed Potatoes Green Beans[3] Hot Rolls[6] Cake Coffee Milk
Wednesday	Orange Juice[3] Cereal Milk Raisin Toast Peanut Butter Coffee Milk	Creamed Tuna on Toast Tomato Juice[2] Cake[6] Milk	Baked Meat Loaf Scalloped Potatoes Mixed Vegetables[3] Lettuce Salad Bread Butter Cherry Pie[6] Coffee Milk
Thursday	Bacon and Eggs Toast Jam Coffee Milk	Cold Cuts Cheese Bread Butter Carrots and Celery Sticks Oranges Milk	Fried Chicken Mashed Potatoes Corn[3] Cole Slaw Ice Milk Coffee Milk
Friday	Grapefruit Juice[3] Cereal Milk Coffee Cake[6] Coffee Milk	Scrambled Eggs Tomato Juice[2] Toast Vanilla Pudding[4] Cookies Milk	Baked Haddock Mashed Potatoes Spinach[3] Lettuce Salad Hot Rolls[6] Peaches[2] Cookies Coffee Milk

[1]Milk should be served to children at all meals, to adults at two meals.
[2]Canned.   [3]Frozen.   [4]Instant product.   [5]Mix.   [6]Ready-made.

others would be similar, simply to permit those that are more costly. Breakfast can sometimes include bacon; it can also include eggs frequently. Lunches can sometimes include meat dishes, and dinner may follow the traditional pattern of meat, potatoes, vegetables, salad, and dessert—perhaps omitting bread. Butter may be served at the table, and half-and-half cream may be provided for coffee. Cooking is not as lean as the low-cost plan requires; more eggs, fats, sugar, and extras can be purchased. More convenience can also be purchased, but the budget is not yet sufficient for the extensive purchase of ready-to-eat entrees, ready-prepared breakfasts, and so on. Menus for one week of moderate-cost meals are included.

To summarize, the moderate-cost plan costs about one third more than the basic low-cost plan; the major quantitative difference between the plans is the quantity of meat suggested. The costs differ principally because allowance is made for the purchase of some more expensive foods within food classes, for slightly larger portions of some foods, and for some convenience. As long as the proper quantities of food in each group are purchased, either plan provides a nutritionally good diet. However, the spending of either sum does not guarantee good nutrition. When meat or convenience expenditures are too high, the diet may be nutritionally inadequate because allotments for milk, vegetables, and fruits may have been usurped.

THE LIBERAL-COST FOOD PLAN

Quantitative differences between the moderate-cost and the liberal-cost food plans are shown in Table 13–11. The liberal-cost plan permits the purchase of additional pounds of meat and of fruits and vegetables; quantities of potatoes and cereal products are modestly reduced. The added pounds of meat would permit added portions such as might be included in breakfasts and lunches, or they might provide larger-than-average portions. The additional poundage of fruits and vegetables permits additional servings, especially of fruits. Both additions allow for more waste of food in the home than the other two plans.

The quantities of foods suggested by the three food plans for a family of four are recapitulated in Table 13–12. Note that there is less difference between the quantities of food suggested in each food group for moderate-cost and liberal-cost plans than between the suggested quantities for the basic low-cost and moderate-cost plans. Ultimately, a point is reached when further increases in the recommended quantities in some food groups would be impossible of consumption because of limited human appetites, and decreases in quantities of other food groups would be inconsistent with the goal of good nutrition. The spending of ever more dollars for food is for foods of a different kind, for convenience, and for delicacies of the table. Actually, the quantities of food purchased by meal managers

TABLE 13–12.   *Market Baskets of Three Food Plans for a Family of Four*

Food Class	Low-Cost Plan	Moderate-Cost Plan	Liberal-Cost Plan
Milk, cheese, ice cream (qt.)	19	19½	20½
Meat, poultry, fish (lb.)	10	16	18½
Eggs	22	26	27
Dry beans, peas, nuts (lb.)	1⅛	11/16	⅝
Flour, cereals, baked goods (lb.)	11¾	10¾	10
Citrus fruit, tomatoes (lb.)	8¼	9¾	11¼
Green and yellow vegetables (lb.)	2¼	2½	2¾
Potatoes (lb.)	9	8¼	7
Other fruits, vegetables (lb.)	18¾	21¾	24½
Fats, oils (lb.)	2	2½	2⅝
Sugars, sweets (lb.)	2¾	3⅝	4⅜

Source: Tables 13–2, 13–4, and 13–5.

with generous food budgets may differ little from those suggested in the low-cost and moderate-cost plans because convenience and the choices within the food groups use the additional dollars. The suggested cost of the liberal-cost plan can be easily exceeded.

Choice-making when the liberal-cost plan is used is easy so long as the meal manager does not assume that because cost is liberal, she can purchase anything and everything she finds in the supermarket. The suggested cost of the liberal-cost plan is only approximately 50 per cent greater than the low-cost plan and only about 20 per cent more than the moderate-cost plan. It is a generous budget for food, but it does not permit undisciplined choice in the supermarket. A third of the budget—that is, the suggested cost of the plan—can be spent for meats, including poultry and fish; a fourth can be spent for fruits and vegetables; enough will remain to purchase generously the foods of the other food groups. Some convenient ready-prepared items can be purchased, but not without limit. To avoid overspending for convenience (for entrees, especially prepared vegetables, and ready-prepared desserts), it is suggested that one estimate the cost per portion of the convenience food and compare it with the average cost allowed for the item. For example, if the estimated cost of the plan is $42.00 per week for a four-member family, then $14.00 can be spent for meats. The average allowance per day would be $2.00, and the average allowance per portion $0.50, if only one portion per person per day were purchased. Any convenience entree that costs $0.89 or $0.99 per portion would spend almost twice the average daily allowance and would have to be balanced with one or more low-cost choices. Actually the meat allowance should always pay for convenience entrees; the meat and vegetable allowances, for precooked and frozen dinners; and the vegetable allowance, for especially prepared frozen vegetables. This explains why the menus of low-cost meals and liberal-cost meals can be quite similar—in the latter instance the added cost is for the convenience of ready-prepared foods, whereas in the former, it buys food only.

Specific guides to choice-making when the plan is liberal-cost follow.

1.   Determine how much can be allocated for the purchase of meats. Decide how many portions it must buy. Establish the average daily allowance per portion. Balance any choice that is twice the allowed average with three choices costing less than the average. Balance any choice that costs two thirds more than the average with two less than average in cost. Balance any choice that exceeds the average by one third with a choice less than average in cost. Include the cost of convenience in determining cost per portion.

2.   Determine how much can be spent for fruits and vegetables. Decide how many portions to purchase. Establish the daily average allowance per portion. Do not overspend the daily allowance for this food group. Include the cost of the convenience in determining the cost per portion.

3.   If you have used one third of the budget for meats and one fourth for fruits and vegetables, then you have five twelfths or a bit more than one third of it to buy all the remaining food groups. This will be ample but not unless you use discretion. You can choose some but not all of the following: milk delivered to your doorstep; premium-priced breads, cookies, and pastries; imported cheeses; gourmet salad dressings; premium-priced ice creams and sauces; exotic pickles and relishes; premium-priced jams and jellies; and so on.

The liberal-cost plan can buy an abundant diet and meals that provide eating pleasure. Meal planning per se is easy and less demanding in skill than when the budget is more restricted. Breakfast may occasionally include such meats as bacon, ham, and sausage, and eggs may be served frequently; breakfast fruits may include melons, strawberries, and other fresh fruits in season. Certain meats and fish may be used in luncheon dishes, and the more expensive cuts of meat may be served at the dinner meal some of the time. Meat portions can be larger-than-average portions some of the time. Salad ingredients may include tomatoes, cucumbers, and green peppers regardless of the season, except when they are priced very high. Out-of-season fresh and frozen fruits and vegetables can be purchased.

Menus for one week of liberal-cost meals are presented. Surprisingly enough, the meals do not include many expensive meats, nor many convenience foods. The cost of the plan exceeds the cost of the low-cost plan by about 50 per cent and the cost of the moderate-cost plan by about 20 per cent.

Menus for One Week of Liberal-Cost Meals

	Breakfast	Lunch or Supper	Dinner
Saturday	Grapefruit Juice[3] Poached Eggs on Toast Coffee Milk[1]	Hamburgers on Buns Assorted Relishes Apples Bananas Milk	Grilled Sirloin Steak Baked Potatoes Carrots Lettuce Salad Hot Rolls[6] Cherry Pie[6] Coffee Milk
Sunday	Grapefruit Halves Bacon French Toast Syrup Coffee Milk	Assorted Cold Cuts Assorted Sliced Cheeses Buttered Bread Potato Chips Pickles Radishes Apricots[2] Brownies[5]	Baked Ham Sweet Potatoes[2] Broccoli[3] Fruit Salad Hot Rolls[6] Ice Cream Cookies[6] Coffee Milk
Monday	Orange Juice[3] Boiled Eggs Buttered Toast Coffee Milk	Spaghetti with Meat Balls[2] Celery Sticks and Relishes Bread Pears[2] Milk	Sliced Cold Ham Potatoes Au Gratin Squash[3] Cucumbers in Sour Cream Bread Butter Angel Food Cake[6] Coffee Milk
Tuesday	Orange Juice[3] Ready-to-Eat Cereal Milk Coffee Cake[6] Coffee Milk	Spanish Rice[5] Peas[3] Buttered Toast Brownies Milk	Baked Chicken Potatoes Green Beans[3] Mixed Green Salad Bread Butter Angel Food Cake with Ice Cream Coffee Milk
Wednesday	Orange Juice[3] Bacon Eggs Toast Jelly Coffee Milk	Ham and Cheese Sandwiches Assorted Relishes Angel Food Cake Milk	Grilled Liver Potatoes Mixed Vegetables[3] Tomato Salad Grapes Apples Coffee Milk
Thursday	Grapefruit Halves Cereal Milk English Muffins[6] Coffee Milk	Jiffy Joes[2] on Buns Assorted Relishes Assorted Fruits Cookies[6] Milk	Braised Pork Chops Carrots Lima Beans[3] Apple-Celery Salad Éclairs[6] Coffee Milk
Friday	Grape Juice[2] Cereal Milk Toast Jelly Coffee Milk	Cream of Mushroom Soup[2] Egg Sandwiches Oranges Milk	Broiled Haddock[3] with Cucumber Sauce French Fries[3] Buttered Spinach[3] Tomato and Lettuce Salad Hot Biscuits[6] Ice Cream Cookies[6] Coffee Milk

[1]Milk available for children at all meals; for adults at two meals.
[2]Canned.   [3]Frozen.   [4]Instant.   [5]Mix.   [6]Ready-prepared.

According to the 1965 household food consumption survey, four out of every ten urban families used food at or above the cost of the liberal plan (8). It is a desired plan because it satisfies two wants, namely, convenience and an abundance of meat dishes.

THE ECONOMY PLAN

The economy plan costs 20 to 25 per cent less than the low-cost plan. It is a plan that might be used by families during a period of economic adversity or natural disaster. It is also a plan that low-income families can use to ensure better nutrition than is common when the money value of the diet is that of the economy plan. According to the 1965 survey, less than 10 per cent of diets with the money value of the economy plan were good; less than 50 per cent were fair or better (8). Skill in decision-making, shopping, and meal preparation are essentials when the plan is used. It is not a plan recommended for welfare recipients, who may lack not only these skills but also the kitchen equipment essential for such food preparation as the plan demands. The economists and nutritionists of the United States Department of Agriculture recommend that in public assistance, the budget for food equal the low-cost plan; they suggest that the economy plan may be justified for families receiving such food assistance as donated foods, free school lunches, and food stamps with greater value than the family pays for them (8).

TABLE 13–13. *Market Baskets of the Basic Low-Cost Plan and the Economy Plan for a Family of Four Showing Differences Between Plans*

	Quantities		
Food Groups	*Economy Plan*	*Low-Cost Plan*	*Differences*
Milk, cheese, ice cream (qt.)	17	19	2 less
Meat, poultry, fish (lb.)	6	10	4 less
Eggs	18	22	4 less
Beans, peas, nuts (lb.)	1⅝	1⅛	½ more
Flour, cereals, baked goods (lb.)	13¼	11¾	1½ more
Citrus fruit, tomatoes (lb.)	6½	8¼	1¾ less
Dark green and deep yellow vegetables (lb.)	2¼	2¼	none
Potatoes (lb.)	11½	9	2½ more
Other fruits, vegetables (lb.)	11¾	18¾	7 less
Fats, oils (lb.)	2⅜	2	⅜ more
Sugars, sweets (lb.)	3	2¾	¼ more

Source: Tables 13–2 and 13–6.

TABLE 13–14. *Foods Selections for the Economy Plan with Estimated Costs*[1]

Choices	Quantitiy	Equivalents (Qt.)	Estimated Cost
Milk, cheese, ice cream			
To buy: 17 qt.			
Nonfat dry milk @ 65¢/lb.	2 4/5 lb.	13½	$1.82
American cheese @ 69¢/lb.	1¼ lb.	3	.86
Ice milk @ 59¢/half-gal.	1 qt.	½	.30
Totals		17	$2.98

Choices	Quantity	Approximate Number of Servings	Estimated Cost
Meat, poultry, fish			
To buy: 6 lb.			
Hamburger @ 63¢/lb.	2½ lb.	12 (small)	$1.58
Canned pork loaf, 12 oz.	1 lb. (equivalent)	4	.55
Canned tuna	7 oz.	4 (small)	.45
Liver	1 lb.	4	.68
Bacon square @ 39¢/lb.	¼ lb.		.10
Bologna @ 69¢/lb.	1 lb.	8	.69
Frankfurters @ 79¢/lb.	½ lb.	4 (small)	.40
Totals	6 lb. (approximately)	36 (small to average)	$4.45

Choices	Quantity	Estimated Cost
Eggs		
To buy: 1½ doz.		
Eggs, Grade A, Medium @ 49¢/doz.	1½ doz.	$.74
Totals	1½ doz.	$.74

Choices	Quantity	Estimated Cost
Beans, peas, nuts		
To buy: 1⅝ lb.		
Canned beans @ 15¢/ No. 303 can	3 cans	$.45
Peanut butter @ 39¢/lb.	1 lb.	.39
Totals		$.84

TABLE 13–14.   *Foods Selections for the Economy Plan with Estimated Costs*[1] (continued)

Choices	Quantity or Equivalent	Estimated Cost
Flour, cereals, baked goods		
To buy: 13¼ lb.		
Breakfast cereal, to cook @ 2½¢/oz.	¾ lb.	$.30
Breakfast cereal, ready-to-eat @ 3¢/oz.	¾ lb.	.36
Cornmeal @ 29¢/1–½ lb.	¾ lb.	.15
Flour	5 lb.	.59
Bread, 5 loaves 20-oz. @ 53¢/2	4 lb.	1.33
Macaroni, spaghetti @ 45¢/2 lb.	1½ lb.	.35
Rice @ 21¢/lb.	½ lb.	.11
Totals	13¼ lb.	$3.19

Choices	Quantity	Approximate Number of Servings	Estimated Cost
Citrus fruit, tomatoes			
To buy: 6½ lb.			
Tomato juice, No. 3 cylinder can	46 oz.	12	$.33
Synthetic orange base (Tang)		16	.48
Totals	—[2]	28	$.81

Choices	Quantity	Approximate Number of Servings	Estimated Cost
Dark green and deep yellow vegetables			
To buy: 2¼ lb.			
Fresh carrots @ 35¢/2 lb.	1¼ lb.	7	$.22
Spinach, No. 303 can	1 lb.	4	.21
Totals	2¼ lb.	11	$.43

TABLE 13–14.   *Foods Selections for the Economy Plan with Estimated Costs*[1] (continued)

Choices	Quantity	Approximate Number of Servings	Estimated Cost
Potatoes			
To buy: 11½ lb.			
All-purpose potatoes, @ 79¢/10 lb.	11½ lb.	35	$.92
Totals	11½ lb.	35	$.92

Choices	Quantity	Approximate Number of Servings	Estimated Cost
Other vegetables and fruits			
To buy: 11¾ lb.			
Applesauce, No. 303 can	1 lb.	4	$.20
Bananas, @ 29¢/2 lb.	2 lb.	6	.29
Cabbage, @ 12¢/lb.	3 lb.	12	.36
Celery, bunch	1 lb.	—	.29
Corn, No. 303 can	1 lb.	4	.20
Onions	1 lb.	4+	.21
Peas, No. 303 can	1 lb.	4	.21
Plums, No. 2½ can	1¾ lb.	6	.33
Pumpkin, No. 303 can	1 lb.	4	.23
Totals	12¾ lb.[3]	44	$2.24

Choices	Quantity	Estimated Cost
Fats and oils		
To buy: 2⅜ lb.		
Margarine, @ 22¢/lb.	2¾ lb.	$.55
Shortening, @ 75¢/3 lb.	⅞ lb.	.22
Totals	3⅝ lb.[4]	$.77

TABLE 13–14   *Foods Selections for the Economy Plan with Estimated Costs[1] (continued)*

Choices	Quantity	Estimated Cost
Sugars, sweets		
To buy: 3 lb.		
Brown sugar, @ 23¢/lb.	½ lb.	$.11
Confectioner's sugar, @ 23¢/lb.	½ lb.	.12
Granulated sugar, @ 67¢/5lb.	1½ lb.	.22
Jam, @ 29¢/lb.	½ lb.	.15
Totals	3 lb.	$.60

[1]All prices are discount market prices.
[2]Weight not given because of concentration of synthetic product.
[3]Extra weight because of extensive use of canned items.
[4]Extra weight because of use of nonfat dry milk.

Table 13–13 shows how the low-cost and economy plans would differ for the same family. The economy plan includes more food in the beans-peas-nuts group and the flour-cereal group and more potatoes. It provides for less milk, meat, and fruits and vegetables, but the biggest change is the re-duction in the amount of meat. This reduced quantity of meat suggests that portions be small to average so as to net more servings and thereby provide more meals containing a meat item. Always, the least expensive foods in food groups would have to be purchased; and these could be dif-ferent from season to season. Some recommended purchases are nonfat dry milk for all milk, pasteurized process cheese, and cottage cheese; ham-burger, liver, canned pork loaves, canned corned beef, canned fish or fro-zen fish fillets, and frankfurters; potatoes, carrots, cabbage, and bananas; margarine; breakfast cereals that require cooking; and so on. The market-place would have to be shopped for the best buys. In addition, much food would have to be home-cooked, even some breads and such baked items as cookies, cakes, and pies.

Suggested choices for this plan are presented in Table 13–14. The esti-mated costs are discount supermarket prices for most of the items. The estimated total costs for the food groups follows:

Food Groups	Cost
Milk, cheese, ice cream	$2.98
Meat, poultry, fish	4.45
Eggs	.74
Beans, peas, nuts	.84
Flour, cereals, baked goods	3.19
Citrus fruit, tomatoes	.81
Green, yellow vegetables	.43
Potatoes	.92
Other fruits, vegetables	2.24
Fats, oils	.77
Sugars, sweets	.60
Total	$17.97

To the estimated cost of the plan it is desirable to add an allowance of ten cents per person for miscellaneous purchases; an allowance for the purchase of one and one-half ounces of instant coffee per adult; and 10 per cent of the estimated cost to make the plan feasible even for limited use. That is, choices from week to week may cause some fluctuations in the weekly cost of the plan. Sales tax must be added in states where it is collected on food. Final calculations would be as follows.

	Low Limit of Cost	Upper Limit of Cost
Estimated cost of economy plan	$17.97	$17.97
Miscellaneous allowance (4 persons)	0.40	0.40
Instant coffee (3 oz.)	0.49	0.49
Ten per cent addition	—	1.80
State sales tax	—	—
Total	$18.86	$20.66

As proposed, the plan costs $19.00 to $20.50 approximately; the cost is about two thirds of the cost of the basic low-cost plan.

Plans for meals that might be planned around this assortment of foods are presented. Many persons would not favor them because they contain small quantities of meat and because the meats used are not those generally favored, and also because they contain potatoes and cereal foods abundantly. Actually the number of servings of fruits and vegetables is not less than some families consume, but it is far less than many prefer. The meal plans conform closely to the model for planning nutritionally good meals;

Menus for Economy Plan for One Week

	Breakfast	Lunch or Supper	Dinner
Saturday	Cereal with Sliced Bananas Coffee Cake Coffee[1] Milk[2]	Grilled Cheese Sandwiches Celery Sticks Apple Sauce[3] Cookies Milk	Spaghetti and Meat Casserole Cabbage Salad Rolls Cake Coffee Milk
Sunday	Juice[5] French Toast Syrup Coffee Milk	Peanut Butter Sandwiches Celery Sticks Cake Milk	Liver and Bacon Mashed Potatoes Creamed Onions Rolls Ice Milk Cookies Coffee Milk
Monday	Cereal Milk Toast Peanut Butter Coffee Milk	Tomato Soup[3] Egg Sandwiches Cookies Milk	Smoked Pork Loaf[3] Scalloped Potatoes Spinach[3] Cole Slaw Rolls Cake with Ice Milk Coffee Milk
Tuesday	Juice[5] Cereal Milk Sweet Rolls Coffee Milk	Potato Soup Bologna Sandwiches Carrot Sticks Milk	Macaroni and Cheese Hash Brown Potatoes Cole Slaw Rolls Pumpkin Pie Coffee Milk
Wednesday	Juice[5] Cereal Milk Coffee Cake Coffee Milk	Spaghetti with Meat and Tomato Sauce Celery Sticks Bread Plums[3] Milk	Baked Beans[3] and Frankfurters Potatoes Carrots Cornbread Chocolate Pudding Coffee Milk
Thursday	Juice[5] Cereal Milk Toasted Cornbread Coffee Milk	Potato Soup Bologna Sandwiches Celery Sticks Cookies Milk	Meat Balls Potatoes Corn[3] Bread Fruit Cup Cookies Coffee Milk
Friday	Tomato Juice[3] Cereal Milk Toast Jam Coffee Milk	Cheese Rabbit on Toast Fried Potatoes Cookies Milk	Tuna Noodle Casserole Peas[4] Celery Sticks Hot Biscuits Baked Custard Coffee Milk

[1]Serve instant coffee at two meals daily.   [2]Serve milk to children at all meals; to adults at two meals daily.   [3]Canned.   [4]Frozen.   [5]Tang.

they would provide a nutritionally adequate diet. The menus do not conform to some suggestions for planning meals that people like. They lack the texture contrasts and variety that an affluent society prefers. Good cooking would do much to make the meals acceptable. Cookery would necessarily be plain because funds could not justifiably be used to buy ingredients that would add zest to dishes. The stock of flavorings and adjuncts would consist mainly of imitation vanilla, spices, herbs, onions, celery, cocoa, raisins, and peanuts. Time and energy would of necessity have to be devoted to the preparation of the meals.

Families would eat these economy meals only as long as circumstances required. One could purchase a nutritionally good diet for less by further reducing the quantity of meat and vegetables and increasing the quantity of cereals and beans and peas. Meals would resemble the diet of the European countries during World War II and also of some of the developing countries today in that cereals would become the mainstay of the diet.

ESTABLISHING A FOOD BUDGET

Establishing a budget for food should be comparatively simple; one determines food needs and then decides how they will be purchased. Actually, the decision is not that easy. Buying food needs according to the plans discussed means limiting food choices more or less, depending on the plan selected. The more conservative the plan, the more food choices are restricted; and food preferences and food habits once established are not quickly nor easily modified. Further, the more conservative the plan, the more time and energy the meal manager must devote to meals in planning, shopping, and food preparation and also, the more knowledge, skills, and abilities required. The decision to spend conservatively for food cannot be made out of context—that is, without consideration of all resources and, as we have already noted, of the various factors that affect the way in which families buy their respective food needs.

Nonetheless, it is possible to suggest three approaches to the problem: one is to begin with food needs and to decide objectively how much to spend to buy them; another is to select a spending plan from among the published costs of plans; and the last is to modify objectively the current pattern of spending. To use the first approach, it is necessary to first establish family food needs according to the low-cost plan. Next, the cost of this plan must be calculated, taking into account family food preferences. From the estimate obtained, the cost of all the other plans can be derived. Lastly, from all estimated costs, one spending plan can be selected that is compatible with income and all the other competing demands on income, such as housing, insurance, clothing, car payments, medical care, and so

TABLE 13–15. *Food Plans, by Family Income and Size, 1970*[1]

Family Income (After Taxes)	2-Person Family	3-Person Family	4-Person Family	5-Person Family	6-Person Family
$2,000 to $4,000	Low-Cost	Economy[2] or Low-Cost	Economy[2]	Economy[2]	Economy[2]
$4,000 to $6,000	Moderate-Cost	Low-Cost	Low-Cost	Economy[2]	Economy[2]
$6,000 to $8,000	Liberal-Cost	Moderate-Cost	Low-Cost or Moderate-Cost	Low-Cost	Economy[2] or Low-Cost
$8,000 to $10,000	Liberal-Cost	Moderate-Cost or Liberal-Cost	Moderate-Cost	Low-Cost or Moderate-Cost	Low-Cost
$10,000 to $15,000	Liberal-Cost	Liberal-Cost	Liberal-Cost	Moderate-Cost or Liberal-Cost	Low-Cost or Moderate-Cost
$15,000 and over	Liberal-Cost	Liberal-Cost	Liberal-Cost	Liberal-Cost	Moderate-Cost or Liberal-Cost

[1]From "Cost of a Family's Groceries and the USDA Food Plans," *Family Economics Review*, Consumer and Food Economics Research Division, United States Department of Agriculture, Washington, D.C. (June 1970), p. 12.

[2]For families on very limited food budgets.

on. A suggested model for selection according to family income and family size is given in Table 13–15 (1).

A second approach bypasses the step of establishing food needs. Instead, from the published costs per person of the food plans, the estimated costs for a family according to all the plans are derived. From these estimates, again, it is necessary to choose the spending plan that fits income and spending commitments. It is not possible to state that any given percentage of income should or should not be spent for food; however, a percentage could be more generous for families without children than for families with children. Similar families with similar assets may decide on quite different spending plans for food: one may prefer two homes; the other, two prime rib roasts of beef in the oven.

The third approach to establishing a food budget is to analyze present spending practices to discover how much is being spent and what is being bought. To do this, first keep careful records of all food purchases including soft drinks, ice cream, candies, and nonfood items bought in the supermarket for two weeks or longer. Classify these purchases into the eleven food groups, a miscellaneous category, and a nonfood category. For a careful analysis, describe all items fully, for example, frozen french fries, ready-to-bake cherry pie, canned spaghetti and meat balls, delicatessen potato salad, and so on. These descriptions aid in determining the extent to which convenience is being purchased. A record of the purchases of nonfood items may disclose that spending for food is not what one thought, but rather that items formerly bought in department and variety stores are being purchased in the supermarket. Because modifications of spending patterns are generally downward, one can assume that the analysis of expenditures will be made with the intent of reduced spending. Next, study each food group item by item to discover if there are items you could buy for less either by buying the same item in a different way or by choosing differently. For example, such items as calves liver, frozen ready-baked cake, and frozen peas with mushrooms can be purchased for less without a change in choice: chicken livers, a bakery-made cake, and frozen peas. But items like frozen asparagus, frozen shrimp, and out-of-season fresh pineapple can be changed to frozen corn, frozen ocean perch, and apple sauce to effect reductions in spending. A third possible step in an analysis of spending practices is to compare the quantities of food bought in the different groups with the amount suggested in the different plans. Perhaps more is being bought and wasted than was realized. As a result of a complete analysis of present spending practices, a new budget for food can be established. However, unless all family members will accept the changes deemed desirable and unless someone is willing to spend the time and energy required by these changes, the new budget is doomed to failure.

CONTROLLING SPENDING FOR FOOD

Once a sound budget has been established, the whole family must share the responsibility for living within the limits imposed. Father and the children do their part by accepting the meals prepared and by helping with food preparation and mealtime duties, particularly when much of the food must be home-cooked. The homemaker carries the main responsibility because she plans the meals, does the marketing, and prepares the food. Her skill in performing each of these duties helps determine the success or failure of the budget; the smaller the budget, the more this is true. If any of these duties takes first place, it is marketing. True, meals must be pleasing and food should taste good, but these goals must be accomplished with whatever foods the budget will buy.

With regard to marketing practices, the meal manager must know, first, how much she can spend for partially prepared and ready-to-eat foods, for if she overspends on those, she will wreck the most carefully planned budget. Second, she should know approximately how much she can buy in such classes as fruits and vegetables and meats, particularly the latter. Third, she should know what choices within the food classes are consistent in cost with her budget. To live on a low-cost budget, she must keep in mind the sum she can spend on fruits and vegetables and on meats, that is, one fourth of the budget for each group. To make proper choices, the homemaker should know the portion yield of market units because cost per portion is her best guide to proper selection.

Fourth, for all budgets except liberal ones, the homemaker should be cautious in the number of purchases she allocates to the miscellaneous category. This should not exceed fifteen cents per person weekly for the low-cost plan, twenty cents per person weekly for the moderate-cost plan, and twenty-five cents per person weekly for the liberal budget, excluding coffee. Finally, the homemaker profits from knowing how to shop to advantage and how to recognize a bargain if the budget demands the practice of economies.

With regard to meal planning, meals must please those for whom they are planned. The larger the budget, the easier is the task, for if each member of the family has a good steak, he pays little attention to the other dishes in the meal. The smaller the budget, the more the homemaker is dependent on the science and art of meal planning. She should be aware and make use of the different taste and flavor combinations that are satisfying; she should make sure of texture contrasts; and finally, she should use all means at her disposal to make the food look and taste good. It goes without saying that good cooking is always desirable; it is of prime importance when the budget is limited.

Summary. The goal of controlled spending for food is not easy of attainment because it may require skilled decision-making and it may demand modification of food preferences. On the other hand, the marketplace offers such abundance and such variety that it is possible to spend the dollar so that it will buy food abundantly. It is also possible to spend the dollar so that it will buy comparatively little food. Man's capacity to eat is limited. Spending more or less for food means buying different foods: tender cuts of meat versus less tender cuts; fresh out-of-season fruits and vegetables versus canned or frozen counterparts; superior quality versus fair to good quality; foods with or without built-in convenience; commonplace versus rare and exotic foods; and so on.

Good nutrition can be had at different levels of spending. Four levels are recognized: economy, low-cost, moderate-cost, and liberal-cost. The food plans of the different levels differ in the quantities of food purchased in the different food groups, in the choices made within the food groups, and in buying practices.

Buying practices differ in the extent to which the dollar must buy food, in the extent to which convenience can be purchased, in the extent to which super quality can be purchased, and in the extent to which the luxuries of the table can be indulged in. The meals typical of the different plans, or levels of spending, have certain identifying characteristics, such as the variety of the diet, the variety and number of dishes within meals, the kind and quantity of meat served, and, especially in the 1970's, the number and variety of ready-made dishes. Meals of all levels of spending can be satisfying if they are well planned and well prepared.

Actually, the meals of differing levels of spending may be very similar because in one instance all food may be home-prepared and in the other, all purchased ready-made.

Even with the two incomes of many families of the 1970's, controlled spending for food is a goal in meal management because of the many wants and expenses of families. Other families find controlled spending for food essential because of the scarcity of money.

REFERENCES CITED

1. "Cost of a Family's Groceries and the USDA Food Plans," *Family Economics Review*, Consumer and Food Economics Research Division, United States Department of Agriculture, Washington, D.C. (June 1970), p. 12.

2. "Diets of Low-Income Families," *Family Economics Review*, Consumer and Food Economics Research Division, United States Department of Agriculture, Washington, D.C. (March 1969), p. 3.

3. "Distribution of the Food Dollar by Families in Four Regions and in the Low-Cost Plan," *Family Economics Review*, Consumer and Food Economics Research Division, United States Department of Agriculture, Washington, D.C. (June 1970), p. 13.

4. "The Effect of Family Size on Expenditures," *Family Economics Review*, Consumer and Food Economics Research Division, United States Department of Agriculture, Washington, D.C. (March 1967), p. 14.

5. "Food Consumption of Households in the United States, Spring, 1965," Consumer and Food Economics Research Division, United States Department of Agriculture, Washington, D.C. (1968), p. 2.

6. "Food Expenditures in the South," *Family Economics Review*, Consumer and Food Economics Research Division, United States Department of Agriculture, Washington, D.C. (December 1968), p. 3.

7. "Food Spending and Income," *National Food Situation*, Economic Research Service, United States Department of Agriculture, Washington, D.C. (February 1972), p. 8.

8. "Money Value and Adequacy of Diets Compared with USDA Food Plans," *Family Economics Review*, Consumer and Food Economics Research Division, United States Department of Agriculture, Washington, D.C. (September 1969), p. 7.

Chapter 14

Meal Management Goals— Satisfying Meals

The third goal for meals is that they be accepted, eaten, and enjoyed. For the meal manager—whether homemaker, dietitian, or club steward— this is the most difficult goal to achieve because the same meals are not accepted, eaten, and enjoyed with the same degree of enthusiasm by all persons and because it must be achieved with available resources. And, of course, meals must also provide for good nutrition. The menu card at a restaurant suggests a number of appetizers, entrees, vegetables, salads, and desserts; yet a party of two, let alone a party of eight, does not order the same dishes. In addition to satisfying hunger, the pleasures or delights or satisfactions that may be derived from meals are several: visual, gustatory, aesthetic, social and emotional, and psychological. If meals had only to satisfy hunger, their planning would pose fewer problems, but it would not eliminate them since we have known for some time that even hungry persons reluctantly eat what is strange to them, that is, wheat or corn if their basic staple is rice, and vice versa; or white soup if the indigenous soup is brown.

In this chapter, we shall discuss the food preferences of consumers in the United States, flavor perception, and foodways; and lastly, we shall suggest some guidelines for menu-making.

FOOD PREFERENCES OF CONSUMERS IN THE UNITED STATES

The food preferences of consumers in the United States have been studied. The most extensive studies have been those of food acceptance and food preference of men in the armed forces. These studies have demonstrated that, in general, preference studies predict acceptance—that is, people eat what they like. Further, it has been observed that the preferences of men in the armed forces correspond generally with those of the entire American population with variations due to age, sex, and region of origin (10). In their study of food preferences, Peryam and his co-workers had subjects rate 438 foods and dishes on a nine-point scale from "like extremely" to "dislike extremely." Results of the studies (12) verified what we have long thought we knew about food likes. First, some classes of foods are better liked than others; the least liked were vegetables, salads, and soups. The best-liked classes were meats, breads, and desserts. The ten best-liked and the ten least-liked items as rated by men in the armed forces are given below.

Best-Liked Foods	*Least-Liked Foods*
Fresh milk	Mashed turnips
Hot rolls	Broccoli
Hot biscuits	Baked Hubbard squash
Strawberry shortcake	Fried parsnips
Grilled steak	Creamed asparagus
Ice cream	Cabbage baked with cheese
Ice cream sundae	Asparagus with Hollandaise sauce
Fried chicken	Iced coffee
French fried potatoes	Cauliflower with cheese sauce
Roast turkey	Candied parsnips

The best-liked foods are in the classes of bread, meat, and desserts. The least-liked foods, except for the iced coffee, are all vegetables. Hot coffee, although not as well liked as milk, is liked. Iced and hot coffee do not taste the same; the former is quite bitter and lacks the aroma of hot coffee.

Second, within classes the range in preference may be wide or narrow. For main dishes—including meat and meat, egg, and cheese dishes—the range was wide. The highest preference was for meats in the following order of decreasing preference: grilled steak, fried chicken, roast turkey, roast beef, Swiss steak, grilled pork chops, and baked and grilled ham. The low-scoring items were lamb, liver, fish, stews, creamed dishes like creamed salmon and creamed dried beef, and combination dishes like hash and chop suey. Baked beans and macaroni and cheese were preferred over baked and fried fish. The range in preference for breads was narrow, the highest-scoring items being hot rolls and hot biscuits, the lowest-scoring muffins. Well-liked fresh fruits included peaches, watermelon, cantaloupe, apples, and Tokay grapes; well-liked canned fruits included peaches, fruit cocktail, pears, and pineapple. The best-liked desserts included strawberry shortcake, ice cream and ice cream sundaes, apple pie, chocolate cake, and chocolate chip cookies. Milk was the most universally liked beverage, but hot cocoa, coffee, and tea were also liked. Orange, pineapple, tomato, and apple juices were preferred over other juices.

The least liked of the food classes was vegetables. The best liked ones were corn-on-the-cob, sliced fresh tomatoes, green beans, cut corn, and peas. These are liked about as well as some potato dishes. The least-liked vegetables have already been named. Buttered vegetables were consistently preferred to those cooked with some other ingredient. Those served with sauces were least preferred. Potato dishes in decreasing order of preference were french fried potatoes, mashed potatoes, potato chips, oven-browned and hash-brown potatoes, cold potato salad, and parsleyed and baked potatoes.

Fruit salads were preferred over such vegetable salads as cole slaw, lettuce wedge, and sliced cucumbers. Perfection and asparagus salads had low preference. Combination salads like Waldorf salad, carrot-and-raisin salad, and salads with cottage cheese were less well liked than fruit salads. The best-liked fruit salad was pineapple-apricot-banana salad.

Third, the preference for individual foods is modified by the combinations in which they appear. Combinations are defined as individually prepared foods that are served and eaten either together or sequentially. Combination effects have important implications in menu planning. Eindhoven and Peryam (5) found that some meat-and-potato combinations and some meat-and-vegetable combinations had higher preference than others. For example, baked ham and candied sweet potatoes and baked ham and mashed potato combinations scored higher than baked ham combined with french fried potatoes; but the combination of fried fish and sweet potatoes scored very low, whereas the combination of fried fish and french fried potatoes had high acceptance. Corn had better acceptance when served with chicken than with fish; sauerkraut, with pork than with beef; and cauliflower, with ham than with fish. There are many food combinations that are considered traditional or regional in origin. It would be interesting to know if they are liked because they are traditional or for reasons that have to do with the flavor enhancement of one food in the presence of another.

Fourth, the preference for individual foods is modified by the method of preparation, with the food prepared plain scoring best. For example, grilled steak is preferred over Swiss steak; grilled ham, over ham loaf; buttered broccoli, over broccoli with cheese sauce; and buttered asparagus, over asparagus with hollandaise sauce.

Other studies, of which only a few will be noted, reveal quite similar findings about food preferences. In a study of the dessert preferences of southern urban families (9), the best-liked desserts were pie, shortcake, and cobbler; the next best-liked was ice cream; then cake or cookies. The best-liked ice cream was vanilla, followed by chocolate and strawberry.

In a study of women students fed in a dormitory dining room, it was found that the best-liked vegetables were green beans, wax beans, peas, corn-on-the-cob, and potatoes. The least well-accepted were strongly flavored turnips, broccoli, and red cabbage; also Swiss chard and zucchini squash and yellow crookneck squash. VanRiter (16) noted that disliked vegetables were never tasted or never served at home—that is, they were unfamiliar. This study also disclosed that student dislikes and family dislikes were similar.

In a study of the influence of the father's food habits on those of his children (4), it was noted that 89 per cent of mothers did not serve often the foods that the father disliked. These included fish, liver, lamb, spinach, squash, sweet potatoes, and combination dishes.

An early study (7) attempted to discover what foods were disliked and why. The subjects were students attending three universities, two in the West and one in the Midwest. The disliked foods included the internal organs of animals; buttermilk; three vegetables—parsnips, rutabagas, and turnips; and clams and caviar. What was interesting about this study was the finding that although women were familiar with more foods than men, they had more food dislikes than men. The main reason given for disliking a food was its taste, but texture, appearance, and odor were also mentioned.

The Gallup Organization polled the preferences and prejudices of Americans when they eat in restaurants. The surveys were conducted during the years 1966 through 1969. The findings about food preferences are summarized but are limited to the preferences of 20 per cent or more of those polled. In 1966, soup preferences in descending order of preference were vegetable and any kind of chicken; in 1969, chicken noodle, vegetable beef, tomato, oyster stew, and chicken with rice. Green beans were the only vegetable preferred by 20 per cent of those polled. Preferences were for baked and mashed potatoes, in that order. Favorite Sunday dinners were, in descending order of liking, steak, chicken, and roast beef. Many breads were liked; in descending order of preference they were hot biscuits, Parker House rolls, French bread, garlic-toasted French bread, individual loaves of bread, rye bread, and hard rolls. Some of the salad dressings liked included tangy French, Russian, Roquefort, Caesar, mayonnaise, bleu cheese, Italian, and Green Goddess. The desserts preferred were, in descending order, apple pie, ice cream, fruit desserts, pumpkin pie, chocolate cake, cheesecake, cherry pie, and lemon pie (6).

In a study of the food preferences of sixth-grade children, Zunich and Fults (17) noted that cereals, fish, and cooked vegetables were most frequently disliked. Dislikes included liver, tuna fish, salmon loaf, baked fish; beets, broccoli, spinach, squash; stewed prunes; oatmeal and Cream of Wheat; and vegetable salads. Their study included subjects from Ohio, Texas, and Florida. They noted regional differences in preferences: the

Ohio children had more dislikes and fewer likes than the children in the southern states. The authors hypothesized that because of the climate, children in the southern states have longer exposure to some foods, especially vegetables.

Knickrehm and her co-workers (8), in a survey of food acceptances of college students, found that there were relatively few foods that students wanted to eat twice daily, once a day, every other day, or even twice weekly. The menu items acceptable twice daily were fresh fruits, fruit juices, fruit combinations, and tossed green salads. Fewer than half of the students wanted roast beef and broiled steak as often as twice a week, and, contrary to expectations, only about 40 per cent wanted hamburger on a bun as often as twice weekly. Mashed potatoes would be accepted twice weekly by 60 per cent and baked potatoes by 40 per cent. Forty per cent would eat these vegetables twice weekly: fresh tomatoes, whole kernel corn, peas, green beans, and cream-style corn. Popular desserts were ice cream, fruit pies, cream pies, cake, canned fruit, cream-type puddings, cookies, and Jello. Ten per cent would eat ice cream twice daily and 20 per cent would eat it daily. Dessert flavors, in descending order of preference, were chocolate, vanilla, lemon, butterscotch, and coconut. Some menu items that 25 per cent or more would not eat were corned beef and cabbage, liver and onions, ham loaf, roast lamb, shrimp casserole; a long list of vegetables from acorn squash to zucchini; vegetables-in-gelatin salad; and boiled beans.

Pilgrim (12) has summarized what we know about food preferences. Individuals like or dislike by food classes, that is, vegetables or salads or desserts. The preference for a food changes with the method of preparation. Persons who like a food prepared in a certain way like other foods prepared that way; for example, if a person likes a particular creamed dish, that person likes other creamed dishes. The more that is done in preparation, the less well a food is accepted. Combinations of food score like the less well-liked items. For example, pear-and-cottage-cheese salad is scored like cottage cheese rather than like pears, which are liked. The American male likes plain, simple food. Food preferences change with age; the preference for soups and vegetables increases, whereas preference for beverages, cereals, desserts, and fruits decreases.

Though regional differences in food preference exist, the 1965 household food consumption survey revealed that regional differences are less sharp than formerly. The American diet has become somewhat homogenized since World War II. Food preferences are learned: they are a part of the culture transmitted to all born into a culture. Where food is abundant, all persons do not like all foods equally well: many like green beans, but do not like eggplant or zucchini; others like eggplant and zucchini. Food preferences are shaped by many forces; however, flavor, texture, and color in foods are relevant factors in determining individual food preferences.

Food Flavor

We judge food flavor when we say that something tastes good or bad or that we do not like the taste of a certain food or dish. Perception of flavor is an experience short in duration but long in memory. It is partly sensory, but it is also personal. Man's sensory perceptions are modified by his habits, his customs, his prejudices, his emotions, and his physiological state. Flavor perception varies in intensity among individuals and in the same individual from time to time.

Flavor has been defined as "the sensation caused by, and those properties of, any substance taken into the mouth, which stimulates one or both of the senses of taste and smell and/or also the general pain, tactile, and temperature receptors in the mouth" (10). That is, flavor is more than just what we think of as "taste." It is also the way a food feels in the mouth—that is, smooth or lumpy, slimy or gritty. Food temperature, hot, cold, or lukewarm, is an aspect of flavor, and the sting of pepper and ginger, the coolness of peppermint, the astringency of tannins, and the warmth of cassia are part of the flavor experience.

Aroma

Odor or aroma is the facet of the flavor experience that most influences acceptance or rejection of a food or dish. Compared with the sense of taste, which is a dull one, our sense of smell is keen. The organ for smell is able to distinguish among many different stimuli and is sensitive to odorous substances in very dilute solutions. For example, one ten millionth of a milligram of vanillin per cubic meter of air, that is, one part per ten billion, is perceptible. The olfactory organ is located on the roof of the nasal cavity where it occupies an area about the size of the end of the thumb on both sides of the nasal septum. Volatile odorants reach it via the nostrils during breathing, as demonstrated by the quick recognition of "what's for dinner" when one steps into the kitchen, and via the posterior nasal passages during eating.

The stereochemical theory of olfaction suggests that the olfactory organ contains pores into which odorant molecules fit—a "lock and key" concept. It suggests that there are primary odors, such as camphoraceous, floral, and musky. The number of primary odors is not yet known. Complex odors would be composed from different proportions of primaries in different permutations. The aroma of a food is composed of many different volatile components (2). The interactions and blending of odorants in the production of food aromas are many and varied; they very likely account for the unique character of the dishes prepared by different cooks. Further, they may explain why some food combinations are more pleasing than others. Olfactory acuity is decreased by sugar, alcohol, amphetamines, and aging. Olfactory acuity diminishes after a meal, and is prevented by tartaric, tannic, and acetic acids, bitter tonics, and dry red wines (1). Flavor perception is affected by color, with food having the flavor associated with the color. Flavor identification of uncolored or atypically colored candies or jellies has been found difficult (3).

During eating, odor is perceived both by the smelling of food before it is eaten, while it is in the dish or cup or on the fork lifted to the mouth, and during chewing and swallowing when the motions of the palate and throat create small air movements that send ordorants to the smell organ via the nasopharynx. Flavor perception is experienced briefly on breathing out. Closure of the nasal passages by swelling, as when one has a cold, causes a loss of the sense of smell. At such a time, food has only taste and mouthfeel and we are apt to comment, "It all tastes alike" or, "It is like eating cotton." The pleasure that accompanies the eating of roast beef, fresh homemade bread, spice cake, and all the other foods we like is derived primarily through the sense of smell.

The organ of smell adapts to continuous and repetitive stimulation with a consequent loss of perceptive ability called *smell fatigue*. For example, our sensitivity to the enticing odors of the bakery and to the offensive odors of the fish market is diminished as we wait there. Adaptation to a single odor is more rapid than to the same odor accompanied by other odors. Adaptation to some odors is more rapid than to other odors. There seems to be no point of fatigue for oil of lemon and oil of cloves. The time of adaptation to an odor varies with its strength or intensity—the more intense the odor, the less rapid its adaptation. Intense odors mask less intense odors. And finally, the longer one is in the presence of a prevailing odor, the more intense must the stimulus for its perception be. This last observation causes one to wonder if food eaten in the kitchen, where the prevailing aroma is that of the food just prepared, is as flavorful as the same food eaten in an atmosphere free from kitchen odors.

Some culinary practices and some dining customs can be explained by reference to these observations. The fact of adaptation explains why no two bites of a single dish ever taste the same and why the last bite never tastes as good as the first. It perhaps explains the habits of eating quickly the foods we like and of eating slowly the foods we dislike. In the one instance, we unconsciously hurry so that we may enjoy the flavor of a dish before adaptation to odor is complete; in the other, we unconsciously delay until fatigue diminishes sensitivity. Because the organ of smell recovers rather quickly when the stimulus is removed or changed, enjoyment of flavors is assured when meals are composed of several dishes eaten inter-changeably. Perhaps the lack of enthusiasm for one-dish meals can be explained by quick adaptation to its aroma. The suggestion that foods of similar flavor, herbs, spices, and seasonings not be repeated in meals is sound; repetition would cause rapid adaptation to a particular smell.

Fatigue to the aroma of spices is delayed longer than fatigue to other aromas—hence, the long and colorful history of their use. Used judi-ciously, spices undoubtedly prolong the period of enjoyment of their unique aromas. But the stronger odors of spices, herbs, and seasonings can dominate and prevent the perception of subtle odors. They should be used with a light hand, if the other ingredients of a dish or even other foods in a meal are to be tasted. For example, the delicate flavor of garden-fresh peas would pass unnoticed were they served with a lamb curry. On the other hand, the masking powers of herbs, spices, and seasonings are well recognized.

Aroma is modified by the temperature of food because the odorous particles that stimulate the organ of smell are more volatile at higher tem-peratures. Food that is too hot causes pain so that neither taste nor smell can be perceived. A degree of warmth, however, is essential for the best flavors of many foods. Very cold foods, like ice cream, have more flavor if they are held in the mouth until somewhat warm. Fruits of delicate flavor, like peaches, pears, strawberries, and raspberries, have more flavor when eaten unchilled or only slightly chilled; and some kinds of melons have more flavor when only slightly chilled. The suggestions that the first course not be sweet, that wines enhance the enjoyment of food, and that fruits and vegetables be eaten with meats are in line with our limited knowledge of olfaction.

Taste

The taste receptors are cells of the taste buds. Taste buds are structures present in the papillae of the tongue; they are also present in such areas as the soft palate, the pharynx, and the larynx, where they are embedded in the epithelium of the mucous membranes. The cells of these organs are aroused by different substances in solution. The cells are nonspecific; each responds to evoke several tastes. The number of tastes is numerous, but it is believed that all are combinations of four primary tastes: bitter, salt, sour, and sweet. The salty taste is evoked by some inorganic salts; we add ordi-nary table salt, sodium chloride, to produce the salty taste of foods. The sour taste is effected by the hydrogen ion; all inorganic acids taste alike when they are sampled in equal concentration. Some organic acids, such as acetic, tartaric, citric, and malic, taste more sour than their hydrogen ion concentration would suggest; it is likely that the complex structure of the acid affects the taste mechanism in some manner not yet understood. The sour taste of foods is present in fruits. We add vinegar, wines, and lemon juice to produce the sour taste. The sweet sensation derives from complex organic compounds, including sugar and sugar derivatives, saccharin, dulcin, glycerin, cyclamates, and some other organic compounds. The sweet taste is present naturally in fruits and some vegetables. The bitter taste is chiefly aroused by alkaloids and certain gulcosides and some inorganic salts. Tannins in foods and beverages impart bitterness and astringency. Saccharin has been found to have a bitter off taste for about 90 per cent of persons. The bitter taste is present in fruits and vegetables, especially salad greens, and bitters are added to foods to introduce the bitter taste. Bitterness has a positive quality in coffee, tea, red wines, beer, and some other beverages. Rietz (14) says that traditional flavor combinations balance bitter-salt-sour-sweet tastes, for example, pork with apple. Man's order of sensitivity to the four tastes is bitter, sour, salt, and sugar. If saccharin replaces sugar, then the order of sensitivity is bitter, saccharin, sour, and salt. Taste sensitivity can be enhanced or depressed. Pharmaceuticals make use of flavors to disguise or mask tastes. For example, a salty taste is masked by syrup of orange, cinnamon, and sarsaparilla; raspberry and cocoa disguise bitterness.

Because the taste buds are stimulated by substances in solution, the texture of foods affects their taste. The taste of liquids and foods of fluid consistency is more readily perceived than that of foods that must be chewed. The taste of poorly chewed food may not be sensed. Temperature also affects the taste of food. Not all taste stimulants are similarly affected by temperature. The range for measuring the influence of temperature is from 63°F to 108°F. As temperature rises from 63°F to body temperature (98.6°F), sensitivity to sweetness increases, then decreases. Sensitivity to salt and bitter tastes decreases over the temperature range. For most persons the sensitivity to the sour taste is not modified by temperature; for some persons response to sour is similar to the response to sweet (13). In food terms this means that apple pie eaten warm will taste sweeter than when eaten cold; that hot coffee will be less bitter than cold or iced coffee; that hot soup will taste less salty than cold soup; and that the sweetness of sugar added to tea will not be apparent until the tea has cooled in the mouth to approximately body temperature. Because temperature is a factor affecting the taste of food, we serve hot food hot and cold food cold; we also taste the food we are preparing at the temperatures at which dishes will be eaten.

Taste receptors fatigue or become insensitive to a stimulus that acts for some time. The degree and duration of fatigue depends on the intensity of the stimulus; the weaker the stimulus the more rapid is adaption or fatigue to it. Persistence of taste is longest for bitterness and shortest for sweetness; sourness and saltiness fall in between, with adaption to saltiness coming more quickly than adaptation to sourness. Adaption to one taste enhances the perception of another, as of the sourness of an apple after one eats a sweet. Some interactions of the tastes are interesting. A quinine solution effects fatigue to the bitter taste and reduces sensitivity to the salt, sour, and sweet tastes. Salt solutions reduce sensitivity to bitterness and acid; acid solutions reduce sensitivity to salt and bitter tastes; but both enhance sweetness. A weak sugar solution fatigues the sweet, salt, and sour sensations but a 20 per cent concentration enhances perception of all tastes. Practically, in cooking and food preparation we use a pinch of salt to enhance sweetness as of a melon, a frosting, or a pudding; sugar or a sweet sauce to reduce the saltiness of ham; sugar to modify the bitterness of coffee; a bit of sugar to reduce the saltiness of the soup; and sugar to reduce the sourness of a grapefruit. The particular taste of a food is the result of the concentration of the various taste stimulants and their interactions.

All persons are not equally sensitive in perception of taste, which may explain why saltcellars, sugar bowls, and vinegar cruets have been present on dining tables through the years. Further, it may explain why some persons use two lumps of sugar, whereas others use one lump to sweeten coffee to their satisfaction. Acuity of the sense of taste is not modified by smoking or hunger. It has been reported that acuity diminishes with age, with the perception of sourness being least affected (1).

The acceptance of food is affected by taste and aroma. Food combinations that introduce all the basic tastes and that do not have one in excess are pleasing. The sweet taste is highly prized. Saltiness, sourness, and touches of bitterness all contribute to the pleasures of eating.

The Mouthfeel of Foods

The feel of food in the mouth is the third component of flavor; it is extremely important in the acceptance of food and meals. Mechanical stimulation of sense organs present in the tongue, the gums, and the hard and soft palates results in the judgment of mouthfeel, that is, the texture of a food or beverage. Among the many adjectives we use to describe food textures are crisp, chewy, crunchy, creamy, dry, juicy, fibrous, greasy, hard, soft, moist, tender, tough, stringy, fluffy, oily, sticky, velvety, and gritty. For different foods we demand a different feel in the mouth. We want meat tender and juicy; bread, soft and moist; crackers, crisp and dry; pudding, smooth; and cake, velvety. Further, we like foods combined in ways to contrast texture—for example, crisp crackers with soup; crisp cookies with smooth, soft ice cream; mealy baked potatoes with chewy steak; crisp bacon with liver; crusty hard rolls with spaghetti and meat sauce; and so on. Certain ingredients are introduced in the preparation of foods and in the composing of combination dishes to produce desirable textures, for example, raising in rice pudding, slivered almonds with green beans, almonds in chicken chow mein, water chestnuts with brussels sprouts, green pepper in chicken à la king, and many others.

Some texture qualities like grittiness, fibrousness, toughness, mushiness, lumpiness, and dryness decrease food acceptability. The textures we like include smoothness, crispness, softness, lightness, moistness, flakiness, fluffiness, as well as others. However, softness and smoothness to the exclusion of other textures we reject, as evidenced in the dislike of soft and liquid diets. Control of food textures means control of changes that occur during the cooking and staling of foods. Undercooked foods and overcooked foods lack the sought-for textures. Staling results in dryness, hardness, toughness, and sogginess, depending on the food. Modern packaging attempts to prevent the changes in texture that decrease acceptability.

In menu-planning, the meal manager purposefully introduces liked textures and an assortment of textures. Following are some items that will be recognized as foods introduced as much for texture as for other reasons: salads of mixed greens, cole slaw, crusty rolls, mealy baked potatoes, crisp french fried potatoes, mashed potatoes, smooth and lump-free gravy, crisp fried chicken, and chocolate pudding with whipped topping.

In addition to receptors for taste and texture, there exist in the mouth receptors that are stimulated by substances present in food and condiments that affect the flavor experience. The irritants include pepper, ginger, cloves, radishes, horseradish, peppermint, and the tannins of tea and foods. Overstimulation by them brings pain; mild stimulation produces the burning sensation of pepper and hot curries, the cooling sensation of peppermint, and the astringency or puckeriness of tannins.

Flavor and the Auditory and Visual Senses

There is an auditory aspect of flavor. Certain sounds are associated with certain foods and may have a role in flavor perception for some persons: the crunchiness of celery, the fizz of champagne and carbonated beverages, the sizzling of steak, the perking of coffee, and so on (1).

Color is an important attribute in the judgment of food quality and food flavor. Foods with too little color or too much color in relation to a norm are judged adversely. Color is an aid to flavor perception in candies, jellies, syrups, and frozen desserts. Foods with the same amount of flavor are judged more or less flavorful as color is deep or pale (1).

Flavor Potentiation

Cooks have always added a "pinch of this and a pinch of that" to improve food flavors. Herbs, spices, onions, chocolate, vanilla, citrus rinds, and a whole host of other items are in use to add and improve flavor. The movement of cooking out of the home kitchen and into the factory has produced a body of knowledge on how to improve food flavors through the use of flavor enhancers and flavor potentiators. They are substances that do not have flavor of their own in the quantities in which they are used; but they do affect the ways in which flavor is perceived and they are elements of the stimuli that affect this perception. The flavor enhancer is an intensifier of flavor. A flavor potentiator is defined as a compound that by itself has no sensory effect but that exaggerates the effects of other agents in a system. According to Sjöström (15), monosodium glutamate is a flavor enhancer but it also meets several of the criteria for a flavor potentiator. In the dry form, MSG tastes sweet and salty; in solution, it has all four tastes. It acts on nerve endings in the mouth to affect the impression of basic tastes and on the tactile nerve endings to produce a satisfying feeling in the oral cavity. Flavor potentiators in commercial use include the 5'-nucleotides (disodium inosinate and disodium quanylate; dioctyl sodium sulfosuccinate (DSS); and maltol). The 5'-nucleotides enhance the flavor activity of MSG and spare the MSG requirement in many foods. Alone or in combination, these compounds are important in the production of convenience foods. Here are some of their effects: they protect "freshness" in processed fruits and vegetables; they cover the sour, grainy, and starchy flavor notes of cereals; they reduce the oily mouth effects of fats and oils; they enhance flavor and protect freshness in beverages, especially fruit beverages; they suppress sulfury notes in food flavors; they enhance meaty and brothy flavors, as in bouillon, canned meats, soups, and gravies; and in soups, they give a sense of greater viscosity.

FOODWAYS

Thus far, we have discovered that people eat what they like. They like what they know and what tastes good to them. The knowledge about foods and meals is established for each person by his culture, his family background, and his breadth of experiences, including his level of education. The culture distinguishes the edible from the inedible, for example, that chicken but not guinea pigs and peanuts but not acorns are food. Further, it establishes how food is prepared, that is, as soups, stews, or curries or boiled, fried, or roasted; it determines the number of meals as one, two, three, or more per day; and dictates how food shall be eaten, that is, with fingers, forks, or chopsticks. The foodways of persons in the United States differ within the framework of Western culture primarily, but also of other cultures, because families are of diverse national origins or subcultures, such as Swedish, Italian, German, Dutch, Cuban, Japanese, and Chinese. What a family considers food and enjoyable meals are established by such characteristics as ethnic origin, religious beliefs, region of residence, socioeconomic status, standard of living, and goals and ambitions.

The influence of these characteristics is so well known that they do not require discussion; however, attention should be called to the last one. The attachment of status and prestige meanings to some kinds of foods, certain dishes, and meals of certain kinds is not uncommon. Expensive foods; imported foods like Russian caviar and Roquefort cheese; rare foods like truffles; elaborate or time-consuming dishes to prepare like *Galentine de poulet*, veal Cordon Bleu, napoleons, Dobosch torte, and black-bottom pie; white foods in contrast to dark-colored foods; the serving of wines with meals; and the serving of meals in several courses make meals more or less enjoyable, depending on those for whom they are planned. The broader are experiences, the more people come to know about foods and meals. Travel away from home, whether to far places or to a college campus, adds to food experiences and ultimately affects food preferences and acceptances.

The foodways change. In the United States regional differences in food habits are less marked than formerly. Immigrants adopt new foods and dishes; they in turn introduce the indigenes to new food experiences.

During the 1960's and to some extent during the 1950's, people in the United States became increasingly interested in food per se. Fine restaurants flourished, especially those featuring nationality foods. Experts on food and cooking gained recognition and their names became as well known as those of politicians—James Beard, Poppy Cannon, Julia Childs, Craig Claiborne, Michael Field, Dione Lucas, and Helen McCully, to mention only a few. Cooking schools flourished. *The French Chef* and *The Galloping Gourmet* were top television programs. Cookbooks and books about food and wine were published in great number, and some became best sellers. Formerly little known dishes, such as quiche Lorraine, beef Stroganoff, beef sukiyaki, coq au vin, arroz paella, steak teriyaki, and crêpes, became common fare. The Swiss fondue and the Japanese tempura were adopted and redesigned. Pot-cooking at the table with each doing his own thing became a national fad. Exotic fruits and vegetables appeared in the supermarket.

At the same time, we began eating more meals away from home and more meals each day. Mid-morning and mid-afternoon coffee breaks and the evening snack were added to or eaten in place of the traditional three meals daily. The meal manager's tasks became simpler in many ways. But the fact remains, she does plan many meals; for these, she may have a higher set of standards than formerly.

GUIDELINES TO MEAL-PLANNING

No set of guidelines for planning meals will assure the acceptance and enjoyment of meals by all persons. Some guidelines are based on knowledge of food preferences and flavor perception; others, on recognition that man is not entirely rational or logical about his food and meals. One makes use of art, artifice, and science in meal-planning.

Because food is seen before it is tasted, the eyes have a role in food acceptance. They preview the eating experience. They reveal the identity of foods and dishes; they warn of the strange and unfamiliar. They prejudge the texture and the general quality of dishes. They perceive color. Meals are enthusiastically received or are rejected without tasting because of what the eyes have seen. Planners of meals deliberately plan so that meals have eye appeal. Meals must look good to be tasted, to be enjoyed.

Food and the Eyes

To have meals pass muster with the eyes, do include in meals some foods and dishes that are known and liked by the persons for whom the meals are planned. Introduce the new into meals in small ways and along with very well-liked foods and dishes. Second, have foods prepared in familiar ways: the pot roast with or without carrots and onions, the chicken fried with or without batter, the green beans seasoned with butter or crisp bits of bacon, depending on preference. Third, have the foods and dishes within a meal prepared in a different manner. Do not mash everything; do not cover several dishes with a sauce; do not fry several items. Next, have the different foods and dishes appear different. Do not have small whole potatoes, small whole stewed onions, and meat balls, or macaroni and cheese, French cut green beans, and cole slaw in the same meal. Everything looks too much alike. Have the items seen at one time differ in the shapes and sizes of pieces. Be sure that food looks like what it is; there is little reason to have a tomato look like a rose, a banana-pineapple salad look like a candlestick, or a cake look like a football unless these are for parties for children. Make certain that every constituent of a dish, other than seasonings, can be identified. Dislike of such combination dishes as stews and casserole dishes may have been born out of inability to identify the constituents and hence to know precisely what was being eaten. For the best appearance, have the different items within a food mixture sized and shaped differently. The dish will look better if it does not appear that everything was chopped up at one and the same time. Limit the number of mixed dishes within a meal. For people in the United States, do not serve a meal composed of lamb stew and vegetables, with Waldorf salad, and a mixed fruit cup for dessert; the meal includes too many combination dishes.

Last, use plenty of color. Man likes color in his clothing, in his surroundings, and especially in his food, although he also prizes whiteness, but for reasons other than color. The color of food assists us in identifying food of poor quality: the underripe tomato, the overripe peach, overcooked green beans, and overgrilled steak. Color assists us in identifying food flavors. Some colors stimulate the autonomic nervous system, of which the digestive system is a part; they are yellow, orange, orange-red, bright green, tan, and brown. Purple, red-purple, yellow-green, olive and mustardy tones, and gray are not pleasing (3). We like color and color variety in meals, but we do not like our foods colored artificially. We will eat blueberries but not blue bread, strawberries but not red mashed potatoes. The artificial coloring of food is best limited to such uses as heightening natural colors, like the addition of red color to a cherry pie filling or a strawberry gelatin dessert. Colored frostings on cakes and bright red maraschino cherries we accept because the color is part of our concept of the food. Colored candies we like but not colored mayonnaise or cream cheese.

Some thought should always be given to the choice of the dinnerware on which food combinations are served. Modern ceramic and plastic dinnerwares are bright in color and bold in design; they look magnificent on the colorful linens on which they are so often displayed. However, their function is in the service of food and the food is overwhelmed and disadvantaged by their color sometimes. Salads look good on green plates. White, pink, aqua, pastel green, and yellow are the colors acclaimed as best in food service (3). Black linens and dinnerware are a dubious choice of background for dining.

Food and the Senses That Savor It

To maximize the enjoyment of eating, allow plenty of time for dining —flavor perception takes time. Consider the temperature of foods, the tastes, the mouthfeel or textures, and the aroma of foods. Introduce all the tastes; use them judiciously. The sweet taste is the one to be watched. We like it, but we sometimes overdo it. In general, keep it for the dessert course. Jellies, preserves, and pickled fruits are sweet, sour, and bitter. We use them along with meats. Pickles and pickle relishes are sour and sweet. Olives are salty. Oil and vinegar dressings are sour and can be made salty to enhance slightly bitter greens.

Introduce a variety of textures into a meal and use the liked ones, such as smoothness, crispness, moistness, and chewiness. Use crisp salads and crusty breads to contrast the smoothness and softness of mashed potatoes, meat loaves, macaroni and cheese, or a salmon casserole. Use a crisp cookie to contrast with the velvetiness of ice cream.

Introduce extremes in temperature; have something hot with a cold meal and something cold with a hot meal. Some persons like cold sherbet with a hot entree. Serve hot food hot and cold food cold for optimum perception of food flavors and the tongue taste of foods.

Include a variety of flavors within a meal, so that the organ for perception of aroma does not fatigue. Because the organ of smell adapts to one odor quickly, a meal composed of only one or two dishes may make dull eating. Food flavors range from the very intense to the very delicate. Foods that have intense flavors include garlic and onions; the well-ripened cheeses like Limburger; sauerkraut; many herbs; spices; some sausages; and some kinds of fish. Foods that are delicate in flavor include the staple foods: rice, potatoes, bread, and other cereals; skim milk and cottage cheese; meats like chicken and veal; vegetables like peas, corn, squash, and cucumber; and fruits of delicate flavor, including the avocado, the papaya, the pear, and the banana (14). The blending of flavors in creating dishes and planning meals is an art. Unfortunately, not all, even experts, agree on the rightness of flavor combinations. Individual differences in the ability to perceive tastes and aromas, in past experiences, and in personal preferences would explain lack of universal agreement. Flavor preferences are probably culturally determined to no small degree.

A widely accepted principle of menu-writing suggests that mild flavors come first in a meal, strong ones later. Thus, a meal of several courses traditionally begins with consommé, proceeds through fish to meat or fowl, and ends with cheese and crackers. Few homemakers plan such meals, but this is a useful suggestion for first courses. Keep them mild in flavor, particularly if the main course will consist of delicately flavored foods, such as fowl with wild rice, scalloped oysters, or veal with mushrooms. Mildly flavored foods suitable in the first course include, in addition to fruit juices and thin soups, crackers spread with mild cheese spreads, olives, delicately flavored fish, liver, and meat pastes, and so forth. Highly seasoned foods and strong cheese are more suitably served in later courses, with cocktails, or in cold suppers, unless they are eaten in small quantities.

The real art of menu-planning is in the blending of flavors within a course and within a meal. Although flavor relationships are not well understood, three seem apparent. Some flavors enhance others—butter on bread and vegetables, horseradish on ham, and cream on strawberries. Some flavors mask others, and their forceful character must always be kept in mind. Peanut butter is one; nothing can compete with it. To serve a peanut butter sandwich with cream of potato soup is to lose the flavor of the soup; the sandwich should follow the soup. The blue cheeses mask the mild flavors of the lettuce, watercress, and avocado they so often dress in salads. The decision on whether or not to use a blue cheese dressing depends upon what one wants tasted: if it is the salad greens, the answer is no; if it is the cheese, yes. Mushrooms served with pork sausage can scarcely be appreciated; whereas mushrooms served with veal or chicken will be truly enjoyed. Just as you lose the flavor of the meat in a hamburger if you cover the hamburger with chopped onion, a glob of mustard, a shake of catsup, and a spoonful of chopped dill pickle, so can you miss the flavor of new peas if they are served with Polish sausage. Those who eat many meals in restaurants soon learn the cover-up value of sauces and condiments.

Some flavors are pleasing when eaten together; others are less so. By and large, the traditional combinations that have stood the test of time can be depended on to please. Included in this long list are spinach with tongue, peas with lamb, cucumbers with fish, tomatoes with egg and fish, asparagus with cheese dishes, cabbage with corned beef, onions with liver, wild rice with poultry, carrots and onions with pot roast of beef, and cinnamon with apples. The planner of meals should not feel limited to the use of these; rather, she should try different combinations of flavors. Those that she finds good can be continued; those she finds poor can be abandoned. Of all the cooks in the world, French chefs have best understood the art of blending flavors; perhaps that is why French cooking is so prestigious.

Few individuals are sensitive to subtle flavor relationships; just as few are sensitive to the qualities that make one painting a work of art and another just one more picture. Yet everyone enjoys some meals more than others, even when the quality of the food is the same. Could it be that careful blending of flavors makes one meal taste better than another? The homemaker who wishes to plan pleasing and satisfying meals will consider flavors, making certain that the ones she wants appreciated are not lost because stronger ones mask them.

Planning a Meal

The best menus are planned around a single food item, either a food like roast beef or baked beans, or a combination dish like tamale pie or chicken chop suey. This item becomes the focal point of the meal and all else either is subordinate to it or complements it. Usually meals are planned around the main dish of the main course, but they could be planned around salad, dessert, or any other dish. All other foods and dishes are then thoughtfully selected so that they enhance that important dish. Food textures, tastes, aromas, and colors are all manipulated to make the most of that dish and to give pleasure in eating. Desserts should always be planned in relation to the main course. When the latter is light, the dessert can be sweet and filling; when the main course is rich and filling, the dessert should be light and possibly tart. The first course should be planned in relation to both main and dessert courses, but it should be light—it should whet the appetite and not satisfy it.

The sequence of decisions in planning a meal are something like this. First, decide on the main dish of the main course. Next, select the staple to serve with it, like rice, potatoes, bulgur, or Yorkshire pudding; however, such a staple is sometimes omitted and two vegetables are included. Next, select the vegetable or vegetables; choose them for texture, aroma, and color. Then, decide on a salad; the best salads are simple mixtures of greens with or without added vegetables or fruits. Dress the salad with a tart dressing. Lastly, plan dessert and the first course simultaneously to avoid repetitions in foods and flavors.

Summary Guidelines to Meal-Planning

1. People eat what they like. Include in meals the foods and dishes they know. Prepare them in the ways people know.

2. Include foods of different colors. Preferred colors are yellow, orange, red-orange, pink, bright green, browns, and white. Use purple, yellow-green, olive and mustardy tones, and gray sparingly. Use artificial color only to enhance natural colors.

3. Limit the number of mixtures, that is, combination dishes, in meals. Always have the ingredients of mixtures identifiable.

4. Plan so that the mass, shapes, and sizes of food items differ.

5. Introduce several food textures so that the feel in the mouth changes during eating.

6. Introduce all tastes. Use the sweet taste sparingly until toward the end of a meal; balance it with the other tastes.

7. Avoid repetitions of foods and modes of preparing foods.

8. Introduce several food flavors. Avoid repetition of similar flavors. Combine foods in accordance with preferred flavor combinations.

Summary. In summary, the goal of satisfying meals is not easy of attainment. It must be achieved within the limits imposed by planned uses of money and time. Not all persons like the same foods and the same meals. Foods and meals are prejudged before they are tasted; they must look good, but this does not imply elaborate garnishing. Flavor perception is a complex of sensations; acuity of perception differs among persons. In planning meals, use art, artifice, and science to have food both look and taste good.

References Cited

1. Amerine, M. A., R. M. Pangborn, and E. B. Roessler, *Principles of Sensory Evaluation of Food*. New York: Academic Press, 1965.

2. Amoore, J. E., "Stereochemical Theory of Olfaction," in *Handbook of Food Additives*, edited by Thomas E. Furia. Cleveland: Chemical Rubber Company, 1968, Chapter 4.

3. Birren, F., "Color and Human Appetite," *Journal of Food Technology* 17:45 (1963).

4. Bryan, M., and M. Lowenberg, "The Father's Influence on Young Children's Food Habits," *Journal of the American Dietetic Association* 34:30 (1958).

5. Eindhoven, S., and D. R. Peryam, "Measurements of Preferences for Food Combinations," *Journal of Food Technology* 13:379 (1959).

6. *Gallup Survey—The National Poll of Patron Preferences, Prejudices, and Trends,* Volumes 1 and 2. Madison, Wisconsin: *Food Service Magazine* (1967, 1969).

7. Hall, I. S., and C. S. Hall, "A Study of Disliked and Unfamiliar Foods," *Journal of the American Dietetic Association* 15:540 (1939).

8. Knickrehm, Marie E., et al., "Acceptance of Menu Items by College Students," *Journal of the American Dietetic Association* 55:117 (1969).

9. Moore, M. E., and J. E. Pond, "Dessert Choices of Southern Urban Families," *Journal of Home Economics* 58:659 (1966).

10. "News to Note," *Journal of Food Technology* 23:1360 (1969).

11. Peryam, David R., et al., *Food Preferences of Men in the U.S. Armed Forces,* Department of the Army, Quartermaster Research and Engineering Command, Quartermaster and Container Institute for the Armed Forces, Chicago (1960).

12. Pilgrim, F. J., "What Foods Do People Accept or Reject?" *Journal of the American Dietetic Association* 38:439 (1961).

13. Rietz, C. A., *A Guide to the Selection, Combination, and Cooking of Foods, Vol. 1: Selection and Combination.* Westport, Conn.: The Avi Publishing Company, Inc. (1961).

14. Rietz, C. A., and J. A. Wanderstock, *A Guide to the Selection, Combination, and Cooking of Foods, Vol. 2: Formulation and Cooking of Foods.* Westport, Conn.: The Avi Publishing Company, Inc. (1965).

15. Sjöström, Loren B., "Flavor Potentiators," in *Handbook of Food Additives.* Cleveland: Chemical Rubber Company, 1970, Chapter 13.

16. VanRiter, I. G., "Acceptance of Twenty-Six Vegetables," *Journal of Home Economics* 48:771 (1956).

17. Zunich, Michael, and Anne Carol Fults, "Food Preferences of Children from Lower-Socioeconomic Groups—A Geographic Study," *Journal of Home Economics* 61:47 (1969).

Chapter 15

Meal Management Goals— Controlled Use of Time

Four general goals for meal managers have been established. Three have been discussed: good nutrition, planned spending, and satisfying meals. Although we have left the discussion of the use of time and energy until last, it has the first place in the management plans of many homemakers. Perhaps it would have been wise to discuss it first, for often all else hinges on the meal manager's decisions on her use of time and energy. If she cannot or will not give much time and energy to meals, then they are what they are and they cost what they cost for that reason.

Some studies that have been made of the use of time by housewives for household work and food-related activities are summarized in Table 15–1. As would be anticipated, full-time homemakers spend more total time on household tasks than employed homemakers. But what would not be anticipated is that the science and technology of the past decades have not altered the workload of the housewife. In fact, her workload has expanded, probably, because she has less paid help and less assistance from children than earlier in the century. According to these studies she is spending a third to almost half of the time spent in household work on food-related activities. Actually, it is more time than she spends on any other household task. Though it has been established that husbands assist with household work, the average time given to meal-related activities by them was six to twelve minutes per day, depending on the weekly hours of the housewife's employment outside the home (10).

A survey made in 1968, by Social Research, Incorporated for *Better Homes and Gardens* (12) suggests a division of time use in food-related activities. Data were derived from a survey of one thousand homemakers and are presented as median hours spent. Data are recapitulated here.

419

Time Spent in Average Week	Median Hours
Shopping for food	1.7
Putting away purchases	.5
Baking	1.8
Cooking	9.0
Setting table	.9
Washing dishes and tidying up	7.1
Planning meals	.9
Total	21.9

Of the total of 21.9 hours, 17.9 hours were spent in food preparation and dishwashing and tidying up. These are the big time-costs of meal management.

Table 15–1.   *Time Used by Urban Housewives for Household Work and Food-Related Activities*[1]

Studies	Full-Time Homemakers[2]		Employed Homemakers[2]	
	Hours per Week All House- hold Work	Hours per Week Food Activities	Hours per Week All House- hold Work	Hours per Week Food Activities
USDA, 1920 (4) [3]	47.1	13.3	—	—
USDA, 1944 (7)	47.1	14.1	—	—
Wiegand, 1952 (11)	51.8	18.2	28.7	13.3
Anderson, 1960 (1)	49.0	20.0	31.0	15.0
Bailey, 1962 (2)	—	25.2	—	19.53
Walker, 1969 (9)	56.0	16.1	37.1	11.2
Hall, 1970 (4)	54.0	19.6	42.0	16.8

[1]It is possible that this includes only food preparation and dishwashing in some studies, but it also includes shopping and care of food in others.

[2]Classified as *full-time* if homemaker worked 0–14 hours per week for pay and as *employed* if she worked 15 hours or more per week for pay.

[3]No distinction made on employment status; probably full-time housewives.

Another study (6) estimated that of the 99.6 hours that the typical non-working housewife spent per week on household tasks, 23.8 hours were devoted to meal-related tasks: 1.2 as dietitian, 3.3 as food buyer, 13.1 as cook, and 6.2 as dishwasher. The money value assigned to these tasks was per hour: dietitian, $4.50; food buyer, $3.50; cook, $3.25; and dishwasher, $2.00. The dollar value of the total hours that the typical nonworking housewife spent on meal-related tasks was $71.92.

Until well into the twentieth century, the affluent purchased time through the hire of servants. The affluent housewife of the 1970's is forced to seek other ways of acquiring time.' Convenience foods, fast foods, and dining out are time-savers, they are also dollar-users. Because dollars are not always available, it is necessary to explore other ways of controlling the use of time. In the discussion that follows energy will not be singled out for attention. Except for the elderly and the unwell, the resource of energy is a less worrisome problem than is time. We have the habit of speaking of them as one and are likely to conclude that time-saving means energy-saving and, contrariwise, that time-consuming tasks are energy-consuming.

The amount of time the meal responsibility requires is established by such factors as family size; standards for meals; food preferences; the efficiency of the kitchen and its equipment; the knowledge, skills, and abilities of the meal manager; and her dollar budget for food. The control of time use depends on knowledge of the diverse ways in which time is spent on meals.

How Time and Energy Are Used in Meal Management

Following is a listing of the ways we use time in meal management. Not all meal managers use time in all of these ways, nor does a given meal manager use time in all of these ways every week.

1.   Planning menus for meals; this may include time looking for ideas in books and magazines. Planning may precede or follow shopping or both. It may also occur during shopping.
2.   Planning shopping; this may include time spent in looking at store ads for information, for specials, for coupons, or for ideas.
3.   Shopping.
4.   Care and storage of food.
5.   Meal preparation, that is, actual cooking and baking; may include time spent in looking for recipes.
6.   Setting the table; however, this is usually done during the period of food preparation.
7.   Waiting on the table.
8.   Clear-up and clean-up after meals.
9.   Care of the kitchen and its furnishings.
10.   Care of the dining area and its furnishings.

It is an impressive listing of activities and provides opportunities for leaks in the use of time. It also provides opportunities for controlling time use because minutes saved from a few activities each day will add up to hours in due time.

The meal manager's problem in setting limits to the use of time for meals is complex. The best approach to the problem is to discover how much time is being used and how that time is put to use. One may discover that too much time is being spent in shopping, or too much time is spent in decision-making about menus, or that too much time is spent in cooking. When excessive uses of time are recognized, it is possible to seek alternatives to the use of time and to seek ways for saving time. We shall discuss the former first and then discuss ways of maximizing time use.

ALTERNATIVES TO THE USE OF TIME

Alternatives to the use of time include money; knowledge, skills, and abilities; and lastly, time itself. That is, all of the homemaker's resources are alternatives for the use of time; the extent to which she can use them depends on her supply.

Money

Money buys time easily and in many ways. Unfortunately, the supply of money is often too limited for many persons to rely heavily on it as a time-saver. Here are some ways to buy time.

First, and most obvious, is the purchase of ready-made foods and dishes, such as carry-in fried chicken, ready-baked pastries, ready-to-heat dinners and breakfasts, mixes, easy-use ingredients for cooking (such as gravy mixes and instants), and so on *ad infinitum*. According to a *Better Homes and Gardens* survey, an average of 58 per cent of the respondents to a question-naire said that the time-saving characteristic of convenience foods was the most important; only 24 per cent said that the work-saving factor was the most important. Sixty-five per cent of the working housewives in contrast to 55 per cent of the nonworking housewives said time-saving was most important (3). Time-saving products come and go on the market. Those that we have found suitable stay; we spend dollars for them and buy the time we would otherwise spend in cooking and baking. All meal managers cannot use convenience foods extensively; either they do not have the dollars or there is opposition to their use in the home. The money cost of convenience and the time-saving value of convenience have been discussed (see pages 135 through 142). When the supplies of money and time are limited, it becomes imperative that the convenience forms bought provide maximum convenience, that is, time saved, for the dollars spent. The increased spending for baked products during the decade 1955–1965 is evidence that housewives recognize how well their dollars buy time in those purchases.

Second, money can buy time and energy in the kitchen by being used to make it a more efficient place in which to work. An expensive investment might involve the total remodeling and updating of the kitchen. However, there are many small investments that can improve the efficiency of a kitchen. New and/or better appliances, such as a dishwasher, a garbage disposer, an electric mixer, an electric or battery-operated cutting knife, and a pressure cooker, can save time. Not all appliances are equally valuable to all homemakers, because each cooks and works differently in kitchens that may appear quite similar. Certainly, no appliance or gadget should be purchased until the would-be purchaser has studied it to discover what it can do for her. New and/or better cookware, such as pots and pans with tight-fitting lids and/or no-stick linings, and those that are matched to the size of range units, may take some of the risks out of cooking and may save time. Good tools for preparing food, like good measuring equipment, cutting knives that hold a sharp edge, a cutting board, kitchen scissors, tongs, and effective tools for stirring food, save time. Paper goods, aluminum foil, film in rolls, film bags, throwaway cookware, and special cleansers and polishes all save time. Unquestionably, all throwaway items should be conservatively used in the interest of ecology.

The improvement of storage facilities for appliances, cookware, kitchen gadgets and tools, and food can make work in the kitchen easier and save time. Portable storage cabinets, portable storage shelves, on-the-door storage units, and the peg board that permits within-arm's-reach storage of frequently used equipment are some suggestions in this category. Easy-care appointments for the dining table, such as no-iron cloths and mats, paper napkins, stainless steel flatware that requires little care, and plastic or glass-ceramic dinnerware and plastic beverageware that can be quickly handled without danger of breakage, are all ways of spending dollars and buying time. Lastly, money buys time when it hires help to come in and prepare and serve meals and clean up after them; and to clean the kitchen and the dining area. There are many ways that dollars buy and save time. The meal manager uses dollars to help her control her uses of time and energy; how extensively they can be used depends on her supply. When she decides to limit the use of dollars for meals, she cannot at the same time decide to limit the use of time and energy. She must spend the latter to compensate for limited use of dollars.

Knowledge, Skills, and Abilities

The knowledge, skills, and abilities that the meal manager brings to the meal responsibility are among her most valuable resources for controlling the use of time. Among her assets are her knowledge of when to shop, where to shop, how to shop, how to choose from among the eight thousand or more items on the shelves of the supermarket, how much items cost, how to cook, what cooks quickly and what requires long cooking, how to organize the kitchen for efficient work or step-saving, how to schedule the preparation of meals, how to plan meals that satisfy, and so on. Much is gained through experience; much can be acquired through effort: the use of books, magazines, radio and television, and the help of friends, relatives, and neighbors. Knowledge, skills, and abilities are alternatives for time and also for money.

Time

Lastly, time can be invested to save time or control the use of time. A constructive use of time is to study and analyze one's own use of time; such a study points to leaks in time use and suggests ways of saving time. The use of time in planning ahead is rewarding. Time spent in organizing the kitchen into an efficient place in which to work is well-invested time. A kitchen may have to be arranged and rearranged several times before the most effective plan of arrangement is achieved. The maximum use of time in the kitchen to produce as much food as possible is desirable. Prepare a roast large enough for two or more meals; make up juice for tomorrow's breakfast, sandwich fillings for tomorrow's packed lunches, salad or dessert for tomorrow's dinner while preparing and cleaning up after dinner today. Make two pies and freeze one; make enough of a favorite casserole for two meals and freeze half. There is much that can be done here. Time in the kitchen is both busy time and watching time; often the latter is wasted. Use it for food production. Lastly, time spent in menu-making per se can earn the meal manager time. It permits efficient shopping, the strategic placing of thirty-minute meals, and the investment of time in cooking when it is available.

Some Deterrents to Time-Saving.   Not every meal manager can reduce the use of time for meals and not all would wish to. Malloch (5) in a study of the most- and least-liked household tasks found that cooking was a most-liked task. Ronald et al. (7) found that 43 per cent of the housewives interviewed rated cooking as their most-liked household task. Many persons like to cook; for them cooking and serving meals is what gardening or flower arrangement may be to others. Possibly the first deterrent to saving time is simply the lack of a desire to do so. Some wants and needs of some homemakers are satisfied through the various decisions and activities that meal management provides: the need to be creative, or the need of a reputation as a good cook, or the joy in the approval of spouse and children of the meals served. Do-it-yourself cooking requires time and energy and those who want it that way cannot save as much time as others can. Family food preferences may also be a deterrent to time-saving. Those who were born after World War II have adapted to instants and ready-mades. Those who are older remember homemade dishes; they are often adamant to change.

The lack of knowledge and skills precludes time-saving by beginners;

however, conscious effort to acquire knowledge and skills can result in ever-diminishing investments of time in meal management. Lastly, the most significant deterrent to reduction in the use of time is lack of money. Much can be accomplished to control the use of time without it, but having money to purchase some convenience foods and improvements in the kitchen is a boon.

How to Make the Most of Your Time

The following statements summarize what has been said and at the same time give emphasis to guidelines in the use of time, the resource that so many feel they have too little of.

1.   Study and observe your uses of time: know how you use it, then seek ways to curtail its use if necessity demands.

2.   Set limits to the use of your time; budget it just as you budget your dollars. Spend it extravagantly one day, then stingily the next several days —that is, plan and serve thirty-minute meals as well as meals that require long cooking.

3.   Use other resources as alternatives to time to the extent their supply permits.

4.   Become proficient in the art of timing or scheduling the production of meals (see Chapter 16).

5.   Keep records of good menus, recipes, buffet arrangements, brand names of good products, names of satisfactory cuts of meat, and any kind of information you use. File it systematically. Meal managers use a lot of time seeking information that they could have at their fingertips.

6.   Keep a bulletin board in the kitchen; note needs as they arise.

7.   Limit your shopping trips to the minimum consistent with storage facilities. Shopping can be a thief of time.

8.   Learn the floor plan of the market(s) you patronize. Order your shopping list to your traffic route through the market.

9.   Buy the largest size that you can conveniently store and use. Buy in multiples the items you use often.

10.   Put everything you use routinely within your easy reach. Put staples and things you use less often on the hard-to-reach high or low shelves of your cupboards.

11.   Hang things up. Hang on a pegboard all the gadgets and pots and pans that you use often, especially knives. If you have two working areas in the kitchen, have equipment in both areas.

12.   Store supplies where you use them.

13.   Use the oven for as much cooking as is practical: soups, stews, chili, in fact, any dish that cooks slowly. In the oven, it requires no watching and no active time.

14. When you prepare something, make enough for two or more meals; have all cooking time pay dividends.

Finally, to control the use of time, be receptive to new ideas. Try new menus, new recipes, new methods of cooking and baking, and new products. Change old habits by adapting to the new when goals require it.

REFERENCES CITED

1. Anderson, E. D., and C. Fitzsimmons, "Use of Time and Money by Employed Homemakers," *Journal of Home Economics* 52:453 (1960).
2. Bailey, Betty W., *Food and Management Practices of Employed and Unemployed Homemaker Families*, Bulletin N.S. 98, Georgia Agricultural Experiment Stations, University of Georgia College of Agriculture, Athens, Georgia (June 1962).
3. *Better Homes and Gardens Consumer Questionnaire*, A Better Homes and Gardens Report, in *Indices*, Des Moines, Iowa (1970).
4. Hall, Florence R., and Marguerite P. Schroeder, "Time Spent on Household Tasks," *Journal of Home Economics* 62:23 (1970).
5. Malloch, Francille, "Characteristics of Most and Least Liked Household Tasks," *Journal of Home Economics* 55:413 (1963).
6. Porter, Sylvia, "Housewives' Worth Defined," St. Petersburg Times, February 14, 1972, p. 3-D.
7. "Research on Time Spent in Homemaking, An Annotated List of References," ARS 62-15, Agricultural Research Service, United States Department of Agriculture, Washington, D.C. (1967).
8. Ronald, Patricia, et al., "Rating Scale for Household Tasks," *Journal of Home Economics* 63:177 (1971).
9. Walker, Kathryn, "Homemaking Still Takes Time," *Journal of Home Economics* 61:621 (1961).
10. ———, "Time-Use Patterns for Household Work Related to Homemakers' Employment," Talk at the 1970 National Agriculture Outlook Conference, Washington, D.C., Agricultural Research Service, United States Department of Agriculture, Washington, D.C.
11. Wiegand, E., *Use of Time by Full-Time and Part-Time Homemakers in Relation to Home Management*, Memoir 330, New York State College of Home Economics, Cornell University, Ithaca, New York (July 1954).
12. "Women and Food," A Better Homes and Gardens Report, in *Indices*, Des Moines, Iowa (1970).

Chapter 16

Timing Meal Preparation

Meal preparation is doing many small tasks sequentially and simultaneously to the end that arrangements for dining will have been completed and all dishes of a meal will be at or near the peak of perfection and ready to serve at the desired moment in time. This is not an easy accomplishment. The question is what comes first, second, and last.

To time the preparation of meals means to order tasks systematically and assign a time for doing each. This ordering is decision-making and precedes action. Experienced meal managers do the ordering of tasks as they proceed with meal preparation; their knowledge and skills permit it, because they have established work habits. The beginner in meal management may acquire the knowledge and skills by trial-and-error learning; however, she will acquire both more quickly by learning how to anticipate and schedule the tasks essential for the preparation of a given meal; that is, she can learn how to order and time the production of a meal.

There are at least four reasons for developing skill in timing meal preparation. The first is to have all tasks completed at the desired and designated hour. For example, the potatoes mashed at the moment the steak is done, or the table set and the salad ready so that last-minute attention can be directed to the mashing of potatoes, the broiling of steak, and the preparing of a vegetable for serving. A second reason is to have the different dishes of a meal of excellent eating quality. Some foods lose quality when held; they dry out, harden, or toughen. For many dishes there is a peak of perfection. We try for that moment. The third reason assumes that, in the long run, the total time spent in the preparation of a meal is less when tasks are carried out in a directed order than when they are done in a hit-and-miss fashion. Our last reason assumes that the preparation of meals is less frustrating when one proceeds with the knowledge that all tasks have been anticipated and planned for. It is nerve-wracking to discover that one forgot to start cooking the peas, to make the salad, or even to set the table.

THE CHARACTERISTICS OF TIME SCHEDULES

First, the schedule that results from ordering tasks differs with menus. Some begin with cooking; others begin with setting the table. Some, such as that for the thirty-minute dinner presented later in this chapter, concentrate the cooking in the twenty minutes just before food goes to table. Other menus have long-cooking items; the meal manager can leave the kitchen for some time after they begin to cook, as she can when using the second menu presented in this chapter. These latter menus result in broken schedules; they start, stop, and start again. In between these extremes is the menu that includes fried chicken or braised porkchops, some item that comes first in the schedule of tasks and all other tasks can be accomplished within the time allocated for the cooking of that item. What we are really saying is that there is no one schedule that works for all meals; schedules are tailored to menus. This fact makes it possible for the meal manager to tailor her menus to her established limits for the use of time.

Second, the schedules of different homemakers for identical menus will differ to some extent; they will reflect differences in skill in the kitchen, the efficiency and organization of kitchens, and the size of the families for which meals are being prepared. Further, schedules reflect the personality of the homemaker, her idiosyncrasies and habits. Third, the time schedules of different persons planning the same meal for the same number of persons will have some constants: the specific hours when different foods are put to cook on the range or in the oven; and certain tasks like setting the table, making the salad, and placing the dinner plates to warm. Last, a schedule should be specific and detailed enough so that, as with a bus schedule, one knows where one is at a given moment. To carry the analogy further, a followed schedule should bring one to the defined destination.

TIMING MEAL PREPARATION

Essentials for timing the preparation of meals, that is, making a schedule for their preparation, are

1. Either a cookbook or a recipe or knowledge of the time required for the cooking of the different menu items.
2. Some ability to estimate the time required to accomplish the different tasks required in preparing menu items for cooking and serving and in completing preparations for dining.
3. A pad and pencil for step-wise problem-solving.
4. A clock for careful timing.

Steps in Preparing a Schedule

1. List the items of menus one under the other on the left side of a sheet of tablet paper. Add table setting. Itemize the tasks of table setting if they are not yet habit. For example, you might include under it: lay flatware and napkins, place filled tumblers, place bread and butter, and so on.

2. Record in four vertical columns the estimated time in hours and minutes that each item will require (a) for preparation for cooking, (b) for actual cooking, (c) for preparation for serving, and (d) for totals of these estimates. Estimate realistically, especially for small tasks, such as the time you will require to make a salad, trim fresh green beans, or peel potatoes. See Table 16–1.

3. Arrange all items in decreasing order of total time required as in Table 16–2. This listing gives you two kinds of information: first, some idea of the total meal-preparation time and, second, the order in which different dishes of the menu should be prepared. Very often a meal may be prepared and the table set within the time assigned to the dish requiring the longest preparation and cooking time. Frequently, as when a stew or Swiss steak is to be prepared, time in the kitchen is much less than the cooking time of the dish requiring the longest preparation and cooking time. Again, when cooking time is short for all dishes, as it would be if

TABLE 16–1. *Steps 1 and 2 in Timing Meal Preparation*

Menu Items	Prepare for Cooking	Allow for Cooking	Prepare for Serving	Total Time in Minutes
	Time in Minutes to			
Broiled sirloin steak or hamburger patties	5	15[1]	5[2]	25
Mashed potatoes	5	5	2	10
Peas	5	10	2	15
Tossed mixed greens	—	—	5[3]	5
Bread and butter	—	—	4	—
Milk	—	—	4	—
Ice cream	—	—	5	—
Cookies	—	—	4	—
Coffee	—	5	5	5
Table setting	—	—	10	10

[1]Thickness of one inch.
[2]Includes time for serving up potatoes and peas also.
[3]Assumes greens and dressing are ready for use.
[4]Included in table setting.
[5]Done between courses of meal; coffee is an instant product.

steak were to be broiled and frozen vegetables used, time in the kitchen will be longer than the longest required cooking period.

4.   The last and final step is the ordering of the tasks. Begin with the established hour for dining and clock cooking times backward from this; for example, if dining will be at seven and one hour is required for frying chicken, put the chicken to cook at 5:50. This one hour and ten minutes allows one hour for cooking and about ten minutes for serving up the chicken and making gravy. Calculating in this fashion, establish the time to put to cook and to remove from the range or oven all the other items that are to be cooked. Remember that food is best when it is just done and when it is served at the appropriate temperature.

Now decide when you must enter the kitchen. Next work in and around the already established tasks, the various other tasks you must accomplish. See Table 16–3.

To illustrate, we will go through the four described steps for the following menu.

A Thirty-Minute Dinner

Broiled Sirloin Steak or Hamburger Patties[1]
Mashed Potatoes[2]   Buttered Peas[3]
Tossed Mixed Greens
Bread and Butter
Milk
Ice Cream   Cookies[4]
Coffee[5]

---

[1]Choice would depend on budget for food.
[2]Use potato flakes.
[3]Frozen product.
[4]Purchased ready-made.
[5]Instant.

As the name of the menu implies, the meal is quick and easy to prepare. It is the kind of meal a young homemaker who works outside the home might serve. Table 16–1 shows steps 1 and 2. The items of the menu are listed, and estimates of the time required for cooking the meat, the potatoes, and the vegetable, and for other tasks, are given. The estimates are based on the assumption that the meal manager is preparing the meal for two persons and that the prepared foods are served onto two dinner plates.

In Table 16–2, the menu items and the meal tasks are listed in descending order of the total time estimated. It is the kind of menu that telescopes cooking into a short period of time. Further, it prepares foods that must go from range to table quickly for good eating. It is the kind of meal for which one does almost all the tasks but the cooking first, then cooks the food. The total time is so short that water, milk, and salad can go to the table as soon as prepared, although one might wish to chill the salad until the last minute as the completed schedule suggests.

TABLE 16–2. *Step 3 in Timing Meal Preparation—Tasks Listed in Descending Order of Total Time Required*

Tasks	Total Time in Minutes
Meat	25
Peas	15
Potatoes	10
Table setting	10
Tossed mixed greens	5

To prepare the final schedule, the time of dining has been set at 6:30. And although dinner is called thirty-minute we are allowing the meal manager forty-five minutes in the kitchen. We can assume her kitchen is small; she does not take many steps between sink and range, refrigerator and sink, and range and refrigerator. Below we have worked out the schedule for the food preparation tasks of the schedule; it is helpful to do this first, then schedule other tasks around these. Table 16–3 shows the entire plan of work—one that permits the meal manager to move leisurely.

6:10 Place steak or patties under broiler unit and set water to heat for cooking peas and preparing potatoes.

6:15 Put peas to cook.

6:20 Or earlier, turn steak or patties. Prepare potatoes and leave on warm unit.

6:30 Approximately, serve meat, potatoes, and peas onto two warm dinner plates.

It is best to limit specific timings in a schedule to critical moments in food preparation; too many are confusing. It would be dishonest not to admit that the best of plans can go awry. A dish may cook in less than the anticipated time; then either one holds it or modifies the rest of the schedule. Or a dish may not be done in the anticipated time, in which case one can hold all else and wait.

TABLE 16–3.   *The Time Schedule for Preparing the Meal*

5:45	Line small broiler pan with aluminum foil. Place steak or patties on it.
	Measure out peas and put into small saucepan.
	Prepare salad, dress, toss, serve onto plates, chill.
	Measure out potato flakes; set by range.
	Place two dinner plates on range where they will become warm and will be available at serving time.
	Get out bowls and underliner plates for ice cream and set on counter near refrigerator. Put cookies on plates. Place cups and saucers on counter near range.
	Set table, including placing bread and butter, pouring water, pouring milk.
	Have milk and butter at range for peas and potatoes.
6:10	Place steak or patties under broiling unit and water on for peas and potatoes.
6:15	Put peas to cook.
6:20	Or earlier, perhaps, turn steak or patties. Prepare potatoes.
6:25	Drain and season peas.
6:30	Approximately, serve food onto dinner plates and take to table, with salads.
6:45	Or later. Put water to heat for instant coffee. Clear table. Serve ice cream into dishes and take to table. Make coffee and take to table.

A second menu, with more and different tasks to be accomplished, is suggested. Steps in arriving at the final plan and the final plan itself are given in Tables 16–4, 16–5, and 16–6. Assumptions used in timing are dinner at 6:30 and preparations for four persons.

Dinner for Four

Pot Roast of Beef[1]

Potatoes   Carrots

Cole Slaw

Hot Rolls

Milk

Apple Crunch[2]   Coffee

[1]A chuck cut weighing 4 pounds.

[2]Fresh, sliced apples with topping of flour, sugar, butter, and spices.

Table 16–4. *Steps 1 and 2 in Timing Meal Preparation*

| Menu Items | Time in Minutes to | | | Total Time in Minutes |
	Prepare for Cooking	Allow for Cooking	Prepare for Serving	
Pot roast of beef	30	180	10[1]	220
Potatoes	5	90	—	95
Carrots	5	90	—	95
Gravy	5	—	5	10
Cole Slaw	—	—	20	20
Rolls	5	10	5	20
Milk	—	—	—[2]	—
Apple crunch	15	40	5[3]	60
Coffee	3	12	—	15
Table setting	—	—	15	15

[1]Includes time for serving up potatoes, carrots, and roast and for slicing roast.
[2]Included in table setting.
[3]For serving and adding whipped topping.

Table 16–5. *Step 3 in Timing Meal Preparation—Tasks Listed in Descending Order of Total Time Required*

Tasks	Total Time in Minutes
Pot roast	220 (3 hours, 40 minutes)
Potatoes	95 (1 hour, 35 minutes)
Carrots	95 (1 hour, 35 minutes)
Apple crunch	60
Cole slaw	20
Rolls	20
Coffee	15
Table setting	10
Gravy	10

This latter menu with suggested timing is typical of broken schedules, those that send the meal manager into the kitchen for doing some tasks, free her for a period of time, then return her to the kitchen for the final tasks in meal preparation. Pastries, gelatin salads and desserts, and numerous kinds of main dishes for meals are prepared according to such broken schedules. Preparations for a guest dinner often require several schedules

TABLE 16–6. *The Time Schedule for Preparing Dinner for Four*

2:50	Brown roast in Dutch oven. Peel potatoes and carrots.
3:20	Roast into slow oven.
4:50	Potatoes and carrots put into Dutch oven with roast. Prepare apple dessert.
5:10	Dessert into oven.
5:50	Dessert out of oven. Make and chill cole slaw. Make paste for thickening gravy. Prepare rolls for heating. Set table. Place dinner plates on range. Have dessert service ready on counter. Prepare coffee maker.
6:15	Salads to table. Rolls in oven. Put roast and vegetables on platter. Slice roast. Keep warm.
6:20	Make gravy. Plug in coffee maker.
6:30	Dinner served.

for the preparation of the different dishes of the meal and for completion of the arrangements for dining.

No magic enables us to have everything included in a meal ready at a designated time. Timing based on estimates of required allotments of time are helpful. Each of us learns by experience, and much is learned only through experience. The period when detailed planning is essential is short for those who know how to cook. Sooner or later we reach the stage where only the final schedule is made. Even experienced hostesses and cooks who appear to do things easily make these schedules when preparing special meals.

The use of heat-and-eat dishes does not eliminate the need for timing, however much it may simplify and shorten the period of meal preparation. We repeat: it is very important to heat all frozen precooked foods at recommended temperatures and for the directed time to have them safe to eat.

In summary, timing the preparation of meals means ordering systematically in time the tasks associated with meal preparation. Knowledge of how to prepare food and the ability to estimate how fast one can work are prerequisites to the task.

Chapter 17
Styles of Meal Service

Man dines in diverse ways: some ways are casual, like the picnic; others are formal and elaborate, like state dinners at the White House. Between the extremes of casualness, and of elaborateness and formality, we choose degrees of both. During this century the serving of formal and elaborate meals in the home has all but disappeared because servants are prerequisites to them. The formal meals we now enjoy we generally eat at fine restaurants.

The styles of meal service we use are just new models of traditional styles that we inherited from the hoi polloi and the elite. From the beginning of recorded history, some individuals, because of wealth, power, and social position, have deliberately dined in modes that set them apart from the lesser members of their respective societies. However, the deep urge in some men to rise to high position has made some men want to dine like kings, if not at all times, at least some of the time. Historically, the mode of dining became a means for the display of wealth and refinement. Rare and expensive foods and elaborate dishes were offered at table. Luxuriously decorated dining rooms, beautifully appointed tables, and liveried servants were considered essential to the proper service of meals. A remnant of this idea remains; it can be seen in the custom in some families of serving different foods and dishes to guests than the family customarily eats. It may also be seen in the use of special dinnerware, beverageware, flatware, and linens; in the use of a different pattern of table service; and in the use of different table manners when guests are present. One set of customs was practical and comfortable; this set was followed when the family dined alone, however "wrong" it would have seemed if viewed by the outside world. The other set of customs was showy and considered refined; this set was considered "correct" and was followed when guests were present. Only in recent years has there been a trend away from the duality of customs relating to meals in the home.

Meal service styles differ in three ways. The first is the manner in which the diner receives food. There are three ways in which we receive food: we take it from a common pot or serving dishes; it is brought to us served up; and it is served to us at table. Second, meal service styles differ in the number of courses offered; that is, the items of a meal may be served sequentially, as in Russian service, or in one or two courses, as in family dinners. Third, patterns differ in that some require a servant to wait on table; in other styles the hostess, the host, or another person who dines at the table waits on the table. Eight styles of, or patterns for, serving meals can be described.

AMERICAN SERVICE OR COUNTRY-STYLE SERVICE

American service, or country-style service, is the oldest pattern. It is not originally American. In all ages men have helped themselves to food from a common pot. Perhaps it is named *country-style* because meals were served this way in rural regions of the country long after the pattern was modified by Americans who left the farm and moved to the cities. This pattern remains in wide use in both rural and urban communities.

For this service, individual places at the table are completely laid, including the dinner plate. Serving dishes of food are placed on the dining table or, if the dining table does not accommodate them, on a side table placed at either the host's or the hostess's right. Each serving dish of food is passed from hand to hand until all at the table have served themselves. Someone at the table removes the main course and serves the dessert course. The dessert may be brought in from the kitchen in individual portions, it may be served at the table, or it may be passed around the table as was the main course. This pattern of service is often used for public meals like the church supper, in which situation, those who wait on table do only that and dine after the public is served. Some restaurants feature this style of service.

EUROPEAN SERVICE

European service is also designated as *formal service, Russian service,* and *continental service.* It is truly formal, and it is elaborate and dignified. It can be carried out only in the home in which there are well-trained servants and in which all the other essential resources are available. European service has always been limited to an elite. The service or offering of food is from the side and not from the table. No dishes of food appear on the table other than compotes of fruits and candies, or nuts in cups at individual covers. The serving of food is accomplished by the placement at

Cover of formally set table. (*Courtesy of Baccarat Crystal.*)

covers of plates onto which food has been served or the placement of empty plates at the covers of guests who either serve themselves from serving dishes of food proffered by a servant or the food is served onto plates by a servant. When diners are seated at the table, there is at every cover a service plate—a large, beautifully decorated plate. The plate holding a cold first course or a first course served in a stemmed glass and the hot soup plate can both be placed on the service plate. The service plate is removed with the soup plate, but it is replaced simultaneously by the plate of the next course. Sequentially through the courses of the formal meal, plate replaces plate, through the serving of the salad course. The salad course precedes the dessert course. The salad course is removed and for the first time during this formally served meal the cover is empty of both plate and flatware. The plate and flatware for the dessert course are placed next; then the desserts are brought; and perhaps fruits and candies follow. Finger bowls may be brought in with the service for the dessert course, or they may follow the serving of the dessert. Coffee is not offered at the table but is served in the living room. In only a few homes are meals served in this style; but we occasionally see this style of meal service, or a reasonable facsimile of it, when we dine at a good restaurant.

ENGLISH SERVICE

Originally, English service was only slightly less formal than European service. It, too, was used in the homes of the privileged who had servants. The host and hostess participated in the serving of the food of the main course. The platters and serving dishes of food were placed in front of the host and hostess; he carved and served the meat onto the dinner plate, and she served the vegetables onto the dinner plate. A servant took the plate from host to hostess to guest. As use of the pattern spread to the servantless house, plates were passed from hand to hand—from host to hostess, then to those seated at the table. Considerable passing at the table occurs, especially when dessert is also served at the table.

FAMILY OR COMPROMISE SERVICE

This pattern is restyled English service. Stacked dinner plates and meat and vegetables in appropriate serving vessels are placed at the cover of either the host or the hostess, generally the former. The food items of the main course are served onto the dinner plate; the served plates are passed in order from hand to hand until all at the table have been served. Salad and dessert courses may also be served from the table. Unless a meal is limited to one course, the table is cleared and the next course is brought to the table. Some person who dines at the table acts as waiter or waitress.

The use of this pattern of service implies the possession of a dining table sufficiently spacious to accommodate serving dishes and a dining area large enough so that the person waiting on table can, at least partly, move around it. Neither of these is an absolute requirement, however, because an accessory table may hold the serving dishes of food, and the plates to be removed may be passed from hand to hand and placed on a trolley—a table on wheels—or a tray set on a small table from which they can be removed to the kitchen. Compromise service is best used when the group at the table is small—not more than eight—to keep serving time to that which is compatible with the serving of hot food. A person who sits to the left of the host may assist in serving an item of the meal to expedite serving. Because a member of the group, often the hostess, performs the waiting-on-the-table duties, meals served this way are best limited to two courses at the table. Any course served before the main course is best served before the diners come to the table; but if one wishes to serve a first course at the table, the dessert might be planned so that it can be served in the living room.

APARTMENT OR BLUE-PLATE SERVICE

In apartment or blue-plate service, plates are served up in the kitchen and placed on the table just before the diners sit down. Eating begins

A table arranged for the serving of food at the table.

A table arranged for the self-serving of food—American style of table service.

when the hostess signals. A course that precedes the main course is best served before the diners come to the table. Second portions can be served from the kitchen or offered from serving dishes that are passed from hand to hand. However, in the interest of weight control, second portions are far less frequent offerings than earlier in this century. Removal of the main course and service of dessert are by some member of the group at the table. This pattern of service is most frequently used when the group is small, the dining table is small, and the area for dining is small. Serving up any large number of plates is time-consuming and is apt to result in food being cold when eaten. When the number to be served exceeds six, or eight at most, another and more suitable pattern of meal service should be selected unless there is help in the kitchen. The proximity of the kitchen and the dining areas in contemporary homes makes this a much-used service pattern for family meals.

BUFFET SERVICE

The most-used style of meal service for guest meals is buffet service; in fact, it is the only practical service for guest meals in many homes if the number of diners exceeds six. Although the buffet pattern was introduced in the United States during the last century, it was not accepted and not appreciated until the dining area and dining tables became as small as they are and homes became servantless. A buffet is a dining table or other suitable surface, such as a chest, a desk, a kitchen counter, a folding table, or a card table, that will accommodate a stack of plates and serving dishes of food. Guests are invited to serve themselves at the buffet. They dine according to the arrangements of the hostess. There are three possibilities in dining arrangements. First, dining may be at a table. This may be the dining table, or card tables, or individual tables. Tables are fully set with all appointments for dining except the dinner plate, and it may even occasionally appear on the set table. Lacking room for tables, a hostess may provide each guest with a tray that holds plate and beverages and that the guest places on his lap. Eating from a tray on one's lap is fairly comfortable. Sometimes the tray is supported so that it becomes an individual table—that is, a TV tray. Often the only arrangement made for dining is to have plenty of table space on which guests can place a beverage while they sit on chairs and eat from the plate held in the hand. The menu for a buffet meal must be planned to be compatible with the arrangements for dining; that is, the food must be eatable under the conditions established for dining. Because the food is self-served, the buffet table must be carefully and logically set. Buffet service carried out well is excellent and practical for serving meals to large groups. Chapter 22 presents a full discussion on the management of buffet meals.

TRAY SERVICE

The popularity of the studio apartment, the ubiquitous apartment balcony, the universal acceptance of television, and the appreciation of sit-by-the-fire meals have helped make tray service a popular one, though there was a time when breakfast in bed and meals for the ill and the convalescent were the only ones served from trays. Trays are set according to the rules followed for table setting, although some modifications may be desirable for comfortable eating. Food is served onto plates, and they are placed on trays. Trays are then picked up by family members and taken to guests; the meal is eaten wherever the group chooses.

MEALS WITHOUT WAITING ON THE TABLE

Families eat many meals at which there is no waiting on the table; it is a simple, easy way to eat a simple meal. It can be a simple, easy way also to serve a more elaborate meal. Both good and bad can be said of it. The good includes the following: the family remains together throughout the meal; the mother plays only the role of hostess, a role she forsakes for that of a servant when she waits on her own table; and the total time for dining is reduced without the meal becoming hurried. The unfavorable comments might include these: the dining table can become a sea of dirty dishes; poor table etiquette may be fostered; and special props are essential to effect such service smoothly. In general, people do not like, although they may accept, a dining style that eliminates being waited upon. The idea of being served is old in time and old for each person, because it goes back to his infancy. Nonetheless, a homemaker may find it to her advantage to acquire the few desirable props and to develop a technique for managing smoothly meals served without waiting on the table. It is a style she can use for guests as well as *en famille,* particularly during those years when no child is old enough to wait on the table, during those years when she is gainfully employed, and after the children have left home.

The props desirable for such a service are few: a serving table or cart, called a *side table,* which is placed to the right or left of the hostess's chair; possibly a similar table, to be placed beside the host's chair; and an appliance for keeping coffee hot or for making coffee at the table. Given these, it is possible to serve meals of two or three courses comfortably and in good taste without any person leaving the table for the purpose of serving.

The main course could be served according to the American, compromise, or blue-plate styles—preferably the last one, to keep passing from hand to hand minimal. Clearing can take place by the passing of soiled plates from hand to hand to the hostess or host. The dessert and the beverage are passed from hand to hand. For a further discussion see Chapter 19.

Summary.   There are several styles for serving meals. The ones in use have evolved from older patterns. The styles used today are less formal and less elaborate than those possible when homes were not servantless. Actually, the patterns for meal service used in any home will vary from time to time and from meal to meal. They will be determined partly by choice, partly by expediency, and certainly by family values. The size of the home, the size of the dining area, the size of the dining table, the number to be fed, and the menu will influence the pattern of service to be used at a particular meal. The best pattern of service is the least obtrusive one, the one that takes the hostess or her helper away from the group the shortest time and the least number of times, and the one that provides maximum dining comfort with the facilities at hand. Table service is a means to an end. The end is a mealtime free from tension and confusion, one in which to enjoy both food and companionship.

Chapter 18
Setting the Table

The decade of the 1960's witnessed no changes in the fundamentals of table setting. The decade did, however, enrich the supply of things with which to set the table: new designs in flatware, new designs and bold color in dinnerware and linens, more synthetics and fibers for table linens, and, especially, new design and variety in throwaway appointments for the table.

Housewives in the United States, and elsewhere too, have always placed a high value on the appearance of the table they set. The ownership of both everyday and best appointments was, and remains, commonplace. The best may have been used only infrequently; its possession, however, was important. Table setting was definitely the housewife's own sphere of action. Perhaps, in pre-women's-lib days, it was one of few spheres of action in which she made the decisions and, possibly, for that reason she made much of it. Table setting provides some opportunity to be creative, to express personality, to do one's own thing—albeit within the framework of more or less flexible rules.

Table setting is the means to an end or ends, rather than an end in itself; but it must be recognized that not all who set a table have the same ends in mind. Four possible ends are discussed; only two of them may be universal. First, and from the practical point of view, the purpose of table setting is to make the act of eating easy. Some rules of table setting serve this purpose—objects that are to be used in the right hand are placed to the right of the plate centered in a cover: knives, spoons, and beverage containers. The fork is laid to the left of the plate centered in the cover because it was, and still is in some cultures, used only in the left hand. Second, we are uncomfortable and insecure when faced with the unfamiliar. Prescribed procedures accepted and used within a culture engender a feel-

444

ing of security in a recurrent and necessary act, that of eating. Persons from Western cultures are confounded when confronted with Oriental customs of dining, including the use of chopsticks; also by customs of Moslem and African cultures, which prescribe precisely the use of the hand and fingers in eating. Man derives a sense of security not only from what he eats, but also from how he eats. To be asked to eat foreign food in a foreign manner is doubly disconcerting.

Third, there is overwhelming evidence that some men seek an aesthetic experience at the table. Museums are crammed with objects of metal, glass, and ceramics that have been designed for use in dining. A prodigious assortment of table linens, dinnerware, beverageware, and flatware is produced for consumption today. In many, though perhaps not all, homes attention is paid to the selection and coordination of the appointments used on the table to the end that the background for dining will be pleasing to the eyes. Finally, this observation leads to another, namely that sometimes the setting of the table is for the display of objects and the sophistication and wealth that their use reflects.

When objects were created for use in eating, customs governing their use came to be established; they in turn gave birth to the rules of table setting; that is, the rules developed through usage. Existing rules have been in use long enough to be stripped of artificiality and ostentation. They seem to have been refined according to these principles: art, common sense, concern for the comfort of those at table, and courtesy. Each rule of table setting is explainable by reference to one of these principles. Because man's concepts are subject to change, customs also change from time to time and place to place.

Art principles would suggest that individual place settings and the table as a unit present a balanced appearance. Balance means even distribution of weight so that the parts of a composition appear in equilibrium. Balance is obtained by both symmetrical and asymmetrical arrangements. Color, texture, and shape effect balance with dissimilar objects. Small objects of dark color balance larger areas of light color; for example, the small dish of red jelly may balance the larger plate of bread. Small objects of bright luster balance larger objects of dull texture; for example, the glass at the right of the cover often balances the bread-and-butter plate at the left. There are nearly always a few items on any table that can be shifted in one direction or another to give the table balance. A table makes a pleasing appearance when its appointments are in scale with one another and with the table. The luncheon knife and fork, the small dinner plate, and the small centerpiece are best used on a small table. Large tables can be set with appointments larger in scale. Further, it is desirable to keep the number of items on a table in scale with the table. Eliminating nonessentials on the small table avoids a cluttered look. The pattern obtained through the repetition of lines, shapes, and designs within the individual place settings and through the repetition of place settings around the table is pleasing. Straight lines made by flatware and linens are pleasing when they are parallel or perpendicular to a table edge. Orderly arrangement of the numerous objects on a table is pleasing; disorder is confusing. Some rules establishing the positions of appointments and the rule that states that all place settings must be similar are based on art principles.

Common sense dictates that place settings include what is necessary for eating a meal; it also forbids the display of nonessentials. Common sense and concern for the comfort of those at the table require that appointments be placed in convenient positions for use. Courtesy demands that all the tools essential for refined eating be provided and that they be conveniently placed.

Currently, rules allow latitude in table setting. There is no one "right" way to set the table: the pattern of table service to be used, the menu to be served, and the size of the table establish the plan for setting the table. The pattern of service establishes the position of some items, particularly the dinner plates and the serving dishes. The specific appointments to be placed at covers are established by the menu. The exact positions of appointments at covers may differ on small tables and on large tables.

SETTING THE TABLE

Before discussing the rules that guide the placing of appointments on the table, it is desirable to define the cover. A *cover* consists of the dinnerware, beverageware, flatware, and linens to be used by each person; it is the individual's place at the table. A cover may vary in breadth from twenty to thirty inches, depending on the size of the table and the number to be seated, but dining is more comfortable if twenty-four inches can be allowed per cover.

The rules relating to the use of the appointments are discussed in the order in which each is usually placed on the table, beginning with the linens and proceeding to the final item, the food. It is possible to place all the flatware, then all the beverageware, then the dinnerware, in that order —except that when butter spreaders are included in the cover, they are placed after the bread-and-butter plates have been placed.

Linens

The kinds of linens used on the dining tables of the 1970's are diverse. *Linens* means all of the table cloths, placemats, and other table covers and napkins used on the dining table, regardless of fiber and including man-made materials. Easy-care, no-care, and disposable linens have, except for special occasions, replaced the linen damask and the fine linen and lace cloths of yesterday. Some cloths and placemats of man-made materials imitate the traditional ones in design and appearance. The dining counter and the dining table may be so constructed that the surface is impervious to water and heat; such surfaces are often set without linens, except for paper napkins. However, tablecloths, runners, and placemats are used some of the time by some families, and all of the time by other families. Here are some suggestions for the placing of linens.

1.   As unrealistic as it may seem, iron out creases in fabric cloths whenever possible. Lay a cloth so that the overhang is the same at the two ends and the same on the two sides. An overhang of twelve to fifteen inches gives a good appearance. Avoid great depth of overhang at the table where persons are seated for dining because the weight of the cloth against the legs of seated persons may become uncomfortable; also, the cloth may become entangled with legs crossed under the table.

2.   Runners may be centered on a table or they may be laid along the sides as a background for the place settings.

3.   On the square or rectangular table, lay rectangular placemats flush with the table edge or at a distance of one to one and one-half inches from the edge of the table. The position you choose is determined by the placemat, tne table, and the line you wish the flatware to follow. Deeply hemmed and fringed placemats may look better when placed flush with the table edge. Narrowly hemmed mats may appear more pleasing if placed away from the table edge. Regardless of hemming, small placemats, those smaller than twelve by eighteen inches, may look better when placed an inch away from the table edge. On a narrow table, all mats, regardless of hemming and size, may look better when placed flush with the table edge. Conversely, on a wide table, all mats look better when placed away from the edge of the table. Whenever possible, use placemats that are in scale with the table: small ones on the small table and large ones on the large table. Sometimes the fringing or hemming of a mat makes it desirable that the flatware be aligned in relation to that hemming or fringing. In such a situation, the placemat would be placed flush with the table edge so as to have the flatware placed at a comfortable distance from the table edge. When you have decided what looks best and is best, then lay all the placemats in the same way.

4.   In general, place oval, round, scalloped, and other mats with nonstraight edges so that some part of the edge is flush with the table edge. The large, round mat is often placed so that part of it overhangs the table. Place it so that the area on the table can accommodate the objects you wish to place on it and so that the area on the table is at the same time pleasing in relation to the area of the table left bare.

5.   On the round or oval table, lay rectangular mats so that the corners are flush with the edge of the table; this leaves a small arc of the table

FIGURE 18-1.   Formal service—individual cover.

bare in front of each mat. Lay oval and small, round mats flush with the table edge.

6.   The preferred shape for the folded napkin is the rectangle, but the square is also good. The triangle introduces oblique lines that make for a less harmonious whole. The five-sided fold permits the effective display of a pattern or monogram; it is preferred over the triangle. There are fanciful folds of the napkin that are appropriate at times; however, on the traditional dining table the simpler folds produce more artful settings simply because they are not obvious.

7.   The napkin is usually placed to the left of the fork or forks. However, if covers are close together, it can be placed in the center of a cover between the knife and the fork for the family pattern of service, on the dinner plate for the American pattern of service, or to the left of the dinner plate when the fork or forks are laid upon it. In formal service, the napkin is placed to the left of the forks or on the service plate, preferably the latter (see photograph on page 437 and Figure 18-1).

8.   The practice of placing the fork or forks on top of the napkin laid to the left in the cover has come into wide use. The practice necessitates sliding the napkin out from under the fork or forks, and presents an accident-prone situation to those accustomed to tradition.

9.   Place the napkin so that the edge closest to the table edge lies on an imaginary line that the tips of the handles of flatware and the rim of the plate will touch (See Figure 18-2).

10.   The placement of napkins on the placemat is determined by the size of both. It may be placed entirely on the mat, partly on the mat and partly on the table, or entirely on the table. Probably most tables look better when the napkin is entirely on the placemat. Placing the forks on the

FIGURE 18–2.   Alignment of napkin, flatware, and plate within a cover.

napkin is a way of keeping the napkin on the placemat. Lay a napkin so that the design and hem placement are coordinated with the placemat.

11.   Napkins vary in size. The twelve-inch one is usually used for breakfast and lunch. For the dinner meal the eighteen-inch (or larger) napkin is preferred.

Table Decorations

Table decorations ought always to be appropriate for viewing while dining, in good taste, and in scale with the table.

1.   On the dining table that seats no more than twelve, keep the decorations low so that persons can see across and converse across the table. Obviously, for banquets and special dinners for crowds this is not a problem because it is not expected that persons will communicate across a table. If the dining table is placed against a wall, there is no reason why an arrangement may not be tall if it looks pleasing from the sitting position.

2.   Decorations need not always be placed in the center of the table. Small arrangements can be placed at diagonally opposite corners, at all four corners, at the two ends of the table, or at one end of the table, depending on the size and shape of the table and how people are seated at it. Asymetrical arrangements of flowers placed away from the center of the table are handsome when balanced by candles or other objects.

3.   Decorations on the buffet and tea table can be larger and taller than dinner table decorations because they are viewed from above.

4.   With the exception of the tea table, candles are placed and lighted only after dusk. For the comfort of those at the table they should burn above eye level. Both candles and table decorations should be coordinated with the colors of the table appointments.

Laying Flatware

All flatware laid on a table ought to be free of spots and fingerprints. Enough flatware for comfortable and refined dining should be laid at each cover; the use of unneeded pieces is ostentatious and should be avoided. Easy-to-use and effective serving pieces should be laid for all food and dishes served at the table.

Laying Flatware at Covers.   Except for formal service, place all the flatware required for eating the full meal at the covers when setting the table; this simplifies the waiting-on-the-table duties. Lay pieces of flatware in the order of use from the outside toward the plate; this is done both for convenience during dining and because it gives the cover a balanced appearance at all times. Pieces should be laid close together, but not touching. Traditionally (see Figure 18–11), all pieces are laid so that the ends of the handles would touch an imaginary line parallel to the table edge and so that they are about an inch to an inch and a half from the table edge (see Figure 18–12). When the mat is placed flush with the table edge, the line made by the ends of the handles of flatware pieces is an inch or more from the edge of the mat; when the mat is placed away from the edge of the table, the flatware is placed so that the ends of the pieces are aligned with the edge of the mat. Some contemporary table settings show pieces laid in such a way that a line that bisects them is parallel to the table edge because the pieces are laid next to each other in relation to length. This arrangement looks best when the pieces increase in length from the outermost to the innermost (see Figure 18–12).

Pieces are placed in the same position at all covers for order and good appearance. Because the main plate is usually a warm one, the plates are generally among the last items to be placed; however, in laying the other items of the cover it helps one to place a plate briefly or to imagine one in the approximate center of the cover. In the directions that follow, a plate is considered to be in the center of the cover and is so indicated by a broken line.

1.   Lay the dinner knife to the right of the plate with the cutting edge directed toward the plate. All knives are laid with the cutting edge directed to the left, a position that protects the fingers of the right hand as it grasps the knife.

2.   Lay spoons with the bowls facing up at the right of the knife.

3.   Always lay the fork or forks with the tines facing up at the left of the plate, with this exception—a fork for eating seafood is laid to the right of any spoons in the cover because this fork is used in the right hand only. Lay the salad fork nearest the plate and the dinner fork to the left of it if you intend that the salad be eaten with the main course or after it. Lay the dinner fork nearest the plate and the salad fork to the left of it if you

(a)   (b)

FIGURE 18–3.   Possible positions of the dinner fork when no dinner knife is laid. (a) On the right of the cover when only one fork is laid. (b) On the left when a salad fork is also laid.

intend that the salad be eaten before the main course. In most homes the salad is eaten with the main course of the meal.

4.   It is not necessary to provide a salad fork when the salad accompanies the main course.

5.   When no dinner knife will be required for the eating of a simple family meal, it can be omitted from the setting. Lay the fork on the right in the place the knife would ordinarily occupy. Because the fork is used only in the right hand when no knife is needed, the position on the right is a convenient one. But if you wish to lay more than three pieces, then lay the forks on the left (see Figure 18–3). However, do not omit the dinner knife from the cover for the dinner meal except when dining *en famille*.

6.   When you provide salad forks for salads served in salad bowls, make certain that the fork will rest securely within the bowl and that it does not easily fall out. The preference is for broad, shallow salad bowls.

7.   You may place the butter spreader on the bread-and-butter plate in any of three positions; choose the one that looks best on your plates and your table (see Figure 18–4).

(a)   Across the upper edge of the plate in a line parallel with the table edge, the cutting edge of the knife directed toward the center of the plate.

FIGURE 18–4.   Possible positions of the butter spreader on the bread-and-butter plate.

FIGURE 18–5.   Position for the butter spreader when no bread-and-butter plate is placed.

(b)   Across the right side of the plate perpendicular to the table edge, cutting edge directed to the left.

(c)   Across the center of the plate with the tip of the knife a little to the left of the center of the plate and with the cutting edge directed toward the table edge. This is a good position on the coupe plate.

8.   Sometimes, it is intended that the salad plate do double duty and be used also as a bread-and-butter plate. Because salads are cold and the plates for them are frequently chilled, this practice ought to be limited to use with bread that is not hot. Whenever you intend that the salad plate be also a bread-and-butter plate, arrange the salad in a lettuce cup, and leave about half of the plate free for the bread. In this case, eliminate the salad fork and the butter spreader. The salad can be eaten with the dinner fork, and the dinner knife can be used as a spreader.

9.   Occasionally the butter spreader is the only knife provided, particularly in covers for breakfasts and simple lunches. In this situation, lay it on the right when no bread-and-butter plate is provided (see Figure 18–5).

10.   The use of the butter spreader is optional when a dinner knife is laid; current practice is not to use it.

11.   Laying the flatware for dessert is no problem unless the tool for dessert is a fork. When it is a fork, it must be laid so that there is no doubt about its intended use. Should a menu not include a salad, the dessert fork can be laid to the right of the dinner fork. When a salad accompanies the main course and your supply of forks does not permit the laying of three at each cover—one for the main course, one for salad, and one for dessert—lay one fork only on the left. Lay the fork you intend for dessert in the center of the cover above the dinner plate, handle directed to the right (see Figure 18–6). When the fork is laid in this position, it is unlikely that anyone will use it for salad because it is not in the expected position. When a beverage is served with dessert only, lay the beverage spoon above

FIGURE   18–6.   A possible position for the dessert fork and the beverage spoon.

the dessert fork with the handle likewise directed toward the right, because both are used in the right hand. Placing the beverage spoon here,
along with the fork, gives the cover a balanced appearance. Further, it
permits narrowing covers slightly.

Two other procedures are possible. The flatware for dessert may be
laid just before dessert is served. Place both the fork for dessert and the
spoon for the beverage on the right of each cover because both are used in
the right hand. The hostess who is her own waitress should avoid this procedure because it keeps her away from the table longer than is necessary.

Finally, the fork may be placed on the plate with the dessert, both when
it is served from the kitchen and when it is served from the table. When
you choose this procedure, covers will be better balanced if you do not
place beverage spoons in the place settings. Place the beverage spoon on
the saucer with the handle parallel to the cup handle when you pour.

12.   When the flatware for dessert is a spoon, lay it to the right of the
knife as previously directed. There is no cogent reason for laying dessert
and beverage spoons in the center of the cover above the dinner plate;
however, do so if you choose to. It is rather sophisticated to provide both
a dessert spoon and a fork for the dessert course. If you follow this practice, the handle of the spoon is directed to the right; the handle of the
fork, left. The spoon is the tool for eating and is therefore used in the
right hand; the fork is used as a pusher in the left hand (see photograph
on page 454). Because of our custom of serving coffee or other beverages
with dessert, if not throughout the meal, and because we formerly used
cream and sugar abundantly in beverages, beverage spoons have been traditionally laid at covers. It is quite proper to omit the beverage spoon
from place settings and place it on the saucer as one serves the beverage at
the table. Whether or not you use both spoon and fork for dessert service,

Table setting that shows placement of the dessert flatware above the cover. (*Courtesy of Doulton and Company, Inc.*)

do use the dessert or place spoon as much as you can. Make certain that the plate under the dessert bowl is large enough to accommodate it. A plate used under a bowl, a stemmed or footed sherbet, or any dish is called an *underliner*.

13.   Fresh fruits are often served for dessert. Some are eaten with a spoon, some may be eaten with the fingers, but a few require the use of a

FIGURE 18–7. Position for the fruit knife and fork and the beverage spoon.

knife or a knife and a fork for refined eating. When both knife and fork are provided, lay the fork, handle directed to the left, below the knife, handle directed to the right, in the center of the cover above the dinner plate. Lay the beverage spoon for a beverage served only with dessert above the knife, handle directed to the right (see Figure 18–7).

When a selection of fruits is offered from a tray or a large plate, it is acceptable to place the fruit knives on the tray, handles spread in a fan shape. Anyone who will use a knife in eating the selected fruit takes it from the tray. As with dessert forks, the fruit knife and fork or knife alone may be laid on the fruit plate when it is placed by the person acting as waitress.

14. Place the tools for a dessert of cheese and crackers in the center of the cover above the dinner plate as for fruit, or lay them on the right after the main course has been eaten, using right-hand service. Either the butter spreader or the fruit knife is suitable as a cheese spreader.

Serving Flatware. The serving pieces selected when persons at the table serve themselves should lend themselves to quick and easy use. The scissors-type, two-tools-in-one combinations, and tongs are excellent for chops, vegetables like broccoli and asparagus, and salads. Serving spoons larger than tablespoons are indicated for casserole dishes and any other dish that would require several dips with the tablespoon to provide a serving.

When serving is by the host or another person at the table, two serving tools are more effective than one unless the one is a two-tools-in-one combination. Tools that can be used together—one to assist the other in serving—are two tablespoons, a tablespoon assisted by a dinner fork, a meat

FIGURE 18–8.   Serving pieces laid beside serving dishes.

fork assisted by a tablespoon, a shallow flat server assisted by a dinner fork or a tablespoon, and a large serving spoon assisted by a dinner fork or a tablespoon.

1.   Lay to the right of the serving dish or platter one serving tool if only one tool is provided.

2.   When two serving tools are provided, lay the one that will assist to the left of the dish containing food, the one that will pick up the food to the right (see Figure 18–8). These may also be placed to the left and right of the cover of the person serving (see Figure 18–9).

3.   Place the carving fork to the left of the platter, the carving knife to the right with the cutting edge directed to the left or lay them to right and left in the cover of the person who will carve.

4.   Lay the serving tools for small containers of food passed at the table, like butter, jelly, and pickles, to the right of a dish that has no underliner, and on the underliner when one is used.

5.   Lay spoons with the bowls and forks with the tines facing up. Use a small fork like the lemon or pickle fork for butter cut into pats rather than a butter knife.

Placing Beverageware

Some persons prefer to delay the placing of glasses of beverages until they have been filled to avoid a possible accident while pouring at the table. The glasses are placed on a tray, filled, carried on the tray to the table and placed. Common sense would suggest that if you plan this way, coasters for the glasses should be placed during table setting.

FIGURE 18–9.   Serving pieces laid at the server's cover.

1.   Rinse and polish glasses with a lint-free towel to remove fingerprints and smudges whenever this is indicated.

2.   Grasp tumblers and footed ware at the base, stemmed ware by the stem.

3.   Use coasters under beverage glasses whenever humidity and temperature favor the condensation of moisture on glasses.

4.   Place the water glass at the tip of the knife (or fork when placed at the right of the plate) or a little to the right or left of the knife, depending on the breadth of the covers, the width of the table, and the number of glasses to be placed. Place it where it looks best and is easily grasped (see Figure 18–10).

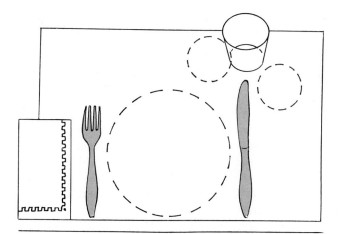

FIGURE 18–10.   Possible positions of the water glass.

5. Ice and water may be put into the glasses about fifteen minutes ahead of serving time. Water is poured to within an inch of the top of the glass.

6. Glasses of milk, when water also is served, are placed to the right and a little in front of the water glass, that is, a little closer to the table edge (see Figure 18–5). This permits the easy removal of empty milk glasses before the dessert service. If no water glass is placed, as is often true in families with children, place the glass of milk or other beverage in the position for the water glass. Place a glass of juice to the right and in front of the last glass, that is, nearer the table edge (see Figure 18–6).

7. Glasses placed in addition to the water glass, such as for wines, are positioned successively closer to the table edge but not so as to modify the position of flatware on the right side of the cover. Generally, no more than three glasses appear within a cover; however, see the photograph on page 437.

8. Place a saucer or a small plate under a glass of iced tea or coffee so as to provide a place for a spoon and also to collect condensing moisture.

Placing Dinnerware

Selecting the plates, cups and saucers, bowls, and platters that will be used in setting the table makes table setting an art. "Mix and match" sets of dinnerware have encouraged the use of plain color with patterned pieces. Although dinnerware is often purchased by the set, individual covers and the table as a whole are more attractive if salad plates are different from dinner plates, dessert plates are different from cups and saucers, and serving dishes and platter are coordinated with the plates but are not all exactly alike.

1. Handle dishes and plates in such a way that you do not touch surfaces onto which food will be served. You can safely carry dishes and piles of plates if you place your thumbs on the edges and your fingers close together underneath.

2. Place the bread-and-butter plate at the left of the cover near the tip of the fork. In this position it balances the glass or glasses on the right of the cover (see Figure 18–11). In addition to serving as a receptacle for bread and butter, it is also used for celery, olives, and other relishes eaten with the fingers. At the small table, sacrifice it to avoid a cluttered appearance. The dinner or luncheon plate, if not overcrowded with food, is a suitable place for bread and butter, especially when the bread is hot. The bread-and-butter plate is used when a table accommodates it, but it is not a "must" in table setting.

3. Unless served at the table, the salad is placed at each cover shortly before serving time. It may be placed in any of several positions.

Figure 18–11.   Position of the bread-and-butter plate.

Figure 18–12.   Position of the salad plate when there is no bread-and-butter plate in the cover.

(a)   If no bread-and-butter plate is at the cover, place the salad at or near the tip of the fork. This is a widely used position and one that allows good leverage in cutting salad vegetables (see Figure 18–12).

(b)   When a bread-and-butter plate is included in the cover, you may place the salad to the left and a little below the bread-and-butter plate; however, unless covers are spacious, such a position is often not possible (see Figure 18–13). Where covers are close together you may move the bread-and-butter plate a little to the left and place the salad to the right of it; in this position, it is above the luncheon or dinner plate (see Figure

FIGURE 18–13.   Possible positions of the salad when a bread-and-butter plate appears in the cover.

18–13). If using both salad and bread-and-butter plates crowds the table unduly, it may be better to omit the latter. Another, but less frequently used, position is to the right of the spoons and lined up with the napkin and the flatware. There are at least three reasons why this position is not popular. First, the salad is less comfortably eaten. Secondly, the long-established custom of having the salad on the left leads to mistaken eating of one's neighbor's salad, except when covers are so spacious that there can be no doubt. Finally, wide preference for a hot beverage with the main course means that the place at the right has been usurped. It may be well to note further that if a bread-and-butter plate is placed in a cover, and if the salad is placed at the right, then waiting on the table becomes rather complicated. These objections should not preclude the use of the position if one wishes to use it. Men like it because their cuffs are not soiled by food of the dinner plate as they may be when the salad is at the left of the cover.

4.   Whenever possible, use the salad-dessert plate for a salad rather than a bread-and-butter plate, but especially for salads composed of crisp vegetables that require cutting, because the larger the plate on which to maneuver pieces, the less likely are pieces to fall on the table. Whenever there is no choice but to serve the salad on a bread-and-butter plate, keep it small and compose it of fairly soft vegetables or fruits or have all pieces bite-sized. An alternative to the use of the bread-and-butter plate is the salad bowl; again, have all pieces bite-sized.

5.   Some hostesses, and some hosts, prefer to dress, toss, and serve the salad from the table. Three positions of the salad service are possible (see Figure 18–14).

FIGURE 18–14.   Possible positions of the salad service at the server's cover.

(a)   The first position requires right-to-left serving of the salad onto the salad plates. Place the stacked salad plates at the position in the cover that the server's own salad occupies. Place the salad bowl above the dinner plate. This arrangement leaves the last salad in the proper place within the cover.

(b)   The second arrangement is similar to the first but the bowl of salad is placed to the left of the dinner plate. This position permits left-to-right serving of the salad. This arrangement also leaves the last salad served in the proper position within the cover.

(c)   Place the bowl of salad above the dinner plate just left of center; place the stacked plates to the right of it. It may be necessary to move the water glass to the right. With the bowl and plates in this position left-to-right serving is easy. When the last salad has been served, it is moved to the proper position within the cover.

6.   The most appropriate tool for serving salad is the two-in-one scissors-type. Otherwise, use two tools, a spoon with a fork or two spoons.

7.   Set the service similarly for any vegetable or food that will be served into side dishes.

8.   Place warm dinner plates last, just before dinner is announced. Put a plate in the center of each cover for the American style of meal service. Put the stacked dinner plates at the cover of the person who will serve when the meal service style is compromise or family service. Place the served dinner plate at each cover when the service is blue-plate.

Laying the Beverage Service

In the 1970's, beverages are very much a part of meals. Soft drinks, fruit drinks, and fruit punches have been added to the milk, coffee, and tea traditionally served. In general, filled beverage glasses are placed on the table within fifteen minutes of serving time. And, in general, glasses are filled to within one inch of the top. Hot beverages are served at the table; they are also served from the kitchen at the appropriate time.

For those who prefer the former practice, the service must be planned and arranged for.

1.   Keeping beverage glasses filled poses some problems. Strictly *en famille*, glasses can be passed at the table and filled from a pitcher that may be on the dining table or on a small side table. Otherwise, the refilling of beverage glasses occurs between courses.

2.   When a hot beverage is to be served throughout the meal and the hostess is to pour, place cups and saucers stacked by twos either to the right or to the left or above the hostess's cover. The exact position depends on the number to be served, the size and shape of the table, and the number of items already in position at her cover. Figure 18–15 shows possible

FIGURE 18–15.　Possible arrangements of a beverage service at the hostess's cover —beverage served during the meal and no tray used.

positions when no more than three or four cups and saucers must be placed. Try out the several possibilities the table offers, and then adopt the one that permits the most comfortable and graceful pouring. If the dining table does not accommodate a beverage service, place it on a side table, perhaps a table-on-wheels, and set it to the right of the hostess's chair.

3.   When the hot beverage is not to be served until dessert, do not place any of the appointments for it on the table; however, arrange the service as a part of table setting. This service may be set up with or without a tray. When used, the tray should be in scale with the table. Set it with cups and saucers, creamer and sugar bowl, and perhaps spoons. For safety, the tray should be carried to the table without the pot of hot beverage on it. It may be set down to the right of or above the hostess's cover, depending on the size of the table and her wishes. After the tray is placed, the pot of hot beverage will be brought in and placed on it. Place the creamer, the sugar bowl, and the beverage pot on the tray in positions convenient for use (see Figure 18–16). The position above the cup and saucer into which the beverage is poured is a good one for the creamer and sugar. Leave the cover off the sugar bowl.

4.   The beverage service is more frequently placed on the table without an underlying tray because tables tend to be small, and trays large enough to be useful tend to be too large for the table. Again, all items for this service should be readied when one is setting the table. Have them on the serving table or on the counter in the kitchen. Chapter 19 discusses how this service is placed on the dining table.

5.   Ideally, the cups, but not the saucers, are warmed for hot beverages in the same way that plates and serving dishes are warmed for hot food. This is especially important when the design of the cup is such that it has a large cooling surface.

6.   The service for a beverage offered with or after dessert can be set up on a side table placed to the right of the hostess's chair.

FIGURE 18–16.   A tray arranged for beverage service.

Placing Accessory Items

Accessory items include bread, butter, jellies and jams, salt and pepper, food dressings, relishes, and so on.

1.   Place individual salt and pepper shakers in the center of the cover above the dinner plate.

2.   One pair of salt and pepper shakers is enough for two or three diners. Place them between covers in the line made by the water glasses, where they can be easily reached.

3.   Place the salt to the right of the pepper shaker so that it can be taken without need for handling both objects.

4.   Place dishes containing such foods as rolls, butter, and relishes to be self-served and passed from hand to hand to the right and left of the hostess's cover or on a side table placed to the right of her chair so that she can assume responsibility for passing and so that she can be the last to serve herself. Such an arrangement permits her to control the positioning of these items on the table—she may prefer that they not remain on the dining table.

Placing the Chairs

When a table has been completely set, except for the food, the chairs, if not already at the table, may be placed. They should be set with the fronts of the seats flush with the table edge. From this position, they do not require much moving when guests seat themselves, a desirable goal when a floor is tile or other material over which the moving of chairs makes noise.

Placing Serving Dishes of Food

It is desirable that dishes and platters be sufficiently large so that service from them is possible without spilling.

1.   Warm or chill dishes as indicated.

2.   When the pattern of service used is American, place serving dishes in positions where they can be conveniently reached by someone at the table. The serving tools should already have been laid in accordance with suggestions.

3.   When the pattern is family service, the filled serving dishes are grouped at the cover of the person who will serve, usually the host. Place the platter, chop plate, or casserole containing the main part of the meal above, but as close as possible to, the stacked plates onto which the food is to be served. Place other dishes containing food to the right and to the left of the stacked plates. If only one additional serving dish is to be placed,

FIGURE 18–17.   Dining table set for service of food at the table.

put it on the left for better leverage in serving (see Figure 18–17). To facilitate serving, particularly when carving is necessary, remove the server's
beverage glass and salad to a small side table. On the completion of serving, the beverage glass and salad are placed on the dining table by the person who served. Emptied serving bowls can be removed to the small side
table from the dining table by the person who served.

4.   To hasten service to a group of eight or more, the person sitting on the host's left, because he or she can freely use the right hand, may assist by serving one or more of the vegetables. The preferred position of the serving dish is above the cover of that person, especially if serving the item requires the use of two hands.

5.   Although side dishes are less frequently used than formerly, some foods are still best served in them. Creamed vegetables, vegetables in cream, and stewed tomatoes are those most often served in this fashion. Place side dishes served in the kitchen at the tip of the fork or lower, depending on what other dishes are already placed at the cover.

6.   Place the first of foods to be eaten successively, such as breakfast fruits and cereals, in the center of the cover; place the one to be eaten second at the left near the tip of the fork. The two dishes are exchanged in position by the diner after he has finished the first one.

7.   Place the dessert of a simple meal, to be eaten without any waiting on the table, to the left of the cover, at the tip of the fork or higher, depending on what other dishes have already been placed at the cover.

SETTING THE SERVING TABLE

The presence of a small chest, tea cart, table, or buffet in the dining area promotes ease and speed in table service, regardless of the meal service pattern followed. Lacking one of these or room in which to set it up, set aside a part of the kitchen counter, and use it similarly. This aid to service is called a *serving table* or *service table*.

1.   Cover it with a runner or one or two placemats to muffle the clatter of dishes and to protect the surface if necessary.

2.   Add a small tray for use while clearing and placing courses.

3.   Place on the serving table the creamer, sugar bowl, and cups (if they are not being warmed) and saucers of the beverage service; the dessert plates and flatware needed to serve a dessert from the table; or the underliners for a dessert served in sherbets or bowls and brought in from the kitchen.

4.   Place the water pitcher and a drip napkin here if you wish.

5.   Place, too, a small plate and a napkin for use in crumbing the table if crusty bread, such as cornbread or hard rolls, is included in the menu.

6.   Do not completely cover the table with appointments, because it has a real function during the removal and placement of courses (see Figure 18–18).

7.   Leave on the serving table the hot pads and salts and peppers you remove from the dining table when you are removing the main course.

8.   The purpose of the serving table is to simplify service; use it to save steps, but do not put food for a subsequent course on it or leave it stacked with dirty dishes if it is visible from the dining table.

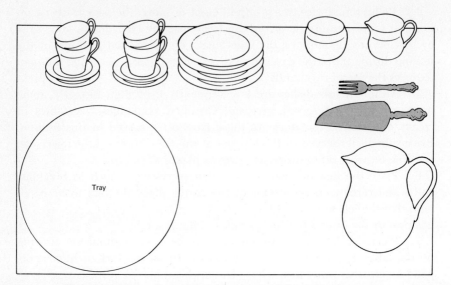

FIGURE 18–18.   A serving table arranged for convenient use.

MISCELLANEOUS

Using a Table-on-Wheels

The small tea cart or table-on-wheels or trolley can be conveniently used in setting the table and in waiting on the table. It reduces the hand-and-foot work of mealtime. Load it with the items you must take from your kitchen to the dining table. If you wish, leave it in the dining area as a serving table if it is of a comfortable height and suitable for such use. Clear the table to it, then roll everything away to the kitchen when you (or another person) wait on the table. To serve you as just described, this table-on-wheels should be of comfortable working height and should have a guard rim to prevent the sliding of dishes as it moves.

"Silent Butler" for Hosts

One last arrangement might be suggested for facilitating the smooth and unhurried service of meals, even though the time devoted to dining may not be long. Place small tables, like TV snack tables, to the right of the host's and the hostess's chair. The host's water glass and salad may be placed there while he carves and serves; his own plate may be placed there while he serves second portions. The hostess may keep on hers some of the items that she will have passed from hand to hand at the table. These small tables are especially valuable when the dining table and the dining area are small.

Summary.   Table setting is the means to an end or ends. It makes eating easy. It provides part of the aesthetic experience associated with dining. Table-setting rules have evolved through usage. They are functional. They are dynamic. They have flexibility that makes it possible for each meal manager to make them serve her purposes.

It has been suggested in earlier chapters that the values of parents, and of the homemaker especially, determine how much of the family's resources of money, time, and energy is allocated to meals. This chapter has been concerned with the setting of the table. This activity makes demands on the money, time, and energy resources and requires knowledge and skills. To maximize the uses of time and energy, it is desirable to use the rules to develop a design for setting the table. When the design has been established, make it routine.

Chapter 19
Waiting on the Table

That the meals of families in the United States are different in the 1970's than they were earlier in this century, no one argues. They are less hearty but more varied; they are often eaten on the run; and they are much too frequently eaten alone. The ritual of family meals at which all were present two or even three times daily has all but vanished. However, a rebirth of mealtime ritual in the 1970's is possible. Alvin Toffler (1) in *Future Shock* suggested that as the pace of change accelerates, greater variety in the kinds of family rituals can be anticipated. Developments that could strengthen the ritual of mealtime are the growing interest, particularly among young persons, in food and wines and the leisure that the four-day work week provides. This leisure will be put to many different uses; it could permit deceleration in the pace of our lives. Eat-and-run meals will not fade away; on the other hand, sit-and-enjoy meals may become more common experiences in our lives.

Sit-and-enjoy meals imply waiting on the table for at least two reasons. First, time permitting, man likes to eat the items of his meals serially, that is, in courses. Perhaps a cup of soup or a shrimp cocktail, a salad, meat and vegetable, dessert, and so on. The availability of so much and of such variety in convenience foods so reduces the time cost of meal preparation that meals of several courses are easy of production, though most of the time we offer only two courses. Second, the eating of meals in courses requires the removal and placement of courses serially.

Waiting on the table is simple and easy in the 1970's. The procedures we follow are adaptations of traditional patterns, they are suited to the times, and they are changeable and changing.

How to Wait on Table

The use of a serving table and/or a table-on-wheels expedites waiting on the table. A large tray can be used between the serving table and the kitchen because both hands are free to carry it; but only a small tray can be used between the serving table and the dining table because one hand must support the tray while the other hand removes something from table to tray and vice versa. Limit the use of even a small tray to the placing and removing of flatware, salt and pepper shakers, creamer and sugar bowl, dressings for food, beverageware, and other small objects.

Order for Removal and Placement of Courses

The order for the removal of a course is this: first, take away the serving dishes; second, remove the plates and the side dishes from individual covers; finally, use a small tray and take away unused flatware and other objects not to be used in the next course. The order of placing a course is the reverse: first, using a small tray, lay the required flatware and such small items as cream and sugar, a pitcher of pudding sauce, or a bowl of whipped cream; second, place any dishes required; lastly, bring the food and/or beverage. For meals for which the table has been carefully set, the removal of a course may entail only the removal of individual covers, as for meals served blue-plate style; and the placing of the dessert course may require only the carrying of served desserts from the kitchen to the table. The menu and the pattern of service establish how many duties must be performed in removing and serving courses.

Left-Hand and Right-Hand Serving

Some of the steps in removing and placing courses are carried out from the left side with the left hand and some from the right side with the right hand. The dinner plate is best removed from the left side with the left hand to avoid a possible collision with the beverage glass or glasses on the right. Any cover that includes a salad plate and/or a bread-and-butter plate must be cleared from the left to avoid reaching in front of persons because these side dishes are placed to the left of the dinner plate. A beverage glass or an unused dinner knife would be removed with the right hand while one is standing on the right; and dessert flatware would be laid with the right hand while one is standing to the right. To serve from the left—left-hand service—stand to the left of the person being waited on so that the feet, heel to toe, are parallel to the table edge; this position brings the left hand closest to the table and puts the right hand in back of the person being served. To serve from the right—right-hand service—stand to the right of the person being served, feet parallel to the table edge; this position brings the right hand nearest to the table and puts the left hand in back of the person being served. Except in formal table service, when standing to the left, use the left hand; when standing to the right, use the right hand. The hand nearest the table should do the work; to use the other hand would be awkward and clumsy and at the same time would introduce the possibility of bumping with the elbow the person being waited on.

In formal service, both hands must be used because removing and placing occur simultaneously. Stand to the left, use the left hand to remove a soiled plate, use the right hand to place a clean plate onto which the next course will be served. Or, still standing on the left, use the right hand to remove the soiled plate, when the plate that will replace it has food served onto it, and place the plate with food on it with the left hand. That is, use the right hand, the one nearest the guest, to handle the plate least likely to have contents that can spill.

Order of Waiting on Persons at Table

The direction of moving around a table is from your left to your right, that is, counterclockwise. You begin at the cover of one of the following persons, depending on who is at table.

1. Begin with the hostess at a family table where parents dine alone with children; at this table the hostess is the honored person.

2. Begin with the woman seated to the host's right if she is a guest, or an elderly grandparent or aunt, or some other elderly person living with the family. A woman guest and an elderly woman are honored persons.

3. Begin with an elderly woman who may be seated to the right of the hostess because of a disability that requires assistance from the hostess. This is an uncommon situation, but one that does exist.

Removing a Course

When all have finished eating a course, if you have been delegated waiting-on-the-table duties or are the hostess and will perform these duties, casually place your napkin to the left of your cover and rise from the table, moving your chair as little as possible. Because few meals routinely consist of more than two courses served at the table, directions are for clearing the main course; but any other course would be similarly cleared. Proceed as outlined.

1. Remove the serving dishes first when these are present on a table or a side table, such as when American or compromise patterns of meal service have been used. The removal of a large platter or casserole may re-

quire the use of both hands; the removal of one or more dishes, left-hand service; a few, right-hand service. Stand to the left of the person in front of whom there is a large platter or casserole that will require the use of both hands; remove it from the left to avoid collision with any beverageware on the right. Take it to the kitchen immediately. Return to the table and remove to the serving table any pad or cloth that may have been placed under the platter or casserole. If one hand can support the serving dishes, stand on the left to remove those on the left. Take one with the left hand and transfer it to the right hand. Take a second with the left hand and then take both to the kitchen. On returning to the table, remove to the serving table any protecting pads that may have been under them. Similarly, remove the serving dishes on the server's right using right-hand service.

2. Next, remove the soiled appointments from covers. Begin with the proper person and proceed around the table in a counterclockwise direction. Exactly what you do is established by the number of plates and side dishes at the covers. Covers may include the dinner plate only or they may include in addition, a salad plate or bowl and/or a bread-and-butter plate.

(a) When the cover includes only one plate, use left-hand service to remove the plate from the cover with which you begin. Transfer the plate to your right hand, and then remove the plate from the next cover with the freed left hand and proceed to the kitchen with these two plates, one in each hand. Avoid stacking dishes in the dining area unless you are *en famille*.

(b) When the cover includes only two items, such as the dinner plate and the salad plate or bowl or the bread-and-butter plate, remove the dinner plate with your left hand, and transfer it to your right hand. Then remove the second plate with your left hand. Proceed to the serving table; now, place the second plate quietly on top of the dinner plate. Clear the next cover in the same manner, and then pick up the plates placed on the serving table and proceed to the kitchen. Continue in the same manner until all covers have been cleared. Take your own in order as you proceed around the table.

(c) When the cover includes three items, such as the dinner plate, the salad plate or bowl, and the bread-and-butter plate, remove the dinner plate first with the left hand. Transfer it to the right hand. Next, remove a salad plate with the left hand and place it as gently as possible on top of the dinner plate. Lastly, remove the bread-and-butter plate with the left hand. Proceed with these to the serving table, where you may place the bread-and-butter plate on top of the others. Whenever a cover includes a salad bowl, remove the bread-and-butter plate after the dinner plate, and place it on the dinner plate. Then remove the salad bowl and proceed as previously suggested. Clear the second cover in the same way, pick up the dishes on the serving table, and proceed to the kitchen. Continue in this manner until all covers have been cleared. Take your own in order as you proceed around the table.

(d) It is necessary in most kitchens to store food as it is brought from the dining area and to stack dishes on the kitchen counter or in a sink or to load them into the dishwasher as they are brought out from the dining area.

3. Finally, using a small tray (one no larger than twelve inches in diameter), remove the salt and pepper shakers, any beverage glasses not to be refilled, and unused flatware and any other remaining items not to be used in the next course. If the table has been carefully set, there will be no unused flatware to remove; should there be, remove it from the proper side—from the left if it is at the left of the cover (such as an unused salad fork), otherwise, from the right. Remove any beverage glasses that will not be refilled from the right, using the right hand. Always use the right hand for removing from the right. All such items can probably be removed in one circling of the table.

4. The course has been removed at this point; however, it may be necessary to perform two other duties: crumbing the table and refilling the water glasses. Crumbing is done only when necessary, as when hard rolls or crumbly corn bread have been served. A plate and a napkin are sufficient equipment. Do this from the left, because the crumbs, by virtue of the position of the bread-and-butter plate, will be at the left of the cover. Hold the plate below the table in your right hand and brush the crumbs onto it with the napkin held in your left hand.

5. It is not customary to refill water glasses during a meal except when a servant waits on the table; refill empty ones at this point, using right-hand service. A napkin, called a drip napkin, held in the left hand, quickly catches the drip from the pitcher as you back away from the table to proceed to the next cover. Do not lift a glass from the table to refill it; if necessary, you may move the glass closer to the edge of the table by grasping it close to its base. Refill the glasses in the same order in which you removed the covers.

Serving the Dessert Course

We serve dessert from the kitchen, from the serving table, and from the dining table. We serve a beverage with dessert much of the time, but we may offer the beverage throughout a meal, after dessert, or only after leaving the dining table. To expedite waiting on the table, especially when hostesses wait on their own tables, we are assuming that the flatware for eating the dessert was included in covers when the table was set.

Serving Dessert from the Dining Table. When a hostess pours a beverage at the table, she may delegate the serving of dessert to the host or another person at the table; on the other hand, she may choose to do all herself. In the following description of how to place the dessert course it is assumed that the hostess will serve. The procedures would be the same if another were to serve dessert; however, the appointments and the dessert would be placed at the server's cover.

1.   Take the flatware essential for the serving of the dessert to the table on a small tray or plate, lay any tools that will assist the functioning tool to the left and the functioning tool—pastry server, knife, or serving spoon —to the right of the hostess's (or server's) cover or above the cover so that they will be beside the plate onto which the dessert was served. At the same time place the creamer and the sugar bowl, if they are needed, in the position selected.

2.   Place the plates onto which dessert is to be served in the center of the hostess's (or server's) cover. Whenever dessert is to be served into bowls, the plates they are to be placed on must also be placed. For such service, place one bowl on top of the stacked plates and set them in the center of the hostess's (or the server's) cover. Place the remaining bowls, stacked one inside the other, to the left of the stacked plates. The person serving places a bowl on each plate when serving the dessert into the bowl.

3.   Place the cups and saucers next. When the beverage is to be served from a tray, carry the already arranged tray without the pot of hot beverage to the table. Place it from the right if the hostess has chosen the position on her right for it. Otherwise, place it from the left to avoid collisions with beverageware. When a beverage is served without the use of a tray, take the cups and saucers to the table either on a small tray or stacked in two's, preferably the former. Place the cups and saucers on the table with

Figure 19–1.   Dessert placed for serving at the table.

FIGURE 19–2.   Possible arrangements of the beverage service at the server's cover.

the handles of the cups directed to the hostess's right for ease in handling the cups. Set the cups and saucers down in any of three positions (see Figure 19–2). If you carry them to the table on a tray, put them down with your right hand (because you support the tray with your left hand). If you carry them by two's, a pair in each hand, put them down this way.

(a) To the left of her cover. Use left-hand service, and set those in your left hand down first; transfer those in your right hand to the left hand, and then place them.

(b) To the right of her cover. Use right-hand service. Place the cups and saucers in your right hand first; transfer those in your left hand to the right hand, and then place them.

(c) Above her cover. Use left-hand service. This position cannot be used if the hostess is serving the dessert. When the number of cups to be laid is odd, the single cup and saucer may always be placed in the position of the hostess's own cup at her cover—it is a convenient position for pouring.

4. Place the dessert in front of the hostess. Place the pot of hot beverage on the hostess's right, either directly on the table or on a tray (see Figures 19–1 and 19–2). Return to your place at the table. Your return will be a signal for the service of dessert.

Serving Dessert from the Kitchen. Much of the time dessert is served up onto dessert plates or into bowls or stemmed ware directly from the kitchen. A variant in the latter situation is to bring the desserts served into bowls or stemmed ware to the serving table on a tray and to serve them from it. Proceed as follows when service is strictly from the kitchen.

1. Place the beverage service on the table according to the option chosen.

2. Bring the desserts from the kitchen, one in each hand. Place from the left the one in the left hand in front of the proper person. Transfer the one in the right hand to the left hand and place it from the left in front of the person next to the right. Return to the kitchen for two more desserts and proceed as above until all at the table have been served.

3. Bring the pot of hot beverage and place it at the hostess's right. Return to your place at the table.

Serving Dessert from the Serving Table. This practice is a possible option when you are serving dessert from the kitchen. Proceed as follows:

1. Place the beverage service on the table in accordance with the selected option.

2. Bring desserts served into bowls or stemmed ware (i.e., ice cream) on a tray from the kitchen, and place the tray on the serving table. You

should have placed a stack of underliner plates for the desserts on the serving table when you arranged it. Place small paper or fabric doilies on coupe plates (plates without rims) as you stack them. This practice prevents the sliding of the dessert dish placed on the plate as the total service is set down on the table. For easy serving of the dessert, put one served dessert on the top plate of the stack and then remove the total service with the left hand. Place a second served dessert on the next plate, remove it with the right hand. Proceed to the dining table and set them down as previously described. Continue in the same manner until all at the table have been served.

3.   Bring the pot of beverage from the kitchen and place. Return to your place at the table.

Strictly About the Service of Hot Beverages

Customs of beverage service differ in different socioeconomic groups, in different ethnic groups, and in different regions of the United States. Hot tea or coffee may be offered with the main course or only with the dessert course. Coffee may be served after the dessert at the table or away from the table. It may be served from the table or from the side. Because it is so much easier to serve it from the table and pass the filled cups on saucers from hand to hand, we have given directions for this procedure.

Whenever a hot beverage is offered throughout the meal, it is customary to refill the cups when dessert is served: the beverage pot is taken to the kitchen and refilled with the hot beverage unless it has been maintained at a suitable temperature. The arrangement for the beverage service should include a spill bowl into which the dregs in cups may be poured out before the cup is refilled. For a spill bowl, use any bowl suitable in appearance and large enough to contain the cold remnants that may remain in cups. Cups and saucers are passed from hand to hand for refilling.

MEAL SERVICE WHEN HIRED HELP IS AVAILABLE

The percentage of families so fortunate as to have hired help available for some or all meals is small; however, some families can hire assistance in the serving of an occasional meal. The use of hired help for the serving of a meal permits us to extend the menu, to use a formal pattern of service, and to relax and enjoy the meal without having to rise and wait on table. The menu can be extended by one or more courses, perhaps a soup might precede the main course, or a salad might follow the main course. Any pattern for serving meals may be adopted that is consistent with one's resources and the skill of the hired help. How much a hostess can relax and enjoy this meal will be determined to some extent by how skilled the help is and how well she has planned the service of the meal and how well she has instructed the person or persons hired.

If she has been able to hire skilled help from a catering service, she has less planning and less instructing to do. If she has hired unskilled help, she may wish to consider some of the following suggestions for having the special dinner or luncheon go smoothly.

1.   Hire enough help to accomplish what you want done, perhaps one person to wait on the table and another to do the kitchen work.

2.   Find out how well trained the person or persons hired are, then plan accordingly.

3.   Plan step by step what you expect done from the moment those hired take over. Explain step by step what you want done and how. Leave written instructions in the kitchen. Try to have it understood that you are to be consulted should anything go awry.

4.   For your own peace of mind have the following clearly understood.

(a)   Who will be served first if the hired person is placing served plates or passing food that guests will help themselves to.

(b)   The order in which those at the table will be served and the order to be followed in clearing each course.

(c)   How you wish a beverage service placed at the table.

When the available help is quite inexperienced, it is probably desirable to use the buffet pattern of meal service for special meals. Inexperienced help fully instructed and assisted can very likely carry out smoothly the simple duties that buffet service requires.

MEALS WITHOUT WAITING ON THE TABLE

People in the United States like two-course meals; they like the main course followed by something, even though that something is only a few grapes or a cookie. These two courses have been served as one. The problem has been that of having the dessert on the table during the main course and of eating the dessert course without removing the soiled dinnerware. Two practices that have prevailed—at least in the Middle West—are these. Individually served desserts appear in the covers as a side dish above or to the left of the dinner plate. Dessert can be eaten without being moved, or it can be moved and placed on top of the dinner plate and eaten. Or else the dessert is taken from a common dish and served onto the dinner plate, or another plate within the cover, from which it is eaten. Neither of these practices is completely satisfactory. A more pleasing procedure suggests that the soiled dishes of the main course be passed from hand to hand to one or both ends of the table, where they are placed on a side table. The dessert is then served from the side table and passed from hand to hand until all have been served. Hot beverages are similarly served. Essential for this kind of service is a serving table that can be placed to the right of the hostess's chair, possibly a similar table that can be placed to the right of the host's chair, and an appliance for keeping a beverage hot or for brewing coffee or tea at the table.

Here are some suggestions for serving meals with finesse without waiting on the table.

1.   Serve the main course in such a way that there is no need to pass plates or serving dishes. Either serve plates in the kitchen or permit guests to serve themselves at a buffet. However, if the host is unhappy when he cannot serve, by all means arrange so that he can. Some way of limiting hand-to-hand passing will suggest itself.

2.   Have no more than two plates at each cover. If a salad plate is used, omit the bread-and-butter plate; if no salad plate is used, a bread-and-butter plate may be laid.

3.   When you offer a salad, avoid serving it from the table; instead, serve it up in the kitchen, and place the salad at each cover. But if you wish to offer the salad as a separate course, the bowl of salad may be passed from hand to hand and served onto the now empty dinner plate. This practice is acceptable, although some people do not favor it. You may also serve the salad course in the usual manner, but remember that this procedure means more passing from hand to hand.

4.   When dessert is to be passed from hand to hand, keep to a food that can be served onto a plate. Avoid the double setup of bowl-on-plate, which complicates passing. Should you use a double setup, place a small doily between the plate and the dish to keep the dish from slipping.

Setting the Side Table

Ideally, the side table should accommodate the dessert service, the beverage service, and the soiled plates from the first course. If it does not, a second side table can be used; one table is used for the solid plates, and the other is used for the dessert and the beverage service. A three-tiered table is probably easier to work with than a two-tiered table, but not necessarily. The dimensions of the table should be such that all soiled dishes can be placed below the top level. There are several optional procedures for arranging the table, depending on its style and size; however, certain principles are fundamental to effective use of the table.

1.   Place the dessert on the second level of a three-tiered table, on the lowest level of a two-tiered table, to keep it out of sight; place the plates and tools for serving it, the cups and saucers, the creamer and the sugar bowl, and the beverage pot on the top level, if possible. As soon as you are

ready to clear the table and will make use of the lowest level, you will bring the dessert up to a higher level.

2.   Because you will stack plates as you receive them, place a basket large enough to accommodate the flatware on the lowest level.

3.   Place accessory items like bread and relishes on the top level or to the right or left of your cover, so that they can be passed around the table and cleared to the serving table with a minimum of passing.

4.   If you intend to serve the salad as a separate course, you may prefer to put the appointments for dessert on the second level and use the top level for serving the salad.

5.   To enable you to use the side table easily and without appearing awkward, use a dining chair without arms.

Using the Side Table

Experience in the use of the side table enhances its value in achieving a smooth, relaxed, and comfortable service for all. Here are some ideas for easy use.

1.   Clear your own cover first or last, depending on whether you need to make room for dessert or beverage service in order to have room for stacking plates.

2.   Ask each person on your left, beginning with the person on the host's right to pass his dinner plate to you. Then, beginning with the host, take dinner plates from those on your right, in turn. Stack them as you have planned but do it quietly.

3.   Next, have salad or bread-and-butter plates passed to you in the same manner as the dinner plates.

4.   Let saltcellars and pepper shakers, unused flatware, and other inconspicuous items remain on the dining table.

5.   If you intend to serve the dessert, place the dessert plates in the center of your cover; put the dessert and the tools for serving it above the plates. Serve the dessert in the order you accepted dinner plates from those at the table.

6.   Set up the beverage service according to your preference, and serve it in the order described earlier, unless you prefer to serve it in the living room.

7.   Both the dessert and the beverage may be served from the side table if you so desire.

8.   Should you wish to serve the salad as a course following the main course, that, too, can be managed. If one side table will not accommodate everything, place a second table beside the host. He will ask that the dinner plates be passed to him, beginning with you and then taking those on his left, then those on his right. As soon as you have given up your dinner

plate, you will place the salad service at your cover. After all dinner plates have been removed, you will serve the salad.

The most serious objection to this particular style of serving meals is concerned with refilling beverage glasses. Strictly *en famille*, there is no reason why a pitcher of milk or water cannot be placed on the table: the members of the family pass their glasses rather than the pitcher. When guests are present, it is desirable to avoid this practice. A solution would be for the host to rise and refill those glasses that are empty or nearly so. Theoretically, the good guest does not drain his water glass in the first few moments of dining; instead, he sips from it, and, if the glass is moderately large, the supply is sufficient for the entire meal, especially when coffee accompanies dessert.

Common sense tells us that exact procedures for serving meals, when neither host nor hostess is to leave the table, will vary with menus and the number served. Until the homemaker is accomplished, one or more rehearsals of the service would be effective in producing a smooth and confident service when guests are present. Some families like this service; others do not. Some homemakers do not like to leave the table when guests are present; others do not mind. When the group is large enough, buffet service is a happy compromise.

Summary.   Telling takes longer and makes the task seem more difficult than actual doing. The procedures described are not the only acceptable ones, nor are they inviolate. The homemaker can modify them to fit her life style and her resources, always remembering to keep procedures comfortable for all and convenient for the person waiting on the table. The fact is that she can ignore all suggestions and "rules" that have been established and follow her own ingenious system, so long as none at the table are made uncomfortable.

REFERENCE CITED

1.   Toffler, Alvin, *Future Shock*. New York: Random House, 1970.

Chapter 20
Etiquette of the Table

Every culture has defined who shall eat with whom, how food shall be taken or received, and how food shall be conveyed to the mouth. Customs of dining and of behavior while dining are defined for a time and a place; those of Western cultures are different from African, Muslim, and Oriental cultures. The body of definitions includes both proscriptions and prescriptions that are part of the folkways. As part of the folkways, the behavior must be taught, it must be learned, it gives order and stability in group interaction, it gives to individuals a sense of security in group situations, and it is supported by the sanctions of the group. Failure to observe the prescribed etiquette brings disapproval, which in the extreme may lead to exclusion from the group.

The origins of dining customs are lost in time; ascribed origins include superstitions, religion, class delineation, and gestures of friendship. Contemporary table manners have been a long time evolving, but much of their refinement has come about during the past four centuries and parallels the widespread adoption of individual eating utensils in Western cultures. The fork was the last adopted of these tools. Although forks were known in Italy as early as the eleventh century, it was the sixteenth century before French society and the eighteenth century before the French middle-class knew the fork. It was not introduced into England until the seventeenth century and it was not until the late eighteenth century that the lower classes adopted the fork. As late as the turn of this century the knife was in use for conveying food to the mouth and a proscription in table etiquette was "don't eat with your knife."

In the same way that setting-the-table and waiting-on-the-table customs are dynamic, so are customs at table. Practices bow to expediency or fall into disuse. Yet, they are folkways modified only by the group. Individuals cannot ignore them without group disapproval. The 1960's produced no perceptible changes in the traditional customs practiced while dining, though they did witness greater use of casual forms—the outdoor barbecue, the patio supper, and the brunch.

In the United States, table customs vary in minor details among different ethnic groups, in different regions of the country, among different socioeconomic classes, and in urban and rural communities. The way of the group will have the sanction of the group. Following are some general definitions for behavior at the table. The order of presentation is the approach to the table; the seating arrangement at the table; the offering of food at the table; the use of the napkin and the tools for eating; directions for eating certain foods; and last, duties and responsibilities at the table.

THE APPROACH TO THE TABLE

Go to the table with confidence in your knowledge of custom. However, if you are unsure, watch your hostess for cues.

1.   Permit older and honored persons to precede you to the table.

2.   Take the position your hostess assigns you. Seat yourself from either the left or the right side of the chair, whichever is easier and less likely to disturb another. Move the chair only if it is essential. In a mixed group a woman pauses to permit the gentleman on her left to assist her as she sits down. A gentleman always assists the woman on his right. He also assists the woman on his left if there is no other person to perform this courtesy. When both older and younger women make up the group, the younger women assist the older women as they seat themselves.

3.   The procedure is to pull the chair out from the table slightly and then to push it gently under a woman as she sits down.

4.   Sit up straight in the chair, do not slouch or lean over the table. Keep your elbows close to your sides to avoid jostling your neighbors. Do not lean with your elbows on the table except between courses and then only if your hostess has led the way.

5.   Do not finger the flatware at your cover, and do not rearrange the appointments at your cover.

SEATING ARRANGEMENTS AT THE DINING TABLE

The seating arrangements at the dining table when guests are present are simply prescribed, with few alternatives possible. The seating arrangements when the family dines alone may be varied and determined by family size, the ages of the children, the arrangements for dining, and family preference.

When the Family Dines Alone

When dining *en famille,* parents usually sit at opposite ends of the family table; children sit in between in positions determined by the amount of assistance needed. The son or eldest son may sit to his mother's right; the daughter or eldest daughter to her father's right. A grandmother or other elderly woman who is a family member sits on the host's, that is, the father's right, unless she is so disabled as to require assistance best rendered by the hostess, that is, the mother of the family. Similarly, an elderly male relative would sit on the hostess's right. When guests join the family table, family members are disarranged to permit the seating of a woman guest to the host's right and a gentleman guest to the hostess's right.

When the Family Has Guests

When there are guests, seating arrangements at the table are established by the number to be seated, the distribution of the sexes, and the composition of the group. In so far as possible couples are separated and men and women are alternated around the table. The host and hostess sit opposite each other except when those at the table are couples and the number at the table is eight, twelve, or other multiples of four. The woman guest, or the most honored woman guest, sits to the right of the host; the gentleman guest, or the most honored gentleman guest, sits to the right of the hostess. When the number at the table is eight or more, it saves time and reduces confusion to have place cards at covers.

1. When the number at the table is even, but not a multiple of four, the host and hostess sit opposite each other and the sexes are alternated, when the group consists of couples, or the sexes are evenly distributed. A group wherein there are more men than women or vice versa is seated so that all persons have compatible dinner companions.

2. When the number at the table is a multiple of four and the sexes are evenly divided, the host retains his position at one end of the table; but the hostess relinquishes her place to the most honored gentleman at the table. She sits at his left; he sits on her right as custom requires. Should the group at the table be unevenly divided as to sexes, the hostess may retain her position at the head of the table and seat the guests in any way she chooses, so long as the most honored guests are seated in accordance with custom.

3. When the number at the table is odd, the host and the hostess sit opposite each other; other persons are seated at the table so that they have compatible dinner companions.

4. When there is no host, a hostess sits at one end of the table. She may ask a gentleman friend to sit opposite her in those situations when a host

would sit opposite her. She would seat an honored woman guest opposite her when the number at the table is a multiple of four, she would likely ask a gentleman friend to sit to this woman's left.

5. When all at the table are women, the honored woman guest sits opposite the hostess, who sits at one end of the table. In some situations, an honored woman is seated to the right of the hostess, the chairman, or the president of a group.

Offering Food at the Table

Food is offered at the table in two ways. First, serving dishes containing food are placed on the dining table or a nearby table; these are passed from hand to hand and each person helps himself to whatever he wants. This procedure is limited in use to small groups and informal meals. Second, the host, the hostess, or another person at the table may serve the food from the serving dishes onto plates, which are passed from hand to hand until everyone has been served or which are placed at individual covers by a servant. This procedure, too, is best limited to small groups, not more than eight.

When Food Is Self-served

When those at the table are to serve themselves, place the serving dishes of food on the dining table or a side table so that the host and the hostess can initiate the passing. In general, when guests are present, dishes will be offered to the woman guest on the host's right first and they will pass from person to person around the table; the host will receive them last and serve himself last. To avoid confusion; the hostess serves herself when dishes reach her; however, when she initiates the passing of dishes, she offers them to the person on her right without serving herself first. She receives them last and serves herself last. The offering of second portions will be initiated in the same manner as the initial offering of food.

When Food Is Served at the Table

When food is served onto plates by the host or another person at the table, the order in which plates are received depends on the composition of the group and on the presence or absence of a servant.

Servant Present. When a meal is strictly *en famille*, parents and children, the mother is served first; plates are then laid at individual covers in turn around the table by the servant, who moves in a counterclockwise direction. When guests are present at the table, the first served plate is placed at the cover of the woman sitting on the host's right; the second, at the cover of the person on her right; and so on. The servant moves around the table in a counterclockwise direction, but he bypasses the hostess and places her plate last and the host serves the last plate for himself. Removal of covers by the waitress is in the same order.

When the hostess serves salad or dessert at the table, a servant places these at individual covers beginning with the woman guest to the host's right and continues to the right around the table; the host's would be the last serving placed.

In Absence of Servant. The procedure will be slightly different when plates are passed from hand to hand. Any arrangements that keep passing minimal are desirable; for example, a hostess may prefer to have salad at covers instead of serving it at the table to avoid the passing of two plates within a course. Here are suggestions for expediting this service.

1. The person serving should always state clearly for whom a plate is intended.

2. At family meals served for parents and children only, the host passes the first served plate to his left to the hostess. All on his left are served in turn, then those on his right (see Figure 20–1a).

3. At meals where an honored woman sits on the host's right, the host passes the first plate to his right to this person. He passes all others to his left, the first going to the person to the right of the honored woman guest. Each in turn around the table receives a plate. It is desirable that after a person receives a served plate he not be asked to pass one. This means that the hostess receives her plate in order and is not the next to the last person served. This practice is a bow to expedience (see Figure 20–1c).

4. Although it is not a common practice to seat her so, an elderly woman sitting to the right of the hostess is served the first plate. It would

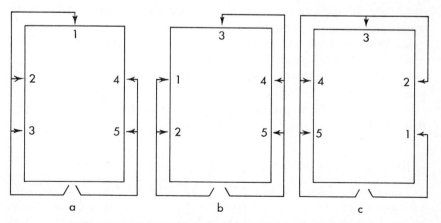

FIGURE 20–1. Order of serving persons at the table.

be passed by the host to his left; he would serve all on his left, then those on his right, beginning with the hostess (Figure 20–1b).

Procedure for Offering Second Portions

Although second portions are taboo for persons who wish to control weight, it is the custom to offer second portions in some places on some occasions. It can be managed this way. As soon as some diners may wish more food, the host moves his own plate to the right of his cover when this space is open, or to a small table placed to the right of his chair, in order to clear his cover. When guests are present, he asks the hostess if he may serve her. It is her duty to ask for a second portion of something, even though she may not want it or may not eat it, to set a precedent. She passes her plate, with knife and fork laid side by side on it, to her right to the host. Her plate is returned to her by the same route. The host asks each person on his left to be served, then those on his right. The order of serving second portions is the same as when the hostess receives the first plate.

Strictly within the family, it is more likely that children and hearty eaters will be served twice or more without the hostess accepting a second portion; when guests are present, however, her acceptance of a second portion signals that others may feel free to do so. Those at the table may ask for whatever they would like, even though food may remain on the plate, since this procedure expedites the serving of second portions.

THE USE OF THE NAPKIN

1. Follow the lead of the hostess. Remove your napkin from your cover when she takes hers. Remove it with your left hand and with the help of the right hand unfold it across your lap under the table. Open a luncheon napkin fully, leave a dinner-size napkin folded in half.

2. Use the napkin as necessary, but always use it before drinking to avoid leaving smears on glasses or cups and after drinking.

3. When you use the napkin, blot rather than wipe with it. Do not remove your lipstick on a fabric napkin.

4. When you leave the table, place the unfolded napkin to the left of your cover. Follow the lead of your hostess here.

5. Follow the same procedures for paper napkins as for fabric ones; don't shred or wad them.

THE USE OF THE TOOLS FOR EATING

To keep the discussion of the conventions for the use of the tools for eating as simple and coherent as possible, the parts of the tools are named. Knives have blades and handles; blades have dull and cutting edges. Forks and spoons have bowls and handles; the parts of the bowl of a fork are the tines.

Follow the lead of the hostess if you are unfamiliar with any tools appearing at your cover. When they have been properly placed, you can safely use them in the order of arrangement from the outside toward your plate.

The Knife and Fork

There are two quite different customs in the use of the knife and fork, the American and the European. The American eats from the fork held in the right hand, tines directed upward; the European eats from the fork held in the left hand, tines directed downward. We favor the use of the fork for cutting whenever it is an effective tool for this purpose. We lay the knife across the rim of the plate when not in use; the European retains it in his hand until he has finished eating the course because he must continually put it to use. Our zigzag style of eating is more leisurely, the European's is more efficient; Americans in Europe tend to copy the Europeans, and Europeans in United States tend to copy us. You may eat according to either style; just make certain that your technique is perfect.

1.   To use the knife for cutting, grasp it in the right hand with the cutting edge of the blade directed downward, thumb extended along the handle, the cushion of the first finger pressing close to or at the union of blade and handle, and the remaining fingers curled around and under the handle, the end of which presses into the center of the palm. When the fork and knife are used together for cutting, grasp the fork with the tines directed downward in the same manner. That is, the index finger presses on the shaft of the fork, the thumb extends along the handle, and the fingers of the hand curl under and around the handle. Do not enclose the handles of either fork or knife with a clenched fist. In order to hold food securely on the plate while cutting, pierce the food with the fork in the manner of a spear. Always keep the fork between you and the knife.

2.   After cutting two or three bites of food, lay the knife with the cutting edge directed toward you across the upper right quadrant of the plate and transfer the fork to the right hand. Hold the fork with the tines pointing upward so that it rests on the second finger, the first finger presses on the edge of the handle, and the cushion of the thumb rests on top of the handle.

3.   To use the knife as a spreader hold it as for cutting but turn it one right angle to the left so that the first finger presses on the flat of the handle and the cutting edge of the blade is directed to your right.

4.   Use the fork in the right hand to scoop food onto it except as it is turned over in the hand to pierce a bite of something. Never put more

than one bite of food onto it; eat from the tip of the fork, tines directed upward.

5.   Use the fork in the right hand for cutting food whenever it is an effective cutting tool. Grasp it in the hand the same way you do the knife so that the edge of the bowl of the fork cuts against the plate, the handle is between thumb and second finger, the first finger presses on the edge of the handle, and the end of the handle presses into the center of the palm.

6.   Use the fork for buttering vegetables including the baked potato. Eat a firm ice served with an entree with the fork.

7.   When not in use, the knife lies across the outer rim of the plate, its cutting edge directed toward you. When not in use, the fork lies so that the bowl is centered on the plate; the handle is directed right about parallel with the table edge in front of you.

8.   When you have finished eating, lift the knife and lay it beside the fork, but keep the fork between you and the knife.

Spoons

The spoon is used in the right hand only. It is a tool for cutting, as well as a tool for eating. It is held in the same way as the fork.

1.   Dip the spoon away from you when eating soup, and sip from the side nearest you.

2.   Dip the spoon toward you when eating soft foods, and eat from the tip of the spoon.

3.   Stir a beverage, or test its temperature with a spoon; always lay the spoon on the saucer after use.

4.   When eating with a spoon, always lay it on the plate under the bowl into which the food was served. An exception to this rule is that a soup spoon may remain in a soup plate. If there is no underliner plate, as when a vegetable in cream or a soft ice is served with a main course, lay the spoon on the dinner plate. Never lay a spoon that you have used on the table.

5.   When iced tea is served in a glass without an underliner and you use a spoon to stir in sugar, hold the spoon aside between your first and second fingers as you drink.

MANAGING GLASSES, GOBLETS, AND CUPS

1.   Take hold of tumblers and small glasses by encircling them at the base with the thumb and the first two fingers; the other fingers either support the glass at the base or withdraw into the palm of the hand, depending on the size and weight of the glass.

2.   Grasp a footed or stemmed water glass at the base of the bowl between the thumb and the first two fingers; the remaining fingers encircle

the stem or withdraw into the palm if the stem is short. Grasp wine glasses by the stem to avoid warming the wine.

3.   Hold a cup by the handle between the index finger and the thumb so that the index finger passes through the handle and the thumb presses on the top of the handle, which rests on the second finger. Drink from the side of the cup nearest you.

4.   You may drink soup from a cup if the soup is of thin consistency, but eat any ingredients that float before drinking; eat heavy ingredients that sink to the bottom of the cup after drinking the soup.

5.   The oriental teacup, a handleless cup, is held in both hands in a precise fashion. The right hand encircles the right of the cup; the cup rests on the fingers of the open left hand, the thumb of which presses on the cup near the rim. Drink from the near side just above the right thumb.

How to Eat Different Foods

Some foods may be taken and eaten with the fingers; these are finger foods. Only foods that do not leave the fingers greasy, sticky, or dripping with a sauce are finger foods. Actually, what is finger food for one person may be fork food for another; individual skill and techniques in eating differ. The following sections describe how some different foods have been eaten traditionally. Confronted with the unknown, use common sense, that is, eat with the fingers only those foods that leave the fingers unsoiled except, of course, when you are dining where the hands are used for eating.

Breads and Pastries

1.   Breads, cookies, slices of cake, pieces of cake without soft frostings, small cakes, doughnuts, and other nonsticky pastries are finger foods.

2.   Eat cake that has a soft frosting, is covered with whipped cream, or has a soft filling between its layers with a fork, or with a spoon if a fork has not been provided.

3.   Eat cream puffs, chocolate éclairs, napoleons, and all other filled pastries with a fork, just as you would always eat pie with a fork.

4.   Many sandwiches are finger foods, but use a knife and fork to eat one served with sauce and to eat some of the triple-deckers. Always break or cut a sandwich, including a hamburger on a bun, into pieces of suitable size before eating.

5.   Spread a tortilla with sauce or butter; roll it; eat it from the end of the roll.

6.   Eat pizza with knife and fork unless for you it is a finger food.

7.   To butter bread, remove a two-bite portion from a slice of bread or roll, and butter the bread while holding it on the rim of the bread-and-

butter plate or the main plate. When this piece has been eaten, break off another piece similar in size, and so forth. Don't butter a whole slice of bread, then bite into it. To butter all or not to butter all is a question that inevitably arises in a discussion of how to eat hot breads. Because hot baking-powder biscuits, corn bread, Sally Lunn, and nearly all hot breads lose eating qualities if not opened and buttered while hot, it would seem that one should do so in deference to the cook. However, break them into small portions for eating.

Fruits

Small fresh fruits are definitely finger foods; the mode of eating large fresh fruits is determined by kind and ripeness or juiciness. Canned and frozen fruits are eaten with a spoon.

1.   Small fresh fruits, such as cherries, grapes, apricots, plums, raisins, dates, and candied fruits and fruit peels are finger foods. The pits of cherries and the seeds of grapes may be removed from the mouth between the thumb and first finger. Eat the flesh from the pits of plums and apricots; the pits should end up in your hand, not in your mouth.

2.   Peel oranges and tangerines, and eat the easily separated sections with the fingers. To peel, score with a fruit knife from stem end to blossom end several times around the fruit, then pull away the petal-shaped pieces of rind. Oranges can be peeled round and round, making a continuous spiral of peeling.

3.   When cut in half, oranges, grapefruit, pears, and avocados are eaten with a spoon, preferably a sharp-pointed one. Eat oranges served sliced or in sections with a fork.

4.   Quarter, and peel if desirable, apples, pears, and peaches. If the flesh is firm, eat with the fingers; if juicy, eat with a fork.

5.   Watermelon is eaten with a fork; other melons, with a spoon. When peeled and served in slices, however, melon is eaten with a fork. Occasionally, fruit knife and fork are provided.

6.   Cut the flesh of cooked plums, prunes, and peaches from the pits with a spoon. The pits end up in the fruit dish, not in your mouth.

Meats, Fish, Poultry

In general, be satisfied with the quantity of poultry or meat that can be cut from the bones and eaten with a fork.

1.   Never chew the meat from chop bones, rib bones, and steak bones, except in privacy. The only bones nibbled from are those of tiny birds and frog legs.

2. Eat chicken or other poultry with the fingers only at a picnic, in privacy, or when granted the privilege.

3. Crisp dry bacon, which shatters under the fork, is finger food. Otherwise bacon is a fork food.

4. To eat clams, oysters, and snails out of the shell, steady the shell with the left hand and remove the edible parts with the small seafood fork provided. Dip a bite at a time into butter or sauce. Use the small seafood fork for removing crab and lobster from cracked shells and claws; gently suck meat from small claws. Again dip only a bite at a time into a sauce.

5. Eat the shrimp of a shrimp cocktail with the small seafood fork; should these be giant size, impale one on the fork, bite off a suitable bite as daintily as you can, and eat in two bites.

6. Use the dinner knife and fork for eating fried shrimp, fried clams, fried scallops, soft shelled crabs, and crab and lobster served out of the shell. However, if shrimp have tails intact, they may be taken with the fingers; the edible part is eaten to the tail, which is returned to the plate.

7. Although people in the United States like gravy on their potatoes, gravy is properly put onto meat. To sop bread with gravy, drop a small piece of bread into the gravy and eat it with knife and fork.

8. Place any accompaniments to meat, poultry, and fish to the side of it. Put it on the meat with the fork.

Vegetables

In general eat vegetables with a fork, but fresh crisp relishes are finger foods.

1. Place vegetable relishes on the bread-and-butter plate, salad plate, or dinner plate in that order of preference when you help yourself to these.

2. French fried potatoes and onion rings are fork foods. Potato chips and shoestring potatoes are finger foods.

3. Don't break open a baked potato and scoop the contents out on to the plate; rather add butter or sauce and eat it bite by bite from the shell. If you wish to eat a baked potato, skin and all, use knife and fork to cut the skin into bite-sized pieces.

4. In general, pickled fruits and pickled vegetables are fork foods. Only small whole pickles and olives are finger foods. Bite the flesh of unpitted olives from the pit while holding the olive in the hand; that is, don't put the olive in the mouth, chew the flesh away, and then remove the pit from your mouth.

5. Eat vegetables served in cream and stewed tomatoes with a spoon.

6. If it is not broken into halves, break corn-on-the-cob into halves,

butter it by row, and eat it by row. Hold the cob between your two hands.

7.   The leaves of the artichoke are taken with the fingers, dipped into butter, and the small edible bit eaten off the leaf. Leaves are laid on the plate. The thistle part is removed with knife and fork and laid on the plate. Finally, the heart is eaten with knife and fork.

8.   Use the knife with the fork in cutting wedges of lettuce or any salad ingredient that the fork alone does not cut. When salads are served as separate courses, forks and knives are usually provided.

MISCELLANEOUS NOTES ON EATING

The Act of Eating

Effort must be made to keep the basic act of eating refined or it can be quite unsightly.

1.   Keep bites sufficiently small so that you can quickly empty your mouth if someone should address you.

2.   Do not drink a beverage when your mouth has food in it, unless the food is burning hot and you drink to cool the mouth.

3.   Do not chew with your mouth open.

4.   To avoid appearing at your very worst, talk only when your mouth is empty.

5.   Do not put your hands on your hair, ears, or face while eating.

6.   Do not use your fingers to push food onto your fork. You may use your knife, held in the left hand in the same manner as held in the right hand for cutting, for this purpose. Do not use bread in your fingers to sop up gravy or sauce; you may, however, drop a piece of bread into it and, using knife and fork, eat it like any other food.

7.   Do not hunch your shoulders over your plate. Move the body forward from the hips, not the waist or shoulders. Lift food to your mouth; do not lower your head to the food.

8.   You may tip soup or dessert dishes away from you to get last spoonfuls.

9.   You may drink thin soups; spoon vegetables and other bits.

10.   Never use a toothpick except in privacy in the United States, although its use is less frowned upon elsewhere in the world.

Individual Casseroles

When food is served in individual casseroles, remove the contents to your plate, a portion at a time, if the casserole has been placed on an underliner and a spoon has been provided for this purpose. Otherwise, eat directly from the casserole. If the casserole has been brought to the table with the cover on it, put the cover on the underlying plate, not on the table.

Removing Food from the Mouth

Remove fish bones and other objectionable bits from the mouth between thumb and first finger and place them on the dinner plate. Make an effort to conceal them if they are unsightly. Remove the pits and seeds of fruits eaten with the fingers, like cherries and grapes, with the fingers to the plate. In general, eat fruits like plums away from the pits; place the pit on the plate. Remove a pit to a spoon if one gets into the mouth while you are eating canned fruits.

Self-service

Never use personal silver in removing food from a common container.

1. Use a meat fork like a scoop and the spoon to steady the portion during the transfer of meat to your plate; use the spoon like a scoop and the fork to assist, when serving other dishes.

2. In general, leave a spoon in the serving dish rather than on the underlying plate.

3. Place condiments and relishes that accompany meat, fish, and poultry beside them on your main plate.

4. Place relishes to be eaten with the fingers on your bread-and-butter plate, salad plate, or main plate in that order, depending on what is at your cover.

5. Help yourself to finger foods so daintily that you touch only the pieces you take.

Finger Bowls

Gently dip the fingers of one hand, then of the other, into the water in the finger bowl; unobtrusively dry them with your napkin. You may moisten your lips casually if you think it essential; blot to dry them.

Smoking

When you are a guest, smoke only when your hostess has made provisions for smoking and only when she suggests that you may. In general, smoke at the table only when it is agreeable to all others at the table.

To sum up, it is not necessary to memorize the specific do's and don't's of table etiquette; it is necessary only to remember not to offend by word or deed. The do's and don't's exist only so that each person will be good company and pleasant to look at.

THE RESPONSIBILITIES OF HOST AND HOSTESS

If meals are to be enjoyed by everyone, each person at the table has a share in making them enjoyable; no hostess, family member, or guest can carry this burden alone. Each one owes it to the others to be pleasant to look at in appearance and deportment; a dirty face, uncombed hair, elbows on the table, and the wolfing of food are never pleasant to see. Similarly, everyone owes it to the others to be good company; kindness, which is at the core of etiquette, should govern personal conduct. The host and hostess always have special duties and obligations.

The Duties of Hosts

Although father is head of the house and mother is head of the table, they share the responsibility of making each meal a happy occasion, whether guests are present or not. Both should be equally alert in sustaining conversation and in guiding it into the right channels. A good conversationalist may be a good listener; nonetheless, given sufficient encouragement, most people like to talk. Good hosts see that each person has a chance to say something at some time during a meal.

Conversation should be kept general enough so that all will be interested, and topics that give offense to some should be avoided. It is a good idea for new and inexperienced hosts to have plans for managing conversation when guests are present. *En famille* mealtime should never be a time for administering discipline or solving family problems, especially budgetary ones.

The Special Duties of the Hostess

The first duty of a hostess is to plan her menu and her work so that she can remain calm, cool, and collected at mealtime, especially if there are guests. She should be present in her living room to greet guests when they arrive, although she may soon excuse herself to complete last-minute preparations for the meal. An experienced hostess plans to serve a few minutes later than she has asked guests to arrive because she knows that someone will arrive late; she does not, however, ask guests for dinner at seven and serve at nine.

In a sense, a hostess leads the way at mealtime, and others follow; they eat when she does and they eat as she does. She is cook, butler, and waitress. Here are special notes for hostesses.

1.   Do enjoy the first course with guests; do not take this time to complete tasks in the kitchen. You may do these while the host and/or the children clear away the glasses and other appointments used in serving the first course.

2.   The hostess invites guests to the table. She takes her position at the table quickly so that she can direct others to their places if the group is small and place cards have not been placed.

3.   Make a plan for seating guests in advance, so that you can do it smoothly. You will seat guests with poise, if you simply place your hands on the top of your chair and say, "Mrs. Boss, will you sit on John's right and Mr. Boss, will you sit on my right? Mary, will you sit beside Mr. Boss, and Robert, will you sit next to Mrs. Boss?," and so forth. By grasping the back of the chair with your hands, you will avoid pointing, which makes you appear awkward, and you will conceal the nervousness that your trembling fingers may display. Use place cards for eight or more.

Now a word about seating guests. First of all, it should be remembered that in most homes seated groups will be small: rarely will they exceed eight in number. It probably matters little to most people where they sit at the table; all guests are honored guests and all cannot sit to the right of the host or the hostess. Except for elderly persons and others of accomplishment, who merit the honor of sitting to the right of host or hostess, seat guests so that each has for a dinner companion a person he will enjoy.

4.   After all are seated, ask someone to say grace, if you wish, but be certain the person asked will not be embarrassed.

5.   Take your napkin and unfold it across your lap. Begin eating at once if served plates are at the covers. Start passing the serving dishes near you, without first serving yourself. Ask to have other serving dishes passed by those who can reach them; be specific in your request, saying, "Will you pass the 'whatever'?"

6.   When food is being served from the table, suggest that the first served begin eating if there are more than six at the table; otherwise, begin to eat as soon as all except the host are served.

7.   When you are serving salad or a vegetable, pace your service to the host's, if he, too, is serving. In serving most dishes, use a spoon as a scoop in your right hand, and steady it with the fork held in the left hand. First, serve those on your left, beginning with the person on the host's right; serve each in order. Then serve those on your right, beginning with the person on the host's left; serve each in order. Serve the host and then yourself. However, in the interest of expedience you may serve the host before serving those on your right. Follow this serving order when you serve dessert and when you pour a beverage at the table.

8.   Have dishes passed or served a second time, if you have planned for it. Accept a second portion so that others may comfortably do the same.

9.   Continue to eat as long as any guest is eating.

10.   When all have finished, signal to the person who is to clear the main course and serve desserts; a nod of the head should do. If you perform these duties, remain away from the table the shortest possible period of time.

11.   Wait for the return of any person who has left the table to remove or bring in a course before beginning to eat or serve.

12.   If you are to serve the beverage at the table, serve its accompaniments also; this avoids some passing at the table. Use tongs for serving lump sugar and a small fork for lemon. If you have neither, you may use a small spoon. When you do not know personal preferences for cream and sugar, ask what they are. Unless the beverage pot has a hinged cover, pouring is safer when the left hand holds the top securely in place. Pour by tipping the beverage pot, rather than by lifting it, whenever this is possible. Separate cups stacked by two's by taking the top cup in the right hand, lifting with the left hand the saucer on which the remaining cup rests; place the cup in the right hand on the remaining saucer, transferring the cup and saucer in the left hand to the right hand, and placing it in position for pouring. You will appear more graceful if you pour into a cup resting on the table. Pouring from a pot held in the right hand into a cup that rests on a saucer held in the left hand looks clumsy, but it may be the only possible procedure with some beverage pots and carafes.

13.   When you are certain that all have eaten and drunk their fill, give the signal for leaving the table by suggesting that all find more comfortable chairs or that they look at John's roses, or pictures, and so forth.

14.   When guests offer assistance, you may accept it if you are certain it is sincerely offered. Graciously refuse if you prefer.

The Special Duties of the Host

The host is the sole dispenser of hospitality when the hostess is absent from the room or the table. He greets guests at the door and assumes the responsibility for coats and hats. He may serve, or at least assist in serving, a first course in the living room. When the pattern of service permits the service of food from the table, this is the host's very special privilege. Here are special points for the host.

1.   When you have guests, take the woman who will sit on your right in to dinner and seat her at the table. Pull her chair away from the table slightly and then push it under her as she sits down.

2.   Be prepared to serve food from the table, if the pattern of service requires it.

3.   Serving food from the table is very easy once you get the feel of it.

Develop skill by requesting the privilege of serving meals when guests are not present. You will want two serving tools or two-in-one tools for serving almost all dishes. One tool does the work; the other supports the first during the transfer of food from serving dish to plate. The tool that does the work is used like a scoop in the right hand.

4.   Learn proper carving procedures. Carve enough portions for all at the table before beginning to serve, unless the platter is so crowded with food that carving is difficult until at least some of the surrounding food has been served. Carving all portions before serving any saves time and continual handling of the carving tools.

5.   Serve meat plus any garnish present, potato, and vegetables in that order. Lift carved meat between the tines of the fork (pointed downward) and the blade of the knife. Use a spoon to assist a fork in serving meat that needs no carving, such as chops or patties. Use the spoon assisted by the fork for other services. Servers resembling pancake turners may be used to serve many items from platters and chop plates. They are particularly useful in the service of such soft foods as meat loaves, for which they may be cutting tools as well as serving tools. Do not make portions too large or crowd the plates.

6.   Pass filled plates in proper and logical order at the table, remembering to state for whom a plate is intended if any doubt can exist; remember, too, that once a person has accepted a plate, he should not have to pass another beyond him. The first plate may:

(a)   Be passed to your left to the hostess.

(b)   Be passed to your left to a special woman guest seated on the hostess's right.

(c)   Be passed to your right to a special woman guest seated on your right.

Decide with the hostess whom you are to serve first. If you are to serve her or a guest on her right, serve those on your left, then those on your right. If you serve a woman on your right first, pass all other plates to your left until all have been served.

7.   When the person on your immediate left is assisting you in the service of food, pass all plates to her. When all those on the left side of the table, except your assistant, have been served, you and she will exchange plates until all, including you, have been served completely filled plates.

8.   Lift the plate while placing food on it if it seems easier. Use the two serving tools provided for ease and comfort in serving when this seems appropriate. You will probably favor the scissors type of serving tools.

9.   Watch guests, and offer second servings as soon as some are ready; begin by asking the hostess to be served. Ask those on your left, then those on your right, if you may serve them. Avoid use of the words *more* and *again*. It is difficult to explain why they should be avoided because second

portions are obviously "more." However, it is considered better to say, "May I serve you this or that?" or "Would you like this or that?" Perhaps in doing so we avoid implying that guests are greedy.

10.   Keep alert for lapses and awkward turns in conversation, and carry part of the conversational burden; no hostess should have to do it alone.

11.   When the hostess is her own waitress, assist in the duties of removing one course and serving another. Follow her instructions. Remain at the table while she is away from it.

12.   Serve the dessert from the table if such a procedure is desirable. Serve it in the same order as you served the main course.

SUGGESTED REFERENCES

1.   Aresty, Esther B., *The Best Behavior*. New York: Simon and Schuster, 1970.
2.   Bracken, Peg, *I Try to Behave Myself—Peg Bracken's Etiquette Book*. New York: Harcourt Brace Jovanovich, Inc., 1964.
3.   Carson, G., *Polite Americans—A Wide-Angle View of Our More or Less Good Manners*. New York: William Morrow & Company, 1966.
4.   *Emily Post's Etiquette*, 12th Revised Edition, edited by Elizabeth L. Post. New York: Funk and Wagnalls, 1969.
5.   Free, Anne R., *Social Usage*. New York: Hawthorn Books, Inc., 1969.
6.   Haupt, Enid A., *The New Seventeen Book of Etiquette and Young Living*. New York: David McKay Company, Inc., 1970.
7.   Miller, Llewellyn, *The Encyclopedia of Etiquette, A Guide to Good Manners in Today's World*. New York: Crown Publishers, Inc., 1967.
8.   Moore, Charles, *George Washington's Rules of Civility and Decent Behavior in Company and Conversation*. New York: Houghton Mifflin Company, 1926.
9.   Roosevelt, Eleanor, *Eleanor Roosevelt's Book of Common Sense Etiquette*. New York: The Macmillan Company, 1962.
10.   Schlesinger, Arthur M., *Learning How to Behave: A Historical Study of American Etiquette Books*. New York: Cooper Square Publishers, Inc., 1968.
11.   Shaw, Carolyn, *Modern Manners*. New York: Fawcett World Crest Books, 1970 (Paperback).
12.   Vanderbilt, Amy, *Amy Vanderbilt's New Complete Book of Etiquette*. Garden City, N.Y.: Doubleday & Company, 1967.

Chapter 21

Managing Guest Meals

The decision to have guests to meals is a commitment to use the resources of money and of time and energy. The decision presupposes some knowledge of local customs, some skills and abilities in the preparation and serving of meals, and assumes the availability of the required equipment in the kitchen and of the appointments essential for dining. Put in another way, guest meals are planned on the basis of resources. These establish the size of the group invited, the menu, the pattern of meal service used, and so on. However, before the decision was made to have guests to dinner, there was a reason for having guests. This reason is important; it justifies the commitment of resources, and it affects the decisions on the menu and the style of dining. There are many reasons why we have guests to share our food: the offer of friendship; the meeting of obligations; the desire for belonging to the group; the desire for the approval of the group; the display of wealth, prestige, sophistication; the honoring of persons; the celebration of events; and others. Our reasons differ from time to time; the more compelling they are, the more likely we are to use our resources for them.

The meals to which we invite guests are dinner, brunch, and lunch, but most often dinner. Whichever meal it is, the guest meal has something special about it. The food may be different, and there may be more of it than we customarily serve. The style of dining and the appointments used on the table may be different from those we use from day to day. And we ourselves are different—we are less family-centered and more other-directed.

Guest meals are easier of accomplishment in the early 1970's than they were in the early 1960's. Obvious reasons for this have to do with the food per se: the vast assortment of available fresh, partially prepared, and

501

ready-prepared foods; supermarket services that include the bake shop, the delicatessen shop that will prepare a bird or roast, the wine cellar, and the gourmet shop; fast food shops that offer delivery or pick-up service of ready-to-eat fried chicken, barbecued meats, Chinese dinners, Mexican dinners, pizza, and so on; catering services that bring in not only the food but also the tables and the dining appointments. Other reasons include the availability of easy-care table appointments; the dishwasher in the kitchen; the acceptance of paper table appointments and of throwaway or single-service dinnerware and beverageware for informal meals; the trend away from formally served dinners to informal buffet suppers, brunches, patio meals, and outdoor barbecues; and finally altered expectations—of guests that meals will be formal and elaborate; of hosts that they are committed to serve formal and elaborate meals to guests.

The fact that guest meals can be easy has not made decisions on them easier to make, nor has it made these decisions any less significant. Not all persons make decisions in the same order; some will begin with money, some with the use of time, others with the guest list. Though few decisions are made independently of others, we shall discuss decisions in this order: the number of guests, the use of money, the meal service pattern, the use of time, and the menu.

Common sense suggests that the number of invited guests be limited to that number of persons who can be physically comfortable in the available space and to a number for which one can conveniently prepare and serve food. The decision on the use of money affects each that follows: the meal service pattern, the use of time, and the menu. If there are no limits to the use of money, help can be hired to prepare and/or serve a meal, food can be purchased more or less ready to eat, use of time can be greatly curtailed, and the menu can be composed of just about anything desired. Though there are families who place no limits to the use of money; the great majority do. The limit may be one dollar per person at table, or more, or less. Often the true reason for having guests encourages over-spending.

Limits on the use of money tend to eliminate the hiring of help to serve the meal. If the number will be eight or more, it is desirable that the meal, whether dinner, lunch, or brunch, be served buffet style. Even with six at the table, the main course is often offered from a buffet. When the group is small, compromise, blue-plate, or American styles can be used. When the hostess waits on her table, she should think through the service and seek ways to keep the waiting-on-the-table time minimal.

Few decisions stand alone. A decision that puts limits on the use of money requires the use of time and energy. Conversely, a decision to limit the use of time and energy requires increased spending of money in the purchase of partially prepared, ready-prepared, and quick-to-prepare foods. The decision to use throwaway table appointments is a decision to use the money resource—perhaps, to save time, perhaps for other reasons.

The number invited and the style of service decided upon affect the use of time. Common sense suggests that it takes longer to prepare dinner for eight than for four, and that it requires a greater investment of time and energy to set the table for a formal dinner for eight than for a buffet supper where guests will dine from the plate held in the hand. The fact is, the decision to have guests to dinner is a decision to use time and energy as well as money. The use of time can be controlled and with careful menu-planning the use of it can be spread over several days, a real boon to the homemaker following a career outside the home. The truly efficient manager of her time decides how much time to use and then tailors menu and all else to it.

Although one can spend much time in menu-making, it is the least time-consuming task associated with guest meals. Unless help is hired for the occasion, the meal is best limited to two courses at the table, the main course and the dessert course. Serve the first course in the living room or the family room, or the patio, or wherever guests will gather. Delay planning the first course until you have planned the main and dessert courses, however, to avoid repetitions and to introduce foods appropriate to the rest of the menu.

PLANNING THE MAIN COURSE AND THE DESSERT

Compose the menu so that it is right for the proposed budget, so that it fits your skill in cooking, so that there is little required last minute cooking, so that it is coordinated with your planned use of time, and so that it takes into account your facilities: oven, refrigerator, freezer, pots and pans, and table appointments. And, of course, consider the rules and guidelines of menu-making.

A meal consisting of excellently prepared baked beans, buttered carrots, tomato cole slaw, crisp relishes, rolls, and Indian pudding can provide wonderful eating and at the same time cost relatively little. The world is full of good things to eat. Prime rib roast of beef, thick porterhouse steak, broiled lamb chops, roast duckling, and turkey are good. But baked pork chops, spareribs with sauerkraut, lamb stews, Swedish meat balls, and broiled hamburger patties are also good. Your best selections are the dishes you prepare especially well, not exotic dishes, new and different. Do not be timid: serve cheeses and crackers or fresh fruits or both for dessert; commercial sherbets, ices, and ice creams; cheesecake made from a mix; cakes made from mixes; ready-made cakes and pastries. However, if you make a wonderful cherry pie, date pudding, or caramel custard, by all means plan your menu around your specialty. But do not plan so that you have to spend two days cooking unless you want it that way. Do plan so that you can prepare one or more dishes on one or more days in advance, such as gelatin salad, dessert, or even the entree that you can refrigerate or freeze until the day of your dinner. And do plan a menu that frees you of kitchen duties like broiling steak or making sauces the moment guests are expected to arrive. Last-minute preparations should only be the unavoidable ones like taking salads to the table and putting vegetables to cook. Do not finalize the menu without checking on the use of the oven previous to serving time; the needed roasting pans and saucepans; and the needed table appointments.

PLANNING THE FIRST COURSE

First courses are part of the image we have of special meals. Tradition has it that the purpose of the first course is to whet the appetite, a purpose that common sense discounts in the 1970's. In a weight-conscious era, many persons do not eat a first course, or a dessert either for that matter, except at special meals when they rationalize their behavior in a personally satisfying manner. It would be a pity to forego the first course in guest meals.

Favorite first courses are clear soups, fruit cups, shrimp cocktail, fresh fruits like melon, fruit juices, tomato juice, canapés, and savory hors d'oeuvres. The predinner cocktail is almost an established custom for guest meals. With the cocktail a great variety of tidbits and savory items is suitable and offered. What is offered differs with socioeconomic groups and from place to place. Low-calorie items like crisp vegetable relishes served with seasoning salt or a cheese dip are in favor at one place; smoked oysters, smoked clams, shrimp with a hot sauce, sour cream and cheese dips, smoked sausage cubes, mixed salted nuts, and so on, in another place. Plan a first course that follows local custom, and that looks, smells, and tastes good; avoid repetitions of foods in the other courses. For example, do not include seafood in the first course if it will appear in the main course, do not serve tomato juice if tomato will appear in the salad, and do not serve fruit cup or a fruit juice if the dessert will be fruits.

SOME SUGGESTED DINNER MENUS

Suggested dinner menus suitable for service from the table or from the kitchen follow; menus suitable for buffet meals appear in Chapter 23. No first courses are suggested for these dinners because they are a matter of custom and personal preference; each hostess would wish to plan this course herself. Some of these meals would be fairly expensive to serve; others would be quite inexpensive. Bread is suggested in all menus, but this item would be omitted from the main course where weight-watching has high priority; or bread might be retained in the menu and potatoes omitted. The broiling of meats requires last-minute attention and creates smoke and odors in poorly ventilated kitchens. It should never be attempted unless all disadvantages can be controlled. Broiled meats are well suited to patio or backyard meals; especially if a host specializes in meat cookery.

Menu I: Patio Dinner
Broiled Sirloin Steak
Twice-Baked Potatoes
Green Beans
Mixed Green Salad
Hot Rolls
Assorted Cheeses   Crackers
Assorted Fresh Fruits
Coffee

Menu II
Braised Stuffed Pork Chops
Squash   Peas
Mixed Salad of Lettuce, Celery, and Apple
Hot Rolls
Lemon Pie or Lemon Soufflé   Coffee

Menu III
Spaghetti with Meat Sauce
Assorted Crisp Relishes
Assorted Olives
French Bread
Assorted Fruits or Lemon Sherbet
Coffee

Menu IV
Prime Rib Roast of Beef
Yorkshire Pudding
Brussels Sprouts
Salad of Bibb Lettuce and Belgian Endive
Crème de Menthe Parfait
Coffee

Menu V
Roast Leg of Lamb
Mashed Potatoes
Asparagus
Mixed Green Salad
Assorted Relishes
Cherry Pie   Coffee

Menu VI
Swedish Meat Balls
Mashed or Scalloped Potatoes
Broccoli
Jellied Fruit Salad
Crisp Relishes
Rye Bread
Rice and Raisin Custard   Crisp Butter Cookies
Coffee

Menu VII
Baked Fish Fillets with Egg Sauce
Baked Potatoes   Beets with Lemon Butter
Tossed Green Salad
Hot Rolls
Coconut Cake   Coffee

Menu VIII
Baked Stuffed Chicken Breasts
Peas and Onions
Tomato Salad
Hot Cornbread
Caramel Custard
Coffee

SERVING THE FIRST COURSE

Serve the first course in the living room or the family room, or on the patio, to reduce waiting-on-the-table duties and to leave the kitchen uncluttered for serving the main course and the dessert course. You can serve almost any kind of food you might wish to offer in this informal fashion. Served food and/or beverage may be taken to seated guests, or food may be arranged so that guests serve themselves. A table-on-wheels is valuable in serving this course, to transport it to and remove it from the living area and, in between, it can serve as a buffet. A desk, a lamp table, or a card table can be set up as a buffet for the food if desirable. Here are a few specific suggestions.

1.   When the first course is a fruit juice or other beverage and no food will be offered, arrange a proper number of glasses and napkins on a tray. Spread the napkins enough so that each can be easily picked up from the tray. Fill the glasses to within an inch of the rim. Hold the tray low and offer it to each guest in turn (see Figure 21–1).

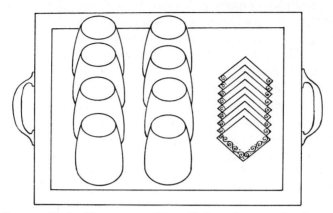

FIGURE 21–1.   Tray arranged for offering a beverage in glasses.

2.   Offer soup in the same way. Arrange on your tray a suitable number of cups and saucers, lay a spoon on the saucer parallel with the cup handle. Place the proper number of napkins and a small basket of salted wafers on the tray. Fill the cups no more than two thirds full. Carry the tray to the living room and set it on a table. Ask someone to assist you by offering the wafers as you offer the served soup to each guest in turn.

3.   You may also serve the soup from a tureen or a deep casserole or a pitcher from a table. Arrange the cups and saucers and the container of soup on a tray. Place the napkins and spoons nearby. Serve it to the guests, who come to the table for it; each takes a spoon and a napkin from the arrangement.

4.   Arrange the service of a hot food to be served from a chafing dish similarly. Place the chafing dish, a basket of toast or pastry shells for food

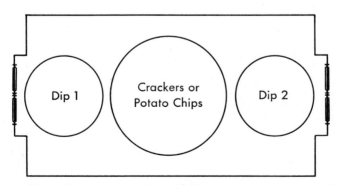

FIGURE 21–2.   Tray arranged for offering accompaniments to a beverage.

in a sauce, and plates on a tray. Arrange napkins and forks. Either serve this yourself or ask the guests to serve themselves.

5. Arrange an assortment of tidbits in bowls and on plates on a tray that you place on a table or directly on a table, desk, or card table. Place napkins and either small plates or small cocktail trays (four by six inches approximately), and picks for items that are not finger foods and that do not have picks inserted (see Figure 21–2). The plate or tray should accommodate food and a beverage glass whenever the group will be milling around. Offer seafood cocktail, as a bowl of shrimp, crab, or lobster, with a bowl of sauce for dipping.

6. Offer a fruit cup as a bowl or tray of fruits that have been trimmed and cut into pieces of suitable size. Have plates of suitable size and offer forks or picks.

SERVING COFFEE IN THE LIVING ROOM

A custom that adds glamour to guest meals is that of serving coffee in the living room, particularly when one has a fireplace around which all can sit.

Coffee may be served both with dessert and in the living room if one so desires. It may be served from a tray or from a serving cart. Demitasse or coffee cups may be used, whichever are more suitable for the group present. If the small cup is used, then the correspondingly small spoon must be used. Cream and sugar are offered unless the local custom is always to drink coffee black. See either Chapter 18 or Chapter 23 for information on how to arrange a tray for serving a beverage. See also Figure 21–3.

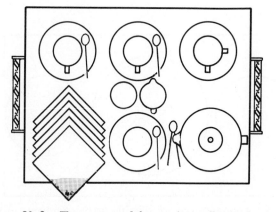

FIGURE 21–3. Tray arranged for serving coffee in demitasse.

Brunch

Brunch is defined in *Webster's New World Dictionary* as, "A combined breakfast and lunch." The hours when this meal is served vary, but between 10:00 A.M. and 1:00 P.M. is usual. It may follow church on Sunday or such active sports as golf or sailing on Saturday or Sunday. The menu usually consists of some or all of the following: fruits and/or juices; such breakfast dishes as eggs with bacon or sausages; such creamed dishes as chicken, sweetbreads, and chipped beef, accompanied, perhaps, by a hot vegetable; griddle cakes or waffles; hot breads and coffee cakes; assorted jams and jellies; and coffee. The meal is actually a very substantial late breakfast. Local custom determines whether or not cocktails or other alcoholic beverages are offered. Always offer coffee as soon as a guest arrives.

Any style of meal service may be followed; however, buffet style with table service is commonly used. For small groups, family service is good. If fruit juices are served before the guests come to the table, the meal can be composed of only one course served at the table. Following are suggested menus for this combined breakfast-lunch meal.

Menu I

Orange Juice

Canadian Bacon   Scrambled Eggs

Hash Brown Potatoes

Buttered Toast   Assorted Jams

Blueberry Muffins

Coffee

Menu II

Fresh Fruits in Season

Corned Beef Hash with Poached Eggs

Scalloped Chicken and Mushrooms

Toasted English Muffins

Coffee Cake

Coffee

Menu III

Fruits in Season

Blueberry Pancakes

Sausages   Ham   Bacon

Orange Muffins

Coffee

Menu IV
Assorted Fruit Juices
Creamed Ham and Eggs on Toast
Chicken Livers and Bacon
Hash Brown Potatoes
Buttered Toast   Brioche
Coffee

MEAL PRODUCTION

After decision-making comes the hand-and-foot work of meal production. Efficient use of time and energy is contingent on thoughtful organization of tasks from shopping to clearing the table. Time spent in anticipating these and in scheduling their doing saves time in the long run and reduces the stress that occasions of this kind generate. Here are some tasks you may wish to plan in detail.

1. The shopping for food, flowers, candles, and any other items you may need to purchase.
2. The selection and preparation of the appointments you will use on the dining table: linens, dinnerware, flatware, beverageware, and perhaps serving dishes.
3. The selection of appointments and the plan for serving a first course.
4. A time table for getting all of the above accomplished.
5. A time table for the preparation of the food of the meal.
6. A plan for waiting on the table.

In conclusion, we like to be guests and we like to have guests. These occasions are something special in our lives. They demand the commitment of resources, especially of time and energy. They require decision-making and hand-and-foot work. Experiences at home and elsewhere enrich our resources of knowledge, skills and abilities. In time, planning menus compatible with resources becomes easy; the planning for serving meals poses fewer questions; and finally, the preparation of the meal becomes easier. The more decisions made and the more planning done before the hand-and-foot work begins, the less stress is generated.

SUGGESTED REFERENCES FOR THIS CHAPTER AND CHAPTERS 22 AND 23

1. Alberson, Sarah D., *The Blue Sea Cookbook*. New York: Hastings House Publishers, 1968.
2. Bracken, Peg, *Peg Bracken's Appendix to the I Hate to Cook Book*. New York: Harcourt, Brace & World, Inc., 1966.
3. Brown, Helen Gurley, *Helen Gurley Brown's Single Girl's Cookbook*. New York: Bernard Geis Associates, 1969.

4. Child, Julia, *The French Chef Cookbook*. New York: Alfred A. Knopf, 1968.

5. Corinth, Kay, and M. Sargent, *All About Entertaining*. New York: David McKay Company, Inc., 1966.

6. Courtney, Marion, *Brunches and Coffees*. Chicago: Reilly & Lee Company, 1960.

7. Crutcher, Minnie Selvin, *The Single Girl's Hostess Handbook*. New York: Grosset & Dunlap, 1969.

8. Dariaux, Genevieve A., *Entertaining with Elegance*. Garden City, N.Y.: Doubleday & Company, Inc., 1965.

9. Ervin, Janet Halliday, *The White House Cookbook*. Chicago: Follett Publishing Company, 1964.

10. Gilbert, Edith, *All About Parties*. New York: Hearthside Press, Inc., 1968.

11. Hirsch, Sylvia, *The Art of Table Setting and Flower Arrangement*. New York: Thomas Y. Crowell Company, 1962.

12. Ivens, Dorothy, *Glorious Stew*. New York: Harper & Row, Publishers, 1969.

13. Jeffries, Ona Griffin, *In and Out of the White House from Washington to the Eisenhowers*. New York: Wilfred Funk, Inc., 1960.

14. Jervey, Phyllis, *A World of Parties, The Busy Gourmet's Guide to Exciting Entertaining*. Rutland, Vt.: Charles E. Tuttle Company, 1964.

15. Kroh, Patricia, *Contemporary Table Settings*. Garden City, N.Y.: Doubleday & Company, Inc., 1966.

16. Lee, Nata, *Complete Book of Entertaining*, Revised Edition. New York: Hawthorn Books, Inc., 1968.

17. *Michael Field's Cooking School*. New York: M. Barrows & Company, 1965.

18. *Michael Field's Culinary Classics and Improvisations*. New York: Alfred A. Knopf, 1967.

19. Morse, Theresa A., *The Best I Ever Tasted*. Garden City, N.Y.: Doubleday & Company, Inc., 1969.

20. _____, *Never in the Kitchen When Company Arrives*. Garden City, N.Y.: Doubleday & Company, Inc., 1964.

21. Perl, Lila, *Red-Flannel Hash and Shoo-Fly Pie, American Regional Foods and Festivals*. New York: The World Publishing Company, 1965.

22. Price, Mary and Vincent, *A Treasury of Great Recipes*. Princeton: Ampersand Press, Inc., 1965.

23. Roberts, Patricia E., *Table Settings. Entertaining and Etiquette*. New York: Viking Press, Inc., 1967.

24. Rombauer, Irma S., and Marion Rombauer Becker, *Joy of Cooking*. Indianapolis: Bobbs-Merrill Company, Inc., 1964.

25. Roosevelt, Nicholas, *Good Cooking*. New York: Harper & Brothers, 1959.

26. Ross, Anette Laslett, and Jean Adams Disney, *Cooking for a Crowd.* Garden City, N.Y.: Doubleday & Company, Inc., 1968.

27. Smith, Georgiana R., *Table Decoration: Yesterday, Today, and Tomorrow*. Rutland, Vt.: Charles E. Tuttle and Company, 1968.

28. Sullivan, Lenore, *What to Cook for Company*. Ames, Iowa: Iowa State University Press, 1962.

29. *Thoughts for Festive Foods*. Boston: Houghton Mifflin Company, 1964.

30. VanBibber, Jack, *Fast Feasts—A Cookbook for Hurried Gourmets*. New York: Funk and Wagnalls, 1969.

31. Wason, Betty, *Bride in the Kitchen*. Garden City, N.Y.: Doubleday & Company, Inc., 1964.

32. _____, *The Everything Cookbook*. New York: Hawthorn Books, Inc., 1970.

Chapter 22
Managing Buffet Meals

In a relatively short period of time the buffet pattern of meal service has been accepted; we have adapted it to our homes; we have created appointments especially for use on the buffet; and we have become fairly comfortable with it. Reasons for preference for buffet meals in the 1970's are several: waiting-on-the-table duties are reduced for hosts; larger numbers of guests can be accommodated than with the small dining table in the small dining area; and the informality that people in the United States value is fostered. Steps in the management of the buffet meal will be discussed in the following order because decisions are best made in that order: planning the dining arrangements, planning the menu, setting the buffet table, and planning for service.

Planning Dining Arrangements

Three patterns for dining are possible when meals are offered from a buffet. The homemaker's decision on which to use for a particular buffet meal will depend on her facilities, her wishes, the occasion, and the number to be present. The first choice is *table service*, that is, guests are seated at tables for dining. A second choice is *tray service*. For this plan, guests are provided with trays on which plate, beverages, and appointments are arranged. The tray provides a sort of table from which to dine. Third, guests may be expected to dine from the plate held in the hand, an arrangement we call *plate service*.

Table Service

Whenever possible, it is desirable to arrange for guests to dine at table. Some possibilities for table arrangements are these. The dining table may be used for dining and the buffet arranged on a chest, a serving table,

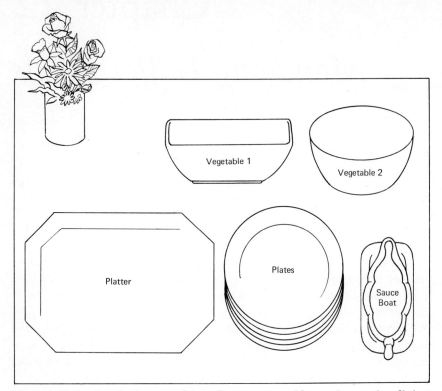

FIGURE 22–1.   Small chest set for buffet supper—table service at the dining table.

or any other suitable surface in the dining area, or even in the kitchen. When the area for dining is small, the buffet pattern of serving is ideal because it minimizes serving problems. The most frequently planned arrangement for dining is the use of card tables. Although they normally seat four, they can be enlarged to seat six by the use of round pads made especially for that purpose. Individual tables for dining and folding snack tables offer other possibilities. In general, the dining table serves as the buffet in the latter instances.

The tables for dining are completely set with the proper appointments: cloths or mats, flatware, beverageware, such accessories as butter, jelly, and saltcellar, cups and saucers, and accompaniments for any beverage served. When arrangements for dining are so completely made, the buffet may be quite small, since it need hold only dinner plates, serving dishes, and food (see Figure 22–1). However, when small tables of the collapsible variety are used, the buffet or some other table will have to present the appointments essential for dining. Since these collapsible tables require arrangements similar to those for trays, they will be discussed in the next section.

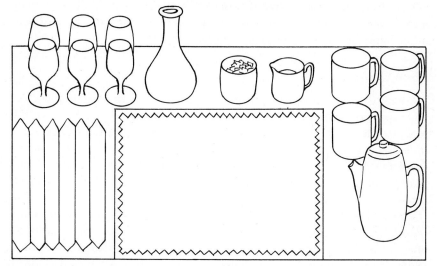

FIGURE 22–2.   Small chest or table set with trays, appointments, and beverages.

Tray Service

Lacking room for setting up tables, hosts may decide to provide guests with trays. Trays for this purpose usually measure about twelve by eighteen inches. The tray holds plate and beverages and is placed on the lap for quite comfortable dining. Here, as in the use of table service, the buffet need present only plates and food; the guest ought not to acquire the tray until he has served himself. This situation is not like that in the cafeteria where food is served for the patron. It is best to place trays, beverages, napkins, and flatware on another surface near the buffet (see Figure 22–2). After serving his plate, the guest places it on the top tray in the pile; next he places the beverage or beverages, the napkin, and the flatware on the tray; he then removes the tray and proceeds with it to the place indicated for dining.

It might be pointed out that dining from a tray held on the lap is not as comfortable as dining at a table and that there are people who like it less well than dining from the plate held in the hand. To minimize hazards, cover the trays with mats to prevent the slipping of dishes; use short tumblers for water, and mugs for a hot beverage; avoid drippy, spattery foods; and be sure that food that must be cut is fork tender. All of these precautions will reduce, if not eliminate, accidents resulting in soiled garments, carpets, and furniture. Trays and their appointments should be coordinated and should make an attractive setting for the meal.

When folding snack tables, actually trays on supporting stands, are used, appointments and beverages must be provided on the buffet or on an accessory surface. Someone in the family or a guest should set up the folding tables while guests are serving themselves. Sometimes this kind of arrangement is made for male guests; women guests may dine from a plate held in the hand, or they may be given regular trays.

Plate Service

Often, the only arrangement a hostess can make is to provide plenty of table space on which guests can place beverages while they dine from the plate in the hand. Table space may be provided by nested tables, stack tables, end tables, the coffee table, the corner bookcase or desk, folding snack tables, or any other available surface—except the floor. When the number of guests is large relative to available space, one may have no choice but to use this plan for dining.

At wedding receptions, late suppers, and similar occasions where large numbers are present and when a beverage does not accompany the food offered, no special arrangements are made; guests are expected to stand while dining, although some chairs may be made available for elderly persons.

When plate service is used, the buffet or an accessory surface presents the following, in addition to plates and food: forks, napkins, and beverages. Common sense dictates that guests must have both hands free for serving food and holding the plate; they cannot hold onto anything else until the serving of the plate has been accomplished. The practical and logical arrangement of the appointments on the buffet is exceedingly important, as one realizes while observing a guest making his way along or around the buffet. A guest probably serves some food onto the plate before he takes it if two tools are required for serving a dish; otherwise, he takes a plate with his left hand so that he can help himself to dishes with his right hand. When he has finished serving his plate, the guest places a fork on it and takes a napkin, which he slips between the plate and his left hand; he can then take a poured beverage, or he can even pour his own, since he can still use his right hand freely.

Considerate hosts will always avoid the use of tray service or plate service at black-tie functions. If guests are to be formally dressed, it is not only highly desirable, but almost a must, that they be seated at tables for dining.

PLANNING THE MENU

Only when the plans for seating guests have been made and arrangements for dining have been decided upon can the homemaker plan the menu for a buffet meal, because the dishes she can serve are largely determined by these arrangements. All the rules for good menu planning should be observed in planning the buffet meal; and, in addition, special considerations require that dishes be easy to self-serve and easy to eat. When guests are to be seated at tables where they can have the usual assortment of knives, forks, and spoons, there are few restrictions on the menu a hostess may offer. However, guests should not be expected to carve for themselves; roasts and birds are carved in the kitchen or at the buffet. When guests are to dine from trays, the hostess may offer almost any meats she chooses; however, because it is awkward to use the knife at the level of a tray held on the lap, it is desirable that meats be fork tender. It is also very important that the dishes be free from sauces and juices that can drip as bites of food are lifted to the mouth. This last qualification is also important when guests are to dine from the plate held in the hand. In addition, the food must be fork cuttable, and all bread should have been buttered for this service. Spaghetti dishes must be made from the elbow variety if served to guests who are not dining at a table.

The dishes on the buffet table should lend themselves to attractive service, be easily self-served, and maintain proper temperatures during the serving period. Casserole dishes containing meat, potatoes, and vegetables are good choices for the buffet menu, although some people do not like them. The ingredients of a casserole dish should be compatible and identifiable. If a salad is served with a casserole dish, it should be simple in composition; it ought not to be another mixture of many ingredients. It is possible to avoid the appearance of mixture by casual arrangement of a few fruits or vegetables in lettuce cups. Molded gelatin salads and salads of mixed greens are highly acceptable. Trays of relishes on which there may be a half-dozen or more choices may replace a salad or be served in addition. Relishes are not only widely acceptable, but are also easily prepared in advance of mealtime and, since they are usually finger foods, easily eaten. Cakes, tortes, and pies are favorite desserts, especially when guests are permitted to cut pieces of the size they want. A hostess can serve any dessert she wishes; however, she will be wise to plan one that requires only one dish for adequate service lest confusion arise and a guest be embarrassed by failing to place a bowl on the proper underliner plate. Although the dessert may be brought to the guests, almost all persons enjoy returning to the buffet for dessert. This practice also frees hosts from serving duties.

Except for the smorgasbord, the well-planned buffet menu will be simple; all the food of a course, including bread, will be served onto one plate. This plate will look neater and be easier to eat from if it is not completely filled. An exception is the occasion when guests serve themselves from a buffet and dine at the dining table, on which individual salads have been placed at covers.

Two courses, the main course and the dessert course, are all that should be served from the buffet table. If a first course is offered, it is best served in the living room as already suggested.

Here are some special suggestions for the planner of buffet meals.

1.   For your own sake, try to have some dishes that can be prepared a day in advance. Do, however, prepare cakes, pies, and tortes the day of the meal to ensure excellent quality. Some desserts, such as chiffon pies, Bavarian creams, Spanish cream, and icebox desserts, can and should be made the day before.

2.   Remember the capacity of your oven; also remember that an overloaded oven lengthens cooking times.

3.   Unless you are very sure of the food preferences of all your guests, offer an alternative to your main dish if it is made from any of the seafoods; many persons do not like them, and others are allergic to them. The same is true for dishes made with lentils, black beans, and other legumes.

4.   Be sure that all foods to be eaten from the plate held in the hand, except finger foods, can be cut with a fork; have the bread buttered. Jam or jelly may be put onto bread with a fork at a buffet meal, although this method is not acceptable when a knife is available.

5.   Hot rolls, biscuits, and muffins cool very quickly; unless you have a warmer for them, other bread choices provide better eating and are easier to manage. Thin slices of fruit, nut, or brown breads, both the baking powder and yeast varieties, provide excellent eating and the advantage of being preparable well ahead of serving time. Vienna bread and French bread, as well as plain loaves of bread, can be cut, buttered, and heated, and because of their size, they remain hot.

6.   Relishes may include apple wedges, cucumber fingers, green pepper fingers, cauliflower florets, prunes stuffed with cheese, pickled fruits, pickled beets, and pickles of all kinds, in addition to the familiar celery and carrot sticks, radishes, and olives.

7.   Avoid dishes with thin sauces or dressings that may spatter during serving or eating.

8.   Plan so that most, if not all, hot dishes can be finally heated in casseroles or other heat-holding containers unless you have special appliances for keeping food hot.

9.   More than enough of everything should be provided, so that all may feel free to help themselves to as much as they want.

The following menus are suggestions. The kind of dining arrangements each requires is indicated.

Menu I
(Suitable only when dining at a table)
(Roast carved at buffet)

Prime Rib Roast of Beef
Twice-Baked Potatoes
Broccoli
Assorted Relishes
Buttered Hot Rolls
Crème de Menthe Parfait
Coffee

Menu II
(Suitable only when dining at a table)
(Roast carved at buffet)

Roast Leg of Lamb
Eggplant Casserole
Mixed Green Salad
Thin Whole Wheat Bread Sandwiches
Assorted Cheeses and Crackers
Fresh Fruits
Coffee

Menu III
(Suitable when dining from table or tray)

Baked Boned Chicken Breasts
Corn Pudding
Green Beans and Water Chestnuts
Assorted Relishes
Toasted Sesame Seed Loaf
Toffee Angel Cake
Coffee

Menu IV
(Suitable for any mode of dining)

Chicken Rice Casserole
(Chicken, rice, mushrooms, ripe olives, almonds, sauce)
Baked Tomato Halves
Assorted Relishes
Herb-Buttered Bread
Lemon Chiffon Pie
Coffee

Menu V
(Suitable for any mode of dining)

Ham Loaf
Potatoes Au Gratin
Brussels Sprouts and Tokay Grapes
Assorted Olives and Pickles
Thin Rye Bread Sandwiches
Pumpkin Pie with Whipped Cream
Coffee

Menu VI
(Suitable for any mode of dining)

Swedish Meat Balls with Mushrooms
Danish Potato Soufflé
Broccoli
Jellied Fruit Mold
Rye Bread Sandwiches
Boston Cream Pie
Coffee

SETTING THE BUFFET TABLE

These decisions must be made: what surface will be used for the buffet, where will it be placed, and how will it be set or arranged. The dining table provides an excellent buffet; a chest of suitable height, a desk, a card table, a credenza or sideboard, the kitchen counter, or the kitchen table are all usable. Choose the buffet in accordance with your resources and the size of the group. We do not always use the same surface for a buffet even in the small home. Make certain that it will accommodate all that it must present; establish what it will accommodate by a trial setting with all the selected appointments. If one surface does not accommodate all that must be presented, use another to supplement it.

Place the buffet near the kitchen so that it can be serviced quickly and efficiently and so that there will be a minimum of movement among guests to service it. If you use a supplementary surface for trays, appointments, or beverages, place it so that guests will pass it after leaving the buffet. Place the buffet against a wall so that guests pass from one end of the buffet to the other or place the buffet away from a wall at or near the center of a room so that guests move around it (see Figure 22–3). There is less confusion when movement is from end to end of the buffet than when around it (see Figure 22–4). We tend to move more gracefully from left to right and counterclockwise. At clubs, church suppers, and PTA suppers at school

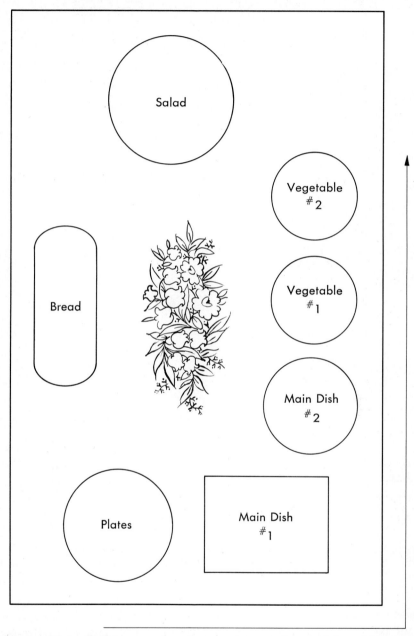

FIGURE 22–3. Buffet arranged so that guests proceed around it—table service.

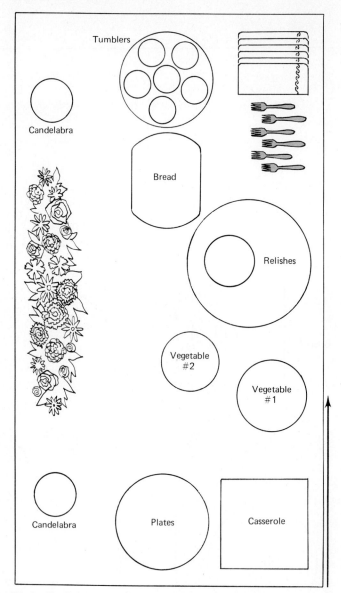

FIGURE 22–4.   Buffet arranged so that guests proceed from end to end—plate service.

where crowds are large, it is expedient to have duplicate buffets. Have a full and complete buffet on the two sides of a table centered in a room; arrange two full and complete buffets on one side of a long buffet table placed against a wall; or, space permitting, arrange two or more identical buffets in different places within a room. The first and last are probably the most satisfactory arrangements.

Guiding principles in setting or arranging the buffet are these: the place to begin should be obvious; how to proceed should be equally obvious, but must also be in a direct line without the need for backtracking; self-service of the food must be easy; and the appointments and the beverages presented on the buffet must be easy to remove and easy to handle. Whatever the arrangements for dining, all buffets present the food similarly. When dining will be from plate in hand, the buffet must present appointments and beverages, but these should follow the food so that no one is attempting to serve food onto a plate and at the same time hold the appointments for dining. It cannot be done.

If we take cues from the behavior of people at a buffet, the starting point is the pile of stacked plates. Almost without thinking we proceed to the stacked plates on the buffet and we take one from the pile. This suggests that every dish on the buffet ought to be servable with only one serving tool. Two-in-one serving tools, tongs, and large serving spoons expedite the serving of food with one hand. The dishes that compose the meal can be clustered or aligned on the buffet. They ought to appear in decreasing order of importance to prevent the filling of a plate before the important items of the meal are taken. A buffet that presents food only can be quite small. Never place the food of the dessert course on the buffet with the main course.

The buffet that offers appointments in addition must be larger, or a second surface must be used to present the napkins, the flatware, and the beverages. When dining is to be from plate in hand, the only flatware present on the buffet is the fork. A guest places it securely on the served plate, takes the napkin and slips it between hand and plate in the left hand, then takes the beverage with the free right hand. He can even serve it himself if you have carefully arranged for this, but it is desirable that there be an open area on the buffet where he can place the served plate while he pours his own beverage. When dining will be on trays, offer trays and appointments and beverages on a table or chest removed from the buffet. When dining is to be at individual tables that are set up as guests are serving themselves, the flatware offered may include the knife. Present the flatware and the napkins in such a way that they can be taken from the buffet gracefully. Display of the flatware on the napkin is usually space-consuming; a tight and neat arrangement of alternating forks and knives parallel with or followed by overlapping napkins uses space more efficiently at the same time that it permits the guest to place knife and fork on the plate, take a napkin in the conventional manner, and finally take the beverage offered. The enclosure of the knife and the fork within the napkin reduces the required space for their display but is a clumsy arrangement for guests who must also take a beverage. Small receptacles that hold forks stacked one upon another and similar receptacles for teaspoons have been designed and made especially for the small buffet.

Buffet arrangement—guests to dine at tables.

Buffet supper table—plate service.

Although our homes and our way of life commit us to the use of the buffet pattern of meal service, we are not yet completely at ease with it: we have not used it long enough. Far too often we have been guilty of just setting out the food and letting the guests carry on from there. The well-arranged buffet and the well-managed buffet meal do not happen by chance. Some specific suggestions for setting the buffet table follow.

1.   The buffet table may be covered with a cloth, it may remain bare, or it may be partially covered with runners or mats to introduce color. For the best appearance, a cloth should extend halfway to the floor or farther.

2.   Provide eighteen-inch or larger napkins.

3.   Floral or other decorations may be taller and larger in scale on the buffet than on the conventional dining table. The arrangement of the plates and the main dishes of the meal gives one part of the buffet greater weight than the remainder; position decorations and candles to effect balance.

4.   For the best appearance of the buffet table, limit the plates, cups and saucers, wine glasses, tumblers, flatware, and napkins on the table at any one time to the number in scale with the table. Additional appointments for the first course should be set on a table, chest, or other usable surface near the buffet table. It is desirable to have the appointments for the dessert course set here too; certainly, they should be collected and readily available on the kitchen counter if the serving table is not large enough to accommodate them.

5.   Use the ten and one-half to eleven-inch dinner plate for the buffet meal when the plate must accommodate all the food of the main course.

6.   When guests dine at a dining table, have salads at covers rather than included in the buffet.

7.   When guests dine at card tables, these can accommodate small salad bowls. Place the salad last on the buffet, bowls beside it; include a two-in-one serving tool so that the salad can be served into a salad bowl with the right hand while the left hand holds the dinner plate. Leave an open area that will accommodate the dinner plate in case someone cannot manage otherwise.

8.   Group two or three dishes of the meal around the stacked plates or align them, depending on the dimensions of the buffet. Arrange them in decreasing order of importance in the meal.

9.   Provide two-in-one serving tools whenever practicable. Provide two serving tools when feasible, but always have an open area on which the guest can place his plate while serving such food. Put serving tools in or on each dish before inviting guests to the buffet.

10.   When arrangements for dining permit the serving of a roast or a

bird, it must be carved at the buffet or in the kitchen. The former practice is preferable.

11.   To expedite service when the group is large, you may invite someone to assist in serving one or more dishes of the meal.

12.   Whenever flatware and napkins are required in the buffet setting, place them beyond the food so that guests will not have to clutch them and serve themselves at the same time. If guests are to dine from the plate held in the hand, place forks only. They are laid close together, but it should be possible to take one without touching another. Never make them a center of interest. Do not enclose the flatware in a napkin, except for tray service.

13.   Put glasses of water or other beverage on a tray. This tray should be the last item in the buffet setting, or it may be placed on another table. The beverage is the last item in a setting because once it has been taken, the guest has both hands full and cannot serve himself further. In general, use stemware for wines only, tumblers or footed ware for other beverages.

14.   Coffee is often served with both courses of the buffet meal. It is easily managed when dining is at small tables where cups and saucers may be placed at table-setting time. You may fill these cups after guests are seated, or you may ask someone to do it for you. The beverage service may also be set up on the buffet table; if it is, the guest serves the beverage and takes it to the small table along with the dinner plate. When dining is from trays, the beverage service appears close to the trays; the guest pours,

F IGURE 22–5.   Arrangement for self-service of a hot beverage.

after placing the cup on the tray and before picking up the tray (see Figure 22–2). When dining is from the plate in the hand, cups of coffee may be taken to those who wish it, or the guests may choose between water and coffee and serve themselves.

15.   Set the beverage service very carefully whenever you expect a guest to pour for himself. Leave a near area empty so that the filled plate can be set down by those who wish to do so. Do not stack cups and saucers by twos or on top of each other. To establish a pouring center, place one cup and saucer close to the edge of the table; set the pot to the right beside it. To the left, lay the spoons directly on the table, on a small plate or tray, or in a small receptacle. A spoon may be laid on each saucer, handle parallel with the cup handle; however, because many people do not use sugar or cream, they will not require spoons. Set the accompaniments above the cup. This arrangement permits the guest to pour into the cup, take any accompaniments he uses, place a spoon on the saucer if he uses one, and remove the cup and saucer from the table with the free right hand. Group the other cups and saucers around this center. Those who follow the first guest will remove cup on saucer to the obvious and convenient place for pouring. Needless to say, the beverage pot should have a hinged cover or one that does not fall out of the pot when it is tipped in pouring (see Figure 22–5).

16.   The table setting for the dessert course is determined by the service planned. If the group is large, it may be desirable to have the dessert and

FIGURE 22–6.   A self-service dessert buffet.

Dessert buffet.

beverage served to guests from the buffet table. Those who serve sit at opposite ends of the table. People probably prefer to receive the dessert before the beverage. The beverage cups may be placed on the plate with the dessert if the dessert is not a frozen one. However, eating is both more enjoyable and more comfortable when the cup is on a saucer, which can be set on a nearby table.

17.   Set up the dessert course according to the same principles followed in setting the table for the main course. Set the dessert plates to the right of the dessert, because service is more convenient from left to right. Provide two serving pieces, so that the piece of cake, pie, or whatever can be steadied on the pastry server while it is being moved from one plate to another; without this steadying tool, people instinctively use the fingers, thereby soiling them. Place the proper tool for eating the dessert directly on the table beside the stacked plates. After taking the plate, the guest takes the tool and places it on the plate. He may then pour his own beverage with the free right hand, or he may set the plate down before pouring. If the beverage is poured for him, he can accept it with the free right hand (see Figure 22–6).

PLANNING FOR SERVICE

One reason for using the buffet pattern of meal service is to keep waiting-on-the-table duties minimal. Some duties remain, however. They are carried out with the least confusion when they have been planned. They include the following: service of or waiting on the buffet during the main course, the removal of the main course, the serving of the dessert course, and the final removal of the dessert course.

Service of the Buffet Table

Replacements of food and table appointments must always be made. Additional appointments include the plates, flatware, and napkins not included in the original setting of the buffet table. Ideally, they are available from some table or chest near the buffet table; if not, they can be brought in from the kitchen, where they should have been made ready. All appointments, except plates, are best carried on a tray to the table to avoid excessive handling. The plates are supported on the open hands with the thumbs pressing on the rims of the stacked plates. Because it is customary to ask guests to serve themselves more than once at buffet meals, there should be food in plenty on the table at all times. The hostess, since she knows the supply and its whereabouts, is the logical person to assume the duty of keeping the food on the buffet if she does not have hired help in the kitchen.

Removal of the Main Course

Whatever the mode of dining, the main course is taken from the buffet to the kitchen when it appears that all persons have finished eating it. Unless she has hired help, the hostess with the assistance she requests does this. Some temporary storage of food is imperative in the average kitchen so the competent hostess uses assistance here. The clearance of individual covers depends on the mode of dining.

1.   When dining has been at the dining table, the table is cleared and the dessert is served in the conventional fashion.

2.   When dining has been at card tables, two options are possible. Covers at card tables can be cleared in the conventional fashion; or the guest may be asked to take his plate and leave it on a designated tray or table-on-wheels as he goes to the dessert buffet.

3.   When dining has been plate-in-hand style, the hostess, the host, or a helpful guest may take the plates and place them on a table-on-wheels or a tray and remove them to the kitchen. Again, the guest may simply be asked to place his plate on a designated tray or table as in (2).

4.   When guests are dining from trays, it is best to clear trays as you would individual covers at the table. Use a table-on-wheels on which to collect the plates. Clear the covers of persons dining at individual tables similarly.

Serving the Dessert Course

Whenever the group is at all large, the dessert buffet is the easiest way to offer dessert. It often presents a choice of desserts, a low-calorie and a sweet-and-rich one. When guests dine at the dining table and from trays, dessert is served in the conventional manner; in all other modes of dining, guests can go to the dessert buffet to serve themselves—table by table or in small groups.

1.   Place a single dessert offering on the buffet with serving tools. Place dessert plates to the right for easy left-to-right transfer of dessert to plate. Next lay on the table the forks or other required tools for eating the dessert. Next arrange the beverage service unless the beverage is to be or has been offered at table (see Figure 22–6).

2.   Place the desserts when more than one is offered at intervals on the

buffet. Place the proper serving tools with each. Place to the right of or in front of each dessert, whichever effects easiest service, the appropriate dinnerware and flatware. Arrange any required beverage service so that it follows the desserts. Dessert is always taken before beverage.

3.   Serve the dessert and the beverage to persons dining from trays from a table-on-wheels.

4.   Serve the beverage to guests dining at your dining table from the table.

5.   Refill beverage cups by passing from table to table when the guests are dining at card tables or individual tables; pass from person to person when the guests are dining from trays or from plate in hand.

6.   Set up a beverage service or services in the dining area and permit guests to wait on themselves for beverages whenever space for moving about permits.

Final Clearance

Finally, the dessert buffet and all else must be cleared.

1.   When dining has been at the dining table, clear it or leave it un-cleared, depending on whether or not it is visible from the living area.

2.   When dining has been at card tables, clear table by table using a table-on-wheels. Take the tables down unless they will be used for bridge or other games. Use any assistance offered so that you can stack dishes in the kitchen or load the dishwasher.

3.   When dining has been from individual tables, clear as in (2).

4.   When guests have dined from trays, permit someone to assist you by removing the trays to the kitchen as you stack and so on.

5.   When dining has been from plate in hand, use a table-on-wheels and remove plates, cups and saucers, and glasses to the kitchen.

Permit guests to help you; give them clear instructions; do not try to hurry through either the serving or the removing of courses. Above all, have some plans for doing what must be done. But do not worry if plans go awry. The buffet pattern is still new to us. Procedures are not as stan-dardized as the more conventional patterns for dining; what seems famil-iar to one person may seem strange to another.

ORGANIZING THE TASKS OF A BUFFET MEAL

Organizing the tasks that must be accomplished in the planning for, preparation for, preparation of, and serving of a buffet supper, brunch, or any other special meal, is helpful whether one, two, or twenty are engaged. Many decisions must be made. Following are two plans that detail decisions and schedule the doing of the various tasks, the so-called hand-and-foot work. They are meant to be suggestive only: they will differ as the resources of different meal managers differ. To illustrate, a menu is presented. The following assumptions are made: supper will be at eight o'clock on a Saturday evening; there will be eight in attendance, including the hosts; the hosts will do all the work of preparation and serving; and dining will be at card tables.

Menu for Buffet Supper

Chicken Tetrazzini
Mixed Greens with Italian Dressing
Celery   Assorted Olives   Radishes
Garlic-Buttered French or Vienna Bread
Lemon Chiffon Pie
Coffee

PART 1. *General Plan*

Tasks	*When*	*By*
Plan menu	Before Thursday	Him and her
Make shopping list	Before Thursday	Her
Check table linens	Before Monday	Her
Make plans for preparing food	Before Thursday	Him and her
Make plan for service of meal	Before Thursday	Him and her
Shop for groceries	Thursday P.M.	Him and her
Shop for flowers and last-minute items	Saturday A.M.	Him
Tidy rooms	Friday evening	Him
Get out table appointments and give needed care	Saturday A.M.	Her
Plan buffet setting	Saturday A.M.	Her
Arrange flowers	Saturday A.M.	Her
Set buffet table and card tables	Saturday 5:00 P.M.	Her
Fill water glasses	Saturday 7:30 P.M.	Her
Take food to buffet	Saturday 8:00 P.M.	Her
Take extra food to buffet	As indicated	Her
Clear main course from buffet	As indicated	Her
Take main course plates from guests	As indicated	Him
Set up dessert service	As indicated	Her
Refill coffee cups	As indicated	Him
Clear buffet table and others	As indicated	Her
Take all dishes to kitchen, load dishwasher	As indicated	Him

PART 2. *Plan for Food Production*

Items of Menu	*Steps in Preparation*	*When*	*By*	*Shopping List*
Chicken Tetrazzini	1. Stew chicken— chill	Friday P.M.	Her	2 Chickens Mushrooms
	2. Bone and cut up	Saturday A.M.		Shell macaroni Olive oil
	3. Clean mush- rooms			Cream Parmesan
	4. Sauté mush- rooms			cheese
	5. Cook spaghetti			
	6. Make sauce			
	7. Combine and put in cas- seroles, chill			
	8. Clean up kitchen			
	9. Put in oven	6:30 P.M.		
				Italian dressing
Mixed greens	1. Wash, dry, chill	Friday P.M.	Her	Belgian endive
	2. Tear, chill	Saturday 6:00 P.M.	Him	Lettuce
	3. Dress and toss	Saturday 8:00 P.M.	Him	Bibb lettuce
Relishes	1. Chill olives	Saturday A.M.	Her	Ripe olives
	2. Wash celery and radishes	Saturday A.M.		Green olives Celery
	3. Cut celery and radishes and chill	Saturday A.M.		Radishes
	4. Arrange for table	Saturday 6:30 P.M.	Her	
Garlic bread	1. Prepare garlic butter	Saturday A.M.	Him	2 Vienna loaves Butter
	2. Cut and butter bread and wrap in foil	Saturday A.M.	Him	Garlic powder
	3. Heat first loaf	Saturday 7:30 P.M.	Him	
	4. Heat second loaf	Saturday 8:00 P.M.	Her	
Lemon chiffon pie	1. Make crumb crust	Friday P.M.	Her	Lemons Gelatin, eggs
	2. Make filling	Friday P.M.	Her	
	3. Whip cream and spread	Saturday 7:00 P.M.	Her	
Coffee	1. Measure and make	Saturday 7:30 P.M.	Him	

Chapter 23

Teas, Receptions, and Other Occasions with Refreshments

Full meals are not the only occasions at which families and individuals serve food to guests. The times when one has guests and does not offer something to drink, with or without something to eat, are exceptions, rather than the rule. This is true, not only in private life, but also in the social life of the community; study clubs, committees, professional groups, church groups, and even political parties lure attendance with the promise of refreshments. This custom stems in part from the long-held belief, that to share food is a symbol of friendship.

Occasions at which we offer food are many: morning coffee, afternoon tea, afternoon coffee, receptions, the cocktail hour, "refreshments," dessert parties, and after-the-theater suppers. A common feature of all of them is that the refreshments are of secondary importance; the real purpose is to provide a time and a place for people to come together, either to visit with old friends or to make new ones, to be informed, to work or play, and even to be persuaded.

These occasions with light refreshments may vary in size from "tea for two" to receptions for several hundred. Some just happen; others are preceded by weeks or months of careful planning. The homemaker can manage a tea or reception for fifty or more, if she has good friends to help her, or if she is able to hire one or two persons to work in the kitchen, and if she has enough space to accommodate this number of people. It is more than likely, however, that her experiences with large teas and receptions will, for the most part, be at church, school, and clubs; at home, small, intimate affairs are more to her liking. Discussions of what to serve and how to serve it follow.

WHAT TO SERVE

The light refreshments served at these various functions are similar, in the sense that basically they consist of beverage and bread; but they differ in the items served in addition to bread. The beverages served include coffee and tea, punch, carbonated beverages, cider, and so forth. The bread that accompanies these beverages may be thin slices of buttered bread, sandwiches, coffee cake, sweet rolls, hot breads, cake, doughnuts, cookies, rich pastries, and crackers and similar crisp confections. In addition to bread, sweets and nuts appear on the tea table; savory items, such as olives, seafoods, cheeses, meats, crisp vegetable relishes, dips, and pickles, appear on the cocktail tray and the late supper table; and ices, sweets, and nuts may accompany cake at a dessert party or a reception. There are few restrictions on what may be served with a beverage except those implicit in the time of day, the occasion, and the beverage itself. Obviously, ice cream and cake or pie would be ill-chosen for the mid-morning coffee, and doughnuts and sweet rolls would be equally inappropriate for the dessert party.

At teas and coffees, as we give them in the United States, the beverages take first place, the food, second. For these functions, the menu is planned so that the food items offered are good but do not interfere with the enjoyment of the beverage. When the beverage is to be a sweet punch, a mulled cider, a Bohemian tea, or another sweet drink, the accompaniments should be bland in flavor and never too sweet. The following accompaniments would be good because they would be subordinate to the beverage: sandwiches of fruit and nut breads; sandwiches made with mild cheese, chicken salad, or avocado-butter fillings; short, crisp, but not sweet, cookies; pound cake; or short bread. A similar situation exists when a fine tea with a delicate aroma is served; with it the best choice would be plain bread and butter, although pound cake or sweet cakes and cookies would also be good. When the usual "garden variety" tea is served, the food may be more flavorful, because the tea is almost lacking in aroma. Usually coffee may be accompanied by more flavorful food than tea because coffee has more aroma. Cocktail food is traditionally full-flavored.

Food for Large Teas or Receptions

The number of items on the menu for a tea or a reception is determined by the size of the group invited. As the guest list approaches fifty, the menu may consist of a half-dozen or more items, and as it approaches one hundred, the menu may include a dozen or more items. Coffee and tea may be offered; punch can replace one or be offered in addition.

Principles that guide in the selection of the items of the tea or reception menu follow.

1.   When two beverages are to be offered, plan so that every item on the menu will be appropriate with either beverage, because you can never be certain that a guest will know which items are most pleasing with his chosen beverage.

2.   Plan so that there will be differences in the textures of the items offered, some being soft and others crisp or chewy.

3.   Plan so that there will be some color in the plates and trays of dainties. It may be only a difference in intensity of color, as between plain sugar cookies and chocolate brownies, or it may be a true color difference. Sandwiches introduce true color with parsley, cress, cucumber, green pepper, olives, pimiento, avocado, jelly, and so forth. Limit the use of artificial coloring to frostings on cakes. Color them delicately, and have someone with an eye for color blend the tints; colors as they come from the bottles are too harsh.

4.   Plan so that more than one taste is included. The beverage may introduce bitterness, as in coffee; sweetness, as in punch; or sourness, as in tea served with lemon. The foods served introduce either saltiness or sweetness.

5.   Plan to introduce a variety of flavors and ingredients. Use coconut, chocolate, citrus fruit rinds, dried fruits, nuts, candied fruits, and spices.

Following is a typical menu for a tea or coffee planned for one hundred guests.

Orange Frosted Petits Fours   Chocolate Frosted Petits Fours

Crisp Brownies   Soft Spice Cookies   Coconut Meringues

Nut Bread and Butter Sandwiches   Assorted Open-Face Sandwiches

Shrimp-Butter Pinwheels   Parsley Cream Cheese Pinwheels

Egg Salad Cucumber Sandwiches

Tea   Coffee

The menu could well offer less. In addition to or instead of some of these items, ices may be offered at receptions.

Food for the Small Tea or Coffee

Food for the small tea or coffee may be fresh bread and butter, fresh hot rolls, hot muffins, cake, doughnuts, coffee cake, cookies, or sandwiches; in fact, it may be almost anything one wants to serve and which is appropriate for the time of day. However, it should be remembered that these are occasions for light refreshments.

Food for Dessert Parties

Dessert parties are the proper occasion to serve rich and luscious desserts. When inviting guests to this kind of party, the hostess might well stress the "come for dessert." The refreshments for these occasions may be three-layer cakes heavily iced, tortes rich in nuts and whipped cream, filled angel food cakes, meringues filled with ice cream and covered with fruit or rich sauces, ice cream and cake, cheese cake, chiffon pies, or any other kind of pie, especially when men are to be present. The possibilities are definitely unlimited and a hostess may offer two or more choices.

Food for Late Suppers

The late supper offers breads or crackers with a variety of prepared sandwich fillings, or a variety of meats, cheeses, and seafoods. In addition, pickles, olives, vegetable relishes, and seafood or chicken salad may be included, as well as such hot dishes as Welsh rabbit, cheese fondue; seafood Newburg, and chicken à la king. Perhaps local custom as much as any other factor determines what one serves at late hours.

APPOINTMENTS FOR SERVING LIGHT REFRESHMENTS

Light refreshments are eaten in diverse ways. Guests may be seated at tables, they may dine from trays, or they may be expected to sit or stand informally and dine as best they can. The food may be finger food, it may require the use of a fork or a knife or both, or it may require a spoon. Appointments must be selected according to the kind of food and the manner in which it will be eaten; they must always provide for easy and neat eating. It is conceivable that a hostess might plan refreshments with her store of appointments in mind. Here are some general do's and don't's for selecting appointments for serving food.

1. Use plates large enough to accommodate the food you serve.
2. Provide all the tools essential for comfortable and refined eating.
3. Do not use footed cups, except when guests are seated at tables.
4. Whenever you provide a plate and a cup and saucer, be sure there is ample space for guests to put one or the other down while eating.
5. Refreshment sets that consist of cup and plate, with a well for holding the cup in position, provide a comfortable service if a cup and saucer are too small and a plate and a cup and saucer cannot be provided.
6. When you use cups on plates, place tiny soft paper doilies under the cups to anchor them. These doilies are now available in good design.
7. Serve cakes that guests are to cut on large cake plates so that there is ample room for cutting and serving.

8. Do not fill any dishes to the brim; it makes serving difficult and food may be spilled.
9. If you have a beautiful tray of the proper size, use it for serving sandwiches, cookies, or small cakes.
10. Do not crowd small items onto the serving plates or trays; a guest should be able to remove one item without touching another.

Following are some specific do's and don't's for selecting appointments appropriate to the manner in which food is to be eaten.

Finger Food

1. Do provide a saucer or a plate along with the beverage container. This underliner holds food and frees the right hand for eating and using the napkin. Most persons appear both baffled and annoyed when they attempt to manage simultaneously a cup of punch, a napkin, and even single tidbits, unless the tidbits are passed after the guests are seated with napkins on their laps, or they can gather around the table on which the tidbits are offered, as at cocktail parties.

2. Keep food tidbits in scale with the underliner of the beverage container. Have them bite-sized when it is a saucer or a bread-and-butter plate, but somewhat larger when it is a dessert plate. It is quite important not to overlook the factor of size; accidents occur if the cakes and sandwiches served are larger than the saucer or plate can accommodate; if they are too small, the food looks lost on the plate.

3. Offer spoons with a beverage to which sugar, cream, or lemon may be added and with a punch to which dips of sherbet are added.

4. You may use either tea- or cocktail-size napkins; but tea-size is preferred when a dessert plate is the underliner for a cup.

Food Requiring Fork or Knife or Both

Whenever the food served requires the use of a fork, such as a cake, or a knife, such as hot muffins or scones, it is desirable to provide a plate for the food and a cup and saucer for the beverage. This means that a place to place the beverage while eating must be provided whenever guests are not seated at tables. End tables or snack tables may be used for this purpose. If they cannot be provided, the cup may be placed directly on the plate with the food as at wedding receptions and dessert parties, where cake and coffee are served on the same plate. But this plate must be large enough to hold both cup and food and to permit neat eating. Combine a glass with a plate in this way only with caution. The refreshment set is useful under these circumstances, and the well of the plate will sometimes accommodate a glass.

The fork provided may be a dinner fork or a salad fork; the knife may be a butter spreader if it will be used only for spreading, but should be a dinner knife if it will be used as a cutting instrument. Late suppers or snacks may require luncheon or dinner plates, knives and forks, and cups and saucers.

Use tea-size or larger napkins in all of these situations.

Food Requiring a Spoon

Unless guests will be seated at tables or will have trays, do not serve a dessert eaten with a spoon unless you have coupe plates with considerable depth. That is, avoid a situation where the guest must eat from a bowl, large or small, placed on a plate held in his hand. Fruit shortcakes, cobblers, and sundaes are desserts that should be served in bowls or deep coupe plates and eaten with spoons.

Provide dessert spoons for desserts served in coupe plates and shallow bowls if the dishes are at all large; provide teaspoons for desserts served in sherbet or fruit dishes. Do not use footed ware unless guests are to be seated at tables. Provide tea-size napkins.

SERVING REFRESHMENTS

Refreshments for small groups may be served from a tray, from a table, or directly from the kitchen. Refreshments for large groups are usually served from a table. In general, the service is buffet with guests helping themselves to food, although other methods of service are also used. Guests may receive a poured beverage or they may be expected to pour their own. Much latitude in service is possible; it can be suited to the occasion, the group, the available appointments, and the refreshments, as well as to the room in which they are offered.

Serving from a Tray

When serving coffee or tea to a few persons and when serving finger foods, a hostess sets up a tray with the needed appointments. She carries it to the living room, terrace, porch, or wherever her guests have gathered. She then places the tray on a coffee table or other table at which she can sit and pour comfortably and gracefully. On these occasions she pours and adds the accompaniments to the beverage according to the taste of each guest; she places a spoon, if one is needed, on the plate or saucer, handle parallel to the handle of the cup; she then lifts the cup and saucer from the tray with her right hand, places a napkin between her hand and the saucer, and passes the whole to each guest in turn. Guests seated at a distance come to the table to be served, or the hostess may ask someone to take the services to guests. When the hostess has poured for all, she passes the food, unless guests have helped themselves.

Setting the Tray.   Although size and shape may necessitate variations, all trays set for beverage service are similarly set. The pattern of setting is not unlike that described previously for beverage service from the table and for the service of after-dinner coffee. Here are pointers on how to do it easily. This step-by-step procedure is for cups and saucers.

1.   Place the tray lengthwise on the kitchen counter in front of you.
2.   Place a cup and saucer in the center of the side closest to you.
3.   Place the napkins, spread just enough so that the top one can always be grasped without fumbling, to the left of the cup and saucer.
4.   Place the teaspoons, bowl inside bowl but with the handles spread in fan shape to your right for ease in removal, at the right of this cup and saucer.
5.   Place the accompaniments in back of the cup and saucer for ease in serving. Place cream or lemon to the right of the sugar, because they are taken more frequently.
6.   Place the pot to the right of the spoons with the handle directed to the right if possible, so that you can pour by simply tipping the pot.
7.   Place the remaining cups and saucers by twos, if possible; if not, stack saucers and place cups by twos. Have the handles directed to your right or directly toward you, whichever you prefer.
8.   If you are left-handed and not ambidextrous, your tray arrangement will be the mirror image of the one described. This reversed arrangement is, probably, the only one in table setting that is modified for the left-handed person.

Figure 23–1.   Tray arranged for afternoon tea or coffee.

9. If space permits, cups and saucers may be set singly, with the spoons placed on the saucers parallel to the cup handles.

10. Place the plate of tea dainties on the tray. If space does not permit, remove the pot from the tray and try to fit the plate of tea dainties onto the tray—remember it is safer to carry the tray without the pot of hot beverage. If the plate of tea dainties cannot be fitted onto the tray, it may be necessary to bring it in separately. The plate of dainties and even the napkins can be removed from the tray to the table once the tray has been set down. Slight rearrangements will usually allow for easy and graceful pouring (see Figure 23–1).

Serving from a Table

Refreshments for tea or coffee, dessert, or supper may be offered from a table. This table may be a dining table, a card table, a lamp table, a tea cart, or other small table; the size of the group to be served will determine which table to use. A cloth may or may not be used, depending on personal preference and the condition of the table; if one is used, it should be suitable to the occasion and in harmony with the appointments and the room. Fine lace cloths, embroidered linen cloths, sheer organdy cloth over solid colored cloths, satin cloths, and cloths of novelty weaves and fabrics are often used. The overhang of a tea cloth is greater than that of a dinner cloth and may even reach the floor. Unless a cloth is appropriate and adds something to a setting, it may be better to leave the table bare. Whatever the occasion for which the table is set, the table should be as beautiful as one can make it.

At teas, coffees, and receptions, guests help themselves to food, although the beverage is poured for them. At the dessert party or the late supper, the service may be similar, or the guests may pour for themselves. Infrequently, both the food and the beverage are served to the guests. Tables must always be set with these two goals in mind: the comfort of the person or persons pouring or serving and the comfort of guests who must serve themselves.

The Small Tea Table.   The hostess pours at the small tea table. Guests usually go to the small tea table to be served. Place the table on the perimeter of the room and arrange it so that you will face the group.

1. Plan the setting or arrangement of the tea table well in advance of tea time. Do a trial run of the beverage service; then proceed as you plan guests to, to make certain that it all works.

2. Set the beverage service on a tray or directly on the table, whichever you prefer; but if the tea cloth is a fine one, use a tray to protect it from stains. Place the cups and saucers within your easy reach. Plan to

Tray arranged for afternoon tea or coffee.

Small table arranged for afternoon tea.

serve the accompaniments of the beverage. Plan to lay a spoon on each saucer with the spoon handle parallel with the cup handle except when the food is finger food.

3.   After you have arranged the beverage service, plan for placing the food on the table; three possibilities exist, depending on the kind of food offered. To do this, move to the side of the table opposite the pouring service.

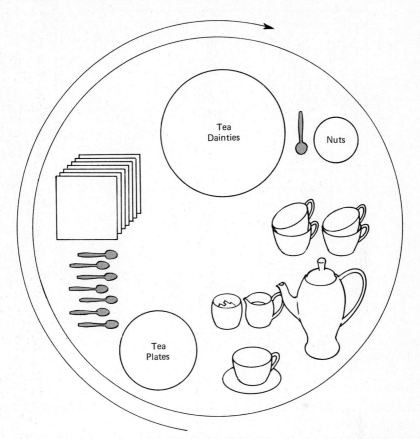

Figure 23–2a. A small table arranged for tea or coffee—finger food.

(a) When the food offered will be finger food, place the teaspoons and the napkins near the pouring area, on what is now your right. Place the plate or plates of tea dainties so as to give the table a balanced appearance (see Figure 23–2a). Guests will approach you on your left as you pour to receive the poured beverage. They next take a spoon and a napkin, then food.

(b) When the food is to be fork food, place the dessert on the table on your left, lay the serving pieces in position, and then place the dessert plates to the right of the dessert for easy left-to-right transfer of the food to the individual plate. Next place the dessert forks on the table, then the napkins. After serving herself, the guest approaches you on your left and receives the poured beverage with her free right hand (see Figure 23–2b).

(c) If the food is to be hot muffins, hot coffee cake, hot scones, or other food requiring the use of a butter spreader; put individual plates on your left and the plate of food to the right of them. Place the butter and the jam next; then the butter spreaders and the napkins. After serving herself,

FIGURE 23–2b. A small table arranged for afternoon tea or dessert—food requires the use of a fork.

the guest approaches on your left and receives the poured beverage (see Figure 23–2c).

4. If trays are to be provided, stack them on a nearby table because they detract from the beauty of the tea table. Each guest in turn places her plate and cup and saucer on the top tray, removes it, and returns to her chair. When the food requires the use of a knife, always provide trays.

5. Arrange to have plenty of table space on which guests can place their plates and/or cups and saucers. Folding tables are excellent for this purpose.

6. Place an arrangement of flowers or some other decorative object on the table if space permits.

Setting the Table for a Dessert Party. Dessert may be served from a buffet or offered to guests seated at a table, either card tables or the dining table. Setting the dessert buffet is similar to setting the dessert course of the buffet meal or setting the small tea table. The tea cart provides an excellent buffet at the same time that it permits a hostess or an assistant to pour the beverage. The dining table may be set for full self-service of dessert and beverage, or one or both may be served for guests.

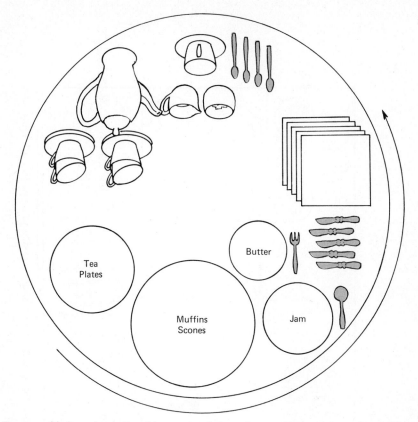

FIGURE 23–2c. A small table arranged for afternoon tea or morning coffee—food requires the use of a butter spreader.

1.   When the food is to be self-served, set the dessert plates to the right of the dessert to provide for easy left-to-right movement in serving. Provide two serving tools. Next, lay the forks and then the napkins.

2.   When the beverage is to be self-served, set the service as previously described in Chapter 22. Have the beverage service follow the food service closely. Remember, cups and saucers should not be stacked by twos in this arrangement.

3.   When the beverage is to be served for the guest, set the service at one end of the table as previously described. Have the person who pours serve the beverage accompaniments and place a spoon on the saucer as indicated.

4.   When food is to be served for guests, set this service at one end of the table. Place the dessert plates so that they will be directly in front of the person who will serve. Place the dessert in back of the plates to allow for forward movement in serving. Provide two serving tools, so that the

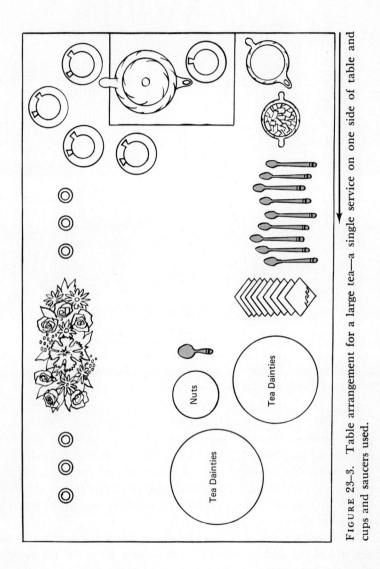

FIGURE 23–3. Table arrangement for a large tea—a single service on one side of table and cups and saucers used.

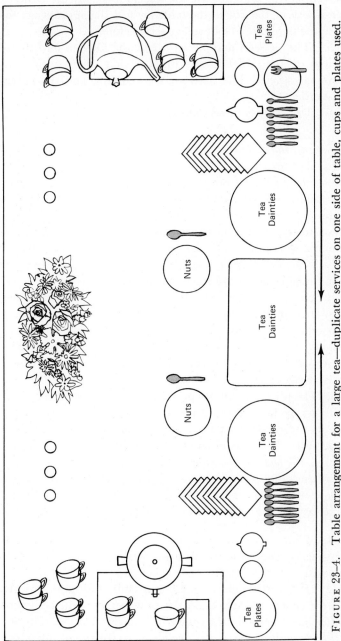

FIGURE 23-4. Table arrangement for a large tea—duplicate services on one side of table, cups and plates used.

person serving does not use the fingers to steady the dessert on the pastry server. Along the side of the table lay first the appropriate tools for eating, then the napkins. The beverage service follows.

5.   The desserts may be served in the kitchen and the served desserts placed on the buffet in any number that seems suitable to balance the beverage service. The flatware, the napkins, and the beverage follow in that order.

6.   Dessert may be served from the kitchen to seated guests.

Setting the Large Tea Table.   When the group invited to tea exceeds a number for whom the hostess can pour, the tea table is large. Large tea tables vary in size from the usual small dining table in the home to the enormous one put together from several tables in the schoolroom, the church parlor, or the club room. The tea table may be against a wall or away from a wall to permit traffic around it (see Figures 23–3 and 23–5). The persons responsible for serving can work most efficiently when the table is near the kitchen; at the same time the tea table ought to be in the handsomest part of the room. Compromise between these two sites is usually necessary in selecting the site of the table. Whatever the site and whatever the size, the table, when set, should present a well-composed picture. No other table—not even the buffet table—has so much potential for beauty, whether the appointments include exquisite linens, fine china, silver service, and orchids or peasant linens, pottery, and zinnias.

Beverages may be served from one or both ends of the table or from one side. The arrangement of appointments for those who pour should be carefully worked out so that they can perform with grace and poise. Arrangements for guests must be made so that they serve themselves easily and gracefully. The accompaniments for the beverage when these are self-served, the spoons, the napkins, and the food must be conveniently placed for them. Two patterns of arrangement now prevail: either guests receive the beverage first, or they take food first and receive the beverage last. Specific suggestions for setting the table for large teas and receptions follow.

1.   Plan the setting in detail well in advance of the actual hour of table setting. Whenever possible, do a practice setting with the appointments to be used.

2.   Decorations may be elaborate, tall, and large in scale; they should be the center of interest on the table, except when the wedding cake or other motif becomes the center of interest. The position of the flowers or other decorations may vary according to the site of the table and the number of beverage services at the table.

(a)   Center a single arrangement on a table that has two beverage services and that will have traffic around it. Place two arrangements on this table for good effect.

(b)   Decorations are not always centered on the table placed against a wall. Instead, they are placed on a lengthwise line that divides the table into thirds midway between the two ends of the table at which there are two beverage services, away from the center at the table with one beverage service.

3.   Candles can be placed on the tea table. Use them in colors coordinated with the decorations. Use them in different heights and place them for the best effect. Always light them.

4.   Whenever possible set the beverage services so that the guest receives the beverage at the left of the pourer who is pouring from a beverage pot to avoid having the beverage pot between the pourer and the guest. A table placed against the wall and at which there are two beverage services has one service at which the beverage is received on the pourer's right, a situation the pourer can cope with. The use of a samovar or a silver urn at the left end of the table expedites the service. The samovar or urn must be coordinated with the table appointments and must be in proper scale. The urn-style coffee maker that would be appropriate in some situations would be quite unsuitable on this table. When punch is the second beverage offered, offer it at the left end of the table.

5.   Any of the previously described patterns for the service of a beverage may be modified for use on the large tea table. Modifications differ, depending on whether the guest is to be served the beverage first or last. We shall call it Plan A when the guest receives the beverage first and Plan B when the guest receives the beverage last. The beverage service may be laid with or without a tray, but the tray is preferred.

6.   Here is how you go about setting the table according to Plan A— when the guest receives the beverage first. Details may differ from table to table, but in general all tables are similarly set.

(a)   *Cups and saucers used.*   Sit down at the table where the pourer will sit. If a tray is to be used, place it in the center of the area close to the edge of the table. Place a cup and saucer in a position comfortable for pouring. Place the beverage pot or pots to the right of it, but place in back of the saucer an urn or a kettle on a swivel base that tips for pouring. Place a suitable number of cups and saucers, stacked by twos, within easy reach, either above the single cup and saucer or to the right of the beverage pot if the guest is to receive the beverage on the pourer's left. The size and shape of the table will determine the better position for the cups and saucers. Place the cups so that the handles are parallel to the table edge and directed to the pourer's right (see Figures 23–3 and 23–5).

When the beverage is to be received at the pourer's right, place the cups and saucers on her left, with the handles directed to her right for ease in separation.

When an urn is used, place the cups and saucers on either the right or the left, depending on which side the beverage will be received from.

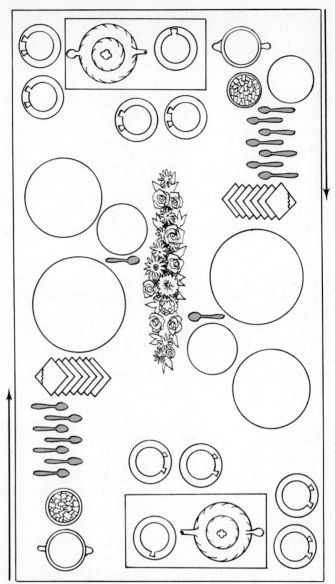

FIGURE 23–5.   Table arrangement for a large tea—duplicate services on the two sides of the table, cups and saucers used.

(b)   *Cups and plates used.*   Place the tray, one cup with or without an underlying saucer, the other cups, and the beverage pot or urn as above, but place a pile of plates to the pourer's left. She places the filled cup on the top plate of the stacked plates and hands the plate with the cup to a guest. Use the tiny doilies now available to keep cups from slipping (see Figure 23–4).

(c)   Place the remaining appointments away from the beverage service in this order: the accompaniments for the beverage, the spoons, and the napkins. Finally, place the plates or trays of tea dainties. Double service from one side of a long table frequently has one plate or tray of tea dainties in common (see Figure 23–4).

7.   According to Plan B, the guest receives the beverage last. Two possibilities in appointments exist: the cup may be placed on the plate; or both a cup and saucer and a plate are used. Some persons frown on the use of the cup on the plate unless the plate has a well to accommodate the cup. The disadvantage of having the cup on the plate can be partly overcome by the use of a tiny doily under the cup to keep it from slipping. Expediency sometimes leaves no choice but to use cup and plate.

When a plate and a cup and saucer are provided, stack tables, folding tray stands, or other table space must also be provided.

Here is how you go about setting the table according to Plan B.

(a)   *Cups and plates used.*   Sit down at the table where the pourer will sit. Place a tray close to the edge of the table in the center of the area. Place a cup in the proper position for pouring. Place the accompaniments for the beverage behind this cup; place the beverage pot or pots and the kettle of hot water if one is used to the right. Place an urn behind the cup and the accompaniments to the right or left. Then, keeping the area empty on the side where the guest will approach the pourer, place a suitable number of cups—handles directed to the right—stacked by twos within easy reach on the tray or the table. According to this plan, the pourer—usually, but not always—adds the accompaniments for the beverage and then places the filled cup on the plate extended by the guest, who takes a spoon and lays it on the plate if he needs one (see Figure 23–6).

(b)   Place everything else in this order, away from the pouring station: spoons, plates and trays of tea dainties, napkins, tea plates. The napkins are sometimes placed between the stacked tea plates, particularly if the table is small. The guest starts at the place where the plates are stacked and proceeds toward the pouring station.

(c)   *Plates and cups and saucers provided.*   The only change this provision introduces is that the saucers and the spoons are introduced into the setting at the pouring station and that the pourer will pass the cup and saucer of beverage with the spoon laid on the saucer parallel to the cup handle to the guest.

It would be difficult to say which plan is better, as each has an advantage and a disadvantage. Service is quicker by Plan A than by Plan B; with Plan A, however, there is the possibility that an unwary guest may be jostled while at the table, thus causing an accident. Regional customs determine which plan to use.

8.   Always place at the pourer's station a napkin of generous size, so that she may be protected while she is pouring.

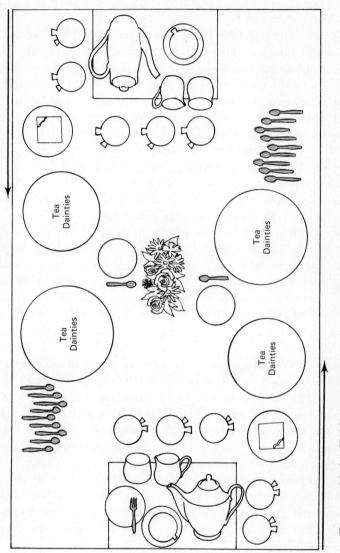

554

FIGURE 23-6. Table arrangement for a large tea—guest takes food, then receives beverage.

Large table arranged for afternoon tea.

9.   Place on the table at one time only the number of cups and saucers or plates that is in scale with the table.

10.   Avoid elaborate arrangements of napkins and spoons that would make them the center of interest. Spread the napkins only enough so that each can be taken in turn without fumbling. The spoons may be laid directly on the table, or they may be placed in a basket or a bowl, or on a plate or a tray, or in a receptacle designed for that purpose.

11.   Do not place large numbers of plates or trays of tea dainties on the table; instead put several items on one plate or tray and keep the number of plates or trays compatible with the size of the table. The total setting is improved when there are differences in the sizes or shapes of the plates or trays used for the tea dainties. One plate or tray may be common to the two services of a table set on one side for dual service.

Setting the Service for Punch.   The setting for punch service is somewhat different from that for a hot beverage. The person who pours may sit or stand. Punch is ladled with the right hand into a cup grasped by the handle with the left hand. Whenever food is offered, the cup is then placed on the plate and the whole transferred to the guest. If no food is offered, the pourer will transfer the cup from the left to the right hand and offer it with its handle directed toward the guest. Here is how you might set the service.

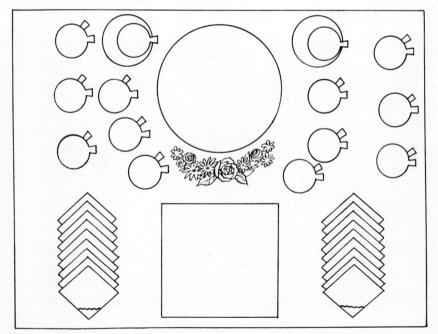

FIGURE 23–7.   Table arrangement for serving punch.

1. Stand in the pourer's position. Place the punch bowl on a large plate or tray to catch any condensing moisture. Set it close to the edge of the table, and arrange decorations around the base of the bowl. Place a pile of small plates on both sides of the bowl. Place the cups, stacked by twos if desirable, in symmetrical arrangement around the bowl, but not so far to the front that they will be difficult to reach or will spoil the effect of any decorations. Direct the handles to the left.

2. Place the napkins and the plates of food to give a balanced appearance to the table. Spoons will also have to be laid if sherbet is put into the punch cups (see Figure 23–7).

3. If punch is being offered without food, as it frequently is at weddings, the service may be set on any small table, as described, but there is no need for plates.

Serving Refreshments Directly from the Kitchen

Refreshments may be served directly from the kitchen in several ways. Some persons prefer this kind of service because it seems to be less bother, few props are required, and setting a tray or a table can be avoided. On the other hand, except when the guests are seated at tables, movement among the guests to serve them can become a nuisance unless an effort is made to control said movement. Perhaps every service has advantages and disadvantages.

1. The most widely used and popular service from the kitchen is that used when guests are seated at card tables for dessert before bridge or other games. These tables are completely set with linens, flatware, beverageware, the accompaniments for the beverage, cups and saucers, and small table decorations. The dessert and the beverage may be on the tables when the guests are seated, or they may be brought later, depending on whether the group is large or small. A similar service is used when refreshments follow an afternoon or evening of cards.

2. Trays completely set with the dessert or other food and the beverage can be brought to the guests. The accompaniments for the beverage must then be passed; they are offered from a small tray or plate.

3. Often, plates of food are brought directly to the guests. They may or may not be offered from a tray. The beverage cup may be on the plate with the food, or it may be offered separately, in which case a place to set the cup and saucer while eating must be available. End tables and the small snack tables can provide this space. Accompaniments for the beverage are offered from a small tray as in (2). Napkins may be offered with the plate or from the tray, depending on the manner of presenting plates.

4. When refreshments consist of a beverage and finger food, a tray that offers the poured beverage, its accompaniments, and napkins is offered to

Table arranged for serving punch.

each guest. After all have accepted the beverage, the food is served by the hostess or someone who assists her.

Except when guests are served at small tables, these serving patterns are very informal and casual; their use is best limited to small groups. Service from a tea tray or a table has more dignity and is more ceremonious.

Maintaining Service

At large teas and receptions where serving continues for several hours, a crew of workers is required to maintain service at the table. In her home, the hostess may depend partly on her friends and partly on hired help; organizations appoint committees to perform the various serving duties.

Plans for Service

The following duties must be performed, and the number of workers required to carry them out is determined by the number of guests anticipated.

1. One or more persons should be available to move between the kitchen and the tea table to carry additional appointments, newly arranged plates of food, and all the other items needed on the table and to return plates that need rearranging to the kitchen. The people performing this task might be called runners.

2. One or more persons remain in the kitchen to keep a fresh supply of the beverage or beverages ready, to refill the plates of food, and to wash dishes. They might be called the kitchen helpers.

3. One or more persons should be responsible for taking cups from guests and stacking them in a designated place. These persons might be called cup bearers. Hostesses at large teas should not be expected to have this responsibility.

4. One or more persons should be concerned solely with greeting guests, talking with them, introducing them to other guests, and so forth. This job is for the hostesses.

At small functions, the hostess, by herself or with the help of a friend or the host, manages all these duties.

Techniques of Service

Here are some suggestions that lead to effective service, whether one hostess or a committee makes the plans.

1. Make definite assignments of specific responsibilities.
2. Organize the kitchen so that a place is assigned for each task.

3.   Have food set up on trays, cookie sheets, or other large containers. Use one tray for each kind or for several similar kinds of food. Cover all trays of sandwiches and other foods that dry out quickly with a film wrap.

4.   Have duplicate sets of all serving appointments, except punch bowls and urns. When an object is removed from the tea table, another like it must be set down in its place. Urns and punch bowls can be filled from pitchers without being removed from the tea table; they need not be duplicated. However, the pitchers should be as thoughtfully selected as all other appointments.

5.   The plates and trays of food should be replaced frequently, so that the table presents a pleasing picture at all times and all plates and trays offer a generous assortment of dainties at all times.

6.   Appointments like cups and saucers, flatware, and napkins should be brought to the table on trays to avoid fingerprints and excessive handling. Stacked plates are more safely carried when grasped in both hands.

7.   Set up a serving table near the tea table whenever possible. From it, additional cups and saucers, plates, spoons, and napkins can be taken to the tea table. Used cups and saucers can be stacked on trays on the serving table for later removal to the kitchen.

8.   It is not necessary to use linen or paper doilies under the tea dainties; the gleam of silver or the color of plates may be part of the beauty of the table. Glass plates may need frequent washing to stay presentable.

9.   Instruct those who work with food in the kitchen to handle it with spatulas and tongs whenever feasible.

Appendix A
Format for Menus

1. Capitalize all words except articles and prepositions.
2. The items that compose meals should be grouped by courses, beginning with the first. The items of courses are presented in order of greatest consequence. For example:

Broiled Sirloin Steak

Baked Potatoes   Sour Cream

Broccoli

Hot Rolls

3. When an item on the menu has a special accompaniment, you may either place the main item to the left and the accompanying item to the right, or you may center the main item and write the accompanying item underneath. For example:

Braised Pork Chops   Applesauce

or

Braised Pork Chops

Applesauce

4. When a dish is accompanied by two or more items, center the former and space the latter on the same line to the right and left, or write them on the line below. For example:

Sesame Seed Wafers   Chicken Consommé   Saltines

or

Chicken Consommé

Sesame Seed Wafers   Saltines   Ry-krisp

5.   The beverage appears as the last item of the course with which it is served.

6.   Such items as butter, cream, sugar, or salad dressing are not written on menus unless they are particularly interesting or different. For example:

Head Lettuce with Thousand Island Dressing

or

Oatmeal   Thin Cream

7.   Plan the spacing and arrangement of the items on the menu so that the written menu is symmetrical. Allow extra spacing between courses; this extra space is often omitted in menus printed in books, magazines, and newspapers, in order to save space. Following is a menu for a meal of three courses.

French Onion Soup

Celery Sticks   Whole Wheat Wafers   Assorted Olives

Prime Rib Roast of Beef au Jus
Potato Soufflé
Asparagus with Hollandaise Sauce
Mixed Green Salad
Hot Rolls

Lemon Ice
Coffee

Appendix B

Quantity Food-Purchasing Guides

Quantity food-purchasing guides become increasingly unimportant with each passing year. This is true for several reasons, some of which are proposed. Food is extensively processed and packaged in an assortment of packages of different sizes. Labeling regulations stipulate that the contents of all packages, with a few exceptions, must bear a statement of the contents in pounds and ounces for some products and in fluid measures for others. The aphorism "a pint's a pound the world around and a pound fills a pint" has only a few exceptions. One-half cup of many different foods is considered a serving, that is, one pint or one pound will often be enough for four persons. See-through packaging permits rough guesstimates of numbers of servings, that is, of how many persons the package will feed. Trimming practices in the marketing of fresh vegetables have all but eliminated waste. Trimming practices in retailing meats have reduced both the fat and the bone contents of meats. Some food items are packaged as single portions; others, as family units. Many food purchases are made by count: pot pies, ready-to-eat dinners, apples, oranges, bananas, artichokes, fresh pears, chicken legs, eggs, and so on.

The almost universal concern for weight control means that few persons want jumbo food portions or second portions of any food, except steak perhaps. Estimates of how much meat to buy, except when one is buying by the unit, are only guesses at best. A rule of thumb that works much of the time in buying meat is bone in, two, and bone out, three portions to the pound. It must be recognized, however, that when using this rule, one can overbuy because the amount of bone and fat will vary from cut to cut and time to time; also, such boneless buys as ground beef and stew can yield four portions per pound. Another rule of thumb that works most of the time in buying fresh vegetables suggests that one pound will provide

TABLE B-1.   *Guide to the Use of Foods in Cooking and Meal Preparation*

Item	Comment
Apples	One pound yields about 2 cups of peeled and sliced apples and will make about 2 cups of apple sauce. It takes $1\frac{1}{2}$ to 2 pounds to make a 9-inch pie. Allow $\frac{1}{3}$ pound per person for baking.
Bread	Slices are not equal in weight. Two ounces will make 1 cup of soft bread crumbs; 1 cup of dry bread crumbs weighs 6 ounces.
Celery	One buys a bunch; each part is a rib.
Cereals, breakfast	Allow 1 ounce of cereal per person, regardless of kind and whether cooked or ready-prepared—except for puffed cereals and the concentrates added to cereals to enrich their nutrient content. For the latter, follow manufacturer's directions. One-half ounce of a puffed cereal fills the usual cereal bowl.
Cereals, milk for	Plan to add $\frac{1}{2}$ cup of milk or cream to each portion of ready-prepared cereal; $\frac{1}{4}$ cup to cooked cereals.
Cereal pastes, pasta	Noodles swell some during cooking, macaroni and spaghetti double in volume; a pound of any of these yields about 8 cups when cooked and serves from 8 to 16 people, depending on use. Italian spaghetti (the long kind) does not swell as much as the regular kind; 1 pound serves 4 to 8 people, depending on the kind and quantity of sauce served. Cereals absorb between 2 and 3 times their original weight in water during cooking.
Chocolate, cocoa	Three tablespoons of cocoa plus 1 tablespoon of fat are equivalent to 1 ounce of chocolate.
Citrus fruits	One grapefruit or orange yields 8 to 10 sections. Three medium oranges yield 1 cup juice, that is, 2 4-ounce portions.
Coffee	To brew coffee for 2 persons, use 6 tablespoons of ground coffee and 3 measuring cups of water for a brew of medium strength; this volume of beverage yields 4 servings in as much as most coffee cups have a capacity of $\frac{2}{3}$ to $\frac{3}{4}$ cup (the measuring kind). One ounce of instant coffee makes 12 to 24 cups of beverage depending on desired strength of brew. To make coffee for 50, use 3 ounces of an instant coffee or 1 pound of ground coffee.
Flour	Two cups of flour made up into pancakes, baking-powder biscuits, muffins, or yeast bread will serve 6 people. One cup of flour made into cake or cookies will serve 6 people.
Lettuce	Medium heads of lettuce weigh about 1 pound.

TABLE B–1. *Guide to the Use of Foods in Cooking and Meal Preparation (Continued)*

	Individual portions served as slices or wedges weigh about 2 to 2½ ounces. The weight of the lettuce used as underliner in a salad is approximately 1 ounce. The percentage of waste in lettuce varies from 0 to 15 per cent for a quality product.
Milk	In reconstituting nonfat dry milk, 1 pound yields 5 quarts of fluid milk. Whole milk contains approximately 3.5 per cent butterfat. The fat content of 1 quart of milk is 1¼ to 1½ ounces.
Potatoes	Allow ⅓ pound per person when baking; otherwise, ¼ to ⅓ pound is adequate. Follow directions of manufacturer when using instant products; however, these instructions may provide small portions.
Prunes	One-half pound of prunes cooked will yield 1 cup of pitted, chopped prunes.
Relishes	In preparing relishes, allow ½ rib celery, ½ carrot, 2 radishes, ¼ dill pickle, ½ sweet pickle, or 3 olives per person. How many of them will be eaten depends partially on the assortment available.
Rice	Rice triples in volume during cooking—cook ⅓ cup to obtain 1 cup of cooked rice.
Salad dressings	Allow 1 tablespoon French or similar dressing per portion of mixed salad. Allow ¾ tablespoon French or similar dressing per individual salad. Allow 2 tablespoons mayonnaise or "salad dressing" per serving of fish, chicken, or similar salad. Allow 1½ tablespoons mayonnaise or "salad dressing" per serving of cabbage, mixed fruit, head lettuce, or other arranged salad. Allow 1 tablespoon mayonnaise per serving in preparing sandwich fillings.
Salads, mixed green	Two ounces of mixed greens are the usual portion. There is often considerable waste to heads of endive, escarole, and romaine; only the inner portions are suitable for salads. The outer, less delicate leaves are often cooked and served as green vegetables.
Salads, mixed vegetable	The total weight of ingredients varies from 2 to 3 ounces per dinner salad. One tomato, ⅓ cucumber, and 6 to 8 ounces of lettuce will be sufficient for a tossed salad of these ingredients for 4 portions.
Shrimp	Raw, headless shrimp are about 30 per cent waste. One pound serves four if the shrimp are mixed with other ingredients; otherwise, it serves only 3. Cooked, shucked, and deveined shrimp provide 5 to 6 portions per pound.

TABLE B–2. *The Measure of One Pound*[1]

Items	Approximate Measure of One Pound (Cups)
Almonds, shelled	3
Butter	2
Cheese, cheddar, grated	4
Cheese, cottage	2
Coconut, shredded	5
Coffee, ground beans	5
Coffee, instant	8
Cornmeal	3
Cornstarch	3½
Crumbs, cracker	6
Crumbs, graham cracker	4
Farina, wheat	3
Flour, cake	4½
Flour, general purpose	4
Flour, light rye	5
Flour, pancake	5
Flour, whole wheat	3
Lard	2
Macaroni	4
Margarine	2
Noodles	6–8
Pecans, shelled	4
Rice	2
Shortening	2½
Spaghetti	4
Sugar, brown	2¼
Sugar, confectioners	4
Sugar, granulated	2
Sugar, granulated brown	3
Tea, leaves	6
Walnuts, shelled	3½

[1]For more information see *Family Food Buying: A Guide for Calculating Amounts to Buy, Comparing Costs,* Home Economics Report No. 37, Agricultural Research Service, United States Department of Agriculture, Washington, D.C., 1970, and *Handbook of Food Preparation,* American Home Economics Association, Washington, D.C. (1971).

four portions. Exceptions are few and are readily learned if one buys those vegetables—fresh greens, podded vegetables, and hard-shell squashes. Actually few persons desire to eat jumbo portions of vegetables: should a pound provide small portions, probably most persons would not care. For this reason, the No. 303 can and the No. 2 vacuum can of vegetables and the ten-ounce and the twelve-ounce packages of frozen vegetables will, in general, provide four suitable portions.

Though shopping for food in the 1970's is complicated, the quantitative aspects of the shopping are not. Only three tables are included in this appendix. Table B–1 includes some bits of information useful in meal preparation. Table B–2 gives the measure of some staples that remain in general use. Table B–3 gives the measure of some cans in which foods are commonly packed. It is quite probable that the 1970's will see some reduction in the numbers of can sizes used in canning foods. Further, there will come about some standardization with regard to the size of can used in packing different food products; for example, concentrated tomato products may come to be packed in only two or three container sizes.

TABLE B–3. *How Much There Is in a Can*

Cans by Name	Approximate Weight (Ounces)	Approximate Measure (Cups)	Products Commonly Packed in Can
No. ½	6½–7	1	Tuna, shrimp, crabmeat, lobster
8Z Tall	8	1	Fruits, vegetables, tomato products
No. 1 Picnic	10½	1¼	Condensed soups, tomato products
No. 300	15	1¾	Ripe olives, dry beans, tomato products, some soups
No. 303	16	2	Fruits, vegetables, pie fillings, specialties
No. 2 Vacuum	12	1½	Vegetables
No. 1 Tall	16	2	Salmon
No. 2	20	2½	Juices, pineapple, pie fillings, dry beans
No. 2½	28–29	3⅓	Dry beans, fruits, a few vegetables
No. 3 Cylinder	46	6	Juices, dry beans, fruit drinks

Index

Adulterated food, 87–88
After-dinner coffee, 508
  to set tray for, 508
Afternoon tea (*see* Tea, Teas and receptions)
Agriculture and food in the 1960's, 58–60
American style of meal service, 438
Apple varieties, 260–61
Artificial color in food, 71, 90, 102, 105, 106, 414

Beef
  corned, 184
  cuts, 158–62, 188–89
    less expensive, 162
    less tender, 162, 188–89
    more expensive, 158–60
    tender, 158–60
  grades
    quality, 171–73
    yield, 171
  hamburger, 162–87
  how to cook less tender cuts, 159, 203–204
  how to identify cuts, 155–57, 159–62
  how to judge quality, 170–72, 174
  quality grades, 171–73
  roasts, 160–61
  steaks, 160–62
  tenderness in, 158–59
  yield grades, 171
Beverage services, how to set up
  for after-dinner coffee, 508
  for first courses, 506–508
  for punch, 556–57
  on buffet table, 527–28
  on dining table, 462–64, 475–77
  on tea table, 542, 551–56
  on tray, 508, 541–42
  on serving table, 467

Beverages, 276–81, 313–18
  coffee, 314–16
  fruit, 276–81
  instant versus brewed, 316
  tea, 316–18
Blue-plate style of meal service, 438
Bread-and-butter plate
  position at cover, 458
  position of butter spreader on, 451–52
  use of, 458
Brunch, 509
  menus for, 509–10
Budget for food
  factors affecting, 357–62
  how to adhere to, 397–98
  how to establish, 394–96
  how to revise, 396
Buffet meals, 513–34
  dining arrangements for, 513–16
  menus for, 519–20
  planning menus, 516–20
  service of, 530–34
  setting the buffet for the dessert course, 528–30
  setting the buffet for the main course, 520–28
Buffet style of meal service, 441, 513–34
Buffet tables, 321–29
Butter, 243–44, 254
Butter spreader
  position of on bread-and-butter plate, 451–52
  position of on dining table, 452
  when to use, 452
Buying information
  bakery products, 304–307
  breakfast cereals, 308–309
  butter, 243–44, 254
  cereals, 310–12
  cheeses, 206–17, 223–32

Buying information (cont.)
  cheese products, 217–23
    cheese food, 219–20
    cheese spread, 220–21
    process cheese, 218–19
  coffee and instant coffee, 314–16
  coffee creamer or whitener, 245
  convenience foods, 135–46
  cream, 338–39
  dressings for foods, 319–20
  eggs, 247–52, 254
  fats and oils, 318–20
  fish and shellfish, 179, 191–95
  frozen desserts, 242–43
  fruit beverages, 276–81
  fruits, 256–76, 282–83
    apples, 260–61
    canned, 271–74
    chilled, 275
    citrus, 262–65
    fresh, 258–70
    frozen, 274–75
    melons, 266–68
    pears, 268
  jams and jellies, 320–21
  macaroni products, 310
  margarine, 246
  meat food products, 195–97
  meats, 155–205
    beef, 158–62, 173–74
    cured, 182–84
    ground, 187–88
    lamb, 164–65, 175
    pork, 162–64, 174–75
    sausages, 184–87
    veal, 164, 174
  milk, 235–38, 253
  nondairy topping, 245–46
  poultry, 154–55, 166–67, 176–78, 200–201
    chicken, 166–67, 176–78
    turkey, 176–79
  poultry food products, 197–99
  salad dressings, 319–20
  tea, 316–18
  vegetables, 284–301
    canned, 294–95
    fresh, 287–93
    frozen, 297–99
    onions, 290
    potatoes, 290–93
    salad greens, 289–90
    squashes, 293
    tomato products, 295–96

Candles
  at teas, 451
  use of, 449
Cheese and cheese products, 206–32
    cheese food, 219–20
    cheese-making, 208–11
    cheese spread, 220–21
    cheese varieties, 211–16, 228–32
    cold-pack cheese, 221
    cold-pack cheese food, 221
    dictionary of cheese, 228–32
    how to serve, 226–28
    how to store, 226
    process cheese, 218–19
    ripened cheeses, 210–11, 213–17
    unripened cheeses, 210, 212
Codex Alimentarius, 117–18
Coffee
    cost of brewed versus instant, 316
    demitasse, how to serve, 508
    how to serve at table, 498
Coffee cream, 238
Coffee creamer or whitener, 245
Combination food store, 35
Compromise style of meal service, 438
Consumer behavior, 39–54
    choice of food store, 40–42
    frequency of shopping, 42
    how influenced, 53–54
    shopping habits, 44–52
    store loyalty, 43
Convenience foods, 129, 135–46
    composition of some, 146, 195–97, 197–99
    cost of convenience of, 138–42, 144–45
    palatability of, 142–43
    time saving of, 136–38
Convenience food store, 34
Cost of food as influenced by
    built-in service, 129, 138–42
    convenience, 129, 138–42
    grade, 130–31
    market patronized, 122–24
    packaging, 131–33
    quality (grade), 130–31
    sales, 133–35
    specials, 133–35
    supply, 133–35
Cover
    definition, 446
    dimensions of, 446
    items of, 446
    position of items (see Table setting)
Crumbs, removing from table, 474

Dairy products (see also Milk, Cheese and
      cheese products)
    butter, 243–44
    cheese and cheese products, 206–32
    cream, 238–39
    frozen desserts, 242–43
    half-and-half, 238
    milk, 235–38
    whipping cream, 238

Decision-making in meal management, 6–13

Decorations, table, 449
  for buffet table, 449, 526
  for dining table, 449
  for tea table, 449, 550–51

Definition and standard of identity, 91–98
  authority for, 91
  examples of, 92–93, 95–97
  labeling of defined foods, 94
  promulgation of, 91–92

Dessert
  flatware for, 452–55
    how to lay, 452–55
  how to place dessert course, 474–78
  how to serve at table, 481, 497
  party, 538–40, 546–50, 557
    menu for, 538
    setting tables for, 546–50
    ways to serve, 547–50, 557

Dietary standards, 241–44

Discount food store, 32–34

Eggs, 247–52, 254
  Fresh Fancy quality, 249–51
  grades for, 247–51
  inspection of, 81
  sizes of, 251–52

English style of meal service, 438

Etiquette of the table, 483–500
  buttering bread, 491–92
  drinking from cups, 490–91
  drinking from glasses and goblets, 490–91
  duties of host, 498–99
  duties of hostess, 496–98
  finger bowls, 495
  finger foods, 491, 492, 495
  how to eat
    breads, 491–92
    chicken, 493
    French fried potatoes, 493
    fruits, 492
    meats, 492–93
    pastries, 491–92
    relishes, 495
    salads, 494
    shellfish, 493
    vegetables, 493–94
  how to use
    forks, 489–90
    knives, 489–90
    napkin, 488
    serving tools, 488–89
    spoons, 490
  offer to assist hostess, 498
  order of serving persons at table, 472, 486–88
  passing at table, 486
  removal of food from mouth, 495
  seating a woman, how to, 484
  seating of persons at the dining table, 484–86
  sitting down at the table, 484
  smoking at the table, 495

Family style of meal service (see Compromise style of meal service)

Fair Packaging and Labeling Act, 81, 102–108

Fats
  butter, 243–44, 254
  lard, 318
  margarine, 246
  oils, 319
  shortenings, 318–19

Finger bowl, 495

Finger foods, 491, 492, 495

First courses for meals, 504, 506–508
  how to serve, 506–508
  what to serve, 504
  where to serve, 506

Fish, 116, 169, 179–80, 191–92
  grading of, 179
  inspection of, 80, 169

Flatware
  demitasse spoon, 508
  laying on table, 450–56
    beverage spoon, 450, 452
    butter spreader, 450–51
    carving tools, 456
    dessert fork, 452–53
    dessert spoon, 452–53
    dinner fork, 450
    dinner knife, 450
    fruit knife and fork, 455
    salad fork, 450
    serving tools, 455–56
    spoons, 450

Flavor enhancer and flavor potentiator, 64–70, 410–11

Flour, 309–10

Food additives, 67–72, 100–102

Food and Drug Administration, 108–110
  inspection function, 109
  laws administered by, 108
  promulgation of definitions and standards of identity, 92–98
  promulgation of standards of fill of container, 99
  promulgation of standards of reasonable quality, 98–99

Food and Drugs Act of 1906, 79, 82–84

Food buying information (see Buying information)

Food, Drug, and Cosmetic Act of 1938, 81, 84–99

Food, Drug and Cosmetic Act (cont.)
  amendments to, 99–102
Food flavor, 69–70, 405–11
  aroma, 405–407
  taste, 407–409
  texture, 409–10
Food laws
  Egg Products Inspection Act, 81, 82–84
  Fair Packaging and Labeling Act, 81, 102–108
  Food, Drug, and Cosmetic Act of 1938, 81, 84–102
  Food and Drugs Act of 1906, 79, 82–84
  McNary-Mapes Amendment, 80
  Meat Inspection Act, 78, 79, 110, 168
  Poultry Products Inspection Act, 81, 111, 168
  Wholesome Meat Act, 78–80
Food packaging (see Packaging)
Food plans, 362–94
  basic low-cost plan, 371–78
    food choice for, 372–76
    how to spend for fruits and vegetables, 375
    how to spend for meat, 372–75
    menus for, 377
    table of individual food needs, 363
  differences and similarities of, 368–69
  economy plan, 387–94
    food choices for, 388–93
    menus for, 393
    table of individual food needs, 367
  liberal-cost plan, 383–87
    food choices for, 384–86
    how to spend for fruits and vegetables, 385
    how to spend for meat, 385
    menus for, 386
    table of individual food needs, 366
  low-cost plan for southeastern states, 378–79
    table of individual food needs, 364
  moderate-cost plan, 379–83
    food choices for, 380–83
    how to spend for fruits and vegetables, 381
    how to spend for meat, 380
    menus for, 382
    table of individual food needs, 365
Food preferences, 400–404
Food safety, 72–76
Food stores, types of, 19–35
  combination, 35
  convenience, 34
  discount, 32–34
  specialty, 19
  supermarket, 21–32
Foodways, 411–12
Forks

dinner
  how to place on table, 450
  how to use, 489–90
  salad, how to lay on table, 450–51
  for seafood, where to place, 450
Formal meal service (see Meal service, European style of)
Frozen desserts, 242–43
Fruit beverages and juices, 276–81
  citrus, 277–280
  diluted, 278
  orange juice concentrate, 277
  synthetic, 279–80, 281
Fruits, 258–76, 282–83
  apple varieties, 260–61
  canned, 271–74
  chilled, 275
  citrus, 262–65
  frozen, 274–75
  grapefruit, 264
  grapes, 266
  guides to purchase of, 282–83
  melon varieties, 266–68
  nectarines, 270
  orange varieties, 263–64
  pineapple varieties, 269
  tropical and sub-tropical, 269–70

Goals and meal management, 10–12, 13–17
Grace, saying at table, 497
Grade labeling, 113
Grading food for quality, 113–16
  agencies for, 113, 116
  definition of standards, 113
Guest meals, 501–12
  after-dinner coffee, 508
  first courses for, 504, 506–507
  how to plan, 503–506
  management of, 501–506, 510
  menus for, 505–506, 509–10, 519–20
Guides to shopping for food (see Buying information)

Ham
  canned, 183
  curing of, 182
  fully cooked, 183
  Smithfield-type, 184
Host
  duties of at table, 498–99
  order of serving at table, 487–88, 499
Hostess
  duties of at table, 596–98
  how to serve beverage at table, 497
  how to serve salad at table, 497
  seating guests at table, 497
  when to begin eating, 497
  when to cease eating, 498

Imitation food products, 95, 237, 239, 243, 246
Inspection of food
  agents responsible for, 109, 110–11, 116
  eggs, 81
  fish and seafood, 116
  meat, 79, 110
  symbols of, 111–12
  when mandatory, 110–11
Iced tea
  how to serve, 458
  what to do with spoon for, 490

Jams and jellies, 320–21
  definitions of, 321
  labeling of, 320

Knives
  butterspreader
    when to use, 452
    where to place, 451–52
  carving, where to place, 456
  dinner
    how to use, 489–90
    where to lay within cover, 450
    where to place when not in use, 490
  fruit, where to place, 455

Label, definition of, 86, 104
Label requirements, 88–91, 105–106
  of enriched foods, 341
  of net contents, 89–90, 106
  of nondefined foods, 90, 106
  when number of servings in package specified, 106
Lamb, 164–65, 175
  cuts, 157, 164–65, 175
  definition of, 175
  grades, 175
  identifying cuts of, 165
Legislation (see Food laws)
Liberal-cost food plan (see Food plans, liberal-cost plan)
Linens, 446–47, 526–27, 541–42
  cloths
    for buffet table, 526
    for tea table, 542
    how to lay, 447
  definition of, 446
  napkins, 448–49, 488, 527, 541
    folding of, 448
    paper, 488
    placing at cover, 449
    sizes of, 449
    unfolding at table, 488
  placemats, 447–48
    oval, 447
    placing on table, 447

round, 447
  size of, 447
Low-cost food plan (see Food plans, basic low-cost plan)
Low-cost plan for Southeast, 378–79

Macaroni products, 310
Maid, meal service by, 478–79
Meal management
  decision-making and, 6–8
  definition, 6
  goals, 10–12, 13–16
  resources, 8–10
  values and, 12–13
Meal planning, why, 15–17
Meal plans (see Planning meals)
Meal service
  setting the table (see Table setting)
  styles of, 435–443
    American, 436
    apartment, 438–41
    blue-plate, 438–41
    buffet, 441, 513–34
    compromise, 438
    English, 438
    European, 436–37
    family, 438
    formal, 436
    Russian, 436
    tray, 442
  waiting on the table, 470–82
  with hired help, 478–79
  without waiting on the table, 479–82
Meals away from home, 5, 327, 353–55
Meat analogs, 189
Meat cuts, 155–67
  beef, 158–62
  lamb, 164–65
  pork, 162–63
  poultry, 166–67
  veal, 164
Meat extenders, 189
Meats, 150–204 (see also according to kind)
  beef (see Beef)
  buying for the freezer, 180–82
  cured, 182–84
  cuts (see Meat cuts)
  grades
    quality, 170–75
    yield, 171, 174, 175
  how to cook, 203–204
  how to store, 201–203
  identity standards for meat food products, 196–97
  identity standards for poultry food products, 197–99
  inspection of, 79, 81, 110
  Kosher, 188

Meats (cont.)
 lamb (see Lamb)
 pork (see Pork)
 quality grading of, 170–75
 quality in, 170–75
 sausages, 184–87
 simulated, 189
 spending the food dollar for, 369, 372–75, 380, 384–85
 tenderizing beef, 188–89
 tenderness in, 170–171
 veal (see Veal)
 yield grades, 171, 174, 175
Melon varieties, 266–68
Menus
 brunch, 509–10
 buffet suppers, 519–20
 economy, 393
 guest dinners, 505–506
 how to plan, 345–52, 412–17
 how to write, 561
 liberal-cost, 386
 low-cost 377
 moderate-cost, 382
Milk and milk products, 235–42
 condensed, 239
 cost as affected by form of product purchased, 234
 cost as affected by size of package purchased, 234
 cultured, 236
 evaporated, 239
 filled, 237
 Grade A, 235
 homogenized, 236
 how to buy, 253
 imitation, 238
 low-fat, 240
 nonfat dry, 240
Minimum Daily Requirements, 341
Misbranded food, 88–89
Moderate-cost food plan (see Food plans, moderate-cost)

Napkins
 folding of, 448
 how to use, 488
 placing on buffet table, 526–27
 placing on dining table, 448
 placing on tea table, 545, 553, 556, 557
 placing on tea tray, 541
 unfolding at table, 488
New food products, consumer acceptance, 37, 51–52
Nondairy products
 coffee creamer or whitener, 314–16
 imitation milk, 238

margarine, 246
topping, 245–46
Nutrients
 calories, 330
 minerals, 335–37
  calcium, 336–37
  iodine, 336
  iron, 335–36
 protein, 332–35
 vitamins, 337–41
  ascorbic acid, 339
  niacin, 340–41
  riboflavin, 340
  thiamine, 339–40
  vitamin A, 338–39
  vitamin D, 337
Nutrition and meal planning, 345–52

Oleomargarine, 246
Onion varieties, 290
Orange varieties, 263–64
Orange juice products, 277–80
Order of
 passing at table, 446
 placing a course, 471–72, 474–78
 removing a course, 471–74
 serving those at table, 486–88, 499
  by host, 487–88, 499
  by hostess, 497
  by servant, 472, 486–87

Packaging
 requirements for, 64–66
 label requirements, 105–108
Pasta, 310
Pineapple varieties, 269
Place cards, 497
Placemats, 447–48
 placing on table, 447
  oval, 447
  rectangular, 447
  round, 447–48
 size of, 447
Planning meals
 reasons for, 13–17
 to fit a budget, 358–94
  basic low-cost plan, 371–79
  economy plan, 387–94
  liberal-cost plan, 383–87
  moderate-cost plan, 379–83
 to meet nutritive needs, 345–52
 to provide satisfying eating, 400–17
Pork, 162–64, 174–75
 cured, 182–84
 cuts, 156, 162–63
 grades, 174–75
 identifying cuts of, 156, 157, 158, 163

Pork (cont.)
  judging quality of, 175
  yield grades, 174
Poultry, 166–67, 175–79, 197–99
  chicken
    broiler, 176
    capon, 176
    cuts, 166–67
    fryer, 176
    roaster, 176
    stewing, 176
  classes, 176
  grades, 177–78
  inspection of, 81, 110
  poultry food products, 197–99
  purchasing guides for, 154–55
  quality in, 177–78
  Rock Cornish game hen, 176
  turkey
    fryer-roaster, 176
    roll or roast, 167
    yearling hen or tom, 176
    young hen or tom, 176
Portion sizes
  fruits, 258
  meat, 154–55
  potatoes, 287
  vegetables, 286–87
Punch
  how to serve, 556–57
  setting table for serving, 556

Quality-grading of food, 98, 130–31
  attributes of quality, 113
  grading agencies, 112, 116
  standards for, 112–13, 116
Quantity-purchasing guides, 563–67

Receptions (see Teas and receptions)
Recommended Dietary Allowances, Table
    of, 342–43
Resources and meal management, 8–10
Rice, 311

Salad bowl
  position within cover, 459–60
  removal of, 473
Salad fork
  laying in cover, 450–51
  use of, 451
Salad greens, varieties of, 289–90
Salad plate
  position in cover, 460
  removal of, 473

size of, 460
Salad service at the table, 461–62, 480, 481
Salt and pepper shakers, 465
Sausages, 184–87
Seating arrangements at the dining table,
    484–86, 497
Second servings, how to offer, 488
Serving procedures
  at teas, 542–57
  by host at dining table, 487, 498–500
  by hostess at table
    beverages, 497–98
    dessert, 497
    salad, 497
  when serving self, 486
Serving table, 467–69
  how to arrange, 467–68, 480–81
  how to use, 473–74, 477–78, 481–82
Serving tools, 455–56, 495
  how to use, 495, 499
  placing on the table, 455–56
Shellfish, 193–95
Silverware (see Flatware)
Smoking at table, 495
Spending for food
  eaten outside the home, 5, 355
  as influenced by family size, 357–58
  as influenced by income, 359–60
  as influenced by region of residence,
    361
Spill bowl, 478
Spoons
  placement of
    on saucer, 540, 544
    on dining table, 450
    on tea table, 545, 553, 556
    on tray for serving beverage, 541
Standard of fill of container, 99
Standard of identity, 92–95
Standards of quality, 98, 112–13
Styles of meal service (see Meal service,
    styles of)
Substitute foods, 66–67
Superette market, 19
Supermarket, 21–32
  definition, 19
  development, 21–23
  history of, 21–23
  margins, 24–25
  number of items stocked, 30
  organization, 23–24
  promotions, 28–30
Supermarket shoppers, 39–54
  choice of store, 40–42
  number of weekly trips, 42
  number with shopping list, 44–45
  purchases of different socioeconomic
    groups, 45–47

Supermarket shoppers (cont.)
   store loyalty, 43–44
   time spent per shopping trip, 44
Synthetic foods, 66–67

Table decorations, 449, 526, 550–51
Table linens, 446–49, 526–27, 541–42
Table service styles (*see* Meal service,
      styles of)
Table setting, 444–69
   principles for, 445–46
   how to place
      beverage service, 462–64
      beverageware, 456–58
      bread-and-butter plate, 458
      dinner plate, 462
      flatware, 450–56
      linens, 446–49
      salad plate or bowl, 458–60
      salad service, 460–62
      salt and pepper shakers, 465
      serving dishes of food, 465
Tea
   dainties, 536–37
   kinds of, 316–18
   tables, how to set
      large, 550–57
      small, 542–56
   tray, how to arrange, 541
Teas and receptions, 535–60
   decorations for, 550
   menus for, 536–37
   service of, 559–60
   setting table for, 550–57
Technology and food in the 1960's, 60–76
Time schedules for meal preparation, 427–
      34
   how to prepare, 428–34
Trading stamps, 28–29, 49
Tray
   beverage, arrangement of, 464, 540–41
   setting for tray meals, 442
   use in waiting on the table, 467, 474, 475
Time management, 419–26
   alternatives to use of time, 422–25
   deterrents to saving time, 424–25

how to save time, 422–25
maximizing use of time, 425
uses of time in meal management, 5,
      419–22
Time spent in meal management, 5, 419–22
Tomato products, definitions of, 295–96

United States Department of Agriculture
   inspection function, 110–12
   promulgation of definitions and stan-
         dards of identity, 110, 195–199
   promulgation of quality grade standards,
         112

Values, influence of in meal management,
      12–13
Veal, 164–174
   cuts, 164
   definition, 174
   grades, 174
   identifying cuts, 156, 157, 158, 164
Vegetables, 284–301
   grades
      canned, 294
      fresh, 288
      frozen, 298
   onion varieties, 290
   potato varieties, 291
   salad greens, 289–90
   selection of fresh, 300–301
   squash varieties, 293
   tomato products, 295–96

Waiting on the table, 470–78
   left-hand service, 471–72
   order for removal and placement of
         courses, 471
   order of waiting on persons at table, 472
   placing the dessert course, 474–78
   principles, 482
   removing a course, 472–74
   right-hand service, 471–72

Yield grades, 171–72, 174, 175